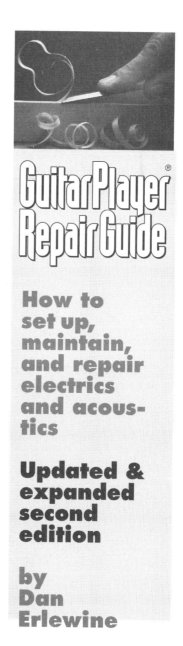

GuitarPlayer® Repair Guide

How to set up, maintain, and repair electrics and acoustics

Updated & expanded second edition

by Dan Erlewine

Backbeat Books

San Francisco

Published by Backbeat Books
(formerly Miller Freeman Books)
600 Harrison Street
San Francisco, CA 94107
www.backbeatbooks.com
Email: books@musicplayer.com
An imprint of Music Player Network
United Entertainment Media, Inc.

Distributed to the book trade
in the U.S. and Canada by
Publishers Group West
P.O. Box 8843
Emeryville, CA 94662

Distributed to the music trade in the U.S.
and Canada by Hal Leonard Publishing,
P.O. Box 13819, Milwaukee, WI
53213

Library of Congress Catalog
Card Number: 93-80493
ISBN 0-87930-291-7

Printed in the United States of America
04
12

Dedication

Dedicated to Joan, Meredith, and Kate—with love.
Also thanks to:
Tom Erlewine Design—the book looks great!
David Vinopal and Jon Loomis—for helping me over my writing hurdles.
Jas Obrecht, the greatest editor a guy ever had and a patient amigo.
Bryan Galloup's Guitar Hospital in Big Rapids, Michigan, where many of
the photos were taken. And to all my customers: thanks for breaking your
guitars!

Editors: Jas Obrecht and Jon Loomis
Design/Illustration/Photos: Tom Erlewine   •

Photo Credits
We would like to thank Brian Blauser of Athens, Ohio for his photos from
road trips with Dan to check out the guitars of the stars. Thanks also to
Al Blixt of Ann Arbor, Michigan for his photos on pages 53 and 219.
Thanks to the following companies for providing
the instruments shown at the start of each chapter:
Page 1:   Klein Custom Guitars
Page 3:   Robert Steinegger
Page 23:   Fender Musical Instruments
Page 43:   Erlewine Guitars
Page 79:   Gretsch Guitars
Page 115:   Santa Cruz Guitars
Page 129:   Paul Reed Smith Guitars
Page 137:   Fender Musical Instruments
Page 191:   Gibson Guitars/Elderly Instruments
Page 193:   CF Martin Guitars
Page 219:   ESP Guitars
Page 233:   Rickenbacker Guitars
Page 261:   MV Pedulla Guitars
Cover: Paul Reed Smith courtesy of Darrel Marvel

**TABLE OF
CONTENTS**

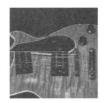

Foreword

Among material objects on this earth, few possess the mysterioso voodoo of the guitar. From the moment we first pick it up, there's something about its feel, its look, its heft, that whispers—or screams—to us. Before long this intriguing stranger becomes a friend, even an extension of ourselves, and we feel the urge to nurture it, to take care of it, to caress it. Or maybe to rip out its pickups, bolt a whammy bar on there, and spray it with metalflake green enamel.

We can't keep our hands off the guitar. If we're not playing it, we're polishing it, adjusting it, altering it, or wondering about it. Why does it buzz when I bend a string? Would it get more sustain with a brass nut? How come it doesn't play in tune anymore?

Whether you want simply to maintain your guitar in performance-ready shape or hot-rod it into a radical new incarnation, Dan Erlewine is the ideal guide, guru, and godfather. He's a player, he's an extraordinary repairman, and he gets to the point.

Erlewine's credentials run deep. He was co-founder of Erlewine Instruments and proprietor of Dan Erlewine's Guitar Hospital in Big Rapids, Michigan, and is currently the author of *Guitar Player*'s popular Repairs & Modifications column, as well as Director of Technical Operations for Stewart-MacDonald's Guitar Shop Supply in Athens, Ohio. He's also produced numerous acclaimed how-to videos.

This is Dan's personal edit of his Guitar Player columns—adding in new stuff and removing out-dated information. And far more than that, too: it's the product of thousands of hours spent hunkered over wounded guitars, a smoking soldering iron in hand. It's the product of experimentation and improvisation, endless hours poring over books and manuals, consultations with top repairmen, and countless weekend seminars, trade shows, and lutherie conventions. In short, it's the life work of a talented craftsman who loves his work. You'll find the good advice that all guitar owners need to know, plus loads of up-to-minute tips on new-generation whammies, finishes, acoustic pickups, and a whole lot more.

Over the years Dan's clients have included gifted, demanding players like Mike Bloomfield, Clarence White, Otis Rush, Johnny Shines, and Ted Nugent. Jerry Garcia owns one of his Strat-style electrics, and Albert King was pictured on the cover of *Guitar Player* with Lucy, the V-shaped electric blues machine that Dan custom-built for him.

Dan Erlewine has helped all these players and many more to get the most out of their guitars. Now it's your turn.

Tom Wheeler

Tom Wheeler
Editor
Guitar Player Magazine

Introduction

Every guitarist wants an axe that plays easily, stays in tune, looks and sounds good, and is set-up correctly, right? And when things go wrong, important repair decisions must be made. Who'll fix *your* guitar? Should you get a second opinion? Since 1985, my *Guitar Player* column Repairs & Modifications has looked at guitar repair and set-up from many angles. This book updates those columns for the '90s, condensing and organizing them into a manual for guitar players and repairmen. It teaches do-it-yourselfers to fix guitars, helps players keep their axes sharp, and gives advice that will help you choose a good repair shop when the chips are down.

The Set-Up and Maintenance section is for players of all levels. Beginners suspect that learning to play is easier on a well-set-up guitar, and they're right. Professionals discover that by personally setting up their own guitars, they finally realize every inch of its potential—but only after making such fine adjustments as setting the intonation and adjusting the "action" themselves. The Acoustic and Electric Guitar Repair section is for everyone—take what you need. Fellow repairmen are sure to find new tricks of the trade, and players: just *knowing* about guitar repair may keep you from the heartbreak of seeing your guitar ruined by inexperienced hands.

Dan

PART 1
SETUP AND
MAINTAINANCE

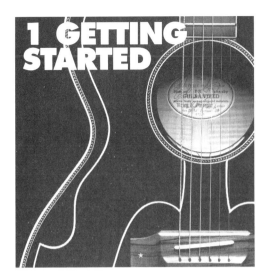

Cleaning the finish

Imagine that you've just bought a great used guitar. It's filthy and out of adjustment, but underneath the crud you know it's in excellent condition. I've come across many such guitars over the years, and to get them in shape I always follow the steps outlined in this chapter. First clean the finish, to start out fresh and see what you've got. Then, before installing a new set of strings, clean the fretboard and any dirty or rusted metal parts (most often the bridge). String it up and adjust the neck. If the bridge is adjustable, set the intonation. At this point, if your new axe plays great and satisfies your needs, you're done! If it doesn't play great, you may have uncovered a number of problems during the basic maintenance stage. The rest of this book will help you take care of those problems. Good luck!

Cleaning and polishing a guitar is the most basic maintenance task of all, and every player should know how to go about it. Maintaining a new instrument's clean good looks is simple if you keep it up from the beginning. But the lucky player who "discovers" a vintage piece that's perfect except for a finish that's been dulled by years of sweat, dirt, and exposure to barroom smoke and the elements may need the helpful information in these pages.

Guitar finishes become dirty and hazy because dirt particles come to rest on the finish, which always has a thin film of oil on it no matter how often you clean it. Some of these oils come from your body, while others become suspended in the air from cooking, manufacturing, pollution, etc. The oil and dirt create a "build" on the finish, which hardens in time and is quite tough to remove. When you remove the dirt, because of its abrasive qualities, you could be removing the finish too! That's why using the right cleaning technique is important.

The tools needed for cleaning and polishing new or used guitars are few, simple, inexpensive, and easy to use. Clean soft rags are the most important tool, and depending on the situation, you may also need any of the following: naphtha, liquid guitar polish, "swirl-

If you would rather not use chemicals to clean your guitar, try the moist-breath trick or use a saliva-moistened rag wrapped around your fingertip.

Remember: Don't rub your guitar down too much, even with just a rag. Polishes are more gentle than cleaners, and be very careful when working on old finishes!

mark remover," liquid abrasive cleaner, warm water, and elbow grease. First, I'll describe each cleaner and explain why it's used, and then follow with a few cleaning tips. As you'll see, lemon oil and silicone products are to be avoided.

EVERYTHING YOU'LL NEED

■ Clean, soft rags head the list. With several rags and plenty of time, you can clean the dirtiest guitar without polishes or cleaners, although polishes and cleaners help you do a faster, better job. The three best cleaning rags are: used, well-cleaned baby diapers, cotton T-shirts, and 100% cotton flannel. The soft rags that many manufacturers imprint with their company logo and include with a new instrument are made from flannel. You can also buy a yard of flannel at any fabric store for $3.00. Most other rags and fabrics are too coarse for delicate guitar finishes.

■ Naphtha (lighter fluid) is a great, all-around guitar cleaner. It's a de-greaser for finishes, pickguards, fingerboards, bridges, tailpieces, and metal parts of all kinds. Used lightly on a rag (more dry than wet) it won't harm a delicate lacquer finish, and certainly not polyurethane or polyester finishes. Naphtha leaves a flat, dry haze on a finish, but it's generally used first in the cleaning process, so guitar polish or a dry rag brings the sheen right back.

■ Guitar polish. The creamy stuff in the little plastic spritz jars is a *cleaner* because it's a liquid with an extremely fine abrasive. The liquid washes, and the abrasive lifts dirt. It's a *polish* because there's wax in it that protects and shines. The right polish won't scratch a finish. Martin makes a good polish/cleaner, and you can trust them to recommend something safe for high-quality guitar finishes, especially lacquer.

■ Swirl-mark remover is similar to liquid polish, but without the wax; it's actually a cleaner with an extremely mild abrasive. Swirl-mark remover is used in the auto industry for the final polish of newly-sprayed finishes. A good brand is Mirror Glaze #9 —it's a delicate, excellent cleaner that even without wax leaves a nice shine. I have found that #9 does not give

good results on water-base finishes. It may dull them—not the desired effect!

■ Liquid cleaners are light-duty buffing compounds made with a mild abrasive but no wax. Cleaners are best for dirtier finishes, since the absence of wax allows unlimited cleaning time without the wax drying (along with the dirt) at every polish-stroke. The abrasive is coarser than swirl-mark remover or guitar polish, so it does a good job of removing heavy dirt buildup. Cleaners won't leave scratches, but as soon as the dirt lifts, switch to a milder polish or swirl-mark remover—you don't want to rub away more finish than needed! Two good cleaner brands are Mirror Glaze #7 and Martin Seynour's Buff-eez #6355.

■ Lemon oil, while not on the list, is highly touted by some as a polish for guitar finishes, but I avoid it because it feels as though I'm wiping kerosene onto the finish. I believe that lemon oil works its way into and under the finish, especially on older vintage instruments with a lovely checked patina. This could cause the finish to lift and the wood to become saturated with oil—possibly dampening tone. Lemon Pledge should not be used on guitars!

■ Silicone is definitely not on the list, but it's added to some polishes and cleaners. Polishes or cleaners with silicone should be avoided! ArmorAll, which has silicone, is used by many music stores to keep guitar cases looking spiffy, but they should avoid it. Lacquer, glue, stain, and all sorts of guitar repair items just don't get along with the slippery aftermath of silicone, and subsequent repairs to an instrument exposed to silicone will be a hassle.

■ Warm water, used sparingly (your cleaning rag should be slightly damp—not sopping wet!), works wonders. Don't force water into checked, dry, or weathered finishes. Saliva is an excellent cleaner, too (seriously)—but only if you're working on your own guitar. Elbow grease needs no introduction, so let's get on with the work.

Polishing is what you do to a guitar that isn't really dirty, and the process doesn't have to involve *polish* at all. A clean, dry rag may be all you need to keep a new guitar's finish in shape by wiping off sweat and oil before they get a chance to build up and oxidize. Occasionally use the liquid guitar polish for its protective wax coating—but only on newer finishes which aren't weather-checked. Before polishing or cleaning, be sure to wipe, vacuum, or blow any *gritty* particles from your finish; otherwise you'll drag them around on the surface, causing scratches you'll never get out!

Polishing an extremely dirty guitar doesn't make sense. You don't polish dirty instruments; you clean them first and *then* polish. Since guitar polish is also a cleaner, it takes care of both jobs at once if the finish isn't too bad. But cream polish also puts a nice shiny film on top of the dirt if you're not careful. And with polish *or* cleaners, it's easy to just move the dirt around without transferring it to your rag. Remember, getting dirt off the surface of the finish and onto your rag is the object! There's a knack to getting dirt to transfer, especially on old guitars where it's heavily oxidized. Here's how you do it.

CLEANING

Take a 4" x 6" section of a clean, dry rag, fold the corners into the center, and grab the rag like a "knuckle-ball" (bunch the corners and loose parts into your palm, so that the fingers and thumb are pinching the rag into a ball shape as in the photo below). In the finishing world this ball of cloth is known as a tampon, "frenching-pad" or "pad," and is used for French polishing, which is the art of applying a shellac finish by hand-rubbing. This ball of cloth is a good tool for cleaning and polishing your finish. Use it with polish, naphtha, water,

or cleaner, or use it clean and dry. A true French-polishing pad has a ball of cotton in the center to hold finish and to help the pad hold its shape. The best pads are made from lint-free cloth (old linen bed sheets are great if you can find them).

There are no strict rules for cleaning, but here's the "hi-tech" method I generally start out with: Get very close and blow your warm, moist breath on the area until it fogs up, then quickly polish off the dirt; it'll transfer to your rag. If the "moist-breath" treatment doesn't remove all the dirt or haze, follow with a pad dipped lightly in naphtha, since it breaks down grease and sticky residues. Then follow with a pad dipped in water (it's a toss-up which to start with, naphtha or water). What naphtha or water won't remove, a polish or cleaner will. *Note: Naphtha is a petroleum product, and you should wear plastic gloves and safety glasses when using it. Work in a well-ventilated area and keep away from sparks, electric heating coils, or open flame.* Give the whole instrument (or any area to be cleaned) a light wiping with naphtha before switching to a polish or cleaner.

After the naphtha-wash, use polish or cleaner (depending on the situation) and work small (4" to 6") areas at a time. As the dirt starts to loosen or "move," pick it up onto the face of your tampon with a quick upward twist of the wrist. When one side of the rag gets loaded, switch to a clean part; otherwise you'll put the dirt right back onto the finish. Remember, the finish, rag, *and* dirt are all warm from the friction of

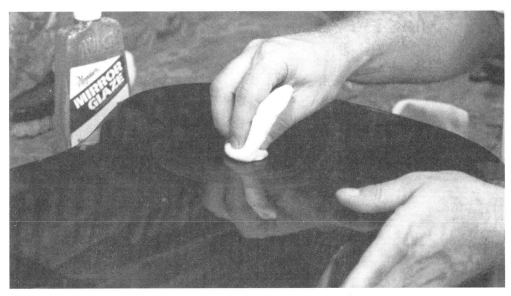

rubbing, which allows the dirt to either lift away from or return to the finish. Another cleaning trick is to move the dirt off to an edge, where you can pick it up more easily.

Let's look at a typical cleaning job. Let's say the top edge of your Les Paul is sticky and showing some dirt where you rest your arm or picking hand. This type of hazy buildup can usually be removed without polish, using only a clean dry rag, so always try the dry rag first! Rub lightly in either a straight or circular pattern (circular motions blend in best). If you're not getting the dirt onto your dry rag, pour a dab of polish onto the rag's face or directly onto the finish and continue rubbing, following the directions on the bottle (some polishes are wiped on and left to dry, some are rubbed off immediately).

Vintage guitars must be given special consideration. Often the "moist breath fog" is the best technique for extremely thin finishes that are riddled with finish-checks, since you don't want to work polish or cleaner down into these crevices. A *light* naphtha wiping is okay—"light" meaning that you tamp off the wetness onto another rag and wait until the naphtha starts to evaporate before wiping.

Warm water has its place in cleaning vintage instruments. If I use water, it's only to *dampen* the rag, which is wrapped tightly in one thin layer around my index finger. Sometimes a barely damp rag can be a big help in removing dirt or haze from a vintage piece where you're afraid of working any petroleum-based chemicals into a checked finish. You must be cautious of working water into a crazed finish, so it's a judgment call. Use the same light French polishing motions that you used with the tampon, just barely hitting the surface to pick up the dirt. And I hope this won't gross you out, but when nothing else works, saliva (spit!) can often dissolve the weird globs or specks fused to a finish! Of course, I'd never use spit on a customer's guitar—only on my own instruments.

Beware of soft finishes! This rare phenomenon occurs with lacquer, varnish, or the shellac-based French polish which was used on most instruments made before the 1930s. It's still used today on many of the world's finest classical guitars. Have you ever sat in a nice wooden-armed chair and felt that sticky, gummy surface that wants to stick to your skin? When you *know* that if you dragged your fingernails along the finish they'd be loaded with sticky, grimy sludge, *that's* a soft finish.

Finishes get this way because there are natural plasticizers (triglycerides) in your body that transfer through the skin—especially your hands. Lacquer "breathes," allowing moisture and certain chemicals such as polishes, cleaners, and plasticizers to migrate through it. The plasticizers go right through the finish and make the wood their home. Once a finish is softened this way, there's no cure except letting it totally air dry, and even then it may never be truly hard. The most common area of a guitar to suffer from this is the part of the body where you rest your arm when playing, although you may also see it on the neck or other areas. It's most common on dirty guitars that weren't cared for, since the oxidized dirt acts as a lid, holding the plasticizers down in the finish so that they can't migrate. If your axe suffers from these symptoms, I'm sorry, but don't try to rub, clean, or polish it away—it'll just make it worse.

POLISHING SCHEDULE

How often should you clean and polish? When should you use a liquid cleaner or guitar polish rather than just the dry rag? I haven't seen your guitar, so I can't tell you. I can only offer you some ideas:

Polyurethane or polyester (catalyzed) finishes seem impervious to anything; I suppose you can clean and polish them until the cat comes home. New guitars with lacquer finishes (ask your dealer what type of finish is on the instrument) can stand up to cleaning or polishing quite well, since the finish surface is smooth and unchecked. Remember that lacquer "breathes," so when you rub polish onto your finish, you're rubbing it *into* the finish as well. Regular polishing helps keep the finish new-looking and makes it less prone to checking, because of the chemical nutrients in the polish.

I always clean a used guitar right after I buy it, since I haven't found a clean one yet, and I don't like someone else's dirt on my guitar. When possible I clean with naphtha and a dry rag, but often a liquid cleaner is necessary. I don't use commercial guitar polish, because I'm afraid of the wax penetrating a thin vintage finish. After the initial cleaning, I may not use polish or cleaner on a used guitar for up to three years—sometimes longer. But I will use a dry rag every few months, or whenever the finish gets sticky. I really can't get too excited about rubbing any sort of liquid *onto*—or *into*—a thin vintage guitar finish, since I don't want to do anything that might change them. Polishes are for new guitars.

Polishes and cleaners are formulated to penetrate a finish and rejuvenate it to a certain extent, adding essential nutrients that keep it softer, shinier, and more flexible. Polishes and liquid cleaners help to delay the aging process, and can keep your finish from becoming overly brittle. However, I happen to *like* a dried-out finish on a 1930s Martin. And I *like* a dried-out finish on my 1944 Gibson J-45!

I believe that dryness and brittleness are part of the reason old guitars have killer tone, so if you clean and polish a new guitar regularly, after 30 years the finish is less likely to be dry and brittle. It will look better, but may not sound as good as a guitar that was dry-polished (or given the moist-breath treatment) somewhat regularly but liquid-polished or cleaned only occasionally.

You now know enough about finish cleaners and techniques to handle anything. Keeping the strings and fingerboard clean after playing is important, too—that's coming up next, and it's not nearly so complicated!

Cleaning your fingerboard

The condition of a guitar's fingerboard is essential to the quality of music that the instrument can produce. Although a warped neck or bad frets are often best left to your repairman, there is one job that any player can perform—cleaning the fingerboard. A clean fingerboard produces clean-sounding music; dirt, however, hampers smooth slides and fast

playing. Dirt can also destroy, slowly rotting the wood and eventually causing the frets to work loose. Whenever I change strings, I always give the fingerboard at least a quick cleaning. There is a fine balance between a dirty fingerboard and one that has absorbed just the right amount of natural oil from your skin. A too-clean fingerboard wouldn't please many players. Decide for yourself; but if you need to clean your fingerboard, here's how.

KEEPING YOUR STRINGS CLEAN

When grime and dirt have built up along the edges and between the frets and the wood itself, the board requires a thorough going-over. However, if you wipe your strings clean after playing, there will be less chance for dirt to build up. Years ago, when I was playing six nights a week alongside a pedal steeler, I noticed that he would clean each string at the night's end, using a special rag called a Blitz cloth, which was commonly used by the Army to polish brass. I started using one, too, and found it to be the greatest string cleaner I'd ever seen. An Army surplus store was the only place I could find them. Since that time I have seen them in music stores being sold as String Care by Blitz.

When cleaning strings after playing, be sure to lift each one out of the nut slot and off the bridge saddle, wiping that part of the string with your Blitz cloth, too. You may have to tune down slightly to do this. Once the strings are wiped and still a little slack, get in between them with a soft rag (not the Blitz cloth) and wipe down as much of the fingerboard as you can reach to get rid of the sweat. Occasionally use your thumbnail to press the rag into the crevice along the fret/fingerboard joint. This is where the wood can rot, since the fret slot (the groove that a fret is set into) has exposed end-grain and will soak up any sweat and dirt that work their way under the fret. If you clean your strings faithfully—especially after a night's playing in a club or a long practice session—your fingerboard should only require an occasional polish with a soft, dry rag.

REMOVING HARDENED DIRT

Cleaning a filthy fingerboard is a different story. *(Note: If you own a guitar with a maple fingerboard, read the caution below before*

proceeding.) If the grime has accumulated for a long time, it may have hardened, and steel wool alone won't remove it. In this case, you'll have to scrape it off carefully. Be sure to use a scraper that won't cut into the wood and leave marks. In some cases you may wish to soften the dirt before trying to scrape it away. Use a Q-tip dipped in naphtha to wet the dirt and help loosen it. Then follow with your scraping tool—I prefer a plastic radius gauge of the type used for measuring fretboard arc (radius gauges are explained early in chapter two). Held at an angle, the radius touches all the board at once and removes the dirt like a snow plow removes snow (photo above). Also, its sharp tip is perfect for getting into that tight fret/fingerboard corner where most of the dirt cakes up. We'll talk more about a radius gauge under "Setup" and "Fretting."

CLEANING AND POLISHING WITH STEEL WOOL

Pinching a ball of 0000 steel wool the size of a golf ball between your thumb and index finger, push down with your thumbnail against the fret/fingerboard joint. This will clean right into that corner and smooth and polish the fret edges. 0000 steel wool is quite gentle—but still, try to avoid making excessive crosswise marks in the wood fingerboard. Since you've already steel-wooled the fret/fingerboard joint, the fret is partially polished (on the sides). To finish the

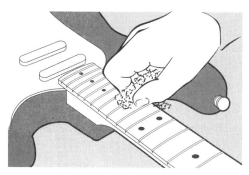

job, press your index finger on the steel wool again and rub back and forth on top of the fret to bring it to a good shine. This fret polishing is done along the fret's length (crosswise to the fingerboard). Finally, to remove any slight crosswise marks left by the fret polishing, use a fresh ball of wool to rub the entire fingerboard—wood and frets—in one direction, going with the grain along the entire fingerboard's length. Now the board should have a smooth, satiny look. Remember: Use only 0000 steel wool; nothing else is fine enough.

Two cautions: 1) When polishing frets across the grain, I lay down not-too-sticky "drafting" tape (a type of masking tape available from art supply stores) to avoid cross-marks in the wood. When removing the tape you could pull finish from the fingerboard edges. Refer to the chapter on dressing frets for more in-depth information! 2) If you own a guitar with a maple neck—i.e., a maple fingerboard with a clear finish—don't use steel wool or a scraper on the finish! Use only a soft rag. For hardened dirt, dip the rag in a little lighter fluid if necessary; mostly, you will need a lot of elbow grease. And don't use the lemon oil mentioned below on a maple neck—it doesn't need it! Tape off the lacquered wood with masking tape while cleaning the fret/fingerboard edge or polishing the fret tops. You may use steel wool on the finish, but it will remove the gloss and leave a dull, satiny finish. Some customers ask me to "degloss" their fingerboards in this manner, since they feel it leaves the surfaces more comfortable to play.

CONDITIONING THE FINGERBOARD WITH OIL

After the cleaning operation, I occasionally apply a dab of lemon oil to the fingerboard, using a soft rag. I'm not advising you to use the oil every time you change strings; use it only when the board is in need of it—several times a year for the average player. If the wood seems exceptionally dry after cleaning, it needs the lemon oil. Likewise, don't use steel wool each time you clean. Don't overdo it. I change strings every week when I'm playing on the weekends, but since I always clean my strings after the last set, I need to steel-wool the board only every month or so.

Here's a tip for tool lovers. Take a rubber squeegee (a 3M product used to remove water when wet-sanding cars, available at auto supply stores), and cut out a piece 1½" by 2½". With a small round file, make a slight groove

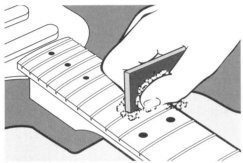

on the long edge. Wrap the steel wool pad around your new homemade fret polisher, and use it as you would your finger (above). This tool saves a lot of wear on your fingertips and thumbnail when working the steel wool.

. . . .

Cleaning and de-rusting metal bridge saddles

At one time or another, most of us run into rusting, dirty, and corroded "adjustable" bridge saddles that no longer move. As a result of wear, sweat, or corrosion, some bridge parts may be beyond repair. But many bridges, saddles, screws, and springs end up being junked unnecessarily when, with a little care, they could most likely be made to work. Here's advice on breaking rust joints, removing caked dirt, and on cleaning, degreasing, and lubricating metal bridge parts in general. I'll use the Fender bridge as my example, since it is both height- and length-adjustable, and therefore has

more parts that may require cleaning. But all electric guitars, from Gibson to Ibanez, are prey to the dreaded crud monster. These techniques for cleaning, rust-breaking, and lubrication work on all metal electric parts (not just bridges) and won't harm a vintage piece when used with care.

There are two likely rust problem areas for electric bridge saddle inserts: at the height-adjusting screws that raise and lower the saddle and control the string height, and at the length-travel screws that are used for setting the intonation. Of course, the basic bridge body, which is usually a stamped or die-cast housing that the saddles sit on or in, needs to be cleaned, too. This is much easier to do if you can remove the parts first.

Whenever possible, remove the bridge from the guitar (with a Tele, gently remove the pickup first—or clean the bridge in place). Then, before trying to disassemble any parts, preclean them with naphtha (lighter fluid). Pour some into a jar and apply a wet coat to the saddles, screws, and springs with a small, stiff brush or toothbrush. *Remember to wear safety glasses, and work in a well-ventilated area!* You may submerge the whole bridge in naphtha if you wish. After the parts have soaked awhile, remove as much crud as possible with a dry toothbrush. An air compressor can be a great help in blowing out dirt, if one is handy. Next, apply more naphtha with a little light oil added to it—the two mix together, with the naphtha thinning the oil and helping it run down into rusted threads.

Now, before turning any screws, clean the Phillips or flat-bladed screw heads. Remove as much dirt and rust as possible. I use the sharp end of a straightened-out dental probe to scrape the walls; a pin, needle, or sharp X-acto blade also works. Slot heads are easy to clean, but the Phillips type require more work. Often the Phillips' criss-cross slots are partially stripped from removal attempts made when the head was packed with dirt. In this case, even cleaning the head won't allow the screw-driver to get a grip. Screw extractors work best in this situation, or you can try blunting the tip of the screwdriver on a grinder (as in the following drawing). By shortening the sharpest part of

Don't get carried away with polishing to the point where you wear out your fingerboard and frets. Be reasonable, and just don't be a total slob.

All bridge parts can be cleaned with lighter fluid and treated lightly with sewing machine oil or Teflon lube.

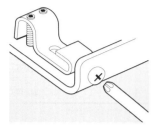

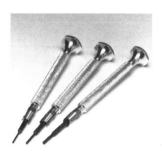

the tip, the screwdriver can then get a grip on what's left of the original slots. Don't fight the hard-caked dirt. Scrape a little out, and then soften the remainder with naphtha. If you're dealing with rust, dab a little Liquid Wrench or WD-40 onto the rusty area. Eventually you'll get the length-adjusting screw to turn, and you can back it out of the saddle.

The height-adjusting screws on Fender-type electrics—in particular the Allen-head type—may be frozen with rust and dirt. It takes a very small, sharp tool to scrape the dirt from the screw's six corner walls. Careful soaking and scraping will, nine times out of ten, finally allow your Allen wrench to slide in properly. Don't try to turn the screw until you're sure the wrench is in far enough that it won't cause stripping!

In some cases, even with the wrench well fit into the Allen slot, the screw still won't back out. Try going forward all the way through. If this doesn't work, don't get rough with the part. If the part's free of the guitar, apply a little heat with a propane torch, which causes the parts to expand and contract and often breaks the rusted bond. Do this gently, since overheating could cause premature cracking of the plating, although this has never been a problem for me. *Caution: Be sure that all solvents and explosives are removed from the area, that the part is completely dry, and that there is plenty of fresh air.* If the screw still won't budge, relax and try the following.

With a small pair of Vise-Grip pliers, grip the very end of the screw from the underside of the saddle. With the saddle clamped or held firmly, remove the part slowly down and through the saddle. If a small bit of thread becomes crushed from the grip, either rethread it with a 4-40 thread-cutting die, or leave it alone, reinstalling it from the bottom up after it's cleaned. This way the crushed thread won't get hung up in the saddle's tapped hole or cause damage to the saddle threads.

If the screw's head is so stripped or rusted that you can't get it to work (and you can't find a replacement, would rather use the vintage part, or have to play in an hour), try this: With the smallest razor-saw blade (.012") or a .010"-.016" nut-slotting file, file a screwdriver slot on the bottom of the screw. Use the new slot to

help remove the screw for cleaning. Then when you replace the screw, reinstall it upside down . This modification switches the Allen head to slot head, with the part now being adjustable with a screwdriver, like with Tele-style bridge saddles. This works great!

Once all the parts are disassembled, submerge them in naphtha. I like to keep all the parts from each saddle together, so they don't get mixed up. Try using a plastic ice cube tray for this, marking the separate compartments *E A D G B E* with an indelible marker. After a good soaking, dry the parts and brush them well with a toothbrush before reassembly. You probably won't even need to oil the parts to get smooth movement after cleaning, but if they're still a little stiff, lubricate the threads with sewing machine oil, Teflon lube, graphite, etc.

Sometimes the effect of a good cleaning causes a height screw to become so clean that it vibrates loose and allows the saddle and string to drop in height, lowering the action (this can happen even if you haven't cleaned the parts). If this is your trouble, adjust the saddle to the proper height and fingerboard radius, and then back each screw out slightly. Use a toothpick to put a drop of glue on the threads right where they enter the saddle itself. Then readjust the screw to the desired position and let it dry. While not actually a bond for metal to metal, the glue will set the threads and stop them from coming loose. A good product for this is the Titebond or Elmer's Carpenter variety of white glue. I've also seen saddles that have a dab of clear silicon bathtub caulk spritzed on the underside around the loose screw. This is a sure-fire method, but it might dampen the tone.

When cleaning parts, don't expect every bit of color or rust to disappear. Metal and plating that have been extensively corroded will never appear new. Just try to get the parts functioning again. Once you've reassembled all the saddles and reinstalled the bridge, put a very light coat on the threads, using any of the lubricants mentioned earlier. Brush the parts off periodically—say, every few months (depending on how much you sweat), or during a change of strings.

Install strings correctly, and they'll stay in tune

Now you can string up—once all the working parts are clean, and before you've adjusted the neck and action. Be sure to use your preferred string gauge. Proper string installation has a lot to do with whether or not you'll be able to keep in tune later. Learning to tune a guitar or electric bass isn't easy—especially if you're starting out. It's hard enough, in fact, that you'll want to know for sure that your guitar isn't working against you and causing tuning hassles that could be avoided. Outside of your ear, training, and playing experience, several factors determine whether your guitar can get in tune and stay there: the shape of the nut and bridge saddle(s), the quality and condition of the tuning keys, and how the strings are installed. Here are several tips that could help you out.

First off, the nut's string slots must not be too deep, and the slots shouldn't pinch the strings: This could cause a string to return flat after a string bend or tremolo dive, and may produce a catchy, "chinking" sound as you tune. If there are notches or grooves in your electric guitar's bridge saddles, be sure they're well-defined (but not too deep), smoothly rounded, and gradually tapered to the saddle's peak. In other words, each end of the string's "speaking length" must have a clean, neat contact point. Adding a tiny drop of lubricant such as Tef-lube, Vaseline, or powdered graphite at each of these points makes good sense, too.

I'm a firm believer in keeping vintage guitars stock, but I also know that replacing the tuning keys may be necessary. Your local music store can help you find exact tuner replacements (some retrofits have the same hole spacings, but better gears and a finer gear ratio). Be sure to save the original parts!

If "vintage" isn't an issue with you, installation of replacement tuners with locking string-posts will eliminate a great deal of tuning hassles. Some stock tuners' mounting holes will show after installing replacements—however, a good repairman can make these almost invisible. In fact, if you're not particularly skilled in guitar work, you'd be wise to have most tuners installed by a pro, unless the tuners are exact retrofits. Locking tuners are available from Schaller, Sperzel, and Gotoh.

With stock, non-locking tuners, how you install the strings may be the key to tuning troubles. With unwound strings (and sometimes a light, wound *G*), I run the string through the slot, pull it toward headstock center, loop it back underneath the string, and then up against the post, thus wrapping it against itself as seen at left, below. This "locking tie" is more difficult with the thicker wound strings. Some people do it, although it can cause kinks, slipping, and string breakage in the heavier wound strings. Try it and see.

For many wound strings, especially the lighter *D*, *A*, and some low-*E* gauges, make the first wrap *over* the string as it comes through the post, and the other wraps *under* as shown. With heavier gauge *A* and low-*E* strings—especially on acoustic sets—just run the string through the post and make all the winds downward. Always wind it tight and neat.

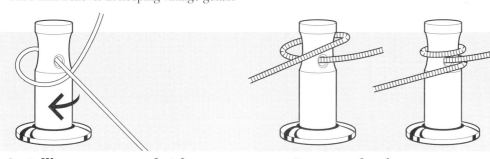

Installing an unwound string
1 Pass the string through the slot in the post.
2 Loop it toward center.
3 Bring the string end back up under the string and begin winding. String is held tightly against post.

For wound strings:
1 First turn wraps the string over itself.
2 Second turn wraps underneath

Some string brands sound better and tune easier than others, but you have to make the choice. Try all the major brands, using your favorite string-gauge set, and expect to take a year or so finding what's best for you.

If you have locking tuners, run the string through the post hole in a natural, straight line. Hold it taut, not tight, while you tighten the string-clamp. Then, in less than a turn, you'll be at pitch. Locking tuners make sense, and I won't be surprised to find them as standard equipment on many guitars before too long.

HOW MUCH STRING SHOULD YOU WIND ON?

For Fender-style guitars (depending on string gauge), wind enough string to keep the angle from the tuner post to the nut somewhere between five and twelve degrees. This angle is less critical for non-tremolo guitars, but too great an angle will cause a string to bind in the nut slot when a tremolo's in use. Too shallow an angle will cause a string to pop out of the nut slot on Fender slab-style necks or other necks with a shallow peghead angle. String "hold-downs," commonly used for the *E*, *B*, *G* and *D*-strings, create the right string/nut angle for you.

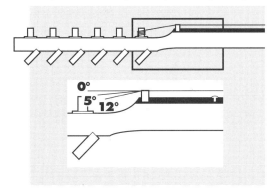

The simplest way of determining how much string to wind on a Fender guitar is to pull the length of string 2 ½ string posts beyond the post you intend to use (that's about 2 ¼" of extra string length), and clip it to length. Then, one method of installing the string is to shove the end of the string down the hole of the slotted "Safeti-Post" vintage-style tuners, and make your string windings downward.

My friend Stan Dixon, the "Wise Master of the Scientific Mystical Guitar Repair Method," is a scientist and a great guitarist from Columbus, Ohio. He never goes out of tune. He taught me another method for stringing up a Strat or Tele with "Safeti-Post" tuners:

1 Line the tuning key slot parallel with the line of the string.

2 Pull the string tightly around the tuning post and, keeping constant pressure, wrap around three times—going from bottom up.

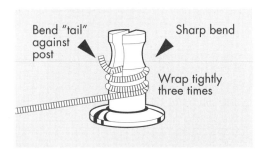

3 After three full wraps, hold the string against the post with your finger, and with the other hand pull the string tightly through the slot. Finish this with a sharp bend in the opposite direction—making a "D" with a tail at the bottom. Then right at the bend, press the "tail" against the tuning shaft with the flat side of your wire cutters to make it hug the post, and clip it close. Tune to pitch.

Stan Dixon on traditional tuners (with a hole in the post): "Measure the string two tuning posts longer than the post for which you are stringing. Make a hard 90-degree bend in the string with your fingers. Thread the string through the post hole. Hold the bend of the string tight against the post; with the other hand, pull the short end of the string tightly forward, making another 90-degree bend in the opposite direction from the first. Still holding the string tightly at the first bend, begin winding (making the windings go down the post). The key here is to keep the string tight and all bends at sharp right angles. This lets the edges of the tuning key hole grab the string to keep it from slipping."

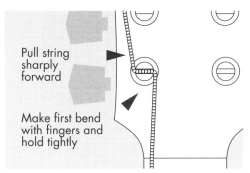

MARTIN STRING INSTALLATION SPECIFICATIONS

Acoustic or electric guitars with traditional *angled* pegheads (Martin, Gibson, etc.) require a different number of string winds than bolt-on "slab" necks. You'll find what's right for you after going through a few sets of strings. As an example, here are the Martin factory specifications for string installation: "Bass side strings passed through the string hole with string wound half way around post under longer portion of string, bent backwards over string and wound counter-clockwise two to three wraps around post toward the headplate. Follow this same specification for the treble strings with three to four wraps clockwise around the post."

ONE FINAL TRICK...

This is a bit of work if you change strings often (and a labor of love if your repairman does it for you). Using a hot soldering iron with 60/40 resin-core solder, tin each string's wrapping at the ball end. This keeps it from slipping or tightening like a hangman's noose at the tailpiece. "Tinning" is the process of lightly pre-coating an electrical lead with solder and letting it cool before making the final solder joint. Well-tinned string wraps should shine like silver and never be gloppy or heavy with solder. The use of a 40–45-watt iron will enable you to get on and off the string in a flash, without overheating it. The low-wattage (15–25-watt) hardware store soldering irons will not work as well.

Note: Don't do any soldering on, over, or near your guitar! Molten solder drips, splatters, and spits—and can make a beautiful finish look horrible. It's not good for your eyes, either, so wear safety glasses!

Neck evaluation and truss rod adjustment

Neck adjusting is simple—you tighten or loosen a nut. Knowing when it's adjusted correctly is the trick. The methods shown here are extremely important and will be used again and again in the remainder of the book—especially in the chapter on fretting.

What follows is an in-depth look at evaluating a neck using straightedges: first I'll show you how to "read" and understand different neck configurations, and then I'll describe the many types of straightedges often used for the job. Finally, we'll go through a typical adjustment using a bass guitar as an example, since they're often the most difficult to adjust.

When customers arrive at my shop wanting a guitar neck adjustment, it's usually for one of the following reasons: the strings buzz on the frets, the "action" is too high (that is, the strings are too far from the fingerboard), or the strings buzz on the upper frets along the "tongue"—the part of the neck that overlaps the body. Sometimes the notes aren't playing clean, or the instrument has intonation problems despite having a perfectly calibrated bridge. All of these are symptoms of a neck that needs adjustment. With an understanding of the basics of neck rod adjustment, action evaluation, and fingerboard straightness and relief, you're on your way to getting your instrument to play its best. Always use your favorite gauge of strings, tuned to pitch, for these adjustments.

SIGHTING THE NECK AND ADJUSTING THE TRUSS ROD IN THE PLAYING POSITION

First, "sight" the neck. Place your nose close to the headstock and look along the fingerboard edge from the nut toward the body. You're looking for straightness, humps, up-bow (often called forward-bow), back-bow, and high frets. Up-bow pushes the surface of the fretboard *away* from the strings, while backbow pulls the fretboard *toward* the strings. Check both the bass and treble sides, since they may look different; I wear safety glasses in case

When I interviewed B.B. King for *Guitar Player*, I found that he installs the *entire string*—winding up all the slack onto each post. It seems like a lot of work, and I would never have thought of it, but Mr. King seldom goes out of tune—and he "invented" string-bending!

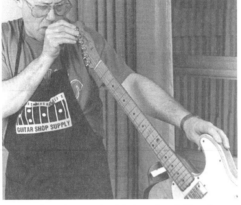

a string breaks. Neck sighting should be done in the actual "playing position," with the guitar on its side. Also in the playing position, double-check what your eye tells you with a good straightedge. The best entry level, inexpensive straightedges are a 12" steel "combination" square (the handle slides off, leaving only the blade) and a "rafter square," which has two edges—a 16" and a 24". These three lengths are adequate for most neck evaluations on guitar or bass. Read on and you'll learn where, and why, to use each length.

Most necks are adjustable by tightening or loosening a truss rod nut. These neck rod adjusting nuts are located at the end of the headstock or recessed into the body at the very end of the fingerboard. Some acoustic guitars are adjustable under the fingerboard, accessible through the soundhole. Find the adjusting nut and choose the proper tool for turning it; this will usually be an Allen wrench, socket/nut driver, or a screwdriver.

Loosen the truss rod by turning the nut counterclockwise.

To tighten, turn the nut clockwise

Tightening (turning clockwise) straightens an up-bow and removes relief. Loosening counterclockwise allows some back-bowed necks that warp *away* from the strings to pull straight, or into relief (see illustration). An old rule for tightening a nut that sounds silly but works is: "righty-tighty, lefty-loosey."

On a workbench or tabletop, set the guitar (strung to pitch) on its side in the playing position with the neck unsupported. You'll need backlighting for the straightedge test (experiment to find the best placement), and I use white shelf paper on the benchtop—it makes an excellent visual background. Set the straightedge on the fingerboard between the third and fourth strings. It should run from the

1st fret to the 17th, covering most of the fingerboard. Hold the straightedge with one hand and, while adjusting the truss rod with the other, watch the light under the straightedge.

Don't despair if your straightedge isn't long enough. Any string becomes an excellent straightedge when depressed between two frets (in this case the 1st and 17th). In fact, at the Fender company, they always install a capo at the first fret, for adjusting neck straightness and relief or for setting the string height. The capo eliminates the nut height as a factor and frees up one hand for measuring relief and adjusting the truss rod. You can read more about this in the "ten-step" method for setting up a Strat in the "Strat Setup" section.

If the straightedge "rocks" on the fingerboard due to back-bowing, loosen the nut counterclockwise, watching for the fingerboard to come into level contact with the rule. If the strings are pulling the neck up in a slight curve, slowly tighten the nut clockwise until the rule rests flat on (hopefully) all the frets. If you loosen it now, the curve or bow will return to the fingerboard. This slight, controlled bow is called "relief." Remember how relief looks. When tightening a nut, it's best to first loosen it completely, then slowly tighten until it begins to grab and feel snug without exerting any real pressure. From this point, a quarter- to a half-turn usually straightens a neck against string pull. It would be rare to take a full turn. A squeak is a telltale sign that you are at the limit—stop there! Overtightening can strip the nut, neck rod threads, or both. As you'll see shortly, it's always a good idea to clean and lubricate the threads of the truss rod and nut.

Caution: Some necks adjust more easily than others. If you sense trouble or have doubts, find a trained person and pay the small cost for an adjustment. Ask if you might look on. A trained hand knows immediately if the rod is working properly.

UNDERSTANDING RELIEF

Relief is often the key to low string height, few buzzes, and comfortable action. If you pluck a string, especially a wound one, the greatest movement occurs toward the center of

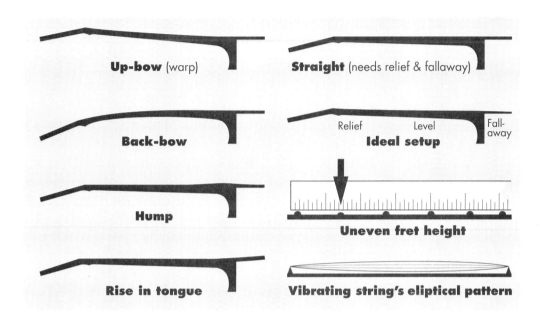

the string length. The string moves in a long, elliptical pattern. By loosening the rod, the fingerboard gains relief, allowing a greater clearance for the vibrating portion of the string between the fretted note and the bridge. Relief can also eliminate buzzing on open strings near the nut and the first few frets, where the strings are lowest. Different amounts of relief are necessary depending upon a player's style and preferred string gauge, differing scale-lengths, and the height of the action. Experiment with adjusting relief in and out of the neck. Be sure to play the guitar at each stage to see the effect.

Expect that you may have to raise or lower the bridge saddle height after a neck adjustment. In fact, a pro will adjust the neck and string height simultaneously—tighten or loosen the rod, raise or lower the bridge—back and forth until the action is set. We set the string height separately in the next section of this chapter (later you'll use all the techniques together in a smooth, flowing operation with experience as your guide).

All instruments don't need relief—in fact I always try to get an instrument to play with a perfectly straight neck first, and only add enough relief to eliminate unmanageable buzzing. Straight necks have lower, faster action—necks with relief play a little stiffer and mushier toward the center of the neck. Necks with too much relief and low action may buzz in the upper register. It's important to under-

stand how relief relates first to the fretboard as a whole and secondly to the upper part of the fretboard, which I call the "flatten-out" area.

Relief is measured by inserting a feeler gauge in the maximum gap between the top of the frets and the bottom of a straightedge. Measure at the approximate halfway point of the neck—not the fretboard—between the nut and where the neck joins the body (normally between the 6th and 9th frets). Factory specifications for relief are listed elsewhere in this book, but as a rule relief will measure as follows: guitars—from .004" to .012"; basses—from .008" to .018".

For guitar, it's best to check relief with an 18" straightedge—or one that will reach at least to the 15th or 17th fret (covering most of the fretboard). For bass you need a 24" edge. Study the illustration to understand how a "perfect" neck looks in both the straight and the relieved, configurations. Relief should gradually disappear as the straightedge is slid further up the neck. You can demonstrate this best by clamping a somewhat flexible but dead flat board to a tabletop, laying a straightedge on it, and pulling up on one end. You should see a curve that gradually disappears as the straightedge is slid further up the "neck." There should never be a hump or a rise at the end! It's OK if the last portion falls slightly away from the straightedge. This slight "fallaway" in the last few frets would *guarantee* no buzzing in the upper register, but it's not a must—either dead flatness, or else fallaway, is correct. Whenever the upper register of the fretboard (called the "tongue," or fretboard extension) rises instead of being flat or falling away, you have a symptom called "rising tongue" (covered in the fretting section).

So relief really needs to be measured *first* with the long straightedge to see the whole board, and then *double-checked* with a shorter edge to view the flatten-out area from the 7th, 8th, or 9th fret up. If the flat area shows a gap where it should read flat, then you really can't measure the whole board's true relief because of this "secondary relief," caused by the rise or hump. Many necks have this problem, and the only solutions are:

■ playing with some buzz on upper frets
■ raising the string height
■ filing the rise out of the frets
■ removing the frets, flattening the wood properly, and replacing at least the last 6 frets (a partial fret-job: refer to the Fretting chapter).

When you have symptoms such as humps and rises, it's far easier to isolate them using a notched straightedge. Several of my favorite straightedges are notched to fit *over* the frets, allowing me to read the fretboard instead of the frets (which may be worn in one area and not another, or poorly seated, and won't give a true picture of fingerboard flatness). I've named this technique the "MacRostie Method" after my good friend Don MacRostie, who invented the notched straightedge and presented me with my first set.

After adjusting a bit of relief into your guitar's neck, rest a normal (unnotched) straightedge on the board and slide it one fret at a time toward the body. The edge should drop from fret to fret as it moves, indicating that each fret is slightly higher than the one following it. As you slide the rule, it should quit dropping and level out between the 7th and 10th frets, and remain flat the rest of the way. As we said earlier, it's OK when the frets from the 15th on up fall slightly away from the rule. I call this "fall away," and it ensures clean notes in the upper register.

Note: When trying to view the flat area with a too-long straightedge, you may find that it runs

Don MacRostie using the notched straightedge

into the pickups and/or bridge before you can slide it onto the area you're after. Yet another reason you need straightedges of different lengths.

STRAIGHTEDGES: A PROFESSIONAL'S TOOLS

Inexpensive hardware-store straightedges can only give you a ballpark reading of a neck. Professional repair shops invest hundreds of dollars in *precision-ground* straightedges of different lengths. At the entry level, you can get by with the straightedge and rafter square mentioned above (for guitar and bass), but when you really want to know what's happening, check into professional straightedges. When I can find them, I prefer straightedges with one beveled edge since they give more accurate readings. High quality precision-ground straightedges have a thickness proportional to their length—the longer, the thicker—to keep them from being "sprung" from end to end (not straight along their flat side) because of flimsiness. An edge this thick, however, won't give a reading to suit me—so all of my longer straightedges must be beveled. Beveled or not, I use the following lengths:

■ 2"—Fret rocker.
■ 3"—Fret rocker. These first two lengths are for setting across any three frets (on guitar or bass) to "rock"—looking for high spots. These straightedges are 1½" wide. When set on end, they act as rockers for close frets.
■ 8"—Reading the area (on guitar) from 9th fret to fingerboard end.
■ 12"—General flatness, guitar or bass (also good from 9th fret to fingerboard end on bass).
■ 15"—Same as above (slight differences).
■ 18"—To look for relief/check flatness on guitar or bass.
■ 24"—Check relief and flatness on bass.

Notched, beveled one edge:
■ 18"—Notched short scale (24¾"/24.9").
■ 18"—Notched long scale (25½"/25.4").
■ 24"—Notched standard scale bass (34").

Of the above three notched straightedges, I took one of each length and cut it at the 9th fret. With these half-length notched edges I can read either the upper or lower portion of the fretboard independently.

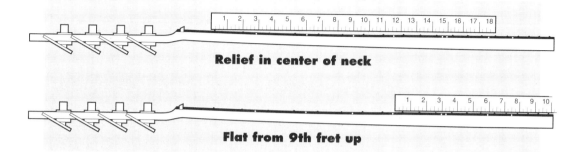

Relief in center of neck

Flat from 9th fret up

A TYPICAL NECK ADJUSTMENT SCENARIO

Neck adjustment problems common to all acoustic or electric guitars and basses are most exaggerated on the Fender electric bass because of its long, slim neck. So the electric bass makes an excellent teaching example for neck adjustments as a whole. The techniques shown here apply to all guitars and to every scale length—basses just tend to need a little more help than guitars. I borrowed this section on bass setup from the Summer '90 "Red Hot Equipment" issue of *Bass Player* magazine— because it's the most thorough article I've written on truss rod adjustment (for our purposes, the word "instrument" or "guitar" has been substituted for the word "bass"). Here I'm reprinting most of the article even though it repeats some of the steps just mentioned.

Guitar necks can be straight, back-bowed (convex fingerboard), up-bowed (concave fingerboard), or somewhere in between. The straighter the neck, the closer the strings can be to the fingerboard for easy action—but you must play with a light touch close to the bridge to avoid buzz or fret rattle. Conversely, if you play close to the neck and dig in, you'll need some relief to avoid buzzes.

A "perfect neck" is one that, under string tension, adjusts straight for low action and easy fret dressing, has a slight back-bow when desired to counteract heavy strings, and loosens from straightness into controlled relief. A properly relieved neck (see illustration above) shows a gradual up-bow going from around the 9th fret toward the nut, but remains straight from the 9th to the last fret. The overall curve in the fret tops between the 1st fret and the body joint mimics the string's long elliptical

pattern as it vibrates when plucked. This eliminates a lot of fret buzz.

Sighting a neck is the simplest way of checking if it's straight, back-bowed, up-bowed, or in controlled relief. Hold your guitar on its side in the playing position to get a true reading from the neck. Support the body, not the neck. Sight from the nut toward the body, and if you have trouble looking along the fret tops, sight along the glue joint between the fingerboard and the wood of the neck, using the line as a straightedge. You can also check by holding down a string at the 1st fret and at the body joint, since a tight string is a good straightedge. Or, to get a truly accurate reading, use a precision-ground straightedge for comparison. This sighting of the neck determines if, and how, any adjustments should be made.

Most necks are adjustable by tightening or loosening a truss rod nut. These neck rod adjusting nuts are located at the end of the headstock or recessed into the body at the very end of the fingerboard. Some acoustic guitars are adjustable under the fingerboard, with the adjusting nut accessible through the soundhole. Find it and choose the proper tool for turning it; this will usually be an Allen wrench, socket/nut driver, or screwdriver.

Tightening—turning clockwise—straightens an up-bow and removes relief. Loosening counter-clockwise allows some back-bowed necks that warp away from the strings to pull straight, or into relief. An old rule for tightening a nut that sounds silly but works is: "righty-tighty, lefty-loosey." Keep these few thoughts in mind when making any adjustments, and follow these steps in order:

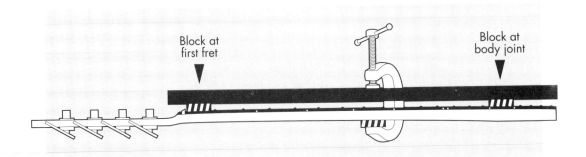

Block at first fret

Block at body joint

■ The adjustment nut on many bolt-on, slab-style necks is at the body end. It's usually accessible only after loosening the strings and removing the neck.

■ Always *loosen* the truss rod nut first, since it may already be as tight as it goes. You'd hate to break it before even getting started. In fact, remove it completely and brush or blow any dirt from the threads of both the rod and the nut. Follow with a *tiny* dab of lubricant on the threads inside the truss rod nut (use Tri-Flow, Vaseline, Magik Guitar Lube, or oil), being careful not to get any on the bare wood. Lubricating the threads makes for a smoother adjustment, especially on older instruments.

■ Without putting tension on it, reinstall the nut until it's just snug. Then make a small pencil or pen mark on both the nut and the neck. When the marks line up, that's your snug starting point—a nice reference when making adjustments.

■ One half-turn on a truss rod nut is a lot. Once a nut reaches snugness, tighten it one eighth- to one quarter-turn and then check your progress. Expect to remove and install the neck several times during this process.

■ The effect of a rod adjustment can take days or weeks to be complete. You may adjust a neck perfectly, only to find a day later that the neck has kept moving from the rod's tension—becoming *too* straight or even back-bowed. Don't panic if this happens; simply readjust it.

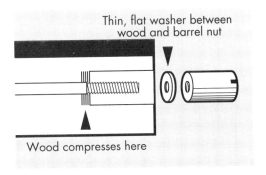

Thin, flat washer between wood and barrel nut

Wood compresses here

■ If the truss rod barrel nut is extremely tight on the rod or recessed far into the hole, watch out! It was probably overtightened by a previous owner or amateur "repairman." Some ill-informed people really crank those truss rods, which is a great way to break them, causing your bass neck to become permanently non-adjustable. Overtightening can also cause the wood to compress without straightening the up-bow. In this case, follow the removal, cleaning, and lubrication steps above, and then add one or two thin washers before threading on the nut. Often this will give the nut a new grip on life and allow the rod to adjust further.

■ With a stubborn neck, sometimes it's best to loosen the rod completely, clamp the neck into straightness (or even a back-bow as seen above), and *then* tighten the truss rod nut. This method generally works when all else fails.

Setting intonation

Repairmen are often asked: What is the reason for the different saddle positions on tunable bridges? Why are some bridge saddles closer to—or further from—the nut? These questions bring up the subject of string-length compensation (most players refer to this as "setting the intonation"). This is an essential part of setting up both acoustics and electrics.

UNDERSTANDING STRING LENGTH "COMPENSATION"

To begin with, accept the fact that fretted string instruments are accurate to a point, but they are not perfect and never will be. With its fixed frets, the guitar is known as an even-tempered instrument. The fret scales are compromised so that a guitar plays closely in tune in all keys but, alas, never perfectly in any. Many players can hear the out-of-tune notes in the even-tempered scale, and it drives them (and their repairmen) crazy.

At best, proper intonation is a compromise among many factors, and at a certain point guitarists must accept some degree of out-of-tuneness or give up the guitar. Too often the repairman doing the setup is blamed for not getting a guitar "perfect," and that's not fair.

Understanding the compensation factors that determine the need for intonation adjustment is tricky, and here experience is the best teacher. Your repairman is doing a lot more than turning a couple of screws. He's checking to be sure that all other important adjustments—such as truss rod, action height, fret dressing, nut and bridge saddle shape, string gauge, etc.—have been made before setting the intonation. That's important!

Many factors contribute to the need for compensation, and most are confusing to the layman (and occasionally to repairmen, as well!). I like things simple, so here are some basic facts regarding string-length compensation as I understand it. Any combination of these factors can cause a need for compensation, so try to look at the whole picture.

When we discuss a string length, or scale, we're referring to the distance from the nut to the center of the saddle, measured in a direct line down the center of the fingerboard and body. A Strat, for example, has a scale length of 25½". But the bridge saddles may actually measure as much as ⅛" to ³⁄₁₆" more than that, depending on string height, string gauge, etc. This addition to the string's length at the saddle is known as compensation. A basic understanding of compensation is necessary before the guitar's intonation can be properly set. Compensation is the adjustment that changes the mathematical (measured) scale of a guitar by altering the string length—almost always at the bridge saddle. This procedure sets the intonation, and is crucial for proper noting. Compensation has been accounted for at the factory on most non-adjustable acoustic guitars and is seldom a serious problem. Most acoustic guitars with problems suffer from *sharpness* and need to be compensated by adding to the string length. Occasionally, though, flatness caused by overcompensation is found on acoustics on which the bridge has been installed out of position.

Although acoustic guitars are compensated at the factory, do not expect them to play in perfect tune, intonation-wise. This job must be completed after the sale to suit the individual player's needs, and it's governed by the many factors listed here.

When setting intonation, we try to get a string to play the same note when fretted at the 12th fret as when played open, only an octave higher. In theory, the distance from the nut to the 12th fret is the same as the 12th fret to the saddle, since the 12th fret is the octave and halfway point of the scale (scale length equals the measurement from the nut to the 12th fret, times two). In practice, the string length must be increased to offset the sharpness that results when the string is pressed down during playing (remember—the mathematical distance of the scale runs in a straight line from the front edge of the nut to the saddle's center). The string, however, runs up and away at an angle to this line. When pressed to the frets during playing, it becomes stretched, which causes it to

Pressing a string down into the fingerboard too hard can cause a sharping problem, especially with tall frets. This can be corrected by changing your playing style.

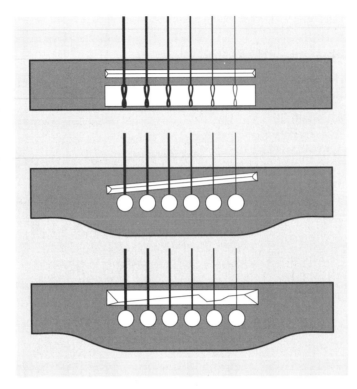

uses .010 strings or lighter, often searches far and wide to find a repairman to set the intonation.

Wound strings need more compensation than plain ones. Because of their extra weight and slower, low-pitched vibrations, wound strings need more clearance from the fingerboard to avoid buzzing. The extra clearance is gained by raising the string height from the fingerboard for wound strings. This increase in height causes the strings to go sharp more than the unwounds when depressed. This is why bridge saddles slant toward the bass side on steel-string acoustics or electrics.

go sharp. This is the basic, and the most easily understood, explanation of the need for compensation. Add it to the factors below, and you'll see why the seemingly simple job of setting the intonation can cause you to tear your hair out before you finally take the guitar to a repair shop, so they can tear their hair out!

STRING-LENGTH COMPENSATION

The closer the strings are to the fingerboard, the less compensation is needed, since the strings go sharp less when pressed. However, guitars with lighter strings generally need more compensation than heavier ones, since as string tension decreases (going from heavier-gauge strings to lighter), the compensation need increases. Therefore, the lighter the strings and the lower the tension, the more need for compensation. So, perhaps one cancels out the other. Confusing, but you can prove it for yourself by trying this test:

Using an electronic tuner, check your guitar's intonation on the low-*E* string at concert pitch. Retune the string to *D*. It will intonate sharper, which indicates the need for more compensation, or added string length. That's why the modern electric player, who

I like the term "speaking length" of a string. Franz Jahnel's comprehensive *Manual of Guitar Technology* refers to the mathematical string length as the "true" length (the measured distance from nut to bridge saddle), and the actual vibrating length as the "playing," or speaking, length. A string, especially a wound one, doesn't actually start vibrating, or speaking, until it gets a certain distance from the nut or the saddle. So, part of the string's "length" (in terms of sound) is always lost—another reason for compensation.

Notice that classical guitars have saddles with no slant (top illustration above). Why? The wound strings have a stranded core rather than a solid one, and sharp out at a rate similar to that of the solid nylon treble strings. Classical strings have a more even tension across the fingerboard than steel strings. Therefore, they require close to the same amount of compensation per string, and in general are more uniformly spaced from the fingerboard in terms of height. You may find saddles that have been slightly filed off-center (compensated) under the *B* and *G* strings on some classicals.

Instruments with longer scales need less compensation than shorter-scaled ones, because the longer string must be tighter to reach the same pitch. Thus the longer string is less apt to be sharp when fretted and needs less compensation (the higher the tension, the less a string goes sharp). The two most common scales are long and short. Long scales are 25½" or thereabouts (these include Strats, all their clones, and many Gibsons; Martin uses a 25.4" and Guild a 25⅝", but we lump them all together as long scale); short scales are 24¾" or thereabouts (Gibson Les Pauls, ES-335s, smaller Martins at 24.9", etc.). Classical guitars have long scales. There are many other scales, but only a few really common ones: a "medium" 25" scale is used on Danelectros and PRS guitars (I really love this scale); a "Three-Quarter Scale" (23") is used on the Gibson Byrdland and the ES-350-T; and Fender's Duo-Sonics, Mustangs and Musicmasters use 24" or 22½" scales.

SETTING ELECTRIC (ADJUSTABLE) BRIDGE INTONATION

Setting the intonation on guitars with adjustable bridges (which even some acoustics have) is simple. All that's needed is a small Phillips or flat-bladed screwdriver or an Allen wrench. If a string sounds sharp at the 12th fret, move the saddle back—away from the nut—to increase the string length. If a string sounds flat at the 12th fret, move the saddle forward—toward the nut.

THE "BASIC RULE" FOR SETTING INTONATION

■ If the string notes sharp, move the saddle back—increasing the string length.

■ If the string notes flat, move the saddle forward—shortening the string length.

SETTING ACOUSTIC (NON-ADJUSTABLE) BRIDGE SADDLE INTONATION

Acoustic guitars tend to shrink over the years because they're made of wood. Add to this the effect of the string's pressure pulling the nut and saddle toward each other, and you lose a bit of string length—measured in thousandths of an inch, perhaps, but it all adds up. Even solidbody electrics suffer from string tension compression on the neck and lose some string length over the years.

Differences in a string's gauge, quality, and physical makeup drastically affect intonation. As a string's cross section (diameter) increases, so does the need for compensation: hence the saddle slant toward the bass side on steel-string guitars. A string's elasticity, or ability to return to its original position after being deflected, is also a compensation factor, and stiffer strings go sharp more when depressed. You'll have to try many brands and gauges before settling on the right strings for you. The sad thing is that by the time you find the set you like, your playing style may have evolved to a new level, requiring that you start all over again! (*Frets* magazine published in-depth string articles in the Nov. '84 and Aug. '87 issues; check your library for back issues.)

The standard factory-installed slant saddle on acoustic guitars is usually sufficient compensation to please most players. The saddle slants approximately ⅛" in a 3" length, toward the bass side (middle drawing on facing page). If the intonation doesn't please you, ask your repairperson about a compensated saddle (where a wider saddle blank is inserted and then filed to staggered peaks under the different strings, as in the bottom drawing at left). If you're interested in compensating your own saddle, study the books listed at the end of this section—in particular those written by Don Teeter.

All of these are factors when it comes to setting your guitar's intonation by compensating. Their interrelation is complex, and the slightest change in any factor (especially string height) can throw the whole deal out of whack. Be sure that the important adjustments described earlier have been made before setting the intonation. An electronic tuner is a big help, also. The following approximate compensation is usually added to the scale length of any guitar:

■ Most electrics and steel-string acoustics—from ⅛" to 3/16".

■ Classical saddles—from 1/16" to 7/64".

■ Electric bass—from ⅛" to ¼".

I hope this information helps you understand how even a top-quality guitar can play out of tune, and why it can be so tough to get it right. Support your local repairman!

You'll find that an electronic tuner is a big help when you're setting the intonation.

Special thanks to William Cumpiano and Dick Boak from Martin Guitar's Woodworker's Dream—two expert luthiers who were very helpful with technical information. Woodworker's Dream has a great selection of rare hardwoods and guitar parts, and their catalog is a must for aspiring luthiers.

More information on this subject may be found in Don Teeter's *The Acoustic Guitar, Vols. 1 and 2*, Hideo Kamimoto's *Complete Guitar Repair*, Franz Jahnel's *Manual of Guitar Technology*, the Guild of American Luthiers' *Data Sheets*, and *Guitar Making: Tradition and Technology*, by William Cumpiano and Jon Natelson. A list of suppliers for these books, and more, is given at the end of this book.

That's it for cleaning and minor adjustments for a guitar or bass. I hope your axe is playing as good as mine! If not, go on to the setup chapter.

2 ACTION ADJUSTMENT AND SETUP

What is a setup?

OK. Your guitar is clean, lubricated, and strung to pitch. You can set the intonation, and you understand neck adjustment. Now, at the setup stage, you'll adjust the overall action—working with neck, bridge, and nut adjustments. For most electric guitars, the action height is adjusted by raising or lowering the entire bridge if it's a Gibson Tune-O-Matic style, or by adjusting the individual bridge saddles of Fender-style bridges. If you need to adjust the action of an acoustic guitar at this stage by raising or lowering its typically non-adjustable "bone" saddle, you'd have to reshape or replace the saddle entirely (this is covered in the Acoustic Adjustments chapter). Some other problems which might temporarily stop you at this stage are:

■ Strings buzz open. The nut needs to be raised (shimmed) or replaced.

■ Buzzing frets which need to be replaced or dressed.

■ Inoperable bridge saddles on acoustics or electrics which will require re-fitting or replacement.

■ An acoustic bridge that needs to be reglued.

■ A bridge that can't be raised or lowered.

If you have such symptoms, you'll have to solve the problem before going further. For the novice, even replacing a bridge saddle on a Tune-O-Matic can be a problem, so it's OK to jump ahead to the chapters on Electric or Acoustic adjustments to find the solution you need. But if you *do* jump ahead, don't *stay* there—come back and finish this section after you solve the problem that held you up.

Those of you with fully functional guitars should stay right here. Remember that we're either setting up a used guitar (which except for needing a little cleanup and adjustment was actually in pretty good shape), or else we're fine-tuning a brand-new axe which has gotten slightly out of factory adjustment. It's fair to assume that a large number of the better instruments will fall into this "healthy" guitar category: i.e., an instrument that plays well after a good cleaning, restringing, neck adjustment, a simple raising or lowering of the action and setting of the intonation.

The object of adjusting the string height is to get the action to feel comfortable with the neck adjustments you've just made. Or, as I mentioned earlier, you may need to adjust the action *while* you adjust the neck. Besides, it's pointless to get on with setting the intonation until the action is where you want it. If the strings are either too high or too low, any fine-tuning of the intonation goes right out the window if you have to readjust the string height afterward.

In a shop situation, the technician does a setup by thinking of neck, bridge, fret, and nut adjustments as a whole. Experience dictates which jobs need to be done, and in what order. For example, a professional wouldn't make a neck adjustment, restring, fine-tune the nut, set the action and intonation, and then go *back* to dress the frets. If a professional is in the middle of a setup and discovers a bad nut, he or she will stop, make the nut, and then catch up to the leaving off point. Some of these side-trips involve repair work, such as shimming or replacing the nut, replacing an acoustic saddle, and replacing or dressing frets. These jobs are covered in appropriate chapters. So the remainder of this Setup section assumes that:

■ The guitar is clean and strung to pitch.

■ The frets are level and OK.

■ The neck is adjusted to what you *think* is right (the following setups may change that slightly).

■ The nut is not in need of replacement (it may be too high—lowering that can be part of setup, but replacing it is not).

■ All bridge parts are functional.

A basic way to set action, and the method I used for years when I didn't *have* any factory specs, is to just lower the bridge until the strings buzz, and then gradually raise the bridge until the buzzing either stops or is no longer bothersome. In other words, set your action "by eye" until it feels good. Develop your own opinion: the factory specs only give you a good place to start from, or return to, when setting up a guitar.

THE BIG THREE

Setting action is a subtle task, and the different manufacturers each have their own specifications for a correct factory setup (there are so many guitar manufacturers and individual builders that I'd never attempt to list the factory specs of even a tenth of them). I use the "Big Three": Martin, Gibson, and Fender, as setup examples for steel-string guitars, acoustic or electric, throughout this book. Excepting nylon stringed classical guitars, most contemporary guitarmakers have followed the example set by the "Big Three." (Guitars equipped with Floyd Rose, Schaller, Kahler and other locking-nut, fulcrum tremolo bridges follow many of the same setup procedures shown here. For specifics, refer to the tremolo section.)

A factory setup is "middle of the road" enough to satisfy most players and to remain in basic adjustment after being shipped around the world to many different climates. Changes in climate—especially humidity—can cause an otherwise straight neck to become either back- or up-bowed—that's one reason why truss rods are installed.

FRETBOARD AND BRIDGE SADDLE RADIUS

These excerpts from a *Guitar Player* column explain how the fretboard and bridge saddle radius are related:

Before taking our vows, we repairmen have learned from experience that a certain amount of buzzing comes with the job—metal strings on metal frets buzz a little. Proper neck adjustment and fret-leveling removes 90% of most buzzes. The remaining 10% should be accepted as normal and will play themselves out in time. Of course, any buzz can be eliminated by raising the action high enough, but this won't satisfy most players.

One cause of string buzz that's often overlooked, however, is the improper matching of the shape of the bridge saddle's curve to that of the fingerboard. Most steel-string guitars have curved (arched, or radiused) fingerboards, although the amount of radius differs among manufacturers (Martin and Gretsch seem to have the flattest fingerboards). If the bridge saddle curve is significantly flatter than the fingerboard's radius, the middle strings will be

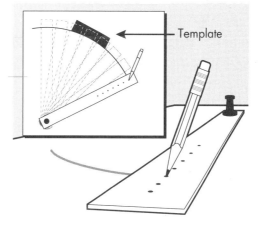

Template

closer to the frets than the outer ones, causing buzzes. Correcting this poor saddle adjustment often immediately eliminates buzz, as well as the need for fret-leveling. You'll also find that a proper bridge setup makes for a more comfortable axe, especially when you play chords. Here's how to make and use a simple tool—a radius gauge for setting your bridge saddles.

MAKING A RADIUS GAUGE

It's not much trouble to make a radius gauge, so if you're unsure about which size you need, make them all and see which fits. The most popular fingerboard radii are: 7¼"—vintage Fender; 9½"—some current Fenders; 10"—Kramer and many replacement necks; 12"—Gibson; and the 16" to 20" range for Jackson, Martin, Gretsch, and others with a flatter fingerboard. I made my radius gauges from Plexiglas, so that they'd last through years of use. Cardboard or thin wood work fine if you're only occasionally setting up your own guitar.

Start with a piece of stiff cardboard or thin wood about 24" long and 1" wide. Draw a center line on this piece and make a mark 1" in from one end—this is your starting point, axis, or center. From your axis mark, measure the correct distance for the radius you want (7¼", 9½", 12", etc.), and make marks accordingly. Next, lay the marked-out strip on a large piece of stiff posterboard (smooth-faced cardboard) and press a sharp pin through the center, pinning the strip to the posterboard below. Now if you poke a second pin through any of the measured "radius" marks, you can scribe the different radii onto the posterboard (above).

The gauges should be 4" in length—or long enough to lay out an acoustic or electric guitar saddle. Cut out the templates with a sharp blade in the shape illustrated by the shaded line in the

drawing. Thin wood or cardboard can be hard to sand or shape, so make your first cut accurate. If you do need to custom-fit your gauge to the fingerboard, reinforce the wood or cardboard gauge by saturating it with Hot Stuff original formula super glue. Once it's dried, you'll find that you can carve, file, or sand the thin material much more effectively. *Note: Always wear safety glasses when working with Hot Stuff or any super glue!*

Use the gauge first to measure the fingerboard radius with the strings removed, and then sight across your guitar's bridge saddles, lengthwise from E to E. On most electrics or acoustics, you should see a gentle rise through the A and D strings, going back down through the G and B to the E. This curve should approximate the fingerboard's curve. Some guitars have a curve built into the bridge (as in Gibson Tune-O-Matic and "Nashville" bridges), rather than using up/down adjustable saddles. With this Gibson type of bridge, variations in the saddle radius can be controlled by the depth of

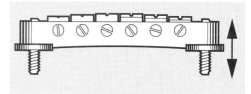

the saddle slot filed into each bridge saddle insert (see the section on Gibson Tune-O-Matics in the next chapter), while *overall* string height is tailored by raising or lowering the bridge's treble and bass sides, by adjusting the thumbscrews on either end. Most Fenders and many of their clones, on the other hand, have saddles that easily move up or down. Take advantage of the adjustment to set your strings exactly to the fingerboard.

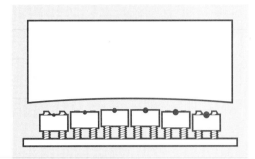

SETTING A FENDER ADJUSTABLE BRIDGE RADIUS

Adjust the outside E strings to the action height that you like by using the 6" steel rule to measure the gap between the bottom of the strings and the top of the 17th fret (see the factory setup that follows). Now place your radius gauge on the two outer E strings just in front of the bridge saddles, and raise or lower the four middle strings ($A\,D\,G\,B$) until they, too, just touch the gauge—it's really simple. Your bridge saddle curve will now match the fingerboard curve. It may not feel exactly like you want it, but it's the correct starting point from which to personalize your action, and it's much more accurate than eyeballing it.

With Fender's individually height-adjustable bridge saddles, the radius is automatically determined when you set the height of each string the same distance (clearance at the 17th fret) from the fretboard during the factory setup. But it's hard to read that scale (ruler) and make the adjustment—so you might find it easier to use the radius gauge to get close, and then use your ruler.

When you sight across the bridge by eye, the curve may look right even when it's not. Often the middle strings are on too flat a curve and too close to the fingerboard, causing buzzes. Also, when the saddle curve matches that of the fingerboard, you'll like the feel of the action, especially for chords. Best of all, you'll usually find that you've eliminated that final 10 percent of annoying string buzz.

Acoustic players may use the radius gauge as a guide for laying out the proper shape onto a poorly shaped saddle, and then filing or sanding the saddle to the correct shape. Saddle making is covered in the Acoustic Adjustments chapter, but I don't mean to sound too casual

about the ease with which this saddle shaping can be done—don't screw up your guitar! Take care when removing and replacing the saddle into its slot, and if you lack experience, have the saddle reshaped by a professional.

 Whether on acoustic or electric, most saddles are shaped so that the strings gradually rise higher on the bass side. This compensates for the extra thickness of the wound strings and their wider, floppier vibration when struck. For this reason, I consider the perfect matching of the bridge curve as a starting point. Once the proper curve is reached with a low to medium-low action, expect to slightly raise the three lowest strings to get perfect results.

CUSTOMIZED RADIUS GAUGES

Stewart-MacDonald's radius gauge set is the perfect tool for determining the fretboard radius of most guitars, the saddle radius of an acoustic bridge saddle, and for setting the bridge saddle radius of height-adjustable bridges like Fender uses. But it doesn't fit every bridge, so:

■ I cut the corners off of my radius gauge to fit between the metal walls of a Tele bridge, and to keep from hitting the bridge base on Gibsons.

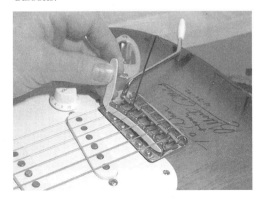

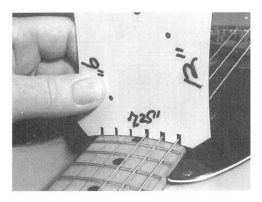

■ If you're really picky (which I am) the only *true* way to set any bridge saddle radius is to check the radius from *underneath* the strings—since measuring from the top doesn't take the height of the strings into account. On a piece of white plastic (or cardboard), use the standard radius gauge to layout the appropriate radius for a "below the string" (convex) gauge.

■ Another nice trick is to notch the Stew-Mac gauge so that it fits *over* the strings (photo above). Then you can measure a fretboard radius—or a saddle—with the strings on!

WHAT SETUP INCLUDES

All setup specs include the following measurements where applicable:

■ Maximum relief, or "forward bow."

■ String height over the fretboard (controlled by adjusting the bridge saddle height).

■ String height at the nut.

■ Bridge, tailpiece, and tremolo adjustments.

■ Pickup height adjustment.

All string height measurements (over the fingerboard, at the nut), relief measurements, and pickup height measurements are made by measuring the clearance between the bottom of a string and the top of a given fret (or polepiece) with a small 6" ruler which reads in 64ths.

Also, the following adjustments for both acoustic and electric guitars should be made (or at least checked) in the *playing position.* The measuring tools needed are a small 6" ruler or "scale" which reads down to ¼₄" increments, and a set of feeler gauges.

Along with the factory specs, I include a second set of "custom" setup measurements when possible. These measurements (marked

Mine) are taken from guitars that I know, either mine or a good friend's, and that are extremely good playing guitars. The second measurement always represents a lower-than-factory-action, and in my opinion is the best that you can reasonably expect from a given type of guitar.

Factory setup specifications for Gibson electrics

For long (25 ½") or short (24 ¾") scale guitars. Sample instruments used were a factory-fresh 1993 Les Paul, and my 1961 ES-345.

Gibson Neck Relief/String Height		
Neck relief at 7th fret	Factory	Mine
On all strings:	.012"	.004"
String height at 12th fret	Factory	Mine
On the bass E string:	5/64"	3/64"
On the treble E string:	3/64"	3/64"
String height at the nut	Factory	Mine
On the bass E string:	2/64" (.030")	(.015")
On the A string:	2/64" (.030")	(.014")
On the D String:	1-1/2/64" (.022")	(.013")
On the G string:	1-1/2/64" (.022")	(.012")
On the B string:	1/64" (.015")	(.010")
On treble E string:	1/64" (.015")	(.009")

The nut height is adjustable too. files and techniques shown in the Nut Work chapter to lower each string individually. Gibson measures the clearance between the bottom of the string and the top of the first fret using a ruler. Here I've given the distances in thousandths as well, since I use feeler gauges to take these measurements.

BRIDGE AND TAILPIECE ADJUSTMENTS

At the factory, Gibson uses a "crowbar" to quick-raise the bridge while the thumbwheels are spun up or down to raise or lower the bridge body. It's made from steel which is heated and bent to a crowbar shape and then padded with thick felt on the bend to keep from harming the top as the bridge body is pried up. If you lack this tool, you may have to de-tune the strings in order to get some thumbwheels to move (especially when raising the bridge).

The bridge saddle radius should match, or be slightly flatter than, the fretboard radius. This can be checked with a radius gauge. Most Gibson electric fretboards range between a 10" and 12" radius, and factory bridges have a radius of 12". By cutting the string notches slightly deeper on the middle strings, a flatter radius is achieved. The same files and techniques used for lowering the nut can be used for bridge saddles (see Gibson Tune-0-Matics).

Stop tailpieces adjust by screwing the two "studs" in or out until the strings just clear the back of the bridge body. Many players go beyond this point and tighten the stop-bar snug against the body to increase sustain, but it's not proven that this works (try it). It does seem that every model, and even individual guitars within model-types, has a perfect tailpiece height where the strings and action feel best (and you get the best tone). Raise your tailpiece up and down to find the "sweet-spot." I like to see the strings clear the body of the bridge (see photo above right); they often don't when the stop-bar is screwed too far down. Trapeze tailpieces are not, for all practical purposes, adjustable.

PICKUP HEIGHT

Pickup height adjustments are best made with both volumes wide open. Switch back and forth between pickups while adjusting the height, until the volume of both is equal. Then *back off* the neck pickup a little bit to boost the power of the bridge pickup (the bridge pickup is located close to the end of the string length, where the string vibrates with less power). As a rule, when depressing the two outer *E*-strings at the last fret and measuring from the bottom of the string to the pole-piece tops, you should get the following readings:

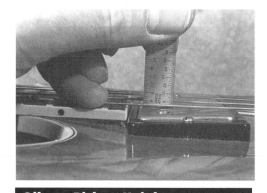

Gibson Pickup Height		
Neck pickup	Factory	Mine
On the treble side:	3/32"	3/32"
On the bass side:	3/32"	3/32"
Bridge pickup	Factory	Mine
On the treble side:	1/16"	1/16"
On the bass side:	1/16"	1/16"

Factory setup specifications for Fender electrics

THE TUNE TEST

Here are the setup specifications used at Fender to adjust most of their bass and guitar models during the "tune-test," or final setup stage of production. The tune-test adjustments include:

■ Bridge height (for tremolo instruments only—clearance between bottom of bridge plate and face of guitar).

■ Neck bow (Fender's term for relief).

■ String height (clearance at the 17th fret).

■ Nut height (clearance at 1st fret).

■ Pickup height (strings pressed at last fret).

TIPS TO MAKE FENDER SETUPS EASIER

■ Sight neck: Even with strings removed you can often get a good idea of how the neck is adjusted by flexing it and sighting it. Sometimes you can make an adjustment before you string up, and it'll be correct when you get to pitch (sometimes).

■ Check electronics: At Fender, the very first check is to ensure that the guitar works when it's plugged in! A dud, or one that mis-fires, goes back to the starting gate.

■ The capo trick: The string height and relief measurements are made with a capo installed at the first fret to eliminate the nut as a factor when setting up. Also, when capoed at the first fret, the string becomes a straight edge when pressed at the 17th fret as well (and you've a free hand to take measurements). This "capo technique" is an important part of setting up Fender instruments, and can be used to set up any guitar.

■ Preset the intonation: Fender pre-sets the bridge saddles to an approximate "correct intonation" pattern to make the final intonation adjustment faster. This insures that the strings won't be kinked in front of the saddles in case you have to move the saddles *back* while setting the intonation. For guitars or basses, set the highest (treble) string so that the center of the saddle is the exact scale-length measure-ment from the front of the nut. (25½" for Strat and Tele, 34" for Precision and Jazz Basses, etc.) Then "rough in" the other saddles to the appoximate intonation pattern shown at right. Now begin the setup using the Fender "factory specs" given at the end of this section.

EIGHT-STEP SETUP FOR NON-TREMOLO GUITARS OR BASSES

All measurements of string height (over the fingerboard, at the nut), relief, and pickup height are made by measuring the clearance between the bottom of a string and the top of a given fret (or polepiece).

1 String to pitch.

2 Install capo at first fret.

3 Adjust relief at 7th fret (sometimes it's the 9th fret, especially on basses) by pressing down a string at the last fret (string becomes straightedge). Expect to take the neck on and off a few times before you get it right (unless your neck is adjustable at the peghead end). NOTE: I tend to adjust my neck almost perfectly straight at this stage and go on to setting my string height. Then if it's too buzzy, I'll loosen the rod and introduce relief gradu-ally. At the factory they adjust in the relief, period. Try both ways.

4 Set the string height across the fretboard at the 17th fret (use your ruler and follow the factory specs). Raise or lower the strings by adjusting the saddle height with the proper tool: a .050" (4-40) Allen wrench for Strats and some Teles, or a small screwdriver for other Teles and bass models. Fender saddles have two threaded set-screws; raising one screw more than another will change the spacing between strings, while at the same time raising or lowering the saddle. Keep an eye on the string-to-string spacing. The radius gauges mentioned earlier can be a big help for setting the string height/bridge saddle radius quickly.

5 Remove the capo, and set the string height at the nut (this only applies if the nut is too high—in which case you can use the tools and techniques shown later in the Nut Chapter to lower the strings. If the strings are too low, you must raise the nut with shims or replace it.

6 Set the height of the outer two polepieces to the factory specs using your ruler. Press the outer two strings at the last fret, and check the clearance.

7 Play the guitar at all frets, checking for buzzes.

8 Fine tune the intonation, and you're done!

TEN-STEP STRAT SETUP

Now here's the same setup as above with some added steps for dealing with the tremolo. I learned this setup in May of '92 while visiting Fender. My tour guide was Albert Garcia, a long-time friend and Fender employee. Having set up thousands of Strats, Albert knows a few tricks, which he uses on his own guitars, that are not used at the factory. Before beginning, make note of the following four pointers:

■ Again, before starting be sure that the electronics are working.

■ No springs are installed on the tremolo.

■ The tremolo claw should be quite loose (1" from the rear wall of the tremolo rout) to allow for easy installation of the springs later.

■ The intonation is "pre-set" as stated previously.

1 String up lightly, but not nearly to pitch. Use .009's for the American Standard, and .010's for the Vintage.

Fender's pre-set bridge saddle pattern

Albert Garcia

2 "Block" the tremolo in the middle position so it can float in either direction. Use a hardwood block measuring 1" wide and 2" long that tapers from ¼" to ½". Shove it in between the rear of the tremolo block and the guitar body until you get a gap of about ¹¹⁄₃₂" . Now string to pitch, and the tension will hold the block in place. Shove the block in, or pull it out (re-tuning as necessary), until a gap of ³⁄₃₂" shows between the bottom of the bridge plate and the face of the guitar. Once tuned to pitch the bridge can't go anywhere—it's "blocked".

3 Install a capo at the 1st fret.

Measuring relief with a feeler gauge.

4 Adjust the neck. In the playing position, depress one of the wound strings (I use either the *D* or *A*) at the 17th fret. Adjust the neck to the proper relief, or straight if you prefer it that way. (Both Albert and I prefer a neck to be almost straight, or maybe with just a *little* bit of relief—.004" to .006".)

If you have a neck which adjusts at the body end, you may have to remove the neck a number of times to complete the adjustment. At the factory, they seldom have to take the neck off more than twice—they're good at it!

5 Set the string height. With the capo still on, adjust the string height at the 17th fret to match the specs in the chart—you can do that one of two ways, with the same result: A) set the outer two *E* strings to the correct height and use the radius gauge to set the remaining bridge saddles; B) use the ruler to measure and adjust the height of each string until it shows the same clearance all the way across at the 17th fret (bottom of string to top of fret). The factory clearance is ⅘₄"for guitars, but Albert sets his bass *E* string slightly higher to ⁵⁄₆₄" and

then blends that into the ⅘₄" height using the radius gauge.

6 Remove the capo.

7 Lower the string height at the nut to match the factory specs. This is generally set between .022" and .020", but if you really want to be exact, there is a range from .018" to .022" depending on whether you're working on a guitar or bass. You'll notice in the chart a plus (+) or minus (-) figure. The (+), when indicated, gives the measurement for the low bass string, the (-) indicates the treble string setting. For example: .020" (-.002") means that you set all the strings at .020", but the treble *E* string *could* measure as low as .018" (guitar). Or, .020" (+.002") means that all the strings are cut to .020", but you *could* leave the low *E* string as high as .022" (bass). It's always best to go with the tallest measurement and "fine-tune" the nut by degree. Follow the techniques for making and fitting a nut in the "Nut Work" chapter.

8 Adjust the pickup height. Use the measurements in the chart; and fretting the outer two *E*-strings at the last fret, measure the gap between the bottom of the string and the top of the *E*-string polepieces. Albert prefers to set his pickups slightly farther away from the strings than the factory does, to avoid overtones and possible intonation problems and to give that "clear as a bell" Strat tone.

9 Play the guitar and check for buzzes at every fret (there could be a need to dress the frets—or perhaps only one—on any guitar, at any stage). Albert sets his final intonation at this stage, while the tremolo is still blocked—it's quicker to do it now (before the tremolo springs and string-tensions get involved).

10 Install three tremolo springs and begin tightening the "claw." For heavier gauge strings, or a stiffer tremolo, use more springs. Strats come with five springs if you want to use them all (Stevie Ray did). Because the wooden spacer block (wedge) isn't too wide, you should have access on each side for the long Phillips-head screwdriver used to tighten the spring claw. And since the claw is loose, nothing will happen to your set-up because the springs won't pull on the tremolo block until they get close to the right adjustment. On

Factory Specs For Fender Setups

Model	Pickup Height*	String Height**	Bridge Height	Relief at 7th fret	Nut Action***
Amer. Standard, Vintage, & SRV	1/8" bass side 3/32" treble side	4/64"	3/32"–1/8"	.012"	.020" (–.002")
Ultra, Plus, Beck	1/16" both sides	4/64"	3/32"–1/8"	.012"	.020" (–.002")
Burton Tele, '52 Tele	3/32" bass side 5/64" treble side 10-12/64" middle	4/64"	n/a	.012"	.020" (–.002")
Malmsteen	1/8" bass side 3/32" treble side middle flush w/pickguard	4/64"	3/32"–1/8"	.008"	.020" (–.002")
Clapton	1/16" both sides	3/64"–4/64"	flat on body	.008"–.010"	.020" (–.002")
SRV	1/8" bass side 3/32" treble side	4/64"	3/32"–1/8"	.012"	.020" (–.002")
Floyd Rose Classic	1/8" bass side 3/32" treble side 3/32" both sides for humbucker	1/8" use pivot screws to even out action	7/32" (±1/32") top of bridge plate to top of body (4/32" ±1/32") measured at pivot screws	.012"	.020" (–.002")
5 String Bass	7/64" bass side 5/64" treble side	3/32" (±1/64")	n/a	.014"	.020" (+.002")
Amer. Standard & Vintage Bass	1/8" bass side 3/32" treble side	3/32" (±1/64")	n/a	.014"	.020" (+.002")
Ultra & Plus Bass	1/16" both sides	3/32" (±1/64")	n/a	.014"	.020" (+.002")

On American Standard type bridges, the saddles on strings 1 and 6 should be 1/32" to 3/32" above the bridge plate. Saddles on strings 3 and 4 should be 3/32" above the plate, and the other two fall in-between.

* Pickup height refers to the gap between the string and pickup when the string is pressed at the last fret
** String height measured at the 17th fret
*** Nut action measured from bottom of string to top of first fret

 most Strats, the tremolo claw is in the approximate correct adjustment range when you have around a 21/32" to 5/8" clearance between the claw and the cavity wall. Once the springs get to the right tension, they take control of the bridge and the wooden block loosens (no longer "blocking" the trem-olo), and pulls right out. You're done! The block will loosen at the *exact* moment the springs come into play.

If you've done everything correctly, you should have a great-playing Strat! If you didn't fine-tune the intonation after Step 9, do it now or play it the way it is (the factory's "rough" setting is actually quite close).

Electric Bass Setup

Although the eight-step setup just mentioned applies to both guitars *and* basses (and not just Fender basses), here's some more setup info just for bass players. I borrowed this from the pages of *Bass Player* magazine.

The electric bass has come a long way since Leo Fender introduced the Precision Bass in late 1951. You might say the electric bass has come of age, with companies such as Pedulla, Tobias, Steinberger, Modulus Graphite, Ken Smith, Alembic, and others *specializing* in electric 4-strings and offering extremely high-quality 5-strings, 6-strings, headless, fretless, and other models as well.

Bryan Galloup using the neck jig

A neck jig is a big help in fretting and setting up the electric bass.

Bass players have evolved along with the instrument, with a whole new range of percussive and/or melodic styles of playing. Now more than ever, proper setup is the key to getting the best bass for the buck. When your bass is set up properly, it means that the nut, bridge, and neck have been adjusted to obtain the best action possible for your playing style and choice of string gauge. With a little practice, you should be able to make most of these adjustments yourself. Here's an outline for getting your bass to play its best, followed by a description of the important steps:

1 Install the strings you prefer. If the bass is new, play it awhile to get the feel of its action.
2 Sight the neck; look for straightness or relief.
3 Make basic neck adjustments before adjusting the nut or bridge.
4 Adjust the bridge and nut together.
5 Re-check the neck adjustment.
6 Adjust the pickup height.

With Fender slab-style necks that have no headstock angle, install the strings with enough downward wraps to create good pressure on the nut. Basses with angled headstocks require fewer wraps to achieve good down pressure. Expect to go through several sets of strings until you find what's right for you. Begin with the manufacturer's string recommendation, and go from there. These basics may help you choose a set:

■ String tension is important. Equal tension from string to string gives a balance that feels right to both the fingering and plucking hands. For hard-to-adjust necks or those that tend to have up-bow, choose a light-gauge, low-tension string. Within a given gauge (regular, medium, light, etc.), flat-wound strings have the highest tension, half-rounds the second highest, and round-wounds the least tension.

■ Round-wound strings are bright in tone and easy to intonate, but cause finger squeaks. They have the most fret buzz.

■ Flat-wounds eliminate finger squeaks, but trade off tone and brightness. They're harder to intonate, but have a good ol' upright sound.

■ Half-rounds combine flat and round shapes into a string with low finger noise, decent brightness, and good intonation.

■ Core-contact (or "taper-core") strings have an exposed *core* that contacts the saddle rather than the outer string wraps. Some bassists feel that these are easier to intonate.

■ If you're a 5-stringer looking for the optimum low-*B* string, D'Addario's Jim Rickard, noted expert on all matters related to guitar design and construction, recommends a .145" gauge.

String height at the nut is critical. If the nut's string slots are too deep or the nut itself is too low, the heaviest strings are sure to buzz against the 1st fret. With a little luck, after any neck adjustments are made, you'll still have a nut that's slightly tall, allowing you the option of lowering the strings a bit. But if the strings are too *low* at the nut, have a new nut made or the original shimmed. Removing a nut without breaking it can be difficult, so leave this work to a professional.

Measure string height at the nut between the bottom of the strings and the top of the fret. A *low* action measurement taken this way would read: *E*–.035", *A*–.030", *D*–.025", *G*–.025". When I make a new nut, I stop lowering the strings at .050" on the *E* and at .030" for the *A*, *D*, and *G*. From that point I prefer to lower the strings gradually, with a customer's specific attack and playing style in mind.

Players with a strong attack, especially those using slap-style techniques that pull the string up and almost out of the nut slots, should use a fairly low-profile nut with string slots that aren't too deep. This way, the edges don't break off as the string is strained in its slot. From half to a third of a string's diameter is a good depth for the string slots. While bone is a preferred nut material for guitars and many basses, if your style is hard-hitting, stick to resilient plastic, graphite, or phenolic materials, which have a reduced chance of breaking.

Bridge adjustments aren't hard to make but are certainly no piece of cake, either. Expect to spend several hours getting things right, and if your first attempts aren't perfect, it's worth your while to keep on trying. A delicate balance exists between neck, nut, and bridge, and their combined effect determines your action. Bridge setup controls the height of the strings, matches the curve of the saddles to the fingerboard radius, and sets the intonation. Here are the basics:

■ String height is raised or lowered at the saddle by adjusting small set-screws with an Allen wrench or screwdriver.

■ Lengthwise saddle travel controls intonation. If a string notes sharp at the 12th-fret octave, move the saddle back away from the neck. If a note is flat, move the saddle forward toward the neck.

■ Matching the arch of the saddles to that of the fingerboard makes the action comfortable to both hands. A radius gauge for measuring fingerboard and bridge comparisons is a handy setup tool.

■ For low action and the least fret rattle, combine these approaches: 1) Get the neck as straight as possible with very low action, and then eliminate any buzz by loosening the truss rod to add relief. 2) Straighten the neck and then eliminate buzz by raising the bridge inserts. Once you see the effect of both methods, *combine* them for the best action and least buzzing.

■ Remember that some buzz between metal strings and metal frets is normal.

String height measurements vary from manufacturer to manufacturer. I discussed bass setup particulars with a panel of experts: Michael Tobias, Ken Smith, Roger Sadowski, M.V. Pedulla's Brett Carlson, and Bob Malone at Alembic. All of their string height measurements are between the bottom of the string and the top of the fret, and here's what they had to say:

Michael Tobias: "We never measure, because each bass is different. But our setups *start out* with ⅛" at the last fret all the way across, following the fingerboard radius (15" to 17"). This gives a height of 1/16" to 3/32" at the 12th fret. When you press a string at the 3rd fret, it should clear the 1st fret by .010" or .012". No bass will play without some relief. As a measure, hold down a string at the 1st and 15th frets—you're using the string as a straightedge—and adjust the neck until, at the 8th fret, you can just slide a Fender thin pick in between the string bottom and fret top; that's

your relief. Our stock strings are private label in .040", .060", .080", and .100" gauges."

Ken Smith: "I use taper-core Ken Smith strings on all but the *G* string, in gauges of .044", .063", .084", and .106". You must have relief, between 1mm and 2mm at the 9th fret, even up to 1/16" at times. Really, all basses must be set up on an individual basis. I don't actually measure string height at the nut, but prefer an action where a player can depress a string without having to press hard, and with no buzzing on an open string. I consider a *low* height at the 12th fret to be 1/16" all the way across."

Roger Sadowski: "I shoot for a mostly straight neck with a *little* relief, and prefer a string gauge of .045", .065", .080", .105". My standard setup is for the string height at the 12th fret to be on the fat side of 5/64" for the *G*, and 3/32" for the *E*—measured from the bottom of the string to the top of the fret."

Brett Carlson: "We use relief, except on fretless models—with those we get the neck perfectly straight. Our relief, measured by holding down a string at the 1st and last frets, is set at .015". String height at the first fret is .025" under each string, and at the 12th fret I shoot for 3/32" under the *G* and 5/32" under the *E*. All our nuts are brass, so we don't have a problem with the string slots breaking. Our standard strings are D'Addario round-wounds in the .045", .065", .080", and .100" gauges." (Brett's .015", by the way, is a *slight* relief.)

Bob Malone: "In a setup you can't go beyond what you have to work with. It all comes down to how straight you can get that neck. If you can get it straight to begin with, then your setup can go from there. I like a very slight relief, but I don't measure it; it's all by feel. For nut height, when a string is pressed at the 3rd fret, it should just barely touch the 1st fret. Alembic basses are built with brass nuts."

Finish up by adjusting the pickup height to suit your tastes (just don't raise them so high that the strings either slap against them, or get pulled into the upper frets by the magnets). Remember that none of us learned these tricks overnight, so be patient.

That's it! If you've followed these basic setup

Bass necks are the hardest of all to adjust, keep straight, and refret. They're so long, it's hard to expect a truss rod to keep all that straight.

tips, you've also encountered most Strat, Tele, and Fender Bass problems, eliminating them as you went along. Problems other than these and certain custom modifications—even fret work—can involve altering a vintage instrument. In cases like this, the choice is yours. There is certainly no disputing the fact that collectors of vintage Strats want them as mint and untouched as possible, and some are broken-hearted if you've even blown the dust off the pickups or from under the bridge saddles. So you could drastically affect the value of your guitar by performing anything other than stock maintenance. If in doubt, contact a pro, and basically don't remove from, or add anything to, a vintage piece without first getting permission.

Special thanks to Jim Werner, who was extremely helpful in steering me toward many of the repairmen and collectors contacted on the subject of Strats. If you're interested in Jim's list of Fender instrument serial number and neck dates, contact him at R.R. 1, Box 236, Letts, IA 52754. Jim works hard to preserve the past, and we can all thank him by sending him any information on Fender instrument serial numbers, neck dates, models, colors, and other pertinent features that help date an instrument to a specific era.

Fender Guitar Neck Profiles

Here are two articles that ran in *Guitar Player* and *Bass Player* magazines respectively, that will tell you all you need to know about the shape of bolt-on necks. Fender set the standards for bolt-on neck guitars. If you look around the industry you'll find that every manufacturer copies the depth, width, and "feel" of Fender necks (many would copy the peghead shape too, if they could get away with it). Understanding the cross-sectional shape, or "profile," of Fender necks will help you choose an instrument—new or used.

TALKING NECK SHAPE AT THE CUSTOM SHOP

During a visit to the Fender factory and Custom Shop in Corona, California, I *finally* understood the terminology used to describe Fender neck shapes (or "profiles"), something you must know when buying a guitar. A neck's shape, front-to-back thickness, and fingerboard width determine whether or not the guitar feels good to *your* hand and style.

LETTER-STAMP DESIGNATIONS

Many different terms, such as "boatneck," "V," "oval," and A, B, C, and D designations, have been used to describe Fender necks. Custom Shop master builder Jay Black helps clear up the mysteries: "The letters A, B, C, or D that were stamped on the end of necks from the early '60s until around 1973 refer to neck *width* at the nut—not shape. So when people say they've got a 'C' neck—referring to its shape—they're wrong, although early-'60s Fender necks *are* somewhat C-shaped in profile. But we call that 'oval.' The *only* letters we use when talking shape are 'U'—the shape of that real early '51 to '53 Tele—and 'V' for the triangulated shape. Neither of these letters were ever stamped anywhere on a Fender neck. The corresponding nut widths for the old letters are: A=1 ½", B=1 ⅝", C=1 ¾", and D=1 ⅞". Currently, all production vintage necks have the B nut width, while the American Standard is slightly wider, falling between the B and C measurements at around 1 ¹¹⁄₁₆". In the Custom Shop, we'll make anything you want."

"Boatneck," an archaic term used for describing certain neck profiles, is a misnomer because it's been used by too many people in too many ways. As Jay explains, "When Fred Stuart, one of our master builders, uses the word boatneck, he's referring to the older Martins, Washburns, and many big V-necked guitars, so we're trying to drop the word from our vocabulary. But if you *have* to use the word boatneck, you'd be talking about a #4 or a #1056 neck."

THE FIVE BASIC GUITAR NECK SHAPES (PLUS ONE)

Due to the use of less-sophisticated machinery and subsequent hand-shaping, old Fender neck profiles are so subtle in their differences that it would be virtually impossible to produce them all. So Fender has agreed upon five basic "generic" neck shapes based on specs from the '50s and '60s. "Today's production necks are made from specific templates on machinery that is very consistent," Jay Black explains. "This is especially helpful with production models because the neck on any new SRV model will be identical in feel to Stevie's 'Number One.'

"Right now the Custom Shop will shape any neck that a customer requests, but most players want one of the five basic shapes. By using these generic shapes as a reference point, we can cover everything from 1950 all the way up to '62. Anything other than that is usually made from an oversize blank and hand-shaped to what the customer wants, using the five shapes as a means of communicating with the customer. Some players have a qualified local luthier measure a favorite neck and send us the specs to work from."

PRODUCTION NECK SHAPES

Here are Fender's basic neck shapes:

No. 1. Essentially a round, chunky, '53 Tele shape—the "U" shape, with lots of shoulder.

No. 2. Also called the "54" or "soft V," it has *some* shoulder, but less than No. 1. It's not quite as deep from the top of the fingerboard to the back of the neck, but it's still a fairly chunky neck. Vintage '54 necks varied quite a bit. Eric Johnson's '54 Strat has one of the smallest front-to-back dimensions Jay's seen.

No. 3. The 1960 and '62 "oval" shape. Thinner, front to back, at the 1st fret than at the 12th, it has a very oval (or you *could* say "C"-shaped) bottom. "We can alter the No. 3 to produce the '63 or '64," says Jay. "This is a slightly beefier version of the same shape, except the 1st-fret dimension becomes thicker by .030" or .040"."

No. 4. Different from the large, soft No. 2, this is a "hard V" that's .030" thinner front to back. You'll find this neck on Strats from late '56 and '57.

No. 5. The contemporary "heavy metal" style neck. Not used too often, it's similar to the '80s necks on Jackson, Charvel, Ibanez, and other models. It's a much flatter, very non-traditional

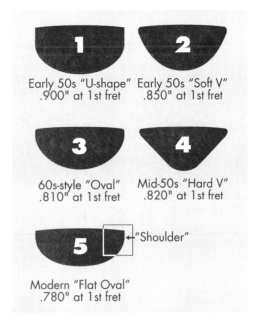

1 — Early 50s "U-shape" .900" at 1st fret
2 — Early 50s "Soft V" .850" at 1st fret
3 — 60s-style "Oval" .810" at 1st fret
4 — Mid-50s "Hard V" .820" at 1st fret
5 — Modern "Flat Oval" .780" at 1st fret — ←"Shoulder"

neck, and its shape changes as the trend changes.

No. 1056 (not pictured). Patterned from a "10-56" neck (referring to October, 1956), this is a very big V neck. '56 necks generally had a small V, but they made plenty of chunky ones too. "If anything could be called a boatneck," says Jay, "it would be this."

MORE ABOUT NECK SHAPES

Fender Custom Shop builders John Page, Jay Black, and Larry Brooks went on to answer some other questions that I had.

Are most Fender Strat necks based on one of the five basic "generic" shapes?

John Page: Yes. With modern machinery and setup techniques, we can alter the patterns slightly to make one model quite different from another—consistently. So one pattern can be responsible for a variety of shapes. Our most popular Custom Shop neck shape is the #3, and most production necks are based on that pattern too. Our model "1962" Strat has a neck based on the #3 pattern, but with a slight alteration in dimension from top to bottom to make it thinner and different-feeling from the American Standard or SRV models, which are also made from the #3 pattern. The American Standard Strat, designed by Dan Smith, is a #3 variant that's wider at the nut and has a little more shoulder (the area from the fretboard edge to about a third of the way down either side of the neck).

Above: Larry Brooks with SRV signature Strat.
At right: Art Esparza, Steve Boulanger, Ralph Esposito, Fred Stuart, Dan Erlewine, Jay Black, Yasuhiko Iwanade, Larry Brooks, John Page.

Larry Brooks: The "Stevie Ray" also starts with a #3 pattern, but we flattened the fretboard radius from the vintage 7 ¼" to a 12" curve, which removed some of the fretboard's thickness and changed its feel. And we added a little more meat to the shoulder to fatten it up—more like a '63 or '64 vintage Strat. Stevie wanted a Custom Shop Strat to take the place of "Number One," which had been broken too many times. The neck shape was critical, especially the "round-over" (edge of the rosewood fretboard in the shoulder area). It had to be smooth, polished, and as worn-feeling as the original.

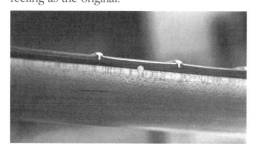

Do production SRV models have that worn round-over?

Brooks: They are machine-shaped like Number One's worn shoulder, but without the hand-shaped and polished vintage round-over along the fretboard. Not every customer would want that worn, vintage round-over, since it removes wood and reduces the neck's dimension and longevity. I did shape it on Stevie's, though. You could take a new SRV model to a good luthier and have the edges smoothed and rounded-over quite easily.

Why did Stevie want a 12" fretboard radius, when Number One was made with the 7¼"?

Brooks: Rene Martinez, Stevie's guitar tech of many years, had refretted Number One so often that the fingerboard evolved into the flatter 12" radius, a result of minor sanding and leveling of the board when the frets were removed. A flatter radius means less noting-out during bends, and Stevie liked that. And Stevie had played—and enjoyed—Bonnie Raitt's brown Strat, which also has a 12" radius. So he requested a 12" radius and the tall Dunlop #6105 fretwire. Rene sent the guitar back to us after Stevie's death so that we could get the production model exactly right.

Jay Black: The Eric Clapton model's neck shape combines the #2 and #4 patterns. It's as large as the #2, but with a little more "V" like the #4. It has a 9 ½" radius for easier blues bending and is fretted with a thin vintage-style wire measuring .085" wide by .045" tall—much like Stewart-MacDonald's #148 fretwire." (Author's note: All Custom Shop and American Standard products feature a 9 ½" radius fretboard. The only Fender guitars currently being built with the old-style 7 ¼" radius are the '62 and '57 vintage Strats and the '52 vintage Tele. In fact, Jay Black says that over the past four years and 500 guitars, he's only had three customer requests for vintage 7 ¼" radius necks. The 9 ½" radius is a nice compromise for most players.)

I've played fatter '50s necks that seemed to have more shoulder on the bass side, and almost none on the treble.

Black: Because of the amount of hand-shaping done back then, you'll find some old Fenders with an asymmetrical shape. That extra shoulder gives good support to some hands. It's often a real help to sufferers of carpal tunnel syndrome. A hard "V" on the bass side doesn't please a player with carpal tunnel, whereas the chunky shoulder supports the hand.

Fender bass neck profiles

A bass neck's shape (or profile) is as important as good fretwork in determining whether or not a bass feels good, plays well, and suits your style. To better understand Fender Page (again), the head of Fender's Custom Shop and

R&D department. He directed me to the neck specialists on his staff: senior R&D engineer George Blanda, and Custom Shop master builders Jay Black, Mark Kendrick, Fred Stuart, and Yasuhiko Iwanade. Yasuhiko, in turn, introduced me to his friend and "bass mentor," Albert Molinaro of Guitars R Us in Hollywood. Among the seven of them, there's not much about the Fender bass that isn't known!

THE FOUR BASIC SHAPES

Fender recently specified four basic neck shapes for bass, based on specs from the '50s and '60s (chart, page 42). Any Fender neck—whether it's vintage, production, or custom-made—relates somehow to these shapes. In one of several conversations, Fender's Jay Black reminded me that "the four shapes didn't exist during the vintage years, but we realized that the neck builders in both production and the Custom Shop needed to be speaking the same language. And since the Custom Shop will make almost any neck you want, it was even more important to set shape standards for communicating with our customers. So we selected the four most popular neck shapes, ones that would cover everything from the '50s through the '60s—the necks made later were simply variations. The satisfaction of our bass-playing customers proves that we chose the right shapes."

A BRIEF HISTORY OF THE BASS

Yasuhiko Iwanade (his friends call him Yas) handbuilt the '51 Precision reissues made by the Custom Shop in 1991, a short "production" run of 82 instruments. He even hand-wound each pickup! Word is that it couldn't have been done better by anyone, and that Yas is an acknowledged expert on Fender history—basses in particular.

Yas got to know Leo Fender himself before Leo's death in 1991, and he told me what the company's founder explained to him about the early days. "Even though the same cutters were used to shape both guitar and bass necks, the shape of guitar necks and bass necks made even on the same day in 1954 would be quite different from one another," Yas notes. "This is because P-Bass necks are wider than guitar necks, and the machine's cutter couldn't reach as far toward the center

of the back of a bass neck. Therefore it carved them differently.

"Of the four generic profiles" continues Yas, "the neck shapes that most Fender bass players talk about are the round or U-shape, the soft-V, and the oval. I've seen only a few hard-V bass necks, but you should ask Albert Molinaro about them."

Yasuhiko Iwanade

Albert has a collection of 75 vintage Fender basses, so I checked in with him next. "Fender set the standards for neck shapes that bass guitar manufacturers worldwide would follow," notes Albert. "As they went through the '50s, the necks evolved from big, round, and chunky to flat, wide, and smooth—possibly to accommodate the changes in music. There definitely were hard-V necks on basses, although I haven't seen many. I have two of them, both made in 1957 (photo at right). I don't like the feel of them too much, though—they're too skinny."

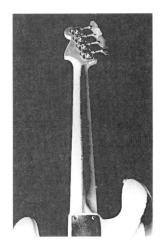

Yas and Albert compared notes to decide what to call two other profiles (not from the "generic four") that were used during the '70s and early '80s. "Both shapes are simply variations of the round, or U, profile," explains Albert, "with the later bass having a sharper round-over."

STILL HANDMADE

"Handmade" is a term often used to describe a quality musical instrument. With the use of more sophisticated machinery and the four standard shapes to control consistency, I wondered if the handwork that made the old necks special had become a lost art. George Blanda works closely with production, so I asked him: *George, is there any hand-shaping on production necks today?*

"In essence," he responded, "our necks *are* handmade, when you get down to the details. The machines remove everything but the critical few thousandths of an inch that are still done by hand. All transitional areas, such as the headstock, butt, and fretboard wrap-around—any place where a machine cutter enters or exits the wood—are still finished by hand. In other words, the things that really give the neck its feel are done by hand. In fact, neck-shaping is one of the most important positions in our guitar factory. We use the most experienced employees; many have worked here for twenty years or more. The machinery just gives these skilled people a more consistent piece to start with.

"Currently all production P-Basses have the B [1⅝"] nut width, except for the Vintage Precision reissues, which have the C [1¾"] width. And Yas is right about the oval profile being the most popular shape—it has now become the standard shape for *all* production bass necks, including the Vintage Precision reissue. The Jazz Bass, whether a Vintage reissue or contemporary, still has the A [1½"] width, and it never strayed from the oval shape, even in the '70s and '80s, when the Precision changed. A player wanting the old U, V, or other shape can contact the Custom Shop."

BASS FUTURES

I asked George Blanda and Fred Stuart about the future direction of the Fender bass. "The Urge (Stuart Hamm model) represents our current thinking on bass design," said George. "It began as a Custom Shop project; as it developed, there was a lot of excitement, and production got involved.

"It's good for us to do new things. It was always true that if you could have only one bass it had to be a Fender, and we'd like to keep it that way. We recognize the requirements modern music places on electric bass, and we're offering instruments to fill that need. Take the P-Bass and J-Bass Plus instruments—these basses are very reminiscent of their predecessors, but they have 22 frets, downsized bodies, and Lace Sensor pickups. We knew that players who didn't play our traditional basses tended toward smaller

instruments, so we responded to that."

Fred Stuart has made lots of basses at the Custom Shop. "Most of them have been left-handed ones," he says. "The typical left-handed bass player is buying a Fender for the historical significance: perhaps he had a P-Bass back in the '60s and wants to recapture that. Being a lefty makes it that much harder to find a bass on the vintage market, and Fender isn't offering the Vintage P-Bass or J-Bass reissues for lefties. We've gotten so many orders we even have a standard price for a left-handed bass ordered through the Custom Shop.

"The Jazz Bass and Precision have their own sounds—and that's what many people are looking for. When they think of a contemporary bass they don't always think of Fender, but perhaps they should. I guess it's just a matter of time—we need to let people know what we've got and that we're serious about it. At this point, we've got a lot of the elements in place for reaching a new market, so a first-time bass player who doesn't go for the Jazz or Precision can still start out with a Fender bass. There's something special about that!"

Many thanks to Albert Molinaro of Guitars R Us, 7404 Sunset Blvd., Hollywood, CA 90046; (213) 874-8221. Albert was a big help as I was writing this article, and he loaned us the beautiful photographs of basses in his collection.

THE EVOLUTION OF THE FENDER BASS NECK

Fender has changed the shape of its bass necks five times over the years. Here's how Yasuhiko Iwanade of the Custom Shop charts the development:

Early '50s: U shape. Round and chunky.

Mid-'50s: Soft-V shape. That is, a more rounded V than the hard V, which had a pronounced ridge down the center. Some hard-V necks are found on basses from late '56 and into '57, but they're quite rare.

Late-'50s to Mid-'60s: Oval shape. These were the widest of all Fender P-Bass necks: 1¾" at the nut. The depth (thickness) was reduced considerably, so they feel very flat and wide. Although the Jazz Bass, which first appeared during this era, shared the same oval shape, it feels more like a U in the lower positions due to its narrow (1½") nut. The oval

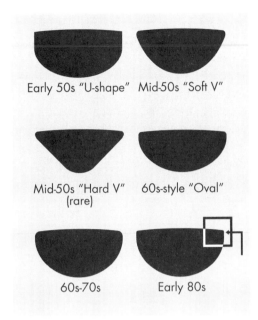

Early 50s "U-shape"   Mid-50s "Soft V"

Mid-50s "Hard V" (rare)   60s-style "Oval"

60s-70s   Early 80s

is the most popular of all Fender bass necks.

Late '60's through '70s: A variation of the original U shape—narrower than the '60s oval necks, not quite as chunky as the early-'50s U shape and with no hint of a V.

Early '80s: Very similar to the '70s U variation just mentioned, but sharper on the fingerboard edge, or "round-over." The early '80s necks became very wide again, reminiscent of the early '60s P-Bass but with a different shape.

1985: All bass necks returned to the oval shape—still used in production today.

Acoustic guitar setup using factory specs

The measurements about to be given apply to all Gibson flat-tops made from the 1930's to the mid-'60s, and for those made in Montana from 1990 until the present—the eras when Gibson made (or makes) great flat-tops. I "skip" the late '60s, the '70s and '80s because those were not the best years for Gibson flat-tops, and many flat-tops (not all) made during that era did not, and could not, conform to these "factory specs." If you'd like to understand why, and learn more about Gibson flat-top history, read the book *"Gibson's Fabulous Flat-Top Guitars—An Illustrated History & Guide"*

written by Eldon Whitford, David Vinopal, and myself (published by Miller Freeman Books).

GIBSON FLAT-TOPS

"Gibson Montana," the company's new acoustic guitar division, was established in Bozeman, Montana in 1989. There in Bozeman, Gibson is building even better flat-tops than during the "Glory Years" of the 1930s—and that's saying a lot! The following measurements came by way of Ren Ferguson, a master builder and head of Gibson Montana's "Custom Shop." Ren, and his right-hand man John Walker are the builders responsible for resurrecting Gibson's flat-top heritage. These factory specs apply to all good Gibson flat-tops. The "Mine" specs are taken from an original, well broken-in 1940 J-35, and reflect the lowest "normal" action you'd expect from a well set-up Gibson flat-top played by an acoustic, not an electric, player. Two acoustic checkpoints which weren't needed for an electric are: 1) "saddle protrusion," or the amount of saddle height above the top of

Factory Specs For Gibson Flattops

Maximum neck relief at 7th to 9th fret	Factory	Mine
On all strings:	.012"	.004"

String height at 12th fret	Factory	Mine
On the bass E string:	6/64"	4/64"
On the treble E string:	4/64"	2-1/2/64"

String height at the nut

These measurements differ from Gibson's Nashville electric setups. The strings are left somewhat high so that final adjustment to suit the customer can be made by the music dealer after the sale. Measured from the bottom of a string to the top of the 1st fret with a feeler gauge, the strings are factory-set to .030". On my guitar, the treble side is .012", and the strings follow a radius to the bass side: .020".

Bridge saddle protrusion

The saddle should have from 1/8" to 1/4" showing above the top of the bridge at its highest point (the saddle will vary in height because of its radius). I consider 1/4" to be the *absolute limit* in saddle height for any acoustic guitar, and 3/16" is a better limit. My J-35 measures 7/32".

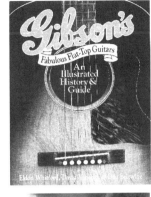

Ren Ferguson

John Walker

the bridge (because a good string angle over the saddle is important to achieve tone and power), and 2) the thickness of the bridge.

I always prefer as straight a neck as possible—especially on flat-tops. That isn't to say *you* won't need, shouldn't try, or won't like, relief. But experiment with getting the neck perfectly straight first. If there are no buzzes, and you like the feel, cool. If you've got problems with string buzz, *slowly* add relief until you're happy.

OBSERVATIONS (AND OPINIONS) ABOUT GIBSON FLAT-TOPS

■ Vintage Gibsons, unknown to some, have become as highly prized by many of us as Martins. Be careful what jobs you attempt on them until you know what you're doing—less is better.

■ The Gibson 12" fretboard radius is a good average between the vintage 7 ¼" Fender and the 16" Martin.

■ For me, the short-scale Gibsons make better blues guitars than their long-scale models.

■ Most older Gibsons (1930s until the late 1950s) seldom need neck resets.

■ It's common for a Gibson to have loose braces, and as a rule, the top and back braces of vintage instruments are not tucked deeply into the "kerfing," or lining that connects the sides to the top and back. Because of this, the braces often come loose, especially toward the ends (this allows the top or back to crack).

■ Gibsons don't normally have the severe "bellying" problems around the bridge sometimes found in other steel-string guitars. Instead, Gibson flat-tops usually have a graceful arch in the top, until the early '60s (from the '60s until 1983, Gibson tops have shown a considerably higher percentage of loose bracings and top problems in the bridge area).

■ The interior structure, design, and bracing of Gibson flat-tops made during the "bad" years mentioned above can be horrendous (huge plywood bridge plates, enormous braces, sloppy work, warped tops, horrible neck sets, impossible action, and poor tone are just some of the symptoms).

■ Most great Gibson flat-tops, with the exception of several models like the Advanced Jumbo and the SJ-200 (J-200), and certain Hummingbirds made during the 1960s, have short (24 ¾") scales. The short-scale "Great Gibson Flat-tops" I'm referring to include (to name just a few) the L-0, L-00, Jumbo, J-35, J-45, S-J, J-50, and others. Although the bodies of the "Jumbo" or "J"-models are comparable in size to the Martin dreadnaughts, the string length isn't. So don't expect them to play like, or sound like, long-scale guitars. For playability, compare these guitars (if you must) to the short-scale (24.9") Martin "0," "00," and "000" models. Even then you can't compare the two guitars since the Gibson has a larger box! It's important to understand this when trying to relate to a customer, or if you're looking to buy an axe.

■ Gibson is making better flat-tops now than ever before—thanks to the guys shown here.

Larry English, Gary Burnette, Ren Ferguson, and Robi Johns.

MARTIN FLAT-TOPS

It's not true that "Only A Gibson Is Good Enough." In 1961 I bought my first really good flat-top guitar—a Martin 00-28 K. It was a lovely guitar made from Koa-wood, a type of curly mahogany that grows in Hawaii. Since that time I've owned at least 30 Martins and loved them all. To this day I'd hate to have to choose between my Gibson J-35 and my old D-18. I just couldn't do it. They're different guitars and I play differently on each of them.

For playing some of the old country music which I love (tunes by the Stanley Brothers, Louvin Brothers, the Blue Sky Boys, and of course Bill Monroe), I prefer the long scale, the tight crisp tone, the definite volume, and that

Jim Trach records in the log as Ellsworth Bush makes the interior inspection.

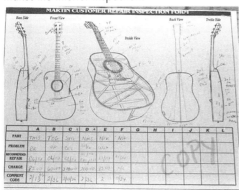

Martin repair log.

certain country sound of a Martin Dreadnaught. If money weren't an object, I'd own many different Martins (my dream is to someday custom-order a 12-fret OOO-45). As it is, though, I always seem to settle on a D-18. I like mahogany, I guess.

Martin guitars are set up a little differently than Gibsons. If you're looking at getting into the guitar repair business and you happen to be a Gibson lover, or don't know much about Martins, don't ever set up a Martin like a Gibson (or vice-versa)—you'll lose a customer! Notice that the C.F. Martin factory has several actual "check-points" for jobs which Gibson either does by eye, or has no written measurement for (note also that Martin lists measurements differently than Gibson). Some of the following

Martin Factory Specs

Maximum neck relief at 7th to 9th fret	Factory	Mine
On all strings:	.010"	.005"

String height at 12th fret	Factory
On the bass E string:	3/32"min~ 7/64"max
On the treble E string:	1/16"min~ 5/64"max

String height at the nut	Factory
Measured from the bottom of a string to the top of the first fret.	Bass E: .024"max Treble E: .016"min

Bridge thickness	Factory
	5/15", 11/32" or 3/8"

Bridge saddle protrusion	Factory
	3/32"min~ 3/16"max

Bridge saddle shape

The radius of a Martin bridge saddle is slightly flatter than the fretboard, and the saddle rises gradually in height toward the bass side to eliminate buzzes on the bass strings.

String inset	Factory
Distance between edge of fingerboard and the *outside* of both E strings.	3/32" ± .016"

Bridge pin height

All pins must be a uniform height above the bridge surface, and measured from bottom of the "ring," must be .032"min~.062"max.

String installation

Bass side strings passed throught the string hole with string wound halfway around post under longer portion of string, bent backward over string, and wound counter-clockwise 2-3 wraps around post toward headplate. Follow same spec for treble strings with 3-4 wraps clockwise around the post.

adjustments, such as bridge pin height, would never be incorrect on a *new* Martin because they're an integral part of final inspection. But you may need to make adjustments on numerous used instruments, especially if they've had a replacement bridge installed by an untrained hand.

Some modern builders use American Flyer sled runners for T-bar replacement, since Martin's T-bar is no longer available.

OBSERVATIONS (AND OPINIONS) ABOUT MARTIN GUITARS

■ The fretboard radius will vary from 16" to 20". A 16" radius is most common.

■ The action will go lower than the factory specs if the frets are properly levelled.

■ Because of the flatter fretboard radius, Martins may not feel as comfortable as instruments with more arch in the fretboard do when you play chords. However, many players feel that you can get more power without buzzing on a Martin than on a Gibson, because of the flatter board.

■ Models made before 1985 do not have an adjustable truss rod. Certainly the newer Martins with adjustable rods are easier to set up than the old ones. I still prefer the old "T"-bar Martins (pre-1969) for stiffness and tone.

■ Martins seem to need neck resets more often than Gibsons (especially vintage pieces of the same era). Do not try to account for an underset neck by planing the fretboard or whittling down the bridge on vintage instruments!

■ Instruments made between 1969 and 1985, with hollow "square tube" truss rods, often develop more up-bow than the older instruments (see the Fretting chapter).

■ A "bellied" top (an arch in the top around the bridge) is not necessarily *bad*. Most flat-top guitars are supposed to have a nice gradual arch in that area since the top is *built* with an arch in it. Do not hasten to "flatten" the top, or let someone talk you into it.

■ A slight "bubble," or rise in the top behind the bridge, and a dip in the front, is not uncommon with Martins. It isn't normally severe enough to warrant serious interior structural work such as bridge pad replacement—but can be in extreme cases. Severe kinks are often caused by loose bracing (especially the X-bracing in the bridge pad area).

■ I think the Martin company is too generous to their customers by offering a lifetime warranty on an object made of wood. Many owners take advantage of the warranty by expecting Martin to repair problems that are caused by nature or neglect. Martin, however, is unfailing about taking care of their customers. Give them a word of thanks sometime—they deserve it!

A final note on setups: With any guitar, electric or acoustic, after all adjustments are made, I will often straighten the neck completely (if it's adjustable) and see how the guitar plays with a straight neck. I generally prefer a straight—or almost straight—neck to one with relief.

3 PRO SETUPS

Low action and the blues

During all my years spent repairing and setting up guitars, low action without buzzing seems to be what most customers are after (at least electric players). Somehow, electric players get it into their heads that the strings should be close to the frets—*real* close—and they expect this low action without buzzing. Always a blues player, even when blues wasn't as mainstream as it is today, I've tried to convince customers that by having the action a little higher, they could get better bends and more sustain, and make the guitar sing. But often customers would misinterpret this as a cop-out on my part because I couldn't (or wouldn't) give them the low action they thought they should have.

I realize that there are many guitarists whose style requires low action in order to execute certain passages fast enough. And many hot country pickers that *don't* do much string-bending can have a slightly lower action than players that do bend. But more often than not, when you get the rare chance to play a top professional's axe, you'll find the action higher, and the strings stiffer, than you might have guessed. I believe that this is because more players today incorporate blues styles—in particular the singing blues bends made famous by B.B King and Albert King—into their playing. Where would Jeff Beck or Stevie Ray Vaughn's music be without the blues? What made Eric Clapton and Cream famous? How did Hendrix drive crowds wild? With certain traditional jazz guitarists as an exception, I don't know of many great guitarists who can't, and don't, play the blues; and players like Eric Johnson, Vernon Reid, and Steve Morse have taken blues to new heights. None of them are wimps, and neither is their action.

With this in mind, I took advantage of every opportunity to check out the setups of some of the world's great blues players. These interviews ran in *Guitar Player* over a period of several years.

Stevie Ray Vaughan and Jeff Beck

Great guitarists have the ability to make their instruments talk. Doing so takes a special gift, a lifetime of practice, and a great guitar. Haven't you always hoped that the guitar had *something* to do with it? Wouldn't you guess that a great player's guitar is set up to play really well? If you're like me, you'd like to know just how their guitars are set up (and I don't mean simply with what gauge of strings, or whether the action is high or low). You wonder how *their* guitars might feel in *your* hands. Would you play better?

In November 1989, I had a chance to try out the guitars of Jeff Beck and Stevie Ray Vaughan when these great guitarists played the Ohio Center in Columbus. I was anxious to see how their guitars would measure up to my expectations. Then I decided to do just that—measure them—so that you, too, would have a chance to adjust, set up, and compare the feel of your guitar to those of these top players.

Before the show, I spent the day with Jeff's and Stevie's guitar techs—Geoff Banks from Witley, England, and Rene Martinez of Denton, Texas, respectively. Geoff has worked with Trevor Rabin of Yes, Robert Plant, and most recently Jeff Beck, Phil Collins, and Genesis. Rene honed his skills for years as a repairman for both Charley's Guitars and Zack's Guitars in Dallas. I was interested in the simple but subtle setup and action adjustments—the everyday stuff of being a tech for a guitar mogul. Of course, I was all ears for any other tips, tricks, and secrets Geoff or Rene might divulge. Here's what I found out:

Jeff and Stevie Ray were traveling with nine guitars, all of them Strats. Jeff's four included a yellow Vintage reissue model made by Fender's George Blanda in '86, as well as three custom-ordered Strat Plus models recently handcrafted and set up by ace guitar man Jay Black of the Fender Custom Shop. The Strat Plus models are equipped with Wilkinson nuts, Lace Sensor pickups, and the American

Rene Martinez using a Dremel Moto-Tool on Stevie Ray Vaughan's Number One.

Standard Tremolo, and are actually prototypes of a Jeff Beck Signature Model. One significant change is the size and shape of the neck. Jay Black notes: "Jeff wanted the biggest necks he could get—like baseball bats—so I patterned them after a 1935 Gibson L-5. Each neck is big, but different in size, shape, and feel. The seafoam green one, which Jeff favors, is an inch thick all the way down."

Stevie's guitars are all pre-'63 models, except for "Charley" (outfitted with the Danelectro "lipstick tube" pickups, it was made from kit parts at Charley's Guitar Shop in 1984). They all have names, too: Number One, Red, Butter Scotch, Charley, and Lennie. The only significant change from stock on these Strats has been the addition of 5-way switches and a good coat of shielding paint in the control cavities. Number One, the beat-up sunburst that we all know, is Stevie's main squeeze.

NECK ADJUSTMENT

With all the guitars, neck straightness is the first thing I checked, sighting down the fingerboard. A fingerboard should either be dead-flat or have a slight up-bow, known as relief, in the direction of the strings' pull. Stevie's guitar had approximately .012" of relief around the 7th and 9th frets, and then leveled out for the remainder of the board. Jeff's fingerboards are flat—adjusted straight as an arrow. Jay Black said, "I gave them a *little* relief, but .007" at the 7th fret would have been generous."

STRING GAUGE

Stevie tunes his guitar to *Eb* and uses GHS Nickel Rockers measuring .013, .015, .019 (plain), .028, .038, and .058. On this particular day, Rene had substituted an .011 for the high-*E* to keep down the sore fingers that blues bends can cause. Jeff performs his acrobatics exclusively on an Ernie Ball set gauged .009, .011, .016 (plain), .026, .036, .046. Both Geoff and Rene change strings every show for each guitar that gets played.

Geoff Banks strings up Jeff Beck's Strat while Dan takes measurements at the bridge.

PHOTOS: BRIAN BLAUSER, ATHENS, OH

FRETWIRE

If you're trying to evaluate action, it's nice to know what size and shape of fretwire is used. Number One's frets measure .110" wide by .047" tall. These frets would have started out at .055" tall when they were new, and were probably either Dunlop 6100 or Stewart-Mac-Donald 150 wire. Jeff Beck's frets aren't quite as big. According to Geoff Banks: "Jeff went with the Custom Shop's recommendation of a .098" wide by .050" tall fret. This is what Fender now makes as a 'vintage' wire, although it's taller than the wire used in the '50s and early '60s."

STRING HEIGHT

I measured the distance from the underside of the strings to the top of the fret at the 12th fret on both E strings. Rene Martinez describes, "I set up all of Stevie's the same: ⁵⁄₆₄" on the treble E string and ⁷⁄₆₄" at the bass E." Geoff Banks: "Actually, I don't measure them. I do it by feel, and what I know Jeff likes." (I measured slightly over ³⁄₆₄" on the treble side, and ⁵⁄₆₄" on the bass. Later, Jay Black told me: "I set them up at ³⁄₆₄" [treble] and ¼₆₄" [bass], but I did this with the string fretted at the 1st fret; I like to eliminate the nut when making this measurement."

FINGERBOARD RADIUS

Knowing the fingerboard's radius can help in setting up a comfortable bridge saddle height and curve. Stevie's Number One was somewhat flatter than the vintage 7¼" radius. Rene has refretted the neck at least twice, and in the process the fingerboard has *evolved* into a 9" or 10" radius in the upper register. This isn't the result of a purposeful attempt to create a compound radius, which allows string-bending with less noting-out; it just happened. Jeff's custom Strats have a compound radius, too, starting out with Fender's currently popular 9½" radius, but flattening out further on up the board. Jay Black hand-shaped them, and from about the 12th fret up they flatten out to an 11" radius.

BRIDGE SADDLES

The bridge saddles on Jeff's green custom Strat Plus were set at the Fender Custom Shop to the same 9½" radius as the fingerboard. The new-style Fender saddles are formed with a

Plastic tubes protect Stevie's strings from breaking.

Stevie's polepieces are highest on the bridge side.

His standard vintage tremolo uses all five springs.

No other guitar —not even the Les Paul—has been so popular for so long. I've been fixing the darn things for almost thirty years!

smooth groove to follow the string angle and support it gradually up to the point where the string takes off at the saddle's peak. While these saddles aren't overly prone to string-breaking, Jeff did manage to break a D and high-E string or two later that night. This was more a result of his exuberant attack, though, than evidence of any bridge saddle troubles.

Stevie's Number One, however, wants to break high-E and B strings at the saddle every chance she gets. Rene showed me why the strings break, and how he takes care of the problem: As a string comes out of the vintage Strat tremolo block/bridge top plate, it "breaks over"—or contacts—the metal directly; this causes a slight kink that weakens the string.

With the bridge saddles removed, Rene uses a Dremel Moto-Tool to grind the hole's edge until the lip is smooth and gradual, and any binding is eliminated.

Number One uses vintage replacement saddles (the originals wore out long ago), and they're not all alike—some have a shorter string slot than others. The high-E and B strings may contact the front edge of this string clearance slot as they rise toward the takeoff point at the saddle's peak. The kink formed by the contact stretches onto the saddle peak during tuning and breaks right at the crown. Rene elongates the slot, again by grinding, and then smooths any rough metal edges. Finally, he slides a ⅝"-long piece of plastic tubing (insulation from electrical wire) over each string to protect it from the metal break points. He uses the heaviest piece of tubing that still fits down into the tremolo block hole. Even with this, the high strings still cut through the plastic quickly, and strings break—sometimes in only one set. Rene plans to try a Teflon wire insulation if he can find the right size.

NUTS

Jeff's Vintage reissue has a standard Fender-style nut. The three custom Strats are set up with Fender/Wilkinson roller nuts, like those used on the Strat Plus. Stevie's Number One, Lennie, and Charley have standard Fender-style nuts, but Rene makes them from bone. Stevie prefers the sound of bone, although for studio work he had Rene make brass nuts for Scotch and Red.

TREMOLO SETUP

Measured at the rear of the tremolo plate, Jeff's American Standard Tremolo shows a healthy ³⁄₁₆" between the bottom of the plate and the guitar top. He uses three tremolo springs mounted in the two outer and one center hole in the tremolo block. The springs connect to the middle three fingers of the claw and are tensioned so that when he plays, say, the 3rd fret of the D string, it provides one whole-step if the bar is pulled up until it stops. His standard Vintage tremolo is mounted with all six screws and uses all five springs. It's tensioned so that the plate returns flat onto the top; I measured ⁷⁄₁₆" between the spring claw and the cavity wall where the claw is attached.

Rene prefers the durability of the stainless-steel Fender tremolo bars. He puts a small wad of cotton at the bottom of the tremolo block hole to keep the bar from over-tightening and becoming hard to remove if it breaks. He emphasizes the importance of lubricating all the moving parts of the tremolo system, preferring a powdered graphite-and-grease mixture (the grease holds the graphite in place where it's needed). He lubricates everything that moves: mounting screws/plate, all string breaks and contact points (including the saddle peaks) where the springs attach to the block and claw, the nut slots, and the string trees. Many other lubricants work: Vaseline, Magik Guitar Lube, Tef-Lube, etc.

PICKUP HEIGHT

As a reference point, I laid a precision steel straightedge along the frets for making this measurement. Jeff's Lace Sensors have little magnetic string pull, and therefore can be set quite close to the strings; in fact, they work best that way. On the treble side, the pickups were all within ³⁄₆₄" of the straightedge; on the bass side, they touched it.

Stevie's pickups were raised fairly high. I measured from the straightedge to the pole-piece tops: On the treble side, the bridge pickup touched the straightedge, the middle *almost* touched the straightedge, and the neck pickup was ¹⁄₁₆" away. The bass side measured ¹⁄₃₂" at the bridge pickup, ¹⁄₁₆" at the middle, and ¹⁄₃₂" at the neck.

TUNING MACHINES

We've covered about everything except tuners, and there's nothing secret here. Except for the yellow Vintage reissue, Jeff's Strats are equipped with either Sperzel or Schaller rear-locking tuners. Stevie Ray's tuners are the originals, and each has three full string winds for the best angle at the nut.

Well, that's the end of this story. You'll need an accurate 6" ruler to do the set-ups, and you can get one at any hardware store (General makes a good one). Don't be surprised if you go through a few sets of strings while you experiment. Good luck, and I thank Geoff and Rene for all of us! I had a lot of fun gathering this information, to say the least, and I hope you find it useful.

Setting up for slide: the Mooney innovations

If you're into slide but have never heard John Mooney, catch his act if he comes anywhere near your town. One of the few guitarists to master the true feeling of Delta slide guitar, the "Moonman" comes mighty close to capturing the Robert Johnson sound. John spent his late teens and early twenties learning firsthand from Son House. Now, after living in New Orleans for 15 years, he plays "second line blues," combining the best of the Delta style with the infectious rumba boogie and funk rhythms made famous by Professor Longhair and the Meters.

Recently John Mooney's Bluesiana (David Lee Watson on bass, Herman V. Ernest III on drums) visited Athens, Ohio, on their way to do the *Mountain Stage* radio show. I found that when it comes to guitars, John's a skilled do-it-yourselfer with some revolutionary ideas concerning slide setups for Strats. I wouldn't suggest these modifications for a vintage piece, but for newer Strats or the many copies, you could have some fun.

Onstage John uses two early-'50s National wood-bodied electric arch-tops, as well as two real Fender Strats (a white '65 and a seafoam-green '62 vintage reissue) and three extremely high-quality Japanese copies made by Artex. The Nationals have *great* tone, but at certain volumes they feed back too much (unusable feedback, that is, since John points out that some feedback is good for electric slide). He started using Strats because they're easy to travel with, they can take a beating, they make a great blues guitar, and they don't feed back.

Except for the '65, John has dramatically customized his standard vintage tremolo bridges. Using wood, bone, and fossil ivory, he either alters the metal bridge saddles or replaces them entirely. "The *typical* Strat sound is not what I'm after," he says. "Strats, with their metal bridge saddles, are just too tinny. There's not enough tone generated by the slide. I like a more woody sound. By using different combi-

nations of wood and bone at the bridge saddle, I capture enough of the National tone to keep me happy. A wood bridge adds warmth and a physical presence to the strings' vibration that interacts with the slide to give the response and tone that I need."

■ One alteration is the filing of square "holes" through four of the metal saddles, into which hand-carved bone inserts are super-glued. John uses this setup on his standard-tuned Artex.

John Mooney

PHOTOS: BRIAN BLAUSER, ATHENS, OH

■ The complete bridge "overhaul" involves entirely replacing the metal saddles, springs, and adjustment screws with a handmade, compensated wood bridge (some ebony, some rosewood) to mellow out the treble. Mooney describes, "The ebony or rosewood bridge saddles removed too much brightness from the treble strings, so I capped the saddle with bone inserts super-glued under the *E, B,* and *G* strings to balance the brightness. When I make these wood bridges, there are no adjustment screws to save me if the bridge saddle height gets too low—it won't go back up. So I lower the action slowly, stopping at various stages to play it for a couple of days, until it's just right. Then I set the intonation. I fret notes too, so it's not like playing certain lap-steel styles where the strings never contact a fret and the fretted intonation is less important. "You'll notice that when I replace the standard metal saddles, I restring through the bridge plate holes that previously held the saddle's six length-adjusting screws. Stringing up through the tremolo block in normal fashion creates such a steep angle that the wood saddle would slide forward or fall over. This creates a different sound than stringing through the tremolo block, but I like it.

"At first I tried using wood arch-top bridges on the Strat. I'd use the top saddle part, cut off the ends, and shorten the height. But with my high, stiff action, I had a rough time getting these 'store bought' compensated wood bridges to play in tune—the saddle peaks reach correct intonation in a different spot. Now I'm carving my own, which is better. With heavy strings and the high pitch of open-*E* or open-*A* tuning, you get a good, strong note when you compare the 12th fret octave to the harmonic—it's much easier to hear than a low-action, light-stringed ax. I carve the saddle peaks close to the right intonation by ear, super-glue the bridge in place, then finish up using a tuner to tell me where to remove wood with a file."

Mooney further "Deltarizes" his Strats by chiseling an increased "sound chamber" into the body wood under the pickguard and installing a solid mahogany pickguard. "I hear a big difference in sound with the solid mahogany pickguards," he notes. "Even acoustically, the sound is great." John's first Strat, a '63, had no pickups when he got it, so he chiseled the body out to accept a pickup from an old Present Company brand guitar. "I was a kid, you know, and I just wanted it to work. Later I put a mahogany pickguard on it, a Tele pickup at the neck, and a humbucker at the bridge—more chiseling. It sounded great! I realize now that part of the sound I liked was from the body being routed, so I'm trying to recapture that sound that I remember from a long time ago. I don't remove a lot of wood, but it makes a difference. The Artex factory routed out the two most recent guitars after they'd seen the one I chiseled out, but they took out a little too much, so I've been filling them back in with scraps of wood."

John keeps six guitars onstage in order to have a pair each in standard tuning, open *A*, and open *E*. He sometimes brings a seventh along for *G* or *D* tuning as well: "I like to sing in *G* and *D*, but I prefer playing with the higher

I couldnt resist giving you this! This is John Mooney showing how it's done: a little bit of bona fide delta sound. It's worth your time to mess with these two examples. "Walkin' Blues" is the original Son House version!

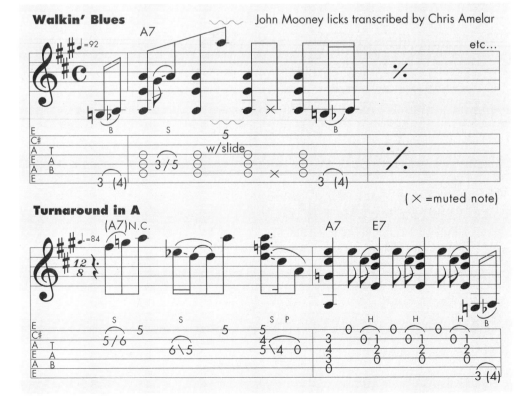

tension of the *A* and *E* tunings. So I only use *G* on four or five songs a night. I use specific gits for specific songs, because they sound and play different in different keys. If you play in five tunings and only have one or two guitars, you'll be tuning up all night. Besides, a guitar properly set up for open-*A* tuning won't play just right if you drop it to open *G*. And the string gauges are a little different for each tuning." John uses bronze-wound D'Addario mediums or GHS Boomers. For open-*G* tuning, his gauges are .016, .018, .024 (plain), .034, .046, .059. For open *A* or open *E*, he uses .016, .018, .024 (plain), .032, .044, .058. Guitars tuned standard are strung .013, .016, .019 or .020, .030, .044, .058.

All of John's guitars have a bridge saddle radius that's quite flat (ranging from 14" to 20"), even on the 7¼" vintage radiused Strats. To get good contact from one string to another with the slide (especially on the treble strings), he flattens the radius on the treble strings by putting the high-*B* string at almost the same height as the *G* string and the high *E* as tall as the *B*, so it's not as round as the fretboard radius would dictate. He flattens the bass side a little too. "The National steel has a fairly flat fretboard radius—about a 16"—and that's what I'm used to. So setting the high-*E* and *B* strings a little higher than the radius calls for lets me hit them really hard and get better tone. And using a .016 for an *E*, you can really lay into some stuff. I think Bob Brozman uses an .018! The .016 works good for me. Even on my standard guitars, I set the high *E* up a bit because I hit it so hard." Mooney's fretboard/bridge radius combinations on the National arch-tops are 10" board, 14" bridge. On the Fender Strats, it's 7¼" board, 12" bridge. The Artex have a 16" board, 20" bridge.

All of John's necks have some relief, and he sets up his standard-tuned guitars a little lower than the sliders: "When you tune up to *A* or *E* tuning with fairly heavy strings," he points out, "the truss rod really has to work to keep the neck straight. In time, a neck can even take a 'set' from the string pressure—they all pull up into at *least* .010" of relief, and sometimes as much as .018". That extra up-bow gives good clearance in the middle of the fretboard for slide

playing, without your accidentally fretting the string with the slide."

John's string height wasn't as high as I would have guessed, considering his clean tone. His heavy strings and high tunings create lots of tension. Measuring the gap between the string bottoms and the top of the 12th fret, I found that all of John's guitars measure about ⅛", give or take ¹⁄₆₄" in either direction. The National arch-tops are set the highest because they have the same 24¾" "short" scale as many Gibsons (Les Paul, 335, J-45, etc.), so their string tension isn't as stiff as the longer-scale Strats, which measure 25½". John sets them up higher to make up for their lower tension. "Since I do most of my slide work on the treble strings," he adds, "I set the treble strings on the Nationals higher than the bass. Scale length makes quite a difference in string tension." Mooney's nut is another reason his slide sound is so clean: "I like a good stiff nut height for slide playing—around ³⁄₆₄" clearance between the string bottoms and the top of the 1st fret all the way across."

Mooney points out that since his playing style evolved on the National steel, he tries to recreate the National's action (and in many ways its sound) when he sets up an electric—the Delta sound is in his blood. He doesn't travel with the National because it's hard to amplify and doesn't take a beating as well as the others. He did have it along on this trip, however, and it looked like it sure had taken a beating—especially the wooden bridge saddle. John describes a repair he often performs: "With some National steels, it's common for the low *E* in particular to pop out of the bridge saddle slot. You can super-glue match sticks on top of the wood saddles to hold the strings and keep them from popping out. Several have broken loose and need to be replaced. Got any super glue?" (Are you kidding?)

Mooney keeps his white '65 Strat tuned standard. "This is the least-customized of all my guitars," he explains, "and it has the only stock Strat bridge. I wired the pickup selector switch backwards, because I hit it when I play. That way, since I almost always use either the neck or neck/middle combination, I can just leave the switch pushed down out of the way of my picking hand. I've also raised the *B* string's polepiece by pushing it up from the bottom. It'll move about a ¹⁄₁₆", and I set it even with the high-*E* polepiece. I need that extra power on the *B* string to keep up with the higher-pitched .016" *E* string." Please note: *This is not a good idea!* It will work, but it may just as easily cause the pickup to quit working entirely. It's better to have custom-made pickups with the pole-piece set this way.

For his slide, the Moonman uses a piece of brass pipe that came out of an old house in New Orleans. "It's different than the brass you can buy today—it's pitted, and the texture reacts to the string differently than smooth brass. Like Son House, I put the slide over the first two joints of my pinky. It just goes to the second knuckle. See, a big part of Son's slide style was damping the strings behind the slide."

· ·

Albert Collins: talking guitar with the Iceman

PHOTOS: BRIAN BLAUSER, ATHENS, OH

Albert Collins' unique Texas swing blues guitar is refreshingly different from Chicago blues. Albert's "simple" style, brilliant tone, and organ-like phrasing have earned him the title Master of the Telecaster and made his patented licks a part of any blues player's arsenal—from Robert Cray to the late Stevie Ray. As his many recordings and live concerts show, Albert is a strong vocalist and killer showman, so don't ever miss him if he plays near you!

Albert's bus broke down as he pulled into the Columbus, Ohio, hotel parking lot. He drives his own bus and sometimes fixes it too, so my first in-person glimpse of the Iceman was of his black leather coat, pants, and boots sticking out

from under his vintage Greyhound tour bus!

Who takes care of your guitars?

I take care of my own. There's only two, my original Telecaster and the new model Fender made for me, which is a copy of the old one. Changing strings, cleaning, or little stuff—it doesn't need much. Oh, sometimes my little *E* will rattle, stuff like that, and I'll adjust it at the bridge with the little Allen wrenches.

You've had some heavy-duty work done on your fretboard, including having a ³⁄₁₆" maple "cap" laminated over the worn neck from the end of the fretboard all the way to the 3rd fret.

That was done by Guitars R Us, which is down the street from the Guitar Center in L.A. But now the stuff on it—the neck finish— makes my hand break out with a fungus. It doesn't do it with my right hand, but it makes me break out on the left one. I guess it's from the type of finish used. It's been happening quite a while now.

Do you carry any special guitar tools?

Allen wrenches and stuff like that, in case one of my screws comes loose. Or I used to have the problem of where you plug it in at the input jack, and it would fall out all the time. The whole jack would fall out, so Guitars R Us fixed that for me.

Do you set up your own action and intonation?

Not too much. I just take it to a guitar tech— somebody who can work on it.

You must have had problems over the years with fret wear and buzzing. Do you ever adjust your own neck?

I don't ever really have that problem very much with my guitar. And the humbucking pickup was already on it when I bought it used in '68 or '69—it's a 1961 Telecaster. The first time I heard a humbucker in a Tele was on the one I got now—I liked it, and I got it.

Those big frets on it weren't available in '69. What made you choose them?

I wanted the big ones since I saw Stevie Ray —he had a guitar with the big frets on it. Stevie said, "Put some of them on there—it'll last longer," so I had them put in there in '82. And he was right. I used to wear them little small frets out. They didn't last me no time— I'd just keep wearing 'em down. You know, I used to put 'em in myself a long time ago!

No kidding! You did your own refrets?

Mm hmm. I'd go buy my frets, they'd give me the stuff to put 'em in, and I'd set it like I want it. That was on a '59 Tele—that's the one that got stole from me when I first got to California. Yeah, I miss that one. I refretted it two times through the years. I'd just go down to Parker Music Company in Houston where I lived—I'm really fond of Houston—and he'd say, "If you leave the guitar, man, you can have it back in two or three weeks." I'd say, "No, I'll do it myself. I can't wait so long—I gotta play!" He gave me all the stuff [tools] to do it with. He basically told me what to do. I didn't have no problem.

During the past 10 years, have you had the big frets worked on?

Nope. I've just had the guitar strobe-tuned, and that's all. Nothin' on the frets. And I used to take the necks off. When I first started playing, it was on an Esquire; I couldn't afford a Tele-caster. So I went and bought a Telecaster neck and put it on an Esquire. I did that myself too.

How does your old Tele—the famous one—feel to you these days?

It feels pretty good, but I want to redo it again just to make it look a little better. It's pretty worn in places.

How does your new Albert Collins model compare with the old Tele?

I need to break in the new one, and it'll be fine. Like all guitars, even though it's a copy, it's still different. I don't say better or worse—just different. I had both my guitars weighed, and the new one is heavier. Since that time the actual production Albert Collins model has been lightened to match the original.

Do you break strings very often?

Every now and then I break 'em when I get, like, a sweat on. So I change strings twice a week if I'm playing six nights. I'll break two strings at once sometimes—at the bridge, the middle of the neck—it don't make no difference. I break my little *E* string the most.

Can you recommend a brand of string?

Well, I've been playing the Fender Rock 'N Roll 150 set a long time. I use .010, .013, .015, .026, 032, .038. I used to play the Black Diamond strings. Man, they were so thick they used to make my fingers bleed. I've tried a .009, and I can't use them; they're too light for me. [*Albert tunes to an* Fm *triad:* F, C, F, Ab, C, F, *low to high. He often capos.*]

Your high tuning and use of a capo must make it tough to bend strings.

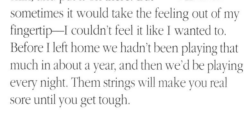

Sure. My hand sometimes gets so sore I can't hardly touch them strings, but you gotta play anyway. We used to get that stuff you call "new skin" [mole skin] and put it on there. But sometimes it would take the feeling out of my fingertip—I couldn't feel it like I wanted to. Before I left home we hadn't been playing that much in about a year, and then we'd be playing every night. Them strings will make you real sore until you get tough.

Which pickup position do you use the most?

Most of the time I'm in the middle. Sometimes I will use the bridge position for a real hard sound. But I get the hard sound in the middle because I use my fingers—not a pick.

Do you have many other guitars?

I got a '67 at home—I don't carry it now here—but I'm gonna take it out next time and try it. It doesn't have the humbucker, but it could make a good sound.

Why is your sound called Texas swing blues?

They call it Texas swing blues because I use a horn section—it's just different than in Chicago, where the guys from Mississippi would migrate up. We didn't have no harp players or slide guitar players come out of Texas. I was raised up with [saxman] Illinois Jacquet and others. Where I come from, the bigger the band, the

better it is—that's just the way it was. At one time I had nine pieces, and I carried that for about two years. But some of my favorite guys didn't work with a big band. Lightnin' Hopkins was a cousin of mine, so I was around him more than anybody. I remember when him and Little Sonny Jackson used to run around together, and I think they did some time together in prison. Lightnin' used to live in Dallas, and he was the only legend I ever knew well.

VITAL STATISTICS

■ String gauge: Albert says he uses Fender strings gauged .010-.038, but the strings I measured read: .009, .011, .013, .025, .031, .037. It seems strings never measure out to be exactly what the package says, so it's a good idea to own a pair of dial calipers to measure different brands.

■ Neck width: 1.553" at the nut, 1.920" at the 12th fret.

■ Fret size/height: Approximately 108" wide by .047" tall—probably a Dunlop 6100 or Stewart-MacDonald 150 fretwire worn down from the normal .055" height.

■ Pickup height (measured from the top of the pickups to the bottom of a straightedge laid on the frets, with the guitar in playing position):

Pickup	Bass Side	Treble Side
Neck	1/16"	3/64"
Bridge	1/32"	1/32"

■ Nut height/string clearance (with the guitar in the playing position, measured from the bottom of the string to top of the 1st fret): The clearance between the bottom of the outer E strings and the top of the 1st fret for both guitars was .010" under the high E, .022" under the low E.

■ Neck relief (measured at the 7th and 8th frets with guitar in the playing position and a long straightedge laying on the frets): .003"—quite a straight neck!

■ String height at the 12th fret (bottom of outside E strings to the top of the 12th fret): Medium-low action measuring $\frac{5}{64}$" at the low E, graduating to a little more than $\frac{3}{64}$" under the high E.

■ String width at the nut (measured with dial calipers from the outside E to E): approximately 1.281" to 1.310".

Buddy Guy: my guitar is almost like my love

Ever since his first road trip in 1968, when he played out of this world on a '57 Stratocaster, Buddy Guy has been inspiring Strat players everywhere. These days his tone is better than ever, and there's arguably no finer blues player alive than Buddy Guy. We met to talk guitars, and then I took the setup measurements of Buddy's signature-series Fender Stratocaster and his trusty Guild Nightingale.

How does your Strat feel right now?

It feels great. My guitar's almost like my love.

Is the Buddy Guy model the only Strat you play these days?

No, no, no. Now they just sent me another one they made—the Stevie Ray Vaughan model. But I want to go back to as close as they can get to the original sound that those guitars had when Leo [Fender] first made them.

How do those Lace-Sensor pickups compare to the ones on your old Strat?

I don't have no choice. Let's put it like this: If you had an accident in a car now, would you rather have it in one of these new ones or one made in 1940? Because you could bump in 1940, and you wouldn't dent it. All that was stone chrome on those cars back like that. So there's just no comparison to that. I think it's the same thing with amps, but they did do pretty well with this new reissue of the Fender Bassman. And they're doing a *tremendous* job with the Fender guitar, but I don't think you'll ever compare to the old sound. I don't want to put the scam out on nobody, but when Fender went haywire there in the '60s and went out of hand, I think it was a rat-race for the *look* of the guitar—not the sound. They come out with all the different pretty colors and was just settlin' for the color.

Why don't you just put the old-style pickups in your guitar?

I don't have them! You can't find 'em. They can make the new one look like the old one,

but it's not there. The engineers and everybody else know it's not there.

Do you work on your own guitars?

No, the only time I work on them is when I hook them son-of-a-bitches up—any other way, no. Oh, sometime if I have to adjust something on it, I know how to do that, but I won't fool with the neck or nothin' like that. But the bridge I would—especially on the Strat. Sometimes I have to fool with that. I never learned that much about fixing it. I put most of my time on learnin' how to *play* it better—each and every day, as I still do now. And when it needs some work I'd rather send it to someone else while I hold the other one in my hand and try to learn. If I knew how to play like B.B., I probably *would* learn some technique about adjusting and so on. About the worst thing I *will* do is the height of my strings. Sometimes I think I play them too low, 'cause I like to play with one hand, and the lower they are, the more you can get out of one hand. So that's the quickness and the snap that gets me to the frets. You snap, and it notes more clearly like that.

The Strat you used early in your career only had a 3-way switch, whereas Fender later decided to go with a 5-way switch.

No, no, no. *We* finally set that switch in between those two things and got that sound. *Then* they heard about it and came up makin' that switch like that. When they first come out, it's like you said, they had a switch for each pickup. Then we found that sound in between both of them [*two pickups wired in parallel*]. And that got back to Leo or somebody, so they decided to make that switch many years later. Now all of 'em got it made on the switches.

So on your old Strat, you used the in-between position?

A lot, a lot. Towards the front—between the front and the second pickup. That's what I was usin' when I went into Chess and started playin' a lot of sessions with Muddy and the rest of them. And that's what sound I used on the *A Man And The Blues* album. That was on my original Strat—the vintage which they call it.

Do you know what year that Strat was made?

I borrowed the money to buy that in '58, so I'm sure it was a '57 or a '56—at that time I don't think they was even keeping up with the years on the guitar. They kept up with the years on a car, but guitars wasn't as famous.

Buddy Guy in Michigan, 1968

But all of a sudden all the numbers and things started comin' out on guitar and things like that. When I first knew anything about a guitar, all that there was was a cutaway Fender. And I only knew two that was there—a Telecaster and a Strat. And then later on in the years they started doing the guitar like they do the automobiles. But I never go into that with a guitar because that number don't mean nothing to me if the guitar don't sound right.

Do you favor your shorter-scale Guild for a certain sound?

Ah, yes, when I want to sound more like B.B. And I got quite a few of those Guilds. When I first got one, B.B. came in and said, "I heard you got a Lucille." He came back in the dressing room and played it, and I just kept that with me at all times. And now, if I really want to imitate B.B. as *much* as I can, I'd have to go get that guitar. It's impossible to imitate him, but I do the best I can. That guy deserves way much more than he's gotten credit for. He's doing okay, but I think B.B. should be as well known as Eric or Beck or anybody like that, man, because we all playing his licks. Nobody was squeezing that string until he came out. Then I got it, somebody heard it from me, and it just went on and on.

Do you keep in touch with each other?

Of course. I still got a key to his house in Vegas; I never took advantage of that, though. He can have mine, too! He can go in my house any time he gets ready. If I'm not there, he can go on and go to sleep. I'd tell my wife get out of the bedroom and leave him alone. Let him have the master bedroom.

Speaking of B.B., is it easier to bend strings on the Guild because of the short scale?

They are easier to bend on the Guild, and I guess that could be why. Because that's my style of playing, bendin'. I break more strings, I think, than any guitar player I know.

You break them on the Guild?

I break 'em on *anything*, if you give me time out there. Because I figure if you don't break 'em, you're not playing 'em. But I do feel embarrassed when I break too many in one night, and sometimes I do. I use a light string, and that even makes it worse. But if I get to the point where I'm making people happy, I don't care. Then I get a smile. I'm fortunate now to have enough guitars out there to not hold up the show, and I got a great guitarist with me, Scott Holt from Tennessee, so if I break 'em all, he can make you forget I'm gone!

Which string do you break the most?

The first one. And I break 'em everywhere, even the middle of the string. Sometimes I get to bendin' on a string, and I just don't have no end. I just don't think it should stop being bent. That's the feeling I get. I think I read somewhere where Eric made a crack where I was bendin' whatever's in it out of it [*laughs*]. I know I like to see the first and the last string touch one another sometimes.

As you bend, do you slide your fingernail under the neighboring string?

Aaah, no. Well, actually I don't even know, man. If it comes under, it's alright; if it comes over, it's alright. You know, I'm not a technical guitar player. I make a lot of mistakes. But when I do make a mistake, I try to come out of a mistake on time. I make a lot of mistakes, because I never go home and practice. I don't think I could sit down and practice. I just go on the stage, and it comes to me and says, "Let's go, go, go, go." Like a rubber band—you stretch and stretch, and you know sooner or later it's gonna break.

Can you recommend a string gauge?

Yes, I'm an endorser for Ernie Ball, and normally I use a .010 or .011 on the number-one string, but on *Damn Right I've Got The Blues* my first string was like .015, which is a big one. I was trying to not break a string if I got a good solo while cuttin' the album. You know, a lot of times you get a groove making an album, and if it's good you may not never get another one that big, because everybody gets too tense. They say, "Oh, we can do it better, we can do it better," but it looks like it gets worse, worse, worse. So by using the heavier strings, I was making sure of not breaking any. Stevie Ray Vaughan played a heavy string tuned down; Hendrix did too. They both tuned to *Eb*. And Stevie's guitar felt like barbed wire, like it was strung with hay wire. Strong hands—oh man, I don't know what that guy had in his hands. But like I was saying, on that album I used a heavier string, and I tuned down the guitar too for recording—first time. I said, "If they gonna tune to *Eb*, then *I'm* goin' all the way to *D*—which I did.

Have you got many guitars at home?

I got every guitar I ever had in my life at home, except the ones that got ripped off.

Do you have any old Strats like the one you used to play?

No, those the ones they go after most. If they would break in the house and see the ones that's *not* Strats, I guess they'd say, "I can't get rid of that one" and don't take 'em. The Strats I got now is the ones they just made—an Eric Clapton, a Stevie Ray, and mine, the Buddy Guy. And I got another one from the '70s. The Buddy Guy model has got the same pickups that Eric's been using—that's the pickup that use the battery, which is fine.

Is the Strat your main guitar?

I favor the Strat because I went into Chicago with it, so I guess I made my little name with it. Plus, I'm not a guitar player of B.B. King's caliber. I was always a wild man with my guitar, and a lot of times when you play like that, the guitar has to be rough. And a hollowbody guitar is not rough. If you drop it in the wrong place, you through for the night—and I couldn't afford two guitars. So I said, "Give me the one that if I accidentally drop it off my neck, I won't break the neck off." I may break a string, a volume knob, or something, and I can replace that. But it'd be hard for me to replace the guitar. So I went after the Strat, and I've had it fly off the top of a car going 80 miles an hour in Africa. The case bust open, it fell out, and I went back and there wasn't but one key out of tune. If I'd have had a hollowbody, I wouldn't have seen anything but splinters on that highway.

How do you prefer your action?

Low, low on the Strat. Sometimes I think I keep 'em *too* low, but that's good for the one-hand playing. But the Guild has a higher action—on purpose.

Do you have any acoustic guitars?

Yeah, they gonna make me play it on my next outing. I got a Guild. You didn't hear the new album *Alone And Acoustic* [Alligator]? There's no band, and I'm playin' 12-string acoustic and singing with Junior Wells. I don't even have the album—I haven't heard it—but it's out there, and it's doing pretty well. Man, I cut it over 10 years ago, and they just released it this November.

What's the extent of your record collection?

I had more than I got now. My kids started going up there, and I started missing records. Then after you get pretty well known, friends come by and tell you, "You don't need it because you can sing it when you get ready." So a lot of my records disappeared like that—which I've changed now, because I'm back into collecting records. A lot of jazz, a lot of piano playing. I love great old piano players. I don't just listen to guitar players. When Bill Doggett's "Honky Tonk" came out, man, the horn solos was like, "I gotta learn that." And I recommend to all guitar players: If you get

hung up on just guitar players, you've missed something. I like to play piano solos, harmonica solos— if I can—and whatever. Don't ever get to a point where you just gotta be a guitar player. You hear something, go try to play that note and sound as much as like that as you can. And who *wouldn't* want to sound like the late Little Walter, man—oohhh!

Were you ever tempted to play slide?

I came to Chicago with a slide because I wanted to really do like Muddy Waters. And before I got a chance to get to know anybody, Earl Hooker shows up with this slide, and I gave him mine. On Muddy Water's boxed set, if you search through there you'll find a cut with Hooker on it—somethin' about the birds singing—and I've never heard anybody take a slide and do that before in my life. I didn't want to even attempt at the slide after Earl, so I gave it to him. Every song that came out of the Top 10, whether it was country-western or what, and he could play the melody with a slide. And he didn't tune his guitar like a lot of slide people do—cross-tune to where it'd slide just right—he played everything in the regular tuning.

Do you ever use open tunings?

No, I don't even know how to tune it like that. I know how to drop my low string down to just an open *D*, but I can't play the open stuff like Bonnie Raitt and them do.

What amp did you record with in the early days?

I always had the Fender Bassman, except when I recorded at Cobra [in the late '50s], I didn't have no Fender amp. I went there with a Gibson with four 10s in it. I forget the name of it now, but I loaned that to a friend of mine and that disappeared. Damn near everything I had disappeared in Chicago, because being from the South I didn't know nothing about stealin' and takin'—but I learned that will happen to you in Chicago, because just about everything I went there with come up missing from me because I was kindhearted. I would loan it to people like the late Earl Hooker, the late Bobby King, and a lot of great guitar players at that time which didn't have guitars, didn't have amps. And they would come to me: "If you're not working tonight, let me use your amplifier," and so on. And I would say, "Okay, man, just make sure you play, because I intend to hear you and steal some licks." So I was always loaning some amps. And if I let anybody have it for any time, they'd never return it. On a couple of cuts on *Hoodoo Man Blues* with Junior Wells we used the Leslie speakers for the organ. A lot of kids would ask me what was that when I had that little funny sound, but the rest of the album was all Fender Bassman. But let me take you back for a minute.

The first time I got an endorsement was from Guild. Guild was makin' amps then, and they came to me and said, "You come to the factory, and we're gonna' make you what you want." And they told me to bring my Fender Bassman amp in. And they kept it for two years, and then called and the engineer said, "You come and get it, because I can't reproduce that." They used to put it on the monitor, and every time I'd strike the guitar to show what the amp's doing, it was like a speeding automobile, hiding the needle, while those other ones was scufflin' trying to get it up to 60, 80, or whatever points they wanted on the monitor. So they never did reproduce the Fender Bassman that Leo had made. Maybe there was something in the transformer they never did get. And then now people tells me it was the material, the wood, and so on, and I believe that.

What amp are you playing through now?

A Fender Bassman. They reissued the Fender Bassman, and I'm very proud of that; because to me, that's the guitar sound. Otis Rush had it. In the earlier days when I went to Chicago, Muddy Waters and Howlin' Wolf was giants in my book—there wasn't no Rolling Stones, no Beatles, there wasn't no super rock groups or nothin' like that. And we used to travel with the whole band in a car, because two guitar amps and a bass amp would fit in the trunk. And the little P.A. system with two speakers in it would fold up like a little suitcase, and all that went in the trunk along with your own personal microphone. And when you'd get there you set the two little

speakers on each side of the stage and set your mike up. All the guitar amplifiers were so small, but when you played the blues you could hear it very well. 'Course we wasn't playing in as big of places as we are now.

And then came along the Fender Bassman, which was a little larger than the ones we had then. That stayed until the '60s, when the British got it and the amplifiers started getting larger and larger. And then you needed an extra man to carry your amp. [*Laughs.*] As small as I was, I couldn't carry the big amplifiers they was makin', so I had to have somebody really love my music just to follow me and help me carry—otherwise you stayed at home.

What are your stage settings?

On the Bassman everything's wide open but the bass—no bass at all. That amplifier don't have that much to open up no-ways, you know. It's simple, just like the old Strat guitar.

Do you still own your original Bassman?

I got my old Bassman saved. Actually, I would love to have it installed in the wall of my house, so if somebody do happen one day to decide to break in, they would say, "It's too much trouble to get that." Yeah, I've still got the same covering on it, but I don't play at home. When I sound good, I want somebody else to share it with me. I don't want it to sound good just to me. I want to bring my sound out there and look at the expression on your face and the other fans, and let them say "wow!" Then I go home and feel good.

See, I don't say, "I'm the best guitar player" —I don't do that. If somebody else says it, fine, but I don't never say that. Because they got too many great guitarists, just like they got good-looking men, good-looking women all over the world. Every time I go to different country, I'm saying, "I thought I saw the best looking woman in the world." And it comes better and better wherever you go—every time you go somewhere, man. So I'm just happy living and looking and learning and watching all this from the music on down to the human beings. If everybody felt like me, wouldn't nobody in the world have a problem, because they would just listen to good music—guitars, pianos, drums, and everything. They'd just smile and say, "I want to come back tomorrow for more so I can smile again. I'm tired of being mad at the world."

Thanks to the staff of the Newport Music Hall in Columbus, Ohio, for their assistance in facilitating the Buddy Guy and Albert Collins interviews.

VITAL STATISTICS

Buddy's Strat gets more play than the Guild, but you can't prove it by the hole worn in the Guild's top from strum- ming. Buddy had it filled with clear epoxy to protect the wood.

PHOTO: BRIAN BLAUSER

■ String gauge: On both guitars, Buddy uses Ernie Ball strings gauged .010, .011, .015, .028, .034, .044.

■ Neck width: Strat—1.685" at the nut, 2.055" at the 12th fret. Guild—1.703" at the nut, 2.070" at the 12th fret.

■ Fret size/height: Buddy agreed that his Fender needed fret work soon, and he'll send it back to the Custom Shop. Since Buddy plays so much, bends like crazy, and covers the entire fretboard, his Strat frets were worn uniformly flat, creating a sharp burr at the front edge of each one. You could almost cut yourself. Normally, a fret crowning would do the job, but his frets are also worn so low that the instrument needs a refret. The Guild's frets are still quite round and have a decent height.

Strat: .080" x .042" "vintage" wire measured .028" at the 7th fret and .032" at the upper frets—pretty low!

Guild: .108" x .045" Gibson-style fretwire averaged .030" to .035" all over.

■ Pickup height (measured from the top of the pickups to the bottom of a straightedge laid along the frets, with the guitar in the playing position). Note: Being Lace Sensors, the pickups can get closer to the strings without the magnetic pull common to tradi- tional Strats (this magnetic pull can cause "Stratitis"—a difficulty in obtaining true intonation in the upper register).

Stratocaster:

Pickup	Bass Side	Treble Side
Neck	touching	touching
Middle	³⁄₆₄"	³⁄₆₄"
Bridge	³⁄₆₄"	³⁄₃₂"

Guild Nightingale:
I didn't measure these. They're EMG pickups, which can be very close without noise—and they were close!

■ Nut height/string clearance (with the guitar in the playing position, measured from the bottom of the string to top of the 1st fret): The clearance for both guitars was .010" for the high *E*, .022" for the low *E*.

■ Neck relief (measured at the 7th and 8th frets with guitar in the playing position and a long straightedge laying on the frets):

Strat: .011"   Guild: .016"

■ String height at the 12th fret (bottom of outside *E* strings to the top of the 12th fret):

Strat: *E, A, D*—all ⁵⁄₆₄"
        G, B, E—all ¹⁄₁₆"
Guild: *E, A, G, B*— a heavy ³⁄₃₂"
        High *E*—⁵⁄₆₄"

■ String width at the nut (measured with dial calipers from the outside *E* to *E*):

Strat: 1.437"

Guild: 1.421"

After reading Buddy Guy's interview you know why it's appropriate to run the King Of The Blues next. I truly believe that B.B. King is the man responsible for modern electric blues playing.

B.B. KING: talking about Lucille

B.B. King would sound like himself on any guitar, because it's the man and his music—not so much the guitar—that's truly important. But on behalf of those of us who've spent hundreds of hours listening to this great bluesman and learning his style, I thought it would be beneficial to actually play Lucille and report on the type of action and response that lets B.B. do his thing. Perhaps these measurements and observations will help other players—especially blues newcomers—find what's right for them. At first B.B. seemed a little apprehensive about answering questions about the guitar rather than music. He began our conversation with a disclaimer:

"I'm like a test pilot for the airplane—he don't know much about it, he just flies it. An amp and a guitar, I don't know much about 'em. I just play—or at least try."

Have you ever been a do-it-yourselfer, adjusting and setting up your guitars?

Not too much, but some. I've been pretty satisfied with the way they're made by Gibson. I have done some little things, like setting the bridge intonation.

Did you help design Lucille?

PHOTOS: BRIAN BLAUSER, ATHENS, OH

Yes, a few little things. The ES-355 is practically the same thing, except that I wanted a thinline, semi-hollow, but also *solid*-body guitar with no f-holes, and they did that for me. So Lucille's like the big brother to the Les Paul. At one time I suggested that they narrow the neck a bit, and they did that for me. Also, the nut was a little different—I believe it was made of brass. With the current model they've returned to the usual white Gibson nut. And that's one of the things that's a little different.

How many Lucilles do you own?

Well, this is Lucille the 15th. I've given some of them away, and been ripped off for others—I mean, people have stolen them. Couple of times, they've come in the dressing room when I'd be talking to someone, and Lucille'd be in the next room. The last time, somebody went in that next room and got it. But luckily the sheriff was able to find it. A young fella had taken it home, and the funny thing was, when the sheriff came up to his house, he said, "Oh, did you come for the guitar?" [*Laughs.*] Yeah, that was the last time, but I've got about five or six of the Lucille model at this time.

Do you own any acoustics?

I've got two or three of them around home. One is an old National with the tin body and a resonator. I've got another one, but I can't think of the name now. The Gibson company is planning to give me one—at least one of the gentlemen there said they were going to.

One of the new flat-tops from Montana?

Mm-hmm, and that's what I want—one that's acoustic, but that you still can amplify. [*Author's note: Ren Ferguson, the man credited for the excellent guitars being built in Montana at this time, is making B.B. a very special J-2000*

with extensive abalone inlay. The flat-top will be a soft-shouldered, round cutaway with rosewood back and sides and a spruce top. The scale length will most likely be 24¾", like Lucille. This new "Lucille" will have a bridge transducer pickup and on-board electronics.]

Do you play acoustic at home?

Not often, but I do. I would rather play it at home [*laughs*] than let anybody hear me trying to play it out.

Do you play fingerstyle at all?

Oh no, I'm not that good—always a pick. In the early years I didn't have a pick. You know, I'm not as talented as a lot of people are; they can take the plectrum or use their fingers. It's all I can do to use the plectrum. So if I try to *divide* the time between the two, I don't do so well! I see Chet Atkins and guys like that just go to town with it, but I'm not able to do that.

Do you travel with more than one Lucille?

Yes, but until about a year ago I always just carried one Lucille. Then my manager suggested that I carry two in case something happened.

Is there a favorite Lucille, or one that's the most broken-in?

No, not really. It's like if you were drivin' a car—say, a Ford or Volkswagen, what have you—and you had two of them. They're both the same thing; it's just that one maybe feels a little different than the other. But actually the guitars' necks are pretty near the same.

You played heavy strings for years. In the old days they didn't have the light rock and roll strings.

The only strings I knew about in the beginning were called Black Diamonds, and gosh, it seemed to me that the first *E* string would have been the size of the *G* that I use today.

Could that have been what made your left hand so strong?

I won't say it's *what* made my hand strong, but I can say it probably did help. Then all of a sudden 20 years later somebody said, "Hey, man, have you tried the slinkies?" I said: "What? [*Laughs.*] The slinkies?" A .009 set, you know. So I tried 'em once, and it was like I'm playing with *toys*, so I took them off because

my hands had gotten used to a specific gauge. For another thing, I'm not the best with chords, but I like light jazz. And I like rock—you know, I like some of *all* of it—but I can't seem to get the *sound* of the chords that I want with a real light-gauge string.

Do you ever get sore fingers from bending?

Yeah, my fingers get a little tender, but I don't have corns [calluses] on my fingers, like most people. And the action's pretty high on Lucille, a little higher now than I usually like it to be. I prefer it a little closer. The only time that I'll have a corn is if I don't play for awhile and then pick up the guitar—*then* I'll develop one. But usually my fingers stay very soft on the tips.

What fingers do you bend with?

A lot of people think it's only this one or that one, but I bend with all of 'em, and a lot with the third finger. The way I bend, I don't push it up or pull it—technically, you could say I'm just trilling. I bend with my little finger too. I guess, you know, I'm one of those guys that was never satisfied—never, never satisfied—so I was always tryin' to find something to add to what I was doing. So I didn't spend as much time practicing as I should have—still don't.

The Stratocaster is popular with all kinds of blues players. Have you ever messed around with one?

I had one of the first Fender guitars that came out.

The Strat?

If that's what it was [*chuckles*], I had one. You'll see a few of my early records with me holding it. But I believe it was a Telecaster.

When did you discover the semi-hollow-body guitar?

About '58 or so is when I got the first one, with the long neck—I believe it was called the ED-355 at the time. I got one of those, and I have liked them ever since. But my *first* Lucille was a little black Gibson acoustic guitar, and I used a DeArmond pickup on it to electrify. And my first amplifier, the very first one I ever had, was a little Gibson amplifier with something like about an 8" or 10" speaker in it—*one speaker.*

What amplifier would you recommend for small clubs?

I love the Fender Twin. When they first made the Twin, I used it all the time, because I never found another amp that satisfied me like it did. But when the company changed and went to a different type of amp during the '70s and '80s, then the sound somewhat changed too. So I started searching for something else, and that's when I found this Lab System, which is what I'm using now and which I like very much. Because with the Lab System I got a sound *similar* to the older Fender Twin, so I try to buy every Lab System I can find, because they stopped making them.

No more Fender Twins?

Oh, I still use the Twin too. Because with the Fender Twin, later on they returned to the old way of making them, and I again started to find the sound that I used to hear. You see, I didn't know much about the settings of those other amps, because I'm a three- or four-button guy, you know [*laughs*]. The volume, the bass, the treble, and reverb—and that's about me. So now, in my contracts, if they don't have a Lab System, which most often they don't, our contracts state that they must have a Fender Twin—and that's what I use all over the world. [*Albert Garcia of Fender explains, "The Fender Twins that B.B. didn't like were models where they added things like master volume, gain control, and a more powerful output and power supply that upped the power from 85 watts to 100 and finally to 135 watts. I'm sure he couldn't get his sound with it, because it's too powerful, for one thing. But now we have the '65 Twin Reissue—just like the original—with more simple controls, two channels, reverb, tremolo, and 85 watts."*]

Do you adjust the knobs on your guitar as you're playing?

Well, as you know, the guitar has tone controls as well as volume. The two front controls are volume for both pickups, and the rear controls are treble and bass. I use these controls all the time—up and down— according to the sound of my ear.

How about the settings of your amp?

My amp is turned up to the maximum, usually, as far as volume is concerned. If you were to think in terms of 1 to 10, the volume would be about 10, or maybe 8 or 9—not always *completely* wide open. It's according to how much balls it's got. If it's *really* hot, then about 8 for the volume. Now, I don't like a lot of bass since I can't hear it so well. Generally the bass would be between 5 and 6 most of the time. I have the treble up *all* the way practically, unless it's *very* hot—too hot for me— then it would be like around 7 or 8. But I prefer a lot of treble because I *can* hear treble, and with a good amp it usually cuts through pretty well. I like reverb, but not too much— just so it's not flat. So reverb would be about 2. That's the way I like the settings when it's a good amp, but I'm pretty rough on amps because I play pretty hard and I wear them out.

You wear them out?

Well, with the volume up strong—and I like a lot of feedback from time to time—that's pretty hard on an amp.

How do you get feedback?

I can find ways of getting feedback, which I can't explain really, but there are certain positions in which you can stand. You don't necessarily have to face the amp or have the guitar *toward* the amp. With this solidbody Lucille I can pretty well control feedback like I want. That feedback's pretty hard on an amp.

Do you have a special repairman or tech who works on your guitars, or do they go back to Gibson?

To Gibson, every time. After I've kept it for about a year or two, I usually will send Lucille back whenever she's startin' to wear a little bit. I get them to check her out, especially the frets.

Have you experimented with different fret wires?

No, this is the standard one that comes with the Lucille model [the wide oval, see measurements].

How often do you need a fret job?

About every four or five years, usually. I don't know, even though I slide up and down the fretboard a lot, I don't seem to wear them down like I've seen on some guys' guitars—I guess the frets are pretty good on them. I've known some guys to file their frets down to where the fret is just above the neck. You know, where it's just out enough to fret it. But I don't like that.

You can't bend on those, right?

Yeah, I could. I can bend on any of 'em. Man you get me one and I'll bend 'em [laughs]—I don't care what kind it is.

Your adjustable Gibson TP6 tailpiece has the individual tuning screws removed. Why?

I don't like 'em, because they easily come out of tune for me. I took 'em off and threw 'em out! For some they may be good, but for me to have to reach back here [points to tailpiece] and tune, no! The next guitar, I plan to talk with Gibson and see if they can't just keep 'em off of mine. Another thing I like is the old style of tailpiece that holds on like a trapeze, so you just put the ball end of the string in the hole, and there it is. I'd like something like that. But if you ask about moving the bridge saddles, I do adjust them when the guitar seems to be out of tune with itself at times. I always check them at the 12th fret.

Do you use Lucille's Varitone switch much?

No, I hardly ever use it. Put it on full and just leave it there. To me, I can get a better sound mixing it myself.

Which pickup combination do you use most?

I leave the toggle switch in the middle most of the time. It's supposed to be stereo, right, so it's got two input jacks—one for mono and one for stereo. So generally the mono input jack is the one that I use most times with just a standard cord. It also has a stereo jack that uses a Y cord, so you can use two amps, right and left, and get the stereo sound with each amp working individually.

You mentioned that you like the long neck.

The guitar's got 22 frets on it. With the long neck joining the body way up, usually a guy with big hands like mine has no trouble going from here all the way down there to get it [*slides from the nut up to the high D*]. You got that *D* way up there on the 22nd fret, so you're all the way from here to there with ease.

B.B. likes a stiff action and a fairly heavy string.

What do you wipe your strings with when you're all done for the night?

Most times I'm kinda lazy, I don't wipe 'em down because when I come off the stage generally somebody else brings it off, and a lot of times I forget to do it when I get to my room. When I get to my room some nights, I'm so tired I put Lucille in one corner and I go in the other. But when I can *think* of it, the best thing to do is wipe the guitar down—then it won't corrode or rust. And my hands perspire so much, if I don't wipe 'em down they rust.

What brand of strings do you use?

I use Ernie Ball's light top/heavy bottom. I once used Gibson; I *liked* the Gibson strings, and I'm kind of a loyal guy. But then they started making the wound *G*s, which I *don't* like. A wound *G* is nice if you're playing jazz, but I like to bend the strings somewhat. And the wound *G* doesn't get the sound, to me, when I'm bending. I can bend, but it's not the sound I'm looking for. My high *E* string is a .010, sometimes .011—I like 'em pretty heavy. A .013 generally, for the *B* string, and a .017 on the *G*. For the *D*, a .030—I prefer a .032, but the .030 usually comes in the set. The *A* string is a .045, and there's a .054 on the bottom *E*. That's what I use.

Do you change strings yourself?

Always.

No guitar tech to do it for you?

I can't afford it! No, it's me and Lucille. In fact, I broke a string onstage last night, but I'm pretty good with changing them. Usually I'll change before anybody really knows that I'm doing it.

Right while you're playing?

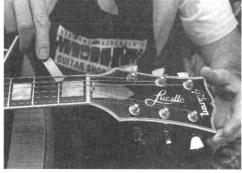

I didn't dare change the truss-rod setting without permission, but a quarter-turn would have significantly lowered the action.

Lucille has lots of string clearance at the first fret.

While I'm playing—never stop. I'll go into something that features somebody else, and if I'm playing a 12-bar thing, in 24 bars I've almost got it together—If it's a slow one.

Do you change strings for every show?

No, it's according to how much I'm playing. If I'm playing every night, about once a week. But if I break one, then I'll change the whole thing. It's like an old story about bears takin' corn out of the fields. If the bear had an armful of corn and he dropped one ear, he'd throw it all down and collect him another armful! [*Laughs.*] So that's the way I am about the guitar. I don't care if I changed last night, if I break one tonight, I'll take 'em all off and put a new set on.

You wind lots of string onto your tuners.

Again, I'm from the old school. We used to break strings so much, so you use it all! You wound it *all* up here [*points to peghead*], then if you break one, you still got more so you can pull it down and tie it on.

Do you run your strings through the post twice or have any special knots or ties?

No, I don't need to because I start to wind the strings from almost their beginning—for instance, like you take the average *E* string and pull it about an inch through—you can wind it about 12 times around there.

Maybe having that many windings is the key to staying in tune.

I don't know, but the tighter your string gets, the more it holds itself. My *B* string has about eight winds, about six or seven for the *G* string, and if I am in a hurry, I can put one on very fast. The only one that gives me trouble is the big *E*. Windin' it together up there gives me a little trouble. But at one time they had—and I liked it—keys with little cranks that you could fold out and wind the tuner very fast. I used to have 'em on the 355. I'm going to get them on Lucille [*Author's note: These M-6 Gold Crank tuners are still available.*]

Do you ever practice or play along to records?

I'm pigheaded. I've never learned that well that way. I read a little slowly, but if I really want to learn, then I buy the lead sheet on it and I sit down and play it. And nowadays I put it in the computer and let the computer play it. But that's the way I learn songs mostly. I've never been able to sit down and play a tune and learn it from that.

Like everybody has with your music?

Well, I guess. I don't have the knowledge of chord patterns like most people do. So, seeing is believing—hearin' is deceiving! [*Laughs.*]

Alone with Lucille: I just know that B.B. King sound's gotta be in there someplace!

LUCILLE'S VITAL STATISTICS

■ Neck width: 1.698" at the nut, 2.055" at the 12th fret.

■ Fret size: .098" wide x .045" (leveled and dressed, the frets range from .038" to .045", with an average height of .040").

■ Polepiece height *(measured with the strings open rather than pressed down):* In the bridge position, ⁵⁄₆₄" at the high *E,* ⁹⁄₆₄" at the low *E.* The neck pickup's polepieces are ⁹⁄₆₄" (almost ⁵⁄₃₂") at the high *E,* ¹³⁄₆₄" (a heavy ³⁄₁₆") at the low *E.*

■ Nut height/string clearance *(measured from the bottom of the string to top of the 1st fret):* .015 for the high *E,* .038" for the low. The open strings don't buzz.

■ Neck relief *(measured at the 7th and 8th frets):* .030". This is a lot of relief. A more normal .015" could be accomplished by slightly tightening the truss rod a quarter-turn or less.

■ String height at the 12th fret *(bottom of outside* E *strings to the top of the 12th fret):* All strings measured ⁷⁄₆₄" in height across the board—a stiff, high action!

■ String width at the nut *(measured with dial calipers from the outside* E *to* E*):* 1.425".

Get ready for the blues

A guitar that's out of tune or hard to play is *not* "close enough for the blues." But blues guitar setups are a little easier than most because the buzzing and dead notes caused by light strings, fretboard radius, and other factors are less apparent when the strings are raised—and most blues players seem to prefer higher action. Here are some points to consider when setting up a "blues" guitar—electric or acoustic—that will not only help you play better but may also influence your next guitar purchase.

SCALE LENGTH

Scale length is worth considering when choosing any guitar. Understanding why it's important will help your blues playing—especially in terms of bends and left-hand reach.

Most electric and acoustic steel-string guitars use either a "short" 24¾" scale (Gibson), the "long" 25½" scales (Fender, Gibson, and others), or something in between (PRS compromises with its 25" scale). Martin's short and long scales are 24.9" and 25.4", respectively. With its reduced string tension, the short scale is easier to bend on, responds quicker to the touch, and enables small hands to span greater distances. Short-scale guitars—electric and acoustic—make the best fingerpicking instruments.

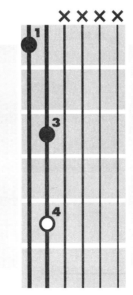

For a boogie rhythm in F: hold fingers 1 & 3 steady while #4 alternates. That 4th finger reach is a tough one on a long-scale guitar!

Fig. 1

Because of its higher string tension, the long scale is louder and more powerful, has better individual note separation and definition, allows for heavier picking attack, and offers brighter, tighter sound. But a long scale is also harder to bend on, and long reaches are more difficult. According to Gibson's Tim Shaw, "When you play a chord on a short scale guitar, like most of the Gibsons used for blues, the strings 'blend' well and sound like a family singing together, like the Everly Brothers. On the other hand, chords played on the long scale sound more like hired professional singers—clean and perfect, but without the blend. As for hand size, when I play the basic two-string blues shuffle rhythm in the key of *F* [Fig. 1] on a long scale, my left-hand 4th finger barely reaches the 5th fret, but I can get it easily on a short scale."

FRETBOARD RADIUS

Your fretboard radius determines how close you can set your strings to the frets while still being able to bend the first and second strings without "bottoming out"— an Albert Kingism for a dead note that has "fretted out." Most vintage Fenders used a 7 ¼" radius while Gibsons used a 12" measurement. Simply put, the more-exaggerated Fender radius follows the hand's natural curve and facilitates barre chords. The same tight curve, however, may cause the aforementioned problems when the bent string runs into the slope of the fretboard, as shown in Fig. 2. Today, many Fenders have a flatter radius, but the company's vintage replicas retain the 7 ¼" dimension. Gibson's 12" radius has always facilitated blues bending with no bottoming out, even with low action. Martin's flatter 16" to 20" radius has never presented bending problems.

Fret size is very important if you bend a lot, and what blues player doesn't? Tall frets are much easier to bend on than low ones. Optimum blues fret height for unworn frets ranges between .035" and .055". Frets lower than .030" begin to give poor bending results, because they no longer hold the string far enough from the fretboard to prevent your finger from slipping off when it grabs and pushes. Fretwire for blues—and most modern guitar playing—falls into two size ranges: "thin,"

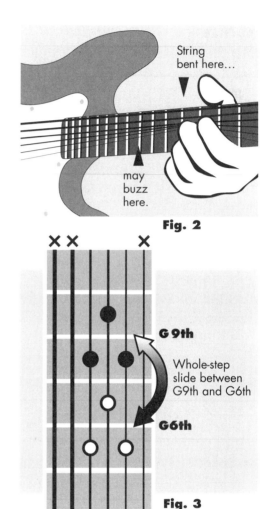

Fig. 2

Fig. 3

.078" to .090" wide and .040" to .047" tall (Fender, Martin, Gretsch, and some older Gibsons); and "wide," .100" to .108" wide and .040" to .047" tall (Gibson and most others). While .055" to .060" extra-tall wire is available in either width and is great for bending, you may consider it too tall for blues chord slides, like the famous "6th to 9th" that we all use from time to time [Fig. 3].

NUT SLOTS

The depth and quality of a guitar's nut slots always affect its sound and playability. (For a guide to making a nut, see the Nut Work Chapter.) Normally, string slots are cut no deeper than one-half of a string's diameter, so that the strings don't become pinched or "muted." A blues setup, though, may require somewhat deeper slots on the treble strings (*G*, *B*, and *E*), since a first-string bend can cause the *B* string to pop out, especially when bending 2nd-fret *F#* up to *G* or *G#*. In this case,

Guitar	1st Fret	12th Fret	Relief
	high E/low E	high E/low E	
ES-345	.010/.024"	1/32–3/64"	None
Strat	.014/.034"	1/16–3/32"	.009"
J-45	.013/.022"	3/32–7/64"	None

Fig. 4

the short section of string between the fretted note and the nut is extremely taut, and you'll pop the string if you tend to slip your finger under the open *B*.

STRING GAUGE

String gauge can affect your style a lot, so experiment with all the gauges—from ultra-light to fairly heavy. But remember that each time you significantly change string gauge, you also change your setup. This will result in either spending some dollars at the local repair shop or learning to do the job yourself. As a general rule, the heavier the strings, the better the resistance to pick attack, so you can play things such as bass-string boogie/shuffle rhythms harder and with more drive.

Gradually grow accustomed to a heavier string gauge. For instance, don't bend a .012"

first string without first toughening up. Otherwise, you risk getting "split nails," where the flesh of your finger pulls away from the nail. Splits are common and take about a week to go away. I've made it through many a night's playing by super-gluing the split, but I don't know if this is medically sound. Stevie Ray constantly glued his split nails.

The late Albert King may have been the most-copied blues player in the world, so he had a good thing going. He tuned way below concert pitch, *C F C F A D*, low to high—which for years allowed him to use Black Diamond silver-wound heavy-gauge acoustic strings and still be able to bend. In later years Albert used this set: .009, .012, .024 (wound), .028, .038, and .050. If you're studying Albert's style, try his strings—he didn't seem to prefer a particular brand—and tuning, and you'll be surprised. Stevie Ray Vaughan also tuned low, but only a half-step. His strings measured a hefty .013, .015, .019, .028, .038, and .058; even tuned down a half-step, you need extremely strong hands to do what he did. On an electric guitar, anything less than a .010 through .046 set is a little light for me, but I admit to occasionally using a .009 high-*E*. For years I preferred Gibson E-340 L Sonomatics (.011 through .056)

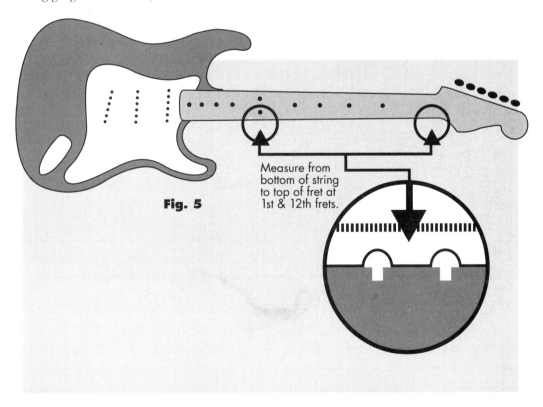

Measure from bottom of string to top of fret at 1st & 12th frets.

Fig. 5

because Otis Rush used them in the early '70s. E-340 L's came with a .019 wound third that sounded great; you could bend it, but it broke all the time. Try substituting an unwound .020 for the *G*, and you'll have a good, fairly heavy set.

For the average acoustic player, light-gauge strings are best for blues, unless the guitar is very old and can't support them. Extra- and ultra-light strings won't strengthen your hands or draw out that "different" style of music inside you. Medium-gauge strings may be too heavy for the tops of many acoustics, so have your local repair shop check out your instrument before you take the plunge. Strong hands are a must for playing blues on medium-gauge strings.

ACTION

Most guitars have adjustable bridges and necks, so setting action is relatively easy. As a precautionary measure, have a pro initially adjust your neck, and be sure to find out if the truss rod is working well. Necks are adjusted either perfectly straight or with "relief," a slight bow toward the strings' pull. Relief makes room for a vibrating string's elliptical pattern and helps avoid buzzing. You straighten a neck by tightening the truss rod, and relieve it by loosening the rod. There are hundreds of variations possible between straight and relieved necks, high or low string settings, and different string gauges, which is why you should learn to adjust your own neck and bridge. You may never know what setup is best until you've tried them all, so here are some helpful tips:

■ Most of us like a neck that's adjusted as straight as we can get away with.

■ You'll need a few simple tools, selected "Repairs" columns, one or two copies of this book, and at least a whole day to experiment.

■ The heavier the strings and higher the action, the straighter you can adjust the neck.

■ Light strings close to the fretboard need more relief.

■ Short scales tend to buzz more easily if the strings are too low, so they need relief more than long scales.

■ Fret buzzes not heard through your amp are okay.

■ Straight necks and low action may work if you play with a light touch and a loud amp setting. Don't expect to bend notes very far with this setup.

■ Gibson action can be adjusted more easily than Fender action because the entire bridge raises and lowers on two thumbwheels, whereas most Fender bridges—Strats in particular—have an adjustable bridge saddle for each string.

■ Most electrics and acoustics should have relief that measures anywhere from .005" to .030" in the 7th- to 9th-fret area.

■ Raising an acoustic's action at the bridge may require reshaping the saddle, which should probably be done by a pro. Sometimes you can simply shim or unshim the saddle's height.

To set your own action, start with the neck straight and lower the strings at the bridge until they buzz badly. Next slowly raise the bridge or individual saddles until the buzzing barely stops, and see how the action feels—you'll probably have a medium-low action that buzzes with relatively firm pick attack. Now give the neck a little relief and recheck the action. The buzzes should stop. The action will be higher, and you may end up liking this setup. If the buzzing doesn't stop, add relief until either it does go away, or the up-bow is so ridiculous that it feels uncomfortable. If you have to start over by re-straightening the neck and re-lowering the strings, try raising the bridge until the buzzing stops. You might like this medium-high strings/straight neck setup.

THREE TYPICAL BLUES SETUPS

The measurements in Fig. 4 were taken from a long-scale '56 Fender Strat, a short-scale '59 Gibson ES-345, and a 1944 short-scale Gibson J-45 acoustic. In each case, the guitars were lying on their sides in the true playing position when I measured them. Using a 6" steel "scale" and a set of feeler gauges, I recorded the distance between the bottom of the first and sixth strings (high and low *E*) and the top of the 1st and 12th frets (Fig. 5).

On the action/playability scale, I rate Fig. 4's setups like so:

1 The Strat is average to medium-high ("normal" Strat action), plays well, and the strings bend easily.

2 The ES-345 has a very low setup. Since it was a brand-new fret job, I was able to get the neck perfectly straight without buzz.

3 The light gauge strings on the J-45 provide enough tension so that the neck can be kept straight. It has low to medium action and plays great.

Pickup preference varies greatly, and I won't rehash pickups and electronics. For a rundown on how various pickups affect a guitar's sound, check out Alan di Perna's "Hot-Rod Your Axe" feature in the Feb. '91 issue of *Guitar Player*. Electric blues is played with humbucking or single-coil pickups and combinations thereof. B.B., Freddie and the late Albert King, early Eric Clapton, and the Allman Brothers all have a humbucking sound—a characteristic of Gibson ED-series semi-hollowbodies, SG's, and Les Pauls. For the single-coil sound, I think of Buddy Guy, Otis Rush, Magic Sam, and most of the current younger players like Robert Cray, Anson Funderburgh, Jimmie Vaughan, and the late Stevie Ray, all of whom use Fender Strats. A Telecaster also offers an excellent single-coil blues sound, but it isn't used as often. Some of the greatest blues guitars are the Gibson arch-top hollowbodies used by T-Bone Walker, Chuck Berry, and many '50s rockers, including the ES-295, the ES-300, the ES-350, and the ES-5 Switchmaster. Many of these early guitars were powered by "soap-bar" single-coil pickups and have a sound all their own.

As a rule, Gibson guitars—even with single-coil pickups—have more sustain, a fatter, thicker overall sound, and more output than Fenders. Strats are more percussive-sounding than Gibsons, but they have less sustain, unless you get them into the distortion mode.

Acoustic guitars draw a different style of blues performance from you, which is why they're so refreshing to play. To me, ideal guitars for playing acoustic blues have a shorter scale length, which leaves out most of the larger dreadnought-style instruments. Of course, you can play blues on a large guitar—think of Brownie McGhee—you just have to work harder. The short scale's lower string tension offers three advantages over the long-scale flat-tops:

1 It's more responsive to fingerstyle playing.

2 It's easier to bend on—even with light-gauge bronze strings, which are quite heavy compared with most electric sets.

3 It facilitates left-hand reach—an advantage if you're trying to play some of the nearly impossible things Robert Johnson did.

My favorite acoustic blues guitars are the early Gibson J-45, J-35, and the smaller L-0 or L-00 series, and all Martin 0-series models in either the 18 or 28 style (Big Bill Broonzy played an 000-28). To my knowledge, the only major company making short-scale guitars is Gibson, which is producing an excellent reissue of the J-45 and an improved X-braced L-1—sure to be a collector's item, since it is the model Robert Johnson played. A builder who makes custom short-scale flat-tops is Bill Collings (Collings Guitars, 1106-A S. 8th St., Austin, TX 78704). His guitars are expensive, but none are finer, and they sound as good as vintage instruments costing $10,000 and up!

Vintage blues guitar expert Dave Hussong of Fretware Guitars says: "Some customers put the cart before the horse when they shop for a blues guitar; if B.B. used an ES-345 with an Ampeg Gemini II amp, they've gotta have the same equipment. But the great players can produce their sound on just about any guitar. Hound Dog Taylor did fine with an Airline. The style overrides the instrument. The best blues setup can only be had after your style has developed. If you're just getting into blues, don't rush out and buy a guitar until you've played for a year or so. Use what you have, unless you're worried about all the great vintage guitars getting bought up.

"Fretwire size has never made much difference to me, but rosewood boards and big frets generally produce a big tone, and maple necks with smaller frets give you the brighter tone. I don't like low action and still subscribe to the Texas school of players like T-Bone Walker,

Lowell Fulson, and others, which means that I use as heavy a string as I can handle. Right now I'm playing an .010 through .050 set.

"My two favorite blues guitars are a 1960 Shoreline Gold Fender Strat, which is on loan to me from Anson Funderburgh, and a 1982 Gibson ES-355 with the wide $1^{11}/_{16}$" neck. If you've been playing a Strat and then pick up the Gibson, it's like a ball player laying down his heavy practice bat as he steps up to the plate. You've got to fight the Strat more, while the Gibson is easier to play. But a Strat has a certain tone all its own. When you're out there playing, you're more committed on a Strat, which means your mistakes will be more obvious."

4 OTHER ELECTRIC ADJUSTMENTS AND MINOR REPAIRS

Fitting and replacing Gibson Tune-O-Matic saddles

A Gibson electric guitar's adjustable bridge occasionally needs cleaning, lubricating, de-rusting, dusting, fine tuning, and calibrating too. Use the cleaning techniques used on the Strat bridge in the previous section which apply to all electric guitar and bass bridges, and not just those made by Fender. Gibson's Tune-O-Matic bridges, however, need certain adjustments that the simple, flat-plate, Fender-style bridges don't. Tune-O-Matics are die-cast, with individual channels for adjustable string inserts. Periodically these bridges need to be dismantled, have their parts cleaned and refitted, or be replaced altogether. Here are some set-up and maintenance tips for owners of these Tune-O-Matic–style bridges.

THE VARIOUS TUNE-O-MATIC MODELS

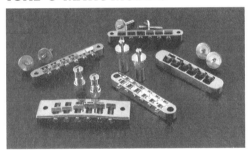

Gibson has offered five different adjustable Tune-O-Matic bridges since the original ABR-1 was first used in 1957: the Three Point, the Top Adjust, the Wide Schaller, the Nashville, and the original ABR-1. Parts or complete bridge assemblies for the Schaller, Nashville, and ABR-1 are currently available; the Three Point and Top Adjust have been dropped, and their parts are no longer available. We'll deal with the bridges and parts that Gibson still offers.

■ A wider bridge provides more travel for the saddles. All three of the current bridges are similar in that they raise up or down and their inserts adjust back and forth for intonation. Since the wider bridge offers more travel for the saddles, there is more latitude for setting

Metal bridge parts can be cleaned with lighter fluid and treated lightly with sewing machine oil or Teflon lube.

accurate intonation when it comes to action height and string gauge. The Schaller is the widest, the Nashville in between, and the ABR-1 is the narrowest. With the original ABR-1, if the bridge isn't mounted in just the right spot (as is sometimes the case), getting the correct intonation is difficult. The other two bridges offer more string-length adjustment, so one way of correcting poor intonation is to mount a wider bridge in the same mounting holes used by the ABR-1. Another method is to first plug the ABR-1 stud holes, and then relocate and redrill the stud holes without switching bridge styles. Note: If you own a valuable vintage piece, think twice about doing this, and then go consult a professional.

■ One of the most solid of all the bridge mounts, the Schaller was introduced in '72 as a stock item on SGs, and then on Marauders, L5- and L6-S models, and other Gibsons. Its height-adjusting studs screw into heavy steel anchor bushings that are pressed tightly into the top. Older Schaller bridges can suffer from flaked plating and metal deterioration caused by sweat, and it's often necessary to replace the pitted bridge saddles and sometimes the entire assembly. The saddles may appear to be permanently locked in by a machine screw with a slot-head on each end, but they're not! One end of the machine screw threads into the other and is super-glued in place. Since you won't know which end is glued (it's usually the backside, away from the headstock), heat *both* bolt ends with a hot soldering iron (40 to 45 watts) to break the glue joint, and then unscrew the bolts from each other. Replacement saddles for the Schaller come in a set (#10176) and are numbered from 1 through 6. Be sure to install them in the right order!

■ The Nashville bridge is the "new, improved" version of the ABR-1. It looks very similar, but it has more travel since it's wider by 7/64", and it doesn't need a retainer spring to hold the saddles into the bridge body. (Neither the Nashville nor the Schaller require the thin wire retainer spring that the ABR-1 uses to keep the saddles from popping out; this is a plus to some players.) It mounts on threaded flanged inserts that are pressed into the body, although the inserts aren't the same as the

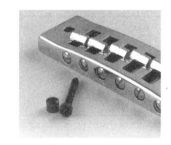

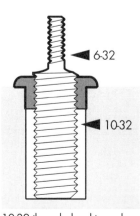

10-32 threaded rod turned on lathe and given a 6-32 thread

heavier Schaller anchor bushings. If your guitar is equipped with the Nashville bridge, you may find that the body anchors pull out too easily; in some cases, they want to fall out. I prefer a tighter fit than this for good tone transmission. You can carefully line the hole in the body with epoxy, white glue, or super glue, let it dry, and then refit the bushing. This tiny increase in the walls of the hole usually makes for a tight fit. If it becomes too tight, you need to scrape the walls slightly to remove excess glue. Working with glue—especially super glue—around a finish can have disastrous results, so be careful. A safer way to firm the bushing is to omit the glue, and instead wrap the bushing with Teflon plumbing tape before pressing it in; or increase the bushing's outside diameter by coating it with glue (instead of lining the hole with glue).

Here's a neat trick for Nashville bridge anchors, taught to me by my friend Bob Pettingill of Carrollton, Georgia. Besides being a top-notch guitarist, Bob is a machinist by trade. He put his machining mind to the task of making the loose anchors on his Gibson Les Paul more solid, and here's what he came up with. He took a short (2" to 3") length of 10-32 threaded rod and turned a small section (about ½") of it down in size to .136" in diameter. He then threaded the turned-down part with a 6-32 tap. Next, by carefully measuring to the bottom of the anchor bushing hole in the Les Paul body and carefully trimming the length of his new part, he got the new bridge stud to bottom out on the wood at the hole's bottom (pictured at lower left), while leaving the new 6-32 threads above the body surface. Now he can raise or lower his bridge with standard ABR-1 thumbwheels used on the turned-down 6-32 thread section. Going through the anchor bushings and down to the wood, the custom studs are very rigid, appreciably improving the tone and sustain!

■ Unlike most imported copies, all three Gibson bridges are available with saddles that aren't prenotched. Be sure to specify that you want them this way. The replacement saddles have no notches, either. This allows the player or repairman to individually notch the strings into the saddles for custom string placement. The imported ones—even Gotoh, which I like—come prenotched, and this is less desirable in many situations.

■ To say that the Nashville bridge is new and improved implies that something is wrong with the ABR-1, which isn't really the case. In fact, when properly located for intonation, I prefer the ABR-1, because it's the bridge I grew up with, it looks "right," and it has a certain tone. While the major drawback (to some) of this original Tune-O-Matic is its narrower string travel, it does have a few quirks of its own. The ABR-1 retainer spring, which holds the saddle inserts into the bridge body, has a tendency to spring upward and buzz against the strings. You can correct this by pressing or "kinking" the spring downward in between the slotted screw heads with a small screwdriver tip.

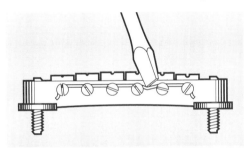

Not all retainer springs cause problems, though, especially on vintage instruments. With the Nashville and Gotoh bridges, you will find some variation of a snap ring or spring clip holding the insert into the bridge body; these must be carefully pried loose before you can remove the bridge screw and saddle insert. This is actually a tricky job, and you need to apply downward pressure to both lips of the snap ring at once, using two pieces of blunt steel as "push-bars". I have often planned on making a scissor-like tool similar to "snap-ring" pliers that would gently squeeze the clip open—but I haven't made it yet! Just be careful, since every slip can chip plating from the bridge parts.

■ Some owners of vintage Gibsons equipped with the ABR-1 may notice a buzzing problem or strange-feeling action caused by a warped bridge. This isn't common, but I've seen it often over the years. Perhaps the problem is caused not only by metal fatigue, but also by a player resting his hand heavily on the bridge while picking. Sometimes you can flatten out the warp, and sometimes you can't.

Don't try it yourself. Take it to a qualified repairman or to a machine shop where the craftsmen are familiar with the metals and stresses involved. With the bridge supported on each end, an arbor press or C-clamp can be used to gently push in the middle until the warp straightens out. You actually have to press the casting past the original point of flatness to get it to spring back true—a tricky task. Too much pressure or too fast a change can cause the casting to crack, so go easy.

■ On older instruments, especially those that were played hard, the studs that support the ABR-1 bridge have a tendency to loosen, bend, and/or lean forward. The most obvious solution to this is to redrill (enlarge) the stud holes and replace them with modern steel inserts and a modern bridge—either Schaller or Nashville. But this could harm a guitar's resale value, and we try not to alter guitar history, right? Here are *some* of the alternate ways to fix worn stud holes, made possible because the ABR-1 mounting hole spacing is so close to that of the Schaller, Nashville, and Gotoh replacement bridges. As a general rule, they're interchangeable. The hole-to-hole stud centers for the various bridge bodies are: ABR-1, 2.891"; Nashville, 2.926"; Wide Schaller, 2.891"; Gotoh ABR-1 copy, 2.891"; and Gotoh Nashville copy, 2.904". There are exceptions to every rule, so always double-check all measurements before making any changes. You might have a *little* trouble getting the Nashville (2.926") and the ABR-1 (2.891") to interchange; it depends on the individual situation. Also, if you're doing any drilling, tapping, or parts-switching, practice the operations on a scrap block of wood to be sure everything fits!

VARIOUS WAYS ABR-1 BRIDGE STUDS ARE REPLACED

1 If the wear is minor and the bridge is just a little wobbly, remove the studs and coat the walls of the holes with super glue, epoxy, or white glue. This not only increases the hole size, but hardens the thread cut into the wood by the stud. Next "chase" (that is, follow a thread lightly with a cutting tool) the threads in the wood with a 6-32 metal tap to re-cut accurate threads, and again coat the new threads with super glue to harden them. Chase the threads one last time with the tap, and you should have tight-fitting studs.

2   Drill-out the worn hole to enlarge it, fill it with a hardwood dowel, then drill a fresh hole and install a new stud (use the 6-32 tap to cut threads into the wood before screwing in the stud). Warning: This drill-and-plug method is quite noticeable if you enlarge too much, unless you can do a very artful touch-up. Give some thought before trying this on a vintage piece!

3   Stay with a metal stud-into-wood design like the original, but switch to the Nashville mounting studs (but without the anchor bushing inserts). These have a larger thread (10-32) than the ABR-1 (6-32), allowing you to quickly and simply oversize the sloppy original hole with a #21 drill bit, and then rethread it oversize with a 10-32 tap; this method eliminates having to use a dowel plug. A Nashville bridge stud fits the new hole, but you'll need to find someone with a metal-working lathe to turn the top part of the Nashville stud small enough to fit the ABR-1 stud clearance holes. The thumbwheel part of the Nashville stud may need turning down a little, too.

4   Using the same oversize tap method, switch not only to the Nashville bridge *studs*, but use the Nashville *bridge*, as well. Again, don't use the Nashville anchor bushings. Mount the new studs directly into the top wood using the appropriate drill and tap listed above.

To get into these drilling, tapping, pressing, and fitting modifications, you're going to need a full drill index with fractional, number, and letter bits, as well as a good assortment of standard and metric taps and dies. You can buy bits and taps one at a time, as you need them. You need a pair of dial calipers, too, and the inexpensive ($25) plastic kind will do fine. Ask your local hardware store for an index that lists the decimal sizes for drills and taps, or check with any good machine shop. If you choose to install the Nashville flanged anchor yourself, note that a "J"-bit fits tight, while a ⁹⁄₃₂" gives a nice press fit. For the wide Schaller anchor bushing, the ⁷⁄₁₆" is a finger-press fit, while ²⁷⁄₆₄" is a pretty tight machine-press fit.

SLOTTING GIBSON BRIDGE SADDLES

Replacing worn bridge saddles is fairly simple, at least mechanically. But once the new saddle has been replaced, cutting a new string notch requires skill and special tools. Many of the techniques in the Nut Work chapter apply to shaping bridge inserts, so look ahead if you wish. Here's a brief rundown on the basics.

While Strat-style bridge saddles don't necessarily require a notch to keep the string in line, the Gibson style does. This is mostly due to the different string angle to the bridge saddle caused by having the separate tailpiece located behind the bridge. I use my nut-slotting files on a bridge although metal saddles are tougher on the tools than the bone, Micarta, or plastic used for nut making. Notch the saddles just deep enough to keep the string from moving to either side as you pick. This should *never* be more than one-half a string's diameter. The four steps for slotting a bridge saddle are:

1 Start a small notch with a nut-slotting file or a razor-saw.

2 Use different file sizes for the different strings (the nut-slotting files have round bottoms, which is nice).

3 "Ramp" the string slot, giving a slight taper toward the front of the saddle. Don't just cut any old "notch"—shape it nicely.

4 Deburr any wire edge, and polish the metal with 2000-grit sandpaper wrapped around a file which is several sizes smaller than the string slot.

Traditionally, the ABR-1 often comes with the treble (*E,B,G*) bridge saddles facing front and the bottom (*E,A,D*) saddles facing rearward for the best intonation. However, it's more difficult to shape the saddle peak that faces the rear because of its sharp edge, and I've found that when installing new saddles on the bass side I can often turn them around (sharp edge to the front) and notch them like the others. I still get good intonation, provided the bridge has been well-placed. Note: If you turn around a saddle that's already notched, you'll probably have to replace it entirely because the notch may be out of line (unless it's in the exact center). File the string notches with a slight taper toward the front edge, and deburr any wire edges left on the saddle. Once you set the intonation, the result should be a clean-sounding, accurately intonated string.

Bolt-on necks

What's the most indestructible electric guitar ever built? Many would bet on the Fender solidbody with its bolt-on neck.

When's the last time you saw a Strat or a Tele with a broken headstock or a cracked body? Aside from the basic setup, fretwork, and occasional electrical maintenance that all electrics require, these guitars can outlast their owners. However, the neck-body joint can be a troublesome spot for bolt-on owners, since its alignment controls the instrument's action and playability. Although attaching a neck to a body by means of four screws sounds simple, by understanding several key adjustment techniques you can get your guitar to play its best. Besides offering advice for vintage Fender owners, these pages on bolt-on necks should be required reading for kit guitar builders about to design and assemble their first instruments, since the biggest problem these new luthiers face is getting the neck set into the body so that the action feels right.

The most common adjustment made on bolt-on guitars is the realignment—or shifting—of the neck. This becomes necessary when the strings are falling off either edge of the fingerboard, even when you're playing the simplest of chords. When you're looking at the guitar from the front, the two outer E strings should line up equally to an imaginary center line, with neither being closer to the fingerboard's edge than the other. Because Fenders are designed with fairly wide bridge spacing and a fairly narrow fingerboard, the outer two strings are quite close to the fingerboard's edge to *begin* with. If the neck is even slightly out of alignment, the high- or low-*E* string will lean too close to either edge.

To correct this problem, slightly loosen the four mounting screws. Then hold the guitar in the playing position, edge down, on a table by gripping the body between your chest and one arm. With your free hand, give the neck a slight sideways pull in the direction that you wish to move the strings. Because the screws are only slightly loosened, enough grip should remain to hold the neck in its new position while you retighten the screws. If the neck still remains out of place after you shift it and re-tighten, you may have to use force to hold it in position while you tighten the screws (this can be tricky if you have only two hands). Some necks can be shifted without even loosening the screws—simply give the neck a quick jerk in the right direction.

A neat trick for keeping a neck in alignment is to slip a piece of metal screen-door mesh (or drywall sandpaper) between the neck and body. The mesh embeds itself into each surface's lacquer, creating a friction that makes it hard for the parts to shift. This slightly raises the neck's height in the body cavity, so you'll have to readjust the bridge and pickup height.

If the fit between the neck and body is so tight that there's no gap on the side you're shifting toward, you won't be able to move the neck without removing a small amount of wood (or excess finish) from the body cavity. If doing this makes you nervous, have a pro do it. But if you'd like to try it, go slowly and carefully. Avoid chipping the finish, removing too much wood, or removing wood in the wrong place. Lay a strip of masking tape on the body close along the neck, with just the amount of body/finish showing that you feel should be

The techniques of filing and chisel-trimming the neck pocket to size can be used for fitting new parts, too. When I get a kit neck and body that fit too tight, I'm happy—I want a snug fit!

removed. (The arrows in the drawing at right show where wood may need to be removed to provide more room for the neck to move from side to side.)

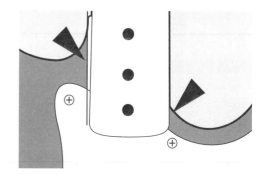

After removing the neck and pickguard, use a smooth file held at an angle to file the paint back to the tape line (middle drawing).

When you've filed to the tape, stop. Switching to a sharp wood chisel held at right angles to the body, pare away small bits of wood until you've removed the proper amount. Use the tape as your guideline as you chisel away the obstructing wood. Avoid touching the paint with the chisel, since paint chips easily. If you have a tight-fitting pickguard, you may have to file a small amount off that, too, before the neck will fit.

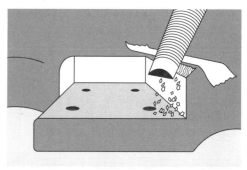

A bolt-on guitar's string height and action is controlled by adjusting the height of the bridge inserts. It's not uncommon to find a guitar with strings that are too high, even though the inserts are as low as they'll go. You may also find one that has strings that are too low, despite the bridge pieces being in their highest positions. In either case, the neck needs shimming. Begin by setting your bridge pieces at the center of their height travel (up or down) and at a radius that conforms comfortably to the fingerboard radius. This way, you'll still have room for fine-tuning the inserts' height after shimming the neck angle.

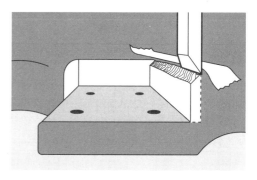

Shimming involves slipping a piece of thin cardboard, wood, or plastic between the neck and cavity. Very little thickness makes a drastic effect in the action. Time-proven shims have been fashioned from playing cards, matchbook covers, and flatpicks. I once even found the tooth of a comb used as a shim. If your strings are too high, making playing uncomfortable, put the shim at the end of the neck that's closest to the inside end of the body cavity (this is where shims are most likely to be needed). If

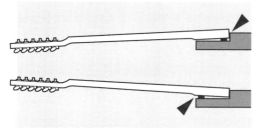

the strings are too low, place the shim towards the front of the cavity, just ahead of the two forward mounting screws. Proceed by trial and error—put in the shim, refasten the neck (holding the guitar as level as possible to prevent the shim from sliding out of place), and retune to pitch. It's best to start off using a matchbook cover; one thickness usually works, and two thicknesses are usually too much. Experiment, and remember that screen-door mesh not only keeps the neck in place, but makes a good shim, as well. You should have a comfortable action when done.

THREE-BOLTERS

Many Strats made during the '70s have a three-bolt neck mount with an adjustable tilt mechanism. These are a little more difficult to get snug, and I advise you to see your repair-man for help. One solution—and I'm not necessarily recommending it—is to install a

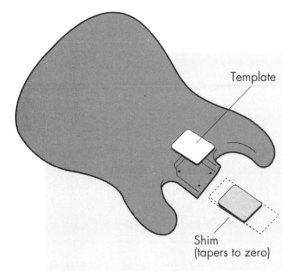

Template

Shim
(tapers to zero)

fourth bolt under the three-bolt plate. This bolt can be countersunk into the wood and completely hidden. Ask your repairman about this and other methods.

Now we'll look at stripped neck holes, mounting a new neck by drilling your own mounting holes, and making a tapered, full-size wood shim.

FULL SHIMS, KIT NECKS, AND STRIPPED SCREW HOLES

Let's take a look at how to install a full-size, gap-filling shim between the neck and body, at ideas for mounting a new kit neck on a body you already have, and at tips for fixing stripped mounting-screw holes in a vintage neck.

First, here's a reference for the drill sizes used in this section: For the four holes in the neck that the screws thread into, use a #30 bit. For the clearance hole where the screw passes through the guitar body, use a $\frac{3}{16}$". A #13 bit is used to enlarge worn-out neck holes in preparation for plugging. Use whatever snugly matches the body clearance holes (usually a $\frac{3}{16}$" bit) as a centering marker for layout of the four holes in the new neck.

The small neck shim described earlier leaves an air space in the joint. This gap may cause an upward warp, "kink," or "hump" in the neck. And many players feel that they suffer a loss of tone unless firm contact is maintained between the neck and body. For these two reasons, a full-size shim that fills the entire gap is often preferred. I make these full shims out of mahogany, which is soft enough to shape easily and hard enough to transmit tone. Before making the *full* shim, first shim the neck with a small sliver of wood as described earlier. This gives

you the proper thickness of the new shim at its thickest part. Measure this test shim with a pair of calipers that read in thousandths of an inch, or use a feeler gauge. Next, trim and fit a piece of cardboard to fit the cavity perfectly (see drawing, left). Hold it in place and mark out the four holes from the rear, using a $\frac{3}{16}$" drill bit. Use this cardboard template to mark out the mahogany shim.

Start with a piece of wood that's $\frac{1}{8}$" thick and slightly larger than the cardboard template. The grain should run lengthwise with the body. Trace around the template onto the wood, drill out the holes, and file, whittle, or sand to shape. Use a few strips of double-stick carpet tape to fasten the shim to a piece of hard, flat wood that's as wide as your shim and about 6" longer. This will be your backing support while sanding, with the extra length serving as a handle. Before sanding, lay out the taper of the shim with a sharp pencil, matching the thickest measurement that you made earlier at one end, and tapering the other to nothing. This line is your sanding guide. Hold the support block with the attached shim in one hand while using your free hand to press it against a belt sander equipped with a medium- or fine-grit belt. Although it may take several tries, you'll end up with a sliver of mahogany matching your thickest measurement at one end and feathered out to zero at the other end—very fragile!

Replacement or kit necks often arrive without the four mounting screw holes already drilled. I prefer ordering them this way, since it allows me to really line things up properly before drilling the holes myself. Set the neck into the cavity and clamp it while you install the two outside *E* strings for alignment. When the strings are in line with the fingerboard's edges, run the proper drill bit ($\frac{3}{16}$") through the hole. You'll feel when it touches the neck. Rotate the bit with your fingers to start the holes; then remove the neck and change drill bits to a #30. Finish drilling the holes, using the starter marks as a guide.

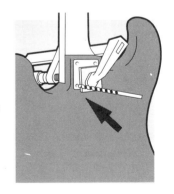

Most neck-mounting screws are standard-size, and the hole they thread into is smaller than the outside of the thread, which leaves enough wood for the screw to bite into. Use an electric hand drill or a drill press and be sure

Here's an important bolt-on tip: When the neck's removed, seal its four neck-mounting screw holes with a drop of lacquer. This keeps moisture from absorbing into the tongue, which can cause a swelling or hump in the wood and frets. Try using a plastic pipette to add a drop of lacquer to the hole, and use an empty pipette to suction out the excess lacquer so the hole can dry. While you're at it, remove the truss-rod nut and seal up the hole bored into the end of the neck, too.

you drill perpendicular holes. If you measure the amount of screw showing through the cavity with the neck plate in place, you'll know how deep to drill without going through the fingerboard. Wrap a piece of masking tape around the drill-bit shank as a depth guide. After drilling the holes, pre-thread each hole with a mounting screw used as a tap. Rub the screw against some beeswax, paraffin, or paste wax to lubricate it before pre-threading each hole. Now mount the neck with the backplate and all four screws. It should line up with the strings.

If the four mounting holes in a used neck are stripped, try coating them with Hot Stuff Super T glue (the yellow bottle). This provides grip for the screw thread. Use a toothpick in each hole to spread the glue around, and let it dry for an hour or use Hot-Shot accelerator to speed up the cure. Repeat this operation several times, and then you can try rethreading the holes with well-waxed mounting screws. This usually solves the problem.

If the holes are too stripped, you need to drill each hole oversize, plug it with a hard-wood dowel, and redrill from scratch. Most worn holes may be plugged with a ³⁄₁₆" (or less) wood dowel (above, right). To ensure a snug fit, you need to drill the oversized hole in the neck slightly smaller than the wood dowel; this is why you use the #13 bit, which is a few thousandths smaller than the dowel size. Whether you use a drill press or hand drill, remember that the neck is usually *hard* maple and may cause the drill bit to run off line, causing the hole to be drilled oversize or out of round. Always clamp an object that you are about to drill—especially maple.

After drilling the holes, cut four pieces of ³⁄₁₆" maple or hardwood dowel (use a larger wood dowel and corresponding drill bit if the hole is really bad) approximately ⅝" deep, or whatever depth you have drilled into the back of the neck's heel. Coat the holes with Super T or carpenter's glue, and slowly press the dowels into the holes, one at a time, with a small hammer. When the glue has dried, trim the dowel ends if they aren't flush, and then clamp the neck back into the cavity and proceed as you would when installing a new neck with no holes. If you've been careful with your work,

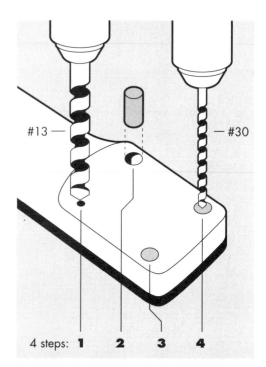

#13 —   — #30

4 steps: **1**   **2**   **3**   **4**

the neck will tighten home snugly and serve for many years of playing.

BOLT-ON QUIRKS

I'm definitely a Strat lover, and I basically agree with vintage experts who advise players not to alter old instruments. But many Strat lovers are caught between the vintage purists and the modern high-tech mechanical marvels. We appreciate the locking nuts and tremolo systems, and we can dig the high-tech sounds offered by electronic advancement, yet we don't want to see that stuff on our Strats. But we also find a need for certain repairs, and in some cases alterations, on guitars that we play and never plan to get rid of. Thousands of players own good but not exactly "vintage" Strats that would be more playable if they allowed their guitars a fret job, for example.

Forgetting twists, serious warps, broken truss rods, stripped truss rod threads (it's usually the easily replaceable nut that's stripped) and other subtle but hard-to-fix problems, we are left with two common Strat neck complaints: buzzing in the upper frets caused by a kinked neck or "rising tongue," and a fingerboard that's too radiused for bending strings without noting out. I, for one, don't think it's a sin to do fret work on a workingman's guitar, and I'll tell you why.

First off, I assume that you'll take your axe to

the best repairperson you can find—someone who's capable of adjusting necks, removing frets, planing out humps, and refretting with barely a trace of the work showing when done. Second, I know that some guitars just can't be played unless some "surgery" is performed. If your guitar is correctly adjusted and set up, yet you're still not satisfied, then the only thing standing between you and great playability (forgetting the electronics, of course) has to be the neck, and the fingerboard in particular. Here's how to go about solving these problems.

Buzzes up the neck are often caused by a swelling or hump that begins anywhere past the body joint. Many bolt-ons have a kink where the neck joins the body, due to the length and slimness of the neck, which is fastened abruptly to the body and placed under constant up-pressure from string pull. Sometimes these forces are more than the truss rod can correct. Also, the neck absorbs moisture through the four mounting-screw holes, as well as through the end-grain of the maple at the body edge. While lacquer is still my favorite finish for the neck and body, it doesn't impede the absorption of moisture as well as some other finishes. This moisture absorption can cause a slight swelling, noticed more often with rosewood fingerboards because of the extra swelling of the glue joint between the maple and rosewood. I've encountered fewer humps, swelling, or rising tongues on the old, pre-'59 maple necks.

A few pages back we mentioned that a shim placed under the neck to change the tilt can cause kinks, too. The thin strips of fill material that are commonly used as neck shims create an air space that allows the pressure of the four mounting screws to act as a clamp, forcing a rising tongue! Combined, these forces—string pressure, moisture absorption, and neck shims —can cause the last 6 or 8 frets to be higher than they should be, since the wood has risen. This doesn't always happen, but it's reasonable to expect it with a guitar made of wood. These problems can be corrected with either a fret dressing, which will remove the buzz from the frets, or by a partial refret, in which the last eight frets or so are removed, the rise is scraped and sanded from the fingerboard, and the

original (or replacement) frets are reinstalled. If you're a novice and any fret work is involved, take the job to a professional. You may be advised to do a complete fret job as long as you're at it.

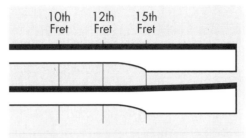

A hump, kink, or rising tongue can be detected by placing a 12" straightedge on the fingerboard alongside any given string. The guitar should be strung to pitch, resting in the playing position, with the straightedge running from around the 10th fret to the fingerboard's high end. When viewed from the side, the fingerboard should appear flat, with the frets level with each other. If you see any gap or relief on this portion of the fingerboard, the tongue is probably high. The drawing above shows two necks: the top neck shows the upper part of a flat fingerboard; the lower one shows the same part of a neck with a rise. Put a small straightedge on the two diagrams and see for yourself—then have your neck checked by a pro.

COMPOUND RADIUS FRETBOARDS

On vintage Strats, bluesy bends that fret out or buzz with a medium-to-low action setup are caused by the very curved 7¼" radius of the vintage fingerboard. Many players like the feel and comfort of the curve when playing barre chords, and country and jazz guitarists find less need for far-stretching blues bends. Most blues and rock players, however, run into bending problems—especially on the high-*E* and *B* strings, and usually in the upper register's 10th to 21st frets. Sometimes the easiest solution is to have metal dressed off the frets in the tongue area under the second and third strings—where the high-*E* and *B* strings end up when bent to their peak. But often this dressing solution is barely acceptable at best. The real answer lies in having a complete refret by an extremely good repairman experienced in *tapering* the fingerboard radius, gradually and subtly

If you have trouble seating a wood dowel into a tight hole (because of the hydraulic pressure created), try this furniture repair trick: With a thin razor saw cut several lengthwise slots in the dowel to let the air and excess glue escape— it will go in much easier!

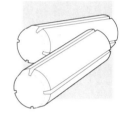

Compound or tapered radius fretboards aren't new. I recently worked on a lovely old C. Bruno guitar from the early 1900s that had a spruce top, Brazilian rosewood back and sides, pearl-inlaid soundhole, and an ebony bridge and fretboard —a compound radius fretboard which began at 5½" by the nut and tapered gradually to 12" at the end of the fretboard!

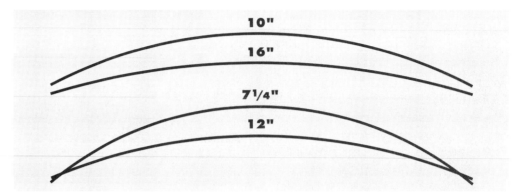

flattening it out as it goes up the neck and ending up with a 12" or 16" radius at the fingerboard's end. This is commonly known as a "compound" radius.

On a 7¼" radius fretboard, take a good look at a bend on the first string (at *least* a whole-step bend). The string is moving at an *uphill* angle towards or over the middle of the finger-board radius; it *has* to buzz! If you really need proof, remove the top strings and set a straight-edge on that same plane—it will rock on the spot that would cause a buzz. Since the strings rise on a long angle up and away from the fingerboard as they head toward the bridge, the fingerboard's radius need not be totally flat to be buzz-free, but 7¼" is pushing it. This is why Fender has begun using a 9" and 12" radius in recent years (only the vintage models still have a 7¼" radius). So, if you play on a vintage Strat (or a copy) your action mustn't be too low, if you want to play the blues.

Repairmen were pleasantly surprised when the Warmoth brothers came out with "Warmoth Radius," compound fingerboards on their re-placement necks. After years of manufacturing necks with 10" radius fretboards, Warmoth switched entirely to the compound radius fretboards. The Warmoth Radius neck starts at 10" at the nut and tapers to 16" at the finger-board's end. While these new necks can't help a vintage guitar's neck problems per se, they can save a lot of worry for players who question, "Should I do that to my Strat?" You can now buy a direct-fit replacement neck with a compound radius, usually for less than a high-class fret job, and try out its blues-bending capabilities while keeping the original neck stock. This can either be done as a test run before having a much-loved neck taper-radiused by a top fretman, or

as a satisfying replacement that allows the original neck to be stored, unaltered and mint, until it's needed. I highly recommend the compound tapered radius for blues playing.

Ken and Paul Warmoth, along with their father, originated the non-factory replacement neck many years ago, and from the outset they perceived that players had some problems  with a 7¼" radius. After discussing the situation with many repairmen, they decided to go with a fingerboard radius of 10", which is between Fender's and the Gibson 12". This 10" radius has since been the standard for almost all kit necks —so much so, in fact, that most locking nuts are made to match that radius. Therefore, if you plan to convert any guitar for a locking nut, check the fingerboard radius. You may find that you'll need to plane and refret the neck for optimum results. The arcs drawn above offer a comparison of different finger-board radii.

Caution: For more detailed information on the compound radius, see the Fretting chapter, and think carefully before flattening, tapering, or altering in any way the fingerboard on a vintage piece!

Tuner basics

There are many devices designed to help tune a guitar and keep it in tune. Electronic tuners and locking nuts have flooded the market, targeted especially at guitarists who use a tremolo. Many players never realize that one of the easiest ways to get in tune and stay there is to replace old, worn-out tuning machines that no longer hold their pitch. First we'll look at tuners in general, and then deal with their installation.

Tuners have three main parts: a plate or casting that holds the gear and shaft together, the drive shaft that's turned by the key or button, and the string-post shaft that's turned by the drive shaft. The drive shaft has a worm gear on one end, which drives the crown gear on the string post. The gears' housing is either the less-expensive, stamped-plate type made of steel, or a solid-metal enclosed unit known as a die-cast. The number of turns needed to cause the string post to go around one full turn indicates a tuner's gear ratio. Today most guitar tuners have a 14- or 15-to-1 ratio, while higher ratios of 20- or 24-to-1 are used on electric basses, which need the finer tuning capabilities due to their low-pitched, heavy strings (a higher ratio makes fine tuning easier).

Judge a tuner's quality by its "backlash"—the amount of free play felt when a peg is turned in an opposite direction without the string post moving. Also check to see if the post moves—thereby changing the pitch—without the tuning key being touched. Backlash is especially noticed by players who bend strings or use a tremolo, since when the constant pressure of the string at the post is altered, the string may not return to the original pitch. The locking nut is a good solution to backlash and post move-ment, but for vintage guitars, I feel that the tuners should be replaced before a locking nut is even considered. By eliminating backlash, you might solve most of your guitar's tuning problems. Better tuners have low amounts of end play (up-and-down movement of the string post) and shaft wobble (back-and-forth string movement in the bushing, washer, or grommet on the headstock face).

For years all tuners were constructed with either open gears or a semi-enclosed, stamped sheet-metal housing. Kluson, Waverly, and Grover were the big manufacturers, with Kluson leading the field. Kluson's Deluxe was not only the most widely used, but often the tuner most in need of replacement. They were notorious for backlash because their gears were made on a screw machine rather than a specialized, more accurate tool known as a gear hobber. Also, they made the worm gear from brass, when steel would have worn longer (all tuners today have a brass crown gear but use steel for the worm). Kluson tuners had a backlash the day they were born, but no one knew enough to complain. There wasn't anything better, so players put up with them until Grover came along with the Rotomatic, the first high-quality tuner. Its die-cast housing enclosed well-machined gears that were lifetime lubricated and completely sealed. In addition, a threaded bushing with extra length replaced the press-in grommet to better support the shaft (right). This tuner became the replacement choice of repairmen around the country—much to the owner's delight—as well as a factory-installed standard on many higher-end guitars. Years later the Rotomatic was copied, then improved upon, by Schaller and Gotoh. Between Grover, Schaller, Gotoh, and the lesser-known but equally high-quality Sperzels, you'll find a size, shape, and style to fit any guitar or bass.

While die-cast tuners are no doubt the most precisely made and offer the least amount of backlash, they are also more expensive. And because of their larger size, you'll have to do some drilling in order to use them as replacements for the old-style tuners with a smaller string-post diameter. They may not be a wise choice for a valuable vintage guitar or bass.

In the good old days, players had few choices when it came to solving tuning-key problems. You'd either install a set of die-cast Rotomatics or buy a new set of stamped factory replacements that were no better than the originals. Today's replacements for those old, low-priced Kluson Deluxe tuners are excellent. Modern

Early Klusons: the "Deluxe" (left), and the "Ideal."

Modern Kluson-style replacements: note Fender style slotted "SafetiPost" and trimmed plate.

Modern Rotomatic die-cast tuner. Note the threaded bushing for extra shaft support.

Sperzel tuner with the solid crown gear housing.

Deluxe styles offer a 14- or 15-to-1 gear ratio, compared to the old 12-to-1, which means closer tuning capabilities. Also, the gears are accurately machined—regardless of which brand you buy—with nylon washers added to support end play on the worm gear, thereby eliminating much of the backlash. That means you're safe using them as an exact look-alike replacement, and you won't have to deface a vintage axe by drilling for the larger die-cast machines. Note: I seem to recall that the earliest Deluxe replacements had larger shafts than the vintage ¼" style—and a larger bushing ("grommet") too. So those tuners wouldn't just "drop right in" the existing bushings since the shaft was too large. In that case, the tuner bushing holes in the peghead face had to be enlarged to accommodate the new replacement bushing— which isn't preferred on a vintage axe! I believe that most of the manufacturers have taken care of this oversight, but be sure to shop around—I know that the Gotoh Deluxe replacements will fit vintage bushings. However, Gotoh's bushings still have a larger bushing O.D. (outside diameter) than the vintage ones by about .012" (.344" vs. .332"). These bushings will slide into some peghead holes but not others. It takes just a few minutes to file down the serrated "teeth" on the bushing sleeve until they fit, however.

Vintage Martin and Gibson guitars often used the Grover G-98. A perfect replacement for that peg is the Waverly W-16 (above). Although expensive, it's the best tuner I've ever used— including any enclosed or die-cast machines. This tuner will fit the plate "footprint" (imprint in the lacquer at the rear of the peg-head), and the mounting-hole spacing, of many guitars. If you're custom-ordering a new guitar, ask the manufacturer to use the W-16 tuners; you won't regret it. The W-16 will fit many Gibsons and Martins from the 1930s through the 1950s.

Waverly also offers vintage conversion bushings with an oversize outside diameter. These bushings fit the enlarged (usually ⅜") holes drilled in many vintage guitars for die-cast tuners, as mentioned above. So, it's now possible to convert back to vintage tuners while still retaining the right look. The Waverly retrofit bushings come in the Martin or Gibson "hex" style and the round Fender or Kluson Deluxe style.

If you want die-cast machines and you don't mind enlarging the holes, read the next section before attempting an installation. Or, since

Waverly W-16 tuners.

many guitars manufactured since the late '60s already have die-cast tuners, replacing them is easy; the hole is already the right size, and no drilling is needed. But even die-cast tuners wear out or eventually suffer from backlash. So if you're shopping for a new set, there are several points to consider. The first is size: Mini die-casts are available for headstocks that won't accept the standard ones (Fender, for example). You can also choose color—from black, gold, and chrome to red and blue. Several other options are available, such as string locks—miniature locks that are actually built into the posts to help control string slippage. Sperzel offers staggered-height string posts for Stratocaster-style headstocks, which keep a good angle at the nut without using string trees; this is a real enhancement when using a tremolo without a locking nut. Perhaps you need Fender's slotted SafetiPost and trimmed plate to fit a Fender. Also keep in mind that some sets are heavier than others, and try to find pegs that match the original shape and mounting screw holes. If properly matched, they'll drop right in, probably even matching the original press-marks in the lacquer.

Many players have no idea of the variety of tuners available today, and since they seldom browse through the catalogs at their local music store, they assume that what they see in the showcase is all that's available. Ask questions and shop around, so you can weigh the facts.

Locking tuners are a great invention. They really help avoid tuning hassles.

**Before drilling
any tuning key
mounting holes,
be sure to read
about over-oiled
tuners on page
88.** People
screw up this
operation all
the time.
If you break
off a screw—
especially in
maple—there's
hell to pay
getting the
broken
part out!

Tuner installation

Those are the basics of tuning machine construction—from costly die-cast tuners to the less-expensive, stamped variety. Almost. any of today's well-made, inexpensive tuners are a good replacement value. Here are a few more tuner facts, with some installation tips.

Not only are die-cast tuners accurate, but they also suffer the least from backlash. This doesn't mean that you can't tune well or won't be satisfied with stamped vintage replacements; you may well be. But die-cast tuners are the best, which is why you see them on most top-of-the-line instruments. (Would you put two-ply tires on a Cadillac?) Now, even die-cast tuners can develop backlash over the years: As the brass crown gear wears, the fit becomes looser. Another little-known fact is that if you tune a string too high—especially a wound string—and it suddenly breaks, the instant release of torque at the string post can loosen the screw that holds the crown gear to the post. This allows slop between the gears, and backlash can result. This explains why one tuner may occasionally develop tuning problems. You can't repair this, because you'd damage the tuner by trying to get inside it. Your music store, though, can often order a single replacement. Most of the various styles are available from Grover, Schaller, and Gotoh at competitive prices, and they are all equally fine tuners. And don't forget the Waverly W-16 if it's appropriate for your instrument!

While researching this chapter, I learned that Sperzel tuners are unique. Their construction features totally eliminate backlash, end play, and shaft wobble. Not only are the machining tolerances extremely close, but the string post and crown gear are a one-piece, solid unit that is locked into the die-cast housing by a cleverly machined collar (see previous page). Also, the bushing threads are outside the housing rather than inside, allowing an even tighter fit between the post and housing and further eliminating any play. Since the string post and gear are solid, there is no screw that can loosen.

Sperzel has been able to drill up through the shaft, thread it, and install a unique string lock that is adjustable with a thumbscrew from the rear; this Trim-Lock is an option. Another option is staggered post heights for Strat-style guitars, allowing the removal of the string trees while maintaining a good angle for the string passing over the nut. Sperzel tuners are a little more expensive, but they're definitely worth looking into.

Replacing stamped "deluxe" tuners is often simply a matter of removal and direct replacement. Installing die-casts, however, sometimes requires the enlargement of headstock holes. First remove the old tuners and mounting screws. Often the headstock grommets are quite snug, and you may have to rock them out, or at least loosen them by inserting a screwdriver shaft inside and gently rolling it in a circle until you feel it loosen. The grommet can then be pushed out from the rear with a blunt tool. Don't overdo the rolling motion, because you could crack the finish. Now measure the housing's diameter: It will usually be around .380" or close to $\frac{3}{8}$", while the original hole will be around $\frac{11}{32}$".

This exact hole size would be important if we were going to use a drill, but we aren't; that's for pros or for people in a hurry. Enlarge the hole by using a tapered reamer (available from hardware stores and guitar shop suppliers). Ream halfway through from the front and from the rear, testing often with the new tuning peg until it fits. If the two reamed sides don't quite meet, leave a ridge in the center (above, right), removing this last bit with a rat-tail file. Be sure to hold the reamer at right angles, clean its blades often, and don't be in a hurry. Each hole may take you five or ten minutes. Wrap a piece of masking tape around the reamer's cutting flutes at the correct width of the new tuners to act as a depth stop.

Once all the holes have been cleared and the pegs slip in easily, install the tuners and tighten down the hex-nut bushing against the washer on the headstock's face. Now you can line up

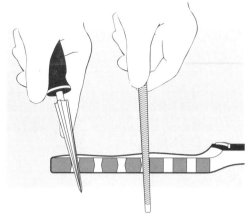

the tuners with the headstock shape in a fashion that both pleases your eye and allows the easiest turning of the keys. When the pegs look right, snug the hex nuts and drill the mounting-screw holes. Use masking tape on the drill bit as a depth guide to avoid drilling through the headstock's face! Be sure to use a bit that's smaller than the actual screw thread, so that the screw can bite into the wood. Thread each screw into the mounting hole to finish the job. The correct way to drill the mounting holes is illustrated and explained in the section on problems caused by over-oiled tuners.

You need to fill the old tuner holes to seal them from moisture absorption and to make the finished job look neat. Remove the tuners to make the job easier. A local guitar shop or cabinet maker can provide small wood scraps (usually mahogany or maple) that match your neck. Carve or file small, round, tapered plugs that are slightly oversize to the hole for a snug fit. Glue them in with a white or yellow glue such as Franklin Tite Bond or Elmer's; use super glue only if you're experienced with it. If you "dry fit" the dowels to each hole, you can see where to trim them to length before gluing them in. This makes cleanup easier and lessens the risk of damaging the finish as you trim. A pretrimmed dowel should push down into the hole until it's flush with or slightly below the surface. Don't expect the color or grain to be a perfect match, and seal the finished plug with a drop of lacquer or super glue as a drop-fill (the section on dents, dings, and scratches explains how). Of course, the plugged holes will be visible unless you totally refinish the headstock, but they should look good enough; besides, that goes along with the installation of die-casts as a replacement for the old-style tuners.

When the finish dries, reinstall the new pegs, put on a new set of strings, and go find someone to play with—you've earned it!

Shrunken heads

Recently I received a note from George Gruhn and his shop foreman John Hedgecoth, warning of a problem that's just beginning to crop up: "We're now seeing an epidemic of deteriorating plastic tuner buttons, pickguards, and body binding on certain guitars built during the early '60s and before." So much for the notion that plastic is forever.

Some plastics used during that era are ticking time bombs with 30-year fuses. The parts most often affected are Kluson "Keystone" and white oval-type tuner buttons; pickguards on older Gibson arch-tops and mandolins; and the pickguards and body bindings on D'Angelicos, Strombergs, Gretsches, and some Epiphones. We are not seeing the same problems with Martin pickguards, for example, or on other instruments that apparently used different types of plastic.

The cause of plastic deterioration seems to be the long-term escape of the solvents and plasticizers used during the manufacturing process (without these, the plastic dries out and crumbles). At progressive stages of this deterioration, the escaping gasses cause fumes that can eat into finishes and wood, corrode surrounding or attached metal parts (turning them green), or exude a sticky, smelly mess that can ruin a clean case. Plastic deterioration may be accelerated by leaving an instrument in a case for long periods of time (not allowing the fumes to escape), by exposure to high heat, or by a combination of high heat and extreme humidity. Oddly enough, not every tuning-key button on an affected instrument may turn bad.

Solutions for this problem range from complete replacement of the faulty part to repairing plastics that haven't completely disintegrated. John Hedgecoth has found that if the material is still all there for bindings and pickguards, super glues can be used to stabilize the plastic, which should then be sanded smooth and coated with lacquer to seal in the solvents. Bindings that are not too far gone can be masked off and sprayed with several coats of lacquer, since generally only the outer layer of binding deteriorates.

"At the time these instruments were made," Gruhn and Hedgecoth write, "there was no way that the manufacturers could have known that these problems would crop up in the future. With today's synthetics, who knows if we are going to face similar problems 30 years down the line."

The repair or replacement of bindings and pickguards should only be attempted by skilled repairers, so take a problem instrument to the best shop you can find. On the other hand, the replacement of Kluson-style tuners with exact retrofit "look-alikes" isn't too tricky: You just need a small Phillips-head screwdriver. Two types of exact, retrofit Kluson Deluxe-style tuners are available:

■ Individual three-on-a-side Gotoh Vintage Kluson-style tuners with single-ring translucent Keystone knobs (as used on Les Pauls, SG's, ES-335s, etc.). These machines feature an improved 15:1 gear ratio and a nylon-bushed worm gear, and they have no name on the back of the housing. They're available from many guitar supply houses, such as W.D. Music Products, Stewart-MacDonald's, Elderly Instruments, Allparts, and C.F. Martin's Guitarmaker's Connection.

■ Allpart's Kluson Deluxe Replica "3 x 3 on a strip" tuners have off-white plastic oval buttons, a 15:1 ratio, nylon bushings like the Gotoh, and "De-luxe" stamped on the back (available exclusively from Allparts dealers).

A third Kluson Deluxe-style individual

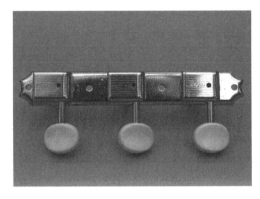

replacement tuner is available from Schaller, but the grommet is not a retrofit (⅜" instead of ¹¹⁄₃₂"), and the Keystone buttons are too green for my tastes.

VINTAGE TUNER REPLACEMENT GUIDELINES

■ Only replace tuners with exact retrofits. Leave the original bushings intact and use the original screws.

■ Remove the rotting plastic buttons from the old tuners. Clean the metal parts, and store them in the case—otherwise they'll get lost!

■ Replacement tuners often work much better than the originals, but another option is to replace only the buttons on the original set.

■ Most important, get the bad plastic out of the guitar case!

There is an alternative to complete tuner replacement. You can repair crumbling plastic buttons or fit new ones onto the original tuners. Read on.

As for "shrunken heads" (the failing plastic knobs on many Kluson-Deluxe tuners from the '50s and early '60s), the simple solution was to replace the entire tuner with easy-to-install, exact-fit replacements. Two Kluson-Deluxe style replacements were recommended: Allparts' three-on-a-strip style with white oval buttons, and Gotoh's individual "Keystone" single-ring tuners. For those who prefer to keep their vintage tuners and repair or replace only the funky plastic knobs, here are some repair and restoration tips.

Crumbling and rotting knobs can often be stopped in their tracks with a bath of super glue. Remove the tuners from the guitar, but if the knobs are really cracked and crumbly, don't even detune them to remove the strings.

Instead, clip the strings off (wear eye protection to do this), since the plastic knobs may crumble to pieces in your fingers.

■ Clean off all dirt, green corrosion, and goo, first with naptha (lighter fluid). Let it dry, and then use alcohol and let it dry overnight.

■ Dip the knob in water-thin, red-label Hot Stuff Original Formula super glue, going slightly deeper than the plastic itself. Immerse for several minutes, and be happy if you see air bubbles.

■ Remove and drip-dry, wiping off any big drop with a Q-Tip or pipe cleaner.

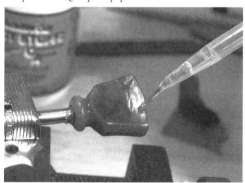

■ Once the super-glue has saturated all the cracks, further fill any other fissures with thicker, yellow-label Super-T Hot Stuff (above). Let dry until hard.

■ For missing corners or chunks, build up layers of brown Fresco powder mixed with baking soda, saturating it with Hot Stuff as you go (top photo, right).

■ Baking soda buildup can be sculpted with files and sandpaper (lower photo, right).

■ Sealed and rejuvenated knobs can be given a final gloss-dipping of super glue, then wet-sanded and buffed.

Until replacement knobs became available, we'd "steal" knobs from newer tuners and "loan" them to vintage ones. And for various reasons, one still might prefer to remove knobs and transfer them to a vintage set. For example, Schaller Keystone replacement knobs are too green for my tastes, so I'll remove the nice-looking Gotoh knobs and use them on vintage tuners, even though it means trashing a new set of Gotohs just for the knobs! Or I'll use the knobs from the more recent Gibson De-luxe keys and saw off the extra "ring." But whether you're stealing knobs or using new replacements, the technique is the same:

■ Remove the tuners from the instrument.

■ Use a soldering iron to heat the shaft (pictured at right is a double-ring knob from a Gibson De-luxe). Pull on the knob as you heat, and the knob will slide off cleanly.

■ Use a razor-saw to convert a double-ring knob to a single (top photo, next page).

■ Clean and then heat the vintage shaft, and slide the new knob on. If you're "stealing" Gotoh knobs, you may need to deepen the shaft hole with a # 31 (.120") drill bit in order for them to slide far enough onto a vintage shaft; the hole should measure about ½" deep.

■ A drop of super glue on the shaft right where it meets the plastic isn't a bad idea, although it's not always necessary.

The photo above shows some knobs that are repaired, some that are replaced.

Cautions: When working with solvents, cleaners, and super glues, be sure to wear protective gloves and safety glasses, and work in a well-ventilated area. And if you're at all in doubt about doing this work, take your axe to a repair shop!

Plastic replacement buttons are available from Gruhn Guitars, 410 Broadway, Nashville, TN 37203 (615) 256-2033, and from Stewart-MacDonald's Guitar Shop Supply, 21 N. Shafer St., Athens, OH 45701 (800) 848-2273.

Removing broken headstock screws

Everyone breaks off the head of a screw at one time or another—even pros. With guitars, it happens most often with tuner mounting screws installed into maple, since maple is hard and the screws are small— their heads twist off easily. If you follow the correct drilling technique for the screw thread and shoulder, you should never be faced with the problem, but don't never say never—I've snapped 'em off more than once when it seemed that everything was going right. Here's a clever trick for removing them, passed on to us by my good friend Paul Warmoth of Warmoth Guitar Products in Puyallup, Washington. It's a combination plug cutter/screw extractor.

At the hobby store, buy a piece of hollow brass tubing large enough to completely surround the broken screw shank and some of the wood that it's embedded into. A $^3\!/_{16}''$ outside diameter tubing has a large enough inner diameter to straddle the screw because the tubing's walls are so thin. Clamp the tubing lightly into a vice and file small teeth into one end (below). I filed the teeth with a small feather-edge file that's used to sharpen the teeth of Japanese Dozuki and Ryobi hand saws, but any small, thin metal file will do. File the face and gullet of each tooth at slightly less than 90°, and the back or rake at any angle—you needn't be too specific—just so it angles back and away from the cutting edge to eliminate friction.

Chuck your new plug cutter into a hand drill, electric drill, or drill press, and drill slightly past the depth of the embedded screw. Then back

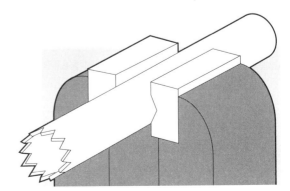

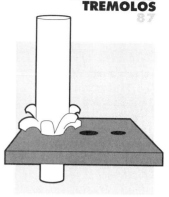

out the cutter and wiggle the plug until it breaks off, which it will do quite easily (or use the cutter—gently, to avoid bending it—to "break" the plug out). The plug that pops out will have the broken screw in it! Now all you need to do is plug the hole with a piece of wooden dowel, and here's how you do that.

The hole you're going to fill is ³⁄₁₆" in diameter, so whittle and file down a ⁷⁄₃₂" or ¼" dowel. When you get in the ³⁄₁₆" ballpark, be very careful to keep the dowel round; you'll probably have to try several times, but dowel sticks are cheap. If you have access to lots of drill bits, and preferably a drill press, there's a better way to size a wood dowel to keep it round and get a good fit.

Using a #9 drill bit, drill a hole through a ¼" plate of steel or aluminum. The #9 bit measures .196", which is bigger by only nine thousandths than the ³⁄₁₆" (.187") hole you wish to plug in the back of the headstock. File or sand a taper on the end of the whittled-down dowel (which is still slightly larger than ³⁄₁₆"), and pound it through the hole drilled in the steel plate. The dowel compresses as it's forced through the sizing hole, allowing it to press-fit into the headstock hole when you tap it in. Then it will swell up tight if you glue it in with a water-base glue such as Franklin's Titebond or Elmer's Carpenter's Glue. Note: Whenever you drill steel, aluminum plate, or anything hard, clamp it down! Especially with steel or aluminum, and especially with a powerful tool such as an electric drill or drill press. When the metal binds to the drill bit—and it often does—it can go whipping around fast enough to cut your fingers off, at the very least! Speaking of drills and drill bits, here's some information you may be able to use:

A full set of drill bits (under a half-inch) is called a drill index and has three types of bits: letter bits from A (.234") to Z (.413"), number bits from 1 (.228") to 80 (.013"), and fractional bits from ¹⁄₁₆" (.062") to ½" (.500"). These bits allow you to drill almost any size hole. Such a drill index was once out of reach for most of us, costing hundreds of dollars; we repairmen would buy just what we needed at a good hardware store. These days you can find the full set (of a lesser quality, but they're fine) for $49

in almost any mail-order tool catalog.

If you can get your hands on a full set of drill bits, try this old-time furniture maker's trick for sizing dowels: drill a series of sizing holes. In our case, start at just under a ¼", with perhaps a "D" or .246" bit, and drill holes at intervals of ten-thousandths until you get to the #10 (.193") size. The holes will actually shave the wood off as you drive the dowel through the plate, not just compress it!

There's a method here for everyone, so for the well-equipped do-it-yourselfer or the serious professional, here's another way to plug that hole in the headstock if you have access to a metal lathe.

Make two plug cutters: one to remove the screw and its surrounding wood, leaving a ³⁄₁₆" hole in the headstock (.187"), and the other with a .196" (#9 bit) inner diameter to cut the plug that fills the hole. The smaller cutter is made from ³⁄₁₆" steel rod, and the larger one from ¼" rod.

Chuck a 1 ⅛" length of the ³⁄₁₆" rod into the lathe, face it off square, and bore a hole ⅝" deep into the end, using a #25 (.150") bit. Remove the #25 bit, put a ³⁄₃₂" (.093") bit into the drill chuck, and bore a clearance hole completely through the length of the rod. This is so you can push the plug out later; we used the smaller bit for the clearance hole so the plug cutter would have some strength. File the teeth, and this is your extractor. It will cut a .150" plug around the screw and leave a ³⁄₁₆" hole in the headstock for you to fill.

Next chuck the ¼" rod and drill a .196" (#9) hole clear through it (a smaller clear-through hole isn't needed here, because the ¼" rod has quite a bit more strength). File the teeth, and this is your plug cutter—it will cut a tight-fitting .196" plug. The beauty of this method is that you can cut a plug out of side grain in any scrap of matching wood (maple, mahogany, whatever you have), and the match can be tremendous. Avoid burning your plug, especially in maple, by cutting slowly—these are somewhat crude, homemade bits (and they certainly aren't hardened)! And all this just from a little tool idea that Paul called me with one day.

Whenever you drill steel, aluminum, or anything hard, clamp it down—especially with a powerful tool like an electric drill or drill press!

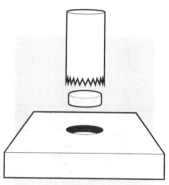

These measurements aren't set in stone. By going smaller on all the sizes, you can cut plugs that can be hidden by the housing of most tuners. I don't always use Titebond glue, either; often it's Hot Stuff.

Damage caused by over-oiled tuners

Something that's often overlooked when people are buying or caring for a used guitar is tuning gears that have been oiled too much. Most modern tuners are permanently sealed and lubricated, so they need no oil. However, I've seen hundreds of good guitars with tuners that have been oiled regularly, and this excessive oiling causes three common problems that can be expensive and aggravating.

The first problem is stripped mounting screw holes. The screws vibrate loose after years of playing, and when the owner tightens them, the soft, mushy wood no longer holds the screw's thread. Second, the finish lifts away around the tuners at the rear of the headstock or on the face of the headstock around the shaft hole. Finally, splits occur in the headstock wood itself. The oil seeps under the tuner, down the shaft hole, and into the wood's end grain. This eventually causes the wood to swell and sometimes split, or it may simply rot. Often these problems can be caught in time and aren't too serious. Before you attempt any repairs, the work area on the headstock needs a good cleaning and degreasing.

Begin by removing the strings and then the tuners themselves. The holes in the headstock —both the shaft holes and the mounting screw holes—are often swollen and mushy. You can remove much of the grease by packing the large shaft holes with Kleenex or cotton balls. Clean the screw holes with a pipe cleaner. The round, tightly-packed cotton wadding used by dentists is an excellent absorber. Soak up as much oil as you can, and then clean the larger holes with some lighter fluid applied with a rag, cotton, or Q-Tip; use a fresh pipe cleaner for the mounting holes. The lighter fluid helps degrease the problem areas. If you're not in a hurry, leave the holes exposed for an overnight dryout. Clean the tuner housings with lighter fluid also, so they aren't reinstalled in their oily condition. When you've cleaned and degreased these, you can begin any necessary repairs.

The worn screw holes can be fixed quickly and easily with some baking soda and water-thin super glue. After you have cleaned and degreased the worn or stripped hole, fill the hole one-third full of baking soda, followed by a drop of super glue into the hole and onto the soda. The glue and soda harden immediately, usually with a puff of smoke. Don't inhale the fumes or let them get into your eyes! Fill the remaining two-thirds of the hole in the same manner, a third at a time, making sure that the glue saturates all the soda. When you've filled the hole flush to the surface, you can redrill it and know that the screw will hold.

It's important to use the proper size drill bit. It should match or be slightly larger than the screw's shaft, but it should not be as large as the outside measurement of the threads themselves (left). Some screws have a shoulder that is larger than the thread. You may need two drill bits in this case—one for the shaft thread, and one for the shoulder if it extends down through the tuner housing and into the headstock. Take the screw to a hardware store and pick out the appropriate bits. Look for number bits as well as standard fractional bits; number bits are available in a much larger selection, graduated in finer increments. Numbered drill bits ranging from #51 (small) to #44 (larger) are commonly used for tuner screws. Hold the screw against a background light and compare the bit to the screw shaft. You want to see thread on both sides of the drill bit without being able to see the screw's shaft. If the screw has a shoulder, choose a second bit that is slightly larger, to allow for clearance.

This super glue/baking soda technique works great on any stripped holes you are likely to come across, such as those for pickup mounting rings, truss rod cover plates, etc.

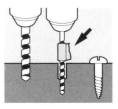

When drilling a hole, wrap a piece of masking tape around the drill bit shaft as a depth guide as shown; this is to stop you from drilling too deep or even through the headstock.

To remedy the second common problem—finish that has lifted from the wood—let a small amount of lighter fluid seep under the finish where it has raised up. Allow it to evaporate and dry for at least several hours. Follow this with a drop of super glue. The glue will run under the finish as you touch the bottle's tip to the loose edge. Hot Stuff's thin, flexible applicator hose is perfect for this delicate work. Press the loose finish onto the wood, using any round, blunt object. If you wipe some wax onto this object, it will be less apt to stick to the finish or to any glue that squeezes out. Never use your finger! Don't use much super glue, and don't try to wipe off any excess. When the glue has dried (usually in a minute or two) you can remove the bead that may have squeezed out at the edges by carefully chipping it off with a sharp, pointed tool; a needle or pin will do. You may be wise to practice first on yardsale specials or a piece of old furniture.

The final problem, splits in wood, should be dealt with by a qualified repairman. If you've noticed any serious separation of the wood at the headstock, get a pro's opinion. Regluing or filling a crack is usually inexpensive, and I advise you not to do this yourself.

To avoid these tuning-gear problems, use the proper lubricant. For the time when it is necessary to sparingly lubricate a stuck gear, use a powdered graphite or the new space-age lubricants such as Magik Guitar Lube, which have microscopic Teflon balls suspended in a solvent that evaporates quickly, leaving no oily film. A dab of Vaseline often works wonders. In most cases, the stuck tuner is an open-back, non-enclosed type. The gears are visible, so make sure that the parts aren't stripped or cross-threaded. If the gear looks worn or damaged, ask your local repairman for spare parts—most repair shops save boxes of old gears and can match parts easily.

Installing the Floyd Rose tremolo

Fitting a guitar with the Floyd Rose Tremolo and its partner, the locking nut, is work. This section begins by presenting the basics of installing a stud-mount, knife-edge tremolo. We'll cover installing the locking nut separately, and then explain setting up and fine-tuning the unit as a whole. If your tremolo is already installed, don't go away—there's something here for everyone!

While making a videotape on tremolo installation and setup, I designed a set of related jigs and templates that require simple, clear instructions. Here are those instructions in abridged form, and I'll read between the lines for you, offering additional tips as we go along.

Routing templates and ball-bearing router bits make tremolo installation fairly simple. The body cavities are routed by using Plexiglas templates mounted to the guitar's face or rear; these templates are screwed to a guitar's existing holes—i.e., pickguard, pickup mounting ring holes, etc.—or held with double-stick carpet tape. Specialized ball-bearing router bits follow the templates' pattern (see illustration at top of the next page). The bearing and router bit are the same size, so the cutter trims flush with whatever the bearing rolls against. Routing templates and ball-bearing bits are available from W.D. Pickguards and Stewart-MacDonald.

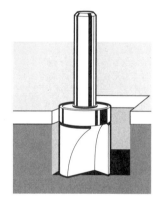

Typical installations involve either a modified rout for guitars with an existing standard Strat-style tremolo (the cavities need only to be enlarged in certain places); or a full rout for guitars that never had a tremolo, for custom-built guitars, and many kit bodies. The same rout depth, width, and clearance measurements used for the full rout apply to the modified rout as well. We'll start by describing a full rout, using the templates mentioned above.

The clear Plexiglas top-rout template is most easily placed if you scribe locating lines on its underside. Scribe a line laterally, when looking at the guitar, through the centers of the two

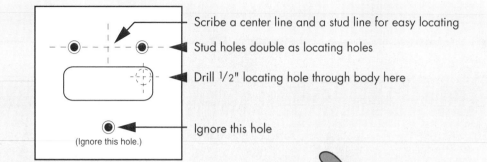

Scribe a center line and a stud line for easy locating

Stud holes double as locating holes

Drill 1/2" locating hole through body here

Ignore this hole

(Ignore this hole.)

mounting holes (right), and then scribe a second line at right angles to it, centered exactly between the holes. This second (longitudinal) line will correspond to a center line taken from the neck and laid out on the body. To find center, use a finely graduated rule and mark the center of the fingerboard at the nut and the last fret. With a long (30") straightedge resting on those marks, transfer the line onto a piece of masking tape fixed to the top in the area where the tremolo will be located. A taut piece of string (and a friend to stretch it) will work if you don't have a long straightedge.

Now locate the template on the guitar top with line B on the guitar's center line, and with line A located the correct distance from the front of the nut. (Exact measurements for the bridge-stud center line measurements are given at end of this section.) Mark exactly the two template mounting holes onto the guitar top; these should be 2¹⁵⁄₁₆" apart, or 1.465" to each side of the center line. Drill the mounting holes with a ⁷⁄₆₄" bit, and use #6 x 1" drywall screws for fastening. The holes must be perpendicular to the top, since later they'll be enlarged and used for the pivot-studs.

Screw the top template onto the body and measure ¼" from each edge of its top right corner, marking this location with a center punch. Remove the template and, using a drill press and brad-point drill bit for accuracy, drill a ½"-diameter hole here, right through the body. This hole aligns the front and rear templates (the modified rout skips this step).

Remount the template. You're ready to rout, using a ³⁄₈" ball-bearing bit. Eliminate plunging into the wood by starting each routing pass with the bit in the ½" locating hole drilled earlier. Rout the front ¹¹⁄₁₆" deep, but go slowly—no

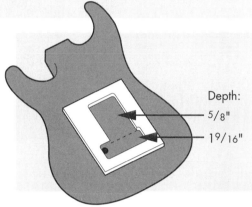

Depth:
5/8"
19/16"

more than ¼" per pass. The first rout is deeper than the others since, for the bearing to contact the template, the bit's full ½" cutting length must make the first pass (unless you shim the template up ¼" to get started, which is a good idea). Once you're ⁵⁄₈" or more deep, remove the template (its thickness might keep the bit from going to ¹¹⁄₁₆"). The bearing will follow the routed wall just created. Tape paper over the finish to avoid scratches from the router base plate. Stewart-MacDonald offers long-shaft bearing bits that permit chucking more shaft into the router collet—a safety feature I like. Never rout with less than ¼" of safely chucked shaft on the router bit!

The rear template mounts by aligning one corner over the pre-drilled ½" index hole (above). Square up the template lengthwise to the body. Drill mounting screw holes or use double-stick tape to attach it to the guitar.

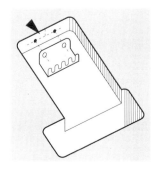

Rout the entire inside shape of the template to a depth of ⁵⁄₈". The rear rout will meet the front rout. Now the spring cavity is complete. Continue routing inside the template to a depth of 1⁹⁄₁₆" for good tremolo clearance. The rear template can now be removed. Center the tremolo-spring claw on the front wall of the rear cavity, with its two holes ³⁄₈" from the back of the guitar (drawing at left). Mark the holes and drill them with a long ⅛" aircraft bit.

Return to the guitar top, and redrill the two mounting holes 1¼" deep with a #10 bit; this is for the threaded portion of the mounting stud. Next, drill the holes again with a letter "I" bit, but only ⅜" deep. This hole gives clearance for the stud shoulder; it's a close-tolerance fit, since it supports the shoulder during use. Install the studs. Note: Press-in anchor inserts with machine-thread pivot studs are now available as a substitute for the original wood-thread studs. These eliminate wood fatigue and the loose studs that can occur with prolonged tremolo use.

The studs, tremolo, claw, and springs could be installed now, but without the locking nut and strings, what's the use? Hold on until we get the nut on, and then we can play a few tunes.

Here are the mounting distances for five popular tremolos, measured from the nut's front edge to the center of the pivot-stud line. Figures for both long and short scales are given. A common installation error is to install the tremolo too far from the nut, causing the guitar to play flat or the bridge saddles to hang over the unit's front edge. You'll be safe with these figures:

Tremolo	25½" Long scale	24¾" Short scale
Floyd Rose	25"	24 3/16"
Schaller Floyd Rose-licensed	24 15/16"	24⅛"
Ibanez Edge	25 1/16"	24¼"
Kahler Spyder	25"	24¼"
Gotoh Floyd Rose-licensed	25"	24¼"

MOUNTING THE LOCKING NUT

Now that you've installed the Floyd Rose stud-mount tremolo, continue by getting the locking nut on. Once you can lock the strings at both ends, your tuning troubles are over.

When we shot a videotape on Floyd Rose installation at Stewart-MacDonald, I was worried about how I'd teach the nut installation so that it could be done with simple tools such as a router. (I'd been doing my installations on a vertical milling machine.) I actually dreamed up the following method right during the shoot, and it works better than I would have guessed at the time! Stew-Mac now sells this jig, and if you plan to do more than one of these operations, or perhaps to get into the business, it would be a wise investment. It's inexpensive and comes with extremely detailed instructions, and you'd need a machine shop to build one as accurate. But for one-time do-it-yourselfers, here are the jig instructions in abridged form, with illustrations to help you fashion your own router jig.

The installation consists of cutting a ledge for the nut to sit on by removing a predetermined amount of wood where the original nut was installed. Then, holes for the nut's mounting bolts are drilled and countersunk. In an experienced woodworker's hands, a sharp chisel could cut the ledge quickly and easily, but a novice should use a Dremel Moto-Tool to slowly machine it. You players who are serious enough about guitar repair to install a locking nut yourselves should welcome an excuse to add a Dremel router to your toolbox.

Installation with chisel or router requires that you accurately measure the depth of the ledge, so that the nut ends up at the right level with respect to the frets. Having it too low causes buzzing, while having it too high creates a stiff action. A pair of dial calipers that measure in thousandths of an inch are a real help. Plastic-bodied dial calipers can be purchased for around $20—another invaluable addition to the tool chest.

When the outer two *E* strings are .010" above the height of the frets as they sit in the bottom of the nut slots, you're in the right ballpark. This is an average, slightly stiff playing height. You'd seldom want a higher action, and you can lower the nut if it feels too stiff. To rout the correct depth, you need one measurement: the distance from the locking nut's string-slot bottoms to the bottom of the unit itself ("A" at right). The nut described here is a Schaller R3 Floyd Rose-licensed model with an "A" measurement of .208". (Floyd Rose and Schaller designate neck/string spacing width with numbers ranging from R1 to R6; they're all slightly different at the "A" measurement.)

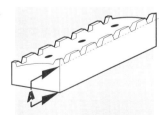

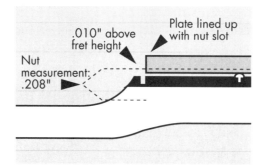

Here's how to guarantee that the nut-slot bottoms end up .010" higher than the fret height.

MAKING THE JIG

Clamp a flat, uniformly thick plate of wood, metal, Plexiglas, etc., to the first two frets, with its front wall flush to the original nut slot (above). Now, the bottom of the clamped plate is level with the fret tops, so if you use dial calipers to measure .010" short of the bottom, that's where you want the nut-slot bottoms to end up. Next, add the one nut measurement we took (mine is .208", yours could be different), and you'll have the distance from the top of the clamped plate to the nut bottom; this is the ledge to be routed.

The plate is more than a surface to measure from, however. With its front edge in line with the nut slot, it acts as a "fence" to guide the Dremel router base, keeping it from cutting into the end of the fingerboard. And routing the end of the fingerboard would change the overall string length—a disaster! The locking nut's front should be flush with the fingerboard end, with the nut bottom at a 90-degree angle to it.

Complete your installation jig by clamping a second platform of uniform thickness to the headstock face. This raises the Dremel Moto-Tool above the surface to be routed, allowing the cutter to be lowered into the wood by

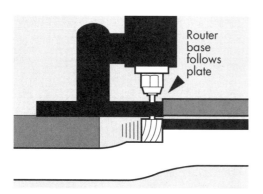

degree. You now have a usable facsimile of the jig I made, which is a single unit made of clear Plexiglas (the upper and lower plates are joined with threads and cap screws). The lower plate has a routing hole machined into it, and a built-in clamp holds it to the neck. There are two types of headstock: the straight, Fender style, and the angled, tilt-back Gibson type. With either, you remove the tuners in order to clamp on the platform (for the tilt-head, shim the table level with the fingerboard).

ROUTING

Use only a #115 Dremel router bit for the cutting. Rout no more than ¹⁄₁₆" per pass, and be sure that the bit cuts flush with the router's base edge. If the bit cuts more than flush, it could trim the fingerboard end. (If this happens, loosen the two mounting screws and wiggle the base into line, or put a couple strips of masking tape along the base edge to shim it away from the fingerboard).

Measure often from the top plate as you rout, and when the ledge is cut, lightly glue the nut body (with string clamps removed) to the ledge. Spray Hot Stuff accelerator on the nut bottom and put two small drops of Hot Stuff Special T super glue on the newly routed ledge. Thirty seconds' drying time will set the nut firm. Then use it as a drill guide for a #30 drill bit. Using a layer of wax paper in between, place a hunk of modeling clay under the rear of the neck/headstock area and press the neck into the clay to form it. The clay supports the wood, allowing your bits to punch through with no splinters! Drill down through the two mounting holes, right through the neck—the nut will hold the bit square. Now tap the nut loose using a block of wood and a hammer. Enlarge the #30 holes with an ¹¹⁄₆₄" bit, again drilling from the top side.

The countersunk holes are most safely drilled by using a step-bit. Stewart-MacDonald makes a step-bit with an ¹¹⁄₆₄" pilot to follow the ¹¹⁄₆₄" hole drilled earlier, and a ⁵⁄₁₆" outer bore that

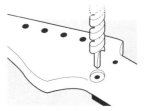

drills a shallow flat-bottomed hole for the bolt heads. Extra care must be taken to avoid the bits' grabbing or tearing the wood by accident. From the rear, countersink the holes until three or four threads protrude through the ledge when the bolt is inserted. This is plenty to hold the nut tight—any more, and the bolt could come through the locking nut's top and touch the string clamps. Go ahead and mount the nut. If your nut ends up too low, it's common to shim it up to the right level. Good shim materials included 3M wet-or-dry sandpaper in the 400, 600, and 1200 grits, or mesh-like drywall sandpaper with a good grip (check your lumberyard).

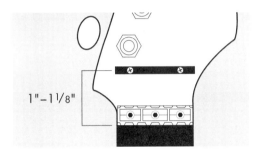

Last of all mount the retainer bar. Locate it 1" to 1⅛" from the front of the nut, and centered from side to side as at right. Drill the two screw holes with a ⁹⁄₆₄" bit marked with masking tape —this provides a visual depth stop to prevent drilling through the headstock! Put your strings on, and check your work. You're done with the worst part. Now we'll troubleshoot any problems, cover setup and fine-tuning, and look at the recessed top-rout made popular by Steve Vai and the Ibanez Jem 777.

Setting up the Floyd Rose

Now you can relax, since the job of setting up your tremolo is easy if you learn these simple set-up basics: Level the tremolo to the body by adjusting the springs and spring claw, set the string-to-fingerboard height by adjusting the two pivot studs, and adjust the intonation. Guitar Player magazine ran Mark Lacey's "Fine Tune Your Floyd" in its Sept. '88 issue, and I suggest you read it; your library probably has a copy. Action and intonation are discussed in the earlier chapters of this book, so I won't bore you with repetition. I'll just skim through the simple stuff, making a few important points as we go. This will leave some space to take a look at the optional recess rout made popular by Steve Vai and the Ibanez Jem 777 series.

Leave the locking nut unclamped while you do the following work. First, level the tremolo parallel with the body by adding or removing springs in the rear spring cavity. Using a Phillips screwdriver, adjust the spring claw in or out until the unit is level. Most players use either two or three tremolo springs for string gauges beginning with .008 or .009, and usually three for .010 and up. Experiment until you get the right feel. Next, the string height from the fingerboard should be set before adjusting the intonation. Most players look for a low action that shows around ¹⁄₁₆" between the bottom of the strings and the top of the 12th fret. However, most players settle for a slightly stiffer action than this—say, ³⁄₃₂". How low you can go depends on the adjustment of the neck and the condition of the frets.

Set the string height by simply raising or lowering the two pivot studs that the tremolo mounts on; this is much easier than with the individual saddle height adjustments common to Strats and many other guitars. Unless your tremolo uses machine-thread studs that adjust with an Allen wrench, use a flat-blade screwdriver with a sharp, well-ground tip that fits the stud slot snugly. This eliminates slippage that can not only mar the slot, but also cause the

You may need extra clearance in the spring cavity (exaggerated here). Note the tapered back wall: the shallow end may be ⁵⁄₈" to ³⁄₄", while the deep end may be ¹¹⁄₁₆" to ¹³⁄₁₆".

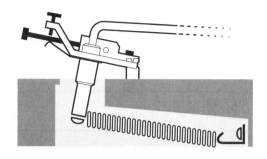

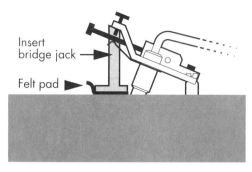

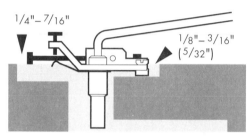

plating to lift away. As a general rule, most players adjust the tremolo so that the underside is from ⅛" to ¼" off the face of the guitar; this provides plenty of forward dump and a fair amount of up-pull.

Keep in mind that a tremolo set close to a guitar's face has little clearance in the rear for up-pull on the bar. A tremolo that's set high off the top may require shimming the bolt-on neck to keep the strings close to the fingerboard (for advice on neck shimming, see the bolt-on neck section of Electric Adjustments). Also, a high-set tremolo may seem uncomfortable for players accustomed to resting their picking hand on or near the body (one solution, the recess rout, is explained later). And, depending on the cavity depth, a tremolo that's mounted high off the body may cause the springs to rub the bottom of the spring cavity. Ibanez and Kramer use a tapered cavity to solve this problem (first drawing, top of next page).

Floyd Rose saddles are made in three different thicknesses or heights. The tallest is used for the *D* and *G* strings, the medium for the *A* and *B*, and the shortest for the two outside *E* strings. This saddle-height combination creates a curve in the bridge saddles that matches the radius curve of most electric guitar fingerboards. Many players find that the "medium" saddle curve of the Floyd Rose plays comfortably with most necks. Custom-tailoring the saddle height is possible by shimming the inserts with thin metal shim stock available from most automotive suppliers, or by carefully grinding the bottoms of the saddles to alter their height (this grinding is a tricky operation and should be left to a professional!). If you wish to experiment, replacement saddles are available directly from Kramer.

Setting the intonation of the Floyd Rose bridge saddles works on the same principle as any other adjustable bridge—if a string notes sharp, move the saddle back away from the nut;

if the note is flat, move the saddle forward toward the nut. Since the string is clamped into the saddle itself rather than into a separate tailpiece, the saddles tend to slide forward from string pressure when you loosen the Allen bolt that holds them in place. This can be annoying if your intention is to move the saddle back, since you have to loosen (detune) the string in order to do so. Try "dumping" the bridge forward and inserting a bridge jack (above, right) to hold the tremolo up, keeping the strings slack while moving a saddle back or forth. I made my jack out of two scraps of hard maple and covered the bottom with felt as a protection for the finish. Of course, an electronic tuner is a help for setting the intonation. When your setup and intonation are correct, clamp the locking nut tight.

Here are a few tips on recess routs, which involve the removal of wood under the tremolo (below the surface of the guitar face). This allows the tremolo to sit fairly close to the top (¹⁄₁₆" is common) while still having clearance in the rear for up-pull. Also, many guitarists keep their palm, hand, or entire arm on or close to the top while picking, and the recess rout keeps the bridge closer to the body for this type of picking comfort. Recess-routing templates are available from some guitar shop suppliers. Most recesses are from ⅛" to ³⁄₁₆" deep in the front portion of the rout, and deeper (¼" to ⁷⁄₁₆") toward the rear for up-pulling (above). Since you can always rout deeper, start with the shallower measurements and follow the ball-bearing routing techniques described earlier.

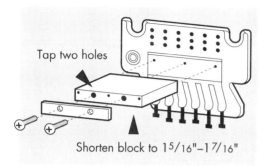

Tap two holes

Shorten block to 1⁵/₁₆"–1⁷/₁₆"

Recess routing may require shortening the tremolo block to keep it from sticking out of the guitar's back. The amount you shorten it depends on how close to, or deep into, the top you want your tremolo. The Ibanez Edge block measures 1⁵/₁₆", while Kramer's shortened block for their guitars with factory-equipped recess routs measures 1⁷/₁₆". I shortened the block on my Floyd Rose-licensed Schaller to match the Ibanez Edge tremolo. Here's how to do it:

With a ¹/₁₆" drill bit, deepen the five spring holes by the amount you plan to remove (up to ³/₈"). Using a hacksaw, remove up to ³/₈" from the block's bottom, and then file it smooth to a length of 1⁵/₁₆" or 1⁷/₁₆", etc. Drill and tap the two spring holes on each side of the center-spring hole to accept a machine screw; I used a 10-32 truss-rod tap that I had handy. Finally, make a ¹/₈" x 2" x ⁵/₁₆" flat spring retainer bar (¹/₈" screen-door aluminum stock purchased at the hardware store and hacksawed and filed to shape) with two clearance holes for mounting the bar to the tapped holes in the block. This will keep the springs from popping out when the tremolo's in use, especially on up-pulls where the springs go slack.

Well, that's about it for the Floyd Rose tremolo. For more information, read Mark Lacey's feature and check the Mar./Apr. '88 issue of *String Instrument Craftsman* for Chris Piles' article on Floyd Rose setups.

Kahler installation and setup

I chose the Floyd Rose tremolo to teach measuring, layout, and routing basics; not only because it's popular, but because it's the hardest to install. If you can mount a Floyd, you're good with a router and can definitely handle any other installations. The most popular and readily available tremolos on the market are the Floyd Rose, the Schaller-licensed Rose, and the Kahler flat-mount. The last section covered installing the stud-mounted "floating" tremolos; now watch how you can apply those same skills to installing another excellent and popular tremolo: the Kahler 2300 series, cam operated, flat-mount tremolo. The 2300 series is the original Kahler tremolo that became popular in the early 1980s.

Several features set the Kahler apart from stud-mount "floating" tremolos. It requires a much smaller body rout (removing less wood, and therefore less mass), and the rout doesn't need to go clear through the body, since it doesn't use a rear-rout for tremolo springs. Instead, the Kahler achieves its smooth operation by way of two small factory-installed springs, ball bearings, and a cam. Not having to rout clear through the body makes for an easy, good-looking installation on bodies that have never had a tremolo before, such as Gibsons, hand-made guitars, Teles, etc. Here's how the Kahler's installed, but first a word of advice before you turn on that router.

My friend and one-time apprentice Charlie Longstreth helped me compile this Kahler information, and he emphasizes a good point: "The first question that should occur to anyone about to install the Kahler or any other tremolo is: Should the installation be done at all? It'd be tragic to modify a pre-CBS Strat, and many Kahlers are mounted on Strats. If you're lucky enough to own one of those rare birds, pick up a newer Strat and put a Kahler on it—and even then, remember that Strats that are new now will be old someday. Maybe you should build a guitar from kit parts." Okay, let's begin.

While Kahler makes a version of its famous flat-mount tremolo that can be installed on the tailpiece studs of a Gibson ES-335 or Les Paul, we'll use the Strat-style guitar for this installation. First, be sure that your neck is lined up to the body the way you want it, especially with reference to the bridge and pickups. Read the section on bolt-on necks carefully, and then remove any parts that could get in the way of your router, such as the pickguard, pickups, bridge, and the volume and tone controls. Next lay a strip of masking tape over the six factory bridge mount holes, and lay out the center line of the body using the same method described for the Floyd Rose. Another way to find center is to use a straightedge long enough to lay along both sides of the fingerboard and extend out onto the body as far down as your masking tape. Mark the straightedge line on the tape and find the center between the two marks.

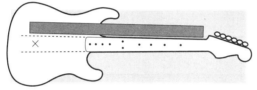

With each tremolo, Kahler supplies a heavy cardboard template to use as a guide for laying out the area to be routed and to locate the mounting screw holes. To ensure correct lengthwise placement and good intonation, this template is located on a line measured out from the nut and marked at right angles to the body center line. Note: This cardboard is not a routing template; it's only for locating the tremolo. If you're using a Plexiglas routing template, the cardboard piece can be omitted, since the Plexiglas template will work for the layout as well as the actual routing.

The front two mounting holes in the baseplate of the Kahler flat-mount 2300 bridge (and the layout templates) are intended to line up with, and screw into, the outer two mounting holes of a standard Stratocaster bridge. You can mount the bridge this way, but if you do, the roller saddles will not be centered with the center line of the neck (and more importantly the strings). The saddles will be closer to the treble side than they are the bass side because the center line of the two mounting holes is not the center line of the roller saddles! I'm unsure

why Kahler designed it this way, and it's not way off, but there is a difference of a healthy $\frac{1}{16}$" at the saddle. To avoid problems, lay out the correct center line of the saddles onto the template and then center to the neck's center line—ignoring the original Strat mounting holes. Here's how to do it right:

All the instructions I've seen for installing a Kahler recommend marking a center line on the template between the two front mounting holes and then centering the template on the guitar. Ignore that incorrect center line and make a new center line on the template which is 1.132" from the center of the bass side hole—not between the two holes.

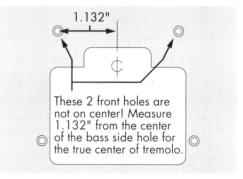

These 2 front holes are not on center! Measure 1.132" from the center of the bass side hole for the true center of tremolo.

When you center the template onto the body's center line, the original outside two Strat mounting holes will not line up. They'll be close, but not right, so plug the two holes and redrill them. (Or you can use the two rearmost holes at the back edge of the template to locate the bridge laterally, because they are centered to the bridge saddles). In either case you'll still have to plug the original Strat mounting holes if you want to be perfect. I had the wrong bridge centering information in the first edition of this book, and I apologize. My error was pointed out to me by Koenraad Strobbe, a repairman in Belgium. Thanks, Koenraad!

Three other considerations when trying to center the Kahler correctly on a traditional Strat are: 1) The pickguard may have to be trimmed on either side of the tremolo. 2) When the tremolo is lined up properly, a small bit of the original tremolo rout may peek through on the treble side. 3) Really, the above centering information is the most helpful for those about to install a Kahler on new work—where there's no good reason not to center it correctly in the first place.

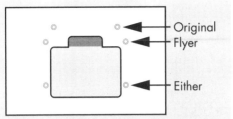

Rout the shaded area to a depth of 1/2:"
The rest of the cutout is routed to 1".
All holes are countersunk.

So on a Strat you can: 1) plug the holes, line the template on the body center line, and redrill the holes, or; 2) go with the two factory holes and ignore the center line you laid out. The safest way to guarantee an accurate placement is to ignore any pre-drilled holes and measure yourself. Here's some help:

To correctly place the Kahler in regard to the string length, measure from the nut's front (where it meets the fingerboard) down to the masking tape on the body, drawing a line at right angles to the center line. This new line is for lining up the two mounting holes of the template; later these holes will be used to mount the actual tremolo, since they're the same holes. If the original Strat tremolo mounting holes don't line up with this line, plug the outer two and redrill them. For a long Strat scale (25 ½"), measure 25 ¼" from the nut. For a short (24 ¾") Gibson scale, measure 24 ⁷⁄₁₆". Once you've located this line, attach the routing template to the guitar body using double-stick tape, or screw the template to the guitar's face with wood screws. The Stew-Mac template that I use (above) has countersunk mounting holes and can be used for either the Kahler Flyer or the Standard flat-mount. The front two holes are for the Original, and the rear/front holes are for the Flyer; the back holes are the same for either tremolo.

Mount the template with wood screws that are smaller than the final mounting screws, and make sure their heads are recessed and won't interfere with the router. After the template is mounted, scribe around the finish along the inside edge with a sharp scribe or X-acto knife. You'll be routing right up to this line, so scoring the finish first helps prevent chips when you remove the template.

Now I can take a break, and you can work. The routing's easy; just follow the directions given a few pages back for the Floyd Rose. The overall depth of the Kahler rout is 1", although many of us prefer to rout only ½" deep on the front part (the shaded area at left, which gives clearance for the two springs) to avoid taking away unnecessary wood, mass, and tone. When you've routed the cavity and vacuumed up the chips, lay a couple coats of clear lacquer on the bare wood to seal out moisture; you can even do this with a rag or a brush. If you want to get fancy, you can tape off the area and spray the new cavity with a matching paint. Sometimes I use black Magic Marker to darken the rout before the clear lacquer. That way, any part of the bare-wood cavity that you could see from the outside can no longer be seen. If your guitar requires a ground wire mounted to the bridge, run that wire now (on new work, you may have to drill a long hole from the tremolo rout to the control cavity, using a long ⅛" "aircraft" bit). You can get an adequate ground simply by screwing the tremolo base plate down onto a ground wire bent up the side of the cavity and wrapped over the edge. Keep this wire away from the workings of the tremolo! Go ahead and install the tremolo now, just to see how everything lines up, and then go on to the locking nut. But don't start playing with that wang bar yet!

Kahler offers the three nut styles shown above, plus one for their 7-string tremolo (not pictured). Two of them, the original Standard and the Deluxe no-wrench, flip-lever nut, are behind-the-nut locks that work together with a real nut. The third is called a Nut-Lock and is similar to the Floyd Rose, which requires that a ledge be routed for installation. We've already covered the Floyd style, so let's briefly discuss installing the behind-the-nut style; it's easy.

With a Strat, the only real work involved is in making a shim to support the nut at the proper height for getting good string angle through the nut slots. As with any nut, too steep an angle causes string binding or breaking in the slots, while too shallow an angle allows the strings to flop around, causing buzzes. Kahler recommends a string angle of 11 degrees between the string lock and the real nut; check this angle with a protractor.

Make the shim from a hardwood such as maple, rosewood, or ebony. Trace around the nut for the outside shape, mark the holes, and then drill them before shaping the shim; this eliminates splitting the delicate shim once it's shaped. Kahler offers pre-shaped and drilled Polystyrene shims that come in two shapes: a flat shim .068" thick (part # 8450), and a curved-bottom one (#8460) that measures .068" at the thickest part of its center but tapers quite thin at the edges of the bottom curve. In certain situations you may wish to stack different combinations of these shims together. The string-lock should be as close to the real nut as possible, while still keeping the right amount of angle to hold the strings in their slots (about ¼" to ⅜" from the rear of the nut). Too much distance between the lock and the real nut tends to store more slack than necessary. To keep from going clear through the headstock, use masking tape wrapped around your bit as a depth guide while drilling the four mounting holes (this is illustrated in the section on over-oiled tuners in Miscellaneous Repairs).

If you pick with a strong attack and are looking for big sustain, you may be interested in recessing your Kahler into the body. John Suhr, of Rudy's Music in New York City, inlays (or recesses) a Kahler flat-mount ⁵⁄₃₂" deep into the body. This allows you to raise the roller bridge saddles to their highest point in order to get a strong string angle over the roller (saddle), without having overly high action. As a general rule, Kahler recommends setting the bridge saddle roller height so that a minimum of .475" and a maximum .625" shows from the bottom of the outer two *E* strings to the guitar body. With the recess method you get the maximum

height (and more if you want), but still retain a normal string-to-body relationship, avoiding the necessity of shimming the neck in the body to keep up with the high rollers. Raising the saddle rollers really high creates better response and tonal quality, but the trade-off is more variance in tuning because you introduce more friction to the rollers with the increased string angle. This doesn't bother most players, though, so try it!

Note: If you recess the tremolo ⁵⁄₃₂", you must move the bridge forward ³⁄₃₂", since as the rollers are raised they also move backward— away from the nut—increasing the string length (just raise a roller saddle up and watch how much it moves). An alternate to recessing the Kahler is to raise the saddles high and then shim the neck to meet the strings; of course, the pickups have to be raised, too, and sometimes you just can't get them high enough. I should point out that Kahler doesn't recommend setting the saddles this high. There's nothing wrong with trying all these different setups and deciding for yourself; that's the whole idea of this book!

Kahler includes a pamphlet called Adjustment And Setup with each tremolo; it does a good job of teaching you how the tremolo works. They've also published a "Trouble Shooting Guide" and "Service Tips and Adjustments." Even if you're not experiencing any trouble, ask your dealer to get you copies of these pamphlets, because they'll come in handy some day. For additional reading on Kahler tremolos, check John Carruthers' columns in the Feb. and Mar. '84 issues of *Guitar Player* and read Chris Piles' setup tips in the May/June '88 issue of *String Instrument Craftsman*.

Fine-tuning a Strat tremolo

With its slab-style body, bolt-on neck, and "automotive"-style construction, the Stratocaster is easy to work on from the repairman's point of view—there's nothing to break! How often have you seen a Strat with a broken peghead?

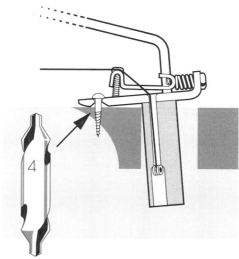

And even though the "Ten Steps" is an excellent approach for basic Strat setup, there are still a few points I'd like to make which are particular to Stratocasters. Understanding Strat quirks and knowing a few tricks of the trade can be a great help in adjusting your guitar for maximum playability.

TREMOLOS

Tremolos have been the rage since the early '80s, when Floyd Rose hit the guitar world with a locking nut and string-clamp "floating" tremolo system which eliminated most of the tuning problems long associated with tremolo use. Still, for many, the most desirable tremolo is that used on the Fender Strat—especially the two-piece unit made from '54 until late '71. Fender has introduced several Strat tremolo designs since then (most notably the "American Standard"), and when used with a properly set-up nut, they all work well. The nut is where most tremolo problems occur, as we'll see in a moment. So if you're a traditionalist not wanting to disfigure your favorite axe, you may wonder, "How can I keep my vintage Strat playing in tune, without installing a locking nut and modern bridge?"

I spent some time with my friend Doug Phillips, a guitar repairman from Norfolk, Virginia, who is a Strat man all the way and a serious blues player. I was impressed by his four unaltered Strats that play beautifully and stay in tune. We spent many hours discussing the fine points of setting up the standard tremolo, and came up with the following modifications and adjustments that not only help the guitar stay in tune but improve its sound as well. And all this is possible without installing any of today's locking nut/bridge systems, all of which require alteration of vintage Strats. These tips will be a help to vintage Strat lovers who are trying to keep up with the modern music world.

SMOOTH TREMOLO ACTION AND BETTER SUSTAIN

Before setting the tremolo, adjust the six mounting screws that fasten the bridge plate—if they're screwed down too tightly, the tremolo won't have the proper freedom of movement. It's a good idea to loosen the screws slightly and then retighten them slowly until they just touch the plate. Sometimes friction between the plate and screws causes jolting, catching, and sticking. One way to track down that problem (and often it's just one or two screws) is to remove the four center screws. Actually, the two outside screws alone are able to hold the bridge sufficiently for playing. Stevie Ray Vaughan sometimes used only two—proof of their strength, considering his high action, heavy strings, and hard-hitting blues attack. Test the tremolo function with only the outer two screws holding the bridge down, and then by replacing the screws one at a time, you'll find the problem. You can remedy this by carefully filing and fitting the holes to the screws:

With the bridge removed, inspect the six holes from the underside. You can increase the bevel by using a #4 counterbore (above). This increased bevel gives more of a knife-edge pivot point to the bridge where it rocks against the mounting screws, and therefore noticeably increases the sustain. Many bridges are beveled properly and need no modification, but it won't hurt to have a look. The bevels should be the same. Concentrate on the rear edge of the hole—the edge that bears against the screw. Bevel (countersink) the underside of the holes until the remaining rim is approximately $\frac{3}{64}$" to $\frac{1}{16}$" thick on each hole. When replacing the bridge, tighten all six screws snugly, and then back off each screw a quarter-turn; this keeps the bridge plate flat to the body while allowing enough room for the tremolo when in use.

A different approach is to hold the tremolo forward in the tilted position, and then tighten the screws against the plate, preventing undue pressure on the screws when the tremolo is in use. Use whatever method suits you. I've known some players who prefer using two

There are many ways to adjust tremolos other than the one explained here. The best way is to sit down and fiddle with your axe for a while to see what you like.

mounting screws, yet would rather keep the middle four screws for looks. This can be accomplished by drilling clearance holes in the plate so that the screws aren't actually touching or holding anything. The instrument is altered, however, which could affect its value.

SPRING ADJUSTMENT

Adjustment of the standard two-piece tremolo involves much trial and error. In the end you must please yourself, and there is no one way to do it. Some players prefer that the bridge come to rest on the body as a positive stop or return point after being "dumped" (pressed downward to lower the strings' pitch). These hard-hitting, string-breaking players often like a positive body stop, so that the remaining strings don't all go instantly out of tune from the difference in string pressure caused by a broken string. The standard factory setup, however, is with the tremolo plate raised slightly off the body at its rear (3/32" as mentioned previously), enabling players to cause the pitch to go slightly sharp by pulling up on the arm.

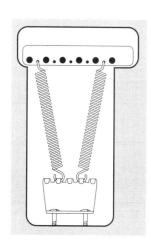

The tension adjustment of the tremolo springs depends on string gauge and desired tremolo action—a personal choice. Many players want the plate to return to the guitar's face after use, but keep more tension on the springs than is necessary. Here's a good test for proper spring tension: Pluck the open low-*E* string and, at the 15th fret, immediately bend your top *E* string one-and-a-half to two steps. If the low-*E* holds true, the spring tension is probably correct. If it goes flat due to the additional pressure caused by bending the top string, tighten the spring claw until the low-*E* is close to remaining in tune. Experiment to find the springs that best suit your style. Not all springs are the same length, size, or material, so shop around. Players using sets beginning with an .008 to .009 high-*E* should experiment with two or three springs; .010s and up play best for me with four springs. Properly adjusted springs should ring clear when plucked, with no dull, plunking sound. A good spring tension and tone are important to a Strat's unique sound, since they create a natural reverb chamber.

No absolute rule exists regarding the number of springs used and onto what claw hook and

into which tremolo block hole they should be placed. Some guitarists who favor light-gauge strings beginning with an .008 use only two springs with the claw backed most of the way out; .009 players often use three springs with the claw still backed out quite a bit. Most players, however, end up using either three or four springs and adjusting the spring claw to get the desired tremolo feel and return point. Some use five springs with medium or heavier strings (Stevie Ray, for instance, uses strings gauged .012, .015, .019, .028, .038, .058). I feel that five springs are too much, and I don't like the way a tremolo plays this way. String gauge is extremely important when adjusting tremolos, and you should decide on a favorite gauge before making any adjustments.

When experimenting with the number and placement of the tremolo springs, try two at first, placed on the second and fourth hooks of the claw and extending to the two outside holes of the block (left). If you want to add another spring—and most players do—place it in the center of the claw and block but relocate the other two springs to the outside hooks and holes. With four springs, simply omit the center one—the idea is to keep the springs balanced.

Here's a common tremolo setup trick that pleases most players: With the strings tuned to pitch, adjust the spring claw tension so that the bridge leans slightly forward, with the plate slightly off the face of the guitar (1/8" maximum). Fret an *A* at the 5th fret on the high-*E* string, and pull up on the tremolo arm until the plate hits the body and stops. Adjust the spring tension until the note played at the 5th fret is *Bb* when the plate hits the body. After this "half-step sharp" test is completed, you'll be able to pull up on the arm slightly. Of course, if you change string gauges or alter the number of springs, you have to start all over again.

ELIMINATING FRICTION

This information applies to any Fender instrument, but in particular to Strats with tremolos. If you eliminate the friction which causes strings to bind, you'll have a better playing axe—with or without a tremolo.

The modern locking nut/bridge system is so popular because it basically eliminates the

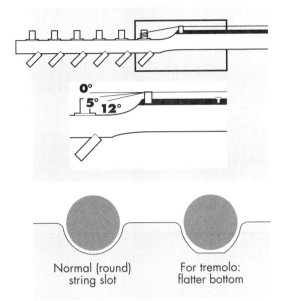

Normal (round)
string slot

For tremolo:
flatter bottom

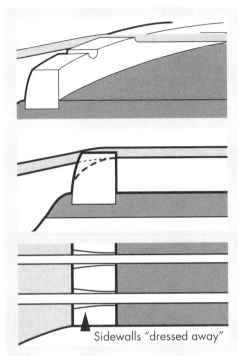

Sidewalls "dressed away"

problem of slack storage—string tension that "hangs up" at the friction points outside the playing area in between the nut and bridge. When you tune a string or run it through the nut and string tree by depressing the tremolo, the friction points (nut, string trees, and less often the bridge) can make the string hang up, causing it to return sharp and throwing the guitar out of tune. The stored slack is held temporarily and usually releases the next time you make a bend or use your tremolo. If you retune this "sharp" string, it will be flat when it releases. Most slack storage occurs at the nut, at the string tree hold-downs behind the nut, and to a lesser degree at the bridge. If you eliminate these friction problems, your guitar will stay in tune. Start with the nut.

For nut-making, I prefer bone over man-made nut blanks of Formica, phenolic, or plastic. Graphite can be a good choice for tremolo nuts, but I don't like the black color and it seems to wear quickly. The string angle, which comes from the tuner or string tree and breaks over the nut, should not be too steep when viewed from the side. A proper angle is between 5 and 12 degrees off the fingerboard plane—no more, no less (above).

The nut's grooves or string slots should be deep enough to hold the string and keep it from popping out when played, but no more than half the diameter of the string in depth. A nut slot should have a round bottom, and the slot

sides should bear slightly away from the string, so as not to bind. On tremolo guitars, some repairmen prefer a slightly flattened bottom for the string slot so that the slot's round shape doesn't grip the string as it moves (above, left).

Occasionally a repairman or manufacturer will hastily file nuts with too sharp a back angle. This puts all the load and friction at one very small point at the front of the nut. While the string should "take off" at the nut's front (where it meets the fingerboard and the actual string length begins), it should have some "meat" or backing behind it and gradually slope up to the front edge. The nut sidewalls should also be slightly dressed away from the string on the back side to allow free movement, and so that they don't pinch the string and keep it from returning to pitch (or cause a muting effect). Slots that are too shallow don't hold a string when it's bent from side to side, plus they can cause a string to pop out when least expected.

As a final step when you finish any nut— especially one designed for tremolo use—give a glossy polishing to the string-slot bottoms with (at least) 1000-grit wet-or-dry sandpaper; this relieves friction and improves tone. A little lubricant in the nut slot doesn't hurt either. Common nut lubricants are pencil lead, powdered graphite, Vaseline, or a Teflon lube such

If you remove your string trees, expect to make an adjustment in your playing style. The upper two strings will probably seem harder to bend.

as Magik Guitar Lube. (The Teflon types are the least messy!) A well-fit and lubricated nut allows the string to travel lengthwise without binding. You may be wise to have a troublesome nut replaced by a repairman who understands tremolo problems and will shape one carefully from a hard material, such as bone. Or, be adventuresome and try it yourself after reading the "Nut Work" chapter.

STRING TREE PROBLEMS

Eliminating the slack storage occurring at string trees can be done in a variety of ways, but the removal of them alone is not a solution, because then there will be insufficient down-pressure, or angle, at the nut, and the strings may pop out when struck. Also, without a decent angle at the nut, a great loss of tone occurs. Roller trees are available from a variety of sources (check your music store— Wilkinson makes several). These are an easy retrofit for the originals, allowing the strings to move smoothly when the tremolo is used.

All Strats have a string tree for the *B* and high-*E* strings; on models made after '59, this tree is supported by a plastic or metal spacer. Often players remove the spacer and screw the tree down to the headstock face—don't do that! The angle becomes too steep, and the spacer is an improvement. Be sure that the string tree is deburred and polished, and use it. Strats made since '71 also have a tree for the *G* and *D* strings. The trees and spacers put enough angle on the nut to keep the string from popping out, but not so much that they cause the string to bind from friction and not return in tune. Combat friction at the trees with Teflon gun oil or Magik Guitar Lube—just a drop on the underside is a help.

With the four highest strings, two or three windings around the tuner maintains a proper angle between the tuner and string tree. If you remove the tree that holds the *G* and *D* strings or own a pre-'59 one-tree Strat, experiment with the number of downward windings (toward the bottom of the tuner post) needed to achieve the correct string-to-nut angle. On the low-*E* and *A* strings, any more than two downward windings cause too great an angle, and the strings will bind when the tremolo's in use. A neat trick is to wind the string up toward

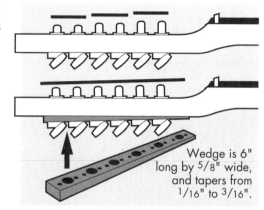

Wedge is 6" long by 5/8" wide, and tapers from 1/16" to 3/16".

the top of the post, to let you control or alter the angle.

You can eliminate the trees entirely by using replacement tuners with graduated shaft heights (above). Sperzel and Schecter offer graduated shaft pegs, so check with your dealer to find what's currently available. Installing these pegs, however, involves enlarging the tuner-shaft hole. Instead of enlarging the holes on his '62 Strat, Doug made a tapered hard-wood wedge, drilled clearance holes for the tuners and screws, and slipped it between the tuners and the back of the headstock. This "wedge" solution works well, doesn't disfigure a vintage instrument, and is a simple way out if graduated shaft height solves your problem. Wilkinson also offers machined aluminum wedges just like Doug's, which work great. If you remove your string trees, expect to make an adjustment in your playing style, because the upper two strings may seem a little harder to bend; you may have to push further to get the desired note. You'll be pleased, though, that the string has a little more resiliency at the top of the bend. Also, this extra resiliency results in a lot less string breakage, since the strings tend to give more.

STRING BREAKAGE

Breakage usually occurs where the string angles over the bridge plate. You can radius (taper) these holes with a small file and sand-paper, or by grinding a radius on one end of the #4 counterbore mentioned earlier and using it in an electric drill to bevel the hole evenly (above, right). This type of counter-bore is generally used by machinists and is available at most industrial supply stores; any machine shop can quickly grind a radius on it. Besides

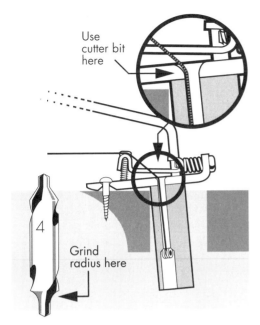

Use cutter bit here

4

Grind radius here

Being extremely stiff, this spring keeps the tremolo arm from being either too tight or too loose. I bought my punch/spring from Holiday Steel Rule And Die in Greensboro, North Carolina, but you should be able to find one at any die-maker's shop."

Roger's idea works great. Note that this will only work on old-style Strat tremolos (made before 1970) that have a bottom to the hole; otherwise the spring would simply fall out. Readers can avoid having to buy a die-punch cutter by finding a hardware or industrial supply store with a good selection of springs; any stiff spring works. Wear safety glasses when using a grinder, and be sure the wheel isn't cracked. Read the strict grinder safety precautions given in "Making your own fret files."

eliminating string breakage, this bridge-plate modification also helps eliminate binding that occurs at the same point. An easier solution is to do what Stevie Ray Vaughan did: Slide a piece of plastic wire insulation over the string at the point of contact at the bridge saddle. This must inhibit some tone and sustain, although you can't prove that by listening to Stevie Ray!

If you follow these tips, you should find that your guitar stays in tune nicely and has marked improvement in tone. For many years, the Strat tremolo has been a great invention; it simply needs a little understanding and care.

A Strat tremolo modification

Richard H. Ruth of Oklahoma City wrote to me: "I converted my tremolo from a face-mount to a semi-floating, knife-edge type. To do this, I bought some brass at a local hobby shop, bent it into shape, removed the tremolo, and mounted the new brass plate to the mounting holes on the body. Since the brass was bent to more than a 90-degree angle, it held the 'knife edge' of the tremolo when I replaced it. The only non-reversible alteration to my guitar came when I filed the underside of the bridge's leading edge to a sharper contact point. This modification changes the tremolo's pivot point

Tightening up a loose Strat tremolo arm

Here's an interesting idea from Roger L. Scruggs of Lynchburg, Virginia: "In regard to Strat tremolo arms going limp, I have a remedy that works well on my '63 Strat. I removed the center spring from a small die punch cutter and ground a ¼"-long piece off from one end. This spring is about ⁵⁄₃₂" in diameter and very stiff. I then dropped the spring into the tremolo arm hole and screwed down the arm until it hit the spring (right). By tightening the arm slowly until it met with resistance from the spring, there was enough up-pressure on the bottom of the arm to keep it from rotating.

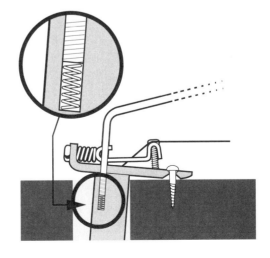

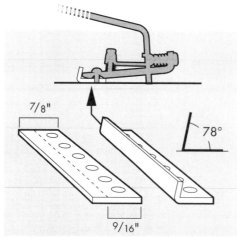

from the mounting screws to the front edge of the unit. The guitar returns to pitch almost as well as an expensive locking tremolo, and the tone is much improved. The only tools I used were a vise, a hammer, a ⅜" electric drill for drilling and countersinking the mounting holes, a hacksaw for cutting the brass to length, and a file. I replaced the original mounting screws with a countersunk variety having the same thread as the originals. The brass plate is ¹⁄₁₆" thick and around ⅞" to 1" wide, and I only needed to cut it to length. For a dollar I got enough brass to make two—and that was a good idea, since I messed up the first one (some experimentation was required to arrive at the proper bending angle so as to retain, but not restrain, tremolo movement)."

I asked Richard if I could borrow the guitar to try it out, and he sent it to me the next day. It works smoothly, and seems to return in tune well. Another nice thing about the conversion is that he enjoyed doing it. Many players love to customize their guitars and are looking for new jobs to do. Richard's idea is fairly easy to perform, and it doesn't really alter the guitar much. If you're squeamish about filing on your stock bridge, buy a replacement bridge/tremolo and use that instead—especially if you have a vintage guitar. A "floating" tremolo is one that doesn't come in contact with the body of the guitar when it returns to pitch, since it's raised up from the surface. This enables the player to pull up as well as push down on the tremolo arm. In some cases, the neck may have to be shimmed in its pocket to accommodate the shimmed-up tremolo unit. Thanks for the tip!

The Trem-Setter

Before concluding this chapter on tremolos, it's appropriate to say a few words about the Trem-Setter, a device that helps keep a tremolo guitar in tune. Designed by David Borisoff of the Hipshot Company, this tremolo stabilizer was first introduced in 1988. Since then thousands have been installed—not only by repair shops on a custom basis, but also at the Fender factory on their Strat Plus, Strat Plus Deluxe, and Ultra Strat guitars. Some players misunderstand the Trem-Setter's use and expect too much from it. So let's look first at what it will and won't do for a wang bar, and then I'll present some tips to make the installation even easier than it already is.

The Trem-Setter is an adjustable, spring-loaded device that replaces the center tremolo spring on locking or standard tremolos. It installs in the rear spring cavity, replacing the standard five-spring tremolo claw with two individual outer spring claws. This leaves the center spring area open for the Trem-Setter, which mounts on a hook (or "hinge-clip," as it's called) screwed to the cavity bottom. A brass pull-rod connects the Setter to the sustain block, so it moves with the block as the player works the tremolo and helps return the tremolo to the same spot after use. It also keeps even tension on the tremolo so that bending or tuning a string doesn't cause the other strings to drastically alter their pitch. The installation and adjustment instructions supplied by Hipshot and Fender are accurate, but a little too technical; they don't say enough about what the Trem-Setter does, or how it's done. So I talked with David Borisoff and Fender's George Blanda, both of whom had a lot to say.

"The main reason I designed the Trem-Setter," says Borisoff, "was to get away from the equilibrium, or balance, of the strings and springs controlling whether a guitar's in tune or not. The standard tremolo is like a bathroom scale—you can get on the scale twice and get two different readings. Or if you stand on the scale and shake, like shaking or bending a string, you'll make the dial flutter on both sides of your actual weight. This is what happens to a tremolo bridge when you bend notes, play certain notes with a strong attack, or even hit certain open strings: You upset the balance, and the tremolo flutters back and forth. The Trem-Setter's like a car's shock absorber; it stabilizes the tremolo."

According to David, the unit accomplishes the following:

1 Improves the guitar's tone by controlling flutter. It stops the tremolo from absorbing or wasting the string's energy as it passes on to the body.

2 Helps the tremolo return to its zero point in tune. This is not true, however, if the guitar has a poorly made nut, inadequate tuners, or improperly mounted strings. Locking tuners and the Wilkinson roller nut work well with the Trem-Setter, of course.

3 Keeps the remaining strings in tune when you bend a string. String-bending adds tension and causes the tremolo to "sag," or lean forward, which lowers the pitch of all the other strings. The Trem-Setter keeps sagging to a minimum.

4 Makes string-bending easier. Since the bridge isn't sagging toward the fingering hand, lowering the pitch, you don't have to bend nearly so far to get a note. Players who don't like tremolo guitars may have a change of heart if they try one with a Trem-Setter.

5 Keeps the strings in better tune if you rest your hand on the bridge or intentionally mute the strings. It's not a big factor, but the Trem-Setter can be set up with this in mind.

6 Helps make up for worn knife edges at the pivot point.

Let me point out the one thing it won't do: It won't keep a guitar in tune if you break a string. It was never intended to. The amount of tension needed to compensate for a broken string would detract from the Trem-Setter's sensitivity.

I asked Blanda if all tremolos have bridge flutter: "At Fender we call it 'warbling' when you get the bridge flutter that David's talking about. Any well-balanced tremolo guitar warbles a little, but that's the trade-off for having a sensitive tremolo that's free from friction and returns to pitch. The tremolo moves to accommodate the different tensions it receives from the oscillation of the strings. This movement is less pronounced with a vintage Strat tremolo, since the bridge plate has a solid rest on the body; it's not delicately balanced on two knife edges like the American Standard. If you want to make a two-point tremolo warble, just to know what we're talking about, pick the G string hard at the 14th fret, or pluck it with your bare fingers, and listen—you'll hear it if it's there. At Fender it's easy for us to take two brand-new identical Strats, one with and one without a Trem-Setter, and compare their sound. You can really hear the difference. The guitar with the Trem-Setter has a better, more solid tone, and any warble is stopped." I've heard that Leo Fender called the tremolo's sustain block an "inertia block" in the original patent drawing, showing that he knew that something was needed to smooth out the string-to-bridge vibration and put the energy to good use.

How much does the Trem-Setter change the feel of a tremolo as it's being dumped or pulled up? Blanda responds: "Not too much, and not at all when you pull up, because the pull-rod moves through the spring on an up-pull, without affecting the tension at all. The tension of the Trem-Setter's spring is comparable to that of a normal tremolo spring. But rather than the spring stretching when you dump the tremolo, it compresses. A factory setup for a Strat Plus uses three springs and usually .009–.042 or .010–.046 strings. A player who wants to use only two springs and .008 strings couldn't benefit from the Trem-Setter, since it's a three-spring system. Besides, we don't recommend using two springs on a tremolo in the first place. I should point out that all springs are not the same tension; springs used on locking tremolo systems are typically stiffer by as much as 15%. In a repair shop, extra springs end up laying all over the place, and if the wrong springs end up being used along with the Trem-Setter, the tension won't be right when you dive-bomb."

Sometimes I feel, or almost hear, a little drag when I press the wang bar on a Strat Plus. "This

Playing a guitar outfitted with a Trem-Setter feels more like playing a non-tremolo guitar.

The knife edges on a new tremolo are sharp, and returning to "0" is not a problem. As wear causes the edges to round off, it may no longer provide the frictionless movement needed to return to absolute "0." The Trem-Setter overcomes that friction.

is not normal," Borisoff explains, "but it can happen. Over time we discovered that if too much grease was used on the brass pull rod, it actually vacuumed around the small stop-collar washer as it moved, creating a suction effect. Dismantle the Setter, clean off any grease, and when you reassemble it, leave the washer dry or lightly lubricate it with WD-40. Be careful not to lose the washer when you take the device apart—the parts want to pop all over the place. We may switch to a fiber washer that not only won't vacuum onto the rod, but will also compress less, eliminating any possibility of slop. If you do take the unit apart, once the small slack spring that pushes against the stop collar is removed, you can see how the brass collar bears against the end of the threaded brass tube that the pull-rod slides through." How much can the nylon thread nuts be tightened or loosened when the tremolo's tension is being adjusted? "You can tighten it a lot," says Blanda, "but you won't want it too tight. You'd never want to see more than ⁵⁄₁₆" of exposed thread on the brass tube: experiment till you find an adjustmnet that feels right. As for loosening it, by temporarily removing the lock collar spring as we mentioned, you'll see that loosening the nylon thumb-nut counter-clockwise too much causes it to hit the brass stop collar—you don't want that! The whole trick in setting up the Trem-Setter is to get the brass stop collar to make perfect contact with the washer at the end of the threaded brass tube when the tremolo is sitting at its balance point. Then any lowering of the tremolo arm puts the Trem-Setter into operation instantly. You can loosen the thumb-nut tension as far as you like as long as it doesn't touch the collar. Hold one nylon thumb-nut while you tighten or loosen the other; otherwise they'll just rotate together, and nothing happens."

I asked Borisoff if he thinks there's a tone improvement when a Trem-Setter is installed: "I don't think there's an improvement, I know it. When the string's energy hits the bridge, you want it to transfer instantly to the body so that the sound comes from the bridge and body together. When a tremolo flutters at the balance point, the tremolo block and springs cancel out and absorb much of the string energy that

you're working hard to get to your amp. The player puts a lot in, but not enough comes out. It's like running in sand, where half the energy just pushes sand behind you, with only half left to push you forward. Get on solid ground, and you can take off with a one-to-one transmission of energy and no waste." Blanda adds, "There's a better coupling between the tremolo block and the body, which produces a difference you can really hear."

One of the big questions, of course, is how well does the Trem-Setter work with a standard Strat tremolo? "Quite well if the guitar is set up right," insists Borisoff. "A vintage Strat has friction at the six mounting screws of the bridge plate, as well as at the nut slots, non-locking tuners, and string trees. Comparatively speaking, a Strat Plus looks pretty good with its roller nut, two-point pivot, and lack of string trees and locking tuners. So setup is crucial on a vintage Strat. All friction points must be smoothed and lubricated so the strings can't hang up and store any slack."

INSTALLATION TIPS

Installation instructions come with the Trem-Setter, so rather than going through the whole operation, I'll just add my notes to what you already have. The installation only takes about a half-hour, and the tools needed are an electric hand drill, a small ruler, Phillips screwdrivers, and such. Adjust the stock tremolo to suit your tastes before you begin the installation, and take the time to set your guitar up right.

Since the original five-hook spring claw is replaced with two individual outer spring claws, you'll be setting the tremolo balance point with two springs instead of three; the Trem-Setter has no effect or spring tension on the tremolo until you depress or lower the strings. This enables you to tighten the spring claws closer to the end of the cavity than you could with three springs.

The hinge-clip has two mounting holes; the front hole (closest to the tremolo block) is located 3 ³⁄₈" out from the sustain block. The hinge-clip mounts at right angles to the block and in line with the center spring hole. Use a center-punch to mark the hole and help the drill bit stay on center. Use a #50 drill bit for soft

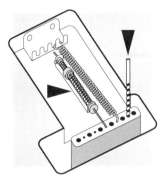

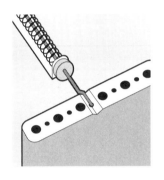

wood and up to a #80 bit for hardwood (the bits vary depending on the type of wood—practice drilling on scrap to be sure it works for you). Drill only the front hole at this time. Then temporarily mount the hinge-clip with one screw, and not too tightly. Now put the Trem-Setter onto the hinge-clip and snap the brass pull into the center spring hole of the tremolo block. Since the hinge-clip is slightly loose, it will line itself up naturally with the tremolo block. When it does, mark it, remove the Trem-Setter, and drill and mount the other hinge-clip screw.

The instructions call for drilling a ³⁄₁₆" clearance hole in the end wall of the tremolo cavity, but they don't tell you that you really should use a long aircraft drill bit. You can order such a bit through a hardware store, or have the hole drilled at your local repair shop. The long bit can create the low angle necessary to allow proper clearance for the Trem-Setter's pull-rod. The bit I use is 12"–14" long. I use a smaller ⅛" bit as a pilot, and then enlarge that hole with the ³⁄₁₆", so there's less chance for the larger bit to run off course.

I was thrown a couple of curves on two recent installations. The pull-rod hook and thumb-nut nearest to it scraped the back cover plate when the tremolo was dumped. The instructions advised rebending the pull-rod hook if this happens, so that its angle matches the angle of the hole in the tremolo block (it won't seat right if the angles don't match). I stuck a #50 (.070") drill bit into an empty hole so I could see the true angle of the tremolo block spring holes, and then bent the pull rod's brass hook to match (upper drawing at right). In one case this was the solution, but in another it wasn't—I found a different problem.

I was working with a replacement neck and body, an original Wilkinson roller nut (not the Strat Plus style), and a real American Standard tremolo that I got in a parts swap. By laying a straightedge across the back while working the tremolo, I could see just where it was rubbing, and that bending the hook wouldn't quite solve my problem. In this case the spring cavity was deeper than that of a real Strat (¹¹⁄₁₆" to ¾" as opposed to ⅝"), causing the Trem-Setter's pull rod to rise at an angle where it

hooked into the block. I used my Dremel tool with an abrasive mesh wheel to grind a groove across the bottom of the block (lower right), so the hook would sit deeper and at less of an angle. I might have been able to shim the hinge clip up ¹⁄₁₆" to ⅛" higher to get the same effect, but I took this route. You probably won't run into this problem, but if you do, you're ready.

One trick Dave Borisoff uses when the brass hook needs to be re-bent is to hammer on the hook with a center punch or nail set while it's in the trem-block; the block acts as an anvil, which shapes the hook to the right fit. I haven't tried this, but metal-working experience tells me it would work. The pull rod is made from a fairly soft brass, so don't hammer too hard—tap it!

In summary, I like the Trem-Setter. Here's what I think it can and can't do:

1 For me, its biggest feature is the way it eases bending strings and the fact that the other strings stay in tune when I get there.

2 It does a good job of helping a tremolo return to zero. It's perhaps 98% successful, so it isn't perfect: you should know that before you start. The slight 2% out-of-tune effect that may remain after dumping the tremolo can be straightened out by shaking the tremolo bar or hitting the bridge with the palm of your hand to settle it back into place.

3 As for the improvement in tone resulting from a better string/bridge/body coupling: if you can make an already great-sounding Strat Plus sound even better, I'm all for that.

4 String flutter or warble is something most players aren't bothered by, but for those who are we've now a way to eliminate it besides "blocking" the tremolo (many players shove a hardwood block between the sustain block and the body to improve tone, eliminate flutter, and stop the guitar from going out of tune).

5 The improved stability doesn't do much to keep the bridge from moving if you rest your hand on the bridge while you pick or mute the strings. It might do a little to help, but when you press down on the back of the bridge, you're pushing in the direction that the Trem-Setter's spring has no control over (this is the only claim of the manufacturer that I disagreed with). But David Borisoff explains that if you slightly loosen the two tremolo springs and then tighten the Trem-Setter's buck spring a little, your bridge should have more stability in the string-raise mode, letting you rest your hand on the bridge more.

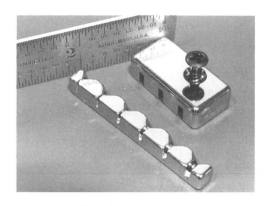

Alternatives to the locking nut

The Wilkinson Original Roller is an excellent tremolo nut that uses roller string trees, and it's offered in a variety of custom options. It's available through dealers and some guitar parts suppliers.

THE WILKINSON ROLLER NUT

Many tremolo users don't want to hassle with a locking nut and don't want to use a tremolo system which can only be tuned with fine tuners. To help guitars with traditional tremolos stay in tune (and help them return to pitch), Trev Wilkinson designed the "Wilkinson Roller Nut." It uses steel rollers in the string grooves, or nut "slots," to help ease the friction that occurs during tremolo use. Wilkinson's roller nut is significant because he also made a variation of it for Fender (the "Fender/Wilkinson Nut") which was Fender's non-locking alternative for tremolo players from 1987 until 1993—and standard equipment on many thousands of Strat Plus guitars during that period. Then, in the summer of '93, Fender switched to the LSR ball-bearing roller nut designed by Bill Turner. Here's some information on the Wilkinson Roller Nut.

Like Floyd-style locking nuts, the Wilkinson nut requires some removal of wood to create the flat on which it sits. Also, the end of the fretboard must be shortened by ¹⁄₁₆" in length so that the nut's rollers are in the correct spot for intonation. So, while the wood removal necessary for either Wilkinson nut is minimal when compared to a Floyd-style locking nut, some routing is necessary, and the need to shorten the fingerboard means you wouldn't be installing these on a vintage axe for sure.

The Original Wilkinson nut is ³⁄₁₆" in width, which means you end up with a nut slot of ¼" on a Fender or a Gibson. The nut comes with a separate "hold-down," installed behind the nut, to keep down-pressure on the rollers. (Fender's Strat Plus nut has six roller hold-downs built right into the nut frame, and that's

why it's significantly wider (½") than the ³⁄₁₆" Original.

Both Original and Fender/Wilkinson nuts have a chrome-plated brass housing that holds six loose-fitting needle-bearing rollers at its front edge. The nut's six individual string slots measure, from treble to bass, .011", .014", .018", .028", .038", and .049". Deduct a half-thousandth (.0005) from each measurement for chrome plating, and you'll know what string gauges fit through the slots (a set of .010 – .046 works best, and an optional nut for .012– .052 strings was available).

The Wilkinson nut, at times, may exhibit any of the following problems: 1) seizing of the rollers; 2) too tight a string notch, which would bind on some strings and not allow it to return in tune; 3) sometimes, rattles or buzzing. Partly because of these intermittent problems, Fender retired the Wilkinson nut in the summer of 1993. According to Dan Smith, Fender's Vice President of Marketing:

"When we first looked at the Strat Plus, we knew we had a great unit in the American Standard Tremolo. We'd made 10 or 11 different tremolos over the past 15 years, and the American Standard was the best—it surprised even us. Taking advantage of this tremolo meant stabilizing what goes on at the headstock between the nut and the tuners. Trev Wilkinson happened along with his roller nut at just the right time. He redesigned it with exclusive, built-in hold-downs to do away with string trees on the headstock face.

"Our first model had rollers on the top three strings only. Soon, we installed them on all six strings to get better down-pressure on the wound *E*-, *A*-, and *D*-string rollers. This eliminated any chance of open-string buzz caused

by either inadequate string angle or from head-stock deflection. It's a little-known fact that a headstock can deflect —or bend up—toward the strings. This changes the down-pressure slightly, but enough to cause a possible buzz. Some headstocks deflect, and some don't, even when made from the same tree. A traditional nut can work well with a tremolo, if everything's perfect and if it's made by a skilled luthier. But those 'perfect' nuts have only a short lifespan before wearing low enough to warrant replacement—another reason we wanted a roller nut on the Plus.

"We were happy with the Wilkinson nut, and of course there are thousands of Strat Plus Strats out there equipped with it—and an equal number of satisfied players. The fact is that less than 5% of those Strat Plus nuts had any problems. However, we never stop looking for ways to improve our products. We found that improvement in the LSR nut designed by Bill Turner."

SOLVING THE PROBLEMS

For those of you having problems with any version of a Wilkinson nut—the Original or the Fender version—here are some solutions:

First, eliminate any binding in the slot. A too-narrow string slot can cause a string to bind (usually the high-*E*), keeping it from returning to pitch or causing a buzz at the roller. The binding may be caused by a warp you could never see or measure, or it may be due to a bit too much plating. I use a "lightning strip" to carefully deburr the back edge of the string slot (above). These thin metal strips are coated with diamond dust; your dentist uses them to clean between your teeth after a filling—ask for one. I also use my .010" Precision Nut File, again on

the rear wall of the nut housing. Don't scar the rollers!

Sometimes there's no binding trouble, but a slight buzz. Most likely, this sitar-like sound is on the high-*E*. If a buzz isn't being caused by string-slot binding, it's generally intermittent and will go away by itself (especially if you try to show it to your repairman). But if it won't play itself out, try these remedies:

■ Simply put on a fresh set of strings.

■ With the strings removed, tap lightly on the problem roller with a sharp-pointed tool such as an awl, ice pick, scribe, etc.

■ Remove the strings and blow out the nut with compressed air.

■ Loosen the nut's mounting screws, let the strings line the nut up naturally, and retighten. Often, just moving it like this solves the problem! Don't overtighten the two small mounting screws—just make them snug.

■ Lubricate the offending roller after it's been blown out with air. To avoid attracting dust, use a non-oily Teflon type of lubricant. A little dab will do you.

■ Rinse out a dirty nut with a spray-type tuner degreaser followed by a blast of air.

■ To alter the nut height, your Fender dealer stocks stainless-steel nut shims in thicknesses of .002", .005", and .010".

REMOVING AND REPLACING THE WILKINSON NUT

Here's how Roger Sadowsky solves problems with the Wilkinson nut. Roger, of "Sadowsky Guitars" in New York City, is in the mainstream of guitar repair and setup. His repair work is renowned, and so are the guitars and basses he makes. Roger offers this solution to problems with the Wilkinson nut:

"I replace it when a customer experiences any problems. The nut really only works its best with .009 strings. As soon as you use .010's, the problem of the string binding in the slot often shows up. And the intermittant buzzes may happen with any string gauge (or not at all). We replace the roller nut with the Floyd-Rose Replacement Nut from Allparts. The Allparts nut is made from "Ebonal," a black, low-friction phenolic somewhat like Micarta, and was

Roger Sadowsky

designed for players wishing to convert back from a locking-nut system.

The truth is, I think most people are not knowledgeable enough about guitar set-up to complain. They don't know that it's not working right. I will say that if Trev Wilkinson himself installs the nut and sets it up, there won't be any problems. But most of us out in the field have met with some trouble. Here's how we take care of the problem:

1 Use a ⅟₁₆" spacer to add back the missing fingerboard length.

2 The Allparts nut has holes for the Floyd nut-mounting screws, but they don't match the Wilkinson holes. We avoid plugging and re-drilling mounting screw holes in the neck by simply super-gluing in the Allparts nut.

3 Mount a string retainer on the peghead behind the nut.

4 Adjust the string grooves in the replacement nut and set up the instrument."

FENDER'S NEW LSR ROLLER NUT

The LSR nut is now a factory installation on the Strat Plus, Deluxe Strat Plus, and Strat Ultra models. This innovative roller nut design features rotating steel ball bearings which are precision-set within a compact stainless steel housing, or "frame." (This frame is smaller than the Fender/Wilkinson nut—about the size of the ³⁄₁₆" Original Wilkinson nut). There are two balls for each string, and the photos here show how it works:

1 The frame's string clearance slots will accept string gauges from .008" to .056" (high-*E* to low-*E* respectively) without touching the strings. The strings' only contact is with the the two steel balls. The steel balls accommodate—

and center automatically—the same variety of string gauges (.008" to .056").

2 Top view (with retainer clip removed, above) shows balls nestled in their respective housings. Notice the half-moon shaped neoprene pressure pads at the rear of the steel balls—these put just enough pressure on the balls as the strings move through them to eliminate ring, buzz, and rattle (but not enough to stop the motion). The top-mounted retainer clip holds the ball bearings and pressure pads in place, and screws down as the nut is tightened home.

Fender is also offering the LSR nut separately for custom installation (through your Fender dealer). This includes a special adapter for an easy upgrade of those models produced before the introduction of the LSR. If you have an older Strat Plus, Deluxe, or Ultra, you can switch to the new nut easily if you wish.

That's it for roller nuts. I'd say more about the LSR, but I haven't been able to find anything to fix on it. Being stainless it won't rust, and lubrication isn't even necessary, according to Dan Smith. An occasional cleaning with a dry toothbrush is the only maintenance chore!

String benders

When Fender Telecasters are mentioned, talk of the late Clarence White and his legendary Stringbender is never far behind. In 1967 Gene Parsons created the first Stringbender for Clarence's Tele, and shortly thereafter Clarence immortalized it on the Byrds' *Sweetheart Of The Rodeo* album, with his buddy Gene on drums.

Beside the Stringbender, the other popular string-bending devices are the Glaser bender (used by Ricky Skaggs and Diamond Rio's Jimmy Olander) and the Hipshot (Hellecaster Will Ray's weapon of choice). All three devices create a "pedal steel" effect by raising a string's pitch (normally a whole step on the *B* string) when a lever is activated. Let's look at what's involved with installing these devices, starting with the original.

THE PARSONS/WHITE STRINGBENDER

Since it involves removing wood from the body, Stringbender installation permanently modifies a guitar. It's available as a $395 kit that includes an excellent 25-page instruction book, but the factory recommends having it installed by an authorized dealer/installation center ($550 installed). Do-it-yourselfers must have advanced woodworking skills, access to a router and drill press, and a good selection of hand tools. Here's why:

■ A rear-routed cavity in the body houses the mechanism (above, right). The pull-lever connects to the guitar strap through the side (shoulder).

■ Connected to the strap, the pull lever is activated by pushing down on the neck.

■ The strap button on the pull lever travels $^{17}/_{32}$" when depressed, creating a whole-step *B*-string bend, and it moves a string-pull "hub" on the guitar's face.

■ The *B* string runs from the pull-hub to the bridge saddle through a clearance slot cut into the bridge base plate. Traditional three- and six-saddle Fender bridges require only the slot. Imported bridges (such as Gotohs) with in-line, solid, flat saddles need additional machine work on the saddles. A new length-adjusting screw is moved over in the base of the saddle. The area vacated by the adjusting screw is ground away so that the *B* string is able to run onto the saddle.

■ Randy Stockwell, a great luthier in Columbus, Ohio, installed two custom-machined

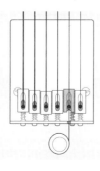

rollers in the saddle shown below: one puts down-pressure on the string, and the other is for the string to roll over. With the down-pressure roller, there's no need to machine a slot in the bridge plate, since the string can run straight through the original hole vacated by the length-adjusting screw. Randy no longer offers this service; he suggests you contact a local luthier with a good machinist's knowledge, and the proper tools, to make the alteration.

The Fender Custom Shop now offers a Clarence White Telecaster equipped with a Stringbender. Asked how a Tele's tone is affected by removing wood from the body, Custom Shop Stringbender expert Fred Stuart replied: "I've installed the Stringbender on two of my own Teles, but not vintage stuff, of course. It may sound strange—and some people don't believe it—but it improved the sound of both guitars. These were guitars I knew, and it just opened them up and made them sound more dynamic."

Fred Stuart

Roy Buchanan. At right: his rare "double-bender" with mechanism activated by both strap buttons.

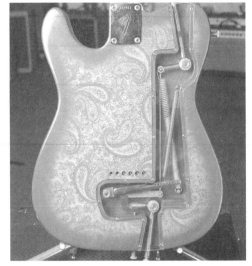

Joe Glaser and Jimmy Olander

THE GLASER BENDER

Joe Glaser of Nashville, Tennessee, made one of his earliest benders in 1979 for Jimmy Olander of the Diamond Rio band. Soon after, Ricky Skaggs made it famous on his Glaser-made "Mandocaster" and guitar. Joe's goal was to make a mechanism that could be installed without having too much of an impact on a guitar's looks or sound.

Joe doesn't offer a kit, preferring to install the bender himself, and he's only recently authorized installers in the field. The price, including installation, is $360. Three new holes have to be drilled into the guitar, removing roughly the same amount of wood required for a 9-volt battery installation.

■ A ½" square hole under the neck plate houses the pull-lever mechanism. This lever extends through a small hole in the plate and attaches to the guitar strap with a StrapLok.

■ A 1"x ¾" oblong hole is milled into the face of the body under the bridge for the string pull.

■ A long (⅜") hole is drilled through the length of the body. This starts at the heel, runs

through the body and oblong bridge hole, and out the guitar's butt end, where the tension adjustment is installed.

■ Fine tuning is adjusted at neck's heel.

■ The link stays invisible by connecting to the underside of the bridge where it comes through the bottom to the saddle's "pull finger", much like the pull-lever of a steel guitar.

■ During a whole-step bend, the pull-lever's travel, or "throw," is about ½" at the strap button. This is the factory-preferred setting, although it can be adjusted much longer.

■ Glaser prefers, and stocks, the Gotoh Tele bridge with six individual saddles, although his bender is compatible with a variety of bridges, including Fender's American Standard and the G&L Asat.

The Glaser bender, like the Parsons/White, is a permanent installation, since wood is removed. However, with the exception of the tension hole on the butt end, it can be removed with no visible effect. On a Glaser, the strap attaches at the neck plate, whereas the Parsons/White connects at the shoulder button in the normal position. "By attaching at the neck plate," Joe says, "the energy of the down-push is efficiently converted. You're not fighting the direction in which the guitar hangs, since the strap pulls in the direction of the lever rather than at a 45 degree angle to it." The B string anchors under the bridge on a hinged finger, transferring all the string pressure to the bridge plate while maintaining original string tension, saddle height, and sustain. The string doesn't slide back and forth over the saddle, thus eliminating friction and the possibility of squeaking. (With the Parsons/White and the Hipshot, the B string runs at a gradual angle to the saddle, which may weaken the tone of that particular string.)

Since 1983, Ricky Skaggs has used a Glaser bender on his "Mandocaster" 5-string electric mandolin. "I didn't start playing electric guitar in the band until '85," Ricky reports, "when Joe made me the first bender guitar, which I still play. In all, I've got five guitars—a '57 Tele, the new Custom Shop Tele, two Glasers, and a G&L that Leo Fender gave me when he first started making them—and they all have Glaser benders. I set the bender for a whole step, and adjust the 'throw' to be a little on the stiff side—maybe stiffer than easy—because I don't want the weight to pull it down and out of tune when I'm standing still.

"Joe's a very creative guy with a real heart for music. He's such a great repairman, too. He does the work himself, and he takes care of all my stuff. Many people don't know the long hours he works to keep the Nashville musicians going. Joe teaches all the young musicians to appreciate a guitar that plays in tune and stays in tune."

Glaser's double-bender is a second string pull (usually the *G* string) housed within the same space as a single bender. Also exiting through the neck plate, the *G*-bender connects to a small cord that attaches to the player's belt loop. Pushing away from ones' body activates the second pull. The cost of two benders is $700. Joe doesn't recommend starting out with two, since the second can easily be added later.

Jimmy Olander is the master of double-bending (just listen to "Meet In The Middle" on Diamond Rio). Jimmy reports, "I have one of Joe's first benders—a complete Glaser guitar, actually—built in 1979. I also have double-benders in a Strat, three Teles, and a bajo sexto from the Fender Custom Shop. I think differently when bending on a Strat—doing a more bluesy than country thing, and playing more single lines.

"With the double-bender, I set the *G* string, rather than the *B*, for the down throw [pushing on the neck], and I use it the most. The tension on my *G* string is set relatively stiff, and both of my pulls are set to a whole step. You can bend double stops in a whole step, or lower and raise the strings at the same time in whole steps. The double-bender was a trick to learn, but worth it! As for which brand of string bender to get, it's what you get used to. My Glaser is the first electric guitar I ever played. I came to Nashville as a banjo player ready to set 'em on fire, and nobody cared. So I picked up a guitar to make a living, and I'm glad I did!"

THE HIPSHOT BENDER

You can install the Hipshot bender yourself in minutes, and it's not "permanent," since no mounting holes are drilled. Designed by David Borisoff, maker of the Tremsetter and the Trilogy Multiple Tuning Bridge, the Hipshot adapts to a Tele, Strat, 335, Les Paul, and many other models. The weapon of choice for Will Ray of the Hellecasters, the Hipshot is easy to install:

■ Temporarily remove the strap button on the butt end. Locate the clearance hole in the Hipshot's trapeze tailpiece over the strap button hole, and remount the strap button, which holds the Hipshot in place (above). It's that simple! A movement of the hip and/or a slight pull on the guitar activates the lever.

■ For additional strength, Will Ray drills two extra mounting holes through the tailpiece and into the guitar's butt end (below). This isn't necessary, but it does make the unit more stable.

It's a good idea if you're not dealing with a vintage piece. (In the photo Will is using a "ring slide" for slide guitar effects.)

■ The hip lever can be located anywhere along the tailpiece bar by loosening two snap rings and sliding it over—a nice feature.

■ The standard Hipshot comes with a "toggle tuner" that drops the low *E* to *D*. It can be moved to other strings, or more can be added (with toggles on the low *E*, *A*, and high-*E* strings, for instance, you could instantly drop into *G*-tuning).

■ A palm lever may be added as an option. The Max Hipshot setup is three toggles, the hip lever, and a palm lever (all strings are loaded except for the *D*).

Will Ray points out: "With the Hipshot, you can have benders on several guitars for the cost of one Parsons/White or two Glasers, or move a bender from one guitar to another. After using it for 10 years, I can install one in about 60 seconds; then I'll spend half an hour getting the lever in exactly the right spot. For smooth operation, lubricate the friction points —the nut, string trees, and *B*-string saddle—with Teflon gel. If you have roller string trees—my G&L has them for the *E*, *B*, *G*, and *D*—you don't need the gel.

"I activate the lever by rocking the guitar, not by pushing my hip into it. I push the guitar with my right hand until the hip lever moves. The Hipshot's sensitive—I set it for whole step bends—but I can bend half steps too, by stopping halfway. It took a lot of practice, but that's the challenge of it."

My string-bending consultant for this section was Mike McGannon, guitarist with the Men Of Leisure band in Columbus, Ohio. A string bender since '78 and an authority on the

Mike McGannon

subject, Mike offers this advice: "Installing a permanent string bender is an expensive proposition that can't be undone. Who you deal with to install it and the kind of service received from those people who take your guitar and 'make it more' is very important. Your guitar will come back as something different, so you must have a positive feel for both the installer and the manufacturer."

Mike recommends these albums for aspiring string-benders: Albert Lee on "Blue Memories," from Patty Loveless' *On Down the Line*, and "Settin' Me Up" on *Hiding*; Mike Warford on Linda Ronstadt's "Willin," from *Heart Like A Wheel*; Marty Stuart's "I'm Blue, I'm Lonesome," from *Tempted*; Ricky Skaggs with Mark O'Connor on "Restless,"from *Nashville Cats*; *The Return Of The Hellecasters* with Will Ray, John Jorgenson, and Jerry Donahue; Jimmy Olander's "Meet In The Middle" and "Pick Me Up" on *Diamond Rio*; and Clarence White's classic "Muleskinner Blues" from *Muleskinner*, and "Truck Stop Girl" on the Byrds' *Untitled*.

6 ACOUSTIC ADJUSTMENTS

Troubleshooting bridge problems before setup

Certain things must be understood about an acoustic guitar before you can even *think* of setups. And some adjustments—often those made to a bridge—fall into the "repair work" category. We'll look at some of those problems here, and then deal with their solutions in the Acoustic Repairs chapter.

FLAT-TOP BRIDGE (AND BRACING) PROBLEMS

No part of the acoustic guitar is more important than the bridge, which transmits sound from the vibrating strings to the guitar's soundboard. And if the bridge has problems, the guitar's tone and volume have problems. Therefore, players of acoustic guitars should become acquainted with the telltale signs of bridge trouble and learn what constitutes proper setup. There are many problems common to the glued-on, flat-top guitar bridge, such as splits, warps, and saddle faults. This bridge overview should help you in evaluating your own instrument, whether you do the work yourself or have it done by a specialist.

Bridges separate from the top for many reasons, not all of which can be detected from the outside. Because of this, I always look inside a customer's guitar before quoting a bridge repair job of any sort. Buy an extension-shaft inspection mirror at a hardware or auto parts store. Then, with the guitar tuned to pitch, use a desk lamp for light and inspect the guitar's insides, paying special attention to the bridge plate (photo above) and the main

The setup of flat-top acoustic guitars often borders on repair work. It's not like electric guitars with their mechanical, easily-adjusted bridges.

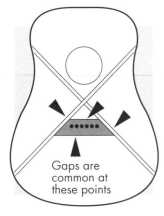

Gaps are
common at
these points

braces. If any braces are loose, you'll see a gap between the brace and the top. Learn to use the lamp and mirror together, reflecting the light source against the top while you look.

On inexpensive guitars and many imports, the two main X-braces often come unglued in the bridge area. This allows the guitar top to bow or hump, and causes the flat-bottomed bridge to pull away from the top's curve. Before regluing the bridge, the braces must be reglued. Sometimes the bridge plates have obvious gaps, or they're made of thin, warpy plywood instead of a proper hardwood. A combination of gluing the braces and replacing the plate can flatten a humped top (see Acoustic Repairs chapter).

In checking for a partially loose bridge, use the flap of any string package as a feeler gauge. Try to slide the paper between the guitar's top and the back of the bridge while the instrument is tuned to pitch. If you can get a ½" length or more of paper under it, the bridge should be removed and reglued. If there is only a hairline gap, often glue can be worked into it while the string pressure helps keep the loose joint open. The strings are then quickly removed, proper clamps and cauls are applied, and the joint is left to dry overnight.

When a bridge has come off entirely, you must choose between regluing the same bridge or using a replacement. I often replace a bridge if one or more of these problems are involved: serious splits in the bridge, a warp in the guitar top or bridge (making a proper refitting impossible), poor intonation, or a cheap original bridge with a saddle that raises or lowers by means of adjustable thumbscrews (I like to replace these with a standard bone saddle). Consider all the facts—and don't be hasty in slapping a bridge back on.

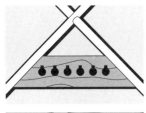

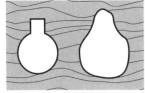

Fitting flat-top bridge pins

Those are some of the common problems that can befall an acoustic guitar bridge, including top and bridge warpage, loose

braces and bridge plates, splits, and other serious ills that may require total bridge replacement or serious repair. Of course, any such work must be completed before you can set up an instrument. Now let's look closer at setup particulars such as shaping the bridge-pin holes and string notches, as well as the various aspects of saddles, including size, shape, and slots.

Flat-top acoustic guitars only sound their best when the strings are correctly installed and well seated in the bridge-pin holes. The bridge has two functions: to hold the strings and to transmit their sound to the body. Any problem in either of these functions results in loss of both volume and sweetness of tone. Every detail counts. For example, on a well-made bridge, the bridge-pin holes should be reamed carefully so that the pin is snug, but not too tight. A string's ball end must fit firmly against the bridge plate on the top's underside. It should never be pulled up into the bridge plate, the top, or the bridge itself. Bridge pins that pop out or "creep" up, string-end windings that pull up onto the saddle, or a dull, muted tone are indicators that things aren't right down below. Also, I prefer to see a slight chamfer (countersink) on the bridge top so that the head of the pin has clearance around it. This chamfer not only looks attractive and allows the pin to sit lower in the bridge, but it also lets you get under the pin's head to pry it out when changing strings.

Use a telescoping inspection mirror to look at the guitar's interior, especially the top, where much of the string pressure is transmitted. Check to see whether the string ball ends are pulled neatly against the hardwood bridge plate as they should be, or instead are working their way up into the plate, top, and eventually the bridge itself.

Most bridge-pin holes have a slight notch at the front edge for the string winding to pull into (the drawing at left compares a cleanly cut hole with a worn one). The pin's job is to keep the ball end shoved forward into this notch when the string is tuned to pitch. Each string, being a different diameter, requires a properly sized notch in the bridge. Theoretically, a properly fit string, notch, and bridge pin would often allow the complete removal of the pin with the instrument at pitch—leaving only the notch to hold the string—but there's no need to try it!

String notches were originally used because the bridge pins of the '30s and '40s were solid —without grooves, or "flutes" (a flute is the groove molded into the pin, which accommodates that portion of the string winding that isn't seated into the notch). With an un-notched bridge, the string and the bridge pin would pop out. In the '50s, when bridge pins became grooved, a smaller string notch was required. I think a slight notch and the old-style solid bridge pins produce the best sound.

Most modern bridge pins are installed with their flutes facing forward, but bridge pins don't ha*ve* to be installed with the flutes forward: With older guitars and instruments with worn, overly deep notches, turning a bridge pin 180°—until the groove faces the rear— helps hold a string in a notch, especially a wound string. This simple pin rotation often keeps a slightly loose bridge pin from falling out all the time, too.

Many bridges (generally on inexpensive guitars) have only very slight notches, or none at all. It's best to create or enlarge these notches until the string locks in. I use a miniature, wooden-handled jigsaw blade for slotting bridge-pin holes. I customized the saw by removing the blade, flipping it end-for-end, and then regluing it into the handle. Now the teeth of this "bridge-pin hole saw" point upward (toward the handle), and cut on the upstroke—avoiding the tendency to tear out bridge-plate wood, which can happen on a

saw's down, or "exit," stroke. After sawing, use a small needle file to smooth and radius the slot's top. The notch should be radiused toward the saddle where the string breaks as it comes out of the hole (arrow at right).

Slotting bridge pin holes is a simple and inexpensive job, but it requires finesse and experience, so consider having it done in a professional shop.

After a bridge is glued onto a guitar, the bridge-pin holes are drilled through the top. A hardwood block should be held on the inside to absorb the shock and keep the drill bit from breaking out wood from the bridge plate as it plunges through. This step is often omitted, especially on cheap guitars or in work done by inexperienced craftsmen. Again, the mirror can tell you a lot in a hurry. If the bridge and plate holes are fractured, punched out, or simply worn out, the string windings will most likely end up on the saddle, and the ball end will pull into the bridge plate, but don't despair— the problem is fixable (see the Acoustic Repairs chapter).

Or, here's a *temporary* solution for badly worn holes. It works well and may even add tone and sustain to lower-quality instruments: slide a plastic, wood, or ceramic "spacer" (a bracelet or necklace bead) over a string's windings and up against the ball end. Now the bridge pin can properly hold the string and spacer against the bridge plate, as in the bottom drawing at right. I took apart a fishing lure—a Mepps Spinner—and used the cone-shaped brass weight as a spacer. It cost me six lures for my set, but they have a great tone, and I use them in my shop during this type of repair. Obviously, after adding a spacer to the ball end, you'll have to string the guitar from the inside, since the beads won't fit through the hole!

Getting a string end to "lock in" at the bridge notch is simple, but requires skill, experience, and the proper tools. Also, this notching of the bridge may require some refitting of the bridge pins to their tapered holes. It's easy to end up with loose bridge pins that fall out after these adjustments. So if all else fails, don't hesitate to take your axe to a pro!

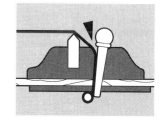

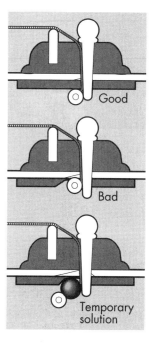

Good

Bad

Temporary
solution

Refitting and replacing bridge saddles

Acoustic players who search for the utmost in tone and volume can't be particular enough about having a well-fit saddle. Made and installed properly, the saddle puts the finishing touch on expensive, high-quality instruments. The same attention to detail in fitting a saddle to a less-expensive model is probably even more important—it's amazing what a tone depressor a poorly installed plastic saddle can be. Here I'll describe symptoms of "saddle sores," and suggest methods for cleaning the bridge slot and fitting a new saddle into it.

Since the saddle is the final stopping point of a string's length, its placement is essential in determining proper intonation. More important, it's the transmitter of sound from the vibrating string to (and through) the bridge, causing the top to move. This creates the sound, tone, and volume that is unique to each individual guitar. In order of preference, my choices of saddle and nut material are: ivory or bone, Micarta, and plastic. Bone is the best all-around material for saddle-making, since it's readily available, inexpensive, and quite hard.

A saddle should be replaced when:

■ It fits loosely in the saddle slot and can be easily moved with the strings removed. This loose fit may not only cause vibrations and slight buzzes, but it also seriously inhibits the guitar's ability to produce volume—not to mention tone.

■ It has become pitted or grooved from years of use. To file or sand out these imperfections would lower the action—time for a new saddle.

■ It is made from plastic, and the player is looking for more volume and better tone. In my opinion, plastic just won't cut it.

■ The slot is too shallow, causing the saddle to lean forward and eventually develop a warp or crack. In this case the slot should be recut deeper before fitting another saddle (more on this later).

Sight across the bridge from the side, looking lengthwise along the saddle. If it looks curved or warped or seems to tilt forward, most likely the saddle should be replaced (and the slot it rests in should be trued, or "squared-up" too). This "squaring the slot" is important, since there is a huge difference in power and tone transmission when the saddle fits well. A saddle should be somewhat difficult to remove, due to its tight fit. In fact, you should be able to grasp a well-fit saddle with a pair of pliers and pick up the whole guitar with it (but don't try it!). However, a saddle that's too tight or forced into its slot could cause the bridge to split.

If you feel like attempting your own saddle work, don't start on a guitar that's dear to you; search out a clunker for practice—they're easy to find. Regardless of whether you work on your best guitar or a yardsale special, record the saddle's height before removing it. Make a mark on the front and back of the saddle with a sharp pencil at the point where it enters the

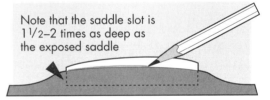

Note that the saddle slot is 1 1/2–2 times as deep as the exposed saddle

bridge. This will help you remember the saddle height after you have installed the new saddle blank and are ready to set the string height. Remove the saddle by gripping it with a pair of end-nippers or pliers, and gently rock it side to side slightly as you pull upward. Don't force anything, and remember that some saddles are glued in. If you have too much trouble, take the guitar to your local repairman. When the saddle is out, mark the bottom on the treble side with a small "X." This will help you remember which side was treble or bass when you're ready to trace it onto a new blank.

Before you can replace the saddle, you must be sure that its slot is well shaped and straight from end to end, with smooth, perpendicular sides that are square to the bottom. The slot should be deep enough to support the saddle well (approximately one-and-a-half to two times the saddle's exposed height above the

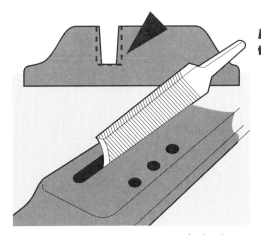

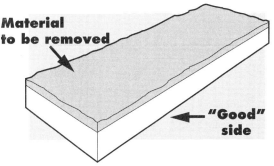

Material
to be removed

"Good"
side

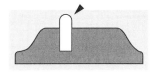

bridge top). It's not uncommon to find sides that are shaped as those at right, with lines that are not perpendicular to the bottom or parallel to each other. Going slowly from end to end with a sharp, long-beveled chisel, you can pare the wood from the sides to square up the slot. A spark-plug file with the tip ground as shown can be used as a scraper on the push stroke, filing at the same time. It's also great for smoothing and straightening a slot from end to end, as well as for cleaning up any chisel marks. If the slot looks good to begin with, try inserting a standard blank into it and don't mess with trying to change its size—I haven't run into this situation enough times, however!

If the slot is too shallow, allowing the saddle to lean or fall over, it must be made deeper. The best method is to rout it with a Dremel Moto-Tool mounted in its router base. Actually a miniature router, this tool is well known by professional repairmen and serious hobbyists. The base can hold the router at right angles to the bridge, and with successive passes of $\frac{1}{16}$" or so, you can quickly reach the desired depth. After routing, clean up any slight marks on the sidewalls with the chisel and file. Wear a dust mask while cutting or sanding bone or hardwoods.

Most saddle blanks range from $\frac{3}{32}$" to $\frac{1}{8}$" in thickness. While some replacement saddles drop right into the existing slot, most are thicker than the original by as much as $\frac{1}{32}$", to account for the squaring-up and consequent over-sizing of the old slot.

I prefer the oversize blanks of bone, and usually size them on a stationary belt sander. Slower but no less accurate results can be achieved by hand. First smooth and flatten

one side by rubbing the saddle against a mill file (the same file used for leveling frets; see the section on making your own files). After measuring the saddle-slot thickness, transfer the measurement to the new blank with a pencil or scribe, measuring and marking off the good, flat side. Remove material from the opposite side until you come to the measured line. This can be done by rubbing on the smooth file or against 180- or 220-grit sandpaper, or by using a scraper blade. C.F Martin repairman Rich Starkey wraps tape around his fingers to hold a saddle which only needs light thicknessing to get the proper fit. When the blank begins to fit, trim it to exact length and round the ends to match the slot's dimensions.

Rather than just dropping in, a well-fit saddle "squeaks" when installed. Support the guitar under the bridge with your free hand while pushing the saddle in from above. A too-tight saddle might eventually cause the bridge to crack, or it may not go in at all. Once in-serted, it's hard to remove for shaping and action work, so practice on inexpensive in-struments if you want to do your own work.

When the new blank fits into the slot, recreate the former string height and saddle shape by referring to the original, which you've marked with a pencil. If you didn't like the feel of the original action, reshape the new saddle to suit your taste, raising or lowering the strings by degree. In general, the saddle should follow the fingerboard's curve some-what, but rise slightly and flatten out a little as it goes toward the bass side. In other words, the bass strings should be higher than the treble strings to avoid buzzing. While roughing in the saddle, always be sure that its top, or crown, is rounded, so you won't be breaking strings each time you string it up to check the action.

The correct shape for the saddle top is smoothly rounded and free of sharp edges. The saddle should be showing ⅛" to ³⁄₁₆" exposure above the bridge. This ensures a string angle steep enough to produce good volume. An over-height saddle exerts too much pressure on the slot, and can cause the saddle to warp. A height much less than ⅛" does not give the guitar's body enough chance to sound.

When you reach the desired action height, final-shape and round the saddle to a gentle curve and polish it with 400 or 600 paper. This final setting of the action is actually extremely tricky and requires much practice.

Evaluating Acoustic Action

Here's a letter from a worried acoustic guitar owner, and his concerns are no doubt shared by many players. It's a good example of some of the problems discussed in this chapter:

Dear Dan:

I've been advised to get some work done on my steel-string, and I'd like a second opinion. The guitar is a good-quality ($900) import with a solid-spruce top and laminated back and sides; I bought it in 1988. The problems are that the action has gotten high and the strings buzz at the lower frets (up to the 5th). I took it to several repair shops without too much satisfaction.

Here's what happened: Adjusting the neck didn't solve the buzzing problem, so the frets were filed, but it still buzzes. A neck adjustment helped significantly with the high action problem, but it was still stiff. The saddle was then filed lower to further bring down the string height, but the strings rattled slightly at the saddle since the angle had been lowered so radically. Then the repairman cut slots in the bridge behind the saddle to steepen and improve the angle as each string came out of its hole in the bridge. I have been told that this is normal and that nothing is wrong with my

guitar, but in the future I may need to have the bridge shaved thinner to further lower the action. Now I have a guitar that has good action, but it still buzzes and has an ugly bridge. Are these techniques standard practice, or is all this work a compensation for poor construction? Why is the guitar still buzzing? And what about this bridge shaving?

P.S. I live in the Southwest, where the climate is very stable and supposedly good for guitars.

All guitars, especially new ones, need adjustments over the years to compensate for any or all of the following: climate; settling of the entire instrument; poor construction; a basically good construction, but with poor design in one area (perhaps the neck-set in your case); average wear and tear. Your problems are common, so let's analyze the repair work that has already been done to your axe.

■ Adjusting the neck can eliminate buzz if the frets are levelled correctly to begin with. Straightening an up-bowed neck (excessive relief) will significantly lower high action. But even a neck with perfect frets can be adjusted either too straight or with too much relief, and you'll end up with buzzes if you haven't matched the adjustment to your playing style and string gauge.

■ Leveling the frets can help eliminate buzz, but if the frets only buzz up to the 5th fret, perhaps they have been worn much lower than the rest of the fingerboard (this is common if you play mostly in the first position). Instead of lowering the remaining 16 frets to the height of the first five, you might have to replace the five frets (a "partial refret") to bring them up to the height of the others. If you're still getting buzz, it could be coming from the bridge saddle. Also, remember that some amount of buzzing is normal for a steel string resting against a metal fret. Don't be too finicky!

■ Cutting slots from the bridge pin holes to the saddle is one way of getting sound out of a low bridge saddle, since it improves the string's break-angle over the saddle. This is not a preferred method, however, and usually the saddle is only low because it's been sanded to improve an action that's too stiff, as in your case. The slotting technique you refer to—

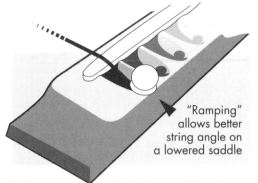

"Ramping" allows better string angle on a lowered saddle

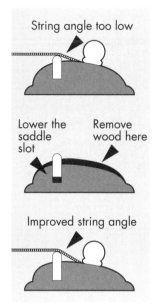

String angle too low

Lower the saddle slot

Remove wood here

Improved string angle

hollowing out wood behind the saddle—is often referred to as "ramping." Ovation uses this ramping technique in the manufacturing process. I don't think it looks good on guitars that weren't designed with it, but on Ovations it looks cool because the guitars are so modern in design. Cutting these slots is acceptable as an inexpensive fix-me-up, but not the preferred correction for a good instrument.

■ If the bridge is ¹¹⁄₃₂" thick or more, it is okay to shave it to expose an almost-buried saddle (see drawings at upper right). The process involves removing wood from the top and re-cutting the depth of the slot that holds the saddle (since it would be too shallow once the wood is removed from the bridge). For the record, the most commonly accepted steel-string bridge thicknesses are ⅜", ¹¹⁄₃₂", and ⁵⁄₁₆", although you'll often see bridges shaved to ¼", which makes me nervous. To many of us, even ⁵⁄₁₆" is beginning to get a little skimpy.

■ In your case, a neck reset may be the best way to lower the action without totally losing saddle height (as well as the guitar's volume and tone). Neck resets are more complicated and expensive than grinding down the bridge/saddle or slotting the bridge behind the saddle. Most imported neck joints I've seen don't reset as easily as Martin, Gibson, Guild, and many other American-made guitars using the traditional dovetail joint and conventional glues.

But now for the crux of the matter. Your repairmen should have advised you to take the guitar back where you bought it so that the dealer could send it back to the distributor. Since many repair shops have little or no experience in retailing, they often don't realize how well most manufacturers back up their products. Often distributors of the more recognized imported brands such as Takamine, Alvarez, Washburn, etc., will even

replace the whole guitar to keep a customer happy, especially with a higher quality instrument. Of course, it's only fair that you must be the original owner. It may not be too late to send it back to the maker, so at least give it a try. Good luck!

Arch-top bridges

Arch-top bridges often suffer from a poor fit of the bridge base to the guitar's top. The best fit can be achieved by hand, using a sharp knife such as an X-acto or a violin-maker's knife. It takes a great deal of skill to do this, however. As a substitute you can tape a piece of 120-grit sandpaper to the top and then slide the bridge base back and forth to contour it. The shape that a knife gives produces the cleanest fit and best tone. Good violin makers are the most adept at this bridge-carving technique. If you can find a person good at violin setups, see if they'll carve a bridge to fit the top; it'd be worth the effort! Some arch-top guitars have a solid, unsplit bridge base, while others are split. In either case, check the bridge fit under normal string tension, since the top and base will flex somewhat. A perfect fit without string tension might be imperfect with the strings on.

I prefer arch-top bridges that do not have metal Tune-O-Matic type saddles; the solid wood top pieces produce a better tone. These solid wooden "saddles" are often staggered for intonation compensation, especially on more modern instruments. The string notches should not be over one-half the diameter of the string in depth—just enough of a groove to keep the string from popping out when plucked. The notch should fit the string's shape and be slightly rounded to a dull peak— not a sharp point— with all burrs removed. I polish the string grooves on rosewood or ebony arch-top saddles with 0000 steel wool to burnish the wood and make it hard.

Arch-top bridges should not be glued into place. They usually leave a mark in the finish, so you'll know where to reposition the bridge

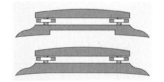

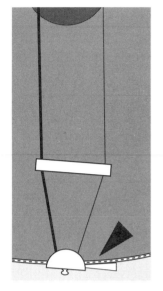

when you remove the strings while cleaning the fingerboard or polishing the instrument. If the bridge seems to pull to either the treble or bass side and the strings won't line up with the fingerboard, the tailpiece may have to be moved slightly to either side. Have this checked by a qualified repairman, since the mounting holes *may* have to be plugged and redrilled. But in many cases, this simple trick often solves the problem: loosen the tailpiece and slide a small shim of wood, paper, cardboard, etc., under one edge of the tailpiece bracket on the same side that you want it to move toward (see drawing at left). The shim forces the tailpiece into position—and it doesn't take much!

While there are some bridge problems that these pages haven't covered, you now know the basics and should be able to see how all the different factors relate. If you have bridge problems, think everything out before trying a repair yourself—and don't be ashamed to get professional help before doing any work that you may regret. For more info on bridge repair, see the Acoustic Repairs chapter.

Setting up a classical guitar

Having the ability to adjust the action on a Fender bass, tweak the truss rod on a vintage Les Paul, or fit a perfect saddle into a Martin D-28 doesn't necessarily qualify a repairman to properly set up a nylon-string classical guitar. There are several major setup differences between steel- and nylon-string acoustics. This section describes classical string installation, correct neck relief, action height at the nut and 12th fret, and the proper shaping of the nut and saddle.

Most of the setup techniques used here apply to adjusting a nylon-string "folk guitar," as well. Braced for nylon strings, these guitars typically have a wider, flatter fingerboard than most steel-strings. Most American and European guitars made before the late 1920s fall into this category, and many of them have

bridge pins. During the '50s folk boom, folk guitars were made by Goya, Favilla, Hagstrom, and other manufacturers from abroad. While these instruments are different from the modern steel-string, they aren't grand concert classical guitars, either. If you understand the setup of both classicals and steel-strings, though, you'll be able to handle the folk guitar.

I've set up my share of classical guitars, and once owned an excellent handmade Yacopi. Like many of my peers, I learned Bach's *Bourrée*, studied the Carcassi method, struggled with Fernando Sor, and ended up playing the blues. So I'm no expert when it comes to the concert guitar, but I know experts. I contacted several of the best to get their opinions on setup: William Cumpiano, a student of Michael Gurian and the founder of Stringfellows in Hadley, Massachusetts; Jeffrey R. Elliott, a master luthier and mentor to a thriving community of guitar builders in the Portland, Oregon area; Thomas Humphrey , a world-renowned classical guitar builder from New York city who designed and builds the "Millennium" guitar; and Richard Schneider, who collaborated with Dr. Michael Kasha on taking the design of the classical guitar to new heights. (After hearing a new Kasha/Schneider guitar, Segovia wrote: "To Schneider, in whose hands is the future of the guitar.")

Richard's guitars incorporate the principles of the Kasha design, and his avant-garde instruments are hailed for their beauty, playability, and superior concert tone. Although he sits at the pinnacle of the guitar-building craft, Richard is more likely to speak about design ideas or his students than about himself. He feels that his main achievement may be that he will one day leave behind him more students trained in his methods than any other builder in history. His students include such well-known builders as Abraham Wechter, Gila Eban, Jeffrey Elliott, Mark Wescott, Gregory Wylie, Peter Hutchison, Charles Merrill, John Mello, Italy's Enrico Bottelli, France's Michel Geslain, and Sweden's Fredrik Gustafsson. Schneider's Lost Mountain Center For The Guitar, a non-profit organization for the education of guitar builders and players, conducts an annual seminar starting the first Saturday of

August; for information on attending, contact seminar manager Eric Hoeltzel at Box 44, Carlsborg, WA 98324.

PROPER STRING INSTALLATION

Nylon or "gut" strings (especially the wound bass strings) are more delicate than steel and must be handled more carefully to avoid kinks, nicks, breaks, and unwinds. To prolong the life of nylon strings, take special care while installing, de-tuning, or removing them. The nut slots and saddle crown must be perfectly shaped to avoid cutting the strings, and the ties used to install them at the bridge and tuners are important, too.

Most wound classical strings have a limp end and a stiff end, while the unwound treble strings often have a plain end and a colored one. The limp end of a wound string is simply a result of the manufacturing process; it is not meant to be tied onto the bridge, although many guitarists mistakenly do this because it's easier to wrap. The limp, loose, wrapped ends break sooner, and will not only mar the tie-block inlay, but scar the saddle as well, causing buzzing and intonation problems. Often the treble string ends are color-coded to identify the string tension (red=high; yellow=super high). Don't tie the colored end to the bridge! As Jeff Elliott points out, "The color can transfer permanently to the finish of the top or the bridge, so I either clip it off or use the uncolored end. Whichever end you use for tying, heat it with a match or lighter to create a small ball end that helps it lock. To avoid burning it, remove the string from the flame the instant it begins to contract. If the nylon looks brown or burnt in any way, it will be too brittle, and break off. In this case, cut it off and try again." Ball-end nylon strings, such as La Bella's Folk Singers, are available through your dealer, but they aren't generally used on fine classical guitars. They're used to simplify string installation on folk guitars or lesser-grade classicals.

For the standard wrap at the bridge, work about a 3" length of string through the tie block and out the back side of the bridge. Then bring the string end up and over the tie block, run it under the string, and loop or twist it toward the back edge of the tie block (shown above).

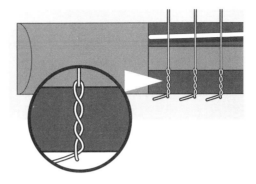

Because the sixth, fifth, third, and second strings have a similar large diameter, two twists are usually enough; the fourth and first strings should have three twists since their diameters are smaller. Regardless of the number of twists, the final twist should be at the back edge of the tie block, where you'll often find a strip of inlay material. The loose end must be tucked in under the string as it exits the string hole in the bridge. This isn't the only tie used on classical bridges, but it's the most common. The sharply trimmed string ends have a tendency to poke into the top after you've completed the wrap, so be sure to snip the string ends to avoid putting dings in the top.

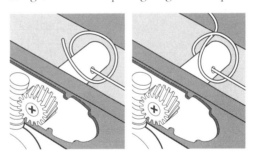

Tying the strings correctly at the tuning key shaft is important, too. For the simplest tie, poke the string through the tuner barrel (roller) twice so that it can't slip, and then wind. This is not the approved method in classical guitar circles, though. Here's the traditional method for obtaining a tie that's good-looking and self-locking: Run the string through the hole, and then back over the barrel and under itself. Then hold the loose end while tightening the string, locking it against itself (first drawing, above). Another similar self-locking tie runs back under itself and then threads up through the loop created by bringing the string back over the barrel (second drawing).

If you work on classical guitars but don't play them yourself, you owe it to your customers to find out as much as you can about proper setup. Visit dealers who handle good classicals, ask questions, and play on the better instruments.

All makers don't necessarily wrap in the same direction or in the same way. William Cumpiano, for instance, believes: "You must have more than one wrap, and it's usually from three to five wraps by the time you get to pitch. Make the wraps around the barrel in the direction that creates the straightest string line to the individual string notches in the nut. Usually the *D* and *G* strings wind toward the center of the headstock, the outer two *E* strings wind toward the outer edges, and the *A* and *B* fall in between." Jeffrey Elliott, on the other hand, says: "Go through the barrel, keeping an inch or two of slack string, and come back up over the top and under the string as shown, but then wrap the string *around itself* twice. Then tighten the tuners, making the wraps around the barrel going *toward* the gears, unless the direction of the string won't get a clean shot from the barrel to the nut. Wrapping away from the gear causes the barrel to act as a lever, putting excess pressure and wear on the gear mechanism and shortening the gear's lifespan by years (especially if the gears are mounted poorly or have any loose components). But different guitars string up differently. The important thing is that a string doesn't touch another string, the channel, or the face veneer while on its way to the nut."

Richard Schneider advises: "Turn the tuning keys until the holes run almost up and down at right angles to the headstock face—maybe with the barrel holes leaning 5° or 10° toward the nut. Run the string down through the hole, up the side of the barrel away from the nut,

and back over and under the string. Wrap around the string twice, and then tighten the key while holding the loose end. I don't worry about undue pressure on the barrel or gears, because the tuners I use have a bearing on the shaft end in the headstock center." All of these methods will work. You'll have to experiment to get the correct number of wraps in the right direction so that the strings look neat and miss each other as they go to their respective slots in the nut.

RELIEF AND STRING HEIGHT

"Nylon strings have greater elasticity," points out William Cumpiano, "and therefore a greater vibrating arc than steel strings. To avoid string rattle, they require greater clearance all along the fingerboard. Fortunately, however, nylon strings are comfortable at a higher action setting, and they also intonate properly at a height where steel strings would play out of tune." Since proper classical setup requires a higher action, the need for relief is less than you might think. In fact, the relief necessary to accommodate the vibrating strings of a classical guitar usually occurs naturally from the string tension (90 lbs. of pull) exerted on a perfectly straight fingerboard. Relief is a very subtle measurement, and most makers expect to see from as little as .004" to as much as .040" when measuring the air space between the bottom of the strings and the top of the fret in the area in the 8th through 10th frets. According to Jeffrey Elliott, "Relief generally runs from a minimum of .004" to an average of .020" at around the 10th fret. More than .040" of relief is excessive, and too little relief can sometimes cause 'back-buzz,' where the string is laying on the frets between your fingering hand and the nut, causing a slight but annoying buzz."

"I like to see a neck as straight as possible," claims Richard Schneider, "but some relief is inevitable and perhaps a help. Too much relief can cause *sympathetic* string vibration on the short string length between your fingering hand and the nut. This is a somewhat rare occurrence and is different than the back-buzz that Jeff's talking about, but it's annoying when it occurs. The average relief would probably measure from .020" to .040"." As a result of string tension, most classical necks take a permanent "set" or forward bow of as much as .020". This doesn't go away even when the strings are removed, so don't mistake this for a warped neck! Again, the higher action is not a problem for the player because of the softer touch used with nylon strings. Some makers may build a slight relief into their necks, while others remove extra wood on the bass side, starting at the nut and running "downhill" to the end of the fingerboard, in the Ramirez and Hauser style. All these methods are correct, and all of the builders questioned approached relief differently.

THE NUT

Bone is the preferred material for making a good nut or saddle for any acoustic guitar. There's no need to go deeply into making a classical nut, since the same techniques described in the section on nut making are used to fit the classical nut. Because nylon strings are so delicate, the correct angle of the string slot to the tuner and a perfectly round shape in the nut slot bottom are even more important than with steel strings. It's especially easy for the wound strings to hang up in a poorly shaped slot, and when they do, they unravel and sound awful—just before they finally break! The classical nut has a flatter top to match the unradiused fingerboard, and like the steel-string, when viewed from the side the nut and string slots must taper at a gradual curve from the back side to the front edge at about a 10° angle.

Correct nut height can best be determined by eye, feel, and experience, but the novice can get close by measuring. Richard Schneider says: "The clearance, or air space, over the 1st fret with the string open and coming off the nut should be a little greater than the clearance over the 2nd fret with the string pressed on the 1st fret. A business card measures .005", so use three business cards to measure under the treble strings and maybe five or six business cards under the bass."

Of course, the overall action and height of the bridge saddle has a big effect on nut measurement. Use the same techniques shown in the nut making and saddle sections, balancing one end to the other and working

the action down by degree. Another general rule for nut height that works for steel or nylon strings is to press a string at the 2nd fret, looking to see a slight clearance between the string and the 1st fret; as long as there is some clearance here, the open strings shouldn't buzz. The clearance should increase gradually from the high- to the low-E, because the lower wound strings must sit from .015" to .030" higher in the nut than the treble strings to avoid open-string buzz. Overall string height at the nut shouldn't get too low, since there's a strong tendency for nylon strings to buzz sympathetically between the fretted note and the nut behind where you're actually playing, just as they would from too much relief! Here's a final general rule for nut height: Measure the air space between the string and the top of the 1st fret, looking for a gap of ½ mm (.020") under the treble-E and around 7⁄10 mm (.030") under the low-E.

A traditional classical guitar fingerboard is flat from side to side, although some modern makers are introducing a very slight radius to make it easier to play barre chords. "This is a very gentle arch that's imparted with a plane," says Cumpiano. "It's not greater than a 1⁄32" offset at the fingerboard edge. It makes the instrument easier to play, and probably lets a player get away with a little bit less technique." The classical guitar's saddle should be flat, too, or match the shape of a slightly arched fingerboard. As with the nut, set the saddle action lower on the treble side, following the same 1⁄32" rise from treble toward the bass. Some makers taper and thin the fingerboard on the base side in order to keep a more regular saddle height across the bridge (this creates a more even angle on the string which exerts a more even tension on the top). Other makers who feel that the bass strings need to break at more of an angle than the treble strings disagree with this technique, since it eliminates that option.

ACTION/STRING HEIGHT

To set the action, use a small ruler at the 12th fret. Measure the air space from the bottom of the string to the top of the fret. Different builders prefer different readings under the two E strings: Elliott's preference is 3 to 3½ mm

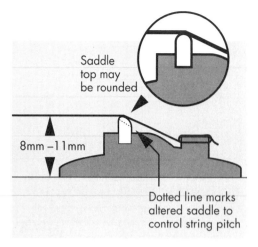

Saddle top may be rounded

8mm – 11mm

Dotted line marks altered saddle to control string pitch

under the treble, and 4 to 4½ mm under the bass, while Cumpiano favors ⅛" under the treble and ⁵⁄₃₂" under the bass. "A high action for a classical," he adds, "would be ⁵⁄₃₂" treble and ³⁄₁₆" bass." Schneider describes: "When fretting the string at the 1st fret, measure 3 mm under the treble and 4 mm under the bass. A good concert player can handle this action, although some prefer to have the action higher. After adjusting the action to these parameters, I make two more saddles: a low one measuring 2½ mm treble to 3½ mm bass, and another one that's 3½ mm treble to 5 mm bass. I also cut a second nut with the string spacing closer by 1 mm. These are put in a little walnut and rosewood box that I deliver with each instrument."

Traditionally, the classical saddle isn't shaped quite as round as a steel-string's, because of the nylon string's tendency to unravel or break when it meets a sharp edge. Instead, the saddle is often tapered smoothly towards the front edge (above) so that the string "takes off" gradually, with full support from the saddle shape to avoid string breakage. This method of shaping is only valid if the exact compensation has been calculated into the placement of the bridge; otherwise the peak of the saddle may have to be slightly altered to get the most accurate intonation. Many classical builders prefer to use a gently rounded saddle top; either method is correct. The saddle should fit snugly into the bridge slot and have a well-sanded and polished top surface for optimum tone. There should be no sharp edges or notches cut into it, although John Williams, a great classical guitarist, has been known to prefer a notched saddle.

Jeffrey Elliott points out that the builder can control tone and string tension by altering the saddle's angle and thereby changing the pitch of the string to the tie block (left). This subtle refinement is probably beyond the scope of our needs, but it's the combination of such little subtleties that make one guitar sound better than another. Jeff also states that the height of the strings from the top is extremely important; from the bottom of the string where it meets the saddle to the guitar's top should measure somewhere between 8 mm to 11 mm for most instruments.

Thomas Humphrey had this to say about setting up the classical guitar: "Dan, what you have to remember is that all guitars move a great deal between summer and winter, especially new guitars. All of the measurements given here are fine, but there are very few players who are going to accept a "factory" setup until they've had time to feel it for awhile. Before people are even out of the shop they want two saddles—a high and a low. They never leave it alone! So it doesn't matter *how* the maker sets up the guitar. As long as a classical guitar is set up within reason (an *average* setup) you're fine. Until a player gets the strings under their fingers, action setups don't mean anything. You have to give a lot of room to the player. The better the player, the more they'll want adjustments made.

"No two guitars play the same way—not even from the same maker. Each may require a slightly different setup. It depends on things like the shape of the neck in the back, the curvature of the fingerboard, and of course the scale length. Long-scale and short-scale guitars must be set up differently because of the difference in the string tension, and there is no scale length standard. 650mm is the most common scale length, 670mm is the longest I've heard of, and the shortest *I've* ever made is 620mm."

STRING RECOMMENDATIONS

What brands are good, and how often should they be changed? Cumpiano points out that a recitalist often changes strings every two or three days, and always before a performance. String deterioration has a dramatic effect on intonation, and sadly enough, classical strings are not only quite fragile, but expensive. Old strings lose pitch accuracy and tone. Cumpiano cites D'Addario Pro Arte Hi-Tension strings as a modern, well-built set, and he also uses Savarez Blues and Whites. Schneider prefers D'Addario Pro Arte, Savarez Crystal Solis, and GHS, which are all high-tension strings. "You might want medium- to low-tension strings for a recording situation," he adds, "because they're easier to finger, and some instruments do sound better with low tension." Kurt Rodarmer plays a Schneider/Kasha guitar and only changes his treble strings every six to eight months, since they get rock-hard and stay that way, creating the best sound. He changes the bass strings every other week during normal practice, and always two days before a concert. (I encourage string manufacturers to market sets of bass strings only, because everyone always has scads of extra trebles!) Elliott favors both high- and normal-tension D'Addario Pro Arte and Savarez Alliance in Red or Yellow, which, he says, "are made of a new material that is smaller in diameter than most others, has less tension, provides a good tonal variety and response, and is extremely accurate and clear sounding." R.E. Brune, a famous luthier based in Evanston, Illinois, has recently begun importing the excellent Hannabach brand. Many players have been extremely impressed with these strings.

For more detailed information on classical setup, read the books listed in the Recommended Reading section, especially *Guitar Making: Tradition and Technology* by William Cumpiano and Jon Natelson.

AUTHOR'S NOTE

Tom Humphrey's 'Millennium' design incorporates a sloping sound-board and an elevated neck. These two factors combine to create a greater string-to-sound-board angle, thus producing a different load on the soundboard (similar to that of the Harp). This angle also creates a more resonant sound, and is one of the features which make Tom's guitar so playable.

The other feature which struck me is the elevation of the fretboard from the sound-board. Because the player's hand is no longer obstructed by the body at the 12th fret, greater access is achieved and the instrument is more playable in the higher registers. Mr. Humphrey recieved a mechanical patent on this innovation from the U.S. Patent Office in 1987. The Millennium may be the first universally accepted new design in the classical guitar since Torres set the standards in the mid-1800's.

PART 2
NUT WORK
& FRET WORK

7 NUT REPLACEMENT

Twelve steps to replacing a nut

Many players are anxious to work on or make their own nut, since it's one of the guitar's most important parts, in terms of action, sound, and playability. While its perfect fit is best left to qualified repairmen where your favorite guitar is concerned, it's OK to develop your nut-making skills on inexpensive imports and old yardsale specials. This chapter describes the necessary nut-making tools (many of which you can make yourself), the best materials to use, and the basic steps involved. If you go about the process slowly, work on instruments of lesser value, and make a small investment in certain specialized tools, you should eventually be able to handle nut making like a pro. Remember, be patient and read the whole story before tearing apart any guitars—and don't wreck a good one while you learn!

Nuts need to be replaced for a variety of reasons: the string slots are too low and cause buzzing at the 1st fret, the string spacing is irregular or too wide or narrow to suit your taste, or the guitar isn't producing a strong, clean sound (this is most often caused by plastic nuts). Perhaps you've found a used guitar that would play, except for a chip right on a string groove at the nut. It doesn't take someone with a Ph.D. in guitar repair to know when the nut has to go—just follow your senses. In most cases, if your guitar plays well on the fretted strings and only annoys you on the open ones, the nut's just worn out. If you were happy with the nut's general shape, you can remake it, trying to copy the old nut's string width and spacing as closely as possible; simply leave the strings higher than before to eliminate buzz. On the next page is an outline for nut making, followed by advice on specialized tools that you'll want.

Bone is white because it's bleached. You'll also find a lot of yellow and off-white bone. I've been very happy with the blanks I get from Stewart-MacDonald and Luthier's Mercantile.

TWELVE STEPS TO REPLACING A NUT

1 Remove the old nut.

2 Clean nut slot of glue and residue, and square it up.

3 Choose new nut material and rough-in the blank to fit the cleaned slot.

4 Lay out string spacing.

5 Rough-in approximate string slots, without going too deep.

6 Trim off excess nut material from top as slots get deeper.

7 Lower and shape string slots, moving strings side to side, if needed.

8 Trim off excess nut material, rough edges, and overhang.

9 Final-sand and contour the nut's shape.

10 Polish with a soft rag and rubbing compounds (especially the bottoms of string slots).

11 Final-check the string height and shape, and string to pitch.

12 Glue in nut (with strings on, for clamp pressure).

TOOLS

The right tools help make the job easier. You can make many of them yourself, and specialized items can be found at the luthier supply stores listed in the back of the book. Other items are available from hardware stores or wood-shop suppliers.

A sharp chisel is great for paring (shaving) and scraping glue off the fingerboard's end; I like a ⅜" or ½" bench chisel for this job. A ⅛" chisel that's ground slightly thinner in width is also good, especially for getting into a Fender-style nut slot (see drawing at left). You'll find a smooth mill file handy for shaping the nut, cleaning away old glue, and helping with squaring-up. A small (6") mill file is also quite handy, since it's thin enough (.115") to file inside a Fender slot for squaring-up, and the file's tang becomes a great scraper, chisel, etc., when sharpened on a grindstone (note the tang-converted file in the drawing). Specialized "nut-seating" files (they fit Fender, Gibson, and Martin slots) are available.

A set of feeler gauges is a help when measuring action height from the string's bottom to the top of the 1st fret. If possible, buy the kind that you can take apart by loosening a screw. In

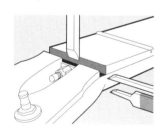

fact, feeler gauges are a must around any shop, for all sorts of uses. We'll use them throughout this book, so buy a full set.

Small "razor-saws" are often used to start nut slots, and in some cases to do the actual nut-slotting. X-acto makes a great razor-saw set with three interchangeable saw blades of .012", .013", .014" in thickness. BLITZ-Saw blades (top photo) come in six sizes ranging from .015" to .040" and can take over where the X-acto saw leaves off. Saws are great for roughing in a slot depth in a hurry, but I prefer to finish up with the round-bottom nut files mentioned below.

An X-acto knife (or other brand) with #11 blades is also a must, since it's used to score the finish around the nut during removal. These saw/knife sets vary in size and price and are available at many hardware stores and guitar supply sources.

Specialized nut-shaping files are available from Stewart-MacDonald, Luthier's Mercantile, and the C.F. Martin company. Custom-made for getting into nut slots, these round-bottomed files have smooth sides that allow you to cut the nut-slot bottom, but not the slot's sidewalls. These "Precision Nut Files" (above) have accurate, well-shaped, round cutting edges, and include ten files ranging from .010" to .058".

Full sets of files are expensive (around $70), but worth the money if you're serious about getting into the business. The ten files that are my favorite can be purchased one at a time, and four which make a good starter set are mentioned shortly under "Cutting String Slots."

Don MacRostie and I have been working on a new nut file with edges coated in industrial diamond. Having no teeth, they don't "run off" the intended line as toothed files will. I hope these become available in the future, because they work great!

You'll need a 6" stainless-steel rule, preferably the hardware-store variety made by General. I've mentioned this tool often; everyone should have one. Notice that the fractions are converted to decimal equivalents on the back side; this is handy for string spacing. A dial caliper is always nice to have, but certainly not a must. Even the inexpensive plastic kind is plenty good enough for our needs. Nut spacing templates, with the string spacing already laid out (see below), are also available.

Whenever you're making or adjusting a nut, remember that string height at the nut is directly affected by the height at the bridge. You may need to work back and forth a bit from the nut to the bridge, by either raising or lowering an electric guitar's adjustable inserts, or by filing, shimming, or replacing an acoustic guitar's saddle. You should be basically satisfied with the action and playability of the guitar as it is (with the exception of buzzing from nut slots that are too low) before making a new nut, so that you don't discover at the job's end that the bridge was too high or low to begin with. Now, on to making a nut.

REMOVING THE OLD NUT

Before removal, score completely around the old nut with a sharp X-acto knife or razor blade. This way, if the finish starts to chip upon removal, the chip will stop at the scored line. Most often the nut comes unglued after being tapped with a block of wood and a hammer. Firmly but gently tap from the front (fingerboard side) of the nut, and then tap from the rear in the same fashion. Do this back and forth until the nut "rocks" out. Once loose, grip it with your fingers and pull it out carefully. I can't

overemphasize the need to watch for finish chipping! It's a risk you'll have to take. Many imported guitars with thick polyester finishes are hard to score—but not impossible. Wear safety glasses while scoring the lacquer or polyester and while knocking the nut loose. With Fender-style guitars, you'll have to grip the nut with some end nippers or pliers after gently loosening it by tapping, and then pull it out like a tooth.

Here's a nut-removal method from Flip Van Domburg Scipio, head of the Mandolin Brothers repair shop in Staten Island, NY:

"When removing a nut from a guitar with a bound peghead—or one with a deep nut-slot or heavy lacquer—I occasionally need to 'collapse' the nut instead of trying to knock it or pry it out. Saw through the nut with a fret saw until close to the bottom and then you can squeeze it together—pulling it away from delicate binding, finish, or wood."

Flip Van Domburg Scipio

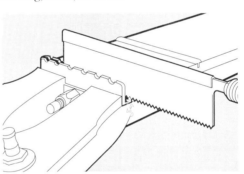

Note: I took a pair of my flush ground fret nippers and ground the sharp jaws flat and dull. This works great as a "crusher" and also as a gripper for pulling saddles too. —Dan

Once the nut's out, clean any glue or residue from the nut slot (the groove that held it in the neck). Even on cheap guitars, the nut slot is generally uniformly shaped at the factory, but it needs to be scraped clean of residue for a good-fitting blank. Common nut thicknesses range from ¼" to ³⁄₁₆" (for Martin, Gibson, Guild, and their acoustic clones) down to ⅛" (for Fender-style electrics). A variety of files and tools will fit in the slots for cleaning. I use a sharp chisel to remove any glue from the fingerboard's end grain and to trim any sticky stuff from the front edge of the headstock overlay. Held vertically and used with short strokes as a scraper, a chisel can be great for cleaning the bottom of

Many new nut blanks have tiny pits and crevices that you might not notice until the buffing stage. These holes may fill with compound or finger dirt, making the finished product look funky. For a smooth-looking job, try filling the holes with super glue before handling them.

the nut slot, too. The nut-seating files described earlier work the best. If you file the bottom of the slot, be sure to lightly file the lacquer's edge first, so that it won't chip as you begin to file the wood. To avoid pushing a chip of lacquer off the neck, always file in from each side toward the center.

ROUGHING IN THE BLANK

I prefer bone as a nut material and no longer use commercial ivory, which necessitates the slaughter of elephants and other mammals with tusks. Don't even mess with sellers of "legal" ivory—they're lying. Bone makes an excellent nut, and synthetic Micarta is also good (begin with Micarta as you're learning—it's cheaper).

Start with a blank that's bigger than the actual slot height, length, and thickness, and slowly bring it down to size. Use the saddle-making techniques described in the Acoustic Adjustments chapter as a guide for squaring up the stock and getting it to fit the slot. (Quick repeat: Flatten one side against a smooth file, mark out the desired thickness, and then sand, file, or belt-sand the opposing side to uniform thickness.) Be sure the bottom is shaped exactly like the slot; Martin nuts, for example, have an angled bottom. Leave a ⅛" overhang on both treble and bass ends to allow the nut to be shifted from side to side as you're laying out and filing the string slots. That way, if you happen to get a bit off on your string spacing, you can tap the whole nut towards treble or bass and relocate the string slots.

The nut should press into the slot and fit snugly. Viewed from the side or end, the blank should be gradually rounded toward the front edge (note the dotted line in drawing below). If it pleased you, copy the shape of the old nut. When the blank fits, trace the fingerboard's shape (radius) onto it from the front side by running a pencil over the fingerboard surface.

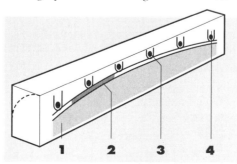

Remove the blank and finish laying out the nut in pencil by adding the thickness of the frets (say .035"), the height of the strings from the fret top, the thickness of the string itself, and a little extra for good measure. Most players prefer an action that's higher on the bass side than on the treble. (This treble-to-bass rise is illustrated in the previous two chapters.) Use care when taking the blank in and out, so you don't chip the lacquer or wood as a result of the tight fit.

This is a good point at which to take a break, and review nut making up to this point. Spend time gathering your tools, and practice a nut rough-in on something that you know you can't ruin. Then we'll cut the string slots and finish the job.

Cutting string slots and finishing up

We just went through the steps for making a nut, described some necessary tools, and got through the roughing-in stage. Now we'll carry on with the job. Good luck!

Before proceeding any further, lay some masking tape over the headstock face and on the fingerboard between the nut and 1st fret to protect the wood and finish from an accidental slip of the file. Use as many layers as possible without getting in the way of your work. On older guitars with brittle finishes, it's best to use the less-sticky draftsman's tape, which won't pull off the finish as badly.

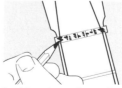

Install the two outside *E* strings as far in from the fingerboard's edge as you like for spacing. Do this by looking down from directly overhead. Mark the outsides of the strings on each side of the nut with a pencil, and file starter notches to hold the strings. The best tool for this is a thin X-acto razor saw; it's also perfect for the actual filing/shaping of the slots for the high-*E*, *B*, and sometimes *G* strings. In general I use a specialized set of nut files that cut only on the thin edge and leave a round-bottomed slot. While

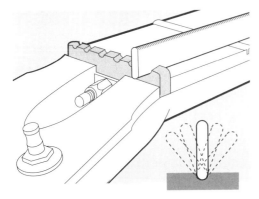

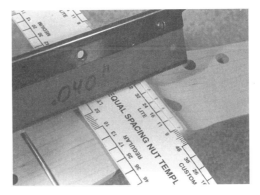

It's hard to find perfect bone blanks, so don't throw out the pitted blanks; just save the really good ones for your primo jobs. And remember: Everyone else is faced with the same situation, so make do with what you have and don't complain to your suppliers—they're doing the best they can!

the full set costs about $70 and is actually a great investment for anyone doing much set-up work, you can begin with three files (.016", .025", and .035"). These can cut most nut slots if you roll the file for extra width as you cut. This "roll-filing" action is the way to file slots. By using a file slightly smaller than the intended notch width and rolling on the forward stroke to widen the outside walls, you have more control and the file won't stick in its own notch.

Once the outer strings are set in position, measure between their centers with the 6" rule or a dial caliper. Divide the distance by five to get an *approximate* equal spacing between all six strings. Use a calculator, because you'll be dealing in decimals—it's rare to find a nut width that's divisible by fractions. For example, if the outer *E* strings measure 1⅜" center to center, the decimal conversion is 1.375 divided by 5, which equals .275 from string to string. I refer to this measurement as *approximate* because the lower wound strings, being fatter, would actually be closer to each other than the unwound treble strings when spaced exactly evenly. Use the *exact* measurement only for the initial layout, file very light starter slots, and then put on the remaining four strings. Now adjust the final between-string spacing by eye, as you file and lower the strings into the nut blank. Note: I repeat, dividing by five gives equally spaced string-to-string *centers*. I prefer equal spacing between the *outside* of adjoining strings, not equal spacing between their centers. A new tool to help you achieve *equal spacing between strings* is the Compensated Nut Spacing Template, which has the diameters of the strings factored into the scale (photo above).

When the slots have all been started just enough to hold the strings so that you can check them by eye, switch to your nut files, X-acto sawblades, and/or ground-down, fine-toothed hacksaw blade. File at a back angle to the nut's front edge, so that the string will have decent downward pressure. To play in tune, the string's actual contact point should be at the very front of the nut. On guitars with angled-back headstocks, which are the most common, you basically follow the angle of the headstock itself. With slab-neck Fender-style guitars, you won't file as steep a back angle, so just file the appropriate angle needed for each string-post.

File the slots one at a time, starting with the high-*E*. Loosen the string and lift it out of the slot as you file. Then replace the string, tune it to pitch, and check your work. Expect to go back and forth from treble to bass several times before the slots get close to their final depth and shape. You'll need to keep filing the nut's top down as your strings get lower into the blank. In general, you want the strings to sit in round-bottomed slots, filed to the shape (diameter) of each string, and no deeper than one-half the string's diameter.

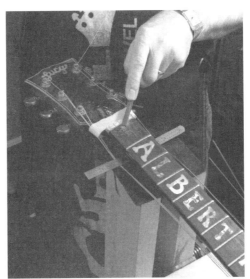

Sometimes you'll work hard making a perfect nut, and right at the end of the job you'll go too low with your file, causing an open string to buzz at the first fret. You'll want to tear your hair out! It's called "blowing the nut," and we all do it. Either shim the nut, or start a new one. Sorry!

Although I've described how to measure and lay out the divisions of the strings before filing, I usually do it by eye. Learn to trust your own eye.

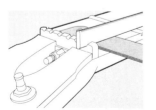

My friend Don MacRostie, who's an ace mandolin designer and repairman known throughout Ohio for his Red Diamond instruments, taught me the following method for knowing when the strings are dropped enough in depth. Here we use the feeler gauges described in the tool list given in the roughing-in section. You need to remove the protective masking tape from the fingerboard to do this.

1 Measure the height of the first two frets, from the fret's top to the fingerboard, by laying a straightedge across the two frets and sliding different combinations of feeler gauge blades under it until they just touch the straightedge. Record this measurement (let's say .035" for an average, somewhat worn fret height).

2 Add to this from .005" to .010", or any figure you come up with after experimenting. New total: .040" (.035" frets, plus .005").

3 Stack up a number of feeler gauges that equal the total measurement (.040"), and hold them against the front edge of the nut while you file at a normal backward angle down to the metal. When your razor-saw, nut file, or home-made hacksaw blade file contacts the hardened steel—you'll feel it instantly—it's time to stop.

The nice thing about this method is that you can control the drop of the string and avoid accidentally going too low. Also, when you find a good measurement for high-*E* and *B* strings that is low and comes close to your final action, you can increase this amount by .002" or so as you go across the radius of the board toward the bass side, slightly raising these strings more than their treble-string counterparts. When you find good average measurements, record them as a guide to use some other time.

When the string slots are well spaced and deep enough, do the final shaping and finishing. Using a very sharp pencil, mark the excess nut-blank overhang and trim it off with your razor-saw (file or sand if you prefer), leaving a slight bit of the pencil line showing so that you can file and smoothly sand it away without chips. For the final time, sand down the top to eliminate any too-deep slots, finish rounding and shaping the nut to look like your original or the picture in your mind's eye, and sand off any scratches using 320-, 400-, and

600-grit wet-or-dry sandpaper, in that order.

If you have any really deep scratches, you may find it easiest to remove them with your smooth mill file. Buff the nut on a soft rag smeared with a buffing compound and then a polishing compound, such as Meguiar's Mirror Glaze #4 and #7, in that order. I like to high-polish the slot bottoms with 1000-grit "Finesse" sandpaper wrapped around my nut files or razor-saw. These buffing compounds and 1000-grit paper are available at most auto parts stores and from many guitar shop suppliers. Finally, dry-buff the nut surfaces on a clean dry rag. Care should be taken when sanding, smoothing, and polishing the nut. Stay on the exposed surfaces and lay off the bone that actually fits into the nut slot—too much buffing here can create a loose fit when it comes to the gluing-in.

To be sure you have the action the way you like it, string the guitar to pitch before gluing the nut. Recheck your string height and the relationship between nut and bridge. Don't be surprised if you have to take the nut in and out of the slot (stringing to pitch, as well) as many as a dozen times while you're learning. Expect some string breakage, too, from the constant tuning down and up to pitch. Most pros usually have a nut in and out of an instrument at least four times before completion, so don't feel bad.

If the final fitting meets your approval, glue the nut into place using a couple of light dabs of hide glue or white glue. I avoid using my beloved Hot Stuff super glue here, because its instant setting time won't allow you to move the nut from side to side when lining it up. Apply the glue lightly to the front wall and underside of the nut, set it in place, and quickly snug up the strings to help hold it. After the glue has set (one hour for a white/yellow glue such as Titebond, and three or four for a hide glue), you can tune to pitch and you're back in the business of making music.

Be sure to read between the lines here, knowing that I can't describe every approach to nut making, nor all the tools that can be used, without writing a book on just that one subject! This is enough information to help do-it-yourselfers do a better job, and to educate those not interested in doing their own setups so they're better prepared to shop for quality work.

8 FRET DRESSING

Loose frets

Before you can learn to dress frets (which is one of the main lessons in this section) you should make sure that you don't have a fingerboard full of loose frets and loose fret ends. It's hard to level and re-crown frets that are loose because they press down as the file passes over them, and pop right back up when it goes by. Loose frets are common, even with good fretwork on great guitars. A lot of fret buzz is caused by loose fret ends, which are hard not only on the ear but also on the fingers. While a complete fret job is sometimes needed to correct buzzes caused by warps, twists, and worn-out frets, just as often the problem can be solved by gluing down the end of the one fret that has lifted. In the old days, the resetting of a raised fret end was difficult and time-consuming. But that was before super glue. Now the average guitar player can easily and safely solve this problem.

A fret end can rise for a variety of reasons. The fret slot may be too big, or the fret tang (the part that's driven into the fingerboard slot to hold the fret in) could be too small. Rising fret ends may also be caused by insufficient glue, or wood that has shrunk: some frets are held in with glue as an aid, while others are hammered in dry, letting the small beads on the side of the tang do all the holding. Dirt, grease, and oils may have loosened the glue or softened and weakened the wood that holds the fret. Here's a quick and easy technique for tamping down those high fret ends:

Begin by finding a wooden dowel at least ¼" in diameter and 6" long. Carve or file a slight notch in one end. This dowel is used for pushing the fret end down flush on the fingerboard while you wax the fret and its surrounding fingerboard area to aid in the cleanup of the glue. The stick also holds the fret in place while the glue sets.

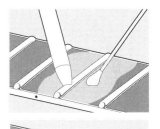

Next, lay a sheet of paper on each side of the bad fret and tape it down to within ½" of the fret. Wax the exposed fingerboard and fret edges, going over the side of the fingerboard

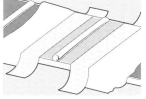

or binding, as well, in case any glue might run over onto the neck. Use a Q-Tip to apply any sort of paste wax. Don't load the Q-Tip with wax; twirl it in the wax and wipe off any lumps. When you've finished waxing, release the fret. It should pop right back up, with no wax having gotten under the fret where you want the glue to do its work.

If you have more than one loose fret end (and often you will), don't try regluing more than one at a time. Use Hot Stuff Original Formula, which is water-thin and able to penetrate deep within the fret slot and tang area. You'll also need a bottle of accelerator to speed up the drying time and cause an "instant" cure. The reason we covered the rest of the fingerboard is so that all the frets don't become activated by the accelerator's effect, which lasts about 15 minutes.

The guitar should be fairly immobile while you're working, so block the neck with some books or something firm for it to press against. Apply a drop of glue to each side of the loose fret along the fingerboard edge as far back as your eye tells you it's loose, and watch it disappear as it runs deep into the problem area. With a soft rag or tissue paper, remove any wet glue that doesn't run under.

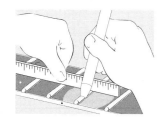

Immediately follow with a squirt of accelerator on each side of the fret, and then quickly but smoothly peel off the tape and paper. While the glue is accelerating, it's wise to have your wooden press-stick in the other hand, ready to press the fret down. While pressing the fret flush to the fingerboard, you can use a straightedge or flat object to help judge when the fret is level with its nearest tight fret. The glue should set within 30 seconds. Don't press the fret lower than the frets on either side, since this will result in a fret that's too low and subject to buzz. The actual gluing and accelerating must be done swiftly and efficiently, so first practice the operation in a dry run. Follow this time schedule: Apply glue and clean up excess—5 to 10 seconds; squirt accelerator—2 or 3 seconds; remove tape— 2 seconds; press fret down and level with straightedge or block—5 seconds.

In less than a minute the fret should hold, sometimes leaving a small bead of squeezed-

out super glue showing along the fret/fingerboard edge. Remove this glue with a sharp-pointed tool (pin, X-acto blade, chisel, etc.). Any glue that might remain on the waxed area of the fingerboard should be removed by scraping lightly (lengthwise with the fingerboard rather than across-grain) with a razor blade, and then polish with 0000 steel wool. If you still have a slight buzz, you may need to slightly level the fret with a smooth mill file or block of wood wrapped with #400 sandpaper, or use the Koontz radius blocks described in the next section.

If you have any trouble getting the fret level or if you feel that you didn't glue it properly, use a soldering pencil to loosen the glue bond and try again. Heat breaks a super glue bond in the same way that it loosens most any glue, including epoxies. Caution: Heat causes some glues to vaporize. Do not breathe the fumes or allow them to get into your eyes! Try to avoid getting into this situation. The second time around on a given fret may be more difficult because the hardened super glue is still under there. Don't use too much glue, and be especially careful not to let the glue run onto the neck. If it does, wipe it off immediately with some lighter fluid, which you should keep handy.

Wear safety glasses when using super glue, and remember that it can bond your fingers together. A short while back, a fret sprung up on me when my push-stick slipped, spitting super glue onto my prescription plastic-lens safety glasses. The glue hardened instantly and permanently. I had to buy a new pair of glasses, but my eyes were spared. Of course, avoid splashing a guitar's finish. Buy a bottle of solvent for cleaning glue from your fingertips and to help separate them in case of accident. Never use this solvent to remove glue from a lacquer finish, since it dissolves lacquer. Practice with the super glue and accelerator on objects that you don't care about before trying a repair. This will give you a feel for the setting time and show you how quickly it runs.

In extreme cases (with much sweat and oil worked under the fret), this method may not work, but it's worth a try; if it doesn't work, a partial or complete refret may be needed.

Fret-dressing basics

Fret dressing is one of the most common reasons a guitar ends up in the repair shop, and while you may never attempt your own fret dressing, this chapter will help you better understand what's entailed in repairing an instrument that plays poorly because of fret problems.

Be sure you understand the fingerboard/ neck evaluation and neck-rod adjustment explanation given in the Getting Started chapter before you attempt any fret work. And before you touch a file to your frets, read this chapter completely, since it teaches the fret-dressing process, as well as helping you determine whether a partial or complete fret job is needed. Even if you're squeamish about dressing your own frets, you can use this information to relate better to your repairman or to help judge a guitar that you are considering for purchase.

Fret dressing refers to the leveling-out and re-rounding (or "crowning") of high, low, or worn spots on frets; these can cause buzzes and "noting out"—notes that won't play cleanly. Basically, here's what's involved in the process: Leveling is first done with a smooth, flat mill file, followed by 220-, 320-, and 400-grit sandpaper for smoothing. Next, the fret tops left flat by the leveling operation are re-rounded with a small triangular file or a fret-rounding file. Any jagged fret ends along the fingerboard's edge are rounded now, too. Finally, a good polishing with fine sandpaper and steel wool gives smooth, buzz-free frets that are a dream to bend on.

Many new guitars come from the factory with the frets leveled, but only a cursory job of crowning has been done. This is often why some factory-fresh guitars play less than perfectly. Since fret dressing is tedious and time-consuming manual labor, a deluxe job at the factory would raise the instrument's price. Crowning is necessary, though, since the flat tops of the frets will otherwise have more surface area for the strings to buzz against as

they vibrate. Flat frets also cause problems in setting the intonation (since the strings can play sharp or flat to either side of dead center) and make the strings harder to bend due to the increased friction.

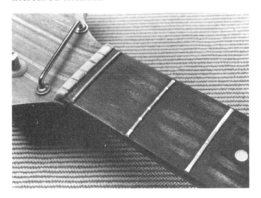

Guitars that have been played on for a while can develop grooves or pits in the frets, especially in the first five (above). If the grooves are too deep, you don't want to file all the good frets down to the level of those few bad ones for the sake of flatness and a level fingerboard. A general rule: When a pit or groove has been worn much lower than a third of the fret's full height (and definitely if the wear approaches the fret's halfway mark), have the guitar looked at by a repairman. You may be advised to have the worn frets replaced with matching fretwire (called a "partial refret") or to refret the instrument completely. Take the repairman's advice, but get several opinions.

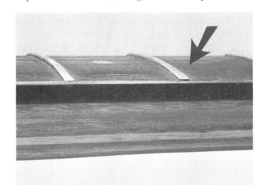

Frets that are worn too flat can be found on any guitar—from inexpensive imports to fine American-made models. Rather than being pitted, the tops of these frets are extremely low and flat (above). This can be caused by years of playing or by a poor fret job that someone tried to correct by leveling without taking the extra time to crown. Although you may

Hot Stuff's yellow-label Super T can be used for loose frets, too. Practice on junkers, by all means. If you use Hot Stuff's red-label Original Formula, you don't have to use accelerator. Try it both ways.

Before touching a file to your frets, read this complete chapter!

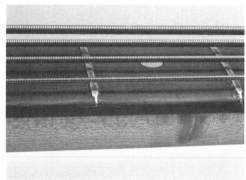

eventually need a refret, these low frets can be rounded with a lot of work. Find a bargain yardsale special with over-flat frets and practice on that.

Loose frets or a fret that is taller than those surrounding it will also cause a string to "note out"—in other words, you can't hear the intended note at all because the string is fretting at a higher fret. In most cases, this is caused by the fret working loose (above); it needs to be reseated. Although this is quite easy to do, I advise you to take your guitar to a repairman. It can probably be fixed on the spot. (Thanks to super glue, instant repairs can often be performed while you wait.) After you've gained some experience, you can try reseating a fret yourself by following the information given at the beginning of this chapter in the section on "loose fret ends."

The opposite of a too-tall fret is, of course, one that is too low, causing the string to note one fret higher. This is most often found on less expensive, off-the-wall guitars. It's usually caused by a fret that was somehow driven into the fingerboard too hard or by a mismatch of fretwire height. These frets should be pulled up to the proper height, or new frets should be installed. I'm not trying to drum up business for the Guild of American Luthiers, but once again, take it to your repairman until you've had some practice. This can be another instant repair, so take care of it before you attempt any leveling.

Jagged fret ends along the fingerboard edge are uncomfortable because they catch your hand as you slide up or down the neck. They are usually caused by the fretboard drying out and shrinking up over time. You may use the flat-leveling file to rebevel the fret ends if

needed, and the triangular crowning file can be used to round and deburr any jagged fret ends. Due to wear or an imperfect fret job, some frets fall short of the fingerboard edge or have jagged ends (above). Don't try to bevel all of the ends to match these; either have the troublesome frets replaced or do your best to deburr the ends and make them feel comfortable until the guitar's refretted.

Fretwire types and sizes

A customer with an old Les Paul "fretless wonder" asks, "Am I really missing anything by using a guitar with short frets?" Another wonders, "Will tall frets cause poor intonation?" The answers depend on the feel that you like and the sound that you want. In the uncomplicated old days, most acoustic and electric guitars came with little variety in fret styles; but today dozens of different fretwires—thin or fat, short or tall, soft or hard—are used for guitars. Generally, a thin wire is used for most acoustics, while a wide, or "jumbo," wire is common for electrics. I like the medium height wires better in either case because you can dress them more times between refrets. They also offer a better sustained note, are easier to bend on, and level and dress easier than low frets. Let's see what's available in fretwire so that you can better choose your new guitar or your future refretting job.

Fretwire is available in three shapes: rounded, squared, and triangular. The most common fret shape, or profile, is the rounded head or "bead." You may have seen square and extremely low fretwire on a Gibson Les Paul or early SG. These guitars were nicknamed "fretless wonders," which they nearly were. This fret offered very low action with little drag on the fingers when moving up and down the board; sustain, tone, and easy bends were traded off for that action, however. Round- or "oval"-type wires (which have different heights, widths, and advantages) are far and away the most common, and therefore the most deserving of our attention here. As for triangle-shaped fretwire, you don't see it often, but it does exist. East coast luthier Phil Petillo manufactures, and uses, a hardened triangluar wire, but it's not readily available and hasn't been used much (if at all) on production instruments.

Tall fretwire ranges from .050" to .065" in height above the fingerboard (about the thickness of a dime). Not many tall wires are available. Here are some advantages: Tall frets are easier for string bends, since the fingertip has less contact with the fingerboard. They also offer more sustain, due to the greater mass and because the string isn't damped by as much finger/fingerboard contact, which draws away some tone, volume, and sustain. While tall frets don't offer the same advantages as the radical scalloped fingerboards described later in this chapter, they lean in that direction more than a short fret does, so you'll get better hammer-ons and pull-offs. They also outlast low frets and withstand more fret dressings between refrets. Some disadvantages: Poor intonation could result from pressing too hard, but this can be corrected with a gentler touch. Until the left hand relaxes, the frets may feel like railroad ties when you slide up or down the fingerboard, and the neck may "feel" slightly thicker, but this is minor.

Regardless of width, medium-height fretwire is the standard that has commonly been used for the last 40 years. Some very wide, medium-height wires are called "jumbo," but this refers to the width, not the height. This wire ranges from .036" to .050" in height. Pros: With jumbo frets, the player can more easily achieve accurate intonation (again, this depends on

touch), since the fingerboard wood stops the fingertip, not allowing the string to be pressed too deeply. Barre chords and slides are easier, and the guitar's tone is softer, since the finger has more contact with the fingerboard. Cons: To enjoy medium-height fretwire at its best, the fret work must be done accurately, to ensure that you don't lose precious height during dressing. Medium-height wire wears out sooner than tall wire, and it allows fewer dressings between refrets. You'll still get years of playing out of medium wire if the fret work is good to begin with. Hammer-ons, pull-offs, bends, and sustain are not as easy as on tall wire, but most of us have been playing on medium wire for years and enjoying it; it's my favorite.

Except for the squared, low fretwire on the "fretless wonders," you probably won't run into low wire (.020" to .034") on a modern instrument. Expect to find low wire on used guitars that have seen much use and are simply worn out from years of playing and fret dressings. They're ready for a refret. While low wire is good for easy slides and fast action, it's not conducive to hammer-ons, pull-offs, string bending, and good tone and sustain. I do not enjoy playing on low wire.

A fret's width, regardless of height, affects playability and tone. Here you'll have to decide what you like. The increased mass of a wide fret offers a more "heavy metal" sustain than a narrow fret of comparable height, and wide frets wear longer than narrow ones. However, wide frets must be dressed more accurately than narrow ones to avoid poor intonation and buzzing caused by the string making contact off center (right), causing poor intonation, or flopping on a too-wide flat. Note: I dress a wide fret in two ways: rounded accurately to center, or semi-round like the top of a school bus (below). The "school busing,"

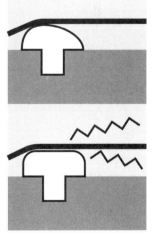

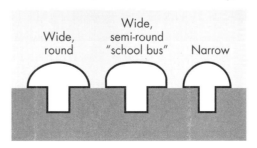

Wide, round   Wide, semi-round "school bus"   Narrow

which is often preferred by my rock customers, wears longer. Narrow frets offer a unique sustain, due to a cleaner contact point between string and fret crown, as well as the most accurate intonation. They don't have any disadvantages that I can think of, except that thinner frets have a crisper sound—clean, like breaking a glass—due to the accurate contact made between string and fret. This clean sound is sometimes misinterpreted as buzzing, and may take getting used to. The choice of fret width can only be decided by you. I prefer a somewhat narrow fret.

Fretwire hardness

A fret's hardness is determined by its composition. Usually the choice is 18% nickel/silver (hard), or 12% (soft). Stick with the hardest wire you're offered—it wears longer. Some classical builders prefer the softer 12% wire, though, feeling that it is more gentle on nylon or gut strings. The most commonly used fretwire for steel-string acoustic or electric guitars is 18% nickel/silver. Harder wire produces more sustain, but a greater advantage is its resistance to string wear. In most cases, the harder wire is the preferred choice (although, from a repairperson's standpoint, soft wire is easier to hammer in, and having less spring tends to "stay down" better than harder wire).

The FretBender

Relative fretwire hardness is a source of controversy in the guitar repair business. I've heard repairmen complain about customer remarks such as: "My guitar was refretted just a year ago, and the frets are grooved already." "My friend's '61 Strat has original frets that still play okay, with few worn spots. Are you guys selling us soft frets so you can get more work out of us?" Believe me, luthiers don't want their customers back in a year complaining of worn frets or expecting free remedies—fret jobs just ain't that much fun!

I checked with the fret manufacturers and found that they haven't changed their alloy specifications (as some of us have wondered).

In the U.S., a 12% wire is considered soft wire, while the industry standard, 18% wire, is comparatively hard. The percentage—12% or 18%—refers to the amount of nickel in a given wire, not silver (fretwire *looks* silver, but it's made of copper, nickel, and zinc—with no silver at all). The alloy mix for an 18% wire is 65% copper, 18% nickel, and 17% zinc.

Fretwire is still made as it always was. It begins as a semi-hard round wire that is heated to anneal (soften) it, and it's then allowed to cool. It becomes "work-hardened" from being drawn through roller dies that compress the wire into a shaped fret. Once drawn, there's no practical way, at the manufacturing end, to increase fret hardness (in experiments, manufacturers found that rolling a too-hard wire, or wire with a nickel content over 18%, caused breakdowns in the machinery).

I sent old fret samples (saved over the years from vintage guitars), along with new ones, to a lab for the Vickers hardness test for precious metals. The results ranged from 184 to 205 points on the Vickers scale, with the modern wire being hardest in each case. The tests showed that large wire was harder than small wire. In the process, I began thinking about how hard copper gets when bent and unbent (those who have run copper water lines know what I mean) and ended up making what, for me, is a significant discovery. By running the fretwire through a Fret-Bender, over-radiusing it, and then straightening it and rolling it again (repeating the process several times), the fret hardness gained from 14 to 20 points on the Vickers scale, which is appreciable. I was able to work-harden a smaller, Strat-size wire until the hardness matched that of the jumbo wires used in the lab test! Tell your repair-man about this technique if he doesn't know it already.

If modern fretwire seems to wear faster than "vintage" wire, it's because modern players are more aggressive than those in the '50s and '60s, utilizing considerable single-note playing, string bending, and a heavier attack, all of which cause more fret wear. Today's harder string windings tend to wear frets faster, too. Also, many of the vintage guitars with original frets "still in good shape" were played with flat-wound strings—which aren't as hard on frets, perhaps accounting for some of the perception that frets aren't what they used to be. The real key to fret wear is playing time. It doesn't matter how old a guitar is; what's important is how much it gets played. Leave it in the case, and the frets will never wear out! Today's guitarists, though, play and practice more than ever.

This basic information should help you understand the different types of frets. If you're shopping for a new guitar, ask the salesman to explain what size, and type, of fretwire has been used. Or if you're looking for a refret, see to it that your repairman uses a hard wire; it lasts longer (a soft wire is fine for classical guitars, though, since the nylon strings won't wear grooves as easily). Here are some of my favorite fretwires:

■ Standard wide frets (vintage "wide oval" Gibson): Dunlop #6130 and Stewart-MacDonald #149 (.103" wide x .041" tall).

■ Extra-tall and wide (modern heavy-metal wire): Dunlop #6100 and Stew-Mac #150 (.110" wide x .055" tall).

■ Thin wires for electric or acoustic guitars (vintage Fender, Gibson, and Martin): Stew-Mac #148 and Dunlop #6230 (.085" wide x .041" tall).

■ Medium width and medium height (Fender 'Stevie-Ray' size): Stew-Mac # 141 (.095" wide x .045" tall).

■ Big Medium width and height (new size): Stew-Mac # 3391 (.092" x .048").

■ Vintage Martin wire: C.F. Martin & Co: All sizes, including bar-style. (See "Compression-Fretting" for details on sizes.)

If you're serious about fret work, you should buy samples of any wire that arouses your curiosity, and check it out for yourself.

Files used for fret dressing

Before getting into fret dressing, let's first look at the specialized files which are used by most repairshops: the "leveling" files which are initially used to "mill" the fret tops flat and level

with each other; and the rounding, or "crowning," files that reshape the fret tops after leveling. Most of these tools are available ready-made, or you can make many of them yourself.

Some of the tools needed for fret dressing you can make yourself. At the hardware store, buy two 10" smooth-mill bastard files (choose ones that aren't warped), a 6" or 7" smooth-cut triangle file, and a "file-card" (a wire file-cleaning brush). Modify the files using my illustrations as a guideline. Caution: Unless you own a grinder with a good stone wheel, and are familiar with the necessary operational safety precautions, have your files ground at a machine, welding, or grinding shop. This is simple for them and inexpensive and safe for you. If there's a high school or trade school nearby, ask the metal-shop teacher if a student needs a small project. Your files can probably be ground while you wait. Note: Few people realize that grinders are dangerous—even those little ones everyone has in the garage. The danger lies in stone wheels that are cracked or otherwise in bad shape. If these come apart while under speed, the exploding fragments could kill you or maul your face. This happened to a friend of mine; he's okay, but only because his father, a surgeon, happened to be home at the time. Don't get me wrong, I use grinders—but only with approved full-face protection, and I'm very cautious. Please do the same.

LEVELING FILES

One of the 10" files should be cut into two lengths, approximately 3" and 6" long. These are the leveling files that will be used to rectify high or low frets and hump or rise, as well as to create fall-away at the high end of the fingerboard. To cut the file into the two lengths, you must grind a V-shaped groove

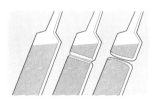

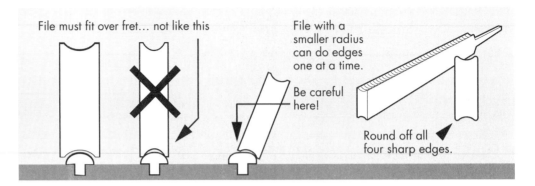

File must fit over fret... not like this

File with a smaller radius can do edges one at a time.

Be careful here!

Round off all four sharp edges.

on opposite sides until the cuts begin to meet in the middle.

Then, with the file clamped to a tabletop or in a vise, break it along the scored line. Grind the broken ends into a smooth, rounded shape. *Always wear safety glasses when grinding and breaking!* You now have two leveling files—a short and a mid-sized one. The 3" one is for leveling one or two problem frets (especially those on the section of the fingerboard that overlaps the guitar's body), and the 6" one is good for mid-size sections of the fretboard (it's also great for smoothing the fret end bevel along the fretboard edge—especially after a refret).

Finally, with the longer 10" (uncut) file, simply remove the "tang" (handle) and the untoothed metal at each end of the file, and then round and smooth the sharp edges. You'll end up with around 9" of good usuable file—this is the basic leveling file used for general smoothing of the whole fingerboard.

With epoxy or super glue, install wooden handles onto all your files.

ROUNDING FILES

These you can't make yourself. They come in several sizes (to accomodate frets of different width) and have teeth which are formed into a convex shape. It's best if a rounding file is larger than the fret size so that it fits easily over the fret crown. A file much smaller than the fret width can cut grooves into the sides. Some files have both a narrow and a wide groove—on opposite edges. Others have the same size groove on both edges. Over the years, I've purchased every fret file there is: call me compulsive, I don't mind.

A rounding file sits over the fret, but the radius of its teeth isn't deep enough to allow the file edges to touch or scratch the fingerboard wood; this could happen with an extremely worn or low-crown fret, however. Sometimes it's effective to use a rounding file with a radius that's smaller than the fret width for rounding just one edge of a flat-topped fret on either side of center, but you must be careful that the edge doesn't cut a groove into the fret top by mistake. These edges of the file where the teeth run into the smooth side walls are often sharp; grind or sand them smooth along the entire file length to avoid gouging the fingerboard on each side of the fret as you're working.

The *type* of cut imparted by a rounding file is round, of course. The file's function is to round off, or "recrown," frets that are filed or sanded flat during the operation of fret dressing or leveling. The *quality* of cut depends on the make of file and how it's used. New files tend to chatter and leave hard-to-remove marks on frets. Here are a few tips for fret rounders: Avoid excess pressure with rounding files. Clogged metal in the teeth causes scratching, so clean them often. Wipe a stick of paraffin over the teeth to act as a lubricant and help eliminate clogging. Practice on scrap to check the cut of a new file.

DIAMOND ROUNDING FILE

These are my favorite. Rather than having teeth, the convex surface is covered with industrial diamonds. These files (coarse and fine grits are available) don't leave scratches that you can't get out, and they cut in both directions! Even dyed-in-the-wool "triangle filers" love this file once they give it a chance. I seldom use toothed files anymore.

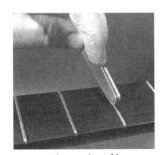

Diamond rounding file

TRIANGLE OR 3-SQUARE FILE

Another great fret-dressing tool is a 6" to 8" slim-taper, three-corner "triangle" file with its sharp edges ground smooth. I learned to use one during my visits to the Gibson plant in Kalamazoo in the good old days. At the time, I had a beautiful flame-top Les Paul, and because I never trusted myself to work on it, the frets were dressed more than once at the factory. (In those days, you could make an appointment to have service done while you waited. I learned a lot by wandering around and watching.)

The triangle file can be used instead of, or along *with* a rounding file to round or crown the fret tops left flat after the leveling operation. It is also used to round over the frets' ends and remove any jagged burrs along the fingerboard's edge. You must remove any trace of a cutting edge on all three corners of

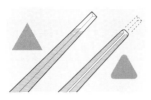

the file with a grinder or belt sander (here's a look at the file before and after). Also, blunt and round the tip, or nose, of the file. A poorly ground triangle file can scar the fingerboard wood on either side of the fret you're working on, even though you have taped off the fingerboard.

A second triangle file is the small extra-slim triangle file from Stew-Mac. Unless I'm "hogging" metal, I prefer this file because it has a finer cut, is more delicate, and can shape fret ends better since it can get in closer .

When you shop for your files, pick up one sheet each of wet-or-dry sandpaper in 320-, 400-, and 600-grits, as well as some 0000 steel

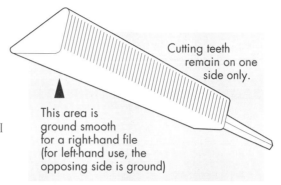

Cutting teeth remain on one side only.

▲

This area is ground smooth for a right-hand file (for left-hand use, the opposing side is ground)

wool and a file-cleaning brush (also known as a file card). My favorite file card has small metal bristles on one side and fiber bristles on the other; buy one if you can find it. Even better than a file card is a brass-bristle mini-file cleaner;they're great for cleaning small, fine-cut triangle files.

CANT SAW FILE

A third file—the cant saw file—is used out in Texas by Michael Stevens and Rene Martinez. Michael Stevens co-founded the Fender Custom Shop along with John Page, and now operates Stevens Electrical Instruments in Alpine, Texas; Rene Martinez was Stevie Ray Vaughan's guitar tech and best friend (see section on Stevie Ray's setup). The cant saw file is similar in cut to the large triangle file, but cuts even faster. These are also available at hardware stores and should be ground to look like the illustration. When the fingerboard is taped off, you can rest the smooth-ground edge of this file directly on the fretboard surface for support (you don't have to balance on the fret as with other files). Because the edge facing down on the fretboard is ground smooth, this file only cuts from one side of the fret to center, so the guitar is turned end-for-end to do the opposite side (which most of us do anyway to get the fret ends). Stevens has both "right"- and "left"-hand files (the file in the drawing above is a right-hand file).

I've been criticized for having too many files for fretwork, but I don't care. *Not* having a wide selection of files is rather limiting (especially if you're in the business of working on frets). I often have quite a selection of specialty files laid out as I work.

SANDING TOOLS

A good tool for sanding and steel-wooling frets after leveling and rounding is a rubber squeegee from the 3M Company. This should

Michael Stevens

Blues-bend buzzing ceases to be a problem with a radius of 9½" and up. This radius, introduced by Fender in recent years, is a good compromise between the curved board of vintage Strats and the modern 10" and 12" fingerboards.

be available at any automotive store selling finish supplies. Buy the smallest rubber squeegee available, and grind or file a groove along one edge of it. Eventually, you'll wrap the steel wool or sandpaper around the edge of this "fret burnisher" to do your polishing (look at the section on fingerboard cleaning for an illustration of how to shape the squeegee).

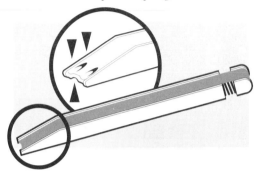

An even better fret burnisher is the "Sand-Stick"—an inexpensive hand held sander with a spring-loaded abrasive belt. I file three slight grooves into the plastic—two on one side and one on the other [ILLU was in trade secret]—which hug the fret's rounded shape. I use three "Sand-Sticks" during dressing: 320-, 400-, and 600-grit.

Finally, pick up a roll of masking tape for taping off the frets while you file and sand them. You should have the light-tack drafting tape as well as standard masking tape.

It will take you a little time to find and modify the proper files and to buy the sandpaper, steel wool, and squeegee. Again, finish this whole chapter before starting work!

Dressing the frets

Now, we're about to put this knowledge to use, BUT—first read the following section on compound and cylindrical shaped fretboards, then you can pick up your file!

THE COMPOUND RADIUS VS. THE CYLINDER RADIUS

Understanding the difference between a cylinder- and a cone-shaped, or "compound," fretboard may be the most subtle—and important—fretting task you'll face. The ability to

use this knowledge during fret dressing or re-fretting separates the novice from the professional, and the clean playing note from a buzz—yet I've never seen it explained!

In my opinion, radiused fretboards are more comfortable for playing chords than are flat fretboards because they follow the natural curve of the hand. A player choosing a guitar should have the fretboard radius in mind. The most heavily-radiused fretboards are Rickenbacker and Fender, but for some reason we always refer to Fender when describing the problems associated with low action and a radiused fretboard—like the vintage Fender 7¼" radius. This radius is very comfortable to chord on, but when you bend the high-*E* string (and to a lesser degree the *B*) the string will often "note out". The solution is to raise the strings higher (which doesn't please most players), or come to grips with the compound radius. If you're a player who never bends strings, or doesn't bend very far, then even a vintage Strat or Tele with a 7 ¼" radius can have a fairly low action without buzz, and you needn't mess with compound fretwork at all.

A flatter fretboard radius offers fewer problems to string benders. Gibson's traditional 12" radius has always been good for blues-bending, and Martin's 16", too. But the flatter you get the radius, the less chord-comfort you have. So an "in-between" radius like a 9" or 10" may be just right. For some, a combination of radii—the compound radius— is the answer.

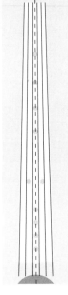
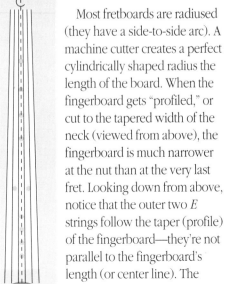

Most fretboards are radiused (they have a side-to-side arc). A machine cutter creates a perfect cylindrically shaped radius the length of the board. When the fingerboard gets "profiled," or cut to the tapered width of the neck (viewed from above), the fingerboard is much narrower at the nut than at the very last fret. Looking down from above, notice that the outer two *E* strings follow the taper (profile) of the fingerboard—they're not parallel to the fingerboard's length (or center line). The remaining four strings follow the same taper but gradually become more parallel to the center line, with the space between the *D* and *G* strings being on dead-center.

Imagine this profiled cylinder-shaped fretboard glued to a neck adjusted perfectly straight. A straightedge set on the board in the lie of the strings (the individual string's line between the nut and saddle), especially the outside *E* strings, will rock from end to end because the *only way a straight line can be in full contact with the surface of a cylinder is when it is parallel to the center.* Take a cylinder—a water glass—and set your straightedge in full contact with the glass' surface lengthwise—from end to end. As soon as you slant the straightedge to the centerline (out of parallel) it loses contact from end to end and rocks on the "hill" in the center.

A fret surface which was machine-radiused at Fender in 1957 was not touched before being fretted. The board—and the fret tops—are a cylinder. The string, following the profile (or being at an angle to the cylinder's centerline) is going to "rock" in the center on the high spot (like the water glass)—especially when the high *E* or *B* is pushed at an even greater angle (out of parallel) to the centerline during string bends. This is why Fender began offering a 9" and 12" radius (only keeping the 7¼" radius on the vintage models).

The only way to avoid this rocking in the center is to shape the fretboard (or the water glass) into a cone. A cone-shaped fretboard simply means that the radius at the nut will be greater than at the last fret—the fingerboard radius will flatten gradually from end to end. In repairshops we have been compounding fretboards for years (when applicable) to give customers low action with blues-bending capabilites and little buzz. Some manufacturers who use, or have used, a compound radius are: Warmoth, Jackson, Collings, Taylor, and Martin.

When preparing the fretboard for a fret job you will sand, file, or scrape the surface until it's straight from end to end across the radius of the board. Note: *If you check your progress with a straightedge resting in the six individual string lies (which is the most common method),*

you are shaping a slight compound taper into the fretboard. In the case of a refret on many factory guitars (Fender, Gibson, Guild, Martin after '93), you're altering the machine-made cylinder which was never intended to have a taper or "profile."

Vintage Martins were compounded this way. They started out with a 16" machine-shaped clylinder fretboard which became tapered to 20" at the end because Martin hand-levelled the board in "the lie of the strings." Martin guitars made after 1993 have cylindrical fretboards with no taper because they changed their fretboard preparation technique (they realized that for a 16" or higher radius, a compound fretboard wasn't too great an issue, especially on an acoustic guitar). As a general rule, the radius of an average compound fingerboard flattens out about 3" or 4" toward the end of the fingerboard.

A QUICK FIX FOR A VINTAGE BUZZ

The quickest fix (although I'm not suggesting it necessarily) for vintage Fenders which buzz when you bend, is to relevel the existing frets until the straightedge sits flat on the top three string lies (the *E*, *B*, and *G*-string lies). You don't need to worry about the bass side because the strings are heavier, higher, and you don't bend them much. You'll be removing the most metal on the edges (*E* and *B* strings) where the string taper is greatest. The first and last few frets will hardly get filed at all because they aren't part of the "hill" which is causing the problem. You're creating a slight compound radius on the fret tops themselves.

After compounding, some frets will be taller than others, but if the frets were fairly tall to begin with the lowest ones usually aren't uncomfortably low. Coupled with the traditionally higher action normally accepted with a vintage Strat, you can now get the blues bends you're after. This solution is only worthwhile on a vintage axe which still has plenty of fret to work with, however, and that's not too common.

A better solution is to put the compound radius into the fretboard itself—prep the board's *surface* that way. Now the tops of the newly installed frets will touch the straightedge (after a normal light fret leveling) because the

Don MacRostie

frets will follow the compound radius from end to end (and the fret height will be uniform). This "compound leveling" is common during a refret, and I fretted guitars like that for years before realizing that what I was doing had a "name" (a compound radius). You can't compound a vintage maple neck without removing most (or all) of the finish however, and neither can you reshape thin "veneer" rosewood Fender boards (there's not enough wood to remove). In all cases—especially the most radiused boards, you have to take inlays and fingerboard side dots into consideration.

It's easy to run into side dots, especially on Fenders. Since Gibson starts out at 12" (sometimes) you have less chance of hitting side dots, but it's still possible. Because of side dots, inlays, and the fretboard thickness/look/feel, a "partial" compound job may be the answer. In other words, you don't go *all the way* (following the formula which is given later), but simply in the *direction* of a somewhat flatter board.

Knowing that I generally "read" and prep a fretboard with my straightedges resting on the lie of the string (creating a cone), I wanted to know what radius I should look for at the fretboard end, and—perhaps even more important to final setup—what is the projected radius when it meets the bridge saddle? I asked my good friend Don MacRostie—head of R&D at Stewart-MacDonald. Working with two other interested luthiers, Gila Eban and Dana Bourgeois, Don worked out three basic fingerboard radius formulas.

The purpose of these formulas is to keep us from removing more wood than necessary while attempting to get the straightedge to sit flat on the fretboard during a refret. The amount of wood to be removed is more subtle than some realize and is determined by the fingerboard's taper (width of the nut and 12th fret), scale length, and starting radius at the nut. With it you can find out what the radius must be at the end of the fingerboard, at any point along the fingerboard (for checking your accuracy with radius gauges as you work), and determine the projected radius at the bridge saddle. It's very useful information!

DON MACROSTIE'S "CONE HEAD" FORMULA: HOW TO DETERMINE A RADIUS AT ANY POINT ON A FRETBOARD

Memo
To: Dan   *From: Don*

Dan: Here you are. Anyone doing a fret job who doesn't understand the difference between a cylinder and a cone is working "blind." If they understand it and choose to ignore it, that's a different story!

Straight lines that run lengthwise on a cylinder and are in full contact with its surface must be parallel, and could never be tapered to each other as guitar strings on a fingerboard are. I have drawn out three formulas for dealing with the phenomenon of string spread over a curved surface. Whenever straight lines eventually converge on a point (the fingerboard tapering from the body toward the nut), and those straight lines lie in full contact with a radiused surface, then the shape of that surface must be conical or some portion of a cone. First we must determine where the lines (strings) converge. I've defined the following:

X = Distance from the nut to the Origin (focal point)

T = Distance from the nut to the 12thfret

Sn = String spread at the nut

St = String spread at the 12th fret

Rn = Fingerboard radius at the nut

Rd = Fingerboard radius at "D" (a certain distance from nut)

D = Arbitrary distance from nut

1 Using the spacing of the two *E* strings at the nut and 12th fret, extend the lines until they converge (illustrated at top of next page). Measure from the point of convergence to the nut and you will have "X" or the focal length. X is then used in the remaining formulas. The formula is marked #1:

1	**2**	**3**
$X = \dfrac{T}{\left(\dfrac{St}{Sn}\right)-1}$	$Rd = \dfrac{Rn\,(X+D)}{X}$	$D = \left(\dfrac{Rd \times X}{Rn}\right) - X$

2 The second formula (see #2 above and illustration following) assumes that you have

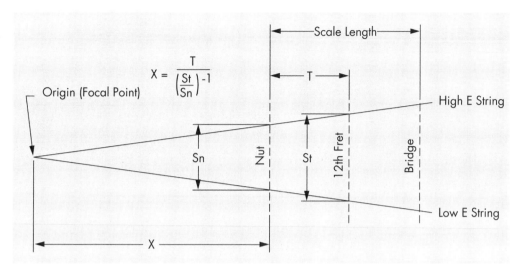

$$X = \frac{T}{\left(\frac{St}{Sn}\right) - 1}$$

already determined (X), the location of the Origin of the cone. This solves for the radius at any point along the fingerboard represented by the value D.

3 The third formula, to find the point D where the radius equals a known value, is written as #3, at left. This formula can be rearranged to solve for any of the values.

All of these formulas are linear and relatively easy to solve and rearrange.

Note: When we were done we discovered that we'd just "rediscovered the wheel." Two similar formulas, overlooked by us, were published in the GAL's *American Lutherie* magazine: "In Search Of The Perfect Cone" written by Tim Earls—Vol. 30 (summer '92, page 44); and "Conical Radius Fretboard Formula" by Elaine Hartstein—Vol. 34 (summer 93, page 46) Check your back issues, or contact the GAL for those articles.

GETTING TO WORK

OK. Enough theory. First check the fretboard radius; if it measures the same at the nut as at the last fret, you have a cylinder-shaped board (*a la* Fender and Gibson). If the radius is flatter at the last fret than it is at the nut, then you have a "compound," "cone-shaped," or "tapered-radius" fretboard. Below are two ways of leveling the fret tops with a file: one for a cylinder-board, and one for a compound. Using either method, the file stroke is always lengthwise with the fingerboard. Until you gain experience at fret dressing, practice on yardsale specials.

THE LEVELING POSITION

Using the neck evaluation and truss rod adjustment section of the Getting Started chapter as a guide, adjust your truss rod to remove any relief. Get the neck straight from the 1st fret to the 12th, using a metal straight-

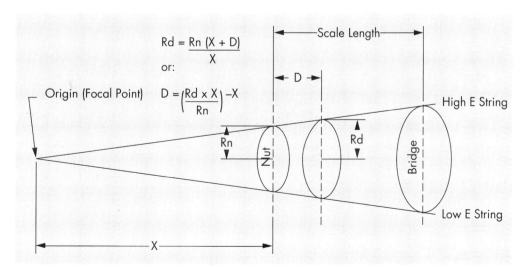

$$Rd = \frac{Rn\,(X + D)}{X}$$

or:

$$D = \left(\frac{Rd \times X}{Rn}\right) - X$$

edge for comparison. Then duplicate this straight, or "leveling," position with the strings removed. Lay a towel or pad on the table top, covering it and the entire work surface with newspaper to catch any metal filings. Rest the guitar's body on the padded part of the work surface, and cradle the back of the neck on a stack of books or anything else that can serve as a support. (I like the "canteloupe" neck rest used by repairman Pete Towers in Chesterton, Cambridge, UK. It's fantastic!)

Any neck support should be padded, and covered with paper as well, because filings will scratch the lacquer on the back of the neck. (To avoid scratching, vacuum or remove the filings often). Check with your straightedge again to be sure that the neck support hasn't altered your neck straightness. If it has, move the support to a different part of the neck and/ or make a slight truss rod adjustment.

Note: Even with the strings removed and the truss rod loose, some necks may tend to back-bow slightly. These necks gain relief from string tension alone. In this case, support the headstock, not the back of the neck, and later you may either put slight pressure on the body or pull down on the neck's heel to straighten the neck as you file.

A better way than pulling down on the heel to get the neck into the "playing," or straight, position was shown to me by Rich Starkey at the Martin repair department. For simulating string tension on a neck—whether refretting or dressing—Rich supports the peghead and then sets two 6 lb. weights on either side of the fretboard on the shoulders of the guitar (above, right). For a non-flat-top (like a Les Paul), use a sandbag or sack of buckshot. The weights add just enough pressure to get the neck of a non-

adjustable Martin (or any guitar) into the perfect leveling position.

TOOLS USED FOR DRESSING FRETS

Here are two lists of the tools used to level and crown (round) the frets. Listed here you'll see the files that were just described. One list is for the beginner, and shows the minimum number of tools needed to "get by"—what you *must* have; the other list describes the tools that *I* get out for "fret dressing." I won't get out all the listed tools if I've just refretted the guitar in question—I know my fretting job was accurate, so I'll only need to kiss the fret tops and polish them. During a regular dressing, however (on someone *else's* fretwork), I get a good number of files out.

"MUST HAVE" TOOL LIST

■ Straightedges—whatever you use—at least a long one for checking general levelness, and a couple of short ones to test individual frets by "rocking" on a high spot (any short flat object can be used as a "straightedge" in a pinch).

■ 10" leveling file, or substitute a 2" x 8" carborundum stone (whetstone)

■ 1 rounding file (diamond, triangle, cant saw, Gurian, etc.)

■ 1" wide x 14" long sanding block

■ 320-, 400-, 600-grit wet-or-dry sandpaper (self-stick, or use double-stick tape). The 320-grit is for leveling, the other two are for polishing out marks after filing.

■ Mini-file cleaning brush—brass bristle

■ 0000 steel wool

■ Masking tape

THE TOOLS I USE

■ 3", 6", and 10" leveling files

■ Carborundum stone

■ Steel leveling block (for sandpaper)

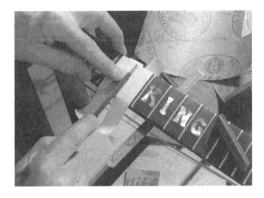

■ 220-, 320-, 400-, 600-grit wet-or-dry sandpaper (preferably Gold self-stick)

■ Small and large triangle files

■ Cant saw file

■ Coarse-grit and fine-grit diamond rounding files

■ Mini-file cleaning brush—brass bristle

■ Three "Sand-Sticks"—with 320-, 400-, and 600- grit belts

■ 0000-steel wool

■ Draftsman's tape, masking tape, and "Flatback" heavy-duty binding tape

■ Small flat file (Stew-Mac Fender nut-seating file #1174 (for removing burr and cleaning up individual fret ends)

■ Straightedges—long, short, notched, and a set of fret "rockers" in 1½", 3" , 4", and 5" lengths

USE PROTECTION AT ALL TIMES

With masking tape, protect any part of the guitar that can be scratched by your files or sandpaper, especially around the fingerboard tongue and the pickups (which, if not protected, will magnetically attract and retain metal filings and steel wool dust). To insure that the tape won't pull off delicate vintage finishes when it's removed, I lay down one course of the less-sticky drafting tape directly on the finish, and then, with regular masking tape, I tape thin (.018") pickguard material onto it as a protector.

REMOVE THE NUT

In theory, the leveling file must pass over the nut slot if the file is to hit all the frets equally. In practice, you can stop your file stroke at the nut as soon as the tops of all the frets have been hit. If the nut can be removed and replaced easily, or has to come out anyhow for replacement, *and* if vintage isn't an issue,

remove it—you'll level the frets more effectively. First, carefully score around the nut with a sharp X-acto knife to break the lacquer. With a block of wood and a hammer, gently tap the nut to knock it loose, as described in the Nut Work section.

HIGHLIGHT THE FRET TOPS

I use blue Magic Marker to "blue" the fret tops before filing. This lets me see instantly what's being removed and is especially necessary if you're doing the tricky "sideways" leveling mentioned later.

Since the file is flat, a number of successive passes are needed in order to cover a *radiused* frets's width. The blue magic marker helps you see how much fret the file is contacting on each stroke. The straightedge must be able to rest flat on all the fret tops (except for a slight fall away of .002" to .004") when the neck is in the straight "filing" position. Note: The position in which you place the straightedge on the frets depends on whether the fretboard you are leveling is a cylinder or a cone!

Caution: Tape off the fretboard to avoid getting marker on the wood—especially on binding, light rosewood, or maple necks! In fact, you probably shouldn't use marker on a maple neck!

GET RID OF ANY HUMP AT THE BODY JOINT

First, check out the fretboard extension: Many necks straighten easily with a truss rod adjustment and have no hump or rise at the neck/body joint or out on the "tongue" (fretboard extension over the body); with these "good" necks, you really won't have to do much filing—you'll only be "kissing" the tops. However, if you have a hump, rise, or high frets on the tongue, *level those frets first* so that they don't cause the straightedge to rise up while you're checking for flatness on the main portion of the board.

To remove a hump or rise, use the short leveling file to work down any small, isolated problem frets. Check your progress constantly—a small amount of filing can make a lot of difference. Note: Many necks are not set at an exact 90° angle to the body, and a straightedge resting on the main fingerboard

Several new fret-dressing tools have become available since 1985 when I started writing for Guitar Player. At Stewart-MacDonald I designed a long and short fret-leveling file with wooden handles and very smooth, long-angled teeth; and also a miniature, super-fine, three-cornered (triangle) file. Another tool, the Sand-Stick, is a small, plastic, spring-loaded belt sander used for sanding the fret tops after they've been crowned with the triangle file.

from the 1st fret to the neck/body joint may be on a different plane from the tongue, with the tongue naturally falling away because of this angle. This is normal, and should not be confused with a "hump," which is actually due to a swollen glue joint or high, loose frets. Usually, the most annoying problem on the tongue is a rise, where the last few frets are higher than the ones preceding them. Sometimes this takes a fair amount of filing to rectify, and in extreme cases it will leave the last few frets quite low and hard to round.

When you feel that you've eliminated any high or low spots on the tongue, restring the guitar to pitch, readjust the truss rod accordingly, and check the relief and/or straightness, and fallaway as described in the neck evaluation section. Once any tongue problems have been eliminated, the straightedge will give you a much more accurate reading on the main fingerboard (1st through 12th frets).

LEVELING THE MAIN PORTION OF THE FRETBOARD

Use the longer (10") file—this file must be the flattest you can find! Your goal is to create an accurate, smooth plane across the tops of the frets, so that no fret is higher or lower than any other. You want to expose new metal, or a fresh "flat," on each fret. With the longer file, begin where the tongue filing ends and file in long, even strokes from the body towards the headstock, applying light pressure. Always file lengthwise with the fingerboard, and because a mill file only cuts in one direction (we use the forward (push) stroke), don't file "back and forth". In theory, the file stroke should continue right off the fingerboard at the peghead end (out into space) so that all the frets get filed the same amount. You don't always have to do this however, and if you do, be careful not to dip the file and hit the shafts of the tuning keys! I usually stop filing when my tool has passed about halfway over the 1st fret. Then I back up and make another pass, continuing in this fashion until I've covered the width of the fingerboard from end to end.

Many repairmen prefer to use a carborundum stone to level the fret tops—especially if the fretwork was well done and there isn't much metal to remove. The Martin repair

shop, and the fretting department, recommend a Crystolon fine bench stone, #FJB8.

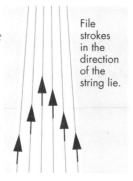

File strokes in the direction of the string lie.

COMPOUND OR CYLINDER: TWO DIFFERENT APPROACHES

1 Compound—The file stroke should follow the 6 individual string lies created by the fretboard profile. Then smooth the flats together using the file in a sweeping arc across the fretboard, working lengthwise and across the board at the same time (do this from the treble side toward center, and then the bass side toward center). The only "straight" file

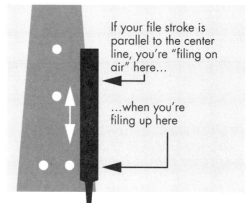

If your file stroke is parallel to the center line, you're "filing on air" here...

...when you're filing up here

stroke is between the *D* and *G* string area that is perfectly straight, or parallel to the center.

2 Cylinder—The file always remains parallel to the centerline. If you start filing on center, part of the file will be "filing on air" as you approach the fretboard edge. If this feels uncomfortable, you can begin on the edge, going lengthwise, but moving the file sideways, toward center, *while* you're moving lengthwise. This is a tricky stroke, but it works great!

Cylinder-shaped boards can easily be compounded during a refret (sometimes by accident), depending upon which of the two methods listed above are used on the fretboard.

REMOVE THE LEVELING MARKS WITH SANDPAPER

After leveling with a file, I use 280- and 320-grit sandpaper to smooth the fret tops and remove the somewhat harsh file marks. Either wet-or-dry (black), or else the "Gold" metal-

In the C.F. Martin fretting department: Carl Frantz levelling with a bench stone.

cutting sandpaper works best for leveling frets. The "free-cut" (blueish gray) lacquer-sanding paper doesn't work as well on frets as it does on finishes or wood—it breaks down too quickly on metal.

For compound fretboards, my leveler is a steel block which measures 1¾" x 1" x 15". I use the 1" edge, which is ground perfectly flat and faced with self-stick paper. The weight of this chunk of steel makes for instant, controlled leveling, but a block of wood or plexiglas would work too if it's flat (the weight of the steel is nice, though).

On cylinder-shaped fretboards, I use radiused sanding blocks (with the same self-stick sandpaper) instead of the heavy flat block. *But they can only be used for sanding on cylinder-shaped boards!* If you level the frets in the compound manner, the radius blocks would just "erase" your work since they can only create a cylinder. Don't mix up the two methods of leveling!

Note: One or two passes lengthwise is maybe all you need for each sanding grit: don't overdo it. The wet-or-dry black and gold sandpaper cuts fret tops like butter. In fact, when the frets only need a light leveling, you can level the frets without files at all—using just sandpaper!

LEVELING WITHOUT FILES (USING ONLY SANDPAPER)

If the frets are in good shape and don't need heavy leveling, you can skip using files entirely and level the frets using just the flat block—or the radius blocks—and sandpaper. Whether you're filing or sanding, use different pressures if you need to blend one section (for example, the 1st through 10th) into another (the 10th through 15th). If you know there is a high fret or a cluster of them, use your 3" or 6" file to work down that area. Follow with the long file to feather it in. A beginner should string to pitch often and readjust the rod to see how the feathering-in affects relief, leveling out, and fallaway. You can always get the neck back into the filing position if—when you begin—you put a mark on the truss rod nut as an index and return to it every time. The approach just described for leveling compound and cylinder *fret tops* is also used to level the wood of a fret*board* during a refret, but with some

different tools (files aren't always the best way to remove wood).

ANOTHER TIP FROM THE OLD WEST

Texas luthier Mike Stevens has this advice: "When all the level-filing and lengthwise sanding is done, I use a 5 ¾" x 2" wood block wrapped lengthwise with 320- or 400-grit sandpaper strips. Cut the sandpaper into strips less than the 2" width of the block, and long enough to wrap lengthwise on the block to stretch it tight—it doesn't sag that way. Go sideways (in the direction of the fret) with the sanding block to remove the final marks. From this point on, all your work will be in the direction that you bend strings—just to add that extra edge."

CLEANING UP THE FRET END BEVELS

Now, feel the fret ends. Sometimes they'll stick out beyond the fingerboard edge because the wood has shrunk while the metal fret hasn't. You can smooth the ends until they're flush with the wood by using the 6" leveling file held flat but lightly against the edge of the fingerboard. Avoid filing the finish any more than you must. If the fretboard edge is straight (you can sight it as if you were sighting levelness of the fretboard) the file will ride smoothly along the finish and cut only the fret ends. If the fretboard edge is irregular, use the 3" file; its shorter length lets it follow the contours. If you find it difficult to get the ends without damaging finish on the fretboard edge, use the small "touch-up" triangle file mentioned earlier.

If you start to remove finish, stop. Then lightly sand any dulled finish with 1000- to 2000-grit wet-or-dry sandpaper, using water as a lubricant, and return the original gloss by polishing with Mirror Glaze #7 to finish the job.

Normally during a fret dressing, you won't have to do much *beveling* on the fret ends, since they were beveled during the original factory fret job. But while you're cleaning up the fret ends, hold the file at the angle of the bevel and kiss them too—being careful not to over-bevel them (you'd remove playing area)! Watch carefully until you see the file just touch the sharp edge of the fretboard and stop! I use a white mat on the bench and a strong backlight to help me see the sliver of light disappear as the file contacts the fretboard.

ROUNDING THE FRET TOPS (HAVE LOTS OF ROOM TO WORK)

My workbench has a repair vice on the two front corners facing me. I work with the peghead to my left (treble side of fretboard away from me)—I call this working "right-handed." For all the frets clear of the body, I do the fret tops and the treble side fret ends in the right-hand position. When I reach the fretboard extension, or tongue, I do half of the fret tops, from the center toward the treble side, and the treble fret ends. Then I turn the guitar 180° ("left-handed") in order to do the bass side fret ends and the other half of the frets on the tongue. Since I have two repair vises I usually clamp the neck firm while I dress—at least I always did until I discovered the canteloupe neck rest (look back to "the leveling position" section).

I have a small pad to protect the part of the guitar body which contacts the bench, and I lay fresh clean paper on the benchtop, under where I'm filing, to catch fret filings and sanding dust (I empty this constantly). I lay the tools out either to the rear of the guitar being worked on, or I'll lay a protective pad over the guitar and use it as a tool "caddy."

PROTECT THE FRETBOARD WITH TAPE

Always tape off the fingerboard on each side of the fret. Use drafting tape, and don't let more than ¼" hang over the fretboard edge (the less tape on the finish the better). You can tape off the entire board at once, before beginning, or tape and file one fret at a time. If you have a tendency to slip, use the heavier Flatback tape (but it has a pretty high tack— you may be wise to put down drafting tape first and the heavy tape on top—especially on a fretboard with finish).

Another good way to protect the fretboard is with a ⅞" x 3 ¼" x .012"-thick stainless steel "Fret Protector". Its .110" slot lies over the fret and protects the board while you work. (Also, check out TJ Thompson's "venetian-blind method" in the "bar refret" section.)

USING THE TRIANGLE FILE

Starting at the 1st fret, hold the triangle file between the thumb and second and third fingers with the index finger on top, using the other hand's index finger to guide the file on the fret. With a forward stroke, apply light pressure, rolling the file to center as you push it across the fret's length. Switch from one side of the fret to the other, using this rolling motion towards center. You are removing the square edge and re-rounding the flat top that you made while leveling.

The triangle file I use most is a small slim one. My fretwork is accurate enough that I don't need a file to hog metal. However, if I'm working on existing fretwork, where the frets are low and need considerable rounding— that's when I'll use the larger "hardware-store" triangle, or the cant saw file.

ROUNDING FILES

You don't have to "roll to center" with a rounding file—they shape the whole fret at once. You can use a rounding file instead of— or along with—the triangle, or any other file. Since the diamond file came along, I seldom use toothed rounding files anymore. If the fret tops aren't very flat—just a sliver of metal—the fine-grit diamond file is better than the coarse (the coarse-grit diamond file removes metal pretty quickly). On my own fret jobs I'm inclined to use my fine-grit diamond rounding file (I have four grits, from coarse to fine) because, as was mentioned above, I don't remove much metal from the fret tops during the leveling (and therefore there's not much of a flat to round). An advantage with the diamond file is that you can get up on the rounded tip to shape one particular area.

Note: Frets which are low (under .030") are

more difficult to round, and if you're using a rounding file (toothed or diamond) don't let the edges mark the board—they can even cut through heavy masking tape.

THE CANT SAW FILE

These files are Mike Stevens' weapon of choice, and they were described earlier under "Files used for fretwork." Mike uses the "right-hand" file the most—for the main part of the fretboard (the easily accessible frets clear of the body). He files all the frets from the body to the nut on his right hand side only; then he flips the guitar end-for-end to do the "left" side. "I'm ambidextrous," he says, "so I could switch to the left hand file and not flip the guitar. But I prefer to see the fret top with the file in my right hand as I'm looking down."

On the tongue frets over the body Mike dresses from the center out (just as we do) toward the treble side, and flips the guitar again to go toward the bass side. But he actually does the frets a "quarter at a time" using the right- *and* left-hand files: first, all the frets from center out with the right hand files; second, all the frets from center out with the left hand file (flip the guitar and repeat the operation). For this "left-hand" filing, he uses his left hand (he's a showoff).

If this seems like a lot of trouble, it's not—I've watched Mike work (and we all have to flip the guitar around a lot during a dressing anyway). The cant saw file is what he learned on, and what he likes. You can't teach an old cowboy new tricks!

THE GURIAN FILE

One tool which can round the whole tongue in the right-handed position is the Gurian fret file (photo above, right). It has an offset handle which keeps your hand free of the top. But it *is* a toothed file. A custom file which I made for my Gurian handle is a chopped-off triangle file ground to fit into the Gurian handle. A diamond-file attachment for the Gurian offset file is in the works. I'll use it!

SHAPING THE FRET ENDS

You'll see the flat top getting smaller as you work. "Round and roll" until the *tiniest* flat is left on the center of the fret. (If you marked the

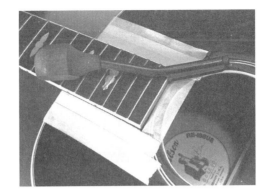

fret tops earlier with a magic marker, it's easy to see when you're ready to stop rounding). When you get to this stage, leave the small flat showing and do a final cleanup on the fret ends with the triangle file, using a downward stroke that follows the fret's beveled end. One light downstroke should polish the bevel,

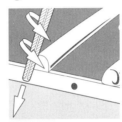 followed by a series of downward strokes, rolling to the center to round the end and remove any burrs. For fret ends, and to remove the final tiny flat, I use the Stew-Mac small triangle file often.

You can round all the fret *tops* that are clear of the body working "right-handed," but you can only get the fret *ends* which are *away* from you because a downstroke is required. So on the bass side, you must turn the guitar end-for-end or walk around your bench to get the fret ends. Also, when you're rounding frets on the tongue, just do one half—from the middle towards the fret ends away from you, and then turn the guitar around to shape the remaining half (from the middle toward the bass side). It's hard to get the correct filing angle otherwise, since the knuckles of your filing hand run into the top (unless the fretboard extension is elevated, as with some arch-top guitars).

Another great tool for fret ends (especially to remove the annoying burr created by the fret-end leveling process) is the small ⅛" "Fender nut-seating" file. Holding it with the smooth edge against the board, you can trim off the wire edge without harming the fretboard. I knocked the sharpness off of the smooth edge on my belt-sander.

Using the neck evaluation and truss rod adjustment section of the Getting Started chapter as a guide, adjust your truss rod to remove any relief. Get the neck straight from the 1st fret to the 12th, using a metal straightedge for comparison. Then duplicate this straight, or "leveling," position with the strings removed. Lay a towel or pad on the table top, covering it and the entire work surface with newspaper to catch any metal filings. Rest the guitar's body on the padded part of the work surface, and cradle the back of the neck on a stack of books or anything else that can serve as a support.

THE FINAL POLISHING

With the frets still taped off, wrap the 400-grit wet-or-dry paper around the 3M squeegee fret polisher (mentioned earlier) with the groove side down—or use the Sand-Stick, which is even better. With a series of back-and-forth strokes, polish the fret top and sides to remove any marks. Switch to the 600 paper and repeat the polishing process.

Now, wrap a thin layer of 0000 steel wool around your fret polisher (or your thumbnail) and bring the fret to a high polish. Repeat this for each fret. When you're through with the polishing, remove the masking tape, always peeling it carefully from the outside edges of the fingerboard towards center; this helps you avoid pulling finish away from the fingerboard's edge.

When all the frets have been rounded and polished, blow or vacuum off any metal dust and steel wool particles, and remove the tape from the body and pickups. Caution: On any guitar with an old, brittle finish, be very gentle in removing the tape to avoid pulling away the finish. As you peel the tape, rub gently with a fingernail on the tape's back just ahead of the bonding point to break the surface tension. String the guitar up to pitch, readjusting the neck rod to give some relief once again. If you use a straightedge now, be very careful not to scar the frets. If you've followed the instructions, you will have the best-playing guitar you've ever touched. Enjoy yourself—you've earned it!

9 REFRETTING

Introduction to refretting

If you keep a guitar long enough and play it often, someday you'll be faced with getting it refretted. Most players get very nervous about letting just anyone pull and replace the frets on their favorite axe, and with good reason: Except for accidental damage, a poor fret job is the surest way to ruin a good instrument.

While lots of my advice in this book is aimed at do-it-yourselfers, I don't recommend that you refret your prewar Martin or '50s Strat; but I'd like to help you understand why fret jobs are needed and what problems they can solve. I'll also describe how I like to see a fret job done, offer pointers on such things as fret-end finishing on bound and unbound fingerboards, and finally compare different fret job prices from around the country. I'm hoping to educate you before you pay big bucks for a fret job, so that you won't end up tearing your hair out afterwards.

A refret is an opportunity to correct many of your guitar's action and playability troubles. Abnormal buzzes caused by worn, high, low, or loose frets can be eliminated. High action resulting from too much relief, up-bow, or just plain old neck warp can also be repaired by actually scraping the wood of the fingerboard itself once the frets have been removed, rather than filing the fret tops. Perhaps a guitar's frets have been over-beveled, causing not only cramped string spacing at the nut but also a tendency for the strings to slide off the fingerboard during play. New frets that are less beveled make better use of the fingerboard's full width.

Head of the Martin Fretting Department, Ben Locicero (left) with Dennis Kromer from the Nut-Making Dept.

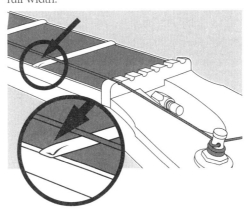

Hard string-bending, overall stiffness, and sore fingers resulting from frets that are too low indicate the need for fret work. Many players will have a guitar refretted not because it plays poorly, but because they're after a different type of fret shape or size to accommodate a certain playing style. As mentioned earlier, tall frets are easier to bend on, jumbo frets have more sustain, etc. Frets can be installed in a variety of ways, but the three most common methods are hammering, pressing, or gluing them in.

Traditionally, frets have been installed by carefully hammering them into the slots with a smooth-faced chasing hammer (this method is still being used—even in many factories). Eventually, to increase production, some factories began using a large overhead press to squeeze frets in (and some of us smaller operations use inexpensive "arbor presses" to accomplish the same task). The most incredible "factory" fret-method I know of was the "sideways" fret method used by Fender until about 1979 (we'll discuss that technique later in this chapter).

Since the mid-'70s, another common fretting method (especially for repairs, or "refretting") has been the "glue-in" method pioneered by Don Teeter: the repairman removes the frets, slightly widens the fret slots with a small hobbyist's router such as a Dremel tool, and then gently presses and glues the frets into place with finger-pressure only—the glue holds them in. The glue-in method is well explained in Don Teeter's important repair book *"The Acoustic Guitar"* (*Vol. One* and *Vol. Two*), but we'll give a nutshell version here. I also have my own variation—the "new glue-in method"—which I'll discuss later.

So there are several ways of going about refret work, and no one method is right. I never fault fret work if it's done neatly and the guitar plays well. I do, however, have flaming fits when I see fret jobs done by so called "repairmen" who do nothing but yank 'em out and pound 'em in, paying no attention to the fingerboard's pre-fret preparation. The prep work separates the pros from the amateurs.

Fretboard preparation

No matter what fretting style you plan to use (sometimes I use them all on the same guitar), the fretboard preparation is basically the same. In some "perfect neck" situations, all we do is pull out the old frets and put in the new ones, but it's seldom that easy. The basic rule? Do as little as possible to alter the fretboard in any way. The hardest part of a fret-job is getting the neck adjusted into the right position so that once the new frets are installed, the neck remains straight (neither back-bowed, nor up-bowed) with the ability to loosen into relief when needed.

Because I use the tilting-table "neck-jig" to prepare (and fret) all my necks, I'm able to control the situation quite well. But I fretted guitars for years without a neck-jig. The neck-jig is discussed later and just understanding how to use it will help anyone do a better fret-job. With or without a neck-jig, you'll need all the neck-evaluation and truss-rod adjusting information given earlier in the book (and all the other books) to "read" a neck correctly and do the best job. Here's how to go about any style of fret-job:

1 Start by determining the customer's complaint with the frets as they are, listening to his or her opinion about what's wrong before forming your own opinion. Pay special attention to the player's style and string gauge. Choose a fretwire shape and crown size that the customer agrees to beforehand.

2 Evaluate and inspect the neck and fingerboard, looking for any problems such as warp, humps, and dips in the surface. Before estimating a fret-job's cost, you must adjust the truss rod (when possible) to its maximum looseness and tightness in order to get familiar with the neck. By checking the action of the truss rod, you determine if a neck has the ability to adjust perfectly straight, yet still offer relief when the rod is loosened. In my opinion, a "perfect" neck is one that can be adjusted perfectly straight under string tension, and yet pull gradually into relief when needed by

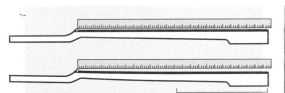

Dead straight neck vs. neck with relief

This section stays flat

loosening the truss rod. Finish this evaluation by leaving the truss rod adjusted so the neck is as straight as it will go with the strings on.

Instruments without adjustable truss rods (especially vintage Martins) are often fretted with too much relief on purpose, knowing that the cumulative effect of the fret tangs will straighten and stiffen the neck; or the opposite may occur (a neck is fretted with a back-bow planed into the surface because it's known that this particular neck will pull straight under string tension). This method, known as "compression fretting," is discussed separately. But in truth, that section and this section are inseparable—they go hand in hand. I only separate compression fretting to keep from confusing you during the traditional hammer-in method coming up. Compression fretting is also used to "help" an adjustable truss rod neck which isn't working well. The neck evaluation which follows is how I go about checking non-adjustable truss rod necks (Martin) for stiffness —but I use the same test on all guitars (adjustable or not).

String to pitch, then rest the instrument's body on the workbench, and while supporting the neck by holding the peghead in one hand, pull down in the center of the neck to see how much "give" or flex there is (see photo above). You may find that the neck is quite stiff, or it may be "rubbery". While at pitch, set the instrument gently on its side (the playing position) and measure the relief at the 5th and/or 7th fret by sliding feeler gauges between the bottom of a long straightedge and the top of the fret (or, use the MacRostie notched straight edge and measure the gap to the fretboard itself). Record your findings.

With the strings removed, repeat the above evaluations (neck flexing, and then measuring the relief in the playing position), and record

those measurements too. The difference between the neck at pitch, and when it's relaxed, tells you a lot about its stiffness, and it helps determine how much, if any, wood you'll remove from the fretboard (and where you'll remove it).

The full effects of truss rod adjustment often take several hours (sometimes even days) to appear. Be sure to allow enough time for the neck to settle after truss rod adjustment, before any frets are removed and replaced. Also allow time for settling after the refret is done, and before the final setup prior to going out the door. There are times when a job must be done overnight for a pro on the road, and occasionally these may need a little redressing after the guitar has settled.

3 If you're fretting a bolt-on neck you should remove it from the body so that it's easier to adjust (vintage-style) and so that you can work on it without damaging the body. Tape off the top around the fretboard of glued-on neck guitars with draftsman's tape, etc. (see the Fret Dressing section for the correct procedure). Remove the strings. If the truss rod was adjusted to keep the neck straight with strings on, the neck will probably be back-bowed—leave it that way since the frets will pull out easier because the back-bow "opens" the pressure slightly on the fret slots.

4 Use a soldering iron to heat each fret before pulling it out with small flush-ground end nippers. This important step helps to avoid chips in the fingerboard by "boiling" oil and moisture out of the wood and onto the fret, lubricating it as it's being removed. The inevitable small chips along the fret slot edge are easily glued back or filled in, but heating the frets does help to avoid chipping. Sometimes large chunks will pull up, the result of poor wood or hasty work. Keep your soldering iron's tip tinned (just as if you were doing electrical work), and the heat will transfer instantly. For a quick heat transfer, it doesn't hurt to put a little solder right on the fret, but be careful on maple fingerboards!

Vintage Fender fretboards are chippier than others (check out the section on Fender "sideways" fretting). Pay close attention to the qual-ity of the wood as you remove the frets. Is it hard or soft? Chippy or solid? Vintage ebony and Brazilian rosewood fretboards are much denser, harder, and stiffer than modern boards. Frets remove more easily from vintage boards, and you can fret them with a smaller tanged wire because they hold a fret better. You need this information later when you select a fret. If you're having fret work done, be sure your repairman is familiar with heating frets.

5 We discussed getting the neck into the leveling position in the "fret dressing" section, but here's some more advice: You're trying to remove the least amount of wood, and to do that you must get the neck as close as possible to where it was under string tension and *then* remove any high or low spots. On adjustable truss rod guitars you'll most likely have to loosen the truss rod to get the fretboard back to the same degree of straightness it had shown under string tension, since now the strings are removed and it will be back-bowed from the compression of the truss rod.

It's easiest to duplicate string tension on glued-on neck guitars because you can rest the peghead or the back of the neck (in the 1st-fret area) on a padded block and the weight of the body will put some tension on the neck. Or you can press down on the body if the neck won't return to its string-tension straightness with the truss rod loose. Sometimes I pull down on the neck's heel while the peghead is propped. Propping the peghead is also a good way to treat non-adjustable necks, such as those on vintage Martins. Rich Starkey, of the Martin repair department, says:

"We put a padded 6 lb. weight on each front shoulder of the guitar top, with the peghead end propped up (see "levelling position" earlier). This puts the perfect average string tension on the neck so that we can see exactly where to take wood off when necessary, while leveling the fretboard. It also puts the fretboard in the string tension position for leveling the frets. And of course some necks are stiffer than others; with the really weak ones you need the larger fret tangs to stiffen them up. Propping the peghead and using the weights is a perfect, and instant, way to check the neck-stiffening progress as we hammer in the frets."

Vintage Fender necks, and many of their clones, must be removed from the body for a truss rod adjustment to avoid gouging the pickguard, the pickups, or the body. For this reason we generally remove them for fret work. But once a bolt-on neck's removed from the body, it's harder to duplicate the string tension than it is with a glued-neck guitar. If your bolt-on neck is adjustable at the peghead end, you may choose to leave it bolted into the body—although it's very hard to fret, nip frets, and file fret ends in the upper register without damaging something. I use a "surrogate body" for bolt-ons. It's a block of wood which the neck bolts on top of—not into. I can work on the frets with ease with all my tools. This block also bolts into my neck-jig.

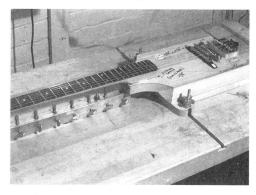

Even without a neck-jig, a surrogate body is handy (and much easier to make than a real guitar body). With your neck bolted into a surrogate body, you can prop the peghead and weight down the body in the same way that Martin does. (Check out the "neck-jig" section too, for the ultimate in neck control).

In general with a bolt-on neck, you loosen

the truss rod completely, and then tighten it a little bit so that you have some tension on it as it's being fretted (you'll still be able to loosen it later for relief). But this isn't always true. Where to leave the truss rod adjustment on any neck is tricky, but with a bolt-on it's trickiest. That's why I like the neck-jig (see "neck-jig" section).

Michael Stevens has fretted hundreds of Strats and Teles. Mike says: "The ideal Fender neck would have a little tension on the rod, and still have some 'negative' (relief) that the fret compression doesn't quite remove when they're installed. Then I can take that last bit of 'negative' out with the truss rod, to make the neck perfectly straight. (And loosening the rod gives back the relief).

"But too often the neck is straight with the rod completely loose—you can't tighten it, or you'll end up with back-bow for sure. In that case, if there's not a finish you can sand a little negative *into* the board. Then sometimes you've got a finish, like on a maple neck, and you can't sand. Then you've got to fret with the rod loose (the nut might even be rattling), and hope you don't get a back-bow. Or you can work down the fret tang so it doesn't compress the neck so much. So, if you have some relief on a Fender neck, don't sand it flat—use it! And if you're removing wood on a vintage rosewood fretboard, to give back the dark polished look of age and finger oil—use Watco's Black Walnut Danish Oil."

6 Remove fingerboard imperfections with files, scrapers, and sanding blocks.

At this point, just as with leveling the frets, you must decide if you're shaping a cylinder or a cone (compound radius). The in-depth theory was covered in the Fret Dressing chapter.

PREPPING A CYLINDER

For working on cylinder-shaped fretboards, my favorite sanding blocks are the radius blocks developed by Mike Koontz of Ferndale, Michigan. These eight blocks (pictured above) are perfectly radiused from 7 ¼" up to 20". Use 3M Stick-It paper to hug the block's contour. A less expensive set of blocks made of wood is available from Stew-Mac (at times I prefer these because they're longer). And another,

the "Handee Fredder" (made of molded polystyrene) is available through Luthier's Mercantile. Choose your weapon! The most common cylinder-shaped fretboards you'll work on are Fenders and Gibsons which have not been refretted since the factory.

PREPPING A COMPOUND RADIUS

With the exception of vintage guitars (especially maple-necks, where I don't want to touch the finish), my fret-jobs are at least somewhat compound. This is because I "read" and level in the lie of each string. When I'm prepping a board with a compound radius, instead of radius-sanding blocks I use either of two long, narrow, flat surfaces that contact most, or all, of the fretboard at once. One is a 1" x 1 ¾" x 15" steel block which I like because of its weight; and the other is a 1" x 3" x 24" maple block, which I like for its length. I use self-stick sandpaper on the 1" edge. With either one I work the board lengthwise, in the six individual "string lies," connecting the six "flats" together with a tapered sweep of the sanding block. This compound-radiusing was discussed in detail at the beginning of this chapter—you must understand it!

You cannot perfectly sand the six "flats" together with a radius block, because the radius block doesn't recognize the tapered edge, or "profile," of the fingerboard—it just shapes a cylinder from end to end. By trying to smooth a "cone" with radius blocks, you'll only "erase" the flats you worked so hard to get. You can use a *progression* of radius blocks to remove the flats, but you'll still have to finish up by hand with a flat block.

Wanting to know how much the "high spot," or difference between a cylinder and a cone, would actually measure on a given set of neck

Mike Koontz

dimensions, I again turned to Don MacRostie. Don calculated the difference between a cone-shaped and a cylinder-shaped fretboard (with all other specifications being equal), and found that on a cylindrical fingerboard the high spot in the lie of the outside *E* strings would measure a maximum of one and a half thousandths (.0015") on a 7 ¼" radius, and only a half thousandth (.0005") on a flatter 16" board. This isn't a lot, but it is the amount that a radius block would remove as it reshapes a cone into a cylinder. This small "high spot" could mean the difference between buzzing or not buzzing, if you have extremely low action. Taking it into account is important if you hope to gain every bit of accuracy possible during a refret.

Most factory-made guitars (Martin, Gibson, Fender, and many others) have fretboards with a cylinder-shaped radius. When their action is set too far below "factory specs," which many customers seem to want, there's more likelihood of fret buzz than if the fretboards had a compound radius. The lowest action without buzzing, with or without bending strings, can be had on cylinder-shaped fretboards with a very flat radius (16" or flatter, like Martin), on compound radiused fretboards, and especially on compound fretboards *beginning* with a fairly flat radius.

So, if you're creating a compound radius during a refret, you might as well be aware of it and work with that in mind. Choose between fretting either a cylinder or a cone, and approach the job in that fashion. You do, of course, have the option of removing the .0015" "high spot" on a cylinder board by filing down the fret tops—this is often the best way to avoid removing material (be it wood, inlay, or lacquer) on a vintage fret-job. Remember: that .0015" high spot is theoretical—actually, you've got to be damn good to flatten a fretboard within .002" or .003"—add .0015" to that and your high spot *really* measures .005" —which is much more typical of what we really run into with strings buzzing on a cylinder fretboard!

As you prep, check the work's progress often by comparing the board to very accurate straightedges. Inlays, especially custom pearl-block types in badly affected areas, must often be removed to avoid being sanded too thin.

They're replaced later just before final leveling.

When the straightedge sits flat on the board—either in the lie of the strings (compound radius), or parallel to the lengthwise center line of the fretboard (cylinder radius)—I usually add from .002" to .004" of "fallaway" into the tongue (the last few frets over the body). Fallaway was discussed in the "neck evaluation" section earlier in the book. So—you're done when the board is flat from end-to-end, or has a little fallaway (but never a rising tongue)!

7 When the board is properly leveled, clean any residue from the fret slots. One good slot-cleaning tool is the back edge of a #11 X-acto knife blade held vertically and used to scrape the crud out of the slot. Some fret slots will have

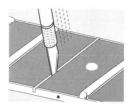

dried glue in them which scrapes out easily. Vintage Fenders and Martins didn't use glue, while Gibson and some others fretted with hide glue.

My favorite slot-cleaner is a small piece of Blitz saw blade (either a .019" or .022" thickness is the most common) with a depth-stop super-glued to it. The short blade (¾") length keeps the saw from cutting where I don't want it to (inadvertently scarring or widening the slot), and the depth-stop follows the contour of the board, giving just enough depth to hold the fret tang—but never going too deep. I "saw" out any residue without widening the slot or cutting it too deep.

If you use a traditional glue-in method, you'd clean the slot differently (see that section).

8 Once the slots are cleaned and you're sure of the proper depth, lightly re-sand the fretboard surface to remove any burrs on the edges of the fret slots. Next run a diamond- or V-shaped file across the fret slot to slightly chamfer (bevel) the edges. This helps the new fret go in, eliminates chipping, and facilitates removing the fret in years to come.

Selecting a fretwire

At this point, the fretboard prep is finished. Choose your fretwire. Measure the cleaned-out fret slot with a feeler gauge. Fret slots vary from .018" (1930s) to .025" (modern imported guitars), but most slots are about .020". I say "about" .020" because the use of feeler gauges to determine fret slot size (or for any measurement) is a subjective art which requires training, experience, and the ability to know when "enough's enough." Since the sense of touch determines your opinion, what feels to me like a .020" tolerance fit, you might squeeze (or force) a .023" feeler gauge into! So let's assume that we could be "plus or minus a thousandth," as they say. The wire you choose is one of the factors which determine the outcome of the fretwork. Experience is the only real teacher, but here are some pointers.

TWO BIG QUESTIONS

Only the manufacturer of a particular guitar knows the answers for sure (and I suspect that some of *them* don't know). First, if the fret tang is the same size as the slot (enough to hold the neck in proper compression so that it can't warp, or "up-bow," because of the weakness caused by 21 fret slots), how large must the barbs be to hold the fret down without back-bowing the neck? Second, did the builder calculate the amount of stiffess (or possible back-bow) the fret tang barbs give to the neck?

SOME ANSWERS

You must learn to match available wires to the existing fret slot in order to get a fit that will hold the fret down without causing over- or under- compression problems that were never a problem at the factory. Factories fret hundreds of "test necks" in order to determine the perfect ratio of fret tang size vs. fret slot size for production. During these tests they determine how much relief to leave in the fretboard so that it will be straight—not back-bowed—when the frets are in. On a refret, you only have one attempt. (OK, maybe two or three. Fretting mistakes are repairable, but you want to avoid them.)

These hassles, by the way, are one of the big reasons that Don Teeter developed the "glue-in method." With Don's method, fret compression (fitting tightly in the slot) does not determine whether or not a fret will "stay down," and back-bow or up-bow because of fret compression is eliminated too.

One problem with fretting a neck in the 1990s that was made in the '50s (or '30s, or '40s), is that modern fretwire is different than what was used back then—most modern fretwires have a bigger tang than those vintage wires did. If you pull the frets on a '56 Tele, and simply replace them with larger ones, you'll often back-bow the neck (from the over-compression of the frets being forced into the slots). And I've pulled frets on 1930s Gibsons that had .016" tangs, very small barbs, and an equally tiny fret slot. I had to enlarge the slots in order to fret it with modern wire. (A solution for this problem is given later. See "Fret Tang Sizer.")

However, if the fret tang (not the barbs) is exactly the same size as the slot—or less, and the barbs are about the same as the original fretwire, you won't back-bow the neck; the frets will go right in, because the original frets compressed the wood of the fret slot downward and to the side as they were driven in. But now, since this is a refret (the second time around), the new fret may not stay down unless you use a wire with a slightly heavier tang, larger barbs, or both, because the wood of the fret slot walls has lost its integrity.

The wood that the fingerboard's made from (normally ebony, rosewood, or maple) also determines what size fret you use for a refret. On a wood-hardness scale, ebony's the hardest, followed by rosewood, and maple can be almost mushy in comparison. So a larger fret may be needed to hold into a maple board (*a la* Fender) than would be needed for ebony or rosewood. Refer to the notes you took while removing the frets.

While your notebook's out, review your thoughts about neck flexibility vs. stiffness and check your relief measurements. If the neck was really up-bowed (too much relief) and "rubbery," you need a fretwire with a larger tang to stiffen the neck (at least to be used at certain frets). C.F. Martin offers replacement fretwire in eight different tang sizes, while the crown remains the same at about .078" wide and .036" tall. These wires are invaluable for choosing a fret several thousandths thicker in the tang, so that it will hold into a worn slot and keep an up-bowed neck (too much relief) straight. Martin wire, being somewhat narrow and not too tall, won't please every player, however; nor is it suitable for many electric guitars. If you're using Martin wire, use the slot-to-tang ratio listed below (or use the same ratio for any fret/fingerboard slot combination). See the Martin compression fretting section for straightening a neck.

FRET SLOT/TANG RATIO FOR REFRETTING

■ Ebony boards: Use a tang which is .001" larger than the slot.

■ Rosewood boards: Use a tang .002" bigger than the slot.

■ Maple boards: Use the same tang (maybe bigger) that you'd use for rosewood (but on a vintage Fender, check into the other problems which are mentioned under "Fretting Vintage Fender Necks").

Note: All the methods used in this chapter apply to new fretwork too—with the exception of fretwire selection. If you're fretting an instrument you made, run some tests (hopefully you'll have scraps of the actual fretboard, or at least wood from the same, or a similar, batch). Decisions must be made: Are you fretting the board before you install it, and if so, how much back-bow can you deal with? Or will you fret it after the board is installed? (I prefer the latter method.) On some new work you may want a fret tang which is slightly narrower than the slot to avoid back-bowing the new wood (see "compression fretting").

OTHER CONSIDERATIONS

■ Frets that are pressed into the slots seem to compress or back-bow a neck less than the hammer method (this is my feeling, but I've never proven it). So the method of fretting helps you decide which size fret to use.

■ Does the neck have an adjustable truss rod? A rod can straighten a neck with too much relief. Or would you rather straighten it with the fret tang, and then loosen the rod to get relief? In the case of Martin guitars made before 1985 (when they started using an adjustable truss rod) the best way to straighten them is with oversized frets (see "compression fretting").

■ Shape and size are important when you're doing vintage work. Many players want non-vintage wire installed on a vintage axe—I don't have any big complaint with that because the work is reversible if it's been well done. Fretwire shape, size and hardness were discussed earlier (but I always go for the 18% nickel/silver content).

■ Martin offers a fretwire with 8 different-sized tangs (the crown stays the same) for "neck-straightening." For vintage Martins with too much relief, this is the best wire to use.

■ If the neck is stable, and can be adjusted nice and straight (even into a back-bow) and can definitely be loosened into relief, choose a wire with a matching tang and just enough barb to hold it. Or use glue and a clamp as a helper (my preferred approach).

The hammer-in method

OK. Now let's do a traditional hammer-in fret job. The fretboard prep is done and you've selected a fretwire. I clean and degrease the fingerboard with naphtha just before fretting, so that it dries while I'm preparing the fretwire. As long as the naphtha's out, use it to clean any oil from the fretwire (clean the wire several times—until any trace of grease is gone). Even if you don't use glue in the fret slots, why introduce grease to the wood? Remember that I keep referring to "compression fretting"—you must become familiar with it since you'll use as much, or as little, compression as the neck calls for with any fret-job. Some compression is a by-product of all fret-jobs, except for Don Teeter's "glue-in" method.

■ Cut the frets to length, leaving about ³⁄₁₆" overhang on each side. Then preshape them so that they have a radius more curved than the fretboard itself. I use my "Fretbender," but a pair of fret pliers will do just as well (pliers

The chasing hammer—
C.F. Martin & Co.

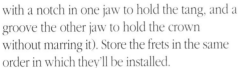

with a notch in one jaw to hold the tang, and a groove the other jaw to hold the crown without marring it). Store the frets in the same order in which they'll be installed.

■ For neck support as you hammer you want something solid to act as an anvil. Good fret-anvils can be made from thick cloth or leather bags filled with buckshot or sand, or curved padded cauls resting on a section of railroad tie, "I"-beam, or steel.

Bob Taylor of Taylor Guitars says: "I've tried every kind of neck support there is—including opening up a bag of shot and remaking my own bags (big and small). The best neck support is a 25 lb. bag of buckshot—left in its original canvas bag, period. Rest that on your neck support. It's what we use in the factory."

■ Hammer in a short test piece (⅜" long) to get a feel of the fit—don't use a whole fret.

■ Start the overcurved fret on both ends. Don't drive the ends completely home, but almost. Now, since the fret is arched more than the fretboard, it is also longer than the board is wide. Since the fret ends are already held quite fast, when you hammer the remainder of the fret home, it wants to "straighten" lengthwise, and to a small degree is pushing its barbs sideways through the wood as it straightens. This helps the fret hold in (and down on the ends) much better than just hammering in a fret that isn't over-arched, or one that hasn't been "tacked-down" at both ends. Some fretters hammer the fret in evenly from the center out, some hammer from the outside in. The Martin factory hammers from one edge across to the other.

■ Since there's plenty of excess fret length overhanging each edge, if a fret end isn't

staying down, give the overhang a tap to snug the edge down. You may even want to "float" a little super glue underneath the end for insurance.

■ I like lots of different fretting hammers. In the photo above, starting from lower left and going clock-wise are: 1) Homemade and fairly heavy, with a 1" x 3½" head made from round brass bar stock; 2) My first "rawhide" fret hammer, which was popular because it wouldn't damage frets (it wouldn't pound them in too well either); 3) The "Dead-blow" shot-filled hammer won't mar frets and it *will* pound in frets; 4) A cobbler's hammer with the back edge sharpened for "mushrooming," or enlarging the tang when it won't hold; 5) Brass/nylon double-faced hammer. You can also use a 16-ounce carpenter's hammer if you're careful!

Bob Taylor

■ The neck area where you're installing a fret should be supported to give resistance to the hammer blow. Use good supports that conform to the neck's shape, such as the buckshot-filled bag mentioned above. Don't just support the headstock and then pound away at the unsupported fingerboard!

■ Pounding too aggressively or too hard in one spot will cause dents or flat spots in the fret as you're going across the board. If this happens, you must remove the fret and either straighten or replace it. Likewise, not pounding hard enough leaves frets that aren't seated against the board. As a general rule, frets that pound in too easily and won't stay down may need to be glued or replaced with frets with oversize tangs. On the other hand, if you're pounding away and the fret isn't going in, don't keep at it. Either the slot isn't deep enough or the fret tang is too wide. Back up and review the situation.

■ On an acoustic guitar, the hardest area to fret is the tongue over the body, since there isn't a solid surface to hammer against. Set the back of the guitar (in the area under the neck block) on your buckshot bag. Here it's essential to hold a metal block or a sandbag inside the guitar under the fingerboard area. It can be very tough to get the frets well seated over an acoustic body. One solution is to use the "glue-in" method only in this area (where fret compression isn't too important). This is yet another reason many of us started using the glue-in method!

■ Bob Taylor's "Fret Buck" is the best tool for supporting the shoulder area under the fretboard tongue. It slides in through the soundhole, rests on the shoulders, and supports the tongue from underneath—enough so that you can hammer frets in normally! You should still rest the guitar body on the buckshot bag.

■ Glue? The decision to use glue to hold in the frets is up to you; even large manufacturers do it differently. Certain repairmen consider gluing frets to be a bad joke to play on a future repairer. I don't feel that way, though, since frets should always be heated prior to removal to break any glue bond. You don't need glue on a perfectly good piece of wood that wants to hold a fret, although the glue's lubrication sometimes helps a fret go in easier. The most common glues for holding hammered-in frets are Titebond (aliphatic resin), hide glue, and shellac. (While not really a glue, fresh shellac does a great job of bonding metal to wood, especially frets. It was commonly used by guitar builders long before we were born.)

The last time I visited the Gibson company in Kalamazoo, they were wiping hide glue into all the slots at once, quickly wiping off the excess with a damp rag, and then hammering-in the frets. At the Martin company, they wipe the fret slot with water to lubricate the fret as it goes in and to swell the slot around the fret. I generally use either hide glue or Titebond, but I've used shellac too. You can't use 'em all at once, so experiment! If you use glue, let it dry overnight before clipping or filing the fret ends.

■ Clip the ends until they are almost flush with the fingerboard edge (leave a little for final-filing to the wood, or you may get nipper

marks on the bare wood or finish). Frets that are hammered in without glue have a tendency to pop up on the ends, so if that happens use a larger fret or check out the section on loose fret ends earlier in this chapter. With or without glue, use a downward pressure as you clip, being sure that you have sharp, flush-ground end nippers. To avoid fret-end pop-up, use a downward motion to clip the fret's crown first, and then the tang.

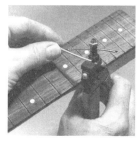

■ I like to pre-cut the fret tang to length (but not the crown overhang) with the Waverly Fret Tang Nipper. Then I have less filing to do on the fretboard edges, and the clipping motion doesn't twist the fret as much.

■ The handles of the ready-made fret nippers are too short for clipping fret ends on the fretboard extension over the body, so you may want to grind a longer-handled 9" pair just for that area (save them just for that job, and they'll last longer). It's hard to get the proper grasp on the short handled ones if your knuckles are banging into the top.

■ Once the frets are in and the overhanging ends have all been clipped, smooth the rough fret ends and file the fret-end bevel (you didn't learn this in the fret-dressing section because the frets had been beveled at the factory).

FILING THE FRET END BEVELS

Novice fretters often "over-bevel" the fret ends; the results of over-beveled ends are: too narrow a string spacing at the nut, too little playing surface overall, and strings that fall off the fingerboard edge. An exaggerated bevel isn't necessary as long as the fret ends are filed smooth and don't catch the hand. A smooth, nicely rounded end is what you're after.

You need to be aggressive on the first file strokes, because the fret ends are so rough after nipping that the file gets caught on them and will barely move. When it does move, it wants to run up, and onto the tops of the new frets, so keep your fingertips against the side of the neck as a guide and "stop." To "rough in" the bevel I like the coarse-cut of the Stew-Mac

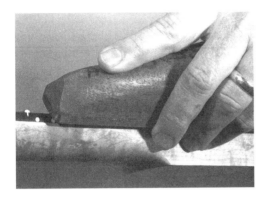

6" fingerboard leveler. As soon as the file is riding smoothly and getting close to the wood (or finish), switch to a smoother cut (the 3" or 6" fret levelers have a perfect cut).

File as much, or as little, bevel as you like. A long bevel (most Fenders) has little drag on your playing hand, but it takes away from playing area. A short steep bevel gives you more fret to play on but will catch your hand. Always use a white backlit surface so you can see what you're doing. Keep filing until the file just contacts the edge of the fingerboard and finish. The sliver of white light which you could see between the file and the neck disappears at the same time that the fret end bevel is finished. To finish the final rounding, shaping, and polishing of the fret tops, follow the directions given in the fret dressing chapter.

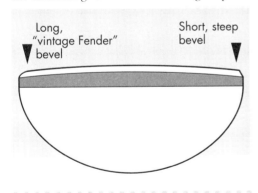

Long, "vintage Fender" bevel

Short, steep bevel

Compression fretting

Actually this section on compression fretting goes hand-in-hand with any hammer- or press-in fret-job. It's not a *method* of fretting, it's knowledge you use while fretting. That's why I gave it a section of its own. The lesson on "neck flexing" in the "fretboard preparation"

section is applied here. Although I tend to think of Martin when compression fretting comes to mind (it was the Martin repairmen who developed this important technique), any guitar will benefit from compression fretting— i.e., where the fret tang matches, and in some cases is greater than, the size of the fret slot. If you understand how compression fretting works on vintage Martins without adjustable truss rods, it will help you deal with any other type of neck. Here's a little history:

The amount of fret compression you need, and in what area of the fretboard you need it, depends on the neck construction (or you could say the guitar's vintage). In general, Martins have very stiff necks from the mid '30s to the end of the '50s and into the 1960s. (Note: There was a period during the war years, in the early '40s, when both Martin and Gibson suffered from lack of materials—both wood and metal. Martin used their old-style ebony neck support during that time, just as Gibsons of the same period have no adjustable truss rod. So necks during that era are not as stiff as before and after. According to luthier T.J. Thompson: "I *know* they made necks with the old-style ebony filler during that time because I've had them apart—as early as 1939"—and during that time Martin did different things on different models. But excepting the war, from the '30s through the '50s, the neck-reinforcing 'T'-bar was very deep—these necks are the stiffest. With them, only slight compression fretting, or planing a drop-off to the nut, is required (if it's required at all).

During the '60s, the T-bar was shallower, and those necks aren't as stiff, but they're still pretty good. Refretting them is not a problem, but the need for compression, and planing a little drop-off toward the nut, is more common. When compression is needed on a '30s through '60s instrument, it's usually in the area of the first 5 or 6 frets (near the peghead where the string pull is greatest).

In the late '60s Martin began using the "square hollow tube" neck-rod. The square tube was used until it was replaced by the current adjustable rod in 1986 (this new truss rod, by the way, is quite rigid). But the necks with the hollow tube can be far too flexible—give them the flex test and you'll see a sag in the fretboard and a hump at the body—no rigidity. Whether you're a player or repairer, you want to know about the square tube neck because four-fifths of Martins ever made were built during that era. So the likelihood of you owning a Martin of this vintage is quite high, if you own one at all. It should be reassuring to know that straightening these necks is commonplace, and nothing to worry about.

It must have been early in the '70s that Martin developed the many different sizes of fret tang—to stiffen, and straighten, these necks. The square tube necks require the most compression in the area from the 5th to 10th frets, and commonly need as much as .015" drop-off (back-bow) planed into the fretboard from the 5th fret to the nut, so that under string tension the neck is almost straight. Both compression and drop-off may be required. Most square tube necks which have been properly straightened will remain quite straight when they're first strung to pitch; then within six months or a year they'll pull into a little relief. So if you have a few buzzes with a newly-fretted guitar, give the neck a chance to settle in.

Dana Bourgeois

I learned compression fretting from Irving Sloane's excellent book "Guitar Repair," where the method is explained quite well (the book is another "must have" for the serious repairperson). But I never fully appreciated this fretting technique, nor neck stiffness in general, until I came to know Dana Bourgeois. After hours of phone conversations, when I thought we'd exhausted the subject, Dana pointed me to T.J. Thompson—describing him as the "repairman's repairman," and master of the "Bar-Style Fret-Job."

T.J. learned the basics of compression fretting as Dana's apprentice, and then refined during his years as head of the repairshop at Elderly Instruments in East Lansing, Michigan. When T.J. left Elderly to build the Schoenberg guitars, he'd already trained a successor in Joe Konkoly. These three men, Dana, T.J., and Joe, are traditionalists when it comes to fretting, and share their opinions with us here. Here's how Dana Bourgeois explains fret compression and judges neck stiffness:

"When you strike a string it drives what's on either end of the neck—the peghead as well as the body. When the peghead is held rigid at the end of a stiff neck, it reflects the energy back up the neck to drive the top. A neck which is too flexible allows the peghead to flap around, which actually absorbs vibration. So flexibility in a neck is not good for tone, volume, or sustain. When compared with compression fretting, the Dremel fret job is more likely to cause a loss of neck stiffness and result in a fretboard that may be flat (straight) and well fretted when strung to pitch, but has no rigidity. Many fretboards are flat under string tension, thanks to a truss rod adjustment and careful leveling of the board, but will have too much give if you apply the 'flex' test. Try this:

"Put the end of the guitar on the bench surface, and sight down the neck. Hold up on the headstock and pull down in the middle of the neck. Look, and feel, for the give. A neck should have very little give, so if you sight a neck and it flexes easily, you know you're losing some tone, even though the fretboard is straight under tension. As a tonal consideration, the stiffness of a compression fret job is distinct from flatness! When fretting, I flex the neck after every fret to check for stiffness. I can watch those weak necks stiffen right up. But you can only get as much stiffness as a given neck, or piece of wood, will allow.

"I've seen glue-in fret-jobs where flatness (straightness) was obviously the only consideration. Stiffness is equally important! Flatness can be achieved by compression fretting an up-bowed neck and improving the tone, or by tightening a truss rod, which does little for the tone. Of course, both methods often require at least spot levelling of the fretboard itself. If stiffness can be retained when using the Dremel method, I have no problem with it. This is possible with careful matching of the slot to the fret and properly mixed, good-quality glue."

There are two ways to approach compression fretting: 1) To maintain stiffness and straightness in a good neck; 2) To add or return stiffness and straightness to a weak or fatigued neck. Use these compression principles with any fret-job—refret jobs in particular.

To maintain straightness and stiffness, measure the wire you took out, and consider following Martin's recommendation for the correct replacement size: use the next size bigger tang for ebony, and two sizes bigger for rosewood so that the fret will hold down (the fret slot has widened some from the force of the original fret being driven in and pulled out). All you're doing is keeping a stiff neck stiff. You need a selection of Martin oversize wire for this job. Martin fret slots measure between .020" and .022", so when replacing a fret, the "next size up" means a half-a-thousandth, since Martin wire comes in half-thousandth sizes (.0185", .0195", .0205", .0215", .0225", .0235", .0245", .0275"). The ability to work in such subtle increments gives you a lot of control. The heavier .0275" is only used in soft fretboards or at select locations on the fretboard, to add a lot of stiffness quick. You wouldn't fret an entire Martin neck with the big wire too often.

When removing up-bow, as Dana pointed out, there's a limit to how much stiffness you can add to a given neck by increasing the fret size. Sometimes you can remove from .010" to .020" of relief from a fretboard by increasing the size of the fret tang alone, but beyond that you must remove wood from the fretboard surface to get it straight, and then rely on the compression of the tang to keep the neck stiff. So with Martin necks, it's common to scrape, sand, or plane a certain amount of back-bow into the fretboard , so that when fretted and strung to pitch, the neck is straight, or has a slight relief (but not an unwanted up-bow).

VARIATIONS

■ I've seen Martins that were compression-fretted too straight, even bordering on back-bow (and I like straight necks). I think that on some stiff vintage necks, by going to the next size tang to keep the fret down, you're adding more tang than you need (when you really only want more barb). I'm willing to use the same size fret (1:1) and glue to keep the fret ends down if I think the neck will benefit.

■ An alternative to the above is to plane relief into the neck so that by using the next size up tang (for holding pressure), you get a straight neck when you're done. It's more

difficult to give a fretboard the correct relief before fretting than it is to give it back-bow or "drop-off," however.

■ Many times it's beneficial to use a "neck heater" or a heat-lamp to heat the glue-joint between the fretboard the neck, and to clamp the neck into straightness or back-bow as it cools. Heat-straightening is used by many to remove excess up-bow. While I don't think it's a permanent cure in most cases (the neck usually goes back into an up-bow), it's a great way of getting a neck where you want it temporarily so that you can keep it there with compression fretting. By heating a neck straight before fretting you can often eliminate the need to remove wood from the fretboard surface.

A typical Martin T-fret installation

At "Symposium '93," the biannual convention held by ASIA (Association of Stringed Instrument Artisans), I videotaped a selection of the country's best repairmen. That tape is available through ASIA and Stewart-MacDonald. The video has a great lesson on compression fretting given by Elderly Instruments' Joe Konkoly. Joe was a student of T.J. Thompson during T.J.'s reign in the Elderly repairshop, and he assumed command when T.J. left to build the Thompson-Schoenberg guitars. Like his mentor, Joe is at the top of his field. Here are a few words from Joe on re-fretting Martin guitars:

PHOTO BY STEVE SZILAGYI

Joe Konkoly

"When the strings are off, I like to see a slight back-bow in the neck—so that a straight-edge would balance in the middle and drop at each end. This particular D-18 we have is a 1943 model with an ebony filler strip in place of the metal T-bar for neck reinforcement (the metal was needed for the war effort). With the strings on I measured .027" relief, and even with the strings off it was .014"—a difference of .012". It would be uncommon to find this much give in a Martin neck made before or after the war until you get to the square tube necks of the '70s. I'd like to see a *back-bow* when the strings are off (not relief). Under string pres-sure, the maximum relief should be .015"—that's the Martin spec. I like less, or almost none. After judging the stiffness of the neck and the density of the ebony fretboard I knew I couldn't simply fret the neck straight with oversize tangs: I had to remove some wood from the fretboard, too.

"Since there was a .014" up-bow without any string tension on the neck, I had to remove that much from the wood right off, just to get the neck straight, then back-bow it to remove the .012" difference between the original two measurements (the bow with the strings on and the bow with the strings off). I very rarely just pound in oversize frets to "straighten" the neck—they're used to *keep* the neck straight. I planed and sanded a .010" drop-off between the 4th fret and the nut, figuring that under string tension, the neck would pull into at least the .002" of relief I didn't plane off and probably another .002" on its own—giving me an almost straight neck under tension. If it came out perfectly straight (no relief), I'd be happy, too. Straight, or a little relief, that's what I'm after.

"So this neck, which is pretty typical of 1940s necks, looked like this after I prepped the board:

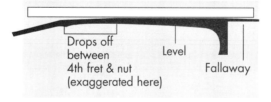

Drops off between 4th fret & nut (exaggerated here)   Level   Fallaway

- A little drop-off from the 4th fret to the nut

- Flat from the 4th to the body

- From the 14th to the 20th fret: a drop-off of .002" ("fallaway").

Of course all the areas are blended in—there aren't any distinct marks where one joins the other, and I recut the slot depth where I took off wood.

"The slots measured .022" and it was a hard ebony board, so I used the .0225" wire (the next size up). I put the 1st fret in at the 11th fret to get the feel in an area that doesn't affect the compression much (the most compression occurs between the 3rd and 9th frets). By testing a fret in a non-compression area I won't

have to remove it if it doesn't feel heavy enough. It wasn't heavy enough, so I switched to .0235" and used it from the 10th fret to the nut. When I got to the 12th fret I switched back to the .0225" for the tongue.

"As a rule I use a half-thousandth over on the tongue in rosewood or ebony, and on the main fretboard I use 1 ½ thousandths over on ebony, and at least 2 ½" thousandths over on rose-wood. Sometimes rosewood is so soft you'll use the big .027"!"

Note: Joe Wisely sticks several rags in the sound hole to deaden the sound, and wears "head-band" ear-protection while he frets.

Martin bar-style fretting

Bar fretwire is the old-style solid wire that was used on guitars until the modern T-fret came along. Unlike the T-fret, bar fretwire is rectangular in profile, meaning it doesn't have barbs or beads. It ranges from .045" to .055" in thickness, and is quite tall (about .160"). Most of its height, however, remains below the level of the fretboard—most bar fret players like a fret height of .040" to .055". Bar frets add great stiffness to a neck (and consequently improve the tone of the guitar), but they are difficult to install. Here, Luthier Dana Bourgeois describes his bar fretting method:

"*Most* 'Bar-fret' Martins that we see are 12 fret guitars, and usually have wide necks, short scales, and a short span, meaning there are 12 frets clear of the body rather than the later 14. Fret compression isn't as important with the shorter necks as it is with the long-necked OM. OM refrets are really hairy because they have a narrow neck, the longer scale,14 frets clear of the body—and they only have *wooden* (ebony) truss rods. And they all had bar frets! Therefore you have to rely on fret compression to keep your neck straight, and the fitting of every fret is crucial.

"Using compression, you can flex a neck too far backward, or not using enough can cause forward, or "up-bow." The typical OM has to be fretted in such a way that it's slightly back-bowed in order for it to be reasonably stiff under string tension. A *plus* with the bar fret job is that because the height is somewhat variable on bar frets, you do have the option of slightly adjusting your height if you've mis-judged the compression vs/ flexibilty ratio (you can take off more metal from the fret tops if you need to). But the bottom line is that refretting an OM is like standing in a boat in rough sea and shooting at a moving target."

Another highlight of the ASIA "Symposium '93" repair video is watching T.J. Thompson calmly pulling bar frets out of a 1931 Martin 0M-45 in order to straighten the neck—he wasn't even nervous! T.J.'s into bar frets—he frets his Thompson OM-style guitars with bar frets, as well as the Schoenberg OM-28 and OM-45 reissues. T.J. knows that bar frets produce the most rigid neck and that their tone is unsurpassed—the guitars he builds prove his point. Here are some pointers on bar refrets:

Because of the massive depth and thickness of bar frets, they exert an even compression on the fretboard and neck (there are no barbs which come into play). If you pull out a couple of bar frets, say at the 4th and 8th fret, you'll see the relief increase. Drive a couple of thick bar frets into a tight-fitting slot, and the opposite occurs—just as with oversize Martin wire, but quicker. So the perfect fit of the fret width to the slot is most important.

When Irving Sloane's book "Guitar Repair" was written in 1973, Martin no longer pro-duced bar wire, and what they had on hand was saved for Martin customers. Because of that the book recommends filling the fret slot with wood and recutting the slots to accept standard T-frets. I disagree with that method, although I have done it.

Martin again offers two sizes of bar fretwire: .051" and .057"—these will take care of any vintage refret, although you must do consider-able filing on the flat sides to match many slots in situations where you don't need extra compression. I have a roll of newer Martin bar fretwire that measures .046", but Martin doesn't advertise it. Perhaps they no longer have it, I'm not sure (but it's mighty handy, and I try to use

it sparingly). Vintage fretboards were fretted with wire ranging from .045" up into the mid-.050"s, and it's not uncommon to carefully pull up (or remove) the old wire, straighten and re-radius it, then reuse it by not driving it in as deep. Here's a brief rundown on how T.J. goes about a bar fret-job.

"I use bar frets in two situations: refretting old work, and for the initial fretwork on my own instruments. With this particular OM-45 we have here, there's too much forward bow (about .015") which I will straighten by removing frets 4 through 9 and replacing them with larger wire.

■ "Use a hot soldering iron to heat the fret before pulling it with your nippers.

■ "With the frets removed, ever so lightly sand the fretboard surface just to clean it (400-grit)

■ "I'm cleaning the slot with a straight-sided dremel burr—but not widening it. These particular fret slots are .050" wide, and I don't intend to widen them because I have a feeling that about a 054" fret will be perfect for the compression I'm after. So in this instance I'm just making sure that it's deep enough for the new wire, and clean. And often, when I take the frets out, I clamp the peghead back to open the slot's compression on the tang and make removal easier. Sometimes I'll reverse the process to put them in, but that'd be a whole 'nother chapter.

■ "Sometimes I will widen the slot slightly to get closer in size to the wire I intend to use. I grind new dental burrs to different diameters to suit my fret slot needs. You need a wide selection of cutters ranging from .002" smaller than the thinnest fretwire you intend to use, on up to .002" wider than the heaviest gauge (and everywhere in between). The .002" undersize bit is used to cut the fret slots in the middle of the neck (maybe frets 4 to 8), and the oversize cutter is used on the fretboard extension over the body where fret compression is undesir-able. On the extension you can lightly hammer the frets in, or press and glue them in (the only instance where I use the 'Teeter-style' fretjob).

■ "You don't need a lot of compression per fret (usually .002" is plenty). It's the sum total of all the frets that give you the desired effect.

T.J. Thompson and Eric Schoenberg

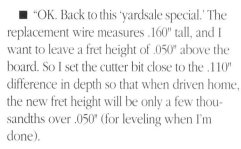

■ "OK. Back to this 'yardsale special.' The replacement wire measures .160" tall, and I want to leave a fret height of .050" above the board. So I set the cutter bit close to the .110" difference in depth so that when driven home, the new fret height will be only a few thousandths over .050" (for leveling when I'm done).

■ "Bar fretwire is rolled on its flat side for storage and is somewhat curved on its flat side end to end—it must be straightened. The Waverly Fret Bender does this perfectly—run the wire, on its side, backwards through the rollers (set to the right gap) and it straightens beautifully.

■ "I think I want the frets to measure .054" wide, so I'm filing the flat side of the .057" down to .054" (I could be routing the slot wider, but I don't remove wood from the fret slot walls needlessly). I'll check the fit often by just pressing the end of the wire into the slot. It shouldn't press in easily, and if you tried to press the whole length in, you couldn't.

■ "Next, cut the wire to length with a little overhang on each side, and file the ends clean and square. It's good that we have this bound fingerboard, because the ends must be notched to overhang the binding, and that's an important step that I couldn't show you on an unbound board (otherwise the actual fretting is the same).

■ "Before notching the ends, curve the wire to match the fretboard radius. I lay the fret on this steel block with a piece of hardwood to support it. I hammer the curve into the wire because the Fret Bender was not really intended to radius the heavy-gauge bar fret. I hammer against the wood to keep from marring the top of the fret (even though I plan on dressing it down anyhow). We hammer the bottom of the fret.

■ "To notch the ends, grab the fret with your nippers so that they're a binding thickness from the end, and the height of the exposed fret (once installed) from the bottom. Hold the wire firmly with the nippers face down on a steel block. File until your file hits the steel-block 'stop' (photo above).

■ "The rest is easy. Hammer in the fret until the notches stop on the binding and the crown is uniform across the width of the board.

■ "Don't bevel the ends at a 45° angle as you might other fret-jobs—leave it perpendicular and flush with the edge of the fretboard.

■ "I shape the ends with a flush-bottom file which has one safe edge (no teeth), against the board. Don't remove as much metal, or shape the ends as round as a T-fret often is.

■ "To dress the tops, lay a piece of venetian blind on one side of the fret and a piece of heavy tape on the other side, in case you slip.

■ "With a triangle file (or whatever you like) shape one side of the fret to center at a time, then reverse the venetian-blind "protector" and the tape. Take your time. If this part of the job doesn't seem like work, and like it's taking forever, you're probably doing it wrong.

■ "Sand the fret tops with 320- and 400- grit paper to knock off any sharp edges. Follow with steel wool. That's it!

"In closing I'll say this: Bar fret wire went out of fashion in the 1930s when steel neck reinforcement came in. This important detail is often overlooked. It's incorrect to say that the early guitars had no neck reinforcement—the frets keep the neck straight! If the frets are too loose, the neck bows forward; if the frets are too tight, the neck bows backward."

After watching T.J.'s demonstration, I still had a couple of questions: Would bar frets be good in a Strat or Les Paul? And what's kept more people from using bar frets? Here's T.J.'s answer:

"*One half* of the reason I use bar frets is to keep the neck straight—and the necks you mentioned have adjustable truss rods to keep them straight. So half the reason would be wasted—unless the owner was only interested in the tone bar frets might produce (because the other one half of the reason for using bar frets is to produce tone). The guitars which I build, and the vintage Martins which I specialize in repairing, do not have truss rods, but they have straight necks, and great tone!

"Most customers wouldn't want to go through the trouble and expense of a bar fret job on something like a Les Paul, that didn't *need* it for straightness, because they'd be *experimenting* on it in a very non-traditional way. And perhaps I make bar fretting sound simple, but it's actually a manufacturing nightmare—what Dana said about standing in a boat is right. And of course I wasn't there at the time (at least not in this life), but I know that Martin had very good reasons for switching to T-frets from a manufacturing point of view."

Thanks T.J.! And I'd be remiss not to point out that T.J. would ask, in his firm yet gracious way (and he has all of our support), to *please leave the vintage instruments to the professionals*. Many times poor work—especially fretwork—is done to a vintage instrument that can never be undone. Don't cut your teeth on something you shouldn't (if it's vintage, even if you own it, you don't really *own* it). Please don't remove forever the integrity of these guitars which are our national treasures!

The glue-in method

If you're serious enough about fretting to have read this far, then you'll thank me when I suggest that you buy Don Teeter's first book "The Acoustic Guitar" (Volume 1). The fretting section shows the original glue-in method in great detail, and the rest of the book is an incredible guitar repair education for the professional. There are few of us that haven't worn out at least one copy of Don's book. There'd be no sense in me teaching you Don's method—I certainly couldn't out-teach him. But I will point out the bare bones of his method and show you how I altered it to suit my needs. The glue-in method uses the same neck preparation we used earlier, and continues after step 7, where we cleaned the fret slots.

■ Widen the slots with small dental burrs and a Dremel Moto-Tool (miniature router) mounted in the accessory router base. Widen the slots enough so that the frets will push in with finger pressure, or with a very light hammering. Only the outer edge of the fret tang barb should kiss the slot walls; the tang itself shouldn't touch at all.

■ With a Q-tip and paste wax, wax off the area in-between the frets. Wax up close to the slot, but leave a little dry clean wood (the width of the fret crown) on each side (and don't get any wax in the slot).

■ Tape off the fretboard with masking tape so that only the fret slot is visible. Then use a thin bladed spatula to pack 24-hour cure epoxy glue into each slot (Don Teeter uses Elmer's 601 epoxy exclusively). Mush the glue into the slot until it squeezes out, and remove the excess.

■ Remove the tape and carefully press the pre-radiused (no over-radius for this method) frets into the slots. The frets can be cut to exact length or left with an overhang that you can clip off later. You will get some glue squeeze-out but this can be chiseled off when it's dry—the waxed board makes cleanup easy.

Dan with Don Teeter

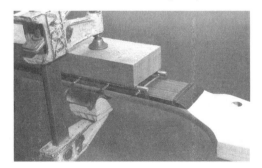

■ Clamp the frets to dry overnight, using a dowel rod on each side and a block of wood as a caul.

■ Remove the clamps, chisel off the glue squeeze-out, clean up the rough fret ends (or overhang), and then level and dress the frets in the normal way.

GLUE-IN VARIATION

In the '70s I used the glue-in method a lot, because it guaranteed better results than I was able to get with a hammer (straightness-wise), helping to avoid the back-bow and up-bow problems caused by fret compression. For me it was a great fret method to use while I slowly learned how to handle fret compression. It's an excellent way to deal with worn out, rotten fingerboards that won't hold a fret, and especially useful on the fretboard extension over the body (the tongue), where hammering is difficult and dangerous. I developed my own variation with a couple of differences. They are:

■ I use 5-minute cure epoxy and fret two frets at a time. While two are drying at the nut end, I go to the body end and install two more—going back and forth from one end to the other until done.

■ I only wax off around the two frets that I'm doing so that I won't inadvertently drag wax into a clean slot.

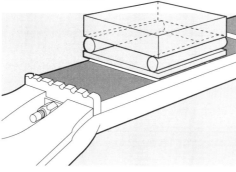

■ I use a different gluing caul. With Don's caul, the pressure applied to the top board with the clamp is crucial—too much pressure can make the fret rise in the center. I use a caul with ½" thick Plexiglas on the top, two ³⁄₁₆" plexi-dowel rods, and a ⅛" Plexi-sheet on the bottom. The Plexiglas is super-glued at three points —the top of both dowels to the ½" block, and on the bottom of one dowel to the ⅛" sheet. This leaves one edge of the sheet loose so the caul can "flex"—curving to match the fretboard radius and holding down the center.

■ Several neck and body cauls are needed to facilitate clamping in the area of a curved neck heel (a little further on, we'll take a look at Bryan Galloup's clamping jig for this purpose).

There are as many variations to Don's original "glue-in method" as there are repairmen and women using it. You must read Don's book to fully appreciate his method before you experiment with your own. Now here's the "new glue-in method," which is the evolution of the above two methods that I often use today.

THE NEW GLUE-IN METHOD

The only reason I even call this a glue-in method is because I do use glue, and because it evolved from my use of (and variations on) Don Teeter's original method. But it really incorporates all the fretting methods described so far.

The three major differences between the new glue-in method and the first two (Don Teeter's and my old variation) are: 1) I don't generally rout the slot at all; 2) I often alter the size of my fret tang to match a particular fret slot; 3) I neither finger-press, nor hammer them in—I press them in. Actually what I'm doing here is a "hammer-in" method without the hammer and using glue. Just as with the other fretting methods, follow the fretboard prep up until step #7.

■ It's important to me that the fret tang is the same size as the slot—with no airspace or gap. I may want an *over*size tang (like the Martin "compression method"), but only in rare cases would I want an *under*sized one. I can live with a gap of .001" to .002" (which the glue fills) if I must, but I prefer not to have even that. To accomplish this, I may widen the slot to the tang size by using the different thicknesses of Blitz saw blades (they range from .015" to .040").

Sometimes I will rout the slot with an extremely thin dental burr, but I'm enlarging for the *tang* (not the barb as with a finger-press, or a medium-press fit). I widen the slot until it's the same size (or perhaps .001" to .002" smaller) as the tang of the modern fretwire that I'm using. I'm looking for the same fit required for a hammer or arbor press fret-job.

■ I use glue, although I'm constantly switching between Titebond, 5-minute Epoxy, super glue, hide glue, and shellac. When the fit is tight (no gap), the type of glue is less important, but I'm still trying to learn. If I have to pick a favorite glue, I'd pick the System Three company's Quick-Cure 5-minute epoxy. This was recommended to me by Steve Anderson—famed builder of arch-top and flat-topguitars,andbeautiful mandolins. This epoxy dries hard and brittle—a quality I prefer for transmitting tone.

■ A significant tang barb is needed for a hammer-in fret job because of the "springback," or recoil, of the fret and the wood to the blow of the hammer. But when the fret tang matches the slot, and you press in the frets with *glue*, the barbs don't have to be as large to hold the fret down (particularly the ends). For this reason I will sometimes remove a fair amount of the barb with my "Fret Tang Sizer and De-barber" to get the right fit of the fret to the slot. Here's how I made this tool:

1 Cut a Stew-Mac No. 864 fingerboard levelling file into two 2 ½" lengths;

2 Clamp the faces (tape protecting the teeth) and grind the edges smooth and somewhat round from end to end;

3 Space them apart with a feeler gauge and clamp them in a vise;

4 Insert the frewire between the files;

5 Draw the wire against the cut of the teeth. Switch feeler gauges every .002" to pare a .034" barb down to the bare tang on three lengths of fretwire in a minute!

With good fret compression and glue, I don't need much of a barb to hold the fret in (and super glue will hold in a fret that has no barb at all). It's as if I were fretting with Martin's old-style bar fretwire, only I have a "T-head", or crown on the fret. This technique gives the best of both worlds: 1) The compression to

retain stiffness; 2) The perfect seating of frets that are pressed or "cauled" in (not hammered), without the barb "overcompressing."

■ When the slot is clean, test a ⅜" sample length of the chosen wire for fit.

■ I'll often give the fret ends a slight "overbend." This helps the fret ends to hold down, especially on the "rolled-over" edges of vintage Fenders and some others. To create the overbend, I use either my fret pliers or a miniature vise with a hand-shaped round in the top and a notch filed into the one end of each jaw. The vise holds the fret tang firm, but the notch lets the end of the fret move as I hammer it into a slightly over-bent shape against the "anvil" (Thanks to Michael Stevens for this great idea).

■ Just as with the hammer-in method, before installing the frets I normally clip the fret tang to length (put not the crown overhang) with the Waverly Fret Tang Nipper. Then I have less filing to do on the edges of the fretboard, and when I clip the overhang the clipping motion doesn't twist the fret as much.

■ Sometimes I over-bend the ends and clip the entire fret to exact length before installing it so there *isn't* any overhang. The overhang may not be necessary, depending on how the frets are going in and holding down.

■ If you use an overhang, you can clip the fret ends anytime they become an annoyance. The longer you wait the better. Sometimes I reclamp with a caul, to keep the fret from twisting as I clip (especially if the fret tang—not the crown overhang—wasn't nipped to length beforehand). Press downward on your nippers as you clip.

■ Another clipping variation, if you haven't clipped the tang ahead of time, is to clip the

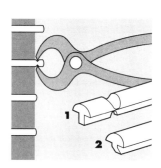

fret crown first, and the tang second. This, too, helps you avoid twisting the fret and making the ends pop up.

■ From this point on my method is much the same as the original glue-in (I put glue of my choice in the slot and press the frets in). But with my method, your fingers *couldn't* press the fret in, and a medium-pressure hammer-tap isn't enough either. I could use normal hammer pressure to get them in, but I'd rather not hit the frets when I can avoid it (and I don't like to hammer in the neck-jig).

■ For glue, if I use epoxy I wax off the board and use the 5-minute cure. I can squeeze Titebond or hide glue into the slots using a syringe, and have minimal cleanup with a damp rag (I don't have to tape off the board).

■ I squeeze the frets in with Jaws, a unique "Vise-Grip" converted into a fret press. The radiused "shoe" presses the fret in. Since most of my fretting is done with the guitar in the neck-jig, Jaws is the only type of press I can use to get in there and get the job done. You can use a drill press or arbor press to install frets on slab (bolt-on) necks, but it's hard to do a D-28 or Les Paul because the body and the tilted-back peghead are in the way. With Jaws I can get quite close to the heel of an acoustic and then take over with a hammer on the fretboard extension if I need to (all in my neck-jig).

■ I have radiused "shoes" for Jaws in these sizes: 6 ½", 7 ¼", 9", 10", 12", 14",15",16", and 20". They are interchangeable so that on a compound fretboard I "change my shoes" every two or three frets. On a cylinder board I use one shoe all the way up.

■ A drill press makes a nice press, though, if you're fretting a bolt-on neck (out of the neck-jig).

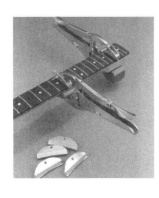

■ A variation of Jaws designed by Brian Galloup is a sliding Bessey bar-clamp. This works great too, and he even has a version which comes in through the soundhole (but that was before Bob Taylor's Fret Buck came along). With the Bessey variation and special cauls, we can fret right through the neck heel/ body joint area with ease, an area where Jaws doesn't always excel.

■ The box-like fixture shown above, and in use by Chicago repairman Charles Avila, gives something to clamp onto (other than the neck) when pressing in frets over the neck heel and body area. It was designed by Bryan Galloup.

■ Jaws was a lot of work to make. If you don't have a shop or all the tools to make Jaws, or Brian's version of it, you can press frets in with the radius-sanding blocks. If you have the wooden ones, coat the face with thin sheet-steel, because they're too soft. If you have the deluxe blocks made by Mike Koontz, you can use them without reinforcement, but the sheet steel wouldn't hurt. The typical hardware-store orange Jorgensen clamp isn't strong enough. Find the more industrial-strength Bessey clamp.

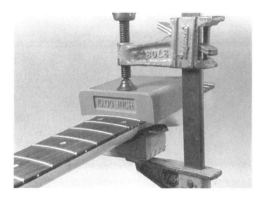

A Bessey used with a radius block caul can press frets into a slot that neither a finger-press, nor a medium-press fit could.

So, if you prepped the fretboard with radius-sanding blocks (cylinder-shape), you can use the same radius blocks to clamp in the frets, but you may need a slightly looser fret slot (or a de-barbed tang) on some rosewood or ebony. I used this method before I had Jaws, or Brian Galloup's version of it. Note: When the fret's height (average of .040") is added to the fretboard radius, the radius has increased (whereas the radius of the block hasn't). So there is a slight mismatch when you use the block as a gluing clamp or caul. But the difference is so minimal that you can ignore it. The ability to use a radius-block as a clamp is one reason you might choose to prepare a cylinder-shaped fretboard.

With regard to the radius mismatch of the sanding-blocks: If you really want to be exact, add a layer of .040" shim stock (or whatever thickness matches the fret height) to the bottom of the radius block *before* you sand the fret-board. Then remove it to use it as a press.

■ Let the glue dry 10 minutes while you bend two more frets at the other end of the fretboard. Also wax and tape off two more slots. By the time these two frets have been installed, you can remove the clamp from the two that are drying and begin the process over.

■ Remove the clamp, and with a sharp chisel pare away the epoxy squeeze-out on each side of the fret. The wax makes this job easy, although many glue-in fretters don't bother with it. Watch out! It's easy to cut into the fretboard with your chisel. As you work, keep the edge of the chisel that's away from the fret slightly above the fretboard's surface

("floating" is as good a word as any).

■ Repeat the process until you're done. Using this method you may run into a problem fitting a caul and clamp around the neck joint. (I rig up something like you see above).

■ After I've pressed in a set of frets, I'll often put the old Plexiglas "conform to any radius" caul on while the glue dries and I go onto the next pair of frets. Sometimes I use my deluxe radius sanding-blocks as a caul to hold the fret as the glue dries. At other times the frets press in so well that no caul is needed.

TO GLUE OR NOT TO GLUE: ARGUMENTS FOR AND AGAINST THE "GLUE-IN" FRET-JOB

Because the fret slots are widened and the frets pushed in with a finger-tight fit and then held by epoxy, this method has created controversy over the years. Some say that using epoxy is a poor trick to play on a future repairperson; others worry about hurting correct intonation by altering the fret slots, and the question of the vintage market comes to mind. I don't feel that the glue-in method is the right way to refret a valuable vintage guitar, but there are circumstances when it's the only way to go (rotten fingerboards which won't hold a fret, and on the fret extension over the body of acoustic guitars where hammering is dangerous). Maybe you won't use the glue-in method for every fret-job, but you should know its history, and how to go about it.

■ If you rout the slot and press in the fret, an air-space or clearance "gap" usually exists between the tang and the fret slot walls. With a finger-press fit, the very edge of the barbs are just touching the walls as the fret is pressed in. A medium-press (hammer) fit forces some of the barb to drag through the wood. With either

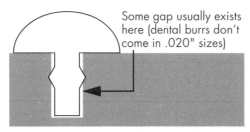

Some gap usually exists here (dental burrs don't come in .020" sizes)

of these press fits, the tang is not touching. That's why we use glue—to fill the gap, and hold down the fret. If a gap is left, and not filled with glue, poorer tone transmission showed in my tests. So the amount of gap, and the type of glue used, becomes the issue (and at times it has become most controversial between many of us). Here are the main points of argument, and some solutions:

■ Those against the glue-in method feel that by routing the slots you create a weak "rubbery" neck, even though the playing surface may be perfectly level (especially on adjustable necks where you can control the neck's straightness with ease).

Solution: Don't use the method, or don't rout the slots too wide, or perhaps not as wide as Don recommends. (Don is very scientific, and has run many tests. He says that the epoxy he uses [Elmer's E-601] makes the neck stiffer than the wood itself—stiffer than before the slots were enlarged and the neck refretted).

■ It's my opinion that over-widening the slot does cause a neck to lose stiffness in some cases—and especially on adjustable-neck guitars. If a neck loses its stiffness, the tone will be harmed—it may play well, but won't sound as good. But I don't believe that epoxy is the culprit.

Solution: Study fret compression, hammer the frets in, or use the "new glue-in method."

■ Glued-in frets can be a nasty surprise for future repairpeople.

Solution: Use heat; the frets come right out.

MORE OBSERVATIONS ON GLUING FRETS

■ Some suggest that epoxy is a "tone-sink," and that fretting with it is like setting the fret into a shock-absorber. Using a tool which measures sound transmission, I ran extensive tests, and found that *not* using glue, even with a traditional hammer-in fret-job, produced a

poorer metered response than using glue on any fret-job. I used hide glue, Titebond, 5-minute epoxy, and four different 24-hour cure epoxies for my tests. Wide slot "glued-in" frets measured lower than tight-slot hammered-in frets with glue, but not significantly.

Epoxy seemed to match hide glue, shellac, and titebond as a fret-holding glue in tight-fitting and loose-fitting slots. I then measured hardened glues by themselves, and epoxy was lower on the list: actually in the same response category as nylon and Plexiglas as a sound transmitter. Therefore, I would not want to use it as a bed for my frets with a finger-press, or a medium-press (hammer) fit, regardless of what the fret tests showed me.

■ You can use super glue to hold a fret in with the glue-in method, but I don't think it fills the gap well enough to insure a tight fit and good tone (unless you fill the slot with slow-curing glue and wait forever for it to dry).

■ Harry Fleishman suggests mixing sawdust that matches the fretboard wood into the epoxy to stiffen the neck and improve the tone. This didn't produce any measurable effects in my tests, but it makes sense, and it's worth doing.

■ Tests on sound, at least the kind that I'm qualified to make, didn't prove much really—so much for science.

When the frets are all installed, level them, bevel their ends, and go about dressing them in the normal fashion. Here's how to deal with bound fingerboards.

Bound fingerboards

Bound fingerboards need special attention. There is seldom a reason to remove fingerboard binding when refretting; yet it's done often, perhaps in an attempt to save the "nibs" at the fret end, as pictured above. It's almost impossible to save the nibs during a fret job. It's best to pull the frets, level the board as if the nibs weren't there, and then fret it by either the hammer- or glue-in methods. Also, removal of the binding involves much touch-up finishing,

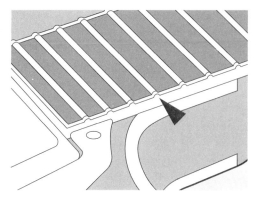

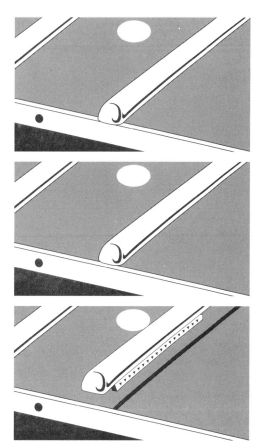

so don't be talked into doing it. (A rare vintage guitar can be fretted with its nibs left intact, but the job is so time-consuming and delicate that you'd best be sitting down when your repairman gives you an estimate.)

The frets can be installed so that the crown overlaps the plastic (at right, top), as with most bound-fretboard Martins, or they may be trimmed flush to the binding and then beveled. Players getting a refret on a guitar with nibs (Gibson, Jackson, Gretsch, etc.) may prefer the fret/binding overlap, since it takes the place of the missing nibs and retains the feel. In the case of the overlap, the fret's tang is notched and filed smooth before installation. The tang is also beveled slightly inward to avoid pushing the binding out (bottom, right). The fret end is then finish-beveled and rounded to the player's taste.

SOME BINDING CONSIDERATIONS

■ When nipping the fretwire for the over-lapped-binding method, Waverly Fret Nippers are a great time-saving device that eliminates most of the filing on notched fret ends.

Slightly back-bevel the fret tang

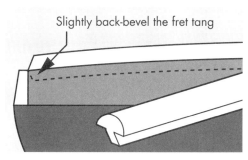

■ Frets trimmed flush to the binding should have the tang slightly back-beveled with a file to avoid pushing the binding out. On flush-to-the-binding fret-jobs, the ends of the frets must be filed at the same taper as the fretboard width (see drawing at right).

■ If you're hammering in frets flush to the binding, don't overbend the radius as much as you would for an unbound board with fret overhang. It's hard to guarantee where the fret ends will end up as the fret seats, finally straightening out to its full length. You could end up with a gap on one end, and pushed-out binding on the other.

■ Overlapped binding is the easiest of the bound fret-jobs because the notched fret hides the tang. Therefore you can leave the tang a tiny bit short at each end with no danger of hitting the binding.

SOME SPECIAL BINDING REPAIRS

If you are rebinding during the job, here's a little advice taken from the pages of *Guitar Player* magazine:

Question: "I'm restoring a late-'50s Gretsch 6120. Everything's original and in fair shape, even the frets, but for some reason there's no fingerboard binding! When rebinding, what's the best way to shape the fret-end nibs, and where can I find the little red dots for the edge markers?"

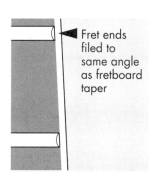

Fret ends filed to same angle as fretboard taper

Answer: Create binding nibs by tracing the profile of the fingerboard and frets onto your plastic. Then cut it close to shape on a bandsaw. Finish the job with a scraper once the binding's installed. Also, drill your red-dot holes (.055" dia.) in the new binding before you glue it on—it's easier than drilling after the new binding has been installed, especially on the fingerboard extension.

As for edge markers—recently, on a similar Gretsch binding replacement, I lost two of the red dots saved from the original binding—oops! The sharp tip of a red drawing pencil dipped in super glue, stuck into the hole, and sawed off solved the problem—you'd never know which dots are fake.

Here's a common, but somewhat complicated, bound fretboard repair which started with this letter from Phil Henderson in Foley, Alabama:

"The original frets on my SG Les Paul 'Fretless Wonder' are so low that it's impossible to bend a note, so it needs to be refretted. The neck is wide, but the strings are really close together at the nut because the frets stop short at the binding. To get more playing area and wider string spacing, I'd like new frets that could lay out over the binding (similar to a Martin), but on my guitar the binding is all rounded over where it meets the fretboard, so I doubt you could overlap a fret onto it. But a friend says that the binding must be removed for refretting anyhow. Is this true? If so, could you put on thicker binding and then fret out onto it? Thanks!"

Answer: Binding is not normally removed during refretting—this is a common misconception! You'd appreciate a refret if you like to bend strings because "Fretless Wonder" frets were notoriously low, even when new. On your Les Paul the binding was over-rounded when the guitar was built, and you're right, there's nothing to fret over (which is something to fret over). This over-rounding isn't "wrong," it's just the way a particular Gibson craftsman chose to file and round-off that particular neck on that particular day. I've seen other guitars just like yours that made good use of the neck's width without the binding being rounded over. I prefer to leave as much

of the neck/fretboard/binding width as possible so that the string spacing can be comfortably wide. Why not replace the binding so that the guitar can be refretted the way you like?

In the case of this particular instrument, it would be OK with regards to the guitar's value as a vintage instrument to replace the binding, since the finish on the back of the neck is in rough shape—even worn to the bare wood in areas. Also, the guitar has been refretted, but with the same low "Fretless Wonder" fretwire—that's why Phil thought it was the original fret job! During that refret the binding was filed on and removed even more, as evidenced by the fact that there are no plastic "nibs" on the end of each fret, which there would be if the frets were original. With the removal of the nibs that had once "capped off" the fret ends, the replacement frets had to be slightly beveled and rounded-over (see the "after the first refret" illustration). This makes the fret's actual playing width even more narrow than it would have originally been.

Another reason that it's OK, vintage-wise, to rebind the fingerboard is that the neck has already been sprayed on and touched up (again, Phil was probably unaware of this because the work was done so well). But looking carefully at the rear of the peghead, I can see different colors of white, yellow, and creamy white from the layering of different paints. My guess is that the instrument had a broken peghead that was well repaired and expertly touched up. The best way to see such finish repairs is to look at the instrument under black light—when you do, finish defects, spot touch-ups, and hidden repairs to the wood that are not visible under normal light show up instantly. Using black light as a means of "reading" a finish is a trick passed on to us by the violin trade. If you're buying an expensive vintage guitar, look at it under black light before you do! I assembled my black light for $30 and one visit to a local electric supply house.

So new binding could be installed and the neck finish could be touched up so that it still looks old and worn, with the different layers of color showing as they do now, and nobody would be the wiser. Then the frets could be notched to hang out over the binding, "Martin"-

style, as we've just seen. The total neck width of Phil's guitar is 1 $\frac{11}{16}$" (1.687"), while the string spacing of the original nut is 1 $\frac{13}{32}$" (1.406"), measured between the centers of the two outer *E* strings. With new binding that is only slightly rounded, and with the frets installed with the overhang method and then correctly beveled, Phil would end up with a new nut-string spacing of 1 $\frac{15}{32}$" (1.468"). The overall difference—.062" ($\frac{1}{16}$")—is a huge amount!

When I followed the above advice, it worked out well. Phil's guitar ended up playing beautifully, with comfortable, wide string spacing at the nut, and nice, tall, rounded frets that are a joy to bend on. Finish-wise, it's hard to tell that the job was done. While I wouldn't recommend such drastic measures for all guitars, in this case it was the right thing to do.

Fretting Vintage Fender Necks

You can use any method you like to refret vintage Strats and Teles, and they've all been discussed. So I'll just add a few pointers here. The one difference with Fender fret-jobs and all others is that until 1982, Fender slid their frets in from the side. Understanding how they were installed will help you remove frets with less chipping, and do a better fret-job in general on guitars made before 1982. Haven't you always wondered why Fender, although they didn't use glue, never had loose fret ends? Here's a little history on Fender's "sideways" fret-job.

THE SIDEWAYS FRET-JOB

I'd heard about the sideways fret job for years but never truly believed it (nor understood it) until James Rickard, Wayne Charvel, and Bob Taylor finally set me straight. James Rickard visited the Fender factory in the early '70s with Wayne Charvel as his guide. James was working for Ovation at the time, and Fender was "jobbing-out" certain custom finishing work and some refrets to Wayne's shop, so Wayne had the run of the place. Here's what Jim and Wayne told me:

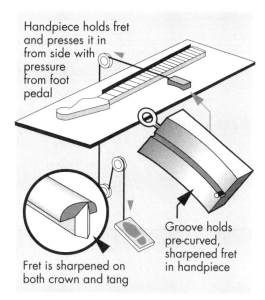

Handpiece holds fret and presses it in from side with pressure from foot pedal

Groove holds pre-curved, sharpened fret in handpiece

Fret is sharpened on both crown and tang

"The neck blank was profiled (tapered from the nut to the end), but still unshaped at the rear. The fretboard surface had been radiused, slotted, 'trued' end to end, and was ready for the frets. The neck lay flat on the work table, and was very stable because its backside was still a flat slab of wood. The table was bare except for a pile of frets and an 8" long piece of angle iron, bolted to the the rear of the table, that served as a 'fence' for the neck to be shoved up against. The angle iron was wrapped with a thick rubber band (about .090" thick) that acted as a cushion and also spaced the neck just far enough off the fence so that the sharp fret ends could overhang the fretboard edge.

"The operator installed the frets from the bass side by working an under-the-table foot lever which pulled down on a cable. The cable was connected by pulleys to a steel handpiece. The handpiece was 3" to 4" long by ¾" wide; the underside was radiused to match the fretboard (7 ¼") and had a groove to hold the crown (head) of the fret. The fret tang was exposed. The machined groove which held the fret was stopped at the operator's end by a hardened steel dowel pin which drove the fret into (and across) the slot. The handpiece was covered with a smooth wooden 'shell' to protect the operator's hand.

"The secret to the operation was that the end of the fret away from the operator—the part that got pulled through the slot—was sharpened on a special jig. The tang edge was sharp

Jim Rickard

as a knife, and the head (crown) was curved up like a ski so it couldn't catch on the fretboard surface. The barbs or 'beads' on the tang created their own groove (like a T-slot) as the fret was pulled through!

"The operator would pick up a presharp-ened, pre-radiused fret in his left hand, slap it against the underside of the handpiece (into the groove), and hold it in place with a finger. Then he'd slide the sharp fret end into the end of the fret slot and stop. Next he pressed the foot lever while holding the radiused handpiece bottom against the fretboard surface. The cable pulled the handpiece across the board, and pulled the fret into the slot. The handpiece was pressed firmly against the fretboard to help keep the fret down. After each fret he'd slide the neck along, keeping the treble side up against the fence.

"Once the fret got started, the fret would sort of hold itself down as the beads 'broached' their own groove into the walls of the fret slot. The fret really *couldn't* come out because the wood above the beads, which would normally be compessed downward and sideways by a hammered- or pressed-in fret, was still there— the fret had never entered through it. The end result was as if the fret had been pushed sideways into a T-slot, except that the fret broached its own T-slot.

"The frets were all the same size, and extra long—leaving plenty of overhang which was rough-bandsawed and then trimmed flush on a pin-router. No glue was used during the fretting operation; however, when all the flush-trimming was done, the neck went under a small press with a radiused shoe that would squeeze the frets down tight, two or three at a time, just for insurance.

"I timed the installation several times. The worker we watched could install 21 frets in 27 seconds! Of course he was putting a show on for us, and the job wasn't done (they weren't trimmed or finished). But nobody could fret a guitar with a hammer or a press that fast. It was a crude process compared to Fender's very sophisticated techniques of today (I toured Fender thoroughly in August and have never been more impressed by any facility—Dan). But the old Fullerton plant was a monument to

how much you could do with very little."

Jim Rickard would rather be known for his knowledge and love of music, guitars, wood, and woodworking than as the metalworking engineer and machinist who has built machines that can take a freshly-made guitar string and wrap it, package it, and store it in a box in 5½ seconds. As manager of engineering and quality control for Ovation from 1968 until 1986, Jim was one of *the* creative forces behind the Ovation guitar, and he invented the under-the-bridge saddle pickup which made Ovation famous. Jim is a problem solver.

After leaving Ovation Jim spent 7 years as manager of engineering with the D'Addario string company, where he designed and built their string packaging machines. His current business, Rickard Engineering—*Integrated Design Solutions,* continues to design tooling and solve problems for the industry. When the big guys need an answer, they call Jim.

Next, I went to Fender's Dan Smith, Vice President of Marketing, to find out what year they *quit* the sideways method: "We quit sliding frets in from the side in '82—I was on the committee that did away with it. It required a lot of skill and went beyond the limits of what we could reasonably expect someone to do, especially if the worker was encouraged to produce a high volume of work. It was one of the contributing factors to the poor fret jobs that sometimes occurred during the '70s. If you pressed too light the fret would be raised above the surface; too hard, and it would cut right into the wood. Each fret could have its own individual height! It was almost impos-sible to get perfect fret jobs unless the operator was really adept."

Then I asked Bob Taylor of Taylor Guitars if *he* knew anything about Fender sideways fretting (Bob seems to know how everything is done), and Bob said, "Oh yeah, *I saw it!* That's the way it was. In fact, I finally figured out that you can drive the fret *out* sideways—they come right out! I'll tell you, Dan—when you try it, you're in for a pleasant day!"

WAYNE'S WORLD

Then I asked Wayne Charvel to add to the picture:

"I talked with Leo Fender a number of times. He was a wonderful man who loved to talk shop. Did you know that the reason Fender switched from maple necks to rosewood fretboards was because Leo was watching a band on TV—all playing Fenders—when he suddenly realized that the finishes were starting to wear through on the fretboards? He thought they looked terrible! They got rid of maple necks in a hurry.

"A lot of people don't know how Fender fretted. Of course, how *could* they have known (who'd have guessed) if they'd never seen it? It's nice to be aware of it when you're pulling frets on Fender guitars made before—what year did you say they quit—'82? With a vintage maple neck, when you pull the fret up and out of the slot with your fret nippers, you get a line of small, evenly spaced chips on each side of the fret slot—these represent the wood displaced by the fret barbs. If the fret had been pressed in, the barbs would have compressed the wood downward and to the side, and then could have been pulled out with less chipping.

"The chips are larger and more severe with rosewood boards because most of them were 'slab'- or 'flat'-sawn. They really want to chip if something imbedded under the surface—such as a fret tang—is being pulled up through it. If you're experienced with vintage maple necks, you'll notice that the removal chips are very small and actually become hidden by the new fret. But with the rosewood boards, they *really* chip—often in long V-shaped pieces much larger than the beads themselves.

"When I pull frets from vintage Fender necks—either maple necks or the rosewood fretboards—I dampen the fret and the fret slot with a 50/50 solution of water and rubbing alcohol. It softens the wood enough to let the frets pull out cleaner, and the alcohol seems to help the water evaporate fast enough to keep from overswelling the wood. We were always afraid to use a soldering iron to heat the frets before pulling them (as you might on frets installed from above), because the heat makes the fret expand and chip the wood even worse, especially on rosewood boards.

"I'll tell you Dan, *way* back I tried what you and Bob Taylor are talking about—removing

the frets sideways. They came out, but it made me nervous, so I didn't pursue it. I probably should have. I'll tell you though, a novice could really cause some damage that way. On thick-finished necks especially, be careful of the finish along the fretboard edge on the bass side—you can pop a chunk out easily. Most of those thick-finished necks have chunks just

waiting to pop loose at the fret ends because of neck expansion and contraction. You've given me confidence though, and I'll try it on the next original factory Fender vintage fret-job that comes in—one fret at a time."

Thanks, Jim, Bob, Dan and Wayne!! Now that I understand how the frets were installed on the majority of vintage Fenders I've worked on, I wish I had them all back (but that's water over the dam). From now on though, we all may consider a different approach to removing them. You have several choices:

1 Use a soldering iron and fret pullers.

2 Dampen the wood with the alcohol/water solution before using the fret pullers.

3 Combine the above methods (a soldering iron and moisture—I don't think you need to worry about watered-down rubbing alcohol catching fire, but to be safe omit the alcohol, use water, and "steam" them out).

4 Drive the frets out sideways, the same way they went in. The difference between a vintage fret pulled out sideways, and one pulled up the normal way (on the same fretboard) is shown in the photos above. Here's how you can do it:

■ Grind a small notch, or hole, in the top of the fret on the treble side (I used a small dental burr in a Dremel tool)—just enough of a groove to catch whatever tool you use to knock it out with.

Wayne Charvel

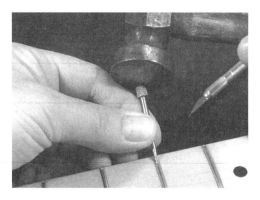

■ I'm using a small machinist's scribe which I press into the groove and tap with my fretting hammer. After it begins to move you can pull it out with fret nippers if you'd rather. Once the frets are loose you can slide them in and out like drawers!

I've been removing frets sideways (toward the bass side) with great results. When you tap out the frets, the top of the fret slot is perfect! You'll have to heat most of the '70s "thick-skin" polyester maple neck frets before they'll move, but you need less heat than if you were pulling them out the normal way, so there's less risk of "burn-marks" on the maple.

Soon I'll try removing the frets out the treble side, since that's the direction the wood grain is pushed. There are two ways to think about hammering frets out: One idea is that removal is easier out the bass side because the fret is retracing the path it cut on entering the slot. The other thought is that removal is easier out the treble side because the wood fibers are already going that way and won't "reverse" and grab the fret as they might with the bass side removal. I suspect it will be more difficult (but possible) going out the treble side. I just don't have piles of vintage necks lying around to practice on! If you can drive frets out to either side, you can go to the side *away* from the player's eye (treble side for a right-handed player, and vice-versa). If you did get a little chip, it wouldn't be noticed until after you'd gotten paid for the work! (Just kidding).

But take Wayne's warning to heart. On all necks, especially the thick-finished ones, be especially careful of the fretboard edge on the bass side. Use heat, a sharp X-acto knife, and a sharper eye to keep the exit of the fret under control. After the first tap, stop and check if either the wood or the finish are pulling outward in the direction of the removal (if so, do something about it and then finish removing the fret). I'm already thinking about a little fixture to keep pressure on the edge of the fretboard, around the fret-slot edge, as the fret comes out.

The small compressed groove below the surface of the fretboard ("broached" by the fret), is not actually cut or broached, but pressed—and I can't *see* it with a 10X lens. But because I know it's there, I wipe a drop of water into the slot (not too much), so the wood can swell back to where it had been in 1956, or whenever.

ABOUT FRETTING MAPLE NECKS

Because of the lacquer finish, refretting a maple neck is more troublesome than working with a rosewood fretboard. Many maple necks are so true and the finish is in such good shape that you just pull out the old frets and stick in the new—the preferred method. Other necks are worn nearly bare, especially on the fretboard. Dealing with the finish on these necks isn't a problem, either, since you can't lose what you never had (some players want to have finish put back on and some prefer the feel of bare wood). Other necks may need to have the fretboard surface leveled before they'll play right, and *then* you're forced to deal with the finish.

We commonly see vintage Strat necks with some, or all, of the original lacquer, along with plenty of nice gray-brown wear spots. Unfortunately, these great-*looking* necks often have the typical hump, or "rising tongue," at the last six frets. If the hump is bad and you want a great-*playing* guitar, you'll have to remove the hump in order to get that portion of the neck surface level with the rest of the fretboard. Since these vintage boards are cylinders, I use a 7¼" radius block and sandpaper to keep the original fretboard contour. Here are some tips on maple neck refrets:

■ If the neck's true, simply remove the frets and refret it, but don't touch the lacquer except to clean it. If you sand, don't use anything under (coarser than) 2000-grit paper.

■ Many maple necks from the '70s and '80s have a hard polyurethane finish ("thick-skin" as

Mike Stevens calls it). There's less chance of harming this finish during a refret, but removing it is a chore if you need to level the board. Also, many of these finishes were too thick, and removing the frets without chipping can be tricky. You may have to cut the finish along the fret, or heat each fret slightly before you can remove it (especially if you plan to drive the fret out sideways).

■ Don't try to sand out the wear spots. Wear spots are cool.

■ Bare wood on the fretboard should be lightly dampened with naptha to raise the grain. When it's dry, any wood fibers that "fir-up" should be sanded or scraped off. Do this before you refret, since it's a little hard to sand later in between frets. You'll want to respray the lacquer over smooth wood.

FRET SLOTS AND TANG-SIZE

■ Carefully clean out the fret slots by pulling through an X-acto saw blade that's thinner than the slot. If you're careful not to deepen or widen the slots, they'll hold the replacement frets and look original. Blow the dust out of the slots.

■ Degrease a dirty board or slot edges by wiping with naptha or lighter fluid (in a well-ventilated place, of course!). Don't use lacquer thinner!

■ If you had to remove wood from the fretboard surface, you may have to slightly deepen the slot to accommodate the fret tang. Don't overdo it.

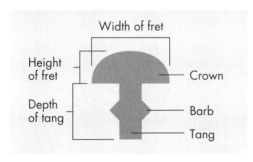

■ Save the old frets for comparison with the new replacement wire. Try to match the original fretwire in height, width, and tang/barb size. Two wires that nicely refret a vintage Strat are Dunlop 6230 and Stewart-MacDonald's 148. Refretters sometimes widen a fret slot for a press fit and use glue to hold in the new wire,

but not on a vintage Strat. You'll be tapping or pressing-in the new frets, so match the size as closely as possible.

■ If the new tang is too deep for the slot, you can grind or file it shorter so that the slot doesn't have to be deepened.

■ To avoid creating a back-bow or warp, it's important that both the tang and the "barbs" are not too large.

■ If the neck was refretted before, the frets may tend to be loose in the slots. In this case, you want a wire with an oversized tang and barb that will hold.

■ Glue may be needed to hold down the new frets or fret ends. Use an aliphatic glue such as Titebond or Elmer's Carpenter's Glue; don't use epoxy or super glue. Fender didn't use glue when they installed the frets, but you may have to.

■ Overbend the fretwire radius to hold down springy ends.

■ My chasing fret hammer has a shaped "claw" to serrate and "mushroom" the bottom of the tang—making it hold better in a worn slot.

■ Level and dress the frets as normal, and touch up the finish if needed.

TOUCHING UP A MAPLE NECK FINISH

At the finish touch-up stage, if the fretboard's bare wood looks much lighter than the amber finish on the rest of the neck, mix an amber water-stain from red, yellow, and brown. Using a cotton applicator, lightly stain the wood to match; this prevents your having to color the lacquer, which can look sort of phony.

■ If the fretboard ended up bare, or was already bare when you got it and very dirty, seal it with a 4 to 5 lb. cut of fresh shellac to avoid silicone problems (4 or 5 parts alcohol to 1 part shellac) before using lacquer. Shellac may give a maple neck just the color you want, so practice on scrap. I fret the neck bare and spray the finish afterward—right over the frets.

■ Then use a thin mixture of lacquer (from two to four parts thinner to one part lacquer), and only spray two or three coats—just enough to protect the wood.

■ The lacquer is easily removed from the frets, so spray right over them. When the finish is dry, sand off the lacquer using the Sand-Sticks that are used for dressing frets.

■ Don't use much lacquer. You can always add more later, even after a few months. See the Finish chapters for more information!

Scalloped fingerboards

Even though the '80s speed-at-all-costs fetish has faded a bit in recent years, some players are still looking for advice on scalloped finger-boards. Should they perform this modification? What does it have to offer? Is it reversible? Does scalloping a neck cause problems in the future? While many of you may be aware that John McLaughlin and Ritchie Blackmore used scalloped fingerboards years ago, I think that most of the current interest has been stirred up by speed-metal phenom Yngwie Malmsteen.

I thought scalloping was a dumb idea until I received a phone call from Pat Patton, a gui-tarist and instructor from Westlake, Michigan. Pat has been playing on a scalloped board for years and doing the scalloping himself. He

came to me for instruction on doing the job neatly and to learn how to refret the neck when he was done. After only five minutes of listening to Pat play, I was totally knocked out! I hadn't been that excited about playing—and learning something new—for many years. You can teach an old dog new tricks after all. Here are the pros and cons of this modification:

Scalloping involves dishing out the wood between frets so that the fingertip has no contact with the fingerboard. It's difficult to do well. If you're thinking of doing the job yourself, be sure to finish this chapter before you start—and you might decide to have it done by the very best repairman or builder that you can find. Expect the scalloping job to be expensive, and don't be surprised if you have to refret your guitar at the same time—this is not an absolute, but a good possibility. Factory-scalloped replacement necks are available from some of the suppliers, which gives you the option of leaving your original board stock—a great idea where vintage pieces are concerned!

When playing with a scalloped fingerboard, you have to develop a whole new touch in order to keep from accidentally pressing the strings too hard and going out of tune. I found that this light touch was easy to get used to. And, for the first time in my life, my fingering hand became so relaxed that I was able to play much faster and smoother, since my fingertips were no longer fighting the fingerboard wood in order to press the string onto the fret. This seems to be in direct opposition to Yngwie's view that "it's much harder to play fast with a scalloped fingerboard because the string action has to be much higher." I don't know why he says this.

The photo shows scalloping as Pat prefers it.

A salesman in a music store tried to tell me, "Scalloping ain't no big deal; tall frets will do the exact same thing." This is simply not true.

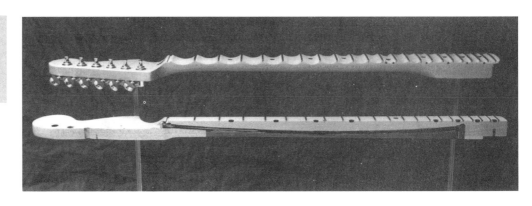

These "radical" scallops are quite deep: ⁵/₃₂" to ³/₁₆" below the actual wood surface of the fingerboard that the fret seats against, and you can add the height of the fret itself to that. The scallops are complemented by either a good fret dress (the tops are filed smooth and round, enabling the string to move smoothly when you press down into the scallop) or a complete refret with a jumbo fretwire. I prefer the scallop to look a little asymmetrical—that is, not a perfect radius—with a little extra removed on the fret side that the finger plays against to accommodate the finger's ball end.

Since the guitar is a very personal instrument, the "benefits" of scalloping are subjective. Playing on one, I noticed the following changes in my playing: My fingering hand was relaxed, allowing me to play faster. Hammer-ons took less pressure in the attack, enabling faster trills and hammered chords. Pull-offs became easier, since the finger's flesh can reach deep down and really catch hold as you pull away, creating a distinctive percussive sound. A pitch bend (pushing straight down with the finger towards the fingerboard) could easily accommodate a semitone, and with a little practice, whole-tones and minor thirds can be done. Using this tech-nique, you can imitate a pedal steel, for example, or even bend whole chords —I can't do that without a tremolo on an unscalloped neck, and then the sound isn't the same.

OTHER BENEFITS

Due to the lack of pressure needed to hold down a chord, scalloping allows you to "rake"—or sweep—arpeggio passages, since your hand is free to move with the chord. This is an essential aspect of Yngwie's style. Bending blues notes has never been easier, since the finger can really get a good grab on the string with no slipping. This makes the wide, full-string vibrato of Yngwie or Ritchie Blackmore easier to achieve. Two-handed tapping techniques are also made easier, especially for the right-hand fingertip that is now able to pull off the string without first hitting the fingerboard. The violin-type finger vibrato also takes on a new sound, since you can alter its pitch with a gentle pressing of the string. With scalloping, I find a more even, clear sound on all the strings in any position,

probably because there is no longer any muting effect from the fingers touching the wood and drawing off some of the sound. Sounds good, huh? Now for the other side of the coin.

I wouldn't suggest that you scallop a vintage guitar if you have any interest in retaining its market value—you'll ruin it forever. Scalloping could considerably weaken any neck (aside from one you may have had custom-built with a scalloped board in mind), since the finger-board is an integral part of the neck's straight-ness and stiffness. After scalloping, a neck might twist or warp, but frankly, I think any good repairman could compensate for this by adjusting the truss rod accordingly or making up for the problem with accurate fret work. Also, since the scallops must be quite deep, the position markers may need to be removed and reinlaid. This is easy for dots, but if you have pearl-block or large, ornate inlays, you may have to settle for dot replacements or foot a very expensive reinlay bill. The side dot markers may have to be moved or eliminated as well.

OTHER CONS

The scallop is non-reversible. You cannot change your mind if you don't like it; the entire fingerboard has to be replaced. The tone of the guitar is going to change somewhat, too, and nobody could advise you as to what to expect there. I'd worry about this more with an acoustic guitar than a solidbody electric, yet even with electrics, I suggest scalloping a bolt-on neck at first. Buy yourself an extra kit neck and have it scalloped, leaving the original intact (or, try the prescalloped Strat-style necks offered by several guitar shop suppliers). And if you're used to playing on strings that begin with a high-*E* gauged .010 or heavier, be prepared to switch to .009s in order to gain the scallops' benefit. I found that my newly relaxed left hand compensated for the switch to lighter strings, and even though I don't enjoy playing on lighter strings, I really didn't notice a difference. (Pat suggests using .009, .011, .013, .022, .032, .038 for acoustics or electrics.) Since standard truss rods curve up towards the fingerboard at each end of the neck (see photo, previous page), the scallop depth must be controlled accurately in these areas. Finally, scalloping is

At first, try scalloping a fingerboard on an extra guitar, not your main axe! If you have any interest in retaining its market value, don't scallop a vintage guitar— you'll ruin it forever!

expensive and comes with no guarantees. A fair price will be in the range of $150 to $200.

Recently a salesman in a music store tried to tell me, "Scalloping ain't no big deal; tall frets will do the exact same thing." This is simply not true. I may not have covered all the pros and cons of scalloping here, but you get the idea— give scallops a try if you've got the appetite.

The neck-jig

The neck-jig is the most important tool in my repair shop. Although only the most serious fret worker would actually build this tool, its basic concept should help all guitarists understand more about neck repairs and fret work. Many repairmen should profit from these pages, too.

Although I currently use the neck-stress jig for all fret work, it was originally designed to help correct problem fret-jobs: necks with twists, warps, humps, and rises, or truss rods

The original neck jig didn't tilt (1975).

The first tilting neck jig (1983).

that don't work well. I wanted something that would duplicate the pressure of a fully-strung guitar, so that as I worked on a neck, it would be under the same stress—and in the same configuration—as when it was being played. Thus, the fingerboard shape had to remain constant. I also realized that because of gravity, the neck's straightness and relief when being held, or hung from a strap in the playing position, is different from when it's lying on the repair bench with its strings removed. By using the neck-jig, it's possible to gain a greater degree of control over any normal neck, and more important, it's easier to salvage the problem necks that are often found on rare and valuable vintage guitars. When not in use (a rare occurrence), the jig doubles as a heavy-duty solid maple workbench. Here's how it works.

The body is first clamped firmly to the table with padded hold-down "dogs" that ride on cross-slots in the table . Padded spacer blocks rest under the body to raise it off the table surface. At this point, the neck is suspended freely with ample space for stringing and unstringing. Now for the most important part: By loosening four lock pins, one on each corner of the table, I free the bench top to spin on centers. Next, the top is tilted in the playing position at a 90° angle relative to the floor, and the guitar is tuned to pitch.

Now the neck is read (analyzed) from the side, using a good straightedge while looking for the proper amount of straightness or relief, depending on string gauge and action height. I use a fluorescent Bright Stick as a backlight (above, right). The light rides up and down on two rods, tilts to align with the fingerboard, and bolts to my rotating table top, following the work wherever it goes.

The tilting table eliminates the gravity factor, making it easier to adjust the truss rod, which controls the fingerboard's shape lengthwise. Note: With a properly working neck, there's always some pressure on the truss rod. With the strings in place, loosening a rod (turning counter-clockwise) gives a straight neck relief, while tightening it (turning clockwise) removes excess relief, or "up-bow."

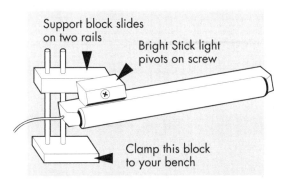

Support block slides on two rails

Bright Stick light pivots on screw

Clamp this block to your bench

Of course, tightening the rod too much causes a back-bow away from the strings. Most players prefer a straight neck or one with a slight, controlled relief.

Once the neck is adjusted correctly, I set the neck support rods (above). The steel rods have plastic protective caps and are set into accurately reamed holes in the jig bar, which is clamped to the table top underneath the back of the neck. First the rods are carefully slid up until they just touch the back of the neck, and then they are locked in place with set-screws. With the rods set, the strings are removed. Without the string pressure, the neck usually rises up slightly off the support rods because of the back-pressure from the truss rod. You must slightly loosen the truss rod until the neck sets back down onto the rods; when this happens, the neck is supported in the playing position. Thanks to the support rods, the table can now be rotated and locked into the level position for working, without gravity playing a major role in the neck's shape. The stress jig eliminates the guesswork in fretting and allows me to control the truss rod, especially in problem cases.

Many fine vintage guitars have problem fingerboards. A great guitar can still have humps, rises, warp, twist, up-bow, or back-bow. These are caused in part by the nature of the wood itself, but especially by years of playing with heavier strings and a tight truss rod. Remember that during the '50s and early '60s, light strings (beginning with a .010 high-*E* and under) were not available, and most players used what today would be considered medium- or heavy-gauge strings, except for a rare few who used banjo strings to get those bluesy bends. Many of these necks have taken a definite "set" after years of truss rod/heavy string stress. This is not necessarily bad, but a fret dress or refret must be done carefully in order to avoid needless planing, sanding, and scraping of the fingerboard. To me, the stress jig is a necessity in these cases.

Imagine the following situation: I received a '62 Fender Jazz Bass with severe problems. The neck was extremely back-bowed, which in itself is unusual, especially since the truss rod was completely loose. Worse still, the owner had tried to correct the problem (in exactly the wrong way) by tightening the truss rod, thereby breaking off the end of the truss rod along with the tightening nut. Suffice to say that I managed to replace the rod with one that worked, which got me back to the guitar's original problem: a back-bow with a loose rod. Here's where the jig helped greatly in solving the problem.

By stringing the bass up to pitch with the table tilted, I could see that the neck would become almost straight, but with none of the relief that most basses need. I supported the neck in this position, yet knew that with the strings removed, I couldn't loosen the truss rod to let the neck back onto the jig's rods. After removing the frets, I ran a guitar string through the empty fret slot at the 7th fret and used it to tighten the neck down with a turnbuckle that held it onto the rods. I was then able to scrape a little here, sand a little there, and by being careful where I worked, I managed to gain a little relief when stringing back to pitch. Next, I put some pressure on the truss rod by tightening it slightly. The neck was straight, and I rejigged it.

This time around, I could set the neck back onto the rods by releasing the truss rod. I then scraped and sanded again, mostly in the middle of the fingerboard, but also a bit on the tongue and some at the 1st and 3rd frets. The next time I strung to pitch, I had good relief with no rod tension, slight relief with some rod tension, and a straight neck with good truss rod tension. At that point, I was able to proceed with a standard fret job. To me, this minor miracle could only have been accomplished with the jig.

The videotape "Don't Fret" covers the neck jig's use in great detail. I shot the video in 1993 at Bryan Galloup's Guitar Hospital (a guitar repair school in Big Rapids, Michigan). We had two neck-jigs in operation at the same time—check it out!

Summing up fretwork

If you've experienced action problems from a warp in the neck or humps in the board, the new fret-job should enable you to set the action much lower without undue buzzing. But remember that a certain amount of clean, metal-to-metal string buzz is normal for any guitar, especially if one plays with a medium or heavy attack on light strings (.010s and under). Keep in mind that repairmen are a sensitive breed. They're known to become offended when, after doing a painstaking fret job and then taking half a day to set up a guitar, the customer picks it up and whines, "It buzzes!" Any new fret-job takes some time to break in, so be patient. It may take as long as a month for playing and fret wear to make things feel normal again.

FRET-JOB PRICING

When discussing price, few customers seem to appreciate the careful and tedious setup involved after the fret work. Often the nut must be replaced or shimmed to accommodate the new, taller frets. Bridge heights and truss rods must be readjusted, and often intonation must be set. This work must be added onto the price of the fret-job itself; there's no way around it. I spoke to several different repair-men from around the country, and they gave me some figures that may help you know what prices to expect when fret-job shopping. I'm

listing the highest and lowest prices for normal fret-jobs, along with prices for set-up and a new nut. As a rule, the highest prices were on the East and West Coasts, with New York being the highest. This list is current as of July, 1993.

Refret Prices

With binding: $125 – $300
Unbound: $90 – $250
Maple w/lacquered fingerboard: $150 – $300
Fret dress: $25 – $80
New nut: $12 – $50
Action and set-up: $18 – $40

Action and setup to involves truss rod adjustment, bridge intonation on electrics, string-height adjustment, and the final fit of the nut. For many acoustics, the saddle has to be refit or replaced by hand to accommodate the subtle action changes after a refret. These prices point out how much can go into an acoustic setup alone:

Acoustic Action Set-up

Truss rod adjustment: same as electric
Final fit of nut: same as electric
Clean, straighten, square up saddle slot: $10 – $30
Install new bone saddle or shim old saddle: $10 – $30
Adjust action to fit the nut: $10 – $20

When shopping for a refret, consider the years of experience and training needed for one to do the job well. Consider the value that it adds to your guitar, and the enjoyment you'll get from playing when it's right. If you can't afford a first-rate refret, save your money. Price is important, but a botched fret-job is much worse than no fret-job at all.

For those of you who aren't intimidated by the complex nature of fret work and wish to learn more, these books are invaluable: Don Teeter's *The Acoustic Guitar, Vols. 1* and *2*, Hideo Kamimoto's *Complete Guitar Repair*, and Irving Sloane's *Guitar Repair*. I've made a videotape that offers an in-shop view of the subject, titled, of course, *Don't Fret*. It's available from Stewart-MacDonald.

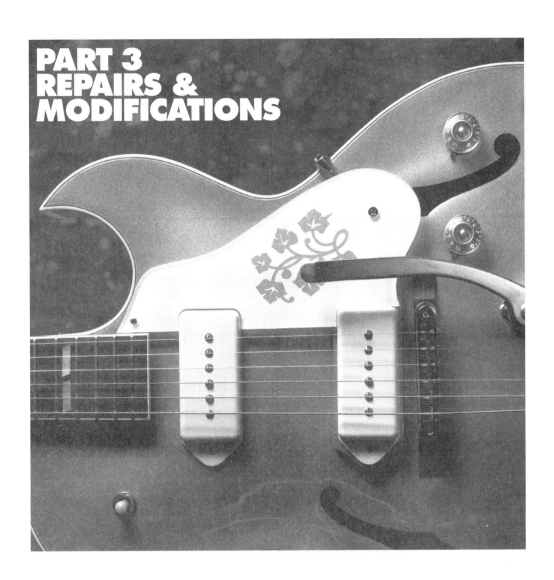

PART 3
REPAIRS &
MODIFICATIONS

10 ACOUSTIC REPAIRS

Read this section on humidity every fall, just before heating season. Then follow its advice —I do!

Dealing with humidity

Acoustic owners need to care for their delicate wooden instruments during the cold, dry months. Paying attention to humidity won't hurt electric owners either, so here's the skinny on chapped lips and cracked guitars.

In the humid summertime, guitars may suffer from becoming too wet, getting such symptoms as higher action (due to a more swollen top, which occasionally causes a bridge to loosen as well) and a flat, "tubby" sound. Solve the high-action problem by having a lower "summer saddle" made for your guitar. The tubby sound goes away by itself in the fall, or whenever you have three or four nice, dry summer days in a row. Summer conditions aren't as dangerous as winter ones, however, since the wood seldom cracks due to over-humidification.

Low humidity occurs in the winter in most areas, and all year long in some desert and high mountain states. Heating your home, especially with forced air, adds to the dryness problem. When a solid-wood guitar dries out, the wood shrinks across the grain. The fingerboard shrinks, and the fret ends poke out from the sides. Tops flatten out or cave in, lowering the bridge and allowing the strings to buzz on the frets. The back may also flatten, and glue joints anywhere can come apart. If the wood dries too rapidly, the finish may check. In extreme cases, braces can come loose and the back, sides, and especially the top can crack. Most of these troubles can be avoided by adding moisture to the guitar's environment.

Use a hygrometer to measure your home's relative humidity; combination thermometer/hygrometers aren't expensive. If you're fortunate enough to have a furnace with a whole-house humidifier, use it; if you don't, consider having one installed. Check out the portable room humidifiers available through Sears and other companies. A natural approach is to leave bowls of water to evaporate on wood stoves and heater grates. Any of these measures will help, but they may not be sufficient protection against the dreaded crack monster.

Ontek's Lifeguard model 100L.

The Ontek Lifeguard in use.

The Dampit system (with humidity gauge).

Like the Ontek, the Dampit covers the soundhole and slowly distributes moisture to the body.

Lately, soundhole humidifiers have gained popularity with many players and manufacturers. Two companies, Dampit and Ontek, manufacture soundhole humidifiers that sell for about $12.00. Simply put, these devices are dipped in water and then mounted in the soundhole when the guitar's not in use, and they slowly distribute moisture inside the guitar body. These humidifiers have soundhole covers that must be used to work properly. With the proper use of these humidifiers in the dry season and possibly a lower saddle in the wet season, your guitar should play consistently all year round. I asked acoustic guitar experts Dick Boak from Martin, Bruce Ross at Santa Cruz Guitar Co., and Bob Taylor from Taylor Guitars for their thoughts on humidity and soundhole humidifiers:

Bruce: "Humidity control is most crucial to newer guitars. Once a guitar makes it through its first four seasons, it comes to terms with itself. Use the soundhole humidifier with care. I've seen them harm guitars, too, from over-wetting, which lets water drip inside."

Bob: "Lack of humidity control is the single source for over 90% of guitar problems. How you wax, clean, play, tote, strum, strap, oil, or loan a guitar is your business. These things don't matter a whole lot—the guitar will stand up to them. But when it comes to humidity, a little attention each time you play your guitar will make it last forever."

Dick: "Guitars sound terrible when they're full of moisture. But sometimes humidifiers are necessary—more so with newer guitars—and we sell both the Ontek and Dampit here at Martin. New guitars need special treatment for the first few years. Mostly watch the heat when it first comes on in the fall—don't 'force dry' your guitar. If all the drying happens in one day, you're in trouble. Keeping it in the case when you're not playing is a big help—with or without a humidifier."

Bob: "Try to keep a new guitar from any real shock (whether dry or wet) for three or four years. Lots of unnecessary and wasteful repair work is avoided by using a soundhole humidifier during the dry months. At Taylor, we include a Dampit with each guitar because it works. The Dampit is almost useless without

the soundhole cover, but magic with the cover. We know of repair shops that use Dampits to fix guitars!"

Don't oversoak the humidifier; be sure to squeeze it out enough. Check the guitar's progress daily. Let your guitar tell you when it needs moisture. If the action's low and buzzy, and the top shows little or no arch, then you probably need to use your humidifier. If you're using a Dampit or Ontek for the first time on a guitar that's already dried out, expect to refill it after the first day—your guitar's thirsty. Keep your axe in the case during weather extremes, and learn to "read" your guitar—it's a great humidity gauge. When needed, use a humidifier from fall till spring. Soundhole humidifiers are inconvenient, but they're better than facing major repairs.

No system is perfect, especially when dealing with delicate wooden instruments that exist in a variety of climates. What's good for my guitar may not be good for yours, but many guitars will benefit from the use of a soundhole humidifier.

Flat-top bridge and brace problems

My cousin David reglued the bridge on his Silvertone by stacking volumes A through F of Encyclopedia Britannica on it, and it stayed on for a month! Not a bad job, eh? Amateurs attempt more top, bridge, and brace reglues than all other serious guitar repairs. That's why these pages are devoted to common repairs for the good old flat-top.

Actually, the term "flat-top" guitar is something of a misnomer, since most flat-tops have a slight curve built into the top. Vintage Martins or Gibsons will show a graceful arch through the entire bridge area, which is normal, and it will become more pronounced as years go by. Only in severe cases would the repairperson try to flatten this arch. If the arch isn't gradual —but more like a 'kink'—the main X-braces may be loose near the bridge (usually a result of too much dryness over a period of time) and they

Some of the gang at the C.F. Martin Co.: (front row, left to right) Dave Musselwhite, Bill Rundle, Amato Alteri, Dan Erlewine, Jim Trach; (back row) Clarence Van Horn, Rich Kroboth, Milt Hess Jr., David Strunk, Barry Henning, Dan Shook, Rich Starkey.

can be reglued. In such severe cases the bridge plate, or bridge pad, may need to be replaced to recreate the graceful arch and to stabilize a kink; but bridge pads are often replaced when they shouldn't be, so you might get a second opinion if a repairman suggests this!

If a top is slightly arched during manufacture, and then that arch increases over the years from string pressure (or from loose X-braces), the flat-bottomed bridge may have difficulty staying glued (a flat can't stay glued to a curve). Often, especially on vintage Gibsons with their somewhat thin bridges, the bridge curves right along with the top. If loose, they can be cleaned and reglued easily. Other bridges, more commonly the thicker Martin ones, often remain flat as the top arches, so of course they won't stay on. I prefer to shape the bridge bottom to fit the top curve—a very subtle arch—when regluing these bridges (when the bridge thickness permits it).

So if your lovely vintage Martin or Gibson has a bowed top, don't *let anyone try to flatten it*. Instead, fit the unglued bridge to the warp. Most often, we flatten tops only on cheaper guitars in order to get the bridge to hold and perhaps to bring down the action. However, it's more likely that the proper method of lowering action on a good old guitar is to remove and reset the neck or by clever fingerboard leveling and refretting.

Other solutions are called for when a bridge is made from poorly chosen wood that warps or curls away from the top. Many repairshops resand the bridge bottom flat, and then reglue it. The problem with grinding a warped bottom flat

is that you'll end up with a bridge which is very thin at each end on the "wings," or one that may later split from its lack of mass and thickness. Warped bridges can be soaked in water and clamped into the proper shape to dry before regluing them, but it doesn't *always* work— wood has a "memory." It may be best to treat the bridge for what it is—a piece of warped wood. Throw it away and make a new bridge.

On any acoustic flat-top guitar, but usually inexpensive guitars and many imports, the two main X-braces will *commonly* come loose just under the bridge area. This allows the guitar top to bow or hump, and the flat-bottom bridge does not want to stay glued to a curve. Before regluing the bridge, the braces must be reglued. Sometimes these guitars' bridge plates have obvious gaps, too, or they're made of thin, warpy plywood instead of a proper hardwood. A combination of gluing the braces and replacing the plate can flatten a humped top and help lower high action at the same time. A horribly warped or severly "kinked" top can be flattened by using a flat or even reverse-warp board, or a caul during gluing.

A method used by Milt Hess Jr. of the C.F. Martin repair department is to saturate the spruce top (and sometimes the bridge pad) with water, and then clamp the wood flat to dry. This is a scary procedure since it causes the finish to buckle (although it does dry back to its original form), and should only be attempted by a highly skilled professional with lots of experience—like Milt!

Minor splits in the top of the bridge, running through the bridge-pin holes or the saddle slot, can be filled with a sawdust/glue mixture or a slip of wood, and usually the repair will last. I advise this method of repair if you own a vintage instrument and wish to keep the original bridge to preserve the guitar's value. However, a skilled repairman can make a perfect duplicate of the original bridge (without splits), and one would never know it had been replaced. Also, some vintage guitars have poor intonation because the saddle is misplaced. If the bridge is already off, this problem can be corrected by making a new bridge with an improved saddle location. An alternate method of correcting a misplaced saddle slot is to fill

If your old Martin has a bowed top, don't let anyone try to flatten it!

Gaps are common at these points

Milt Hess Jr.

the slot with wood and recut it in the correct location (I do wonder if filling and recutting the slot hampers tone, however). Don't be afraid to have a vintage bridge replaced entirely if you have a good repairperson handy.

On many acoustic guitars with adjustable bridges (some low-end '60s and '70s Gibsons and many imports), I find a tremendous improvement in sound from filling the holes in the top and replacing the bridge with a solid-saddle, non-adjustable model. Since these guitars' bridge plates can usually be replaced easily, a repairman can remove the bridge plate and any thumbscrew hardware, plug the holes in the spruce top, replace the bridge plate with a new piece of wood, and custom-make a bridge with a standard saddle and bridge pins drilled closer to the saddle. This gives you a better string angle and bearing on

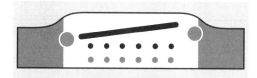

the saddle, and improves power and volume. In this drawing, the dark areas indicate where the new bridge-pin holes are located, while the lighter areas show the original holes to be plugged. Note: Many vintage Gibsons with adjustable bridges should not be altered in this fashion because of their antique value; if you own that type of guitar, discuss your options with a repairman.

Let's look at the specialized clamps that have been developed for repairing acoustic tops, and learn to use them the way the pros do.

Shown above are the five common types of bridge and top clamps: the wooden cam, as

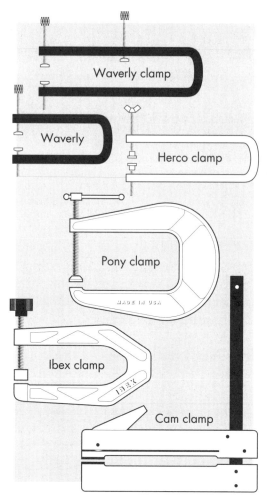

well as models made by Ibex, Herco, Pony, and Waverly. Here's a description of these clamps and the jobs at which they excel that should help you choose the right clamps for your toolbox.

Clamps are chosen for their throat (reach), opening, weight, and strength. Waverly and Herco clamps have an adjustable bottom jaw for getting around bracing—the size and shape of this bottom jaw is important—while the Ibex, Pony, and cam clamps have no bottom jaw at all.

Ibex clamps are cast aluminum, weigh 1 lb., and have a 6 ¼" throat and a 2 ¼" opening. Their lack of a bottom jaw gives them good grip and balance when clamped directly onto a brace or onto an interior caul (this caul is a hand-shaped scrap of wood used to protect against clamp marks, to spread gluing pressure, and to cut down on the number of clamps needed for the job). If I were allowed only three clamps for steel-string bridge

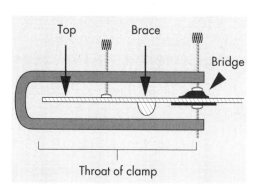

Throat of clamp

reglues, I'd choose the Ibex variety. Note: The most recent versions have substituted a plastic knob for the standard sliding T-bar handle. The plastic knob is not an improvement, and I encourage Ibex to go back to the old style.)

The Klemmsia was the first commercially produced wooden cam clamp, but now several brands are available. Because of their large 8" opening, they perform all sorts of guitar repair and woodworking tasks. They're available in three throat depths: 3 ½", 5 ⅝", and 7 ¾", and weigh ½, ¾, and 1 lb., respectively. Like the Ibex, cam clamps have shallow, non-adjustable bottom jaws that balance and grip well (the cork-padded jaws' large surface area spreads gluing pressure well, and even without cauls, these clamps normally don't leave marks). With appropriate cauls to space around the braces, cams make adequate bridge clamps, and they are excellent for leveling cracks, gluing bracing, and many general shop tasks.

Herco bridge clamps are long C-clamps with a 2" opening, and are available in two throat sizes, standard (6⅝") and long (8 ½"). Each weighs just under 1 lb. Made of ½" x ¼" flat bar stock that's bent to form the "C" shape, these clamps tend to spring apart if too much pressure is applied, so don't over-tighten them. This style of clamp is important because you can fit lots of them in a soundhole, and the adjustable bottom foot allows you to get around the depth of the braces, as seen here. The long model is good for reaching way back to glue bracing, as well as for some bridge reglues on classical guitars. I often use the standard length to help out Ibex clamps during tricky bridge jobs, since they easily squeeze in between other clamps. Herco clamps are best for brace, crack, and bridge pad repair, or when used as helper clamps for bridge reglues. Herco has recently substituted a wing nut for the old knurled thumbscrew (like the Ibex plastic knob, not an improvement). I wish these clamp makers would leave well enough alone!

Ponies are the strongest. These heavy-duty cast clamps are used at Martin for bridge clamping—a long (6 ¼" throat) model for classical bridges, and a short (4 ¾") one for

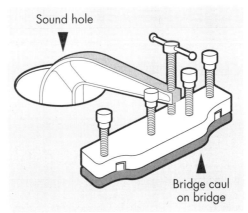

Sound hole

Bridge caul
on bridge

standard models. Martin uses only one Pony clamp per bridge, relying on several styles of special cauls to do the rest of the job (above). Pony clamps have a 2 ¹¹/₁₆" opening, and weigh as much as 2 ½ lbs. Because these clamps are cumbersome and heavy, you would seldom use three, for example, to clamp a bridge. But for certain advanced repairs such as flattening a top, bridge pad replacement, or Martin-style bridge gluing, their incredible strength is just what's needed. Sometimes I'll use one Pony and two Ibex clamps for a bridge job.

Waverly is a newcomer to the long C-clamp market, and its products are available in three throat depths: 4 ⅝" (short), 6 ⅞" (standard), and 8 ¾" (long), with jaws opening to 2 ½". Like the Hercos, they're made of bent steel, but they're thicker and don't spring easily. Built-in leveling jacks are an option on the standard and long models (see drawings, previous page). The levelers support the weight of the clamps by screwing against a caul laid across the top. Best of all, the jacks give extra pressure when needed to get perfect glue squeeze-out at the rear of a bridge. The short Waverly is able to clamp the entire shoulder area, and the area from the bridge in toward the soundhole. Being short, the clamp has more strength than its big brothers, so I'd use this for bridge reglues where I might not want the longer, "springier" types.

Regluing bridges, clamping cracks and loose braces

Inexperienced do-it-yourselfers should never attempt bridge removal and regluing on good instruments—it's hard enough to find a pro who will do it perfectly. Cracks are no different, and again you shouldn't learn on good guitars. A screwed-up crack repair, however, usually just makes a guitar look bad. It lowers its value, but at least you can still play the instrument. Screw up a bridge, and the guitar's finished until you can find a pro to make things right (if possible)! This section focuses on teaching you how to begin bridge and crack work on low-quality instruments, and it should help you communicate with a professional when your guitar needs this type of work.

Bridges that are cracked, warped, poorly placed, loose, or lifted can have a detrimental effect on your guitar's intonation, tone, and playability. Bridge work is tricky and often fairly expensive, so consider the following points before attempting or authorizing any repairs. The most common mistakes made during bridge regluing are:

1 Harming the top wood around and under the bridge during removal.

2 Gluing the bridge on crooked (out of square to the center line).

3 Mounting it too far toward the bass or treble side, so that the strings fall off the fingerboard.

4 Not recognizing when a bridge should be entirely replaced rather than simply being reglued.

5 Trusting that the factory mounted the bridge is in the perfect spot (professionals always measure for themselves).

6 Failure to check inside the instrument for loose braces, etc., before you install the bridge.

7 Not letting the glue dry long enough. Allow a minimum of 24 hours for Titebond or hide glue, although two or three days is best.

8 Underestimating your own ability to do the job well!

9 You must understand the grain makeup of spruce (the most common top wood) in order to remove and replace a bridge correctly. Martin guitar tops are bookmatched—learn to "read" the book!

UNDERSTANDING SPRUCE GRAIN ORIENTATION

Martin repairman Dave Musselwhite offers this advice for determining grain orientation: "Bookmatched spruce is split, opened like a book, and the two edges (the center of the 'book') are glued together. This glueline becomes the centerline of the guitar top. On one half of the centerline the grain often looks darker than on the other. This darkness is caused by a small degree of natural 'run-out' in the spruce. When the top gets bookmatched, the run-out then goes in opposite directions of the centerline.

"When your light source catches the end grain of the runout, it will look darker—this tells you which way the grain is going. Where your light source is

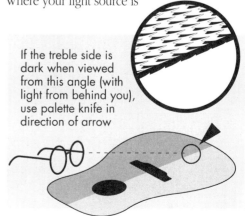

If the treble side is dark when viewed from this angle (with light from behind you), use palette knife in direction of arrow

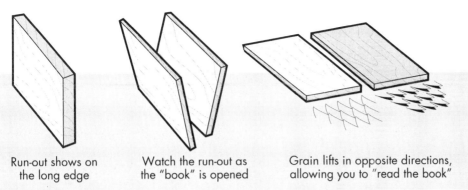

Run-out shows on the long edge

Watch the run-out as the "book" is opened

Grain lifts in opposite directions, allowing you to "read the book"

located, and in which direction you're looking at the top, determines on which side the top will look dark. My light source is behind me, and I look at the top with the peghead toward me . So at my workbench, looking in that direction, if the dark grain of the spruce is on the treble side, I'd attack the bridge from the rear on the treble side and from the front on the bass side. If the dark wood is on the bass side, reverse the operation. This way you will be working with the grain—not into it.

"The grain often lifts up in opposite directions on each side of the centerline. Considerable damage can be caused by pushing your pallette knife under the bridge if you go into and under the grain—rather than *over, and with the grain.* You can avoid potential problems if you know which direction the grain is running, because you can push your knife under the bridge going with the grain and get a clean separation. But it takes a lot of experience to develop your eye.

"Now this won't work on *every* guitar top. Some tops have so little run-out that both halves look the same when viewed from any direction. Then it's hard to know where to enter with the knife. In this case, it doesn't matter as much, because with no run-out, the grain doesn't lift at all. Bridges on such soundboards leave a perfect surface when they're removed. The wood fibers of a tree grow upward (the lengthwise grain). Some trees have straighter grain than others, and spruce is one of the straightest. But all spruce has some run-out, by nature of the way it grows. Run-out can also be a result of how the planks are cut."

Dana Bourgeois, another wood specialist, describes bookmatched spruce like this:

"If the two halves reflect light the same way, you have a top with very little run-out and you

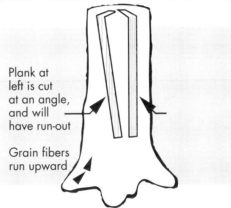

Plank at left is cut at an angle, and will have run-out

Grain fibers run upward

can come either way with your tool. There's no such thing as wood with a perfect level grain matrix; it will always run-in and run-out a little.

"I've removed bridges on tops which reflected light the same in all directions, but still lifted—because right in the bridge area there was localized run-out that I couldn't see. When I can see the darker grain, I anticipate an easy bridge removal because it's so obvious! And Dan, be sure to point out that understanding grain orientation is just as important if you have to remove the bridge pad—maybe more important."

Bridge replacement techniques

Bridges that are only slightly loose at their back edge can often be reglued without being completely removed. This is done by forcing glue into the gap and clamping the bridge in place to dry. As a rule, if you can slide one empty guitar-string package into the opening, take it in for a checkup.

When a bridge is removed, the goal is to break or loosen the glue joint between the bridge bottom and the top wood (usually spruce, cedar, or mahogany). This isn't easy to do, so beginners should only remove bridges on instruments with cheap plywood tops! Here are several accepted bridge-removal methods which are used by professionals:

1   Use heat to warm the glue joint by heating the bridge with the silicon rubber "heat strips" made by the Watlow company of St. Louis, Missouri. These strips are custom-made to the shape of the bridge, fastened to a metal "caul," and controlled by a rheostat. When the glue joint is softened, the bridge lifts off easily with a thin, wide, round-nosed palette knife. This same knife can be used to loosen the tongue during a neck reset. Here Dave Musselwhite of the Martin repair department demonstrates:

Dave Musselwhite shows the tools he uses for bridge removal.

Use the round-nosed palette knife from the rear of the bridge.

2   Strike the bridge/top glue line with a wide chisel to impact or shear it off.

3   Rout the bridge a little at a time with an appropriate router table and top protectors, and then warm up and peel off the last paper-thin layer. This method may sound extreme, but when done properly, there is little risk of damage to the top. Obviously, the router method is only appropriate when complete bridge replacement is necessary, and it should only be performed by a professional.

SOME IMPORTANT POINTS TO KEEP IN MIND:

■ Generally speaking, bridges shouldn't be removed with hot knives, since this method often scars the finish. Telltale marks from a bridge reglue are an unwanted and unnecessary side effect.

■ Some bridges warp up, curling away from the top. Once removed, a warped bridge can often be flattened by heating it, and then clamping it flat to dry into the proper shape. I have straightened a severely warped bridge by first soaking it in water, and then clamping it flat to dry.

■ Cheap guitars may have finish under the bridge, allowing it to pull loose. Remove the finish to get wood-to-wood contact.

■ A bridge may loosen because it's too flat to conform to the top's arch; it's not uncommon to carve the bridge bottom to match the top, or to make a new bridge with an arched bottom.

■ The original glue surfaces must be free of dirt and old glue. A small scraper or the back of a chisel is best for cleaning the bridge area on the top (*sometimes* with a little help from a gel-type stripper).

■ Use Titebond or hide glue (see "Glues" below) for bridge reglues.

■ After the bridge is on, wait at least 15 minutes, looking for any excess glue to squeeze out along the edges. With a damp rag, clean along the glue line until there's no squeeze-out left; you may have to clean the line four or five times.

■ Too much glue is as bad as too little glue—another reason that experience is important for gluing a bridge on properly. Over-gluing or under-gluing can weaken any wood joint; visit a good cabinet shop to get a feel for glue techniques. Spruce absorbs glue into the grain, so practice on scrap.

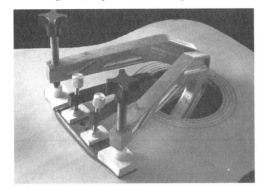

■ When installing a bridge, make cauls that match the bridge shape (above). Cauls spread clamping pressure and protect against clamp marks. It's wise to protect the guitar's interior—especially bracing—with cauls.

■ Gibson Montana uses a unique caul to glue bridges—it doesn't require a clamp. A metal fixture with 2 bolts is placed inside against the bridge pad, and the top fixture (these match the different bridge styles) fastens down tightly on the bridge by means of these 2 bolts. Then the individual pressure screws are tightened, much like the Martin bridge-gluing caul shown earlier.

Speaking of cauls, a sheet of clear acrylic (Plexiglas) in a ⅛", ³⁄₁₆", or ¼" thickness makes a great exterior support for crack and brace work. Being flexible, it can follow a top's arch while still keeping both sides of a crack level (top right; note the extra leveling screw). Its great strength, even in thin (⅛") sheets, gives the top protection from clamp marks and supports the pressure of clamped braces. The

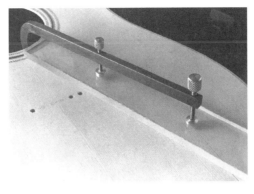

ability to see through a Plexiglas caul is a plus when lining up a clamp with a crack, especially when gluing the interior wooden crack supports known as cross patches. Also, acrylic won't stick to most top-repair glues.

GLUES USED FOR BRIDGE AND BRACE REPAIR

The glues most often used for bridge and brace repair are aliphatic resins such as Franklin's Titebond, fresh hide glue such as Behlen's Ground Hide Glue, and epoxy. Super glue has its place in "el cheapo" top repairs or in special situations, but then only when used by a pro. For the novice, Titebond is the best all-around top-repair glue because it allows the most working time before it sets, and it is not as permanent as epoxy.

Titebond, because of its high water content, causes cracks to swell—so you must be prepared fot that, know what you're doing, and work quickly. The swelling goes away after the glue is dry and the moisture has evaporated. Titebond is good for bridge regluing, and cleans up easily with warm water.

Hide glue is used by many experts for all vintage top repairs, not only because it's historically correct, but also because it dries clear and brittle (like the finish surrounding it) which enhances tone (especially on bridge

Except for normal bridge reglues, many poor bridge repairs end up being done as a way to avoid a neck reset. Why ruin a bridge just because you don't yet know how to reset a neck? Send the guitar to someone who does!

Note the small "cross patch" held in place by this Waverly clamp.

The professional repairperson will often introduce a controlled amount of excess moisture to a guitar or its environment, so dried-out cracks close quickly—then they can be glued and you won't have to wait 'til spring.

reglues). It swells wood less than Titebond, and can be worked easily into cracks. On the downside, hide glue sets into a "gel" very quickly as it cools, so you must be good to use it! The best hide glue is mixed fresh from granules and used hot.

Ready-to-use hide glue such as "Franklin's Liquid Hide Glue" has a shelf life, so always check that it will dry (on scrap) before using it. The chemicals which are added to off-the-shelf hide glue to keep it from going rancid, and to give it more working time, also cause it to lose the ability to dry once the shelf life has expired. I've had some nasty experiences with bad hide glue—be careful!

Epoxy, used correctly, is a great glue for joining cracks and for splints (pieces of wood inlayed into cracks). Never use epoxy for regluing bridges or loose braces, or anything that you might want to take apart sometime. Certain structural repairs can be done with epoxy, but shouldn't be attempted by a novice.

Super glue is great for tiny cracks that don't need to be aligned during the gluing operation. It sets so quickly that I'm not recommending it for most situations. However, many of us use it all the time (and often as a substitute for the glues mentioned above) because we have experience!

Winter cracks

Cracks are among the most common structural problems afflicting hollowbody guitars. Many a person has rushed his instrument to my shop, expecting me to read the last rites over his pride and joy just because of a simple split. While a split on the top, side, or back is certainly not to be ignored, if it's caught soon enough, it can be easily and inexpensively repaired—and quite invisibly, too. Guitars are, after all, made of wood, and wood splits. Of course, a mistreated guitar is bound to suffer damage. Too few people realize that lack of humidity can split even the best of instruments, causing as much of a crack as a sharp blow. In both cases, a simple

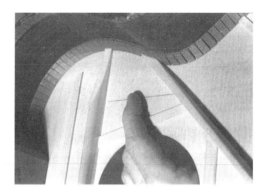

hairline crack is easily repairable, often without the need of a professional repairman.

HAIRLINE CRACKS

These may be very hard to see; often you can only spot one when holding the guitar at a certain position in the right light. Hairline cracks can be mistaken for checks or crazes, which are finish cracks that should be left alone and are nothing to worry about (besides, they cannot be repaired without serious finish work that could hamper a guitar's tone and value). Many of us love a checked or crazed finish and feel that it adds to a guitar's charm and character.

Here's a simple test for determining whether a crack is actually in the wood: Using the ball of your thumb or fingertip, press very gently along the edge of the crack and watch for any movement of the wood. Avoid pressing your fingernail against the wood, since this could leave a mark. If the wood is actually cracked, you will see a slight movement of the wood—most likely on the side of the crack that you're pressing on, since the pressure won't transmit across the split line. For a round-hole acoustic, remove the strings and apply pressure from the inside. If you can reach it, get your fingertip right under the crack, and press dead center (above). This should gently force the split open while you're looking from outside. Remember where you pressed, so that you can repeat the process later while gluing.

CRACK-GLUING METHODS

For the gluing and clamping operation, you'll need a bowl of warm water, some small pieces of clean cloth (3" x 3", some dipped in water and some dry), and good-quality masking tape that has lots of stretch. Squirt a dab of glue onto the fingertip of either hand,

and then quickly use your free hand to move the crack in the same direction as you did earlier, only this time work the hide glue into the open crack. Work in enough so that when you release the pressure, a slight bead squeezes out. Wipe off excess glue with a damp rag, and then wipe the entire area dry in preparation for clamping.

TAPE CLAMPING

At a right angle to the crack's length, apply the masking tape by rubbing/pressing with your thumb two or three inches from one side of the crack. Stretch the tape up and over the crack—without actually touching the tape to the crack—and press it down again about two or three inches on the opposite side. If the tape

is fresh and stretchy enough, the crack will close as the tape attempts to shrink back to size. Practice the taping operation with a dry run (no glue) until you get a feel for the tape's stretching qualities. Use as many pieces across the crack as necessary (sometimes I cover a crack completely for good pressure). If there's a glue squeeze-out each time you apply a piece of tape, wipe it off with a damp rag and redry the area so that the next piece of tape will stick. Let the glue dry at least 12 hours.

When the glue has dried, remove the tape by pulling at an angle (below). Peel it very carefully, since it's possible to remove small

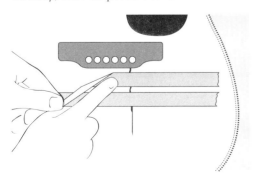

pieces of finish, especially on older instruments with thin, checked finishes. If you see finish coming off with the tape, rub the tape with your fingertip slightly ahead of the point where the tape is releasing from the body. This helps break the surface tension and allows easier removal of sticky tape. If you cleaned the glue bead well when it was still wet, you're done once the tape is removed. However, if there are still any dry glue beads that squeezed out, pick them off carefully with your fingernail or a sharp tool such as an X-acto knife. Buff the area with a soft, dry cloth and add any good guitar polish (Martin offers one).

BAR CLAMPING WITH CAULS—MARTIN STYLE

Instead of using tape you can use cauls to protect the guitar and finish and clamp a crack together. When possible, it's good to use a second clamp from top to bottom to keep the crack aligned. The four photos show Milt Hess Jr., head structural repairman in the C.F. Martin repairshop, clamping a crack. Milt offers this advice:

"With hairline cracks on the top, sides, or back, push on the crack from the inside to open it up, and saturate the crack with water. This 'pre-moistening' of the crack causes the glue which follows to be drawn deeper into the wood for better glue penetration."

1 The crack will close up (the bridge is taped off to protect it from glue and water).

2 After the water, work plenty of glue into the crack, from the outside, until it penetrates thoroughly (look inside with a mirror). Be generous with the glue (Milt generally uses a Titebond-type glue).

3 Clean the excess glue off with a damp rag, and using cauls and a long bar clamp, *gently* squeeze the crack together. The bar clamp rests on a ½" thick clear Plexiglas caul. The Plexiglas keeps the crack level and gives the clamp something to rest on.

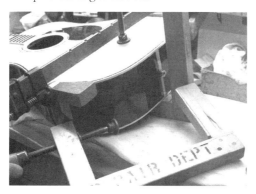

4 A second clamp (like the one in the foreground) and the plexiglass caul keep the two sides of the crack level.

SUPER-GLUING CRACKS

Small "fissure" cracks often look like tiny splits in the finish but are actually in the wood (usually from a lack of humidity in the guitar's enrivonment). These kind of cracks don't really move (you can't wiggle them or open them up), but they don't go away either! They're most common in the sides about 1" from the top or back (where the kerfing which holds the side to the top or back stops and the

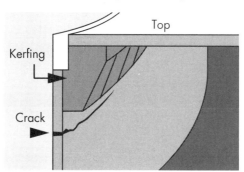

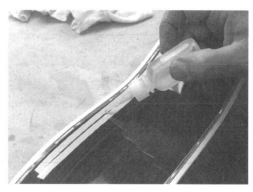

wood is free to move). Wood movement at this point can cause a crack. If the guitar has a healthy lacquer finish, these cracks (and the finish) can be filled with super glue—several coats at a time, letting each coat dry—then sanded smooth, lacquered over, and buffed out. Here is the procedure used by repairman Dan Shook at the Martin repair department.

1 Tape off each side of crack.

2 Run super glue deeply into crack until it builds slightly above finish—let dry (above).

3 Remove the tape—the crack is more than filled with super glue.

4 Scrape the mounded super glue flush with the finish surface.

5 Scuff sand with 220-grit into the surrounding finish.

6 Spray fresh lacquer over area. These coats of lacquer have melted into the original finish (one of the nice things about lacquer—it dissolves itself!), and can now be wet-sanded and buffed. You'll never see the finished crack.

SPLINTING CRACKS THAT WON'T CLOSE

Many cracks won't close easily (or at all) and cannot be repaired using the gluing method for hairline cracks just described. An open split that you can look into may need to be filled with a piece of matching wood. This process, called "splinting," should be done by a professional. Often, but not always, a large crack will close up in the spring as humidity increases, and then it may be glued with little trouble and no splinting. In fact, if the crack was splinted when the humidity was low, the fill might be "spit out" by the wood as it attempts to close and return to normal. Therefore, let a professional determine whether a large crack should be splinted during the dry season, left until spring to swell shut, and then simply be glued; or glued and splinted in the spring or summer (moist months).

Those cracks which *are* wide, stable, and

no longer swell shut in summer should be splinted with a sliver of matching wood (spruce, rosewood, or mahogany on most guitars). Some cracks only need a small thin sliver of wood, while others require a fairly wide insert. Spruce tops are splinted more often than rosewood backs and sides, and are the most difficult to match because of the lighter shade of wood. Most spruce splints are made from the soft wood which occurs between the darker hard grains, since the crack occurs when soft wood splits away from the hard grain.

With the narrower cracks, before gluing in a splint, I use a "crack knife" to clean dirt from the crack and make its edges parallel. It also tapers the walls slightly, to keep the spruce fill from falling through. This crack knife was designed by the Martin repair department. I discovered it on page 48 of Irving Sloane's excellent book *Guitar Repair* (most of the photos in Irving's book were taken in the Martin repair department). It's a wedge-shaped piece of steel that can enlarge and shape an open crack to a wedge, or "V" shape.

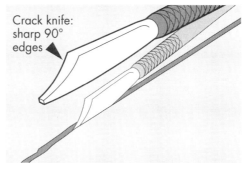

Crack knife: sharp 90° edges

I made my crack knife from a worn Swiss needle file by grinding off the teeth on the sides and bottom, and shaping it as shown in the photo. After grinding the sides of the file smooth, and to a wedge shape, the angular "face" is ground at a 35° to 45° angle and sharpened on a stone, leaving sharp 90° edges to the sides. The knife can be used in two ways: 1) On the push stroke the sharp edges of the face will actually cut both walls (or either wall alone) of a crack at once—creating shavings much like a chisel and shaping the crack's sidewalls to a wedge shape by removing wood. 2) Once the right amount of wood has been removed from the sidewalls to make the crack even in width, the knife can be drawn in the opposite direction along the crack's length, to smooth the "V" groove and slightly *compress* the wood outwards so that it can swell up when the splint is glued in. For more on this technique, see Irving's book—a very important reference book for all of us.

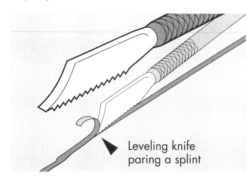

Leveling knife
paring a splint

An off-shoot of the crack knife is a crack *leveling* knife designed by my brother-in-law John O'Boyle, the long-time repairman for Thoroughbred Music in Tampa, Florida. Again, John's is a reshaped Swiss needle file. The face is ground just like the crack knife except that it comes to a distinct chisel point, and the side are not ground to a wedge shape. The teeth on the bottom edge of the file/crack-knife are not ground away—but left alone. What you get is a small, thin chisel with a sharp edge that meets the teeth of the file. With it, and depending on the angle at which you hold it, you can pare down the top of a wood fill, or splint, and file it smooth at the same time! John came up with this tool when working as my apprentice in '72, and we've used it ever since.

Now you've cleaned and tapered the crack walls and chosen a splint of wood, matching the area around the crack in color and grain pattern. Your splint should be slightly wider than the crack: it will then be gently

compressed so that it slides in easily. The wetness of the glue can swell both the crack and the splint, making insertion difficult—the compressed splint goes in easily and then swells up to full size. Once dry, a splint is pared level with (or sometimes lower than) the finish and carefully touched up with lacquer. This can be almost invisible when done by a pro.

Speaking of pros, one of the finest crack and touch-up men I know is Tom Marcell of Islip, New York. Tom spent many years studying with the great John Monteleone, and he's now a much sought-after vintage restoration expert (when he's not building classical guitars—very talented fellow). Tom taught me this method of splinting wide cracks, holes, or punctures:

1   Enlarge the crack on each side of a grain line following the grain's lengthwise pattern.

2   Measure the crack's width at ½" intervals and shape the splint to match any variations (some spruce is perfectly straight-grained and easy to match). Leave the splint wider than the crack by .005" for compressing later.

3   The splint is shaped as in this drawing. The splint is prefinished with several light coats of lacquer to help with color matching the refractive quality of spruce. The finish, which also keeps glue and color off the new wood, is wiped off with thinner after the splint is in, and a proper touch-up is done.

4   Glue the splint in with epoxy which has been colored with a fresco powder that matches the lighter-shaded softwood.

5   Paint surrounding grain lines over the bevelled "head" of the splint.

6 French-polish, drop-fill (see "Finish Repairs") or spray lacquer to blend the finish in.

Tom Marcell and John Monteleone

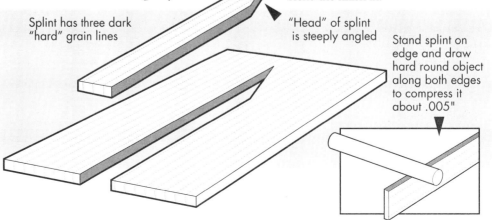

Splint has three dark "hard" grain lines

"Head" of splint is steeply angled

Stand splint on edge and draw hard round object along both edges to compress it about .005"

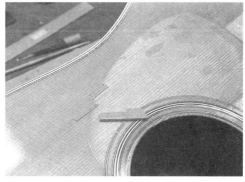

Slide these patches (with their original finish) forward, and they disappear!

SAVE THOSE BUSTED GUITARS!

Martin guitar repairman and vintage guitar expert Dave Musselwhite makes splints and patches from old Martin guitar tops and leaves the finish on. This guarantees a good color match and the correct vintage look. Once the patch is inlaid into the top, and flush with the surrounding finish, French-polishing or a lacquer "melt-in" make the touch-up complete.

TOP CRACKS CAUSED BY CURLING PICKGUARDS

Being a Northerner from Michigan, I had adjustments to make when I moved south to Athens, Ohio—almost to the Mason-Dixon line. Things are different down here. Instead of "hello," we say "hey, bud," and the local term for "yes" is "yeah, boy!" The weather's different, too—an inch of snow closes the schools, and some years it's possible to play golf in February—on grass! But it's not always that way, and when there's cold weather and dry heat, it means trouble for guitars made of wood—especially acoustics.

Besides humidity, another dryness-related problem that affects acoustic guitars with solid wood tops is the shrinking and curling of the pickguard and the damage it can cause to the wood underneath. Martin guitars are especially prone to such troubles, as are most would-be Martin competitors. Here's a list of common pickguard problems, along with their symptoms and suggested repair methods.

Martin pickguards shrink because they're made from either nitrate (until '76) or acetate ('76 until present) plastic. Both are notorious shrinkers, with the older nitrate being the worst. But, along with their good looks, these plastics were chosen because they sound good, too—and Martin's tried them all. The shrinking plastic wouldn't be a problem if it didn't take the wood with it. That's why Martin switched to pickguards backed with double-stick adhesive in late 1987; this modern adhesive allows the wood to move.

Wood needs the freedom to shrink in the dry winter months and swell during the humid summer. Up until 1987, the backs of Martin pickguards were brushed with a solvent to melt the plastic, and "glued" directly to the bare wood before the finish was applied. These glue joints don't move well with the wood, and as a result problems can occur: shrink cracks at the pickguard's inner or outer edges; curling of the pickguard and the top wood, sometimes causing the top wood to pull away from the main X-brace; or the pickguard falling off totally.

Shrink cracks along the pickguard's edge take years to get very big. Some aren't even visible, and lie just out of sight, soaking in moisture, sweat, grime, and guitar polish, all of which make any problem worse. Caught early, a small shrink crack can be sealed with lacquer or glue; this keeps it small and prevents it from absorbing moisture until it stabilizes. The most common pickguard cracks are the ones indicated by the arrows in the drawing below.

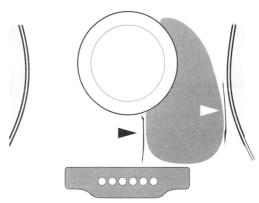

I've seen very few good old guitars with nitrate pickguards that didn't have some sort of shrinkage problem—but it never kept me from wanting them!

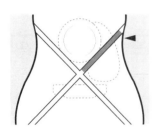

If these cracks are wide, stable, and won't close up, they must be splinted as mentioned above. But usually, if the crack is caught in time, it will reglue nicely, as described here:

1 Clean any lacquer chips or dirt from the crack with a sharp knife.

2 Saturate with water to swell the crack shut and draw in the glue.

3 Pressing the crack open from the inside, work in lots of Titebond from the outside with your free hand.

4 Use a caul, made to fit over the bracing, on the inside.

5 The Plexiglas caul, backed with a rubber block, flattens the crack as it dries (above right).

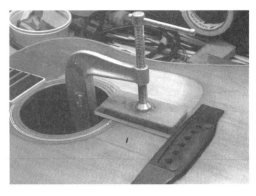

Curling pickguards are upsetting—even mild cases look scary. Severe curling may create a concave dip in the top, pulling the wood loose from the main X-brace (indicated by the arrow on the drawing at far left). By the way, loose braces should be fixed before using the crack-splinting techniques just mentioned. When appropriate, the pickguard can be removed to let the wood relax and flatten before being reglued to the brace. Removing the pickguard without pulling up spruce is tricky, so have it done by a professional shop with prior experience.

The mildest problems are pickguards that come either partially or completely loose of their own accord. The relief of stress often prevents any cracks, curls, or loose braces, so it's nice if nature does the job for you. A pickguard that's only loose around the edges can be reglued (at least temporarily) with white glue or hide glue and then clamped in place to dry. Don't use a permanent solvent-type glue such as Duco or super glue. Usually, it's best to take a pickguard off, then reglue or replace it.

When a pickguard's off, any glue residue should be removed from the top, and the bare wood should be sealed before any remounting is done. I generally seal the bare wood with a coat or two of lacquer or shellac. Once dry and sanded smooth, the hard surface gives future adhesives something to cling to rather than the wood itself. As for the proper remounting glue, follow Martin's lead—use double-stick adhesive, or buy a real Martin pickguard. If you make your own pickguard, mount it with a spray adhesive such as 3M-77 or use double-stick adhesive carpet tape. And don't mount it on the bare wood!

AVOIDING CRACKS

If you heat entirely with wood, keep a large kettle of water on or near the stove at all times to maintain some moisture in the air. Electric home humidifiers that are faithfully filled with water do a good job. There are also several in-case humidifiers available which were mentioned at the start of this chapter. You can make your own in-case humidifier by cutting a piece of kitchen sponge to fit a plastic soap box (the type used for storing soap when traveling) through which several small holes have been punched with an awl or icepick. Soak the sponge in water, squeeze out the excess until damp, and shut it in the plastic box. Kept in the accessory compartment of your case, this helps protect your guitar from cracks due to the excess dryness in winter.

Please, if you have any doubts about your ability to repair your acoustic's top, don't attempt it yourself. It can be fixed—somehow, somewhere, by someone. There are great repairmen (and -women) out there. Choose one who will study the problem and not just do the first thing that comes to mind. A person with the necessary skills, tools, and talent to do a given repair needs only the method—and that's often different every time. Since there's no one "right" way to do any of these repairs, figuring out the best approach is half the fun!

. . . .

Clamping loose braces

With all acoustic guitars, and especially flat-tops, problems can arise which are related to the top's construction and its reaction to the pull of the strings. Aside from accidental damage (punctures and serious breaks) and the normal cracks discussed above, loose bracing is one of the most common structural problems with the acoustic guitar. A good repairshop can take care of most loose braces, and knowing a little about these repairs will help you choose the right shop. I don't recommend that you attempt brace regluing on any good guitar—leave that to the pros because often it's a one-shot deal.

Throughout the 1930s and early '40s, the highly-desirable "Adirondack," or "red" spruce was used exclusively for tops and for braces—until the end of World War II. The war effort used a tremendous amount of spruce for airplane propellers, ship masts, rigging, and the like, so that at war's end the supply of red spruce was depleted. Gibson and Martin switched to sitka spruce at that time (and they've continued using sitka until the present). Repairs on these vintage instruments should be done with red-spruce if they're to look right (another reason shops save smashed instruments—especially vintage ones).

The two main X-braces, in the bridge area, are the first place to look for looseness. Before beginning your inspection, vacuum the interior of the guitar *thoroughly*, and follow with a blow-out using compressed air. Try to avoid blowing dirt *into* a glue joint, however. Vacuum and blow—repeating the operations several times. Then use a mirror and an interior light to check for a gap between the top or back and any brace (this should be done with the guitar tuned to pitch). A loose brace will show as a dark shadow. The best mirror is the 2 ¼" round Telescoping Guitar Mirror which extends to 11". It's really a good idea to inspect your guitar's bracing from time to time.

A good inspection light can be made with a porcelain fixture and a low-wattage bulb. I scrounged my parts at an electric supply—they're probably refrigerator replacement parts or something. You can rig up a similar one by asking a few questions at your local electric shop. I plug the light into the on/off footswitch which I use for my Dremel Tool router. The footswitch leaves both hands free to work, and the bulb (which does generate heat) is only on when I'm actually looking with the mirror. Caution: If you make a lamp, be sure it's insulated at the terminals to protect against shock, and properly grounded.

Gibson flat-tops up until the late '50s were constructed much the same as in the '30s—with thin, light bracing that wasn't tucked into the lining very deep. Because of the light construction, it's more common to find loose (or cracked) brace ends on a Gibson than on a Martin. Cracked brace ends on *any brand* of

Whatever it is, it can be fixed—somehow, somewhere, by someone!

guitar are usually the result of a less-than-perfect piece of wood being chosen for the brace (not well quarter-sawn).

Until the early '60s, Gibsons and Martins were constructed with hide glue, and their braces can be cleaned and reglued easily. Sometime during the '60s manufacturers began using white glues; these glue joints can be cleaned and reglued too, but they're a little more difficult than hide glue. Another nice thing about hide glue is that it can be reconstituted with warm water or fresh hide glue; so if you haven't cleaned the glue from a joint perfectly, what's left inside will soften and help reglue the joint (Titebond doesn't do this as well even though it too is water-soluble).

It's best to remove as much of the old glue as possible from the bad glue joint (the brittle hide glue removes the easiest). I use a variety of spatulas, feeler gauges, thin saw blades, sandpaper strips, and scrapers to remove dirt and glue from between a brace and the top or back. The "Sandplate" files, which are toothed and act like "Steel Sandpaper," make great cleaners if you remove the self-stick backing with lacquer thinner. Sometimes you must fashion a wooden, plastic, or metal "arm" just to reach a loose spot on a particular guitar. Attach the cleaning tool to the arm with super glue or masking tape (later any arm you fashion can be used to apply glue and to hold a cleanup-rag afterward).

BASIC RULES FOR CLEANING GLUE JOINTS

■ Never use a tool that's too thick to fit comfortably in the gap (unless you are purposely "wedging" the brace open while you clean—which I do often).

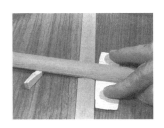

■ If you use an abrasive to clean (sandpaper or "Sandplate"), sand with the grain if it's facing up (to avoid cross-grain scratch marks). I like to reach inside and work sandpaper with my fingers on each side of the brace as shown at left. I use the same technique with thin feeler gauges to apply glue later for good coverage and penetration.

■ Don't force crud into a corner or under an area so that it can't be removed.

■ Vacuum and blow repeatedly one last time before gluing.

GLUE APPLICATION

■ Hide glue or Titebond are the best glues for loose braces, and since hide glue should only be mixed fresh and is hard to use, that leaves Titebond on top. It gives you plenty of working time and cleans up well with warm water.

■ Lay rags or paper inside to protect against glue dripping onto the opposite surface (top or back) while you work.

■ Don't use sandpaper as a palette knife to apply glue, because if it becomes soggy it may tear off and get stuck in the glue joint.

■ Practice all glue application and clamping procedures "dry" (without glue) until you can do it quickly.

■ Use the same probes, arms, and reaching tools to clean up the glue squeeze-out. I tape damp or wet pieces of cloth to the ends of my reaching tools to reach difficult areas.

■ A hypodermic syringe makes a great glue applicator. Slide several pieces of the heat-shrink tubing used for electrical work over the needle as a depth-stop to let you know when you're into the glue joint.

CLEANUP

Most interior repairs can be done with little or no glue smear showing in or around the area. This takes careful planning, taping-off, clever application, skill, speed, and sometimes skinny arms. The best repairers are the ones who don't try the first technique that comes to mind. It may be necessary to think for days about the right way to approach a loose brace, crack, or crunch. There is almost no excuse for a sloppy interior glue job!!

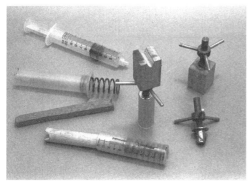

CLAMPING

We use the same clamps on braces that we do for gluing bridges and bridge pads. We also use a variety of jacks, cauls, props, and what have you to push the loose brace against the flat surface of the top or back (above). Again, it can take many "dry runs" to find the solution for a given situation.

BASIC CLAMPING RULES

■ Don't use glue until you know that the clamping setup is correct.

■ Consider training a child or smaller person to apply glue to (or clean) an area which you can't reach.

■ Always use protective "cauls" to keep the clamp from crushing the bracing.

■ Protect the outside surface from the clamp, and use a caul (I like Plexiglas) to spread the clamp pressure evenly.

■ If the clamp won't reach find (or make) one that will. The long 11" Waverly Guitar Clamps will reach most anywhere.

CLAMPING A CRACKED END BLOCK

When a guitar gets dropped on the butt-end, it will probably split through the block if there's a strap button installed. We see this often in a repairshop. The end block will usually split in one of two ways, and it depends on the grain structure of the individual block: 1) Straight split clear through; 2) Angular split. These are pictured at right, above.

It's harder to get glue into an angled split. In either case it's important to glue all the way throught the break. The best method I've found is very similar to what caused the break in the first place: driving a wedge into the end block hole.

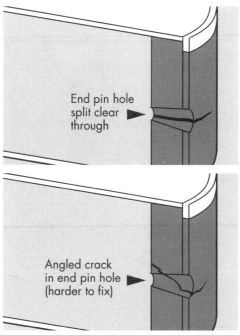

End pin hole split clear through

Angled crack in end pin hole (harder to fix)

1/4" plexi-glas sheet

tapered dowel

threaded bolt

I use a hollow aluminum tapered dowel as a "spreader," inserted from the inside and through the end-block hole. A simple ¼-20 machine bolt runs through the dowel and is long enough that a Plexiglas caul can be slipped over it on the outside. Tighten the bolt and the spreader slowly opens the crack—just enough to make it easy to insert glue with a feeler gauge or with a syringe.

CLAMPING A LONG CRACK IN THE SIDE

Simple cracks in the side are easy to spread open and work Titebond glue into, and can then be clamped with spool clamps. Some cracks in the sides, however, run along one side all the way around (and through) the end-block. Take your time aligning this type of crack, and practice the clamping procedure "dry" many times. You may need two people to align such cracks, and then the other person must have a feel for the job.

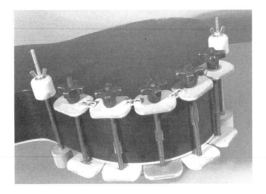

I came up with a "clamping-belt" which enables me to do some of these long cracks all by my lonesome. The particular glue job that required this clamp could not have been done without it, so the hours spent making the tool were well spent (and since that time I have used it often). The point I want to make is that you must go to whatever lengths are necessary to get the job done right. If you're taking your axe to a repairshop, don't be too timid to ask the repair technician how he or she might go about the glue-up. If they don't appear confident, don't leave the guitar!

The bridge pad: repairing worn and jagged bridge pin holes

The bridge pad—also known as the bridge plate—is the reinforcing piece of hardwood glued inside the top of a steel-string acoustic to support the bridge area. The string ball-ends pull against it when strung to pitch. Years of wear, poor drilling during an earlier repair or in manufacturing, and sloppy string installation may cause chips, splintering, wear, and tearing on the pad's underside. The two most common methods for solving bridge pad problems are pulling out and replacing the entire pad, or gluing a thin veneer over a damaged pad. On a quality instrument, the method used, and the execution of that method, should be left to a pro.

Some symptoms of a pad in need of repair are: 1) String slots at the front edge of the bridge pin holes that are overly deep and too close to the saddle slot. 2) String ball-ends that no longer hold against the pad, allowing the string windings to reach onto the saddle. 3) A bent, kinked, warped or collapsed top in the bridge area. 4) The feeling that your guitar should have better tone, volume, and sustain —especially if the nut, frets, and saddle have all been properly fit and adjusted.

■ Removing and replacing the pad is not an easy task. The same type of Watlow silicone rubber heating pads mentioned earlier for bridge removal are also used to heat the bridge pad. The glue softens enough so that the pad can be pried loose. A variety of spatulas, hooks, and scrapers are often needed to coax the stubborn bridge pad out. The commercially made removal tools shown above are a big help—especially the long one with the handle. It is a variation of the one used at the Martin guitar company for many years.

The handle allows you to move the spatula blade from side-to-side while at the same time pulling it into the glue joint (which was heated immediately before). A great deal of knowledge and experience is needed to keep the tool from cutting up and through the delicate spruce top. Note: The same knowledge of grain orientation which is required for clean bridge removal applies also to the bridge pad!

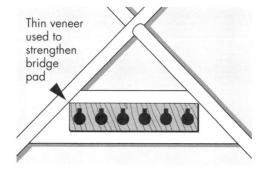

Quarter-sawn bridge pad splits like this

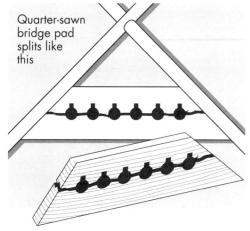

Thin veneer used to strengthen bridge pad

The best replacement wood for a bridge pad is maple or rosewood (Brazilian rosewood, if you can get it). In general, the bridge pad should be replaced with one that matches the original—particularly on a vintage instrument. There are times when a somewhat larger pad is needed to flatten a warped top or give more support (especially on plywood-topped guitars). Traditionally, bridge pads were made of quarter-sawn (vertical-grained) wood which ran at right angles (cross-grain) to the length of the top. The only problem with this design is that if the bridge splits through the bridge pin holes, the bridge pad splits right along with it! Because of this, I prefer to use a grain (it can be flat-sawn, quartered, or in-between) that runs at an oblique angle to the top as in the drawing below. On good guitars, the pad shouldn't be too thick, either—from .090" to .125" maximum (.100" is the average).

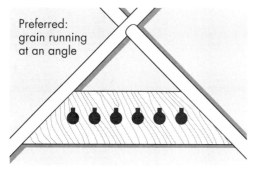

Preferred: grain running at an angle

When replacing a bridge pad, never use epoxy! I prefer hide glue: I think it enhances tone, although I use Titebond often (depending on the age and history of the guitar). And, before you drill new bridge-pin holes through the pad, a backer block should be clamped inside to keep the holes clean and unchipped!

Another accepted repair method for a worn out bridge pad is to veneer the underside of the original pad with a reinforcing piece of wood. This piece only needs to be big enough to add strength, and to give the strings something to pull against. It should definitely not be too thick or it may dampen the tone. A good thickness is from .030" to .070". I generally use Titebond glue for these "veneer" jobs.

A third and simple "quickie" method is to work a Bondo-type filler (represented by black, at right) into the worn or chipped holes. Use a rubber squeegee and wear a rubber glove. Once it is dry, remove the excess filler with small scrapers and sanding blocks and seal the plate's repaired area with several layers of Special T super glue. Then carefully redrill the bridge-pin holes with a backer block inside, and create the string notches using the miniature jigsaw and an upstroke to keep from pulling the new filler out of the holes.

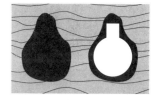

And here's a fourth and somewhat trickier way to repair just the worn areas of the existing pad—the method I used on my own 1944 Gibson J-45. The original small maple pad was terribly worn, but it was still well-glued even after 50 years and had warped gracefully along with the top. I felt that removing and replacing the pad might harm the guitar's tone. (The best time to repair a bridge pad is when the bridge is off—the case with my J-45—but this method can be used with a bridge in place if you're very careful).

■ Make a bridge pad-shaped caul of ⅜" thick pine or soft wood band-sawed to conform to the inside curve of the top. Make the caul wider than the pad by ¼" on both long edges (upper left, next page).

■ Fasten a layer of wax paper to the underside of the pad with double-stick tape.

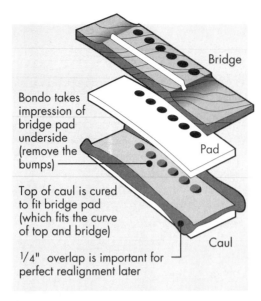

Bondo takes impression of bridge pad underside (remove the bumps)

Top of caul is cured to fit bridge pad (which fits the curve of top and bridge)

1/4" overlap is important for perfect realignment later

Bridge

Pad

Caul

■ Spread a "frosting" of Bondo on the caul and clamp it inside against the wax paper-protected top until the Bondo squishes up against the pad. Clamp it *lightly* so as not to flatten the top's arch at all. The caul being slightly wider than the pad lets the Bondo flow over each edge, and the "impression" taken guarantees exact realignment of the caul later. Note: Spread a rag inside the guitar to catch any Bondo droppings!

■ When it dries—about five minutes—remove the caul and file off the high spots of Bondo where it molded into the holes of the pad. You'll have a perfect imprint of the underside of the pad with six hollow areas, or "pockets," where you removed the high spots.

■ Wax the face of the new Bondo caul, let it dry, apply double-stick tape over the face, and stick a sheet of waxed paper to it. The wax insures that the caul won't super-glue to the pad later.

■ Clamp the caul inside the guitar against the pad.

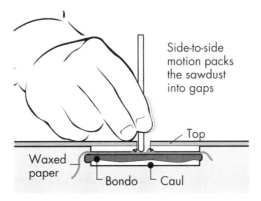

Side-to-side motion packs the sawdust into gaps

Top

Waxed paper

Bondo   Caul

■ File a block of whatever wood matches the bridge pad (usually rosewood or maple) to get a pile of fine sawdust.

■ Sprinkle sawdust down from the top through the bridge pin holes, and with a small, blunt, round-bottomed tool, pack it into the pockets (below). Don't tear the waxed paper!

■ Compressed air blown into a hole with a rubber-tipped blowgun will further force the sawdust down and out into the pockets.

■ Use a pipette to drop water-thin super glue down the hole in a pool and watch as it wicks into the sawdust. Don't fill the hole so deep that the super glue gets out and onto the spruce top, since that could inhibit a good bridge reglue later.

■ After all the holes are filled, drip a little accelerator into each hole to guarantee a cure. Better yet, let the fills dry several hours—the glue-saturated sawdust may need extra time.

■ Remove the caul and check your work. The wear spots should be smoothly filled, so smooth them if they're rough.

■ When the holes are repaired, use the caul as a "backer" when you redrill the holes to keep the pad from tearing out again. The filled area will be as hard as the surrounding wood and can be renotched as if it were new.

The drawback to this last method is that the super glue saturates the top, pad, and bridge—"welding" them together (this could make it tough to remove the pad later). I chose this method for my guitar because it "felt right," and I knew I could get the pad out if I ever had to. Because of this "welding," I'm not necessarily advising this for your guitar (nor would I use it on a customer job without due notice).

Avoid bridge pad problems by installing strings carefully (it helps to use an inspection mirror as you do this). Push each string into the hole and see that the winding and ball end are at the front and pulling into the slot as you put the bridge pin in. Install one string at a time and tune up slowly, watching with the mirror to see that the ball end settles in. And if your bridge pins are bent or worn, replace them.

That's it. Of course you shouldn't try this type of work unless you're well-practiced at it. If not, go to the best repair shop you can find.

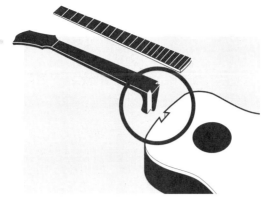

There's a detailed series of articles on neck resetting by William Cumpiano in issues 5, 6, 7, 8, and 10 of *The String Instrument Craftsman*. Find the back issues and check them out!

Neck resets

If you own an acoustic guitar with a stiff, hard-to-play action, or if it isn't as loud as you might wish, don't be alarmed if your guitar surgeon suggests an operation called a neck reset. The life of your favorite guitar may depend on your knowing the basics of this common yet difficult surgery. This is not a "how-to" for hobbyists, but a basic rundown of the neck resetting process as I know it.

The need for a neck reset is generally a natural result of the settling of an instrument's wood and joints. This movement of the top, sides, back, and neck block, coupled with the up-pull on the neck and top exerted by string pressure, can cause the strings to gradually rise further from the fingerboard. Other reasons for resetting a neck include improper fit to begin with (causing poor action that becomes more noticeable and unbearable with age), and glue joint failure (often due to dryness), where the neck is pulling away from the body. If the guitar has great action but isn't putting out the volume it should, it could be due to a low bridge saddle (backtrack to the section on saddle setups for details). Resets are often performed just so a luthier can raise the saddle height and drastically improve a guitar's sound.

A new guitar with any of these problems may be a candidate for factory warranty repair; your repairman will know. In general — especially with older guitars—don't blame the maker, but accept the settling as natural and often unavoidable for a delicately made

acoustic instrument. Whether it's used or new, if you really care about your guitar, be willing to pay for the job out of your own pocket, and have it done by a skilled repairman with whom you can discuss the instrument. Use the following information as a basis for discussing the methods to be employed.

Before work is started, the luthier must determine the best method for separating the neck and body joint. Most often, this involves a "dovetail" joint (above). The preferred method is to first loosen the fingerboard tongue with heat, and then steam the joint apart. This is done by removing the fret just past the body joint, drilling a small hole, and injecting steam into the dovetail joint. This method usually works for Gibson, Martin, Guild, Gretsch, Harmony, Kay, and most traditional American guitars. Some of the joints and glue used on the less-expensive imports, however, have surprised more than one luthier, myself among them. Prior experience and quick decision-making are a necessity for good results.

Luthier Charlie Longstreth, who services both Light's For Music in Springfield, Oregon, and McKenzie River Music in nearby Eugene, came across a neck removal setup that makes for a clean steam operation. It's an Erlenmeyer

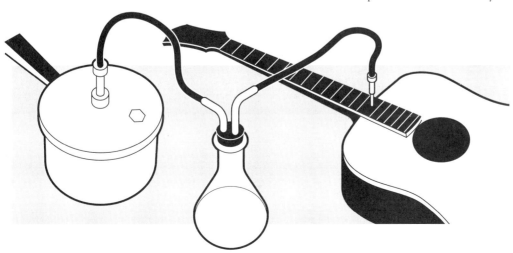

flask from a chemistry lab with two glass tubes in the rubber stopper top—one for the wet, boiling steam to enter (where it leaves much of the moisture behind) and the other for the "dry" steam to exit on its way to the neck joint (previous page). This is not a tool you'd try yourself, but a good one to tell your luthier about if he's using a steamer without a moisture trap. He'll know the safety precautions to take with steam. Dry steam causes less swelling and finish problems than the other methods.

After steaming, the neck is gently pulled up and out of the dovetail socket. Any excess glue is quickly removed while still wet, and the neck/fingerboard and top/neck block joints are allowed to dry (I gently clamp those parts while they're drying to insure that they don't come unglued).

Once the wood is thoroughly dry, a small portion of the neck heel is trimmed away with an extremely sharp chisel, changing the neck-to-body angle and bringing the strings closer to the fingerboard. Much experience and a keen eye are needed for knowing how much wood to remove during this heel shaping. If you get the chance, ask to see and play a completed neck set done by a shop you're looking into.

When I visited the Martin repair department I paid special attention to how they go about neck resetting. Milt Hess, Jr. does most of the neck removing, and then he jobs out the neck refitting to Dave Bosich or Dave Musselwhite. Bosich is the foreman of the neck setting department for production—he's incredible to watch. Here are the 10 steps they follow:

1 An infrared heatlamp loosens the tongue/top glue joint.

2 The bridge removal spatula is used to pry up the tongue.

3 A pressure cooker, mounted under the workbench, provides the steam. The pressure cooker is attached to a strong rubber hose connected to a bicycle-pump needle which is inserted into a hole drilled at the 15th fret to steam the joint, and the neck is worked free.

4 The glue is cleaned from both parts immediately, and the neck and body are left to dry.

5 Lacquer thinner, painted along the heel, softens the finish so that it won't chip when the heel is trimmed.

6 The "cheeks" of the heel are trimmed with a file or chisel.

7 The dovetail itself is trimmed, or else a shim is placed in the female portion of the joint.

8 An aluminum template rests on the fretboard and indexes off the neck—letting Dave Bosich know when the set is right.

9 After a final dry-fitting the neck will be glued in...

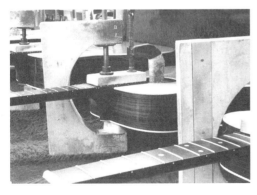

10 And left overnight to dry.

It's not uncommon for a neck reset to require some fret work afterward—either partial or total. The need for fret work can usually be judged beforehand, but remember that when wood is heated and steamed apart, a lot of changes such as loosened frets and swelling can occur. Remember, fret work is often the way of controlling the instrument's final playability. On a difficult neck removal, minor damage to the finish caused by escaping steam may also be encountered, requiring expert touch-up. Finish touch-up (even spraying) is common with neck sets, and often unpredictable!

The easy resets are the older guitars constructed with animal (hide) glue, which requires little heat and steam. The toughies are guitars built with modern glues and those with wide, thin heels (some Guild and Gibson models) that have more glue area. Wide heels tend to swell and crack from the steam, too. Guitars with fingerboard binding require special care to avoid burning or melting the plastic during the reset process. Neck resets aren't so simple, are they?

The principles governing flat-top acoustic guitar resets apply also to arch-top acoustics and electric guitars. As a rule, these guitars don't require resets often, thanks to their adjustable bridges. Exceptions are old Les Pauls with trapeze tailpieces, some mid-'70s SGs and Les Pauls with shallow neck angles, and occasional semi-hollowbody ES models, especially those with non-Bigsby tremolos. Most of these Gibson neck-set problems are solved by slightly grinding down the bottom of the bridge. When you find a Gibson solidbody requiring a reset, expect to lay out some dough, since they aren't easy, even for the factory pros. Early Gretsch guitars are often found to have loosened at the dovetail and fingerboard extension. But don't shy away from buying an old Gretsch because of neck problems—once fixed and set up right, they're hard to beat.

A variation for neck resetting involves removing the fingerboard tongue over the body to reach the joint, rather than removing the neck and fingerboard as one (when this method is used, the fingerboard should be cut

Bryan Galloup designed this fixture for *pushing* the neck out as the steam loosens the joint!

a few frets up the neck—not at the body joint—to keep a strong wood joint). Another way is to loosen only the fingerboard and "slip" the neck by bending it back into perspective; or the back, side, and neck-block joints can be loosened to squeeze the heel in. Of these last three methods, the first is

permissible in some situations, but the latter two "slip 'n' squeeze" methods should only be used on inexpensive quickies.

A neck reset is nothing to fear, but find the right person for the job. Get more than one luthier's opinion. Barring unforeseen problems, a neck reset will probably last 20 years or more—maybe even a lifetime, if the wood has truly finished settling. For getting a less-than-perfect flat-top to play and sound its best, neck resets are as important as good fret work and well-fit nuts and saddles.

11 OTHER IMPORTANT REPAIRS

The last 30 years of guitar repair

Twenty-five years ago, none of us imagined the changes and refinements that the guitar would go through, not to mention the scores of accessories and after-market modifications that are available today. With few exceptions, guitars are being built better than ever, and manufacturers are taking advantage of high technology without losing touch with craftsmanship. Many changes have occurred in the repair business, too, since 1963, with successful repairmen keeping up with the trends and improving their skills along the way. Now more good repairpeople are available than ever before, thanks to repair schools, apprenticeships, and new books and video instruction. *Guitar Player*'s repair columns should take special credit for turning players into knowledgeable, finicky customers, and thereby causing all of us repairmen to keep on our toes and do our best work. Here are some observations on the repair business in general, along with a few good suggestions for those of you interested in this type of training.

Of course, great luthiers have been around for hundreds of years, but in 1963 they were much harder to find. Many of the repair shops grew out of the folk boom of the late '50s and early '60s. Some of the well-known ones included New York City's Folklore Center; the Herb David Guitar Studio in Ann Arbor,

My friend and teacher, Herb David, surrounded by my brother-in-law John O'Boyle (repairman for Tampa's Thoroughbred Music), shop boy David Surovell, and yours truly. Photo circa 1974. Over the years, many excellent repairmen have come from Herb's shop.

Michigan; and the shops of Randy Wood in Nashville, Don Teeter in Oklahoma City, and John Lundberg in Berkeley, California. I got my start at Herb David's in 1963. And unless you were within driving distance of such places, you were in trouble when the bridge popped off your Martin D-28. Nowadays most states have at least several skilled repairmen, many of whom are listed in the Yellow Pages. Most modern music stores offer in-house setups and minor repairs, and personnel can direct you to a qualified repairman for serious problems. It wasn't so easy 25 years ago.

I've known many good luthiers over the years who have called it quits and "gone back to school" in order to provide for a family; they would find a better living to be made in the 1990's. Guitar players and luthiers in general get a lot more respect these days. Because there are more players and more guitars being made than ever before, more instruments get broken or need professional setup. The sheer number of customers out there makes guitar repair a viable way to make a living (not just a labor of love).

Guitar styles have advanced so much in the last few years that players must have far better set up instruments than in the old days, when you used to hear excuses like, "My strings are too high," or "It won't play in tune" every time someone missed a lick. Today's styles call for a comfortable action, well-dressed frets that eliminate buzz, and proper intonation. This type of setup work is usually performed by qualified repairmen after the sale. It depends on personal choice and can take several hours to do properly. I know repairmen in larger cities who do nothing but set up guitars and never get into serious woodworking on broken instruments. A good setup man is usually a good player who gets lots of work by word of mouth. Never be surprised if it takes more than one trip to even the best of repairmen to get the feel you're after; in the old days, players would get rid of guitar after guitar simply for lack of a proper setup specialist.

Thanks to new techniques in woodworking, new glues and tools, and knowledge gained from experience, repairmen have improved each year. The newcomer to our trade finds many roads already paved and is therefore able to reach a higher degree of skill faster, especially after studying such great repair books as Don Teeter's two-part *The Acoustic Guitar*, Hideo Kamimoto's *Complete Guitar Repair*, Irving Sloan's *Guitar Repair*, and a host of building and construction books available at most luthier supply stores or local bookstores. If you are interested in repairing guitars, start acquiring a library on the subject. You can usually find all the *Guitar Player* back issues with repair columns by Rick Turner and John Carruthers on microfilm at a fair-sized library. Another good, simple book is Pieter Fillet's *Do-It-Yourself Guitar Repair*, which is inexpensive and geared for the average player. If you're a video-instruction nut, there are a number of videos on the subject. Video courses are a good substitute for looking over a craftsman's shoulder, but in the old days I'd have given my eyeteeth for Don Teeter's books.

Personal instruction in building and repairing guitars and related instruments is available if you've the time and money to leave home for a month or two. Some repairmen augment their income or take a needed break from shop routine by taking on students for training. Although recently retired from the teaching business, I have taken on at least a dozen students over the years and know that in-shop training can be a great experience for teacher as well as for student. Several schools of lutherie are listed in the back of this book (many of the photos were taken in a repair school—"Bryan Galloup's Guitar Hospital" in Big Rapids, Michigan—Bryan took over my shop and school when I moved to Stewart-MacDonald). I have met graduates of all these programs and have been impressed by their work. Write for these schools' brochures.

A last major change is the incredible availability of specialized tools and supplies for the trade. In fact, many would be of interest to the average player who just dabbles in a little setup here and there. If you're a woodworker interested in building and fixing guitars, send for all the supply catalogs listed at the end of this book. All in all, the guitar repair business is doing better than ever. And best of all, we're hearing fewer horror stories ("I took my guitar in for a fret-job and got it back needing a new neck"), thanks to the larger number of skilled repairmen willing to respect their customers' interests. If you're not into the fix-it business, support your local repairman—he needs it.

Super glue repairs and touch-ups

Super glues can be very versatile when applied to guitar repair. Since several varieties are available, here's a rundown on the different glues and accessories, as well as typical situations in which guitar players, builders, and repairmen can benefit from this glue's instant cure and super strength.

Hot Stuff Original Formula, in the red-label bottle: Its water-thin consistency allows it to "wick" (seep and penetrate) into cracks and hard-to-get areas that are untouchable by other glues. Hot Stuff's drying time is so fast (1-10 seconds) that parts must be prealigned, or they often freeze in place before being perfectly mated. Some typical uses for the red-label Hot Stuff are:

■ Nut repair. Use with bone dust to build up worn slots (see drawing at right).

■ Gluing hairline splits in the top, back, sides, bridge cracks, etc.

■ Fret work. Regluing fingerboard chips caused by fret removal, or fill chips with sawdust. (Notice the piece of plastic shoved in the fret slot as a dam to hold the fill at right.)

■ Holding down loose fret ends.

Super T, in the yellow-label bottle, has the consistency of syrup and is a good gap-filler for ill-fitting parts. It cures more slowly than Hot Stuff original formula—usually 10-25 seconds, depending on the material. I use this most often in cases such as:

■ Finish touch-ups like drop-filling chips or dents on acrylic or nitrocellulose lacquer, poly-ester, and polyurethane finishes. Lacquer fills tend to crater at a chip's edges, while super glue builds up evenly, and even crowns slightly.

■ Gluing jigs and fixtures around the shop.

■ Case repairs.

■ Glue in frets during refretting.

■ Mix with sawdust for filling dents on bare wood projects.

■ Reglue loose bindings. Make a spatula of the desired shape from 1200-grit wet-or-dry sandpaper and use it to work the glue into the gap. Then tape the binding quickly, but gently, into place.

■ Reinforce worn wood threads.

■ Pearl inlaying.

Special T, in the green-label bottle, is an ultra gap-filler that's thick, like cold honey. It dries slower than Hot Stuff and Super T (usually 30 to 50 seconds, and sometimes up to a couple of minutes, depending on the application), so it allows more time for positioning and aligning parts after gluing. It can be used for many of the same applications as the yellow Super T, and therefore doesn't get used as much in my shop. However, occasionally its viscosity is perfect for filling certain gaps and cracks where the red- or yellow-label glues might run out.

Accessory products are available to comple-ment the glues. Get to know them if you want to become a super-gluer. They aren't gimmicks; each one has a practical and valu-able use.

Hot Shot and Kick-It are spray-on acceler-ators that speed the glue's cure time and can add to a glue joint's strength. Accelerator is sprayed on one part, while glue is applied to the other. I spray accelerator on drop fills before applying the glue, to harden it from below as well. Hot Shot is a basic accelerator, while Kick-It is even faster curing and has a longer on-part life (10 minutes vs. 5 minutes for Hot Shot).

Super Solvent is a must. It cuts the super-glue bond, and I've often used it to separate my thumb and forefinger. It ruins most finishes, so bear that in mind. Thoroughly wash your hands with soap and water after using it.

Teflon tubing is handy to insert in the bottle tip for dainty, accurate glue application and control.

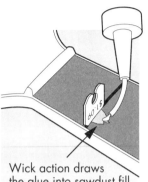

Wick action draws the glue into sawdust fill

Rough up the bottoms of the slots, then use bone dust as a fill

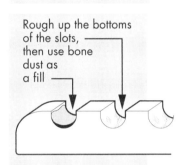

Super glue builds up evenly

Lacquer forms a crater with raised edges

Work glue into gap with sandpaper strip, tape binding

One of the highlights of my career came in 1972 when I built Lucy, a black walnut Flying V, for Albert King.

PHOTO BY PAUL NATKIN (PHOTO RESERVE)

Extra tips aren't expensive, and having them handy allows you to switch to a fresh one when the bottle tip becomes clogged and messy.

Pipettes are clear, 5 ¾" long, plastic micro-applicators with a squeeze bulb. They let you apply glue cleanly and accurately wherever you want it.

Super-glue spears (pictured with pipettes, below) are pinpoint accurate, super-absorbent swabs developed for eye surgery. Use them for sucking up an overrun of super glue during a panic situation.

Most important of all, always wear eye protection and work in a well-ventilated area when using glues and finishes! Rubber gloves are a good idea, although some jobs simply can't be performed while wearing gloves—in that case, just be careful. Always practice on scrap before risking damage to a valued instrument. Follow the manufacturers' instructions, and good luck!

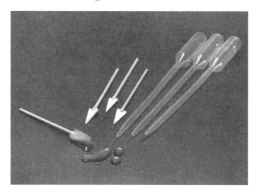

Albert King's Lucy

This column from the September '89 issue of *Guitar Player* has got to be my favorite. My weekend with Lucy really was a typical weekend repair—long hours, high pressure, lots of super glue, and no pay! (I'd never think of charging Albert King!) We did manage to keep our sense of humor, though, me and Lucy…

It was 10:00 on a rainy Sunday morning. I scratched at the 80-grit beard stubble on my middle-aged jowls and sipped a cup of lukewarm coffee. It hit my gut like lacquer thinner. I had the guitar repair blues. I just couldn't face another routine fret job. Then the phone rang. Sounded like *Bb*. I picked it up, and a gravelly voice rumbled through the wire.

"Hello? Is Dan there?" There was no mistaking that voice. It was Albert King, one of the greatest bluesmen in the world.

About 18 months before, Albert's equipment trailer was hit by a tornado and ended up lying on its side in a creek. Most of its contents were replaceable, but Lucy, Albert's main squeeze, was in a world of hurt. The fingerboard and wood bindings came unglued, the neck was loose, and the finish was shot. Rick Hancock of Pyramid Guitars in Memphis did a miraculous restoration job, but over time Lucy continued to react to changes in wood stability and joinery caused by her swim. According to Albert, Lucy wouldn't stay in tune and was bottoming out. Albert told me he was sending her on the next Greyhound.

When she arrived late on Thursday, I found that her neck, which was glued from several pieces, had begun to delaminate. The fingerboard tongue was humped and rising, causing string buzz, and the finish had worn through along the fingerboard edges. Albert was flying to France the following Tuesday, so I was pressed for time. Here's a quick rundown of Lucy's condition and treatment.

Lucy's tuning problem was caused by the nut. Too deep and no longer cleanly shaped, the string slots were pinching the string after a bend, so that the strings couldn't return to pitch.

This problem was compounded by Lucy's fairly light strings—.009, .012, .024W, .028, .038, .050—and her low open tuning of, from low to high, *C F C F A D*. Solution: I filed and contoured the top of the nut to gain shallower string slots (one-half the diameter of the string, as we learned in Nut Work). I also reshaped the slot bottoms, polished them with 1500-grit Finesse wet-sanding paper, and finished up with a tiny drop of Magik Guitar Lube on each slot to lubricate the string.

Bottoming out describes a fretted string that won't sound a clean note (it frets out, notes out, etc). Usually the problem is a high or low fret. In Albert's case, the fingerboard had a rising tongue, causing several high frets. Solution: With Lucy clamped into my bench-top neck jig, I removed the last six frets, planed out the rise in the fingerboard, and inserted new frets of a matching wire—a partial refret.

Later, when dressing the new frets into the old, the 16 original frets chirped as the leveling file passed over them. This indicated loose frets, another cause of string buzz. I waxed the fingerboard on each side of the frets, and ran Hot Stuff red-label super glue under each one. They dried almost immediately and, once solid, could be dressed normally.

Gluing the neck laminates proved to be quite simple, and not as bad as I'd feared. Running red- and yellow-label Hot Stuff into the thin cracks "froze" them in place. Then slowly, in stages, I filled the cracks to the surface with super glue, water-sanding and buffing the glue line when it dried. The glue

blended extremely well with the acrylic automotive lacquer that Rick had used on Lucy.

Albert's hard playing and the large ring on his fretting-hand pinky had worn through the finish on the fingerboard edges, allowing sweat and dirt to decay the wood; it was crumbly in places. With red- and yellow-label Hot Stuff, I saturated the fingerboard edge, building up a super-glue finish. The glue hardened the wood, hopefully making it impervious to Albert's assaults. Once again, the Hot Stuff melded beautifully with the surrounding finish.

Near the neck/body joint, the finish was well-worn on the corner of the cutaway (again, from Albert's ring shaking away on those high bends at the 15th and 17th frets). Here I tried something new: After carefully filling in chips and sealing the light-colored maple binding with thick, gap-filling super glue, I colored the worn corner of the walnut body with yellow-label Special T mixed with a tad of transparent brown sunbursting lacquer. It worked great! The finish was then built up with yellow-label super glue, sanded, and rubbed out.

Since the super-glue repairs were completed on Friday, I was able to spend all day Saturday doing careful fret and nut work. This left Sunday for the final setups, like replacing worn bridge saddles (below), restringing, and setting the intonation in a fairly relaxed manner (this is important, especially when setting up a guitar that's tuned low and played left-handed and upside down by a King of the blues).

Midnight on a rainy Monday night—blue Monday. Lucy's gone. I just can't face tomorrow's tremolo installation. I sip a cup of lukewarm coffee. The java hits my gut like lacquer thinner....

A partial refret was needed: Lucy's last six frets were replaced.

Shrinking Strat pickguards

The UPS man brought me another guitar to fix, along with a note written by a fellow who probably thought he was alone in the world with this trouble. I thought I'd share his problem, along with a solution: "I have a '63 Strat that I dearly love. It's chipped and worn, and ugly to some, but it plays and sounds great. One thing worries me, though. The front pickup is almost touching the strings when I fret the high notes. I tried to lower it by loosening the two pickup height screws, but they move stiffly and the pickup goes nowhere. The pickup and screws seem to be stuck in the pickguard. Also, the pickup sort of leans at an angle. I'm afraid to take the pickguard off, but if I did, what difficulties might I run into?"

I've seen the problem you're describing, and some even worse. First of all, if you're unable to find professional help for your guitar or if you're afraid to mess with the pickguard, shim the neck slightly. This requires the consequent raising of the bridge inserts. The shimming moves the strings up and away from the pickups and helps the fretted string clear the rhythm pickup's plastic cover. If your neck is already shimmed and the bridge inserts are as high as they'll go, or if you simply don't like the idea of a shim, you can fix the problem without too much trouble. You'll have to remove the pickguard, though.

Your best bet is to take your guitar to a good repair shop and let a pro do the work, even though it's not too hard. Face it, your vintage Strat could be worth a couple grand.

If you decide to tackle the problem yourself, the heart of the matter is the celluloid/nitrate material from which the pickguard is made. Nitrate has a tendency to shrink and warp, while the wood body and metal shielding plate remain their original size (a plastic less prone to shrinkage was substituted for nitrate by about 1965). The nitrate's shrinking may cause the following annoying problems, some of which are correctable:

1 A mismatch between the mounting-screw clearance holes in the pickguard and the metal shield. Pulled by the shrinking plastic, the mounting screws slant toward center, often becoming hard to take out or put in. I prefer to leave these as they are. Trying to move or enlarge the holes in the pickguard could harm the guitar's value, and the slanting screws aren't really hurting anything, as long as they'll go in.

2 It sounds like your pickups have become squeezed by the surrounding plastic and are hard to move up or down, and that the height-adjustment screws are stuck in the metal shield clearance holes. These are off-center to the pickup height-adjustment holes, which have in turn shrunk and moved. To seat the pickups smoothly in their holes and make them adjustable again, you need to enlarge the holes in the metal plate as I'll describe shortly.

3 The pickups tilt out-of-square to the strings as a result of the combined warpage and shrinkage. I've never had any success straightening out the warp, and don't recommend trying it on a vintage pickguard. The tilting pickups, however, will straighten up if you get rid of the squeezing plastic and clear out the shield-plate holes as mentioned earlier.

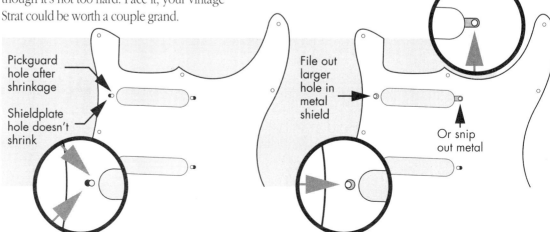

Pickguard hole after shrinkage

Shieldplate hole doesn't shrink

File out larger hole in metal shield

Or snip out metal

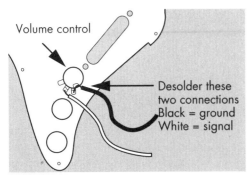

Volume control

Desolder these
two connections
Black = ground
White = signal

HERE'S WHAT YOU CAN DO

You can remove the squeeze and relieve the tension. When the pickguard mounting screws are removed, lift the pickguard/shielding plate up gently, and turn it carefully over onto its face. Have a soft rag handy to place over the body cavity to protect both the finish and the pickguard face. The pickguard often sticks around the heel of the neck and at the bridge surround, so you may have to pry gently.

To make disassembly easier, the entire pickguard assembly can be removed by unsoldering the black (ground) and white (hot) wires at the volume pot (above). Or, if you're careful, you can work with the pickguard still attached, but it's tricky. (The reason I stress taking your guitar to a pro is that experience minimizes the chances of accidental damage to the delicate copper windings.) In order to do this work, you need to remove the pickups and the tone controls from the pickguard and shield.

With a sharp Phillips screwdriver, remove the pickup height-adjustment screws. They may be stiff, but firm pressure will get them out. Be gentle when pulling pickups (still in their cover) out of the pickguard. You may have to wiggle them out. Keep the pickups inside their covers to protect the delicate copper windings, and handle them carefully. When the pickups are out and lying on the clean rag, remove the volume and tone controls. Now your pickguard and metal shield are free, and can be cleaned and worked on separately.

To enlarge the holes in the metal shield: From the underside, look at the mounting-screw holes in the metal shielding plate. Because of shrinkage, they probably are no longer lined up with the holes in the pickguard. Use a small, round needle file to file the holes slightly inward towards the pickup (drawing, left). Or, you

could also simply snip out a section of metal with small wire snips or scissors.

To clean the plastic that surrounds the pickup: Next scrape or file the slightest bit off the sides of the pickup hole. You'll find that it's mostly caked-on dirt, perhaps mixed with a vintage spilled pop or beer. To clean or alter the cutout's round ends, use a ½" wood dowel wrapped with 120-grit sandpaper. Sand small amounts from the rounded ends of the mounting hole; once again, it's mostly grime. It won't take much filing and scraping to get the pickup moving through its hole again. It doesn't even have to move smoothly—just enough to raise or lower. Don't overdo it.

You may also have to enlarge the pickguard's height-adjustment holes ever so slightly by filing outward, away from the pickup. Remember that shrinkage has caused these holes to creep a little closer to the pickups than is desirable.

When you replace the pickups, be as cautious as you were during disassembly. If you've worked carefully, there should be no visible change when all is back together. The pickups will now adjust up or down and sit level, since the rubber grommet or compression spring is able to do its job (pushing the pickup down, eliminating the tilt, and allowing the polepieces to sit level with the strings). Once again, do this work only if there's really a problem. Otherwise, just play the guitar and don't take a chance with its vintage value.

● ●

Broken headstocks

What's the scariest thing that can happen to your guitar? When your guitar's head breaks off, you feel like that's the end! But it isn't. Read on.

Leaving a small bandstand at the end of a performance can be tricky as you step over cords and cables, trying to snake around a ride cymbal while sidestepping a Fender Twin Reverb. Sooner or later, many guitarists watch with horror as their instrument springs from its

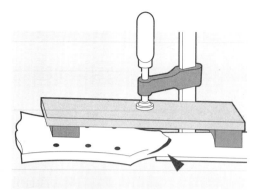

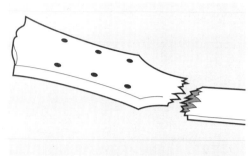

stand and ends up on the dance floor with a broken headstock. The three most common breaks are hairline cracks, heads that are totally snapped off, or those that are cracked severely but still hanging on by the headstock veneer. You also occasionally find one that has been broken in the past and then repaired, with a new break on or near the area of the old break.

In almost all cases, a broken headstock can be made like new again, but this repair is best left to a pro. (Find the best repairperson you can, even if the break is only a "simple" $20.00 crack reglue). Unless you have a great deal of woodworking experience, the best you can do with your damaged guitar is to tune down the strings immediately and place the instrument in its case—where it should have been in the first place. If the head is completely snapped off, clip the strings near the tuners and carefully wrap the head and severed neck end in newspaper; your repairman will want these slivers and fragments of wood to be as clean and untampered-with as possible.

Here are some descriptions of common headstock breaks and how I think you should go about having them fixed. This information will help you in shopping for a repair job to make your guitar as good as new.

Many breaks are initially ignored because they are mistaken for simple cracks in the finish. Although these cracks are hard to open, the wood is usually broken. If the repair is not done soon, sweat, grease, and polish will find their ways into the joint, and the inevitable repair will be much more difficult and expensive. These breaks are carefully pressed open with a clamp, and cauls are used to protect the wood and finish (above). It is then easy to inject glue deep into the break. Ask your repairman if

he intends to use this method.

Some headstocks snap off very cleanly, leaving a long, slanted wood surface showing. While these are easy to glue because of their large surface area, they can be tricky to align because the two pieces may want to slide once clamps are applied. These pieces need to be pinned temporarily during the gluing, thus ensuring proper alignment of the two surfaces. I have seen many headstocks that were glued on crooked; they seldom hold for long.

A headstock that is broken cleanly and hanging by the headstock veneer is easier to repair. Usually this case involves plastic veneer only, because wood veneer faces most often break when the headstock does. This plastic veneer is helpful in holding the two parts in alignment during clamping. Still, I wouldn't advise that a novice even attempt this repair.

The most difficult repair is the clean snap with a very short break line (above). Here the two parts have fingers of wood that slide back together like a locking puzzle. Don't try to put the two parts together. Although it looks easy, you must very carefully remove even the tiniest piece of bent or loose wood. A repairman prefers to do this himself. After years of experience, I seldom even try mating the parts dry before applying glue. I can quickly judge which ones will mate. After applying the glue, I often drive the head home with a hammer tap.

The repairman must deal carefully with a new break around or on a previous fracture. Usually the "rebreak" happens on an old glue line that wasn't repaired properly. All the old glue must be carefully scraped away down to bare wood, since new glue applied over old glue seldom holds.

Often with rebreaks, pieces of new wood

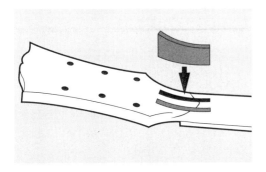

(called splines) are inlaid through the break for reinforcement. I generally use from two to four splines, and always run them well past the break into solid wood (from 1" to 2" on both sides of the break line). The splines should run deep into the neck and headstock, running with the neck's length and grain, and they should be of matching wood (above).

Sometimes, in addition to the splines, we'll put new headstock overlays on the headstock face, or cover the whole back of the headstock with a back strap (a veneer of wood that covers the back surface of the headstock and even runs out onto the neck—a common building technique for fancy banjos and certain higher-end guitars). By putting new wood on the front and back of the headstock, you can "sandwich" the broken area—right over the splines! Either carbon fiber or fiberglas, mixed with epoxy resin, makes good sandwiches too.

Summary: It's hard to ever feel the same about a guitar once the peghead has broken and been repaired. The first repair is the important one, and choosing the right repair method is tough! Follow these rules:

■ In general, especially on new breaks, a simple regluing and minor touchup is best.

■ Resort to reinforcement techniques on rebreaks and breaks that are horribly shattered. But splines and sandwiches don't always hold either!

■ Sometimes the best idea is to replace the neck entirely. This is easy on newer American-made guitars for which parts are available. Vintage pieces may require a custom-made reproduction neck using the original parts (fingerboard, binding, peghead overlay, etc.). This may cost several thousand dollars or more, but there are craftsmen capable of the task.

These techniques take an experienced touch and lots of practice. A repairman should be glad to discuss any technique with you beforehand —it's your guitar. Obviously, a fair amount of finish work has to be performed before the job is complete. Most headstocks can be artfully touched up so that few people would ever know that the job has been done. Once again, shop around. Not every repair shop can handle this job.

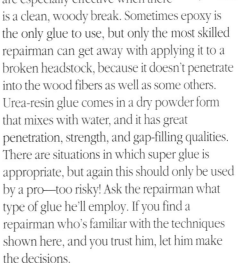

There is no *one* glue for repairing broken headstocks. The repairman should choose a glue depending on the situation. Any of several glues is acceptable. White (which is often yellowish) or aliphatic-resin glues are especially effective when there is a clean, woody break. Sometimes epoxy is the only glue to use, but only the most skilled repairman can get away with applying it to a broken headstock, because it doesn't penetrate into the wood fibers as well as some others. Urea-resin glue comes in a dry powder form that mixes with water, and it has great penetration, strength, and gap-filling qualities. There are situations in which super glue is appropriate, but again this should only be used by a pro—too risky! Ask the repairman what type of glue he'll employ. If you find a repairman who's familiar with the techniques shown here, and you trust him, let him make the decisions.

If you're considering attempting the repair yourself, remember that to do the job right you'll probably need to invest this much in tools and supplies: clamps, $40.00; chisels, $20.00; files, $10.00; Plexiglas for gluing cauls, $4.00; glue, $2.00; wood spline material, $4.00; lacquer, thinner, stains, wood filler, $30.00; finishing equipment using Pre-Val aerosol spray units with extra jars, $20.00 (this is the least expensive finishing method). Total price: $130.00. I don't think you can do a professional job without these supplies and a lot of practice, so use this article as an aid in finding someone willing to do the job right the first time. Better yet, keep your guitar in a case when it isn't in your hands. You can buy yourself a lot of albums with $130.00!

Loose binding

It's important to think about any repair before you jump in and do something that can't be undone.
Patience is hard to learn, and it usually comes the hard way.

One of the most common problems seen in a busy repair shop is loose binding. Bindings come loose along the fingerboard's edge, at the back or top edges where the sides join, on the headstock face, and around the soundhole ring of an acoustic. Most bindings come loose because the wood shrinks in one direction (across its width), while the binding shrinks in the opposite direction (lengthwise). This shrinking, combined with dry glue, climate factors, and in some cases improper glue application during construction, causes the bindings to come loose, which in turn will catch any loose shirt sleeve that passes by. While most modern guitars are bound with celluloid, you might own a guitar with wooden binding. These bindings require a bit more experience to repair or replace, and although many of my tips also apply to wood bindings, this section deals with the more common plastic ones, which can be reglued easily with few tools.

Plastic bindings generally are glued with an acetone-based, plastic-solvent glue. Often this glue melts the plastic into the wood. Usually melted bindings won't come loose in the first place, but if they do, a bit of wood may come with them. If you need this type of problem repaired, have it looked at by a professional. More often, however, the plastic pulls loose with a clean separation, although if the joint has been loose for years, there may be a fair amount of dirt wedged into the opening. This dirt should be removed before the regluing.

Cleaning the binding and the groove or the channel it seats in can be easily done. When

the section of binding is completely separated, gently remove any grease or dirt with a lint-free rag dipped in lighter fluid (I always wear disposable rubber gloves when I'm handling strong solvents). With a sharp X-acto knife, you can cut, chip, or gently scrape any hard, caked-on dirt. Use the back of this blade as a scraper for pulling dirt from a crevice or from binding that is only loose in a section, with the main portion still glued tight (below, left). The idea is to remove foreign matter and grease. In the case of a binding that's loose for only a small area—say, from the 1st to the 5th fret along the fingerboard's edge—stretch masking tape across the point where it's still glued. This way, you can gently peel the plastic away from its glue channel to clean it without further loosening the section that is holding well (below, right).

Binding at the guitar's waist or any area where a sharp curve has to be dealt with, such as a cutaway, is difficult to reglue. So is the fingerboard binding over the tongue. The binding at the waist can shrink and pull away from the body, and because it has shrunk so much, the piece cannot be forced back to its original position. Carefully applied heat can soften the plastic and allow it to stretch into the original shape to cool—not a task for a beginner, though. Heat won't always work, either. Often the binding must be cut and a patching piece fitted into the resulting gap. This patching-in requires some experience, as well as a supply of different binding pieces for a proper match. The fingerboard tongue is somewhat difficult to clamp and requires specialized tools. Don't work on these areas if you're just starting out—leave them to someone with experience. Most other areas are easy to glue, and all you'll need for pressure is a roll of masking tape.

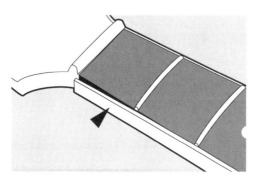

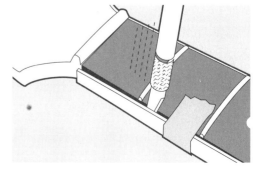

Masking tape is the perfect clamp for headstock, fingerboard (though not over the tongue), and most body bindings. You can apply it near the loose areas on the guitar's side, top, back, headstock face, or back of the neck. For best results, stretch the tape as you go around the guitar's edge. The stretched tape tends to pull the binding into its channel. Caution: On old, checked, thin-finished vintage instruments, be careful not to pull off finish when removing the tape after the glue has dried. Repairs on vintage instruments are better left to a pro. In all cases, remove the masking tape slowly, pulling at a slight angle to the tape's length. Any job that can't be glued using tape for the clamp may also need the pro's touch. It's always good to practice a glue-up "dry"—using no glue—as a trial run.

Franklin's Titebond, their Liquid Hide Glue, and Elmer's Carpenter's Glue are the best and safest for a beginner. When the loose area is properly cleaned, these glues do an adequate job of holding the plastic in place—if left to dry overnight. White glues are water-soluble and offer the advantage of neat, easy cleanup. They usually run into cracks easily, but if you have difficulty, spread the crack with your knife tip and push glue in with a finger. Note: I usually do plastic binding repair with Dupont Duco Cement or super glue, but these glues should not be used by the inexperienced. There are a few areas where these two glues are necessary, and when you've gained some experience, talked to a few repairmen, and studied the subject, you will know when and how to use them.

Don't be alarmed if the binding is a little too short to fill the original gap. Remember that the plastic has shrunk from end to end. In order to stretch binding, you must use a Duco-type cement that actually softens the plastic on contact, allowing it to become somewhat flexible. However, this softening is the reason that I don't advise you to use this glue without experience. Don't try it on your old Les Paul or Martin D-28.

The usual problem with loose soundhole binding is that it pops up and out of its channel, often where two pieces butt together. While holding the piece up with your knife tip,

work white glue in with a finger or by blowing it into the groove. Next, push the binding into place, wipe off the excess, and apply a small C-clamp for pressure. Use a piece of Plexiglas (lightly waxed so it won't stick) as a caul to hold it flat while drying (above). Protect the inside of the guitar from the clamp's jaw with a piece of wood or stiff cardboard. If you drill a few holes into the Plexiglas, the glue area will dry more easily. Leave the clamp on at least four hours. The proper-size clamp shouldn't cost more than $3.00 or $4.00.

Be sure to study the problems mentioned here before attempting any repairs, and certainly don't do anything if you aren't truly confident. If you're at all in doubt, take your guitar to a qualified repairman and pay the small fee that these jobs usually cost. Most repairmen enjoy having a customer to talk shop with—someone who can appreciate the trade.

Fixing a guitar case

Repairmen would have less work—and I'd have much less to write about—if musicians conscientiously kept instruments in cases. It's sad enough to see a scratch, ding, or split on an inexpensive guitar, but the serious and sometimes total damage that I've seen inflicted on caseless vintage guitars would make even a hardened repairman wince. While almost any case is usually better than none at all, to ensure your instrument's safety and to avoid many of the problems I write about, consider several simple points that will keep your case as strong and safe as possible.

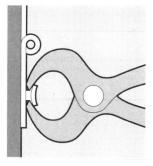

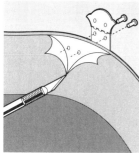

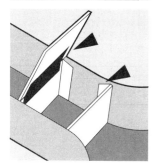

By far the most common problem with an older hardshell or softshell case is the normal loosening of the hinges that hold the top to the body. It may be necessary to remove and replace the rivets that hold a hinge to the case. Usually it's possible to clip off the head of the rivet from the case exterior using an end nipper, which is a common hardware store item (top left). Once the head is removed, use a sharp knife to cut the plush or leatherette lining, and simply peel it back inside the case to expose the remaining rivet (middle drawing). You can then remove the stretched, worn-out rivet and redrill, creating a slightly larger hole through the hinge and the side of the case. (The Tandy Leather Co. is a well-known supplier of tools and parts for this type of job.) The rivet can then be inserted through the new, enlarged hole. Then, holding a solid steel object inside as an anvil, use a hammer to pound the rivet into its seat from the outside.

If the cardboard is worn and spongy in the hinge area of an inexpensive chipboard case, glue an oversized piece of strong cardboard to the inside for reinforcement before drilling and riveting. If a hinge has torn loose and become lost, make your own from a scrap of leather or strong fabric that is wider than the torn area. Glue it on and install rivets for strength. The result doesn't look bad, and an otherwise useless case is salvaged.

Another common problem with cases is the eventual collapse of the accessories box. In a quality plywood (hardshell) case, the walls of the box are usually nailed to the side walls from the outside. These nails probably can be pried out, and then you can rebuild the accessories box by regluing the ends to the sides and inserting longer, stronger nails. If there is a plush lining, remove the parts carefully, but don't be afraid to cut the material in order to get at the problem. Usually, plush lining peels easily from the plywood and is reglued just as easily. To hide any new nails or rivets, put a dab of glue over each one, and then press down a tuft of the "fur" borrowed from a less conspicuous area of the case. This produces an invisible repair.

By carefully disassembling a wooden accessories box, you can reshape its cradle

(the neck-support part), thus raising or lowering the neck's position in the case. I have done this often with cases that won't quite close because the neck is sitting too high on the support. I can generally re-cover it with the same material I peeled back before disassembly. A worn-out cardboard-type box can be easily removed and replaced with a new one constructed of a similar material, which is then glued to the case's sidewalls. A new lid can then be made and glued to the box, using a strip of cloth as a hinge (bottom drawing).

Repairing locks on a case is usually difficult, requiring specialized parts and tools. It is possible, however, to remove many locks and replace them entirely—if not with an exact match, at least with something that works. Locks are generally mounted with either rivets or metal tabs that are bent into the case walls as fasteners. If the lock clasp works properly but the lock is broken, you might consider leaving it as is and forget about trying to lock the case.

Hasps, clasps, and hinges usually cause trouble only when bent, and they are easily fixed by bending or hammering them back into the proper shape. A loose hasp can be reinstalled using the rivet/hammer method. A broken case handle is often just as easy to fix, using the same rivet/hammer method. Sometimes, though, a replacement handle is the only solution. You can find suitable new handles in hardware stores, luggage shops, luthier suppliers, and many music stores. While you may not find a handle that duplicates the old one, perhaps you'll find one that you can adapt, using rivets to hold it on.

Many older plywood cases end up with the exterior leatherette worn away on the corners, and the wooden layers eventually separate. Reglue these plies by deeply injecting them with a slightly thinned mixture of white glue and water; I use veterinary syringes with large needles. Squeeze out any excess and clamp for a few hours. A little touch-up with a matching paint (not too glossy) looks good, especially if you stipple the paint in an attempt to match the case's grain.

The most common case repairs in my shop are rips, tears, and scratches in fairly new cases. I usually perform these repairs gratis, since they are quick and easy to do. A drop of super glue under a raised tear will hold it forever. As the glue sets, you can engrave grain lines into it for an extra touch. Accelerator causes the glue to harden almost instantly, and the reaction can cause it to mound up, looking somewhat like a bubble of leather. Using these techniques, you can get a lot more mileage from your case, and you may find the work is fun and easy to do.

How to ship a guitar

Your '59 Sunburst has so many fret buzzes, it sounds like killer bees are swarming in your amp. Your prize prewar acoustic feels like it's strung with baling wire. Worse yet, your local "repair" shop's equipped with only two tools: a chainsaw and a really big hammer. Or maybe you're buying/selling an instrument, and just want to get it from here to there. What do you do?

UPS does a great job of handling all kinds of fragile and expensive stuff. While recently packing a repaired guitar for its return trip, I decided to pass along some packing tips to those of you who find it necessary to ship a guitar now and then. If you pack 'em right, you won't need a repair book! (Just kidding.)

Good guitars should travel first-class in hardshell cases. If yours has a softshell case, buy a hard one or keep the guitar at home. The same commonsense principles apply to packing acoustic and electric guitars. First, pick up the heaviest guitar shipping box that you can find at your local music store; my favorites are the boxes used by Martin, Gibson, Fender, and Guild. Then follow these twelve steps:

1 Remove any unnecessary items from the case's accessory box, and make sure that the lid can't open.

2 Tune down the strings until they're slack. During a fall, pressure from tuned-up strings can break a headstock.

3 Be sure that the tuners are tight and can't vibrate loose to rattle around inside the case.

4 Protect an electric guitar's fingerboard and pickups by sliding folded paper in between them. With an arch-top, pad all around the bridge with paper pushed under the strings and tailpiece, or remove the bridge entirely.

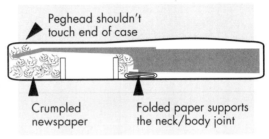

Peghead shouldn't touch end of case

Crumpled newspaper

Folded paper supports the neck/body joint

5 See that the neck rests in its support cradle. The headstock shouldn't touch the case, and it should be supported all around with crushed newspaper rolled into 2" to 3" balls (see the drawing above).

6 For acoustics, fold some paper and support the back of the guitar under the neck block area if there's a gap between it and the case.

7 The guitar shouldn't move inside when you shake the case. If it does, pad the waist and bout areas with paper.

8 Drop a layer of crushed newspaper balls into the bottom of your shipping box, and lower the case into it. Center the case in the box (below) and fill the box snugly on all sides with paper balls; use a stick to push them down where you can't reach.

Crumpled newspaper

Fragile Please!

Fragile

9 If your shipping box still has the original cardboard fillers inside, use them and/or the crushed newspaper. Stiff cardboard placed in the right areas can really firm up a box.

10 Use gummed, fiber-reinforced tape (usually brown) to seal the box when it's full. Wet the gummed side with a damp rag.

11 Clearly print the shipping address on the box. I always print "Fragile, Please" on all four sides (adding the word "please" is important), and draw a picture of a broken long-stemmed wine glass—the international "fragile" symbol (see illustration).

12 Insure the guitar for more than it's worth, pay the UPS person, say your prayers, and you're done. You'll be in good shape.

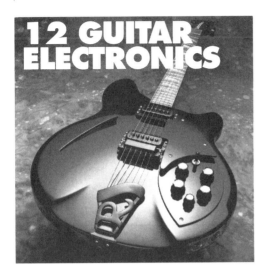

12 GUITAR ELECTRONICS

The basic tools

With the exception of rare, vintage instruments, guitar electronics is one area of repair where a novice usually doesn't do much permanent damage. Sloppy solder joints can always be done over, and even if you burn something up, buying new parts is easy. Electronics never came easy for me, and I'm no Craig Anderton, Dan Armstrong, or Seymour Duncan—but I can teach you the basics, and let you take it from there. Here are some helpful books, listed in what I consider to be their order of importance as they pertain to electronics. They're all valuable, and are available through bookstores, music stores, and guitar shop suppliers: Donald Brosnac's *Guitar Electronics For Musicians,* Adrian Legg's *Customizing Your Electric Guitar,* Hideo Kamimoto's *Complete Guitar Repair,* Melvyn Hiscock's *Make Your Own Electric Guitar,* and Bill Foley's *Build Your Own Electric Guitar.* Let's start by outfitting a basic guitar electronics toolbox, and learn what each tool does. Then we'll put the knowledge to use.

To excel in guitar electronics, you must be able to take guitars apart and put them back together with your eyes closed. Removing control cavity cover plates, pickups, pickguards, bridges, tailpieces, potentiometers, selector switches, and the like is common—even for the simplest repair. Use an ice-cube tray as a parts organizer, since losing parts is the nemesis of many an otherwise well-meaning repairman. And if you don't know guitar parts well, draw a map of which parts went where. Disassembly/assembly tools are the basis of an electronics tool box, and you may have many of them already. On the next page is a list of the basic tools, most of which are shown in the accompanying photo.

■ Small screwdrivers from size 0 to 2 in Phillips and flat-blade.

■ Sockets, open-end wrenches, and nut drivers in the ¼" to ½" range (you'll find uses for these tools in metric sizes, too).

Break open a few pots, mini switches, and other components, and you'll really learn how they work!

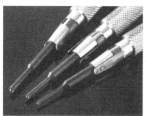

■ Needle-nose pliers, wire cutters, small wire snips, and hemostats.

■ An inspection mirror is handy for finding a problem without removing anything.

■ Screw extractors to remove screws with stripped heads (left). You'll love this tool if you've ever tried to remove miniature screws with slots that are rusted, filled with dirt, stripped and mangled, or a combination of these problems (especially Gibson's Phillips-head pickup mounting ring screws!).

■ Switch-nut wrench (left). This uncommon but valuable tool is used for removing the knurled nut on a toggle switch. Most repairmen have seen lots of vintage switch nuts mauled by slipping pliers or Vise-Grips.

■ Soldering iron. I generally use an Ungar 45-watt pencil type with small and medium chisel tips, and an insulated stand to set it in while hot. With most guitar electronics, you want to get on and off the part fast, and the little 15- or 20-watt pencils don't cut the mustard (but they are handy for some delicate parts like transistors).

■ A desoldering tool, or "solder-sucker," is a mechanical device that cocks like a dart gun and creates a vacuum when you release the trigger. It's used for sucking molten solder away from parts. Another type uses a rubber squeeze-bulb; this one looks like an ear syringe, but it's Teflon-lined so the solder doesn't burn through.

■ Solder. Use a 60/40 resin core in a small diameter (.032"). Never use acid-core solder in guitar electronics!

■ A soldering jig, also known as a "third hand," has a weighted base and adjustable arms with alligator-clip "hands" that keep delicate parts aligned for soldering. Several brands and styles are available.

■ Wire strippers save a lot of time and hassle. Get one with an adjustable stop to control diameter. The simple type sold by General works fine.

■ An X-acto or razor knife with the #11 blade helps in stripping insulation lengthwise and for delicately cutting the insulation of small wire sizes before stripping.

■ Some sort of electronics probe or sharp, fine-pointed dental tool is needed to fish wire through holes, separate braided shielding, etc. The curved dental type can grab around potentiometer shafts and snake them through mounting holes.

■ Heat-sinks clip temporarily onto the leads of delicate parts being soldered or desoldered. These clips absorb heat, keeping it from running up the wire and burning the part. The small (1" to 1 ½") brass, copper, or aluminum alligator clips sold at Radio Shack work well.

■ Jumper cables. Small lengths of wire with alligator clips at each end, these are used for temporarily checking a wiring plan before soldering it together.

■ A curved-bottom file to remove plating or oxidation from the back of potentiometers that won't take solder; 220-grit sandpaper also works.

■ Tuner cleaner and lubricant is used to flush out and lubricate "scratchy-sounding" and stiff or sticky volume and tone controls. Blue Shower and Blue Stuff are good brands.

■ The multi-meter, also known as an ohmmeter or VOM (volt-ohm meter), is the most important tool. It's used to diagnose most of a guitar's electrical ills. A good meter doesn't cost much—from $30.00 to $50.00 buys a nice one. Choose one that reads DC resistances of at least 500,000 ohms. Its main uses in our business are described in the deep guitar electronics section that follows.

These are the basic tools; use this as a shopping list as you add to your toolbox. Now, let's look at supplies such as wire, shielding materials, and switches, and then spend some time working at the bench.

Wire, shielding, and capacitors

One of the best all-around wire types for guitar electronics is tinned, stranded copper wire. Being stranded, it bends easily without breaking, and the tinning (which turns the copper to a silver color) means the wire's ready to solder with no additional tinning necessary. Choose a wire to suit your needs from the following list. Except for the last one, they're all tinned, stranded copper:

■ Single-conductor wire with a plastic insulating jacket. This is usually black, red, or white—your basic "hookup" wire; shielding isn't necessary.

■ Single-conductor, as above, but with Teflon insulation that resists soldering-iron heat. It won't melt in extra-hot situations.

■ Coaxial, or "co-ax," is a single-conductor wire with an insulating sleeve wrapped in a braided shield that protects the inner core from interference. This wire is used as a ground in many situations. Some co-ax types have a

plastic outer jacket, while others have only the wire braid. Most Gibson pickup leads are this type of wire, having a stranded core, black cloth insulation, and an outer braid that's used as the ground.

■ Coaxial, as above, but with non-melting Teflon insulation.

■ Four-conductor with foil shield, a fifth—stranded—ground wire, and a plastic jacket. This "multi-lead" wire is used for four-wire humbucking pickup conversions. The foil shield is the best you can get—90% effective.

■ Last of all, it's convenient to have small-gauge (22 to 25) hookup wire. Usually solid copper, single-strand wire makes a good jumper for short runs such as criss-crossed terminals on mini switches, etc. It also makes a good, strong ground wire.

SHIELDING YOUR GUITAR'S CIRCUIT

This helps give you a hum-free signal. Using shielded wire wherever possible is a good bet, but you can further improve your sound by shielding the body cavities, wire channels, and pickguard with conductive shielding paint or copper foil. The paint is laced with nickel, which creates a conductive barrier that AC hum and radio signals can't penetrate. Shielding paint is easy to use, if you follow these directions:

■ Work in a well-ventilated area and use an OSHA-approved, vapor-barrier respirator.

■ Wear eye protection.

■ Use cheap, throwaway "acid brushes" to apply it.

■ Build up two coats, and test your work using your multi-meter set to its continuity scale. Touch two different areas to see if you get a beep or visual reading.

■ The shield is conductive, so it must not touch any part of the circuit other than the ground, or it could short the circuit.

■ When you're finished shielding, run a wire from the shield to ground. The more carefully you shield, the better your signal will be.

Copper foil is a great shield. Shielding a surface such as the back of a pickguard is easy with foil, and cleaner than paint. But doing a

If you're doing electrical work, make it a habit to double-check your shop when you leave, making sure you haven't left on a soldering iron or anything else that might cause a fire. And if you wake up at 2:00AM wondering if you left something on, get your butt out of bed and go check!

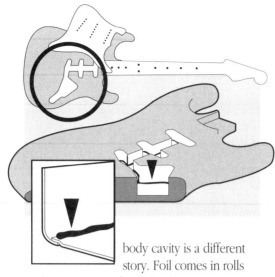

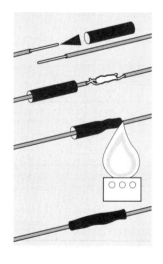

body cavity is a different story. Foil comes in rolls or sheets with a self-stick back; you peel away the protective layer, and it sticks to almost anything (mostly your hands). Shielding a cavity with foil is like making a slip cover for a couch or chair: You cut different pieces to shape (the bottom, sides, etc.) and then "paste" them in place with the self-stick. Let one piece overlap the other by ¼", and then solder each joint—this is the ultimate shield!

Heat-shrink tubing is God's gift to wiring. By sliding it onto one of two wires to be joined (or one wire to be insulated from another) *before soldering*, you can do away with sticky electrical tape or masking tape, which turns stiff, yellow, and crumbly. Heat-shrink, or "spaghetti tubing," as it's known, comes in a wide range of sizes for any wiring task, and it makes even sloppy work look professional. It insulates wires that shouldn't touch, and its stiffening effect strengthens connections.

Choose heat-shrink in a size that not only slides over a given wire, but fits back over the *solder joint* once a connection is made. Always use the smallest size you can get by with, and slide it as far away from a connection as possible while you solder. Wait until the solder cools before sliding the heat-shrink over the new joint; then heat it with a match and watch it shrink and compress tightly around the wires. Rotating the wire as you heat the tubing creates a uniform contraction (professionals use heat-shrink guns similar to small hair dryers). Multiple wires going to a common terminal point can be heat-shrunk together as a unit to make their combined diameter smaller; this makes it much easier to thread wires through drilled holes and wiring channels.

Capacitors play an important part in guitar electronics, since they control your guitar's tone. Older guitars have the "Tootsie Roll" type with multicolored rings to denote their value, while more modern instruments use either thin ceramic disks or the square, plastic-dipped type. The job of the "cap" is to ground, remove, or bleed off the treble (highs) from the signal. Most single-coil pickups (such as those on Strats) use a .05μF (microfarad) capacitor, while humbuckers (Les Pauls) use a .02μF. As Gibson's Tim Shaw points out: "Gibsons have darker-sounding pickups and need smaller capacitors to cut off fewer highs. Our usual guitar capacitor value is .02μF. Fenders, on the other hand, have more top end and traditionally use larger caps to be able to roll off more highs. Fender's guitar caps are usually .05μF. Basses can be .05μF, or even .1μF. These values are for high-impedance circuits only. The lower the impedance, the higher the capacitor value. EMG pickups, for instance, use much higher capacitor values in their tone controls." Changing to a cap of a different value alters your guitar's tone without hurting anything, since you can always get back to your starting point. Learn more about capacitors in Donald Brosnac's *Guitar Electronics For Musicians* and Adrian Legg's *Customizing Your Electric Guitar.*

Troubleshooting with a multi-meter

Guitar electronics runs deep. Only a fool (I saw that smirk) would suggest that the subject could be "taught" in a single chapter of a book. I'll be happy if you just learn these basics here: how to use a multi-meter to troubleshoot problems and test parts, how to replace a simple part like a potentiometer or an output jack, how to shield a guitar, the correct way to solder and desolder, and how to replace a pickup. From there, you can dive on in and swim as deep as you like. Let's get started.

I use the "credit-card"-type multi-meter. The particular model is a Circuitmate DM78,

although I'm sure there are other equally good brands. It's small, inexpensive (around $35.00), has a digital readout (a needle/scale combo can be hard to read, especially on an inexpensive meter), and auto-ranging, which means it finds the correct range automatically, and you don't need a degree from M.I.T. to use it! The meter's four settings are DC voltage, AC voltage, ohm scale (for reading resistance in ohms), and continuity. You won't be needing the AC voltage range for guitar electronics, but the other three settings are used all the time.

The DC voltage scale is handy for checking batteries. A guitar with a preamp, active pickups, or active circuitry needs its batteries checked often. Put the meter's black lead on negative and the red lead on positive for an instant battery check. Any 9-volt battery that reads less than 7 volts should be discarded. Using a meter sure beats laying your tongue across the terminals to see how big a charge you get!

Continuity testing's easy, and if your meter has a beeper, which mine does, you can see and *hear* continuity. In the meter's continuity setting, touching both probes to any conductive surface or surfaces (ends of a wire, copper-foil or conductive-paint shielding, pickup-cover to ground, bridge to ground, etc.) lets you know if there's an uninterrupted connection or a dead short.

Working with the ohms scale always makes me feel like I know something. Use the ohms function to check pickups: Look at the output wire(s) coming from any standard single-coil or humbucking pickup, and you'll see a hot lead and a ground lead. These may be two separate wires, or a single-conductor (hot) coaxial wire with a braided shield used as

On the pickup at left, white is hot, black is ground. At right, the braided shield is the ground and the inside is the hot lead.

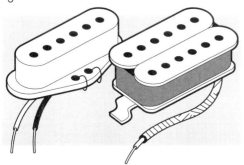

ground. Touch one test probe (red or black, it makes no difference) to the hot wire and one to the ground wire. This gives you a reading of the pickup's DC resistance in ohms. A Strat pickup, for example, should read from 5.5–6.75k ohms, and a standard Gibson humbucker should read from 7.2k to 8k ohms (new ones are 7.6k ohms). Some hot humbuckers, such as Gibson Dirty Fingers and DiMarzio Super Distortion, read twice that—12k to 14k ohms. Since it has two coils, the humbucking pickup is generally more powerful than a single-coil, but not always. A modern 4-wire pickup has four leads coming out of it, and each coil can be read separately; they should read the same. Pickups or coils with weak ohm readings or none at all are defective and must be repaired, rewound, or replaced.

TESTING, CLEANING, AND REPLACING POTS

Because of wear, dirt, spilled drinks, dust, etc., a "bad" pot either doesn't work at all (no volume or tone change), has a scratchy, dirty sound, or only works intermittently. In most cases, simply spray-cleaning a pot cures its symptoms. Two good brands of "tuner" cleaner are Blue Stuff and Blue Shower. Some brands don't do a good job and can actually cause a pot to freeze up—a nightmare on a vintage piece! Stick the cleaner's hose tip into the opening in the side of the pot's case, and spray liberally. Tilt the piece, so the cleaner can run back out as it flushes the pot while you turn the shaft on and off to clean the contacts. If your guitar has sealed pots with no hole to spray into, remove the knob and pull up lightly on the shaft. You'll see a little movement. Squirt here, and the very thin cleaner usually finds its way to the problem. Contact cleaners are available from radio/TV service shops. Don't forget to wear safety glasses, and be sure to protect the guitar's finish and your table top from the cleaner. If cleaning doesn't cure its ills, test the pot with your meter.

Again, set the meter to the ohm scale and practice on a pot that isn't wired into a circuit. Using both probes, touch one to each of the *outer* two lugs for an instant, true reading of the pot's resistance. Now, if you put the test probes on an outer lug and a *center* lug, the

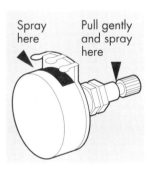

Spray here   Pull gently and spray here

When you find a bad part, throw it out. Repairmen tend to save broken parts such as pots and switches, thinking they'll have some use for them. Eventually the bad stuff mixes with the good, and you have to re-test everything. Chuck 'em!

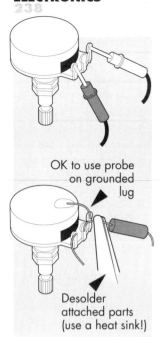

OK to use probe on grounded lug

Desolder attached parts (use a heat sink!)

resistance will vary from 0 ohms to the true rating of the pot (250k, or whatever) as you turn the pot's shaft. You can test a pot that's wired into a circuit using the above method, but note: On a pot with a pickup wired to one lug and an outside lug bent to the case and soldered/grounded (as with most volume pots), you must de-solder one of these two connections—either the pickup or the grounded lug (above)—before you get the pot's reading. Without de-soldering, you simply get a reading of the pickup itself. If there is no pickup wired to a pot, the bent-back/soldered lug poses no problem, and you can test the pot normally. If a pot's good, re-solder the parts you disconnected, and you're back in business. A pot that isn't within 20% of its rating should be replaced.

Soldering techniques

Replacing a pot is pretty easy, if you can get at it. Teles, Strats, and Les Pauls have easy access, but a 335 can be a toughie. You might be wise to make a drawing of which wires or parts went where. Most pots have delicate wires and many have a ceramic capacitor wired to them. Protect these parts by clipping heat-sinks to the leads before desoldering. The operation is made easier if you use a solder-sucker, so it can't reflow and harden as soon as you remove the iron. When the pot's free, remove it and *throw it out*—you don't want to start saving them.

When you solder in a new pot of the same rating, *tin* the connections first; this means adding solder to the lugs and to the metal case before reinstalling the wires (any wires or capacitors are still tinned from the original installation). When parts are tinned before soldering, the actual connection takes place much quicker. Touch the soldering iron to the part, let it heat up, and then flow the solder to the *part*—not the iron's tip. A good solder joint looks slippery, shiny, and silvery—not dull, grayish, and dry. Solder spits, so wear protective goggles, button up your shirt collar (and no shorts or short-sleeved shirts!), and protect

any good finishes nearby (your guitar, the table top, etc.).

HERE ARE SOME SOLDERING TIPS TO KEEP IN MIND:

■ Use a soldering iron rated anywhere from 15 to 45 watts. In a novice's hand, the lighter-duty iron has less chance of burning up a part.

■ It's not uncommon to own and use soldering irons of several watt ratings. The 45-watter is *my* favorite all-around iron, although it's a little hot in some delicate situations.

■ Keep your iron's tip *tinned* (shiny with solder) from the moment you first turn it on, and clean it often during use by wiping it on a damp sponge.

■ A tip that doesn't get tinned the first time it's used may burn up and never do a good job of soldering.

■ Don't forget to use heat-sinks on delicate work.

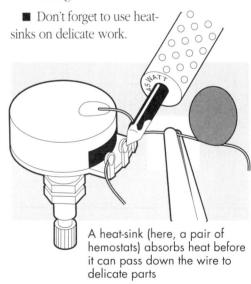

A heat-sink (here, a pair of hemostats) absorbs heat before it can pass down the wire to delicate parts

Mini switches

Still with us? Man, don't let these pages get you too "wired"! If it gets to be too much, take a break and do a fret job or something. Actually, this guitar electronics stuff should be a welcome change from super glue, wood scraps, lacquer, stains, loose bridges, clamps, and dirty hands—there's nothing here but good hot solder, the trusty multi-meter, and nice, clean parts to wire.

ON/OFF ON/ON/ON ON/OFF/ON

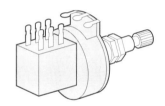

My goal in this chapter is to get your interest, teach you some basics, and give you a good start so you can learn on your own. And to have fun doing it! Guitar electronics *can* be boring—schematics, wiring diagrams, ratings, readings, and (yawn!) so forth. When you start out, you need to tackle some jobs that are *fun*, and leave the heavy-duty studying until after you're hooked. Now, a few more basics—a little more fun—and then the diplomas.

Mini switches are as important to guitar electronics as capacitors, potentiometers, shielding paint, and the like. These little toggle switches control most of the hot-rod and custom wiring options you're likely to try ("dual-sound," pickup phasing, coil cutting, series/parallel, etc.). Because of their small size, you can fit one or more of these switches into most control cavities without having to use a router to enlarge or reshape the cavity walls; and for mounting, you only need to drill a ¼" hole for the small shaft. You can buy double-pole or single-pole mini switches. Double-pole switches have two sets of three terminals, or lugs (pictured on previous page), while single-pole have only one set. I stock double-pole, because even though they're a little bigger, they do anything a single-pole does and more.

The three most common types of double-pole mini toggle switches are on/on, on/off/on, and on/on/on. On/on controls pickup phasing, coil-cut (or two pickups coil-cut at once), or series/parallel. The on/off/on variety puts a single-coil pickup in-phase, out-of-phase, or off, and may be used for pickup selection. On/on/on can work like a Gibson Les Paul toggle switch (lead pickup, both pickups, rhythm). It can give series, single-coil, and parallel selections for a humbucker, or act

as a pickup selector switch for three pickups at once. And these are just some of the functions that mini switches perform. The drawings at the bottom of the previous page show which terminals are "hot" when the lever is thrown.

With double-pole switches, each side (or pole) has three wiring lugs. Each side is independent of the other side, although they can be used together. In fact, it's common to "jump" from one pole to another, like the cross-corner terminals used during phasing, for example (lower right). For short jumpers on mini switches, try this combination: Remove the plastic jacket from solid-copper wire and the Teflon jacket from a stranded wire, and then slide the Teflon over the solid core. This kills three birds with one stone, since the solid core easily pokes through a terminal's hole, it won't fall to pieces like a short strand, and its Teflon won't melt on the criss-crosses and cause a short. When wiring a mini switch, don't rest your iron too long on any one lug, because most switch bodies are made from plastic. In the next section we'll use a mini switch to control the wiring options of a four-wire humbucking pickup.

Installing a replacement pickup

So far you've learned wiring basics, how to read a meter, techniques for clean and safe soldering and desoldering, and which parts are commonly used. Now you may carefully experiment with the electronics of your own guitar, and I'll bet I know what you'll do first— wire in a replacement pickup, right? Since

replacing pickups is the most common job done by do-it-yourselfers, a few pickup-wiring tips are appropriate. Wiring a direct-fit replacement pickup is often simple: Using a wiring diagram, you just unhook one pickup and wire in the other. But there are plenty of pitfalls, too, and you can avoid them by considering the following points before buying a pickup or tearing apart your axe.

■ What sound are you after? If you're adding a pickup to existing pickups, will they be compatible? A well-stocked and knowledgeable music store can help you choose, and Bill Foley's book *Build Your Own Electric Guitar* includes an extensive chart that suggests which pickups sound best for different musical styles. Here's a sample:

Heavy Metal Rhythm/Neck Position

Alembic:	SAE, HB assembly
Bartolini:	1HC, VHC
Dimarzio:	X2N, PAF, Super II, (2) HS2 or 3
Duncan:	Jazz Neck, Invader Neck, Seymourizer II, JB
EMG:	85, 58, SA assembly w/presence control
Lawrence:	M58, XL500 neck, (2) L-25 XL
Schecter:	Monstertone assembly

■ Is the alteration permanent? You often can't go back!

■ Do the polepieces match the string-to-string spacing?

■ Some older two-lead (hot and ground) humbucker pickups can be rewired as four-wire pickups. If vintage isn't an issue, perhaps you can rewire the pickup you have to get what you're after.

■ A direct-replacement pickup should drop right in with no additional routing, an important consideration with valuable vintage instruments. With careful disassembly and measuring, you can know if it fits before it's too late. Replacement pickups often have more depth than the original, so don't be surprised if you have to rout or drill the cavity to gain clearance.

■ Switching from single-coil to humbucking

often requires routing the body cavity. This is easily done with templates, just like installing the Floyd Rose.

■ Universal routing is popular with many kit body manufacturers. These routs accept either single-coil or humbucking pickups, but you still have to enlarge the hole in the pickguard, especially when replacing a Strat-style single-coil with a humbucker. This, too, is done with a router and pickguard cutout templates.

■ Does the new pickup offer functions that the guitar's wiring system can't operate, such as phasing, dual sound, etc.? In other words, will you have to add mini switches, pots, and such. And if so, is there room?

■ If you're going active, you need someplace to put a battery.

■ Would routing a pickup cavity endanger the structural integrity of the instrument? For example, I've seen old Gibson SG single-coil guitars with a humbucker added in the neck position. There wasn't a lot of surface area in the neck/body joint of these guitars in the first place, so when you add some over-zealous routing, the neck falls right off!

If you've read this checklist and still want to hot-rod your guitar, go ahead! Here are a few tips for installing a pickup:

What makes pickups work? In a nutshell, a pickup is made by coiling wire around a set of magnetic polepieces that are held in a frame, or "bobbin." The polepieces pick up string vibrations and "send" them—that is, induce a current—through the magnetic coil of wire that then changes the vibrations into an electric signal. The signal is received and made louder by the amplifier. Understanding how a humbucker works helped me better understand pickup wiring.

A humbucking pickup is a combination of two pickups (coils) in one cover. The two coils are wired together in-series/out-of-phase to eliminate hum. They're also charged magnetically opposite by turning the magnet around in one coil so that the two coils actually end up being electrically in-phase. This describes the traditional humbucker designed by Seth Lover for Gibson in the late 1950s. One set of magnets wrapped with wire makes a single-coil pickup, and single-coil pickups usually hum because they receive interference from AC current in the home, shop, onstage, or wherever. Seth applied for a patent (PAF) on his discovery that two single-coils can be connected together in a certain way with a common output and ground to make up a hum-canceling pickup.

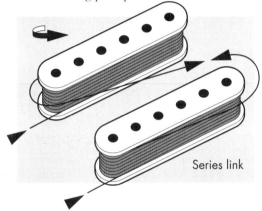

Series link

"In series" means that one coil connects, runs into, or is linked to the other coil end-to-end; this adds the resistances of both coils and gives us the famous humbucking power. The series link always combines matching ends of the coils (i.e., the finish wrap of one coil to the finish wrap of the other, or a start to a start). Most often the two finish ends of the coils are used for the "series link." Although each coil's wire is wound in the same direction on its bobbin, because the end of one goes into the end of the other, this is considered out-of-phase, hence the term in-series/out-of-phase.

At the same time, the coils of a humbucker are also magnetically out-of-phase to each other because the two rows of pole-pieces are on opposite sides of a common magnet. This gives one row of polepieces a "north" polarity, and the other a "south" polarity, which causes the wire of each coil to induce the current

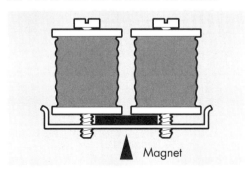

Magnet

(signal) in opposite directions. This phenomenon not only allows the hum of one coil to cancel the hum of the other coil, but it returns the two out-of-phase coils to being electrically in-phase after all! It's the relationship of the north and south polarity and the particular way the two coils are wired together that gives the pickup its hum-canceling ability, its power, and its name. It must be pointed out, though, that the two coils don't have to be in the same cover. Any two single-coil pickups can be wired or switched together to make a humbucker. A Fender P-Bass pickup is humbucking, for example, even though it's split and sitting at different places under the strings.

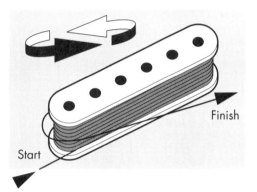

Start

Finish

COLOR-CODING AND START/FINISH WRAPS

When a coil is wrapped, obviously there's a starting end and a finish end of the wire. Knowing which wire is the start and finish allows you to wire it without regard to factory color-coding and without a diagram. Some manufacturers use the same colors but not in the same order, so you can't use a DiMarzio diagram to wire a Duncan pickup! It's no big deal, but each time you discover the start and finish to a certain pickup, keep a record of it. Here's a list of the color-coding and the start/finish wraps for several manufacturers:

	Finish	*Start*
S. Duncan	Red/White	Green/Black
DiMarzio	White/Black	Green/Red
Schaller	Green/Yellow	White/Brown

Learn how to use your multi-meter to determine the functions of two unknown wires coming from a coil by reading page 51 of Donald Brosnac's latest edition of *Guitar Electronics For Musicians.*

With any pickup wiring, it helps to have the factory wiring diagram, since wire color-coding is not the same from manufacturer to manufacturer; one company's green is another's red. If you don't have a wiring diagram, try your local dealer or the books mentioned at the beginning of this chapter.

With a humbucker, usually the smooth-faced polepiece is north and the slotted adjustable polepiece is south. Of course, some pickups have two rows of adjustable polepieces.

SERIES/PARALLEL

Several times in this book you'll see the terms series or parallel used to describe the linking of electric components or the coils of pickups. Series linkage combines two components by wiring them end-to-end. Parallel linkage combines components side-by-side. If you're using these terms with regard to pickups or their coils, you're linking resistances. When two equal resistances are linked in series (i.e., the two coils of a humbucker), the result is the sum of the two; the series sound is powerful and bassy. When the same two resistances are linked in parallel, the result is one-quarter of their combined values. Parallel sound is weaker, but very bright and clean. The series or parallel wiring options are what gives today's versatile four-wire humbuckers their distinctive sounds.

FOUR-WIRE PICKUPS

If your guitar has a modern four-wire humbucking pickup, this means that instead of the coils being permanently wired together inside the pickup with only two leads coming out (a hot and ground), the start and finish ends of each coil are brought outside the pickup casing in a four-wire coaxial cable with a separate ground (either a separate strand or braid of wire). The two coils can be wired together in five combinations: 1) in-series/out-of-phase (a normal humbucker); 2) in-parallel/out-of-phase; 3) in-series/in-phase; 4) in-parallel/in-phase; 5) either coil by itself (a coil-cut). Of course, there are many more options when you begin to combine two pickups together. To learn more about multiple pickup options, read the recommended books and check out the videotape I made for Stew-Mac, *Guitar Electronics And Hot-Rod Techniques*.

The five pickup functions are normally controlled with a mini switch (often supplied with the pickup) or a push/pull pot. At left is a sample Seymour Duncan diagram for wiring a humbucker in-series, parallel, or split-coil using a DPDT on/on/on mini switch. I don't need to give any more space to diagrams, since they're easy to read and the best way for you to understand the different wiring options is to hear

them. Try this test, preferably on a "kit" guitar you're not too worried about screwing up:

Install the four-wire humbucker of your choice in the bridge position, reinstall the strings, and bring the pickup wires out where you can twist (not solder) the leads together in the five different pickup combinations. Then solder two wires, a hot and ground, to an output jack and connect their free ends to two alligator clips. By connecting the alligator clips to the twisted ends of the colored wire combinations, you can plug a guitar cord into the jack and hear the sounds straight from the pickup to the amp. Once you've heard the pickup sounds, you'll be more confident when using a wiring diagram to install the mini switches that allow pickup options to be neatly switched with the flip of a lever!

The following list shows how to wire finishes, starts, and ground to get the five pickup combinations mentioned above. Remember, the pickup has five wires in all (two starts, two finishes, and a ground), and here's how they're designated:

Five Wiring Configurations

(F=finish S=start G=ground)

Series out-of-phase
The standard humbucker.
F+F=series link, S+G=ground, S=hot (output). A powerful sound with lots of bass and not much hum.

Series in-phase
F+S=series link, F+G= ground, S= hot (output). This is no longer a humbucking pickup! Thin-sounding, it has less volume and bass than a humbucking.

parallel out-of-phase
F+S=hot (output), F+S+G=ground. This is a humbucker with a single-coil sound. Quite strong.

parallel in-phase
F+F=hot (output), S+S+G=ground. No longer humbucking, it has a thin sound, and it's not too strong.

coil-cut
S=hot (output), F+F+S+G=ground. One coil is grounded out (shorted) completely. No longer humbucking, but a good, strong single-coil sound.

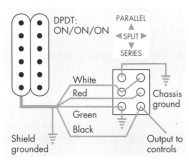

DPDT:
ON/ON/ON

PARALLEL
▲
◄ SPLIT ►
▼
SERIES

White
Red
Green
Black

Chassis ground

Shield grounded

Output to controls

INSTALLING A HUMBUCKER IN A STRAT

Now let's replace the rear (bridge) single-coil pickup of a Strat-style guitar with a humbucker. This is an easy job if you've learned how to use a router and routing templates. You can eliminate the hassle of re-routing the pickguard simply by buying a pickguard with the rear humbucker cut-out already made. These can be purchased from most guitar parts suppliers, and they allow you to save the original for posterity. If you'd rather rout your own, do it before removing the pickguard to rout the body. Lower the bridge pickup until it drops down, so that you can lay out the humbucking outline onto the pickguard. If you have a plastic pickup mounting ring, use that as a template. Otherwise, the usual humbucker rout is 1½" x 2¾" with a ³⁄₁₆" radius in the corners (you could make a cardboard template for tracing). Better yet, use a plastic routing template to lay it out; you'll soon be using it to do the routing, anyway.

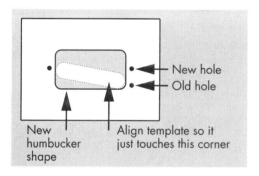

New humbucker shape

Align template so it just touches this corner

New hole
Old hole

With most Strat-style guitars, the rear rout is slanted (above), and you can use the original mounting hole in the pickguard on the bass (low-*E*) side for mounting the humbucker. You'll have to drill a new hole on the treble side, though, leaving the original treble hole showing. These days most bridge-mount humbuckers are installed at right angles to the guitar's center line, and they're easy to lay out. The routing template has six holes drilled in it: The two center ones are for locating the height-adjustment screws, and the four corner ones locate the screw holes of a pickup mounting ring (as used on Les Pauls, 335s, and many others). If you plan on using a mounting ring over the pickguard, you can use the four corner screws to mount the template. If not, use double-stick tape, since you wouldn't want

the holes to show in your pickguard. Note: Screwing down a template is the most solid and safest way to mount it; using double-stick tape works great, but you must be careful not to pull finish when removing the template. To avoid this, don't cover the entire template bottoms with tape. Experiment with routing and removing the template on a scrap of finished wood or on a junk guitar!

Place the template onto the pickguard with the bass-side holes for the height-adjustment screws lined up. Then align the template until its rear edge just touches the original single-coil cutout (as shown at left). Mark lightly on the pickguard in pencil, unfasten the pickups, toggle switch, and volume and tone controls, and remove the pickguard from the body. Now use the pencil marks to align the template as you stick it down to the pickguard with double-stick tape. You're ready to rout.

To do a perfect job, you should lay out and drill a ³⁄₁₆" hole in each of the four inside corners of the area to be routed. This is because the smallest ball-bearing router bit is ³⁄₈", which can't cut close enough to the four inside corners for the pickup cover to fit through the hole. The ³⁄₈" bit will cut a proper size hole for a humbucker without a cover, however, since the corners don't need to be as tight. If you have trouble drilling the lower right corner because there's not enough plastic left from the original single-coil rout to hold the drill's tip, radius the corner with a small rat-tail file. You can do all the corners with a file, if you wish. Go ahead and rout. Routing templates are quite thin (³⁄₁₆"), so be sure that the ball bearing is contacting the Plexiglas as you cut, and that the bearing can't slide up the shaft! If the bearing vibrates up the shaft, the router bit could cut an oversized hole. I use a length of ¼" Teflon tubing slid over the router bit shaft to hold the bearing in place. When the pickguard cutout is routed, replace the pickguard and use the new hole as a template to mark out the body rout.

Routing the body cavity is much the same as routing the pickguard, but you need a different template because the mounting bracket or "tabs" extend beyond the length of the pickup. The hole in the pickguard is smaller and just allows clearance for the upper part of the pickup or its cover. The hole in the body is slightly bigger to accommodate the pickup frame. Install the new pickup into the pickguard and measure its underside to find out how deep the body rout must be. Note: You don't need to make the whole rout as deep as the mounting brackets, as you'll see if you study the situation or look at a factory rout on a Gibson Les Paul. You only need to rout or drill an oversize hole at each end of the cavity for the brackets and height-adjusting screws to fit into; these holes are usually routed slightly oval in shape. For more information on pickup installation, read Mike Metz' article in the Jan./Feb. '90 issue of *String Instrument Craftsman*.

That's it for pickup installation. There's always more to tell, but this gives you a solid start. Now let's learn a little about safety in guitar electronics.

Safety measures

Shock protection should be of concern to anyone playing with an amplifier, especially when you're using lots of high-wattage equipment, playing in a sloppily wired building or in a wet environment, or your equipment is old and rundown or has been worked on by an amateur. Sometimes people are just unlucky. We've heard of players getting shocked, and sometimes killed, onstage. It's not the *guitar* that has the potential to kill; the danger lies in improper wiring and malfunctioning amps or PA gear. Follow these safety steps:

■ Modern electrical cords are equipped with three-prong plugs to ensure that the ground is always connected and to orient the plug so that the hot or "live" prong goes into the right slot in the outlet. *Caution: Never break off or remove the ground prong from your plugs.* This is really stupid! And if you use adapters that allow a three-prong grounded plug to be used in a two-prong outlet without a ground, remember that your amp isn't grounded.

■ For around $6.00 you can buy a circuit

(outlet) checker at the hardware store. Keep it in your guitar case, and check every outlet that you plug into. This little device (shown at lower left) indicates correct wiring, open ground, reversed polarity, open hot, open neutral, hot and ground reversed, and hot on neutral with hot open. You're looking for correct wiring—period!

As far as your guitar and its wiring is concerned, here are some measures you can take to further protect yourself, but none of them are guaranteed:

■ A perfect shielding job allows you to disconnect or "float" the ground wire running from your strings to the ground; this usually runs from the tailpiece to the wiring harness. You could still get a shock from touching metal volume and tone knobs, the output jack, or a metal ¼" input jack on your guitar cord, though. You'll have better luck shielding and removing the ground wire on humbucking pickups than single-coils. Try it, and see if you're happy.

■ Adrian Legg's *Customizing Your Electric Guitar* suggests adding a safety feature between the strings and the ground: Wire in parallel a 220k ohm resistor (colored bands are red, red and yellow, and silver or gold) and a .001 capacitor with a minimum voltage rating of 500 volts. Twist the wires together and solder them as seen below. This can be done out of sight inside the control cavity, and it only lets about 40 volts through to your strings if a shock is headed your way. The normal string ground still functions, too. However, with this safety device you'll still get it if you touch metal knobs, jacks, or guitar cords.

■ You can be safe from volume or tone knob shock if your pots have nylon shafts, such as Fender used to use.

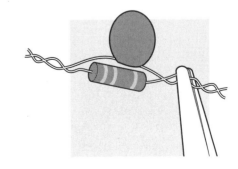

How piezo transducers work, and how they're installed

Now that you're familiar with all the tools and techniques of guitar electronics, turning your acoustic guitar into an electric should be a "piezo cake." This section looks at the new generation of under-the-saddle, piezoelectric "transducer" pickups that are available for do-it-yourself installation. Piezoelectric pickups are being produced by a number of manufacturers, most notably Fishman, Barcus-Berry, Shadow, Ovation, L.R. Baggs, Takamine, Seymour Duncan, Dana Bourgeois, EMG, Highlander, and Dean Markley. The transducer pickup is, in my opinion, very much responsible for the resurgence of acoustic popularity nationwide.

Once a lowly and endangered species, acoustic players are now out of the bluegrass closet, playing on the same stages with drummers and electric guitarists. Moreover, they're actually being heard—without feedback, without rumble, and with a relatively true acoustic sound—all through the magic of piezo pickups. Lots of new guitars are available with factory-installed piezos, including Martin, Gibson, Yamaha, Ithaca Guitar Works, Takamine, Guild, Ferrington, Santa Cruz, Taylor, Alvarez, Collings, Dana Bourgeois, Larivee, Mossman, Seagull, and the entire Kaman family (including Ovation), as well as scores of custom builders such as James Goodall, Don Musser, and James Olsen. Our focus here, though, is not so much on the various *types* of pickups available for installation, but rather on how they work, and most important, how to install them. A piezo's installation isn't actually a piece of cake, but it's as important to the final sound as the transducer itself. But first, here's a little transducer history….

Before the late '60's, when the first under-the-saddle pickup came along, there had been a variety of contact pickups available, but they weren't too great. DeArmond made one of the most popular. Then in '68 Baldwin introduced the first under the bridge saddle transducer pickup, but you had to buy the *guitar* with it (and the guitar was none too great either). About that same time, Barcus-Berry introduced their first pickup, which fastened inside to the bridge plate, or other area of the top. Barcus-Berry seemed intent on making an improvement over the DeArmond top-sensing pickup, and was probably unaware of the Baldwin pickup (which was the first to produce the sound of the *string* rather than the top).

Observing all this was Ovation's James Rickard—one of the great guitar builders, repairmen, and inventors. Aiming to please Ovation-endorsee Glen Campbell, Jim designed Ovation's now famous under-the-saddle pickup. It was second to Baldwin's chronologically, but first musically. This is the pickup that *really* made it possible for players to take their acoustic guitars onstage with an electric band—the same pickup Ovation still uses today, and the pickup which made Ovation guitars famous.

Mr. Rickard says: "The way it happened was, we'd just gotten our greatest endorsee—Glen Campbell. It was in '68 or '69. And then one night Glen shows up on the 'Johnny Carson Show' with Jerry Reed and a matched set of Baldwin guitars—the ones with the earliest transducer. I saw Jerry give Glen the poison apple. Glen probably didn't like the guitar too well, but he liked that amplification. We freaked out, afraid of losing Glen—and we probably would have lost him if we hadn't acted as quickly as we did.

"So at Ovation, we looked at both of those pickups—the Baldwin and the Barcus-Berry. We were very concerned about having a balanced output—getting an even response from string to string. We had to please a real player in Glen Campbell. Glen covered the fretboard from one end to the other, and he was very conscious of dead spots (low output) and hot spots (good, or maybe too much, output). This lack of balanced output was Glen's complaint with amplified acoustic guitars—including the Baldwin. We gave him what he wanted: the even, balanced output of

Unless you're extremely sure of yourself, installing piezo pickups is definitely something you should leave to a pro.

all six strings equally—and not so much from the top. I'd found that the output from top-sensing pickups like the Frap or Barcus-Berry was louder on some resonant frequencies than on others, and that's why some notes, or clusters of notes, had more or less output than others did.

"Where you place a top-sensing-pickup is a problem because there's no 'right' spot. All you do is move the pickup in and out of a guitar's natural hot-spots. A guitar top is full of tonal areas which produce one frequency better than another, but a single pickup can't sense them all at once—there's no place where a pickup can give you the whole spectrum. That's why we went to a pickup that sensed the string. Baldwin had the right idea with their pickup, but the design wasn't as practical as ours.

"Under-the-saddle pickups, which sense the strings, are 'top pickups' as well—they do sense the top. Top-sensing pickups, however, sense only the top, and never the strings. Under-the-saddle pickups, with the piezo element sensing sound from above and below, are therefore louder because they have output from both the top and the string. They don't feed back like a top-sensing pickup does, because the string sound can be loud while the top sound is at a lower volume which doesn't induce feedback.

"Luckily for Ovation, the other companies didn't take us seriously at the time. We produced 30,000 pickup-installed guitars annually for many years before they realized we had something going! Our detractors would say, 'Ugh! A plastic bowl for a back' (actually, it wasn't the back that people first noticed, it was the soundhole rosette and the peghead shape). But the musicians responded to Ovation because we gave them a pickup that allowed them to go onstage and not feed back."

Barcus-Berry then designed the Hot Dots (the rage of the late '70's), which being installed in the bridge body, were still "top-sensors." Finally Barcus-Berry introduced an under-the-saddle transducer *strip*—Martin's First Generation Thinline—that was readily available over the counter. Along with a competitor, the "Shadow" pickup, the Thinline

was very popular, but Ovation still had the best sound onstage.

Takamine soon got into the act with a very good sounding system that was much like Ovation's. Takamine came along in the '70s, around the same time as the Barcus-Berry Thinline strip. Like the Ovation, the Takamine was a functional road guitar that was ready to buy. They became very popular, and one reason was because they were less expensive than an Ovation.

In the early '80s L.R. Baggs and Larry Fishman each produced under-the-saddle transducer strips which were much improved over the original Thinline. I believe Lloyd Baggs was actually the first. From around '85 until '92, Baggs and Fishman lead the field. Currently, however, there are a number of saddle transducers being manufactured—and choosing between them isn't easy. I will say this: Any under-the-saddle transducer will outperform a top-sensing pickup—offering a more balanced output and less feedback.

PIEZO CONSTRUCTION AND DESIGN

Bridge-saddle transducer pickups are all quite similar in construction, although different brands vary widely in sound. Basically, you've got six pressure-sensitive pieces of piezo ceramic that are linked by wire and held together in a strip by various bonding methods (encased in foil, silicone rubber, a brass channel, etc.). These elements transmit sounds by translating the pressure of the plucked strings on the saddle above them into electrical signals. The underside of the piezo elements also sense sound from the guitar top, so in that sense they are "top sensors." The pickup's material makeup, size, thickness, and bonding method all contribute to each maker's individual sound. The manufacturers haven't invented any new technology at all. It's their different 'recipes'—the blend of physical and electrical proportions—that produce the different-sounding pickup.

What this recipe talk means is that since each maker's pickups sound so different, you have to do some research to find the right sound for you. Check with your dealer or local repairman for information. Perhaps you can find out which customers use which pickups, and then call those people to see if they'd mind giving you a quick demo. And many stores have new and used guitars with factory-installed piezos.

Some piezo manufacturers are now using a piezo *film*, rather than a series of piezo elements. An advantage gained with piezo film is that the exact placement of the elements under each string is no longer a factor, since the film sensor is *continuous*. Because of this, the balance of the string ouput is said to be better. Companies using the piezo film are Fishman (Matrix, and Martin's Gold Plus), EMG (AS-93 and AS-125), Highlander, and EMG/Dana Bourgeois.

Over the years, I've known many guitarists who have experimented with piezo pickups, only to quickly give them up, complaining of a poppy, "Donald Ducky," crackling sound that's often joined by unruly overtones, feedback, excess body noise, and unbalanced string response. These discouraged, would-have-been acoustic players weren't aware that these problems could have been caused by impedance mismatch, lack of a preamp, or the wrong amplifier (they hadn't read L.R. Baggs' excellent article in the Oct. '87 issue of *Guitar Player magazine*, "Getting The Most From Your Piezo Pickup"). Last, but not least, is the possibility that the guitars they tried were equipped with incorrectly installed saddle pickups.

So before placing blame on the poor piezo, be sure that your saddle/pickup installation is correct, and keep these five rules in mind:

1 The piezo strip must be located in the slot so that all six elements are under their respective strings.

2 The saddle must be made from the right material.

3 The saddle must be a slip—or "sliding"—fit, and in some cases split in two. Also, the piezo strip should be close to the same width as the saddle, and it should sit directly under the whole saddle.

4 The bottoms of the saddle and the saddle slot must be a perfect match.

5 The best sound is produced when you have a 50/50 installation—50% of the saddle is in the bridge body and 50% is exposed.

INSTALLING PIEZO SADDLE PICKUPS

Now that you understand the basics of how the piezo pickups work, and you know a bit about the history of the various types available, let's begin the actual installation procedure. Installing most under-the-saddle pickups is easy in theory and a little tricky in practice. And it requires certain specialized tools. If you're in doubt, leave the work to a pro; otherwise, here's straightforward advice for do-it-yourselfers.

LOCATION

The transducer must be located with its piezo elements directly under the strings, as shown below. First, the string spacing from *E* to *E* must be taken into account. Martin guitars, for example, have a string spacing at the saddle, from center to center, measuring 2 ⅛". Their pickup is made accordingly. Most conventional steel-string acoustics have string spacing similar to Martin's, and the various pickup brands are made to match. But if your guitar varies more than .050" from 2 ⅛", you should check into having piezo elements custom-installed to match your spacing. Most of the manufacturers I spoke with do some custom work, although some welcome it more than others.

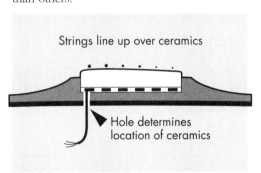

Strings line up over ceramics

Hole determines location of ceramics

Actually, the location of the piezo elements relative to the strings is really determined by where you drill the hole for the output wire (because the six elements are wired together). This hole is drilled in the bottom of the saddle slot, down through the bridge, top, and bridge-plate on its way to the output jack that's usually installed in the end block for added

If you want a built-in preamp, take your axe to the best repair shop you can find; it's a tricky job.

strength. Each manufacturer's installation instructions will tell you the exact location of the clearance hole in the bridge, so just measure carefully. If the hole does get off towards one end or the other, you can enlarge it slightly to compensate.

As mentioned earlier, if your pickup is a piezo film, location of the pickup under the individual strings isn't critical.

SADDLE MATERIAL

I prefer bone or ivory for acoustic saddles, but Micarta, a synthetic, is recommended by the piezo manufacturers as being the best material for transducer installation, since it's more even in texture throughout. It's also more flexible than bone, and it moves with the top, bridge, and piezo when a string is plucked. Bone or ivory may offer a stronger acoustic sound when the pickup is *not* being used, but it won't normally sound as good as the synthetic when you're plugged in (I've done many installations with high quality bone of uniform density which sounded great, however).

THE FIT

To begin with, the piezo strip should be close to the width of the saddle slot, so that the whole saddle sits on it for even pressure. If it is too much narrower, it could end up close to the front or rear edge, or sitting at a cross-angle to the saddle (below). Any of these situations is less than optimum in terms of sound.

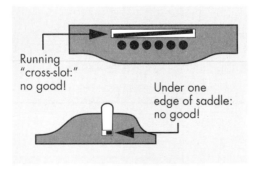

Running "cross-slot:" no good!

Under one edge of saddle: no good!

While most repairmen suggest that a saddle fit quite snugly, this is not true for piezo transducers. The saddle should slide or slip in without force. It shouldn't be loose, wiggly, or falling over, but it mustn't be tight. Admittedly, this is a judgment call that's hard to describe on paper, but you'll get a feel for it after a couple of installations. A too-tight saddle won't exert

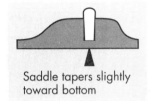

Saddle tapers slightly toward bottom

the proper pressure down on the ceramic and may cause the following problems: no sound at all, unbalanced string response (i.e., sound on some strings and not others, or some strings louder than others), unwanted overtones, lowering of overall output, and 60-cycle hum.

In general, the saddle sides should fit the slot walls with a slip-fit tolerance of, say, .002" to .005". Some professionals recommend shaping a slight downward taper on a saddle to guarantee that it reaches the bottom (left). This is smart if you're unable to get a perfect slip-fit. The saddle bottom should mate with the slot bottom with the same accuracy as the sides. Often it's best to rout the slot bottom to get it flat and then shape the saddle bottom flat to match. This technique, along with a jig you can make yourself for doing the job, will be explained shortly.

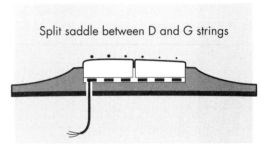

Split saddle between D and G strings

Perhaps you've seen installations where the saddle has been cut in half between the *D* and *G* strings (above). This is the proper method for some piezo saddle pickups, most notably the Barcus-Berry 1440 and the Shadow 1110. These systems utilize balanced phasing, which polarizes the pickup into two halves, like a humbucker. The *E*, *A*, and *D* strings face up (north), while the *G*, *B*, and high-*E* face down (south). If the saddle isn't cut, the *D* and *G* strings "read" each other's plucked string signal and cancel each other out. This can cause a lot of dead notes and bad sounds when the saddle is left in one piece on double-pole transducers.

The Martin Second Generation 332, the L.R. Baggs LB-6, and the Barcus-Berry 1440 SP do not require saddle splitting. The need for splitting the saddle should be considered before installation. Perhaps you simply don't want your saddle cut in two. It's also harder to make a perfect-fit split saddle, since you're sort of making two saddles—and one is hard enough! (Note: The L.R. Baggs Saddle Replacement Pickup comes with the Micarta saddle already bonded to the piezo bottom. In this case the routing and installation fit is the same as the others, except that rather than making a saddle, you shape the saddle that comes on it. Unless you're really sure of yourself, have this pickup installed by a professional, since if you go too far on the Micarta, you're in trouble.)

Installation of under-the-saddle transducers generally involves some light routing of the bridge saddle slot—sometimes widening it and often deepening it. Most important, the routing is done to ensure that the bottoms of the slot and saddle match perfectly. The transducer sits between the saddle and slot bottom and must contact both evenly, so shaping both flat is the easiest method for guaranteeing a good

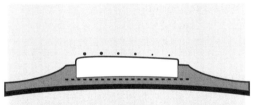

If bottom of saddle slot is curved,
it must be routed flat

contact. Curved bottoms are okay when well matched, but it's easier to be sure of a fit if both are flat. It's best to use a transducer strip that's close to the same size as the saddle, so that it sits directly under the whole saddle—not cross-slot or under one edge.

Most so-called flat-top guitars actually have a slight upward arch built into them. This effect increases over the years from string pull on the top, causing the guitar to visibly belly up. This is not necessarily bad; it's just a fact of guitar life. Realize that the bridge has slowly become curved to match the top, and therefore the bottom of its saddle slot is bent into the same slight curve. Even with the strings removed, the top and bridge remain somewhat curved, having taken a "set." It's best to reroute the saddle slot to create a flat bottom within its curved shape (above). It won't take much, and in so doing, you might also find it necessary to widen the slot as well, so that the transducer drops in without force.

Since most flat-top guitars have significantly more up-bow when strung to pitch, many repairmen use a prop or jack inside the instrument to recreate the top's arch when the strings are removed for saddle slot routing. By holding the top in its true curve, the saddle routing operation is even more accurate. I recommend laying a board or caul over the back braces as a support for a jack or prop, and spreading the load across a large area of the back. With the strings on and tuned to pitch, you can install a prop-stick until it's just snug and no longer falls over in the same way that a sound-post is installed in a violin.

Using a Dremel Moto-Tool and a 5/64" bit, flatten the slot's bottom. Make a routing table cut from 3/8" or thicker Plexiglas or plywood that sits taller than the bridge and gives the router a flat surface to ride over (below). The

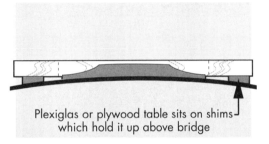

Plexiglas or plywood table sits on shims
which hold it up above bridge

table is shimmed level where needed, and lightly taped to the guitar's face with duct tape so that it doesn't move. If you also don't move while routing, you'll get a flat bottom. Clean up any router marks, and square up the sides with a sharp chisel, following the saddle-making techniques described in Acoustic Adjustments.

The serious transducer installer will be interested in the Vacu-Jig, manufactured by Guitar Systems (at right). This tool uses the power of your Shop-Vac to suction onto a

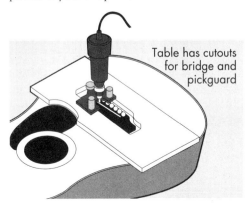

Table has cutouts
for bridge and
pickguard

guitar top. Because it's adjustable, it aligns easily with any saddle slot, and then makes use of the Dremel Moto-Tool for pinpoint routing of the slot. The Vacu-Jig is a flat, stable surface for a Dremel router to ride over, which ensures a flat bottom for the saddle slot and eliminates the need for clamping a makeshift routing table around the bridge. The jig's adjustable fences entrap the router baseplate, guiding it in a straight line during the routing.

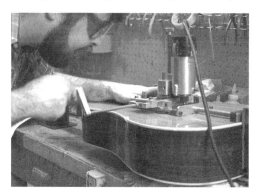

Industrial transducer installers, eat your hearts out! That's what I did when Rich Starkey pulled out the "deluxe" router and jig that they use in the Martin repair department (above). I think I'll ask for one for Christmas!

If you're making the saddle slot a little wider than you started with, measure carefully and keep the walls parallel with each other. It's very tough to work on a saddle slot without widening it a little bit, so expect to replace the saddle with an oversized blank that is filed down to fit. Micarta, bone, or ivory saddle blanks come in thicknesses ranging from $3/32$" to $1/4$", and they must be final-shaped by hand. The Martin Second Generation Thinline, Shadow's 1110, and the Barcus-Berry 1440 and 1440 SP fit into a $3/32$" slot, while the Fishman AG-125 and the L.R. Baggs require close to a $1/8$" slot. Ovation transducers require close to a $5/16$" saddle slot (their non-electric guitars, however, use a $1/8$" saddle slot, as do Guilds, Seagulls, and some others).

There are many repair situations where it's advisable or necessary to widen the saddle more than $3/32$" (compensation, warped slot, etc.). Some repairmen and builders prefer a wider saddle in general. The Fishman AG-l 25 and the Baggs LB-6 are well suited to these situations. It's better not to install a thinner

pickup ($3/32$") in a wider slot. Doing so might cause the piezo to become off-center or run at an angle to the bottom of the saddle.

The correct saddle depth, according to Fishman's Rick Nelson, is "A 50/50 ratio. That seems to be the magic number. We've found that optimum sound results when one half of the saddle is in the bridge body, and one half exposed. Too deep a slot can produce balance problems which we call "ghosting"—where one or more strings have a weaker output than their neighbors. If you have too much saddle in your bridge, and not enough showing on top, shim up the transducer strip from beneath with a piece of hardwood. If too much saddle is out of the slot, rout the slot a little deeper."

When the pickup fits the slot, you must drill a small hole through the bottom of the slot—down through the bridge, top, and bridge pad. This is for the pickup's output wire. The manufacturer's instructions tell exactly where to locate this hole (as mentioned earlier). This isn't too serious a modification, but think twice about doing any such work on a vintage instrument! Next comes a tough part: drilling-out, or enlarging, the strap button hole in the end block to house the output jack (combination output jack/strap buttons are usually installed in the end block).

INSTALLING THE OUTPUT JACK

The hardest part of installing the output jack is drilling the hole through the end block (you'll see some jacks mounted in the side of the lower bout, but this method isn't as strong without clever reinforcement). Most end blocks have a hole for the strap button. This hole must first be enlarged by reaming to accept a large drill bit (.469" to $1/2$"), and then drilled at a perfect right angle through the block. I really recommend that you have this operation done at a professional shop. Go ahead and do your own wiring if you wish, but please, be careful with the drilling! But if you must put the hole through your own block, read on.

When enlarging the end-pin hole, avoid chipping the wood around it, don't split the end block (usually mahogany, which splits easily), and keep the hole straight. A crooked

hole leaves the input jack at an awkward angle, which looks bad and makes it hard to tighten the mounting hex nuts. A drill bit tends to grab into wood, especially when drilling into an existing hole. There are many ways of enlarging the hole with drilling tools (drill presses, hand-held electric drills, bit and brace, etc.), but they're all risky for the novice. The safest method is to use a hand-held ½" tapered reamer to enlarge the hole slowly.

Most hardware-store reamers are about ½" at the widest end of the taper, and may be used straight from the shelf to do the job. They'll make the hole slightly larger than necessary, though, since the outside diameter (O.D.) of the thread on the end-pin jack measures .469"—that is, .031" (¹⁄₃₂") smaller than the .500" (½") hole that the reamer makes. If you want a snug-fitting jack, pay a machine shop a small fee to grind down the reamer's flutes (cutting edges) until they match the thread O.D. exactly. And while you're at it, have the shank ground to the same size, so that it's slim enough to allow the cutting edge to go entirely through the end block (right). Be careful as you work, since a reamer that's not held square can chip the wood or finish just like a drill bit. If your final fit is too snug, use a rat-tail file to finish the job. Once the jack fits easily through the hole, wire in the transducer strip to the output jack—it's easy.

A piezo bridge-saddle pickup must be wired to the jack *before* fastening it home in the end block; be sure you slip the interior hex nut and washer over the wires—in that order—before you run them through the end-pin hole for soldering! I've soldered up more than one jack without remembering the nut and washer; it makes you feel kind of stupid. If you're unsure about soldering, let the shop that drills your end block install the jack at the same time. Or, here's a couple of tricks to help make the jack installation as easy as I say it is:

Solder the insulated (plastic-coated) lead wire to the prong-tip wiring lug, and solder the bare ground wire (or braided shield) to the casing. The manufacturer's instructions tell you which wire goes where (but you *know* that— the hot wire goes to the prong tip, and the braided ground goes to the grounding lug of

the ¼" female input jack). The only pointer that comes to mind is not to strip off any more of the wire shield than is absolutely necessary. If you remove too much shielding, the exposed section acts as an antenna. It then becomes a great source for picking up 60-cycle hum from fluorescent lights, dimmer switches, etc.

For pulling the wires through the end-block hole, run an electric bass string through the hole and into the guitar. Then you can stick the loose wire ends into the large ball end, and use the length of bass string as a guide to pull the ball end and wires through the hole and out where you can solder them. An alligator-clip helping-hand soldering stand makes a good holder while you're soldering.

Probably the toughest part of installing the end-pin jack is getting the hex nut tight against the end block from the inside. I've popped blood vessels while trying to tighten this nut through the soundhole, and those of you with big arms haven't a prayer. I found a solution while visiting the C. F. Martin & Co. factory in Nazareth, Pennsylvania. Martin installs more piezo strips than any of us—in fact, they have a work area devoted solely to installing their Second Generation Thinline by Fishman. To hold the hex nut from the inside while tightening from the outside, they use a hollow-shaft, deep-socket ⁹⁄₁₆" nut driver with a slot milled through one wall of the hex and into the hollow shaft. The slot allows the tool to slide onto the wires and follow along them, over the jack's soldering prongs and onto the hex nut, making it easy to hold the nut against the inside of the block while you tighten the outside nut home. It's a great tool!

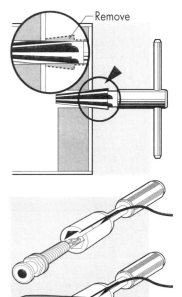

There are also two endpin jacks available that don't require tightening from the inside. One, the "Anderson Stapjack," requires no mounting nuts. It has a threaded exterior and actually screws into the end-block hole, cutting a thread as it goes in. The other, and it's my preference, is the "Guitar Endpin Jack," or "Fast Jack." It was developed by Larry Fishman, and tightens easily from the outside.

All of the manufacturers provide adequate instructions for installation, but none of the manuals are exceptional. Certain points are glossed over, probably to encourage novices

> **Working on anything vintage these days takes nerve, even if it's your own guitar. You should have seen me when my wife Joan and daughters Kate and Meredith gave me a '56 Strat for Christmas '89. I wanted to take off the pickguard and verify its date, but I was scared to death!**

to take the job to a professional, which may head off some customer-service problems. Before closing, I'd like to gloss over one point myself: Some manufacturers install a preamp with volume and tone controls in the side of the instrument near the neck block on the bass side. We're not discussing that installation, nor do I advise you to try it. If you want a built-in preamp, take your axe to the best repair shop you can find; it's a tricky job.

Frankly, it's hard to recommend one pickup over another, because they sound so different. Do your best to locate players with a particular brand installed in his or her guitar and check it out. You might as well expect to invest some dough in at least several different brands until you find what's right for you. I think the smart music store—at least one with an active acoustic clientele—should invest in a half-dozen identical, good-sounding but inexpensive flat-top guitars and install all the different transducers in them. Then customers could make an educated choice. Anybody hear me out there?

TROUBLESHOOTING
UNBALANCED OUTPUT

The most common problem with under-the-saddle installations is unbalanced output. If one string is louder than another, and you're not getting even string response, go back to the beginning and read through again. You probably have a poor fit between the saddle bottom and the bridge bottom.

• Another solution currently being used is placing a thin strip of cedar or spruce between the saddle bottom and the piezo strip. The wood acts as an "equalizer"—eliminating the difference in contact pressure between the individual strings. Note: Eric Aceto at "Ithaca Guitar Works" tried the cedar strip trick and still had a hot string. He looked at the cedar under a microscope and found a piece of hard grain which he hadn't noticed. This hard grain was sitting under the string that was too loud. Eric changed to a piece of poplar, which has the same amount of give but has no differentiation between spring and summer growth, and the problem was solved. The moral? If you use spruce or cedar, select the soft-growth wood in between the hard grain lines (or use poplar

since its grain has no differentiation between spring and summer growth). The cedar should be quarter-sawn.

Other acoustic amplification solutions

Saddle transducers are not the only way to get good amplification from an acoustic axe. Miniature condenser mikes, dynamic field, and transducer/mic combos are gaining in popularity. Contact the following companies for information on acoustic guitar amplification.

Mini-Flex Microphones (Donnell Enterprises): 24 Parkhurst St., Chico, CA 95928-6856 (916) 893-4845

Acoustech Dynamic Field: Harmonic Arts, 841 New Hampshire, Lawrence, KS 66044 (800) 653-1184; also: Guitar Pro Service, 1719 S Bus 65, Hollister, MO 65672 (417) 334-3030

Dana Bourgeois Transducer/Mic Combo: Dana Bourgeois Guitars: 9 Winter St., Topsham, ME 04086 (207) 725-1207

Highlander Integrated Pickup/Preamp: 305 Glenwood Ave., Ventura, CA 93003 (805) 658-1819

Dean Markley Electronics, Inc.: 3350 Scott Blvd. #45, Santa Clara, CA 95054 (408) 988-2456

EMG, Inc.: P.O. Box 4394, Santa Rosa, CA 95402 (707) 525-9941

Seymour Duncan "Woody" Soundhole Pickup and "Sadducer": 601 Pine Ave., Santa Barbara, CA 93117 (805) 964-9610

If you've gotten this far, you definitely have enough information to help you make a wise pickup purchase, even if you don't feel like doing the installation yourself. As always, I remind you that my goal is to educate you, not talk you into doing tough jobs without experience. Installing these pickups is definitely something you should leave to a pro unless you're extremely sure of yourself. Good luck!

Strat pickup quirks

One famous quirk of Strat pickups is that if they are adjusted too closely to the strings, the magnets' strong fields can hold a string's vibration in a vertical pattern, not letting it vibrate freely in a more natural oval or elliptical pattern. This causes the low-*E* string (and sometimes the *A* and *D*) to go crazy. It produces unwanted harmonic overtones that may be perceived as "double notes" or dead notes, and makes the proper setting of the intonation practically impossible. Besides the harmonic overtones, you may notice a general out-of-tuneness on the bass strings, especially as you play up the neck. A pickup that's too close may also cause buzzing on the upper frets, because the magnets actually drag the strings down and against the frets, especially with light-gauge sets beginning with .008s or .009s. This buzzing shouldn't be confused with a kinked neck, rising tongue, or worn frets. Before setting the intonation or string/action height, you should lower the pickups a few turns to eliminate their pull, especially on the bass side. Later, when all the action and intonation adjustments have been completed, you can slowly raise the pickups to find that most of your bad-note problems have been eliminated.

You'll find the right height by experimenting. The overtones described above are found mostly on the bass strings, especially the *E*, and usually further up the neck. Simply keep raising the pickups until the overtone phenomenon begins to happen, and at that point back off a hair. By not getting too close, you'll find a cleaner sound with no bad notes and eliminate potential buzzing in the fingerboard's upper register. Properly set-up Strat pickups are closer to the strings on the treble side than the bass; they actually slant downward across the body. And often the neck pickup is further from the strings than the bridge pickup.

Soap-bar pickups

You don't see many guitarists playing the old single-coil Gibson Les Pauls these days. Too bad! They're a great buy on the vintage market, and they have a killer sound. Here's some advice on caring for the pickups in those great old guitars, brought to mind by this letter from "C.B." in Bowling Green, Kentucky: "I own a '54 or '55 gold-top Les Paul, and I wish it had more output. Routing it for humbuckers would destroy its value on the vintage market (besides, the guitar belongs to my father). Are there high-output pickups that retrofit the same cavity as the original 'soap bar' pickups? Also, I've tried to remove these pickups to clean under them, but they fit tight. Probably glued in, right?"

Even when new, the P-90 pickups in your guitar weren't as powerful or hum-free as most humbucking pickups. Still, there are many of us who prefer their unique sound to that of humbuckers. Replacement pickups with a higher output are available from DiMarzio, Seymour Duncan, and Bartolini. But before you order replacement pickups or remove the originals, consider the following information on old P-90s.

I like to keep things clean, too, and I'll never forget taking out my first soap-bar pickup to really get at the dirt. I removed the two screws that held it down, but like yours, it wouldn't budge. Imagine my surprise when, as I pried out the pickup of my '55 Les Paul, I found that several hundred feet of very thin copper wire unwound right along with it—all over my lap! I managed to scrounge up another pickup, but these days an authentic vintage replacement would be hard to come by.

Normally, Gibson P-90 soap-bar pickups come out fairly easily, but you'll find many that are really tight. If it's just the cleaning that you're worried about, I'd say leave the pickups alone and clean around them as best you can. If you choose to use replacement pickups, consider having the originals removed by a professional repair shop.

If you choose to use replacement pickups, consider having the originals removed by a professional repair shop.

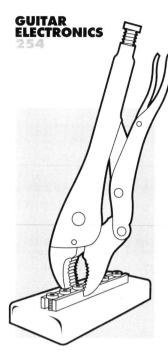

You may rest assured that your P-90 pickups aren't glued in. They're probably stuck because of all the beer that's been spilled onto them in some honky-tonk saloon, where many great guitars have paid their dues. Sometimes pickups stick to the lacquer upon which they sit, especially in humid weather. Perhaps the wood has swollen a bit. To loosen the pickups, raise the polepieces above the pickup surface (protect them with strips of wood as shown), and use Vise-Grips to gently pry or pull them out. Don't just grab the pickup by its cover and pull—this is what caused my catastrophe. Those pre-'55 P-90 coil forms were glued together rather than machined of solid stock like the post-'55 models, and when I pulled the pickup cover, the top plate of the bobbin stuck to it while the rest of the pickup remained snug in the cavity.

So, the pickup covers may or may not come free of the pickup easily, and in most cases there's no reason to ever take them off. Also, plastic covers shrink over the years and grip the pickup tightly. The plastic of both the covers and the pickup are probably brittle from age and may easily crack or break. Therefore, you should leave the covers on original P-90s, and if you get replacement pickups, buy a set of new replacement covers from your Gibson dealer (part number 13949 in black, and 13925 in cream).

Speaking of your Gibson dealer, I'd suggest that before you buy anyone else's replacement pickup, you might check out a set of new P-90s from Gibson. They have a higher output than the originals. It's also possible to "re-charge" your old P-90s: Gibson R&D exec Tim Shaw points out that soap-bars made before 1968 had Alnico II magnets that demagnetize over time and lose power (we used to buy these magnets from Gibson and recharge our pickups with them, but they're no longer available). Tim suggests having your old magnets remagnetized at an automotive or bicycle shop that services speedometers. Ask them to saturate the magnets. This restores much of the original power and sound. If you remove the magnets, mark them so that you can replace them exactly as they came out. The great thing about remagnetizing is that

you can increase your output without doing anything to damage the integrity of a fine vintage instrument—always the best solution!

A pickup for the blues

After interviewing Buddy Guy and Albert Collins, I became interested in the Fender Signature Model guitars used by blues players such as Robert Cray, the late Stevie Ray Vaughan, Eric Clapton, Jeff Beck, and Collins and Guy. I'm interested in things like fretboard radius, neck shape, and fretwire types, but most of all I wondered about the several pickup models available for blues-playing Strat lovers like myself. On a recent visit to the Fender factory and Custom Shop, I had my questions answered firsthand by master builders John Page and Larry Brooks.

The Strat pickups most commonly used for blues are the American Standard Strat, the Vintage Reissue, the Texas Special, and the Lace Sensor. "Around 1978," Larry explains, "the original staggered-polepiece Strat pickup of the '50s and '60s evolved into the American Standard Strat pickup. We designed these flush polepieces for the modern, light, and accurately gauged string sets with an unwound G. The American Standard has the same number of wraps as the Vintage Reissue, but uses a different wire on a different type of bobbin (a molded plastic one, as opposed a two-piece fiber type), giving it a different Strat sound. The American Standard pickup is now our conventional Strat pickup." The reverse wind/reverse polarity of the American Standard's middle pickup sets it apart from others, giving it the hum-cancelling sound of the in-between positions.

John reports: "The Vintage Reissue pickup is made to sound like the average vintage Strat pickup made from around '57 through '62. We redeveloped it to fill the demand created by the vintage market. It has the staggered (balanced) polepieces like the old Strats. But those old Fender pickups were wound on machines with inaccurate mechanical counters, and some pickups would mistakenly have hundreds of more wraps and end up much 'hotter' than other pickups. The new Vintage Reissue is what the old vintage pickups were supposed to be! They're wound on modern machines with accurate counters, holding consistently to the original specs that Leo designed. We're happy with the results. Buddy Guy's next custom guitar—a black and white polka-dot Strat—will probably be fitted with the Vintage Reissue pickup, since he feels he's 'missing' something in tone using the Lace Sensors in the Buddy Guy model.

"The Texas Special pickup is simply an over-wound Vintage Reissue pickup with staggered polepieces, made to look and sound like the pickups in 'Number One,' the well-worn sunburst 'SRV' Stratocaster that Stevie usually played. Number One's pickups, made in '59, are of the non-average, mistakenly over-wound, extremely hot variety, so we purposely over-wound our normal Vintage Reissue pickup to produce that stronger, darker sound associated with Stevie. He asked for a little more crunch without losing the bell-tones that give a Strat that edge."

Fender Lace Sensors are recognized by their smooth plastic cover and lack of polepieces. They differ from any other Strat pickups because of the extremely hi-tech, top secret, magnetic mixture of the material from which they're made. It's called a Sensor because it senses "reality" with no coloration. A Lace Sensor reports what it hears, while Alnico 5 pickups actually create part of the sound you hear, due to their magnetic field. The illustration shows the difference in the magnetic fields of an ordinary pickup versus the Lace Sensor.

"The Alnico 5 magnetic field pattern responds very slowly to the string signal," explains Larry. "On the other hand, activated Lace Sensors respond very quickly. You can't retain the crunch and still be quiet, but you can get 80% of the vintage sound from Gold Lace Sensors. So whatever's 'missing' from the Lace Sensor is what was lost by eliminating the noise of a single coil pickup. It's a much more sterile sound."

The different colors of the various Lace Sensors could be described like this: Gold—

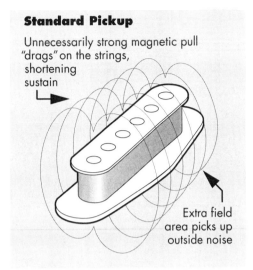

Standard Pickup

Unnecessarily strong magnetic pull "drags" on the strings, shortening sustain

Extra field area picks up outside noise

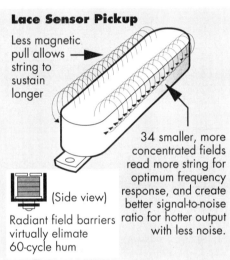

Lace Sensor Pickup

Less magnetic pull allows string to sustain longer

(Side view)

Radiant field barriers virtually elimate 60-cycle hum

34 smaller, more concentrated fields read more string for optimum frequency response, and create better signal-to-noise ratio for hotter output with less noise.

the original Lace, a vintage Strat sound in a quiet pickup; Blue—more of a PAF sound; Red—similar to a hot humbucking or dual-coil sound; Silver—in between the "fat" Strat ¼-pounder sound and the PAF.

Modifying a three-pickup Les Paul Custom

Phil Henderson of Foley, Alabama wrote to *Guitar Player* asking, "I have a 1961 Gibson Les Paul Custom 'Fretless Wonder.' It's a white, three-pickup, SG-type that I understand was the transition between the Les Paul Standard and the SG. Its pickup selector switch allows three pickup combinations: neck, middle, and middle and rear. Frankly, this doesn't give me

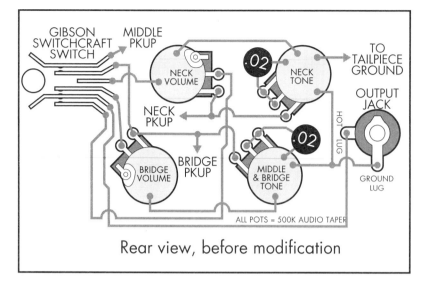

GIBSON SWITCHCRAFT SWITCH

MIDDLE PKUP

NECK VOLUME

.02

NECK TONE

TO TAILPIECE GROUND

OUTPUT JACK

HOT LUG

NECK PKUP

BRIDGE VOLUME

BRIDGE PKUP

.02

MIDDLE & BRIDGE TONE

GROUND LUG

ALL POTS = 500K AUDIO TAPER

Rear view, before modification

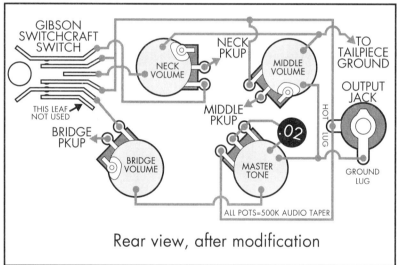

GIBSON SWITCHCRAFT SWITCH

NECK PKUP

NECK VOLUME

MIDDLE VOLUME

TO TAILPIECE GROUND

OUTPUT JACK

HOT LUG

THIS LEAF NOT USED

BRIDGE PKUP

MIDDLE PKUP

BRIDGE VOLUME

.02

MASTER TONE

GROUND LUG

ALL POTS=500K AUDIO TAPER

Rear view, after modification

the sounds I'd like. Can it be wired like a Strat with a 5-way position switch to get each pickup individually and the neck/middle and middle/bridge combinations? Can this be done without drilling any holes or harming its value too much (even though I'd never sell it)?"

Here's my answer: First of all, remember that *anything* you do to alter a "factory" guitar will affect its value on a very finicky vintage market. But sometimes you just gotta do what you gotta do. I've never tried rewiring a three-pickup Gibson the way you want, but thanks to my friends in the guitar repair business, I can usually find an answer to anything. One electronics expert who's helped us before is Mike Koontz, repairman at Gus Zoppi's Music in Warren, Michigan. Mike faxed me the solution to the first question almost before I'd

hung up the phone! He recalled that in the July '78 issue, Jeff Baxter's Eclectic Electric column showed how to rewire a Strat's existing 3-way switch and controls to get most of the combinations of the new 5-way switch that Fender had introduced on Strats in '77. Jeff's modification didn't allow the use of the middle pickup alone, however, whereas Mike Koontz's adaptation does. Shown at left are rear-view drawings of your guitar's wiring before and after modification.

The Baxter/Koontz wiring option will give you a 5-way Strat-style pickup selection—without drilling any holes—by converting the neck tone control to a middle pickup volume control. This leaves the remaining bridge-pickup tone control as a master tone for all three pickups. This modification allows you to operate your guitar like a standard two-pickup Les Paul, with the option of "fading-in" or adding the middle pickup to any combination of the selector switch. Or, by turning down either the neck or bridge volume control in its respective switch position, you can use the middle pickup by itself.

The circuit's also useful for anyone planning to drop a third pickup into a two-pickup Gibson, since it uses the standard toggle selector switch that comes on a two-pickup Les Paul, which differs from the toggle switch used on a three-pickup Les Paul. The three-pickup switch has an extra lug, or "leaf," that you'll notice is not used in the modified schematic. All hot wires must be shielded, of course.

Strat switch modification

Here's a guitar electronics question for you: How many luthiers does it take to change a light bulb? (Answer: Just one, but you've got to be willing to wait six months!) Thanks for letting me say that. Seriously, this letter from a *Guitar Player* reader will put your new-found knowledge to the test: "My Strat has a 5-way switch, which doesn't allow me to use three pickups at once, or the front and rear in combination. Do you have a wiring diagram to modify it so that all seven pickup combinations can be used?"

Here are several ways of doing it that I learned from my friend and fellow repairman, Mike Koontz of Zoppi's Music in Ferndale, Michigan. Mike's an ace repairman at all levels and a whiz at guitar electronics, and he always seems to find an easier way.

A simple method for getting all possible pickup combinations is to install a single-pole/single-throw (SPST—two-terminal on/off) switch in between the neck pickup contact at the 5-way switch and the hot lug of the volume control. This way, the neck pickup is still controlled normally by the switch lever. But since it's also wired directly to the volume control through the on/off switch, you can cut it in or out at will. This lets you use all three pickups at once, or the front and rear together. You can wire in the bridge (rear) pickup instead of the front and get the same combinations.

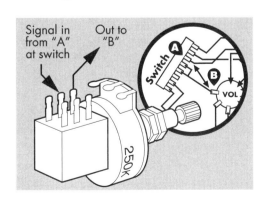

The first drawing below is a wiring diagram for a Strat. Notice points "A" and "B"—you add the switch between these. But instead of drilling a hole in your pickguard and adding a switch, replace the rearmost (middle pickup) tone control with a combination push/pull potentiometer. These are actually a regular pots with a built-in double-pole/double-throw (DPDT) switch. The push/pull acts as both the normal tone control and as the new switch when activated by pulling up on the knob. The

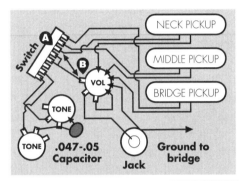

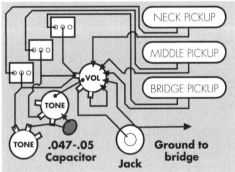

rear tone control is the easiest to wire, since you wire in the new pot just like the one it replaces. Then run a wire from "A" at the 5-way switch into the new piggyback switch and out again to "B" of the volume pot (left). You only use one side (and two lugs) of the push/pull switch.

The 5-way switch illustrated here has all the contacts on one side. This is common with many of the totally enclosed replacement switches available. If your guitar has the Fender switch, the contacts alternate from side to side. With either switch, you must find the soldered contact where the neck (or bridge—your choice) pickup attaches, and go about the simple wiring mentioned above.

Another option that lots of builders and hot-rodders use eliminates the stock switch altogether by installing three mini switches—one for each pickup (second schematic, previous page). This involves drilling three holes in the pickguard. Better yet, have a pickguard custom-made with the standard switch slot eliminated and the holes right where you want them. Each switch controls one pickup, so you can have any combination you wish. You'll see many popular guitars with this setup.

A third choice is to add a Starr Switch digital pickup selector (DPS). The Starr Model 4 has four touch-sensitive buttons that are somewhat like a calculator's. Three of these buttons control the pickup selection, and the fourth button can be used to control optional extras such as coil taps, phasing, or on-board effects. It can also act simply as a master on/off switch, or not be used at all. Switch selection is indicated with LEDs. The retrofit switch installs in the factory switch slot, and it's extremely quiet even at high volumes. A 9-volt battery is needed to power the unit, but there's plenty of room in the wiring cavity for that. Check with your local music store or mail-order supplier, or contact Starr Switch Co.

Perhaps this switch talk, with its single poles, double throws, and ons and offs is confusing—I hate to sound like a nag, but you really should read Donald Brosnac's *Guitar Electronics For Musicians*. This book is the "bible" for guitar electronics. After studying the chapter on switches, you'll be able to shop for the parts to do any of the conversions mentioned here.

Semi-hollowbody wiring

As I said earlier, much of guitar electronics is simple—cleaning pots, switching capacitors, etc.—*if you can get at the work!* Here's advice for Gibson ES-335 owners faced with having to remove the electronics for cleaning or replacement. It's another of my favorite question-and-answer letters from *Guitar Player* magazine: "I own a 1968 Gibson 335. The controls are sticky and hard to turn, and one doesn't work at all. I can handle cleaning and/or replacing them, if I can only get at them. How do they come out? How did they go in? I doubt that they were installed before the top or back were glued on, but they couldn't have fit through the f-holes. I've removed both pickups, but found solid wood and only a small hole for the pickup wire! What's the secret?"

There's no secret. If you simply want to clean the pots, loosen their hex nuts and washers, let the pots fall down into the body, and spray them with a contact cleaner (most aerosol contact cleaners are equipped with small, flexible tube applicators for pinpoint spraying). If you're sure you need to remove the controls, I'd bet they went in through the f-holes, although they shouldn't have. Read on.

Gibson ES-335-style guitars have a solid wood block glued between the top and back, which runs lengthwise through the guitar's center (hence the name "semi-solidbody"). This block not only gives structural support, but considerably enhances the guitar's sustain. From the 335's inception in 1958 until 1961, the center block was truly solid, and the wiring harness was installed or removed through the f-holes. After 1961, the factory machined a good-sized notch in the block (the shaded area in the drawing at right) under the bridge pickup, which helped in the installation and removal of the electronics. A good picture of this type of construction is on page 143 of Tom Wheeler's book *American Guitars*.

Being of more recent vintage, your guitar should have the notched access for the electronics, but if it doesn't, perhaps the block was accidentally flipped over during gluing. This would put the notch on the bass side (look through the bass f-hole to see). You'll have to fish the controls through the f-hole as if it were a pre-'61 axe, desoldering the pickup leads as the pots are pulled through the f-holes. As you can see in the drawing, the wood wall left by the notch isn't too thick (about ½"). A skilled worker could cut through the block on the treble side to give easier access for control removal.

Here are some other helpful tips for working on the electronics of any f-hole electric guitar:

Before removing the volume and tone controls, take off the knobs and mark the top of each shaft as an aid for later replacing them in the right order. Also, you'll have to remove the ground wire from the tailpiece in order to pull the parts out. Unscrew the tailpiece, and you'll find the wire—it may need unsoldering. For a stop-tailpiece 335, unsolder the ground wire as you remove the pots.

If you're replacing the whole harness after the guts have been removed, make a paper tracing of the empty control and toggle-switch holes on the guitar's face. Transfer these to stiff cardboard and drill them out. Flip the cardboard over to duplicate the holes as they'd be on the inside of the guitar, and do your wiring with the pots and switch held in this wiring jig. It makes a great holder for the parts and assures a perfect fit upon reinstallation.

Whether you have access through the rear pickup or the f-hole, you still need to slide your parts carefully—and in the right order—back into the body. Keep from twisting or crossing any wires that later might touch a bare contact and cause a short. I've found that a pair of curved or straight hemostats works great for reaching through a hole in the top and pulling a control shaft into place. Put the washer and hex nut on the hemostats before reaching through the hole (above) and tape them in place. Then you can drop them right onto the threaded shaft while holding it with the hemostats (I've always wished I had three hands when doing this).

Gibson R&D engineer Tim Shaw suggests making a tool for getting an output jack into the mounting hole in a guitar's face or side. This would be worth making for those who plan to do this job more than a few times. Solder or super glue a 12" length of ⅛" or ³⁄₁₆" soft brass to a ¼" plug. Bend the tool gently,

Some of the harder guitars to work on—some Gretsches especially—have all the wiring encased in spiral-wound, stainless steel, flexible cable for shielding. Besides being a wonderful ground and very high-class, the cable has great strength. But if it flips upside down when it's twisted, you have to back out and start over.

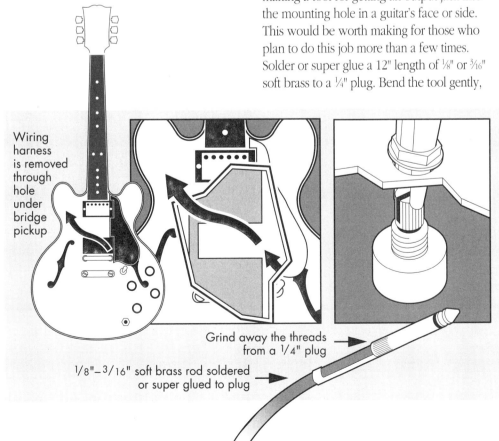

Wiring harness is removed through hole under bridge pickup

Grind away the threads from a 1/4" plug

1/8"–3/16" soft brass rod soldered or super glued to plug

and run it through the jack hole and out the f-hole or rear pickup notch, and plug it into the jack. Now you can pull the jack into place, dragging the rest of the wiring harness roughly into place at the same time.

Tim Shaw also pointed out that when Gibson installed the electronics in those early ES-series semi-hollow guitars such as the 335, 345, and 355, they kept cans of touch-up lacquer of the proper shade (usually cherry or sunburst tones) right at the bench to touch up

the f-holes afterwards. Don't be surprised if you can't get the pots in or out without some degree of scratching—a little masking tape in the right places would help. Good luck with your work.

Easy, right? Actually, it sounds easier here than it really is. Be patient, and you'll get the parts out and back in. You know one thing for sure: Those guitars weren't wired from *inside* the guitar! Someone had to do it.

**PART 4
FINISHES**

13 FINISH PREP & APPLICATION

A basic finishing schedule

Finishing is complex. Read all these pages, and that's just the beginning!

First we'll describe each step and the various finishing products needed to complete it. Then we'll go through the actual steps for some common finishes. Not all finishes require every step, so skip those that don't apply in your case. Just don't change the basic order, and practice every finish operation on scrap wood. Put a complete finish on scrap before tackling the real thing!

STEP 1: WOOD PREPARATION

At this stage, major work such as rough sanding, shaping, binding, scraping, hole drilling, etc., should be complete. All problems in the wood surface are corrected, final sanding is done, areas not to be sprayed are masked off, and the instrument is well cleaned.

Preassemble all parts to make sure everything fits and lines up (neck/body, bridge, tuners, tailpiece or tremolo, etc.). This helps avoid drilling or last-minute "construction" after the finish is on (which often damages the finish by accident or causes lacquer to lift around newly drilled holes). Go ahead and string the guitar up. If the nut is to be finished, install it now. Continue by dressing the frets, especially their ends. You don't need to wire the guitar.

When dry, super glue doesn't take stain, so don't be sloppy while using it, especially for binding.

FIXING DENTS AND CHIPS

Dents or dings in the raw wood can be drawn out with steam, since the wood is still there. Wet the dented area with warm water, let it sit a few minutes, and steam it out using a damp rag and soldering pencil. Use stainable, water-base wood dough to fill small chips. Its ability to accept stain is helpful if you're doing a natural finish, or it can be precolored with powdered Fresco colors before the fill. Larger holes can be inlaid with wood or filled with auto-body filler (but body fillers can't be stained).

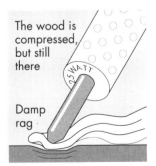

The wood is compressed, but still there

25 WATT

Damp rag

If slowly added to the chip in layers, super glues make a hard, clear fill; I use Hot Stuff. When dry, super glue does not take a stain,

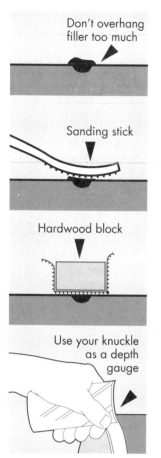

Don't overhang
filler too much

Sanding stick

Hardwood block

Use your knuckle
as a depth
gauge

nor will a stain penetrate through it! So do any staining beforehand, and confine any fill material to the damaged area—keep it off the surrounding wood. Level a dried fill with a homemade, curved sanding stick surfaced with 80- or 120-grit paper. When close to level, switch to a sanding block for smoothing-in.

Scraping with a steel cabinet scraper will remove scratches in side grains, in end grains, and in the cutaways. A scraper is also perfect for removing colored over-spray from plastic binding. An article on scrapers appeared in the May '83 issue of *Frets* magazine—check your library. And there's good info on scraping in the back of the book in the "Tools" section.

SANDING

Some kit parts are so well sanded that they're ready to spray. Most, though, need final sanding to remove marks left by the factory. You can do your own sanding, following these rules: Raise the grain by lightly dampening the wood surface (don't soak it, though). Use a clean rag that's been soaked in clean water and well squeezed out. When dry, the wood fibers will be raised or firred up, making it easier for the sandpaper to cut them off. Dampen the wood, and let it dry, between every sanding to get a really smooth surface. Always wear a dust mask when sanding.

Don't use a sandpaper grit coarser than 120. Use either Fre-Cut silicon carbide or garnet paper. Start with 120-grit and progress through 150 or 180 to 220. A 220 final sanding will satisfy most of us. If not, continue sanding up to 320-grit. Sanding much finer can make a wood surface so smooth that lacquer has trouble adhering. Sand with the grain to avoid crosswise scratches. Block sand flat surfaces by wrapping the sandpaper around a flat-bottomed wood block. This spreads out the sanding pressure, so you won't create hollows in the wood from the roundness of your fingers. Keep moving, or you'll end up with an uneven surface. Don't use electric sanders until you have become proficient by hand. Blow off or vacuum the wood often to remove sawdust.

To remove the invisible sweat or oils left by handling, wipe the instrument with a naphtha-dampened rag before going on to Step 2.

Wood preparation is the most important step of finishing, since the finish can only be as good as the wood, or "substrate," underneath. It's far more difficult to fix a substrate problem *after* finish is on it than fixing it right from the start. Learn to see those problems early!

STEP 2: STAINS APPLIED TO BARED WOOD

Coloring is the most complicated part of finishing new work or repairing old work. We're discussing stain *now* because some of the world's most beautifully colored guitars (especially during the "Golden Age" of the 1930's) would have been stained at this stage (directly after wood preparation, and before washcoating and grain-filling). If you want the color into or directly on the wood, stain it now after reading the advantages and disadvantages mentioned. Otherwise go on to the washcoat stage.

Your three choices at this stage are:

1   Leave the wood bare and go on to the wash-coat stage to protect the wood from stain or filler.

2   Stain open-grain wood, and then seal in the color with the washcoat—before using grain filler. This keeps the stain in the wood, but leaves the filler only in the open pores (a terrific look).

3   Stain close-grain wood (birch, maple, spruce), skip the washcoat and filler stage (filler isn't needed if there are no open pores), and go directly to sealer (a Gibson ES-345-type "cherry" finish comes to mind).

4   Stain the wood, skip the washcoat, and go directly to the wood filler (filling the bare wood). Much of this "base" stain, used before wood filler, will be sanded off when you level the filler, but not all of it. Later when the wood has been filled and sanded, you stain it again for a "double-stained," subtly different look.

STAINS USED FOR GUITAR FINISHING

Electric and acoustic guitars can be finished completely natural (no coloring), in a solid (opaque) color (see Step 6 under "Solid Colors"), or with a variety of transparent stains. The most common stains were red, brown, black, and yellow—usually sprayed in a sunburst—until Paul Reed Smith came along. Using brilliant shades of pink, green, blue, and purple, PRS created a whole new appreciation for coloring guitar woods. There are many types of colorant, a number of ways to apply them, and even more ways to screw them up. As your interest in finishing grows, experience will be your real teacher, and you'll come by knowledge naturally. But for now, I'll do my best to give you a head start.

DYE-STAINS

Some guitar finishes (or parts of them) are natural—crystal clear—with no color added at all. You'll see this most often on the spruce or cedar tops of acoustic guitars, for example. More often, clear-finished guitars have some color in the finish, or on the wood (if only from the wood filler used to level the pores of open-grained woods like mahogany and rosewood). Usually any dark wood is enhanced with stain, and often brilliant stains are used on maple or other light woods to give dramatic effect (PRS, Gibson's Les Paul Cherry-Sunburst or Cherry-Red ES-345, etc.). Unlike pigments, dyes are transparent—you can see through them to the wood. These colors, which let you see the natural wood, are called transparent dyes, stains, or "dye-stains," and are used often in guitar finishing.

POWDERED ANILINE DYE-STAINS

Most of us make our stains from dry powdered aniline stains mixed into the appropriate solvent. These stains can then be used directly on the bare wood, or put *over* the wood by adding them to the clear finish. Powdered aniline stains are available in many colors and in three distinct solubilities: water, alcohol, or lacquer/oil ("oil-solubility" is with mineral spirits). Premixed *liquid* water or alcohol stains are available from well-stocked stores dealing in finishing supplies for woodworkers.

You need red, yellow, brown, and black to produce traditional stained or sunburst finishes, but orange, blue, and green are also handy for altering the tone of a particular shade. Most colors have a *name*—like "scarlet red" or "brilliant green." Scarlet red in water will look different than scarlet red in alcohol or lacquer thinner, and that's *one* reason a

finisher might choose one solubility over another. The solubility of the stain you choose depends on the application, but repair shops need those colors in all three solubilities.

THE THREE SOLUBILITIES

1 Lacquer/Oil-Soluble Stain: Because they bleed so readily, lacquer stains aren't commonly used for direct staining on bare wood, but rather for the transparent coloring of lacquer and some mineral-spirit based polyurethanes (creating "shaders"). Since you can also color lacquer with alcohol stains, you can get along without lacquer stains if you like the color of a similarly named alcohol stain.

Sometimes these anilines, used for their oil-solubility properties, are mixed into colored wood filler to give it a "bleeding" quality. Used without a washcoat, the filler not only fills the pores, but colors the wood simultaneously— and the color springs to life under lacquer because it is also *lacquer*-soluble ("lacquer/ oil"-solubility). I believe Gibson used this time-saving technique on some mahogany SG finishes in cherry-red.

2 Alcohol-Stain (NGR): A supposed advantage of alcohol stains over water-soluble stains is that they are "non-grain-raising," or NGR for short. They also dry faster than water stain; helpful if you're coloring bare wood and you're in a hurry. Alcohol stains are often used for staining bare wood, but they have a tendency to "disappear," not only soaking into the wood, but evaporating at the same time. You may think you don't have enough stain on a piece and therefore apply too much. Later, when you spray on the first coats of lacquer, the solvents in the lacquer (alcohol is one them) cause the stain to pop to life. The color may even bleed out of the wood pores and onto the binding or finish. To combat "bleeding" add a touch of fresh shellac or clear lacquer (say, a capful per cup) to an alcohol stain. This will keep it from soaking in too quickly by giving it "body."

You can't dump *huge* amounts of mixed alcohol stain into lacquer, but you can generally add enough to produce the transparent shader you're after. A rule of thumb is that no more than 10% alcohol stain should be added into un-thinned lacquer (1 part alcohol stain—9 parts unthinned lacquer).

3   Water-Soluble Stain: I like water stains better than alcohol for any bare wood situation (you can't add it to lacquer to make a shader, though). I don't worry about it raising the grain, since I raise the grain several times before staining anyhow (look back to "Sanding"). Water stains are generally "more light-fast than alcohol stains," meaning they don't fade as easy as alcohol; are safer to use and clean up after; don't leave lap-marks because they stay wet longer; come in brighter colors; and don't bite into shellac, lacquer, finish, or bindings.

An excellent brand of premixed water stains, in bright colors, is available from the "Clearwater" company. These are "thixatropic," which means that they are thick (like a gel), and don't run. They wipe on, and don't streak or blotch—even on end grain.

APPLYING STAINS: ON THE WOOD OR OVER THE WOOD?

■ Transparent colored stains are often sprayed or wiped directly onto the wood and then covered with clear finish. You look *through the clear finish* at the colored wood (examples would be vintage Gibson sunbursts from the 1930's, Cherry-Red ES 335's). The wood grain shows much clearer this way.

■ Stains are harder to use on bare wood without getting streaks, blotches, and an uneven look in end-grain areas where the stain soaks in more than on the flat grain. However, used properly, stains give wood the most beautiful look, and they can even make plain-looking wood look exceptional. If time isn't an object, learn to use stains on bare wood. Remember that with factory guitars, production time was a big factor, so they looked for the easiest solution to any given problem when possible.

SHADER

Lacquer-soluble dye (or alcohol-soluble) is often added into the clear finish to produce a "shader," which is a transparent, colored, clear lacquer (think of Fender's "Two-tone" and "Three-tone," or Gibson's Les Paul sunbursts). When shaders are used, the unstained bare wood is protected by several coats of clear sealer, and the shader coat is sprayed on top of that. You actually look *through* the color at the wood (many Gibson Sunbursts from the late '50s until present). Excellent premixed colored shaders in red, blue, yellow, gold, and brown are available under the name "Wolf Transparent Colored Lacquer" from Stewart-MacDonald. Note: Applying color this way can cover or hide the wood grain.

■ Shader is quicker to apply; won't streak or blotch; and if you "sand through" the colored finish you only break into the clear sealer underneath, not into the wood. Sand-throughs to clear sealer aren't too hard to "reshade," but sand-throughs to *bare wood* are tricky (see the "Finish Repair" section).

■ Combinations of stains and shaders are common. Often a dye-stain is used on the bare wood as a color "base," sealed with clear for protection, then sunburst or highlighted with shader coats (before the final coats of clear).

SPRAYING

Spraying is considered by many to be the most uniform way of applying stain. Professional spray equipment will do the best job, but inexpensive, aerosol-powered "spray guns" with removable jars do an adequate job, and these units are self-loading (meaning that the user can add more or less thinner, stain, or lacquer at will). Some common self-loading aerosol brands are Pre-Val, Jet-Pak, and Miller. These aerosol power units will get cold and clog if you use them too long, so watch out for "spitting"!

Hand wiping is a good, quick way to get a base coat on an entire instrument (like that on a red or brown Gibson SG). Yellow bases for sunbursts are often applied by hand. Water stain is the easiest to apply by hand without getting "lap marks" because it stays wet longer, allowing successive passes to dissolve into themselves. Alcohol stains evaporate so quickly ("flash-off") that successive passes, unless perfectly controlled, leave overlapping marks. Retarder added to alcohol stain slows down its drying and helps eliminate lap marks as stain is applied. The traditional sunbursts of the early days were hand-applied, very beautiful, and have a different look from the sprayed-on type.

End grain soaks up more stain than side, or top grain. Presoak the end grain with the appropriate solvent for the stain you're using. Presoaking wets the wood so that it can't take in as much stain, helping to avoid a blotchy appearance. Presoaking—in the right places, and in the correct proportions—isn't a guaranteed effect, however. Like most finishing tasks, it takes practice.

Whether they're sprayed or wiped, liquid aniline stains can be applied straight from the jar, or thinned with the appropriate solvent to weaken the color. If you do use an alcohol or lacquer stain straight, you're begging for a color bleed into the clear topcoats. Water stain, even used straight, won't bleed into lacquer or other non-water base finishes, but will bleed into the new water-base lacquers.

STEP 3: WASHCOAT BEFORE FILLER

Close, tight-grained woods like maple and alder don't have open "pores" and therefore don't need to be "grain-filled" (the step coming up next). But many finished parts of a guitar (especially backs, sides, and necks) are made from woods such as mahogany and rosewood that have large open pores. Finish applied over unfilled open pores will have a pitted look if the pores aren't filled first.

One could fill the pores with repeated coats of clear finish, sanding off what remains on the surface each time, and eventually the pores would be level with the surface wood. But this is a slow process which not only wastes lacquer but pollutes the environment. And it's not a traditional look in the guitar industry (or the furniture industry). Besides, the finish would shrink more than wood filler over the years—showing up as "sinks" in the finish.

Wood filler, packed into the grain and sanded level, is a better solution. But wood filler is not invisible. It's normally colored, generally dark brown (or stained to exotic shades). Even "natural" filler has a light butterscotch color and will change the color of bare wood.

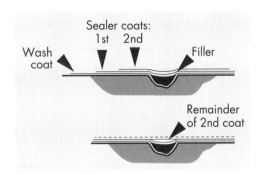

So—stained or natural, open-grain wood is often sprayed with a light "washcoat" of sealer or clear lacquer to keep the paste filler's color from over-staining the piece. Sprayed very thin (3 or 4 parts thinner to 1 part lacquer), a washcoat will follow the wood surface—into and out of a pore—without *filling* the pore. The washcoat acts as a barrier between the wood and filler. One of the best washcoats is "vinyl sealer" (available from C. F. Martin's Woodworker's Dream), sprayed in one thin coat. It's compatible with the nitrocellulose lacquer topcoats we'll talk about later. You may also use clear lacquer or lacquer sandingsealer, well-thinned, for a wash-coat. Martin prefers the vinyl sealer because it does the best job of keeping the natural oils in rosewood from bleeding into the clear finish and onto white binding. (Rosewood bleeds.) Freshly mixed shellac is another excellent sealer.

Note: There are instances when you don't want a washcoat; when you *want* the color of the filler to enhance the wood. Some very dark burgundy or "cherry" SGs got much of their richness from red stain and cherry-red filler applied to the bare wood. In that case, if you washcoated the wood before filling, the end result wouldn't be dark enough.

STEP 4: FILLING THE GRAIN

The Woodfinishing Book by Michael Dresdner has an excellent section on wood fillers. Please read it. Paste wood filler is used to fill open-pored woods such as mahogany, walnut, rosewood, and ash. It eliminates dust and air bubbles under the finish, and creates a flat surface for finishing by keeping the lacquer from shrinking into the pores as it dries. Filler isn't needed on close-grained woods like maple or alder, or on tonewoods such as spruce or cedar. Paste wood filler is available

During the wood-prep stage, carefully seal any holes or areas where wood grain might soak up water.

I'm doing lots of experimenting with water-base lacquer, which will be the way of the future. It's not very toxic, nor a great polluter.

as either an oil-base, or a water-base. Oil base is easier to use because it dries slowly (allowing plenty of working time); but because of the oil, it takes at least several days to dry before you can spray over it without the finish lifting. I'm describing oil base here.

You'll use natural wood filler on light wood, and dark filler on dark woods. Or, you can start with natural filler and color it to match any wood shade in between by using fresco powders, Japan colors, "Tints-All,"or the universal tinting colors (UTC's) mentioned in the staining section. Stir the filler until it's mixed to about the consistency of thick cream. If necessary, thin it with naphtha in a well-ventilated area. Next "paint" the filler uniformly onto the wood and wait for a haze to form—your signal that the filler is dry enough to be rubbed.

When the haze *just starts to form, quickly* remove the excess from the surface with burlap or cheesecloth by rubbing across the grain. The trick is to keep from pulling filler from the pores when wiping, so don't fill too large an area. Do just the back, neck, or one side at a time, since filler that's dried too long is hard to remove (if this occurs, wipe the area with naphtha and start over—you may even have to sand it off). Try to remove as much filler from the surface as possible, without pulling it from the pores.

Protect areas not receiving the messy filler (spruce or maple tops, etc.) with paper and masking tape. Allow 3 days to a week to dry before lightly sanding the filler residue from the washcoated surface with 320 Fre-Cut paper. After this light sanding, filler should remain only in the pores. Filler shrinks about 10%, leaving very slight dips over the pores that will later be filled and leveled with sealer coats.

For an in-depth treatise on filling and sealing, see Michael Dresdner's article in issue #3 of *The String Instrument Craftsman* (available from Pen-Lens Press, 142 N. Milpitas Blvd., Suite 280, Milpitas, CA 95035). I urge everyone to check out this newsletter—it's excellent, and back issues are available.

A NOTE ON FINISH SELECTION

I may *talk* about other finishes in this Finishing section, but I'm *thinking* of the nitro-cellulose lacquer that is the most commonly used finish in guitar repair shops and the woodworking trade in general. You can use automotive (acrylic) lacquer, and in fact that's an easy way to get any solid color you're after (and many transparent "candy" colors). But if you go with acrylic, use *all* acrylic—including the sealer (primer) coat. Don't mix nitro-cellulose lacquer with acrylic lacquer. It can be done, but may cause incombatibility problems.

STEP 5: SEALER

Sealer is simply a clear "primer" for nitrocellulose lacquer—whatever you spray as your first topcoat. It's used to seal in the filler, stains, or sunburst and, when sanded, to create a level surface for the final topcoats. Thanks to its high-solids content, lacquer sanding sealer builds quickly and acts as a "bridge" between the wood and the finish, giving the lacquer something to cling to. The best sealers are shellac, vinyl sealer, lacquer sanding sealer, or clear lacquer used as its own sealer.

Note: Many professionals prefer to use clear lacquer at every stage—even the sealer stage. The result is a clearer finish. So lacquer can be used as a sealer, but it just *takes longer to sand*. Sealer was developed to make the finishing process faster and easier.

Sealer that's been sprayed and sanded correctly leaves a smooth matte finish (a matte finish has a low "sheen," meaning it's not shiny), with few or no shiny specks indicating sinks or dips over the filled grain. Two coats of sealer (don't count the washcoat) sprayed by a pro using an air compressor and professional guns is plenty. Too much sealer (four or five coats) can cause cracking in the harder top coats and can add a slight milkiness to the clear finish. (But if you use the aerosol cans, they don't transfer as much lacquer per coat, so you may need three or four coats to get a true build). Sand sealer coats with Fre-Cut 320-grit until the small dips over the filled grain are gone. Any remaining shiny spots indicate an irregularity or depression in the finish surface. Try to get most of these now, or they'll come back to haunt you during rubbing out! This actually leaves a fairly thin finish, since most of the sealer is sanded off during leveling. Always be careful when you're sanding on sealer sprayed over colors; the risk of sanding through is great!

PRIMER: A SEALER FOR SOLID COLORS

Primer—usually white, brown, or grey—is the "sealer" coat for solid-color acrylic lacquers. There's no need for them to be clear since you can't see them anyhow. If you're using acrylic automotive lacquer, use primer as a sealer now and follow the advice given above.

STEP 6: COLOR COATS

Nitrocellulose lacquer is easy to find in clear, black, or white; but it's hard to find in other colors, especially good-looking ones. If you're after a custom color like "Fiesta Red" or "Surf Green" you want a *pigmented* finish, or *paint*. These finishes are opaque. The Sherwin-Williams paint stores can mix you a pigmented nitrocellulose lacquer in some colors, or an automotive store can mix up acrylic lacquer in a variety of automotive colors.

You can produce pastel shades like Surf Green, Daphne Blue, Seafoam Green and Fiesta Red by starting with white lacquer as your opaque base and tinting it with the appropriate Wolf Transparent Colored Lacquer (white lacquer, and Wolf Transparent Lacquers in red, blue, yellow, gold, and brown are available from Stewart-MacDonald).

For mixing a strong, brilliant color such as orange, you need some form of mixing pigment like paint stores use. Mixing pigments come in several forms. Lacquer "base-concentrates" are thick, pure pigment in a lacquer base (great for coloring lacquer—if you can find them). "Universal tinting colors" (UTC's) are more readily available, and they mix into a variety of finishes—including lacquer. UTC's are what they use at the paint store or automotive supply to mix a color. They start with an opaque base close to the right shade, and then add color drawn from those big silver pots that look like restaurant coffee-makers with a lot of handles. Each handle gives a different color of UTC in very small amounts. You can probably get your

paint supplier to draw off small amounts of different colors if you ask nicely. Stewart-MacDonald sells small tubes of Tints-All, another universal pigment.

Pigments are also available in semi-transparent "wiping-stains," but these are more often used in the furniture business (products like Min-Wax). The closest thing we use to a pigmented wiping stain is paste wood filler, which has a pigmented stain in it (see "Filling The Grain"). Paste wood filler colors the wood much like a pigmented stain does.

SOLID COLORS IN ACRYLIC

For most bright solid colors, it's much easier to use automotive acrylic primer, color, clear topcoats, and thinner (and skip nitrocellulose completely). Just use primer at the sealer stage (Step 5). Also, get yourself a tube of acrylic "Spot Putty"—it's like an easy-to-use Bondo (body filler), and it makes any imperfections in the wood disappear. Spot putty's colored (green or pink), so you can only use it under solid-colors. If you use acrylics, stick with the entire system—never mix acrylics with nitrocellulose wood lacquers!

APPLYING COLOR COATS

Some finishers use just enough color to cover the primer or sealer, and then switch right to clear. Some finishers put on lots of color (4 to 6 coats) and rub out the color coats (no clear topcoats). Using clear over-color gives more depth, and I think a better look. With clear over-color, you must not sand until you're sure you've built enough lacquer to avoid sanding through; this takes two to three coats.

SHADING, TONING AND SUNBURSTING

At this stage a number of things can happen. It's the time to correct any mistakes or sand-throughs into color which may have been applied earlier to the bare wood. An airbrush or miniature spray gun is a necessity for touching-up sand-throughs (the Miller, Badger, and Paasche companies make good, affordable airbrushes). Sunbursts or color coats applied earlier to the bare wood can be be improved now, by "toning," or highlighting, areas with shading lacquer. And some finishers

Remember: never mix acrylics with nitrocellulose wood lacquers!

will tint the binding for an antique look at this time. If you're using a colored transparent finish like a vintage cherry-sunburst, or a PRS-type, spray it now, just before the clear topcoats are applied.

SUNBURSTING

As you learned earlier, most modern sunbursts and transparent colors (PRS) are sprayed at this time—over the clear sealer and under the clear topcoats. One way to imitate a Les Paul "Cherry-Burst," for example, is to spray a coat of clear yellow lacquer (shader) over the clear sealer applied in Step 5. Then spray a coat or two of clear lacquer over the yellow to "seal" it from the red sunbursting shader about to follow. (In a sense you are going back to the "sealer" stage for a moment). Then follow over the sealed yellow with the red, and/or reddish-brown shader to create the sunburst.

By sandwiching the yellow in between the clear sealer coats, you have double protection: the bare top is protected from the yellow shader, and the yellow shader is protected from the red sunburst in case of a sand-through.

Whether spraying a sunburst or simply toning the sides, lay down a number of lighter color coats, one at a time, until you get the desired color build. Don't try to lay all the color on in one pass; it doesn't look as good that way. Experiment with using more than one color, putting one over the other, to get great depth and color in the finish.

STEP 7: CLEAR TOPCOATS

If possible, avoid sanding on any color touch-ups from Step 6. Unlike sealer, you can lay on the clear lacquer; four to six coats of lacquer is standard. Allow a three-hour minimum drying time between coats, and spray no more than three coats a day. To avoid breaking into the color coats, don't sand until after a two- or three-coat buildup. Even then, wet-sand *lightly* . Use water or mineral spirits as a lubricant (if mineral spirits are used, wear gloves and a mask, and have good ventilation), and sand with 400-grit wet-or-dry paper, drying off the finish with a clean, soft rag as you go. You don't have to use a lubricant at all—sand dry if you wish (it just uses up more

Never leave damp lacquer rags lying around the shop. Let them dry outside, and then throw them away.

Mineral spirits makes a great sanding lubricant, if you find that water is causing wood swelling and finish splits. Use mineral spirits in a well-ventilated area, wear gloves and a respirator, and keep it away from sparks or open flame.

paper). Whether you sand between every coat is up to you—some do, some don't—so experiment. Don't sand on sharp, exact edges; unsanded, they'll build up the extra lacquer needed to rub out nicely with the final finish.

Because of its thin viscosity, lacquer sprayed from pre-loaded aerosol cans builds more slowly than lacquer sprayed from spray guns or self-load aerosol units such as Pre-Val, Jet-Pak, or Miller (where the user has the opportunity to control how thick the lacquer is by adding thinner). In general, follow the manufacturer's thinning directions; usually a 50-50 mix (a ratio of 1:1) of thinner to lacquer is required for lacquer to spray smoothly. In humid climates, a dash of retarder should be added to the lacquer to help minimize blushing (the nasty white haze caused by trapped moisture).

STEP 8: WATER-SANDING AND RUBBING OUT

When the final coat of lacquer has dried at least a week (a month is better), wet-sand the finish to a dull, satiny patina prior to rubbing out. With a sanding block (not your fingers), remove the low ("shiny") spots using a *minimum* of 600-grit 3M silicon carbide "wet-or-dry" sandpaper (or 800-grit in the Japanese water-sanding papers, which cut much faster and smoother). Follow with *at least* 1000-grit, and finer if you can. Immerse water-sanding paper in clean water overnight before use. Then during use, rinse the paper often in water to remove scratch-causing finish particles.

Hand rub with a soft, clean rag folded into a pad and held in your palm. Use a fresh rag for each grade of compound. pour a small line of compound onto the finish, and rub both with the grain and in circular motions. I use Meguiar's Mirror Glaze compound in the following grades:

- #4 (Medium-duty cleaner) on 600-grit sandings.
- #2 (Cleaner) on 1200-grit and up sandings.
- #9 (Swirl Remover) to follow #2.
- #7 (Glaze) after #9 for that deep wet look.

In professional shops, two kinds of power buffing machines are used: the large, free-standing "pedestal" buffers used by Gibson and Fender, and the hand-held "right angle" circular "automotive" buffers with lambswool bonnets used at the Martin factory. Each of these buffing methods leaves its own distinctive look—the down-stroke of the pedestal wheel, versus the swirls left by the circular machine. If you wanted to be picky, you couldn't get the "right look" on a Martin finish on a pedestal buffer, and vice-versa. Lots of practice is needed with power buffing to avoid "going-through" a finish—especially on corners, edges, and cutaways.

Pedestal buffers, with large (12" to 18" diameter) flannel buffing pads, are the most common. The width of the buff is controlled by how many 1" pads are stacked on the arbor. The edge of the flannel buff is loaded with bar-style buffing compound in two "cuts"—coarse (reddish-brown), and fine (light tan). The coarse can be used directly after 500- or 600-grit sandpaper, and cuts quickly. The fine brings the finish to a final polish. The coarse wheel does an excellent job of buffing frets, but they turn the wheel black, which shouldn't then be used on a finish.

Until recently pedestal buffers haven't been within the reach of small shops. The buffer shown above is affordable and does a tremendous job. It's available from Stewart-MacDonald, and gives a professional "Gibson" look in a hurry.

The circular buffers at Martin are heavy-duty industrial machines with a lot of weight. Martin uses two compounds, on lambswool pads, for buffing: 3M #05955 Polishing Compound for the initial cut, and 3M Imperial Hand-Glaze #05590 to remove the swirl-marks. Martin finishers, by the way, don't wet-sand the final sprayed coats, but instead go directly to the buffer!

An acceptable "machine-rubbed" look can be obtained by using a variable-speed electric drill equipped with a Meguiar's Finesse Pads (above). Using the same #2 and #9 polishes, these foam buffers have less chance of burn-through than conventional lambswool bonnets, and give you a factory look. With either hand or machine buffing, squirt a thin line of compound onto the area to be rubbed, and pick it up with your rag or buffing bonnet as you work.

No matter how hard you try, some problems will befall you on your first jobs. The fun of solving these problems is what keeps me interested—and learning.

> **These days I use the fine-cutting Japanese Finesse sand-paper instead of 3M. It cuts much faster and smoother.**

Spraying necks and bodies

We just looked at the different steps of lacquer finishing and the nitrocellulose-compatible products needed for doing them. Now here are basic spraying tips and safety measures, along with some specialized spray fixtures that you can make yourself. We'll start spraying with two simple finishes—a basic clear lacquer job for a bolt-on neck (both rosewood fretboards and "maple-necks"), and a solid opaque color on a kit body.

I like to compare finishing to cooking. The novice cook carefully follows recipes that guarantee success, while an experienced chef is more creative, instinctively adding a dash of this and a pinch of that while interpreting a recipe. Practice will allow you to experiment with your finishes, but for now let's stick to our "cookbook." To continue at this point, you

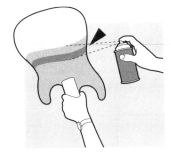

must have digested the information given up until now. Before doing any of the finishes listed here, you should send for the various supply catalogs and acquire some supplies that suit your needs. Don't ruin a nice piece; practice all finishing on scrap wood until you gain a little savvy!

Whether you use a spray gun, aerosol can, or self-load aerosol, overlap the spray pattern of each successive pass from one-third to one-half the size of the pattern. The finish material thins out toward the edges of a spray pattern, so overlapping ensures an equal coat build and a uniform color. When you spray the next coat, spray at right angles to the direction of the first coat for more even coverage. Spray with the can or gun held between 8" and 10" away from the instrument, and tilt what you're spraying away from the spray gun—don't hold it at a perfect 90 degrees. This tilting helps keep the spray from bouncing off the object, and directs the overspray ahead of the spray pattern,so it's covered by the next wet pass.

At times it's an advantage to spray *down* on an instrument that's lying flat. The lazy susan pictured below is easy to make and frees both hands to do operations such as sunbursting and touch-ups. You can spin it as you spray, which is great for spraying along the sides and in cutaways.

A length of two-by-four and a scrap of two-by-two make a portable spray hanger that can bolt, prop, or clamp anywhere. A clearance hole in the two-by-four allows the lag bolt to spin freely, along with the short two-by-two that it's tightly screwed into. A length of ¼" steel rod that's bent into an "S" hook holds the

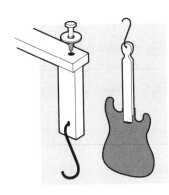

hanging stick for a solidbody, or it can be slid through a tuning machine's hole on a head-stock for hanging. An instrument can also be hung from a screw-eye placed in the butt end's strap-button hole.

MAPLE NECK WITH ROSEWOOD FINGERBOARD

Spraying a clear finish on maple is the easiest to do, since there's no need for stain or filler. Here's the finish schedule for a maple neck with a rosewood fingerboard:

1   Wood prep if needed. Tape off the fingerboard to protect it from overspray.

2   Optional: For an aged look, stain neck with a weak wash of yellow-brown NGR stain. Presoaking end and side grain with reducer keeps these areas from absorbing too much stain. Experiment.

Skip Steps 3, 4, and 6 (which were given in the finishing schedule a few pages back), since no filler is needed on maple, and you're not using a solid color.

5   Seal the neck. This calls for two light coats of shellac, vinyl sealer, or lacquer.

7   Spray four to six coats of clear lacquer, thinned according to the manufacturer's recommendations.

8   Dry one to two weeks. Wet-sand with up to1500-grit sandpaper, and rub out by hand with Mirror Glaze #2 and #9. Care-fully remove the masking tape from the fingerboard.

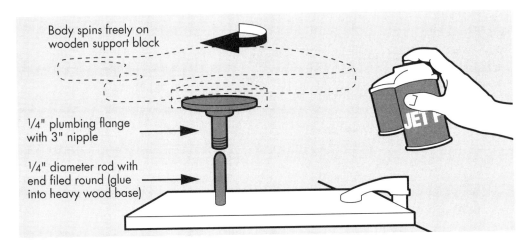

Body spins freely on wooden support block

¼" plumbing flange with 3" nipple

¼" diameter rod with end filed round (glue into heavy wood base)

SPRAYING A MAPLE NECK

This letter from Al Valusek of Ann Arbor, Michigan, brings up the subject of spraying a maple fingerboard—a question often asked: "What kind of finish can I put on my late-'60s Strat's maple fingerboard after refretting? My repairman advised me that the fingerboard would have to be planed in order to remove some trouble spots, but he didn't want to take on the job because he's had poor luck finding the proper material with which to redo the wood (the original finish would be removed in the fingerboard-trueing process). Please help—I need a fret-job!"

There are loads of clear lacquers, polyesters, enamels, etc., that will work when used correctly. I just use plain old lacquer, like Fender always did, and spray right over the frets—the lacquer will chip off during the fret dressing later. If the fretboard must be sanded to the bare wood for the fret-job, consider lacquer for the refinishing. Even aerosol "spray bombs" do a good job. Fender used a thick coat of catalyzed polyurethane or polyester on maple neck finishes of the late '60s and early '70s. Most small shops are not equipped to spray "poly" because it requires special thinners, hardeners (the catalyst), and spray equipment. Unlike lacquer, most catalyzed finishes require the application of two or three coats at 2- to 4-hour intervals, all in the same day—I'd rather spray when it's convenient.

Have you considered using one of the new water-base lacquers? They dry very hard. These non-toxic (even the fumes aren't bad) finishes dry almost as fast as traditional nitrocellulose lacquer and are easy to use—but you can't find them in aerosol cans. Some water-base finishes use a catalyst also. Any catalyzed finish—either "poly" or water-base—should be cleaned from the gun soon after use because they will harden in the gun. With any finish, be sure you have cleaned and degreased the neck and fretboard well!

GETTING A VINTAGE LOOK ON MAPLE

Here's the answer I gave my friend Jim Peat of Laguna Beach, California, when he wrote *Guitar Player* asking,

"Dan the Man,

"I have a bird's-eye maple replacement neck with a rosewood fingerboard. What's the best way to get that ambered 'vintage' look while bringing out the bird's-eye? Should I put amber into my clear lacquer?"

I recently had extremely good luck matching the color on a '61 Strat that needed *only the peghead* refinished. The neck's golden amber finish was original up to the nut, but someone had stripped the peghead's front, back, and sides, polyurethaned it, and stuck on a bootleg decal. All that kept the owner from being proud of his piece was the neck's ugly head, which was whitish compared to the rest of the neck. The method I used to get the aged color is good for both refinishing a vintage neck or making a new one look old.

To get the vintage color, you have to stain the *wood*, not the finish. Apply water-base stain to the bare wood, then use clear lacquer over it. Occasionally I'll add color to the lacquer, but only if the stained wood didn't look right after clear lacquer was sprayed on. (Since clear lacquer shows what stained wood really looks like, first practice on maple scrap.)

Adding color to lacquer is called making a "shader," but I prefer getting the correct color on the wood in the first place. When using shaders, it's easy to sand through a layer of color, which causes a patchy, uneven spot. These sand-throughs are very hard to touch up, even by an airbrush expert, so if you go the shader route, be sure to put lots of clear coats over any color coat. On the contrary, with water stain on wood, if you mistakenly sand through the clear lacquer and remove color, recoloring it with the same stain is remarkably successful: You just wipe some more stain on the bare patch that you sanded into. Shaders have a tendency to hide (rather than enhance) the grain, especially on figured wood. They make the wood harder to see by laying a colored film over it. However, shaders

The secret to finishing a maple fingerboard is not to spray on too much lacquer. Use just enough to soak into the wood, and then build a slight gloss with three or four coats. Spray right over the frets, since the lacquer comes off when the frets are dressed.

You can't always expect the same results when using products such as Fullerplast, since temperature, humidity, and shelf life are involved. Don't blame me if it doesn't work for you; blame yourself for not practicing on scrap!

are good for hiding repair work or creating certain sunburst finishes.

Water stains are made from dry aniline powders and water; I use Lockwood brand anilines. A one-ounce packet of powder makes from one to four pints of stain, which may sit on the average repair shop shelf for years; even the weaker two-quart dilution is very strong. A quart of yellow stain—the base color here—is enough to stain hundreds of necks, so I keep the powder in the packet and mix up only small amounts as needed. To make two ounces of full-strength stain, mix 1¾ grams (a level half-teaspoon) of powder to two ounces of warm water.

The mix ratio of yellow, red, and brown water stain for "vintage maple" isn't scientific. I did it by eye, and ended up with about two ounces of stain, which is more than enough to stain one neck several times. Start with full-strength yellow (¼ oz.) and thin with water (1¾ oz.) until the color isn't too strong when wiped on scrap maple. At this point it should cry out for amber. Then add tiny drops of full-strength red and brown to amber it. If maple scrap is at a premium, test as you go by putting the color on white pickguard plastic; don't test it on paper, since it will just soak in. When you think it's right, test it on some maple. But remember, it won't look right until it's sprayed with clear lacquer.

Highlighting bird's-eye grain is definitely worth the work. One method is to stain the wood and then sand most of it back off. The bird's-eyes will hold the color while the surrounding wood sands back to natural. Sometimes this is done with black or silver stain to really make the grain stand out, and you can "enhance" it several times for a more pronounced effect. Then, when you wipe on your final coat of stain and don't sand it off, the prestained bird's-eyes jump right out at you.!

You can wipe stain on with a clean rag or by spraying; it goes further by wiping. Here are some tips:

■ Water stain will "raise the grain." So before staining, slightly predampen the wood to raise the grain on purpose, and then after it dries, sand off the hairs with sandpaper that's 200-grit or higher. "Damp sanding" is a common wood-working technique for many types of finishing.

■ To avoid streaks and lap marks, quickly wipe lengthwise (with the grain).

■ Stain usually darkens end grains more than either side grains or flat grain, so presoak the end grain using a rag dampened with water. This keeps it from absorbing too much more color than the rest of the neck.

■ Clearwater water stain is a great brand for the novice. With its thick, gel-like consistency, it doesn't soak into end grain as much as conventional water stain, and it won't leave streaks. Clearwater stains are premixed and ready to use, plus colors may be mixed together.

■ The stained wood should dry at least several hours before lacquering.

■ Wear gloves, or your hands will be yellow for weeks!

LAKE PLACID BLUE METALLIC SOLIDBODY FINISH

I've found that the Lake Placid Blue lacquer used on a small number of custom-color Fender Strats in the early '60s is still available at my automotive store in acrylic lacquer (Dupont Lucite 2876-L). If you'd like to try this vintage metallic finish, you'll need one pint each of color, clear topcoat, and primer/surfacer, as well as a gallon of thinner (all acrylic-lacquer products). Spray the primer and color with self-load aerosols, and the clear with self-load or pre-filled aerosol cans (and of course the best job can be had with professional spray guns and an air compressor). I saw an original Lake Placid Blue Strat with the headstock face painted to match the body—it really looked great.

1 Prep wood as normal. Use acrylic spot putty for filling dents; this is available at an automotive supply store.

2 Skip—no stain needed.

3 Washcoat ash or open-grain wood. Alder needs no washcoat or filler.

4 Fill if needed; let dry a week or two.

5 Skip sealer. Prime body with two to four coats of white or gray primer. Sand after the first two coats and after the last two. Allow three to four hours between coats, and let final coats dry three days. Sand the finish level.

6 Spray two to four coats of Lake Placid Blue, or enough to cover. Allow four hours between coats and dry overnight. Lightly sand with 320-grit to remove dust. Touch up with blue if you sand through.

7 Spray four to six clear topcoats. Wait three hours between coats, and only do two coats a day. Sand as needed after first three coats are down.

8 Dry two weeks, wet-sand, and rub out as described above.

FENDER CANDY APPLE RED CIRCA 1964

Here's the answer to an international call for help from Malcolm Coombs of Westville, Republic of South Africa:

"Dear Dan,

"I am keen to restore my 1963 L-series Fender Strat, which is in pieces, to its original state. Could you help me locate the missing parts? Also, the body was poorly sprayed in metallic red. Is Candy Apple Red a vintage 1963 color, and if so, how can I attain it?"

Fender's vintage reissue-Strats use parts identical to your '63, and these may be ordered through an authorized Fender dealer.

Custom builder and repair expert Michael Stevens, who co-founded Fender's Custom Shop and now lives in Alpine, Texas, had this to say about the finish: "I've seen a '64 Candy Apple Red that I *know* was real, and most likely it was available in '63. So it would be correct, vintage-wise, to restore the guitar to Candy Apple Red." Here's how:

1 Color the alder body with a yellow water-base stain or a yellow lacquer sanding-sealer washcoat. This duplicates the yellow "Fullerplast" dipping solution used by Fender in the early '60s as a base for the three-color sunburst (solid colors got dipped in it too).

2 Seal over that with a *white* primer, sanding sealer, or lacquer. Sherwin-Williams Opex

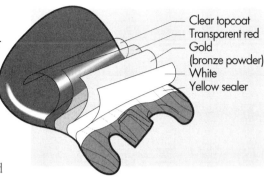

Clear topcoat
Transparent red
Gold
(bronze powder)
White
Yellow sealer

White Primer works well. Sand these white coats smooth and level.

3 Spray a coat of the same gold that you'd use for a Les Paul gold-top (gold bronze powder dissolved in a little thinner and added to clear lacquer). A Sherwin-Williams dealer can order the powder—ask for Crescent Bronze Powder #255 in a 1 oz. jar.

4 Don't sand the gold. Instead, spray over it with a couple coats of clear lacquer to "set" it.

5 Next spray a good coat of transparent red lacquer.

6 Spray four to six clear lacquer topcoats over that, and you're done. After it dries, wet-sand and buff it.

By following the steps in the correct order (yellow, white, gold, red, etc.), any finish wear such as chips, dings, and worn spots will expose the layers of paint in the proper "vintage" order.

Advanced finishes and sunbursts

You're never done when it comes to finishing—there's always lots more to learn. Perhaps you've experimented with some of the different finishing materials and have begun to develop a feel for them. Now you can really put yourself to the test by studying the schedules of two expert builder/repairmen: Mark Erlewine of Erlewine Guitars in Austin, Texas, and John Suhr of Rudy's Music in New York City.

Creator of the Automatic, Lazer, and Chiquita guitars, Mark Erlewine does a great "vintage cherry sunburst" that imitates the faded finish of a 1960 Gibson Les Paul. Mark was the first builder I know of to feature binding and carved tops on Strat-style guitars. John Suhr, besides handling the day-to-day repair needs of his customers, also finds time to create the Pensa-Suhr guitars for which Rudy's Music is famous. John sprayed the finish described here on a guitar made for Mark Knopfler in June 1988.

These two finishes deal with instruments with a mahogany body and flame-maple top. You can do the same type of finish on other wood combinations, such as ash or alder bodies with maple tops, by staining the lighter wood with walnut stain (alcohol aniline) to "imitate" mahogany during Step 2 —otherwise Step 2 is omitted for mahogany. Both of these finishes require the careful taping and scraping of binding, as well as grain filling. They also involve careful, step-by-step planning. I chose them for this reason, figuring that if you can do these, you can do anything.

MARK ERLEWINE'S VINTAGE CHERRY SUNBURST

1 Prepare the wood, mask binding, and protect the flame top with a paper cutout held in place by masking tape (tape the paper up to, and right over, the binding masking tape). Protect the headstock, fingerboard, and neck binding the same way.

Cousin Mark Erlewine

2 This applies to alder or ash bodies only. Stain the back and sides of the body a brownish red, with brown being predominant. Use alcohol stains.

3 Washcoat the mahogany neck and body with lacquer mixed 1:3 (one part thinner and three parts lacquer).

4 Fill the grain with brown-red filler and let dry three days. Spray two coats of clear lacquer to lock in the color.

5 Color the filled mahogany with transparent lacquer shaders. (Wolf makes these premixed, or you can make your own shaders with lacquer-soluble anilines.) Spray two coats of red transparent lacquer mixed with a little brown and a touch of yellow on the mahogany. When these "shader" coats are dry, seal them with two coats of clear lacquer to

help stabilize the color—this isn't the sealer step yet.

6 Expose the flame-maple top, and mask off the mahogany with paper. Run the paper right to the edge so that the tape sticks to the binding, rather than the cherry shader you just sprayed (the shader could pull loose, since it's uncured). Hand stain the maple top with alcohol aniline stain mixed eight parts yellow, two parts brown, and one part red. It looks dull when it dries, but don't worry. It will make the figure of the curly maple bolder, and it comes to life when it's hit with lacquer. Seal this color with two coats of clear lacquer just as you did the mahogany in Step 5. By sealing these colors from each other, you get less "bleeding" between the top and side colors. We're not done coloring yet. After the two clear coats have dried, spray two coats of Wolf Lemon Yellow transparent lacquer (thinned 1:1) over the top. Now watch the flame pop out! When this dries, seal and melt it with one coat of clear gloss lacquer.

Now for the "burst." Use Wolf Ruby Red as is, but thinned enough to spray. Sunburst the edges of the top with your spray aimed off the instrument. Use a small pattern, and hit only the edges while sunbursting—don't spray toward center! Spray this first pass no more than ¾" in from the edge; this creates a fairly strong red. Then, mix the same red with equal amounts of brown transparent lacquer. Spray lighter, but go in 1½" to cover a larger area. Next, use just brown transparent lacquer to lightly mist the entire burst going in 2½" from the edge (this must be done lightly to duplicate the fading of this famous type of sunburst). When this dries, shoot one coat of clear over the burst to set the colors. Remove the tape and paper from the body. Scrape the binding to remove any color that may have bled under the masking tape.

If your headstock is already black (some headstock overlays are black fiber or plastic), remove the masking, and seal it with the rest of the instrument in Step 7. If you need to spray it black, do it now. Tape off the neck around the headstock face and spray enough black lacquer to cover the face. Let it dry, and scrape the paint from the pearl inlays.

7 Seal the entire instrument with two or three coats of clear lacquer (of course, the fingerboard itself should be masked).

8 If you want the aged look, color the binding with some top color that's been lightened with clear and has a dash of brown and red. An airbrush does this best. Don't overdo it, or it'll look fake. I use a homemade lazy susan to rest the instrument on while antiquing. It also comes in handy for spraying sides and sunbursts. There are many times when it's helpful to spray one side of a piece while it's lying flat, especially for avoiding runs. If you do get a run or "sag" in the finish, wet-sand it out with a Finesse block or 400 wet-or-dry sandpaper wrapped around a small Plexiglas sanding block with rounded corners. Rock the block on the bump to "feel" it and sand it level.

9 Spray from four to six clear coats of lacquer, sanding as you wish.

10 Rub out as usual.

JOHN SUHR'S PENSA-SUHR FINISH

Mark Knopfler's guitar has a mahogany body with a flame-maple top and ivoroid binding. The bolt-on neck is made of maple with a rosewood fingerboard that's also bound with ivoroid. The binding runs around the headstock, as well, which calls for quite a lot of scraping. And it's got a unique twist—the Watco Danish Oil. Watch how John's methods fit into the schedule.

1 Prep wood as normal.

Skip step 2.

3 Skip washcoat, but wipe one coat of Watco Danish Oil onto the curly maple top. This keeps the filler from coloring it and brings out the grain. Rub it on, and wipe off the excess.

4 Fill the mahogany with brown paste wood filler—no washcoat—and let dry three days. Clean the binding with a scraper afterwards.

Skip steps 5 and 6.

7 Seal the whole body with one wipe-coat of Watco Danish Oil to mellow out the filler. Wipe one coat of Watco Oil onto the maple neck, too. Let both dry for one day, and then

spray one thin coat of clear lacquer over the body and neck. This melds the Watco with the lacquer. Dry one day, and then finish sealing with clear lacquer mixed 1:1 with thinner. (As a rule, John's thinner is made up of two parts thinner to one part retarder; this is more than the manufacturer suggests, so experiment first.) Spray five or six coats of clear; after three coats, sand between coats with 400 Fre-Cut *Gold* sandpaper, which John says outlasts many others. Final sand until the finish is level. This ends the sealer stage.

8 Mask off the binding and top with newspaper and 3M Stripers tape (a pale green, latex-backed tape that is perfect for this type of work). Mask the fingerboard and neck binding, too. Spray the mahogany back and rims with Wolf transparent red and brown shading lacquer mixed three parts red to one part brown and thinned 1:1 with thinner (add some clear lacquer to this if you want a weaker color). Spray two or three coats. A good way to spray a body is to screw a holding stick in the cavity in place of the neck, and make a hanger as shown earlier. This allows you to rotate the body by hand while spraying or to spray with the body hanging. Let dry two hours, and then scrape and clean the binding. If you let lacquer sit too long (four hours or more), it becomes too chippy, and if it's not dry enough, it drags with the scraper. Two hours is right.

Now for the golden see-through top. Mix a transparent shading lacquer using mostly Wolf Golden Yellow as a base, adding a little Lemon Yellow and brown to suit. Mix in one-fourth clear lacquer, and thin the mixture 1:1. Mask off the sides of the binding, but don't bother trying to mask off the thin top of the binding, since it's easier to scrape that edge. Spray no more than two or three coats for the right color. Wait two hours, and then remove the tape and scrape the binding's top edge. Spray the same golden color onto the maple neck.

Now we lightly shade the binding. Pour off some of your top color, and add clear lacquer and a little Lemon Yellow. Spray the body and neck binding lightly. You don't have to worry about the slight overspray on the surrounding finish, so an air brush is handy for this. This completes the coloring. Let dry overnight.

An affordable (and excellent) little air-compressor/spray outfit is the Miller 2000. I can't say enough about this rig— especially to get you through your first few years.

9 Shoot clear lacquer, thinned 1:1, over the body and neck. Sand after three coats, and then as needed every coat after that. John sprays 10 to 15 coats of lacquer. You probably won't need that much, since your brand of lacquer may not be as thin as John's to start out with.

10 Let the finish dry one month before wet-sanding and rubbing out (following the directions given earlier). John also uses a 3M liquid polish (Prep Team 05939), and his buffer is a Porter Cable 305 that runs at 2000 rpm.

Both of these finishes involve, among other products, the use of clear lacquer that is colored. You can mix these using lacquer-soluble anilines, or they may be purchased ready to spray. The Wolf lacquers mentioned here are premixed; check your suppliers. Clear colored lacquer has always been part of traditional sunbursts, and has only lately become popular in creating see-through tinted finishes over highly figured woods.

For more information and different view-points, read John Carruthers' four-part treatise on finishing in the Feb., Apr., May, and July '83 issues of *Guitar Player* magazine. Other invaluable sources: H. Behlen's *Guide To Wood And Wood Finishing*, Sam Allen's *Wood Finisher's Handbook*, and the appropriate chapters in Melvyn Hiscock's *Make Your Own Electric Guitar*, Roger Siminoff's *Constructing A Solidbody Guitar* and *Constructing A Bluegrass Mandolin* (this has a very good color section on hand-applied sunbursts done with alcohol stains), William Cumpiano and Jon Natelson's *Guitar Making: Tradition And Technology*, and Don Teeter's *The Acoustic Guitar, Vol. 1*. Michael Dresdner's *The Woodfinishing Book* is an excellent reference book (the best yet!). And I have two videos with Don MacRostie: "Spray Finishing Basics" and "Spray Finishing with Colors," produced at Stewart-MacDonald's in 1992.

Well, that's it. I hope you'll profit from this advice. Remember to practice on scrap, and don't set your goals too high at first.

A brief introduction to finish repair

Repairing a finish is more difficult than putting on a new one. You must know a lot about finishing materials in order to proceed correctly, and that's why we saved finishing repairs 'til last. Unlike many structural guitar repairs, you can learn finish repair work by practicing on junk you find at any garage sale: epoxy-finished clocks, ceramics, furniture, fishing waders, you name it. You can can get quite good before you ever touch a guitar. (I'd never advise you to *learn* how to touch-up on a valuable guitar). Here's a brief description of the three most common guitar finishes.

Since the advent of modern spraying techniques, lacquer has been used by many makers, the most notable being Martin, Gibson, Fender (until the late '60s), Gretsch, and Guild. Many modern guitars, especially electrics, are finished in "poly"—polyure-thanes, polyesters, epoxies, etc. These finishes don't redissolve or "melt in" like lacquers and are hard to rub out, but you can do a lot with them. It's important to know about these finish types and to consider which instruments you should or shouldn't work on yourself.

Shellac or varnish is often used on expensive handmade guitars—especially classical and flamenco instruments. Shellac, or "French-Polish," was used on most American guitars made prior to about 1930. (French-polish describes a method of *applying* a finish, not the finish itself). Although French polishing is an important technique for finish repair, it is beyond the scope of this book, and I won't go into it in any detail. I don't advise you to work on shellac finishes—they're hard enough to clean, harder to work on. No do-it-yourself repairs allowed on vintage guitars.

Lacquer finishes are found on most acoustic and many electric instruments made since 1930. Martin, Gibson, Gretsch, Guild, Harmony, Kay, Rickenbacker, Fender, and many other guitars have been finished with lacquer. In general, more recently lacquered guitars have thicker finishes and are easier to work on than vintage finishes which are thin, dry, and brittle (and take very little sanding before bare wood is exposed). All lacquer finishes dent, chip, and scratch more easily than polyester because they are more delicate.

Lacquer is the easiest to repair because it will redissolve itself; the fact that successive coats, or drops of touch-up lacquer melt in completely (even years after the finish was applied), is a real advantage. Always be careful around lacquer finishes because they melt when touched by super glue, lacquer, shellac, alcohol, and lacquer thinner (any of which may be used to repair a lacquer finish).

If the finish on your guitar looks as if the instrument had been dipped into a vat of liquid—thick and glossy—most likely it's some type of polyester, polyurethane, or urethane-enamel. These surfaces are found on most imports and many American electric guitars made after the late 1960s. Once these finishes have cured, no solvent that I know of will soften them—which means that lacquer, super glue, or "poly" itself won't melt in. This inability to melt makes invisible repairs next to impossible on these finishes. For touch-ups, use super glue.

. . . .

Touching-up "dings": chips, dents and scratches

A "ding" is what happens when you accidentally knock your axe into a foreign object, like a chair arm or microphone stand. The *result* of a ding will be a dent, chip, or scratch. Finish dings on the headstock, body binding, fingerboard edges, and the back of the neck (any edge, or convex surface) are easy to touch up, because you can work on them without touching much of the surrounding finish, and they don't show sanding and rubbing in the way that a larger, flat area such as a guitar's face or back does.

Caution: Some professionals will buff the entire surface in order to make even a little

teeny chip go away—the finish will no longer look original. You wouldn't want to do this to any of *my* vintage guitars, buddy! I'd rather have a hand-touched up chip or no repair at all in most cases. So to start out, I'm telling you that many dings just aren't worth messing with!

■ Chips, or "nicks," are usually the result of contact with a sharp object, and leave the wood showing bare. Repair is easiest on a clear, natural-wood finish, but stained wood is usually no problem (in either case, simply apply clear finish over the nick). Some clear finishes, though, have color in them, and these are harder for the amateur to fix because the repair must match the original color.

■ Dents are small pockets in a finish that result from the wood hitting a blunt object— the original finish remains, but is dented-in. Sometimes the dented finish still adheres well to the wood, and sometimes the finish has "lifted," or separated from the wood. Some dents are smooth with no cracks in the finish, and others leave the finish not only dented, but cracked.

■ Scratches occur when a small amount of finish is removed by some sharp object, neither denting the wood nor totally chipping away the finish to bare wood. Scratches come in all shapes and sizes, of course, and may leave an opaque white mark. At other times they are perfectly clear, like V-grooves engraved into the finish.

All chips, dents, and scratches are easiest to repair when they occur in inconspicuous areas. Beware of those that are away from the edges and out on the main body area—these can be tough to fix without showing.

. . . .

Supplies for repairing clear finish topcoats

Many professionals have an extensive array of chemicals for finish repair and know how to use them. We'll keep it simple, using only a few materials for filling in a ding that has been made in a *clear* top coat (most colored guitars are usually top-coated with a clear finish of some sort, so you'll usually work with clear only; dealing with solid colors is explained later). All you need is lacquer, shellac, or super glue. The lacquer should be used on traditional lacquer finishes (choose either nitrocellulose or acrylic lacquer), the shellac on very old finishes, and the super glue on the catalyzed or "hardened" finishes.

■ Lacquer (you'll need lacquer thinner too). Since most lacquers are bottled in quarts or gallons and you only need a small amount, ask your repairman or local furniture doctor to sell you small bottles of clear, unthinned lacquer and thinner. Clear nail polish is almost like lacquer, and could be used in a pinch as a substitute for a minor repair.

■ Naptha (lighter fluid will do) is good for cleaning and degreasing any finish (including lacquer) before attempting any finish repairs.

■ A variation on lacquer is "Transfil"—a lacquer-like dent filler from the Mohawk company. It is sold by several luthier suppliers (Luthier's Mercantile has it). It's sort of like thick lacquer, but has other chemicals which cause it to dry fast (and hard—I think it's a lot like nail polish).

■ Super glue—in the thin and medium (somewhat gap-filling) viscosities. Be sure to get some super glue solvent, and also some "accelerator" to speed up the cure. There are many good brands available—the one I'm most familiar with is "Hot Stuff."

■ Shellac is a wonderful repair tool, but I won't go into it in any detail since figuring out when and how to use it takes years of experience. Shellac is used to touch-up antique "French-polished" finishes, and is often used on vintage lacquer finishes. It also makes a great sealer coat under lacquer. The only shellac I recommend is made fresh from dry flakes; don't use off-the-shelf shellac because it has a notoriously short shelf-life. Sometimes shellac is the perfect choice (especially for its color) for touching up vintage finishes. That's all I'll say about shellac.

■ Colorants—there are a wide variety available. For more information, see the staining section in the previous chapter.

■ An auto-parts supplier is a good source for wet-or-dry sandpaper as well as rubbing and polishing compounds (the compounds that I use are described on page 270). While you're there, pick up a spark-plug file. Finally, you'll need clean, soft rags for polishing and wiping. My favorites are baby diapers or flannelette (soft cotton flannel available at yard goods stores—buy plain, untreated flannel).

Since most dings create a low area in the finish (a spot where the finish is actually removed or dented-in), your job is to fill in the hole, let it dry, and then level and polish it to a smooth finish. Practice on inexpensive yardsale guitars, the edge of worn-out furniture, clear objects such as chipped ashtrays, or even a marble—use your imagination. Be extremely careful with cyanoacrylate glues! Wear safety glasses and latex gloves (available at drug stores), since these glues stick flesh to flesh. Stewart-MacDonald sells a starter super glue kit that comes with a solvent for ungluing fingers if you get in trouble; it can't be used for your eyes, however.

Try to determine what type of finish you have before attempting a repair. To test the finish on most electrics, remove the plate covering the control cavity and test inside—it's the same finish. With an acoustic, remove a tuning machine from the rear of the headstock and practice on the exposed area. If lacquer thinner or alcohol soften the finish, you have either shellac or lacquer. If nothing touches it, you have one of the polys.

● ●

Fixing Chips Using Drop-Fills

Before beginning a finish repair, clean and degrease the area with a rag dipped in naptha, allowing a few minutes drying time. *Caution: Use flammable chemicals only in well-ventilated areas, and never near an open flame.*

Drop-filling is the technique of replacing missing finish by placing drops of finish into a chip or dent until they build level with the surrounding surface. Usually more than one

Be extremely careful with cyanoacrylate glues! Always wear safety glasses and latex gloves while using them, and avoid breathing their fumes.

drop is necessary. Then you sand and rub-out the fill.

■ Poly drop-fills: Use super glue on the catalyzed finishes; it clings the best. Because nothing dissolves these finishes, don't expect a poly repair to look as invisible as one done in lacquer. A clear "crater" always shows after polishing (imagine a drop of clear vegetable oil floating on clear water—that's the look).

■ Experiment by filling in some practice chips with super glue. First fill a chip with repeated light coats of "water-thin" super glue, letting each layer air dry for 20 minutes or so. Then try a different chip with "medium-thickness" super glue. The longer you let the layers of glue dry, the better (and clearer) fill you'll get.

■ Try spraying accelerator on some spots *before* you apply the glue. Let the accelerator "flash-off" (evaporate) for 5 minutes, and *then* add the super glue—it will dry from below thanks to the accelerator. If you overuse accelerator, the glue drop-fill will foam or turn milky.

■ The small squeeze-bulb pipettes sold by Stewart-MacDonald are also a great super glue applicator.

Note: If you're using super glue for a lacquer drop-fill (and I sometimes do), you don't have to use any thinner to melt the edges of the finish as you might with lacquer (see "lacquer" below). Super glue does its own melting as it cures with lacquer.

Caution: When using drop-fills—but especially super glue—to repair a chip on an area such as the binding or the back of the neck, position the guitar so that gravity won't cause the applied finish to run onto an adjacent area while drying.

DROP-FILLING CHIPS WITH LACQUER

On a lacquer chip touch-up, use a brush to apply a small drop of thinner to a chip, both to clean the area and to help the lacquer "melt-in" (the lacquer *will* melt its own way into the finish, but thinner speeds it up and makes for a better melt-in). Follow with a drop of unthinned lacquer as a drop-fill, letting it dry

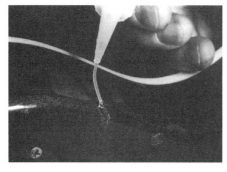
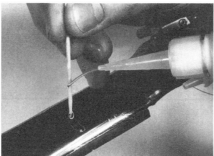
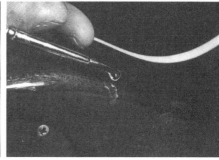

Finish touch-ups aren't easy. To do a job without a trace takes years of practice, and often you can't make a scratch or nick invisible. Whoever said you could mistreat your guitar and get away with it?

Use the flexible Teflon applicator hose to apply just a small drop of glue. Although the applicator hose is handy when precision is needed, you may find that sometimes you can't *stop* the glue from flowing, due to the siphon effect. Try holding a round toothpick in the dent and applying glue to it, letting the liquid run down into the hole. This works for lacquer drop-fills, too.

■ Another way to control super glue flow is to turn the bottle upright, squeeze out some air, and with the bottle still squeezed, turn it back over. The back-pressure from the squeezed-out air will hold back the glue and allow you to control it drop-by-drop.

overnight or until hard (clear nail polish should also dry overnight). When using a brush to apply finish, don't "paint" the finish on. Instead, use the brush to *set* a drop of finish into the hole; it may take several

applications to get a build. If the drop-fill doesn't flow smoothly into a dent, use a toothpick to spread the liquid around evenly.

Note: Professionals often use a form of lacquer retarder, instead of normal lacquer thinner, to improve the "melting-in" process of lacquer. If you get seriously involved with finish touch-up, you might want to shop around for some butyl-cellosolve, which is a very "hot" ingredient of lacquer retarder. It is quite toxic, however, and not to be used in a home shop.

FILLING CHIPS WITH TRANSFIL

Transfil is thick. It clings to a squeegee or spatula without running. Simply wipe it over the area and pack it into the chip. Be careful, because it will dissolve the surrounding lacquer finish. It's amazing how deep a chip you can fill with it, and how fast you can sand it afterwards.

the humped-up mound of drop-fill almost flush with the surrounding area before sanding. The final leveling should be done with #800-grit (and finer) wet-or-dry sandpaper wrapped around a small, flat block and dipped in water for lubrication. As the paper loads up with finish, dip it often and wipe off the particles with your thumb. Feather the spot away from the damaged area; if you just sand right on top of the fill, you'll get a dip. Progress from 800-grit to 1200, and finish with 1500- or 2000-grit.

Note: My favorite wet-sanding papers are the Japanese papers ("Finesse" brand is a good

The photo above shows a chip being filled on the very edge of a headstock—with super glue in this case. Here you have two choices. In method one, prespray the dent with accelerator, wait five minutes, and follow with any of the super glues. Apply the glue sparingly; it sets fast due to the accelerator. You avoid runs this way, and should be able to achieve a full build-up in a matter of minutes by applying several coats. Use more accelerator between coats if the glue isn't drying, but be careful of super glue "foaming." An alternate method (and it works with lacquer too) is to use a piece of firmly attached masking tape to build a dam along the edge. This holds the super glue and prevents it from running. *With this dam method* you don't need accelerator to stop the glue from running, although you'll have to wait longer for each coat to dry. Not using accelerator makes for the clearest super glue fills.

The next two photos show a drop-fill being levelled with a spark-plug file. (The spark plug file is not the only file I use, but it's readily available, has a fine cut; and it has smooth, rounded, "safe" edges that have no teeth). File

one). A little known fact is that these, and *all* wet-or-dry "water-sanding" papers, should be *soaked overnight* for them to work properly. Wet-or-dry paper that isn't presoaked loads up, and wears out, almost immediatley. Presoaked paper doesn't load up because the finish particles rinse out easily. I can use one small piece of presoaked Finesse paper to sand out an entire guitar (where the uneducated finisher would use up several sheets)! Finesse paper should be left in water when not being used, and it will last a week or more before it falls apart.

Even better than sanding blocks and wet-or-dry papers are "Finesse-Blocks"—small (¾" x 1¼" x 2⅜") blocks of pure abrasive grit. Like Finesse papers, the blocks should be left in water, and they last indefinitely. Finesse blocks are designed especially for leveling runs, sags, and imperfections in finishes. They're available in five grits from 400 to 3000.

Follow with one or two grades of Mirror Glaze compound (#2 or #9). If you've sanded to the very fine grits (1200 to 2000), you can begin your "rub-out" with #2 and progress to #9. Use a piece of clean, soft baby diaper or

Make your own drop fill by pouring some unthinned lacquer into a small baby-food jar and storing it with its lid off in a well-ventilated place for a few days. When it's thick and syrupy, it's ready to use.

Don't put too much drop fill into a hole at one time, or it may skin over and never dry clear down to the bottom.

flannelette for rubbing. Don't use too much compound; a small amount will do. Whenever possible, always rub lengthwise with the grain. Don't rub too long or hard, but just enough to get the gloss back. When rubbing, take your stroke three or four inches away from the damaged area to blend in with the surrounding finish. Always use lots of elbow grease. After you've sanded with 2000-grit paper and used Mirror Glaze #2, followed by #9, use #7 to finish the job.

NOTES:

■ Even with fine sandpapers and the right compounds, you can usually tell a finish has been worked on because the sheen of the finish is altered around the repair. This is particularly true of older finishes. Think very carefully before working on any finish—you could ruin a vintage piece that a more qualified person would have done right (or might have left alone).

■ I use lacquer drop-fills on traditional lacquer finishes. Sometimes I may use lacquer on hardened poly-type finishes, but seldom the other way around (there are *some* cases when I drop-fill super glue on lacquer).

■ Lacquer fills, in lacquer, will redissolve the surrounding finish and become invisible.

■ Super glue fills, especially in hardened finishes, will always show when held up to a light (you'll see a faint "edge" around the filled area).

■ Super glue drop-fills in lacquer will *sometimes* be invisible, but not always.

Fixing wood and finish dents

The most common finish dents are small ones that are *only* in the finish. When only the finish is damaged, and is still adhering to the wood, my first approach is to heat the finish in the damaged area with a heat-gun or hair dryer. As the finish warms, the dent will level itself into the undamaged surrounding finish. In many cases water-sanding and rubbing out

won't even be necessary. But don't overheat the finish, or it will bubble. This technique works best with lacquer, but is OK for the poly-types, too. Don't use this method on thin, vintage finishes—stick to the newer finishes with plenty of "build," or thickness.

If the wood is undamaged, but the finish dent won't heat out with the above method, you can simply drop-fill the finish as is. Look at these dents as smooth, clear-bottomed holes that need to be filled with finish—clear over clear. Fill the dent with finish as we did the chips earlier (drop-filling). Lacquer finish dents will disappear using this method, due to lacquer's ability to "melt-in."

Caution: Heating a finish can be dangerous. The finish—especially lacquer—can catch on fire! And the fumes of any finish when heated to a certain temperature can be toxic. Follow strict safety precautions, work in a well-ventilated area, and have a fire-extinguisher present.

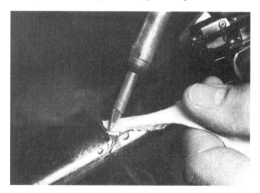

HEATING-OUT DAMAGED WOOD

Deep dents that have crushed the wood fibers can usually be swollen back out with steam. You'll lose the dented finish in the process, however, because the finish has to be removed in order to introduce water to the crushed wood fibers. After chipping out the bruised finish, dampen the wood with a rag dipped in warm water. Squeeze out the excess water from the rag and hold a damp edge against the dent. Carefully steam the rag with a hot soldering pencil or gun, but don't overcook it (I prefer my dents medium-rare). The steam will generally raise the wood close to its original shape—remember that the wood is still there, but only crushed. Allow several hours for the wood to dry, and continue with the drop fill of your choice.

SYRINGE-STEAMING

Sometimes you'll find crushed wood and a solid finish on an instrument (especially a vintage one) that you simply don't want to mess with. Maybe it's in an area of color that you know is hard to match. Using an extremely fine syringe (such as an insulin syringe), inject water under the finish and heat both the wood and the finish simultaneously with a heat gun. Often the wood will swell back with the finish. This is more likely to work on softer woods (especially mahogany), and if it doesn't work, you can always chip away the finish, steam out the dent as we did earlier, and do a drop-fill.

REBONDING A "LIFTED" FINISH

Some dents don't damage the wood, but cause the finish to "lift" or lose its adhesion to the wood. This is most noticeable on dark woods or finishes. The finish gets a milky, whitish cast as if there were air or moisture underneath (which there is). Using a small syringe you can inject thinner or super glue under the finish and press it down gently to dry. Another approach is to slice the finish with a fresh #11 X-acto knife and let the glue or thinner flow down through the cut to redissolve the finish. This works best on lacquer, of course.

. . . .

Scratches

With scratches, there isn't a clear-cut hole to deal with. Most scratches are irregular in shape and quite thin. On a lacquered guitar, brush a thin coat of lacquer thinner along the center of the scratch with a very thin, sharp-pointed artist's brush. This helps dissolve the line before the finish is applied. Apply the finish a dab at a time, once again using the brush tip to set lacquer into the scratch. Don't use a brush stroke; this can smear the work. Start at the farthest end and work your way towards yourself. If you have a good drop of lacquer on a brush tip, run a bead of it from your starting point for a good inch or so, until it runs dry, actually "pulling" the thick lacquer

through the scratch. If a scratch is well filled and doesn't need a second coat, let it dry many hours before leveling with well-soaked Finesse blocks or wet-or-dry sandpaper (1000-grit and up) that's been wrapped around a sanding block and dipped in water. Scratches in hard polyester finish should be filled with the super glue of your choice in much the same fashion, but use a toothpick dipped in glue instead of a brush. Never use a brush you care about with super glue, because you'll ruin it!

REDISSOLVING A BROKEN FINISH

Sometimes a "scratch" is in the form of a cracked or broken finish. The finish isn't removed, as with a chip, but neither is it solid as with a smooth dent. On lacquer finishes, use the "melt-in" method of brushing on a solvent and following with finish. (Note: This type of repair is a situation where BC [butyl-cellosolve] works best).

If the finish *doesn't* choose to melt together well, you may be better off using an X-acto knife to pry under the crushed finish and lever it out of the remaining solid finish. At this point you will have a jagged-edged hole with the bare wood showing—the same as a chip. Be careful not to pry into the wood itself. In the case of a lacquer finish, run a brush tip of thinner, butyl-cellosove, or acetone (not too wet) into the dent to dissolve the hole's edges. Follow immediately with a drop of unthinned lacquer. Use the brush to set a thick drop of lacquer into the hole, but don't try to brush it on with a stroke. The lacquer will probably take all night to harden, and it may shrink a bit, requiring a second coat. Remember that a proper fill should slightly rise above the surrounding finish.

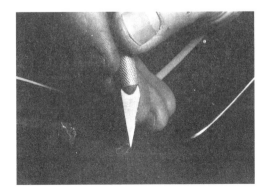

All of the above touch-ups are to be leveled, wet-sanded, and rubbed out. Remember that all of these touch-up methods are most easily performed on the instrument's *edges*, where it's easy to file, sand, and polish. Once again, I caution you not to attempt repairs on the face or back of your guitar unless you have a lot of experience. Sanding and rubbing-out in these areas will contrast poorly with the surrounding finish. Repairs on the sides of guitars (especially solidbodies) are easier, since the curved shape usually offers an easier access for the leveling file and wet-sanding block. The narrow width is also easier to rub out. When working on a side touch-up, wet-sand and rub well away from the repaired area, blending it in with the surrounding finish.

Touching up color

All the techniques described above showed how to fix the clear topcoats. Most often you'll have to match some color, on the wood or in the finish, at the same time. To repair colored finishes, you must understand all the coloring information given in the basic finishing schedule at the start of this chapter. When touching up dings on colored finishes, you'll be confronted with a number of clear finish and transparent, or opaque, color combinations.

PROBLEMS & SOLUTIONS

■ Stain on the bare wood which was covered in clear finish. Most stains bleed out of the wood and into the clear finish to some degree, and a chip of vintage clear finish from an orange-stained Gretsch 6120 may be slightly orangish even though it's supposed to be clear. Water stains don't bleed as much as oil or alcohol stains do. This means that a clear finish may have a weak, or strong, color in it (from bleeding) even if it wasn't sprayed as a shader to begin with. Clear finishes also yellow over the years.

■ Touch up any scratches in the colored wood with water-stain—it's the safest and most forgiving (and it won't cut into the surrounding finish).

■ If color has bled into the original finish, add alcohol or lacquer soluble stain to your clear finish for a matching drop-fill. (Do this if the finish has yellowed, too).

■ Shaders (color in the clear finish). These may have been applied over either of the above bare-wood stains, of course, and may be a uniform color (*a la* Gibson SG red) or a sunburst. Shaders are usually separated from the bare wood by a couple of coats of clear as a "sealer," but not always. Sometimes, color in the finish will migrate into wood (and the wood filler on open-grained woods) that wasn't stained originally!

■ Add alcohol or lacquer soluble stain to your clear finish for a matching drop-fill.

■ If you're working on a non-lacquer finish (poly), you may not be able to find an appropriate clear color to shade super glue—in that case, use shaded lacquer for your drop fill.

Note: Most liquid aniline stains will not mix with super glue, but they can be covered over *by* it. I *have* found that super glue mixes well with certain lacquer "shaders" and with some dry powdered lacquer-soluble aniline stains. In general the more brilliant red, yellow, green, and blue powders will mix into super glue; but the organic "earth-tones" (black, brown, ochre, red-oxide) won't.

■ Dark shaders. Some shader coats (especially the outer edge of a sunburst) are quite dark because many successive coats were sprayed. More often, a small amount of dark pigment (usually brown or black) was added to make the shader almost opaque. This is true of many Fender and Gibson sunbursts. You could lay on coats of shader all day and not get dark enough to match without pigment.

■ To darken a shader quickly, add pigment. Mix in small amounts of the black, brown, red, green, or blue UTC pigment described under "Stains" in the basic finishing schedule. Use "Tints-All," or just add a tad of black lacquer.

Note: with stain, always go lighter than you expect it to turn out. Which *type* of stain you use (pigment or dye) to mix into a finish depends on the original finish and on your experience. Good color touch-up is usually beyond the means and abilities of the D.I.Y.'er.

An easy solution for color finishes is to use artists' felt-tip markers. When the colored ink is dry, follow with the clear drop fill. The colors may change under lacquer or super glue, so experiment. Usually permanent markers do a better job than the inexpensive discount kind that are meant for kids' coloring books. I've worked wonders in a pinch with Magic Markers in yellows, reds, browns, and especially black (great for black headstock-face touch-ups). With any colored pens or alcohol stains, always use less color than you think is needed, since these stains darken in time and look different under the clear drop fill that follows. (For a color test, practice on pieces of glass, ashtrays, mom's furniture, or jewelry.)

SOLID-COLOR FINISH REPAIRS

Solid-color drop-fills are quite tricky to pull off. If the color isn't perfect it sticks out like a sore thumb. Professionals will often spray a large area to get a color match and not even *try* a drop-fill. As mentioned, auto parts suppliers should have practically any color you'd need in acrylic lacquer, and Sherwin Williams can mix some colors of nitrocellulose lacquer.

Note: Used for furniture and guitars, woodworking lacquer is referred to as "nitrocellulose" lacquer and differs from acrylic. In general, the two don't mix well, but small amounts can be used for drop filling, as long as you give the finish plenty of time to dry. To be safe, you can follow an acrylic-lacquer color fill with a "sealer" coat of super glue before switching to nitrocellulose lacquer. Good color matches take lots of experience, so practice on yardsale specials.

Note: no two finish repairs are the same. You need an aresenal of techniques and a broad knowledge base to pull them off successfully!

REPAIRING A CHIPPED FINISH ON A VINTAGE GOLD-TOP

Here's another use for super glue, that fix-all elixir used by so many guitar docs. Super glue has certainly found a place for itself in the guitar repair world. I use it every day—most recently to put a check on a checked finish. A customer wrote: "The finish on my '55 Les Paul gold-top is flaking near the edges, and pieces are falling off! What can I do to stop this?"

First, a warning: Super glue dissolves some finishes—in particular, the nitrocellulose based lacquers used on many American-made instruments. It is this ability to *melt* the finish that makes super glue work so well for the job described here. But if you get any glue on *top* of the finish, forget it—you're in deep trouble. So be sparing with the amount that you use, and practice on scrap or a yardsale special. With a valuable instrument, take it to a pro. And as always, use super glue with care in a well-ventilated area, and wear eye protection!

Now, to the question at hand. After more than three decades, the clear lacquer topcoats on gold-tops can often "cold check" (usually cross-grain), allowing the brittle lacquer to lift away from the dry bronze powder underneath. This flaking is most common near the edges that get the most wear, but you may also have problems near holes, such as the tailpiece anchor holes in the photo below. Try running super glue underneath the loose flakes and pressing the finish down with wax paper until it dries. Of course, this method is only effective around the edges—you can't glue down an *entire* loose finish, since you couldn't reach under it to the center of the instrument!

To get glue under the finish, use a piece of thin 2000-grit sandpaper or a feeler gauge to

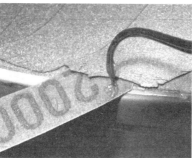

gently lift and probe under the flaking finish. Tilt the guitar body slightly in the direction you'd like the glue to run, and lay a drop of super glue onto the sandpaper probe. The glue will run along the paper and deeper under the finish. Be careful: This is *extremely* tricky business. An instant's hesitation, and the strip of paper will end up being permanently glued under the finish, so don't experiment on a '55 gold-top! Also, prying too hard can cause the brittle lacquer to pop off in large potato-chip size flakes, so be cool. When the flakes are glued tight, seal the peeling edges with a line of super glue to keep them from lifting up again.

Super glue is a generic term that describes cyanoacrylate "instant" glues. It is often incorrectly called Krazy Glue, a brand most commonly found in super markets and hardware stores. Krazy Glue is good *when fresh*, but I'm still using Satellite City's Hot-Stuff brand. Zap is another good brand. For the type of gluing we're concerned with here, you'd choose the consistency of one of these types:

1   The water-thin, original-formula Hot-Stuff (look for the red label) penetrates the fastest and deepest. However, it is also the most dangerous because it sets instantly! Setting time: One to three seconds.

2   The medium-viscosity, yellow-label Hot Stuff Super-T has a more honey-like consistency. It's more controllable and sets much slower—10 seconds to two minutes. As long as it can penetrate well enough, it is your wisest choice.

Only experience will let you know which glue to use in a given situation.

Very important safety information

I realize that finishing products come with specific safety precautions printed on the label. However, I would like to caution you to:

■ Wear rubber gloves when handling most of these products.

■ Use a respirator (available at an auto supply store) approved for organic vapors, and spray in a well-ventilated area (like outdoors—just watch the bugs).

■ Always wear eye protection.

■ Don't smoke around spray products and don't spray around gas flames or pilots, hot light bulbs, or electrical appliances, including fans that aren't "explosion proof."

■ Don't leave damp lacquer rags lying around the shop—the smallest spark can ignite them. Let them dry outside. When they're dry, throw them away.

■ Never pour these chemicals down the drain. Pour all unused chemicals into an empty can with a good lid, and mark it "Used." When it's full, make sure that it goes to the proper chemical waste disposal station—check with city hall or a school's chemistry department to find out where.

Up to date information on finishing—especially finishing guitars—is hard to come by. In 1991 I shot two videos—"Spray Finishing Basics," and "Spray Finishing With Colors," for Stewart-MacDonald. These videos teach musical instrument finishing better than any book on the subject. If finishing guitars is your thing, those two videos are more than worth their cost. And an excellent textbook on finishing, which complements the videos, is *The Wood Finishing Book,* by Michael Dresdner (Taunton Press).

**PART 5
SUPPLIES
& SOURCES**

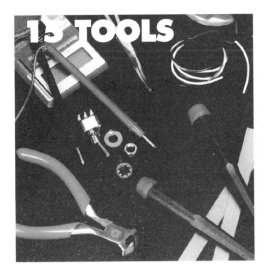

Tools, tools, tools...

The more you have, the more you want. All do-it-yourselfers have a love affair with tools. Before getting too involved with guitar repair tools, I'd like to give you the bare-bones details on sharpening two of our most important ones, chisels and scrapers. I gained much of my sharpening and woodworking knowledge from reading *Fine Woodworking* magazine (Taunton Press, 63 S. Main St., Box 5506, Newtown, CT 06470). If you're a woodworker, subscribe to this magazine! Most libraries have back issues, so read the chisel sharpening article in the July/August '81 issue. It tells all you need to know.

SHARPENING CHISELS

The Japanese are probably best at it. If you're buying your first good chisel, consider buying one of the Japanese versions—nothing sharpens quite as well. The English-made Marples are also a good choice. Woodcraft is a good source for these. I often use a capo on my guitar, and I use a "cheater" for chisel sharpening, too (below). The roller honing

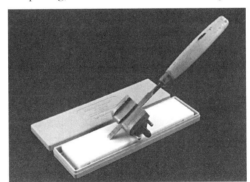

guide allows you to set your chisel at a preferred angle and keep it there as you make smooth strokes lengthwise on the stone. If you're not looking to go big-time into chisels and sharpening (buying lots of chisels and different-grit stones), make your first chisel a ½" one, and get a fine-grit synthetic/ceramic sharpening stone. These stones are easy to clean, don't wear out, and can be used without lubricant.

The most common angle for the bevel of a wood chisel is 35°. When worn-out and blunted, chisel bevels are renewed by first being ground on a bench grinder to the proper angle, and then honed smooth on the stone. (See the caution about grinder safety in "Making your own fret dressing files.") A good trick: If you first grind the initial bevel to a 25° angle, sharpening it to the required 35° bevel is quick and efficient.

SHARPENING SCRAPERS

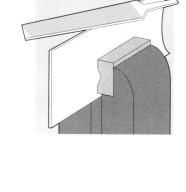

This is an art, and everyone has his own way of doing it. Again, you'll find the facts in *Fine Woodworking* magazine, May/June '86. The idea is to clamp the scraper blade in a vise while you flatten and sharpen its thin edge, making it 90° to the sides. Do this with a smooth-mill metal file like the one used for fret leveling. Then hone the edge on your ceramic stone, holding it at 90° to the flat stone surface. Next lay the sharpened scraper on the edge of a firm surface and stroke the *flat* side of the scraper with a burnisher (a piece of steel that's harder than the scraper), holding it a few degrees off horizontal; this creates a burr on the thin edge. Now "turn" the burr by stroking the *thin* edge of the scraper with the burnisher, and you've got an edge that can cut shavings almost like a plane. A scraper is usually held at an angle to the grain of the wood, and is often bent or curved slightly by flexing it with both hands. If you're lazy or in a hurry, you can use a scraper immediately after the filing stage, skipping the other steps. It probably won't work as well, and it's not *proper,* but I do it all the time with good results! Every third or fourth time, I do it right, following every step for a great edge.

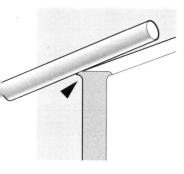

These are the two most important woodworking tools you'll use, along with a slim-handle X-acto knife and plenty of #11 blades. Never be without fresh X-acto blades; if you're in the middle of a job and the blade isn't doing its work, throw it out and grab a fresh one; professionals go through blades in a hurry. It's seldom worth sharpening them, since it's hard to get a factory edge.

Tools of the trade

Intonation getting weird? What about your action? Need a neck adjustment? More and more players are learning to maintain and adjust their own guitars, and it's common these days for them to invest in the simple tools needed for doing their own adjustments, set-ups, and minor repairs. These "case pocket" tools are the basis from which every full-fledged repair shop is built. Here we'll take a look at the tools that keep the guitar world running, from the common ones smart players use to keep their axes sharp to the specialized tools of guitar techs, builders, and repairmen—the tools of the trade.

PLAYER'S TOOL KIT

This should hold everything a well-adjusted guitarist needs to keep his or her guitar from going schizo. The list applies to players of acoustic and electric guitars and basses; if you play only one or the other, you may not need a certain tool, but get it anyway, since you may soon be setting up your friends' guitars, too.

■ **Tuner.** An inexpensive reed-type *A*-440 tuner or pitch pipe, or a six-note pitch pipe (*E A D G B E*) will do. Make your first serious tuner investment an *A*-440 tuning fork; it will last a lifetime. Add an electronic tuner when you can afford a good one.

■ **String cutter.** A pair of small end nippers or side cutters is a must. A needle-nose pliers/side cutter combo makes a versatile string cutter that can handle other jobs, too.

■ **String winder.** Buy two—they're cheap. Keep one in your case and one in your toolbox. Get one with a bridge-pin puller on it.

■ **Inspection mirror.** To check the insides of an acoustic guitar—a must if you're shopping for a flat-top.

■ **Screwdrivers.** Small-sized Phillips and flat-bladed screwdrivers for adjusting bridges and tightening parts on electrics or acoustics. Start with the small sizes and add the larger ones as they're needed for installing or

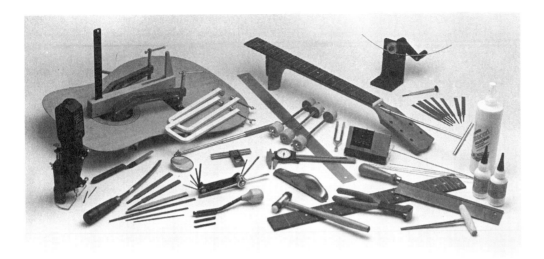

removing strap buttons, tailpiece studs, etc.

■ **Allen wrenches.** You need these for hardware adjustments on most electrics. The most common small sizes for tremolos, locking nuts, and bridge saddles are .050", ¹⁄₁₆", ⁵⁄₆₄", ³⁄₃₂", ⁵⁄₃₂", ⁷⁄₆₄" (fractional), and 1.5mm, 2.5mm, 3.5mm (metric) for imported guitars. Many domestic and imported guitars have truss rod adjusting nuts in the larger ³⁄₁₆" to 7mm size, too. The Guitool combines Allen wrenches, screwdrivers, and a string cutter all in one.

■ **Socket-head nut drivers.** These are needed for truss rod adjustments on many American guitars—most notably Gibson (⁵⁄₁₆") and Guild (¹⁄₄"). Some are a bit too thick to get onto the truss rod nut and into the truss nut cavity at the same time. The long-shanked, "T"-handled, thin-wall wrenches styled after those used by Gibson are my favorites.

■ **Solvent cleaner.** This is helpful for cleaning dirty finishes and hardware. Naphtha (lighter fluid) is good for sticky or greasy spots on most finishes. A good polishing or cleaning is a must several times a year. For cleaning a really dirty guitar, use Meguiar's Mirror-Glaze #7. A light cleaning can be done with any of the creme-type guitar polishes.

■ **6" stainless-steel ruler.** For setting string height. General makes a good one that you'll find in almost every hardware store. It has fraction-to-decimal conversions on the back, which come in handy.

■ **Dial calipers.** A pair of these isn't a must, but it's a nice luxury—great for checking string gauges and action height. An inexpensive but accurate pair can be bought for about $30.00.

■ **A straightedge.** This is for neck adjustments. The two edges of a rafter square (a hardware store item) work for guitar or bass. The more expensive precision straightedges are even better, if you can afford one.

■ **Radius gauge.** Check the section on adjusting the bridge curve with a radius gauge as your guide. Stewart-MacDonald offers an inexpensive set of gauges, or make your own after reading the Electric Adjustments chapter.

■ **Nut file.** Most players would benefit from owning a small, thin nut file for cleaning and reshaping nut slots and bridge saddle grooves. This is not a necessity, but nice. A thin X-acto razor-saw blade can serve as a substitute.

■ **Nail clippers.** Last but not least, this is an essential item for all guitarists. Don't leave home without one!

If you own all these tools and know when and where to use them, you can properly set up your instruments and keep them that way. You may need to visit a professional repair

Robert Cray's Greg Zaccaria (left) and John Hiatt's Andrew Burns— with a truckload of vintage guitars.

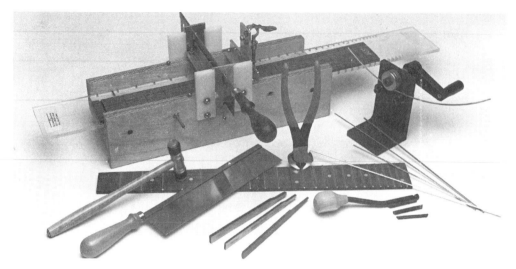

shop for fret work or a new nut, but you'll be relatively independent. If you also have the skills to troubleshoot and solve amplifier problems, set up and fine-tune effects, run a snake through a crowded stage while you're tuning six guitars and restringing a bass, and then have the stamina to pack it all into a semi at 4 AM, consider becoming a guitar technician—better known as a guitar tech.

I've talked with many guitar techs, among them Steve Vai's Stan Schiller, the Georgia Satellites' Steve Winsted, Steve Parish with the Grateful Dead, Robert Cray's Greg Zaccaria, and John Hiatt's Andrew Burns. Their jobs involve a lot more than sitting around changing strings all day. They're responsible for setting up and maintaining anything to do with the guitarists' gear: all effects, wireless outfits, amplifier and speaker setups, and of course, the guitars. "Ultimately," says Stan Schiller, "I'm responsible for any sound Steve Vai makes onstage. I set the sweeps and delay time, and it's not uncommon for me to change settings on the [Bob] Bradshaw board two or three times in one song—maybe more!"

At a Grateful Dead concert, Steve Parish gave me a great backstage "tour de tools." Steve's operation is unusual in the sense that it has about three of every tech tool known to man, and then some. He travels with two tool chests. One's a large wooden one with drawers filled with guitar and bass strings, power cords, wire, outlets, light bulbs, vacuum tubes, capacitors, resistors, power supplies, ad infinitum—replacement parts for any occasion.

It's more of a supply box. The other box with his main tools is a piggyback mechanic's tool chest. The lower drawers house a mini hardware store: crescent, box, open-end, and socket wrenches; Vise-Grips, hammers, hatchets, pipe wrenches, taps, dies, etc.—the large tools needed for tearing down amps and stage props, or for fixing the fuel pump on the band bus, for that matter. In the top drawers are the more specialized guitar tools.

For instance, there's a Dremel Moto-Tool, which, according to Steve, "is good for grinding on any kind of wood or metal. With the right bit or attachments, I can even cut the string groove in replacement metal bridge saddles. And I have screwdrivers of every description—drawers full of them. Miniature watchmaker's screwdrivers are handy for working on so many small electric gadgets. One of the main things most players should have is a good screwdriver set.

"Many of the tools I use are quite common but no less important, such as nut drivers, metric and standard Allen wrenches, scissors, files, drill bits, calipers, and a tape measure. Spray pot cleaner is a must—my favorite is Beaver Cleaner—as are glues such as epoxy, super glue, and Elmer's Glue-All or Titebond. I can't tell you how many times I've fixed something with Elmer's and matchsticks. [Author's Note: Matchsticks dipped in glue and shoved into a stripped hole will hold a screw's thread.] My volt-ohm meter [multi-meter] is important, because if Jerry Garcia's 9-volt battery drops just a little bit below voltage, he can hear it in his tone. So I'm constantly checking batteries. Bobby Weir uses a wireless setup, so we can't go but one set without changing batteries—if you *push* it, you're pushing your whole deal. My meter's a Fluke SM 77. It's completely digital and extremely versatile—the high-price spread. You don't need one this good when you're starting out.

"With the Dead, each tech has his own station—keyboard station, drum station, like that—and each station has its own tools. One of the great things about the Dead has always been that when it comes to buying a tool, we can have anything we need, so I've got a great collection of them. My Paladin wire strippers are special—for $50.00 they should be! We also have a Porta-Sol soldering pencil that runs on butane, like a cigarette lighter. It gets hot fast, and I can use it anywhere. [Author's Note: Radio Shack has a similar soldering tool under its own name.]

"But most special of all is the little kit that I always keep in Jerry Garcia's case wherever he goes, even to sit in and jam at some club. This is in a leather holster, and it includes a Phillips and flat-blade screwdriver, wire cutters, and a string winder—your basic survival kit." Steve keeps a careful eye on all the playing aspects of the guitars, and he prefers to have fret work done by someone who specializes in it. In an emergency, he hires a local repairman: "There's more good repairmen around now than when I started, so it's easier to find help on the road. I used to carry frets on the road and would perform emergency surgery, but now I have spare guitars—it's much easier."

Most of the techs I interviewed don't play the guitar much, if at all. A technical understanding of how a guitar should play enables them to please their bosses. I learned, too, that there's a limit as to the type of guitar maintenance a tech is expected to do; in particular, I was curious as to who does any necessary work on frets and string nuts. While they all carry the specialized files for shaping the nut slots (see the "Repair shop tools" list) or dressing and recrowning frets in emergencies, as a rule these jobs are taken care of by a repair shop chosen by the tech when the band's off the road. An exception to the rule is

Greg "Zak" Zaccaria of the Robert Cray Band.

Having interned with a repairman to pick up the necessary skills, Zak does the nut work, refretting, and fret dressing on Robert's guitars. He also plays guitar well, as does Andrew Burns, who's John Hiatt's tech. They've spent a lot of time together, since their bosses perform a lot of twin bills. Zak's the senior tech, and I got the impression that Andrew was glad to have the opportunity to work with him. I spent an afternoon watching the two of them set up for the evening show.

An electronics wiz who designs mixing consoles on the side, Zak is set-up as well as Steve Parish—a walking hardware/music store/Fender parts supply. He and Andrew travel with some 24 guitars and basses between them (13 for the Cray band, 11 for Hiatt's), all of which must be restrung, adjusted, and tuned for every show.

The guitarists in both bands change guitars often between songs, usually so quickly that the audience hardly notices it. The techs race across the rear of the stage in the dark, switch instruments, and then run back to the work table to replace a string or retune, all the while monitoring the levels of as many as three guitars at once. Robert Cray alternated between three different Strats during his hour-and-a-half show; he switched guitars at least a dozen times—once delivering the guitar to his tech by sliding it across the stage with his foot! Needless to say, the backs of some of Robert's instruments are a little worn.

Both techs operate on top of Zak's custom-made road chest, which folds open to expose drawers of tools and spare parts. The chest's top surface acts as a workbench, and it's equipped with miniature goose-neck lamps that allow quick repairs to be done in semi-darkness during songs. Robert Cray plays hard on heavy treble strings (.011, .013, .018, .028, .036, .046), and quickly wears grooves into the bridge saddles. Zak carries spare saddles and replaces them often. Measuring between the bottom of the strings and the top of the last fret, Robert's guitars have a string height of 2mm (.079") for the first string, graduating to 2½mm (.098") for the sixth string.

All the techs agreed that investing in tools is a gradual process, and the consensus is that a good basic start could be made for several hundred dollars. Expect to invest from $1,000 to $2,000 by the time you're equipped as well as the professionals mentioned here. Such an investment may or may not include a significant amount of non-tool staples, such as cleaners, polishes, sandpaper, batteries, wire, solder, etc.

TECH TOOLS

Any way you look at it, there's a big tool gap between a well-adjusted player and the ready-for-all-emergencies guitar tech. Here's a list of tools that the serious tech carries on the road. I haven't included the player's tools mentioned at the beginning of the article, since a tech owns all of those, too.

- Several 6" and 12" bar clamps for general clamping and repairs—a "helping hand" when you're in need
- Tin snips (just because Steve Parish has some)
- Long and short needle-nose pliers for electrical work
- Vise-Grips (locking pliers)
- Multi-meter for testing circuits, batteries, voltage, etc.
- Desoldering tool (solder-sucker)
- Soldering pencil or gun
- Alligator clips, jumper cables (electrical connections for testing)
- Complete sets of small, large, Phillips, flat-blade, and watchmaker's screwdrivers
- Power screwdriver
- Dial caliper or micrometer
- Dremel Moto-Tool w/bits, grindstones, etc.
- Butane brazing torch (another luxury)
- Electronic tuner
- Complete sets of metric and standard Allen wrenches
- Wire strippers
- Tuner degreaser/cleaner
- WD-40 spray lubricant
- Fret-leveling file, appropriate sandpapers and steel wool
- Fret-rounding files
- Nut-slotting files
- Safety glasses
- ⅜" electric drill (I love the cordless variety by Sears, Makita, Ryobi, Skil, etc.)

- Handsaws in several sizes
- Hand-held electric circular saw (Skil-saw)
- Electric jigsaw (sabre saw)
- Truss-rod wrenches
- Drill bits (fractional, by 64ths, from ¹⁄₁₆" to ½")
- Precision straightedges for checking neck straightness and fret height
- Tape measure
- Hammer
- Crowbar and flat-bar
- X-acto knife (the slim aluminum artist-type with the #11 blade)
- Hacksaw and replacement blades
- Vise for holding parts being worked on (a drill-press vise is quite handy)

REPAIR SHOP TOOLS

Let's add to the list by taking a look at the tools needed to operate a full-service guitar repair shop. Although most guitar repairmen haven't perfected the same electrical skills with amps and effects that a tech has, they use the same tools in repairing guitar electronics, so assume that a repair shop owns all the previously listed tools. I won't relist them.

Repair shops are equipped similarly to shops that do only building, with the same basic power and woodworking tools, spray finishing equipment, and a lot more. In other words, a guitar repair shop is equipped to build almost anything, but not on a production basis. After speaking with scads of repairmen, I've come up with the following list of the tools necessary to operate a complete repair shop.

- Pliers for bending frets (both jaws ground to a basic fret shape for a good grip)
- Small brass hammer for fretting
- Flush-ground end nippers for removing frets and cutting them to size
- Miniature flush ground end nippers for fret removal only
- Dremel Moto-Tool, router base, and assorted bits
- Mid-sized electric drill
- Radius gauges (7¼" to 20" radius templates for bridge saddle curvature and fret work)
- Taps and dies for retapping worn threads, tapping holes, all sorts of fabrication
- Drill index with fraction, letter, number bits
- Straight and curved hemostats for holding small parts during soldering

■ Feeler gauge set for measuring action, fret height, string height at nut, etc.

■ Thin palette knives and spatulas for mixing glues, separating wood joints, resetting necks, etc.

■ Straight and curved wood scrapers for flattening and smoothing wood

■ Vet's syringes and needles for glue injection in hard-to-get areas

■ Infrared heat bulb to soften wood parts for removal (usually used with fingerboards)

■ Pressure cooker for steaming necks out of their sockets

■ Hot plate for heating pressure cooker, boiling water, steaming, cooking lunch, etc.

■ Full set of chisels

■ Full set of diamond nut files

■ Full set of precision nut files

■ Full set of woodworking files—rasps, rifflers, etc.

■ Any fret-rounding files you can find

■ 10" smooth mill file for fret leveling

■ Waverly fret and fingerboard levellers

■ Gurian Three-in-One fret rounding file

■ Diamond fret rounding files

■ 6" triangle file for fret rounding

■ X-acto knife (slim artist knife with #11 blades)

■ Spray guns and air compressor

■ Bridge plate removal tools

■ Bridge pin hole reamer

■ Double-ended pedestal buffer

■ Buffing and polishing pads

■ Air brush

■ Center punch

■ Jeweler's saw and extra blades (for pearl cutting)

■ Respirator

■ Fret-slotting saw

■ Fret tang nipper

■ Fret bender

■ Fret radius blocks for sanding, dressing, and prepping fingerboards

■ Neck heater (for straightening necks)

■ Tapered reamers (large $\frac{9}{16}$" and small $\frac{3}{8}$") for installing end pins and enlarging holes

■ Ball-bearing router bits for template routing

■ Routing templates for pickups, tremolos, etc.

■ Precision straightedges—6", 12", 18", 24", and 30", for testing fingerboard flatness,

nut-to-bridge layout, etc. (I designed a set for Stew-Mac that has the works)

■ Razor saws for cutting nut slots, fret slots, and all sorts of finely detailed work

■ File cleaner to clean the teeth of clogged wood and metal

■ Bending iron for curving wood, patching sides, etc.

■ Scriber

■ Inspection light

■ Small brass spokeshaves for shaping wood (especially helpful for carving necks and bridges)

■ Vise with padded jaws large enough to clamp a neck from side to side

■ Workbenches—the more the merrier

■ Glues (all types), stains, finishing materials, etc.

■ The following 13 varieties of clamps enable a shop to perform all sorts of repairs and building operations. They're used in neck resetting, as well as for gluing cracked sides, headstocks, bridges, and braces.

	Several Jorgensen pipe clamps for heavy gluing
8	6" Jorgensen bar clamps— the basic woodworking clamps for everything
4	12" Jorgensen bar clamps
8	4" C-clamps
12	2" C-clamps
4	6" Ibex cast-aluminum bridge clamps
6	7" Waverly or Herco bridge clamps
4	9" Waverly or Herco bridge clamps
4	5" Waverly soundhole/bridge clamps
4	7½" cam clamps
4	4½" cam clamps
18	small spool clamps
18	large spool clamps
18	small spring clamps

That's a good basic list of the tools a well-equipped shop should have. I'm sure I haven't listed everything—the most obvious omission being stationary power tools. Some shops have everything from thickness planers and sanders to vertical milling machines and are equipped to manufacture almost anything. It isn't a must for a good repair shop to have that many power tools, but all of us dream of owning practically every tool there is. The three main stationary tools seen in most repair

Tom Ribbecke, guitar builder and technical consultant for the Luthier's Mercantile.

shops are a belt sander, a bandsaw, and a drill press. With those power tools and access to a local cabinet or millwork shop for an occasional wood-dimensioning task, any instrument can be built or repaired.

Some tools found in a repair shop are common ones that the average homeowner or hobbyist might own; others are extremely specialized, such as the fretting tools seen in the photo, which shows a Luthier's Mercantile fret-slotting jig, surrounded by a variety of fret tools from Stewart-MacDonald, including a Fret-Bender, brass-faced hammer, nippers, slotting saw, and an assortment of crowning files. Repairmen often customize existing tools, too, especially files (the Fret Work chapter covers making your own fret-dressing files from hardware store items).

Specialty tools that you won't find at Sears or the corner hardware store are available from several woodworking and luthier supply firms. Here is a list of tools, wood, and parts suppliers that can help you set up and maintain a guitar shop, followed by a list of manufacturers that you may need to call on from time to time during the course of your work.

Lutherie suppliers

Allparts
Box 1318, Katy, TX 77492

Buck's Musical Instrument Products
40 Sand Rd., New Britain, PA 18901

Chandler Industries
5901 9th St., San Francisco, CA 94107

Euphonon Co.
Orford, NH 03777

Guitarmaker's Connection
10 W. North St., Nazareth, PA 18064

Harbor Freight Salvage Co.
3491 Mission Oaks Blvd.,
Camarillo, CA 93011-6010

International Luthiers Supply
Box 580397, Tulsa, OK 74158

International Violin Co.
4026 W. Belvedere Ave., Baltimore, MD 21215

Luthier's Mercantile
Box 774, 412 Moore Lane,
Healdsburg, CA 95448

Stewart-MacDonald's Guitar Shop Supply
21 N. Shafer, Athens, OH 45701

Warmoth Guitar Products
6424 112th E., Puyallup, WA 98373

WD Music Products, Inc.
261-D Suburban Ave., Deer Park, NY 11729

Woodcraft Supply
210 Wood County Industrial Park, Box 1686,
Parkersburg, WV 26102-1686

Manufacturers

Acoustech
1302 E. 19th, Lawrence, KS 66044

Alembic
45 Foley St., Santa Rosa, CA 95401

L.R. Baggs
1049 Saratoga Ave., Grover City, CA 93433

Barcus-Berry
5381 Production Dr.
Huntington Beach, CA 92649

Bartolini
2133 Research Dr., #16, Livermore, CA 94550

B.B.E. Sound
5500 Bolsa Ave., Suite #245
Huntington Beach, CA 92649

Dana Bourgeois Guitars
9 Winter St., Topsham, ME 04086

Collings Guitars
11025 Signal Hill Dr., Austin, TX 78737-2834

D'Addario
210 Rte. 109, Box J
East Farmingdale, NY 11735

DiMarzio
1388 Richmond Terr., Staten Island, NY 10310

Donnell Enterprises
24 Parkhurst St., Chico, CA 95928

Dunlop
Box 846, Benicia, CA 94510

Jeffrey R. Elliot / Luthier
2812 SE 37th Ave., Portland, OR 97202

Erlewine Guitars
3004 Guadalupe St., #7, Austin, TX 78705

Everly Guitars (Robert Steinegger)
Box 25334, Portland OR, 97225

Fender
1130 Columbia, Brea, CA 92621

Fishman Transducers
5 Green St., Woburn, MA 01801

Floyd Rose (c/o Kramer)
685 Neptune Blvd., Neptune, NJ 07753

Fred Gretsch Enterprises
Box 358, Ridgeland, SC 29936

Gibson
Box 100087, Nashville, TN 37210

Guild
2550 S. 17th St., New Berlin, WI 53159

Thomas Humphrey
Classical Guitar Builder
37 W. 26th St. Room 1201
New York, NY 10010

Ibanez
Box 886, Bensalem, PA 19020

Jackson/Charvel Guitar Co.
1316 E. Lancaster Ave., Fort Worth, TX 76102

Kahler (APM)
Box 9305, Anaheim, CA 92802

Kamimoto String Instruments
836 St. Lucia Ct., San Jose, CA 95127

Ken Smith Basses
37 W. 20th St., Ste. 603, New York, NY 10011

Klein Custom Guitars
2560 Knob Hill Rd., Sonama, CA 95476

Lacey Guitars
(Mark Lacey's Guitar Garage)
1507 N. Gardner St., Hollywood, CA 90046

Larrivee Guitars, Ltd.
267 E. 1st St., North Vancouver
British Columbia, Canada V7L1B4

Lost Mountain Editions, LTD
(Richard Schneider—Classicals)
754 Lost Mountain Rd., Sequim, WA 98382

C.F. Martin & Co.
510 Sycamore St., Nazareth, PA 18064

Metal Tech Custom Guitar Hardware
422 W. Julian St., San Jose, CA 95110

John Monteleone Guitars
365 Smith Ave., Islip, NY 11751

Ontek
Box 14884, Minneapolis, MN 55414

Ovation
Box 507, Bloomfield, CT 06002

Peavey Electronics
711 A Street, Meridian, MS 39301

Pedulla Guitars
Box 226, Rockland, MA 02370

Pensa-Suhr Guitars
c/o Rudy's Music Shop
169 W. 48th St., New York, NY 10036

PRS Guitars
1812 Virginia Ave., Annapolis, MD 21401

Pyramid Guitars
1985 Madison Ave., Suite 3
Memphis, TN 38104

Rickenbacker
3895 S. Main, Santa Ana, CA 92707

Roger Sadowsky
1600 Broadway, #1000B, NYC 10019-7413

Santa Cruz Guitar Company
Box 242, Santa Cruz, CA 95061

Seymour Duncan
601 Pine Ave., Santa Barbara, CA 93117

Shadow Of America Electronics
Box 1083, Mountainside, NJ 07092

Sperzel Guitar Tuning Machine Specialists
7810 Lake Ave., Cleveland, OH 44102

Starr Switch Co.
1717 Fifth Ave., San Diego, CA 92101

Stevens Electrical Instruments
Box 1082, Alpine, TX 79831

Stringfellow Studios (William Cumpiano)
31 Campus Plaza Rd., Hadley, MA 01035

Taylor Guitars
9353 Abraham Way, Santee, CA 92071

Thompson/Schoenberg Guitars
P.O. Box 1286, W. Concord, MA 01742

Tobias Guitars
3087 North California Street
Burbank, CA 91504

Trev Wilkinson Guitars
4531 E. La Palma, Anaheim, CA 92807

Warmoth Guitar Products
6424 112th E., Puyallup, WA 98373

WRC Music (Wayne Charvel)
7176 Skyway, Bldg. B, Paradise, CA 95969

WD Music Products, Inc.
261-D Suburban Ave., Deer Park, NY 11729

Yamaha
6600 Orange Thorpe, Buena Park, CA 90622

Recommended reading

Here's a list of great books, all of which have been invaluable to me at one time or another. Remember, you only need to find one piece of information that helps make you look good in front of a customer or get the job done, and you've paid for the book several times over. For example, I've used Tom Wheeler's *American Guitars* hundreds of times to find facts about a guitar I'm repairing. I've looked up a vintage amp in R. Aspen Pittman's *The Tube Amp Book* while a customer eager to sell me an amp waited in the other room. Entries marked with an asterisk (*) indicate that the book deals *specifically* with the repair and building trades and should be considered essential for the serious repairperson. It takes a long time to build a library, so don't be discouraged—just add to your collection as time goes by. If you can only buy *one* book, get Don Teeter's *Acoustic Guitar, Vol. 1.* I also highly recommend subscribing to *The String Instrument Craftsman*—better still, buy all the back issues and go from there!

BOOKS

Ken Achard, *The Fender Guitar*, Bold Strummer

Ken Achard, *The History And Development Of The American Guitar*, Bold Strummer

Sam Allen, *Wood Finisher's Handbook*, Sterling

Craig Anderton, *Electronic Projects For Musicians*, Amsco

Tony Bacon, *The Ultimate Guitar Book*, Alfred A. Knopf

Tony Bacon & Paul Day, *The Fender Book*, Miller Freeman Books

H. Behlen, *Guide To Wood Finishing*, H. Behlen & Bros

Ian C. Bishop, *The Gibson Guitar From 1950—Vol. I* and *Vol. II*, Bold Strummer

Klaus Blasquiz, *The Fender Bass*, Hal Leonard.

Bob Brozman, *The History & Artistry of National Resonator Instruments*, Centerstream Publishing

Donald Brosnac, *Guitar Electronics For Musicians*, Amsco*

Donald Brosnac, *Guitar History: The Fender Company*, Bold Strummer

Donald Brosnac, *The Amp Book*, Bold Strummer

Donald Brosnac, *Scientific Guitar Design*, Bold Strummer.

George Buchanan, *Making Stringed Instruments*, Sterling Publishing

John Bulli, *Guitar History Vol. II*, Bold Strummer

Dave Crocker, John Brinkman, and Larry Briggs, *Guitars, Guitars, Guitars*, All American Music

William Cumpiano and Jon Natelson, *Guitar Making: Tradition And Technology*, Rosewood Press*

Michael Dresdner, *The Woodfinishing Book*, Taunton Press.

A. R. Duchossoir, *The Fender Stratocaster 1954-1984*, Hal Leonard*

A.R. Duchossoir, *The Fender Telecaster—The Detailed Story Of America's Senior Solid Body Guitar*, Hal Leonard

A. R. Duchossoir, *Guitar Identification*, Hal Leonard

A. R. Duchossoir, *Gibson Electrics*, Hal Leonard

Tom and Mary Anne Evans, *Guitars—Music, History, Construction, And Players*, Facts On File

Danny Ferrington, *Ferrington Guitars*, Harper Collins/Callaway Editions

Pieter Fillet, *Do-It-Yourself Guitar Repair*, Amsco*

Fine Woodworking Magazine, *Finishes And Finishing Techniques*, Taunton Press

Bill Foley, *Build Your Own Electric Guitar*, German Village Music Haus*

George Frank, *Wood Finishing With George Frank*, Sterling Publishing Co., Inc.

George Gruhn and Walter Carter, *Gruhn's Guide To Vintage Guitars*, Miller Freeman Books

George Gruhn and Walter Carter, *Acoustic Guitars And Other Fretted Instruments—An Illustrated History*, Miller Freeman Books

Guild Of American Luthiers (GAL), *Lutherie Tools*, GAL Publishers

Guitar History, Vol. I, Bold Strummer

Guitar Trader, *Guitar Trader's Vintage Guitar Bulletin—Special Re-Issues*, (Vol. 1, and Vol. 2), Bold Strummer

Richard Hetrick, *Guitar History Volume 3*, The Bold Strummer Ltd.

Melvyn Hiscock, *Make Your Own Electric Guitar*, Blandford Press*

Bruce Hoadley, *Understanding Wood*, Taunton Press.

John Huber, *The Development of the Modern Guitar*, The Bold Strummer, Ltd.

Franz Jahnel, *Manual Of Guitar Technology*, Verlag Das Musikinstrument

Hideo Kamimoto, *Complete Guitar Repair*, Oak*

Beverly King, *Dobroists Scrapbook*, Country Heritage Productions

Adrian Legg, *Customizing Your Electric Guitar*, Amsco*

Mike Longworth, *Martin Guitars—A History*, 4 Maples Press*

Wille G. Moseley, *Classic Guitars USA*, Centerstream Publishing

Tim Olsen and Cyndy Burton, *Lutherie Tools*, Guild Of American Luthiers*

Jose Oribe, *The Fine Guitar*, Vel-Or Publishing

Arthur Overholtzer, *Classic Guitar Making*, Williams Tool Co.

James E. Patterson, *Pearl Inlay—An Instruction Manual For Inlaying Abalone & Mother-of-Pearl*, Stewart-MacDonald

R. Aspen Pittman, *The Tube Amp Book*, Pittman

Jose Romanillos, *Antonio de Torres Guitar Maker—His Life & Work*, Element Books, Ltd.

Paul William Schmidt, *Acquired Of The Angels* (a documentary of John D'Angelico and James D'Aquisto), The Scarecrow Press, Inc.

Jay Scott, *Gretsch—The Guitars Of The Fred Gretsch Company*, Centerstream Publishing

Jay Scott, *'50's Cool: Kay Guitars*, Seventh String Press

Peter Siegel, *The Complete Airbrush Book*, Leon Amiel Publisher, Inc.

Roger Siminoff, *Constructing A Solid-Body Guitar*, Hal Leonard

Irving Sloane, *Guitar Repair*, Bold Strummer*

Irving Sloane, *Classic Guitar Construction*, Bold Strummer.

Irving Sloane, *Steel-String Guitar Construction*, Bold Strummer

Richard R. Smith, *The Complete History Of Rickenbacker Guitars*, Centerstream

Patrick Spielman, *Router Jigs And Techniques*, Sterling

Don Teeter, *The Acoustic Guitar, Vol. 1 and Vol. 2*, Oklahoma Press*

Robert Tice, *Periodicals Index For Stringed Instruments*, Robert Tice Publisher (This extremely useful listing of all articles pertaining to lutherie tells you where to find the information (available from Stewart-MacDonald)

Akira Tsumura, *Guitars—The Tsumura Collection*, Kodansha International

Thomas A. Van Hoose, *The Gibson Super 400: Art Of The Fine Guitar*, Miller Freeman Books

Lester Wagner, *The Martin Repair Manual*, C.F. Martin & Co.

Aidan Walker, *The Encyclopedia Of Wood*, Facts On File

Tom Wheeler, *American Guitars: An Illustrated History*, Harper & Row

Tom Wheeler, *The Guitar Book: A Handbook for Electric and Acoustic Guitarists*, Harper & Row

Eldon Whitford, David Vinopal, Dan Erlewine, *Gibson's Fabulous Flat-Top Guitars, An Illustrated History & Guide* , Miller Freeman Books

Jim Williams, *A Guitar Maker's Manual*, Hal Leonard

David Russell Young, *The Steel-String Guitar: Construction And Repair*, Bold Strummer*

Ed Zwaan, *Animal Magnetism For Musicians*, Bold Strummer.

MAGAZINES

Acoustic Guitar, String Letter Corp.
412 Red Hill Avenue, #15
San Anselmo, CA 94960

Acoustic Musician
P.O. Box 1349, New Market, VA 22844-1349

Bass Player, Box 57324
Boulder, CO 80322-7324

Fine Woodworking, Taunton Press
Box 5506, Newtown, CT 06470-5506

Guitar For The Practicing Musician
Box 2078, Knoxville, IA 50198-7078

Guitar Player, Box 58590, Boulder, CO 80322-8590

Guitar World, 1115 Broadway
New York, NY 10010

Guitarist, Music Maker Publications (Holdings) plc, Alexander House, Forehill, Ely, Cambs CB7 4AF

VIDEOS

I've produced over 15 how-to videotapes for Stewart-MacDonald, covering everything from fret dressing and nut making to installing tremolos, pearl inlaying, and spraying a finish.

Organizations

I belong to both of these organizations, and I wouldn't trade the times I've had at our conventions for anything. Both the GAL and ASIA are made up of people like us, so if you get seriously into guitar repair or building, join up!

**Association of Stringed
Instrument Artisans (ASIA)**
*P.O. Box 341, Paul Smiths, NY 12970 (publishes
a quarterly journal and conducts Symposium,
a semi-annual national convention).*

Guild of American Luthiers (GAL)
*8222 S. Park Ave., Tacoma, WA 98408
(publishes data sheets and a quarterly journal,
and conducts the semi-annual national GAL
convention).*

Schools for guitar repair and building

American School of Lutherie (Charles Fox)
420 Moore Lane, Healdsburg, CA 95448

Bryan Galloup's Guitar Hospital
10495 Northland Dr., Big Rapids, MI 49307

Red Wing Area Voc-Tech Institute Pioneer
Rd. at Hwy. 58, Red Wing, MN 55066

Renton Vocational Technical Institute
3000 N.E. 4th St., Renton, WA 98056

Roberto-Venn School of Luthiery
4011 S. 16th St., Phoenix, AZ 85040

South Plains College
Country-Bluegrass Music Bldg., 1401 College
Ave., Office #105, Levelland, TX 79336

Summit School Of Guitar Repair
Box 55, Beachcomber, R.R. #1
Nanoose Bay, B.C. V0R 2R0 Canada

Timeless Instruments
Box 51, 341 Bison Street, Tugaske,
Saskatchewan, Canada S0H 4B0

**Lost Mountain Seminar for the Guitar
(Richard Schneider)** Contact: Eric Hoeltzel,
Box 44, Carlsborg, WA 98324

Vintage dealers

If you're into the vintage scene, I recommend 3 magazines: *Vintage Guitar,* Box 7301, Bismarck, ND 58502; *20th Century Guitar,* 135 Oser Ave., Hauppauge, NY 11788; and the *Guitar Digest,* Box 1252, Athens, OH 45701.

Here's a list of just *some* of the more well-known vintage dealers—I could never include them all! Many of the dealers operate professional repair services and are also factory-authorized warranty repairmen for major manufacturers. Matt Umanov advises: "Stores with long-standing and well-respected repair departments on the premises are often a good bet, as they can back up the condition and authenticity of their merchandise with information derived from hands-on experience. They can also provide expert service when necessary." George Gruhn, another "old timer" in the vintage business, cautions: "As a vintage dealer, one of the greatest problems I encounter is bad repairs done by owners or amateur repair people. It's much easier to work on an instrument with warps or cracks or other such problems that have never been previously repaired than to try to undo poor work. In the case of vintage instruments, it is often important to know what not to do!"

Airline Vintage Guitars
5601 Airline Rd., Houston, TX 77076
(713) 694-8922

American Guitar Center
11264 Triangle Lane, Wheaton, MD 20902
(301) 946-3043

Angela Instruments
9584 Washington Blvd., Laurel, MD 20707
(301) 725-0451

Bee Three Vintage Guitars (Gary Burnette)
128 Kingsgate Rd., Asheville, NC 28805
(704) 298-2197

Bernunzio Vintage Instruments
1738 Penfield Rd., Penfield, NY 14526
(716) 385-1800

Steve Brown
225 Stanford Ave., Schenectady, NY 12304
(518) 370-2164

Charley's Guitar Shop
11389 Harry Hines Blvd., Dallas, TX 75229
(214) 243-4187

Chris' Guitars
5116 Landershim Blvd., N. Hollywood,
CA 91601 (818) 762-3026

City Lights
139 Easton Ave., New Brunswick, NJ 08901
(201) 846-3330

Dave's Guitar Shop
343 Causeway Blvd., La Crosse, WI 54603
(608) 785-7704

Herb David Guitar Studio
302 E. Liberty, Ann Arbor, MI 48104
(313) 665-8001

Dixie Guitars
560 Windy Hill Rd., Suite F, Smyrna, GA 30080
(404) 436-6642

Donel Music (David Stutzman)
4405 Ridge Rd. West, Rochester, NY 14626
(716) 352-3225

Elderly Instruments
1100 N. Washington, Lansing, MI 48901
(517) 372-7890

Erlewine Guitars
3004 Guadalupe St. #7, Austin, TX 78705
(512) 472-4859

Eugene's Guitars Plus
906 W. Jefferson, Dallas, TX 75208
(214) 942-7587

Fly By Nite Music
425 Fairground Rd., Neosho, MO 64850
(417) 451-5110

Fretted Instrument Workshop
49 S. Pleasant St., Amherst, MA 01002
(413) 256-6217

Fret & Fiddle
809 Pennsylvania Ave., St. Albans, WV 25177
(304) 722-5212

Fretware Guitars
4523 N. Main St., Dayton, OH 45405
(513) 275-7771

Gordy's Music
23263 Woodward, Ferndale, MI 48220
(313) 546-SHIP

Gruhn Guitars
410 Broadway, Nashville, TN 37203
(615) 256-2033

Gryphon Stringed Instruments
211 Lambert Ave., Palo Alto, CA 94306
(415) 493-2131

Guitar Broker
3685 Davie Blvd., Ft. Lauderdale, FL 33312
(305)321-078

Guitar Hospital
10495 Northland Dr., Big Rapids, MI 49307
(616) 796-5611

Guitar Network
27 S. Market St., Frederick, MD 21701
(301) 694-3231

Guitar Emporium
1019 Bardstown Rd., Louisville, KY 40204
(502) 459-4153

Guitars, Etc.
1306 Old Leechburg Rd., Pittsburgh,
PA 15239 (412) 795-8668

Guitar Maniacs
1544 S. Fawcett, Tacoma, WA 98402
(206) 272-4741

Guitars West
10273 Canyon Dr., Escondido, CA 92026
(619) 489-8760

Honest Ron's Guitars
1129 N. May Ave., Oklahoma City, OK 73107
(405) 947-3683

Intermountain Guitar & Banjo
712 East 100 South, Salt Lake City, UT 84102
(801) 322-4682

Koontz Guitar Repair
600 Hilton Rd., Ferndale, MI 48220
(313) 545-8361

Tim Kummer
51 Harbor Green Ct., Red Bank, NJ 07701
(201) 741-2843

Lark Street Music
227 Lark St., Albany, NY 12210
(518) 463-6033

Bernard E. Lehmann
34 Elton St., Rochester, NY 14607
(716) 471-2117

Lone Wolf Guitars
1011 S.W. 44th St. Oklahoma City,
OK 73109 (405) 634-9911

Jon Lundberg
2126 Dwight Way, Berkeley, CA 94710
(510) 848-6519

Mandolin Brothers
629 Forest Ave., Staten Island, NY 10310
(718) 981-8585

Midwest Guitar Exchange
505 Main St., Maple Park, IL 60151
(815) 827-3233

MusicMan
87 Tillinghaft Ave., W. Warwick, RI 02893
(401) 821-2865

Willie Moseley
1200 Woodbridge Dr., Suite D, Montgomery,
AL 36116-3520 (205) 284-1140

Music Emporium
2018 Mass Ave., Cambridge, MA 02140
(617) 661-2099

New York String Service (Steve Uhrik)
233 Butler St., Brooklyn, NY 11217
(800) 333-5589

Norm's Rare Guitars
6753 Tampa Blvd., Reseda, CA 91335
(818) 344-8300

Rainbow Music
Poughkeepsie Plaza, Rt. 9, Poughkeepsie,
NY 12601 (914) 452-1900

Resophonic Guitars (Barbara Sinclair)
Box 2104, Costa Mesa, CA 92628
(714) 545-5172

Rockin' Robin Guitars
3619 Shepherd, Houston, TX 77098
(713) 529-5442

David Sheppard Instruments
1820 Spring Garden St., Greensboro, NC 27403
(919) 274-2395

Marc Silber c/o The Musical Dunce
Box 9663, Berkeley, CA 94709
(510) 843-2883

Silver Strings
8427 Olive Blvd., St. Louis, MO 63132
(314) 997-1120

Soest Guitars
870 N. Eckhoff, Orange, CA 92668
(714) 538-0272

Somewhere In Iowa Guitars
1419 Daniels St. NE, Cedar Rapids, IA 52402
(319) 362-7600

Sound Southwest
2611 N. Belt Line Rd., Sunnyvale, TX 75182
(214) 226-3069

Southworth Guitars
4816 MacArthur Blvd., Washington DC 20007
(202) 333-0124

Stringfellow Studios (William Cumpiano)
31 Campus Plaza Rd., Hadley, MA 01035
(413) 253-2286

Strings West
1305 S. Peoria, Tulsa, OK 74120
(918) 582-3535

Joe Summers
1705 N. Huron River Dr., Ypsilanti, MI 48197
(313) 482-1321

Third Eye Music
1904-A E. Meadowmere, Springfield, MO
65804 (417) 862-5823

The Twelfth Fret
2402 S.E. Belmont, Portland, OR 97214
(503) 231-1912

Matt Umanov Guitars
273 Bleecker St., New York, NY 10014
(212) 675-2157

Tom Van Hoose
1509 Main St. #801, Dallas, TX 75201
(214) 760-8627

Vintage Fret Shop
20 Riverside Dr., Ashland, NH 03217
(603) 968-3346

Vintage Instruments (Fred Oster)
1529 Pine St., Philadelphia, PA 19102
(215) 545-1100

Voltage Guitars
1513 N. Gardner St., Hollywood, CA 90046
(213) 851-1406

Waco Vintage
Box 3413, Waco, TX 76707
(817) 772-1272

Waldo's Music
7406 Sunset Blvd., Hollywood, CA 90046
(213) 851-7129

Washington Street Music
Box 3231, Soquel, CA 95073
(408) 427-1429

Jim Werner
(collects Fender serial numbers)
R.R. 1, Letts, IA 52754

Harry & Jeanie West
3815 Tremont Drive, Durham, NC 27705
(919) 383-5750

Index

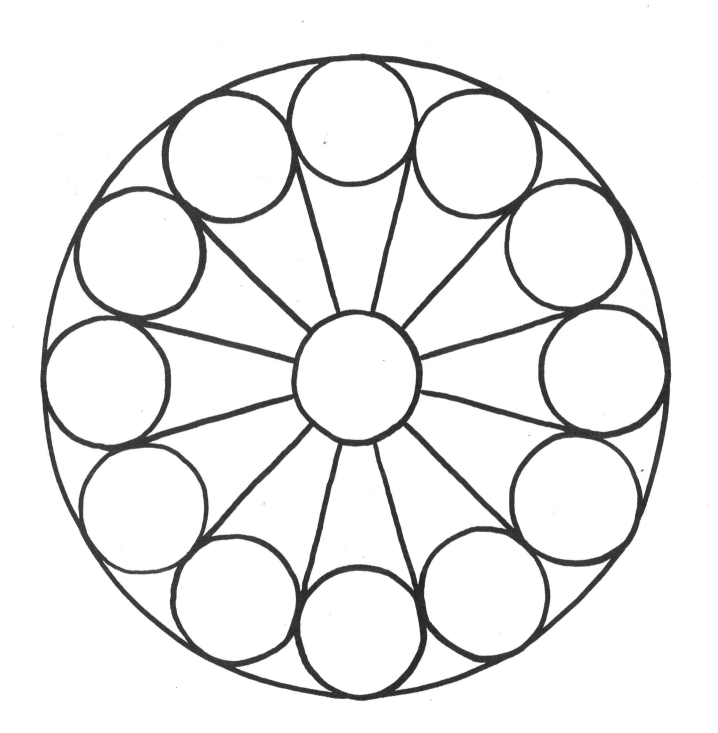

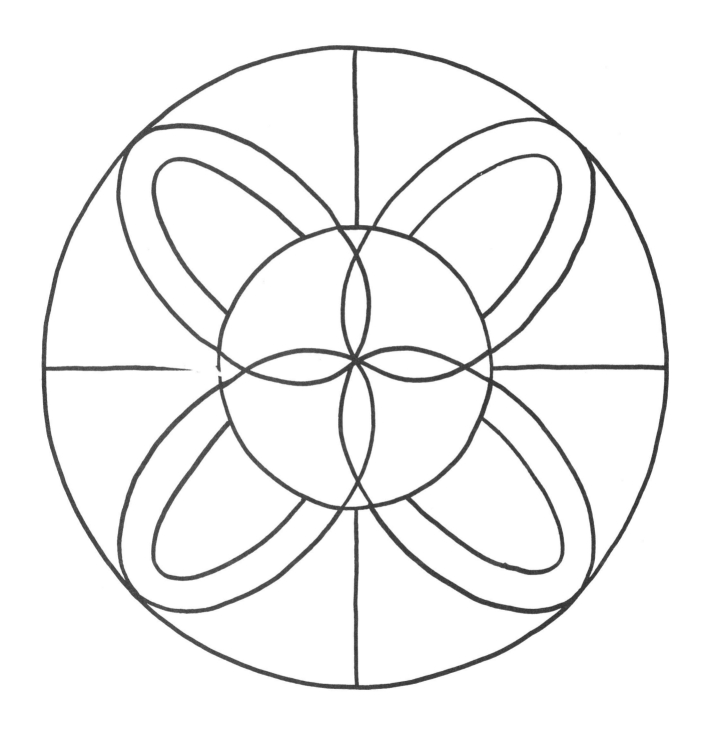

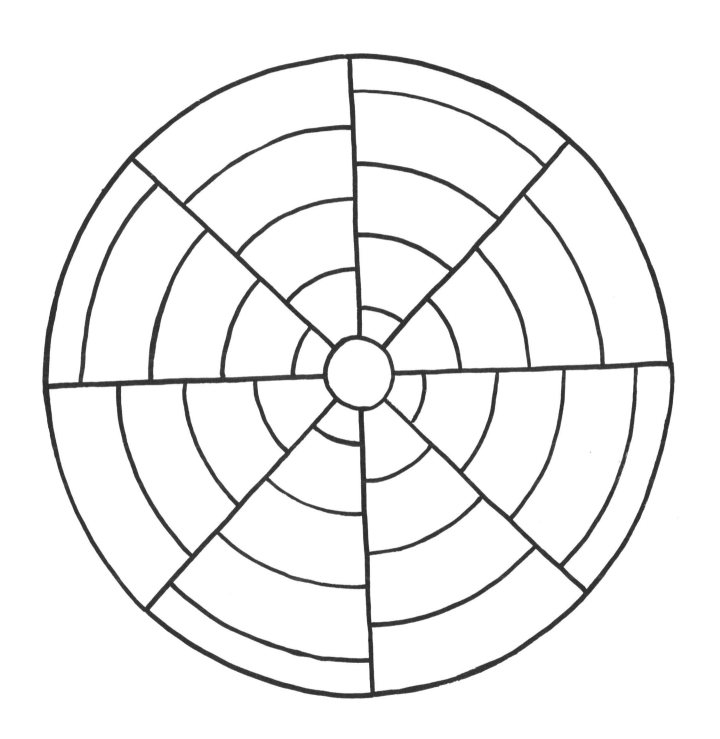

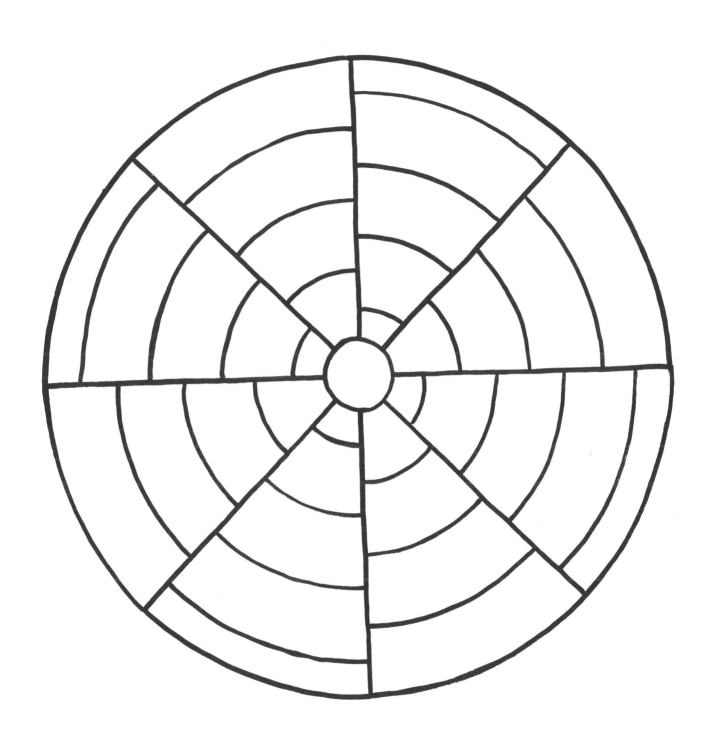

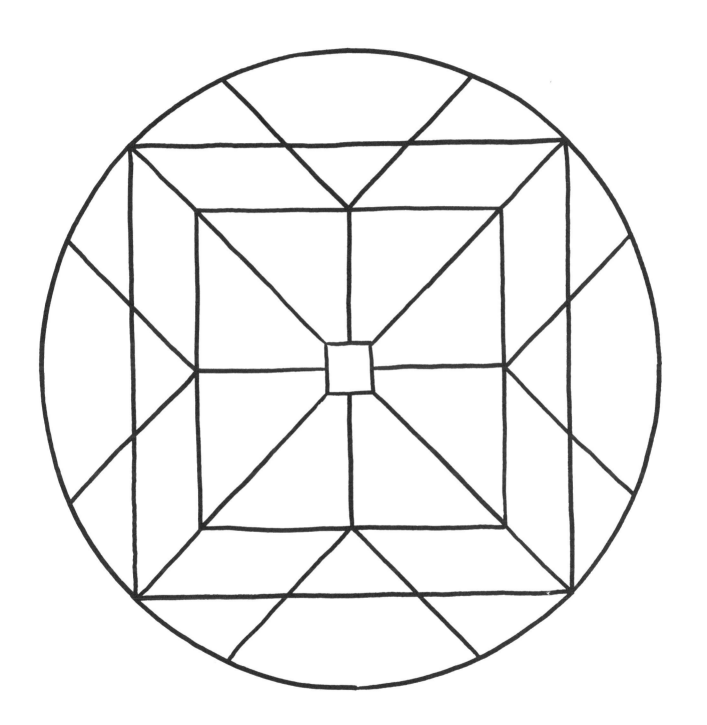

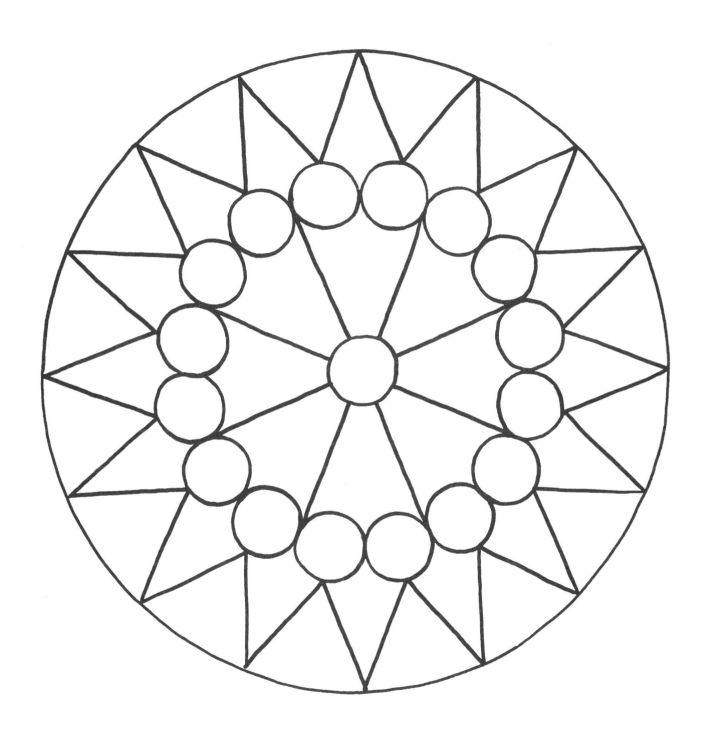

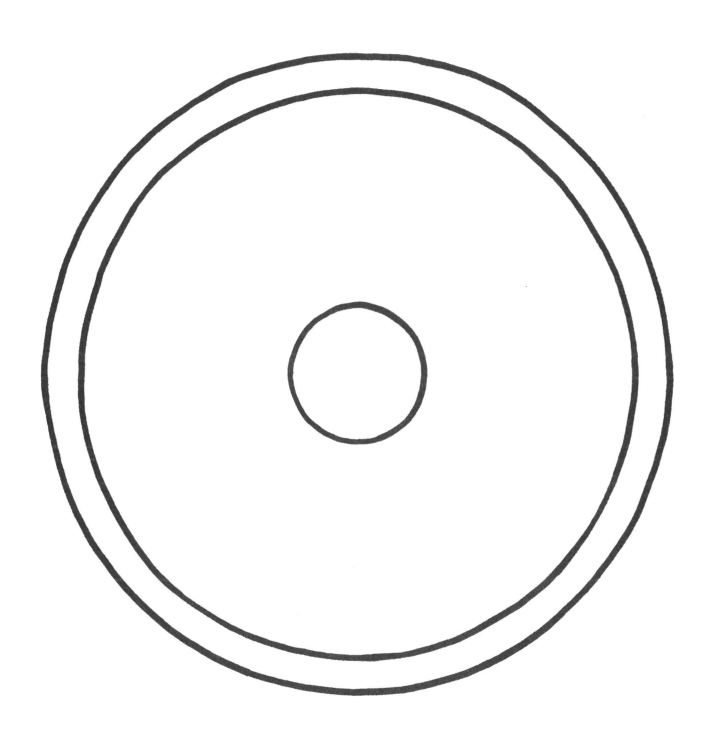

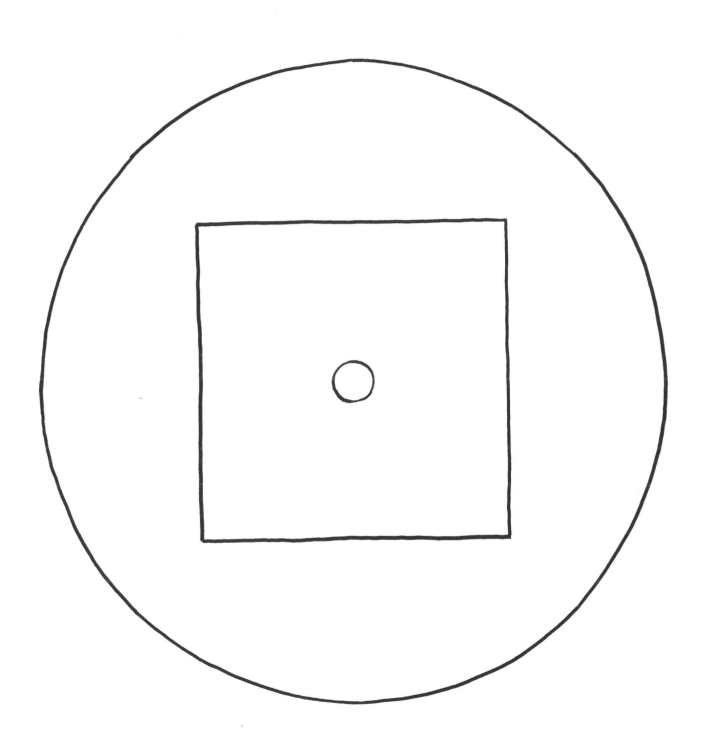